Instructional Technology and Media for Learning

Eighth Edition

Sharon E. Smaldino
Northern Illinois University

James D. Russell
Purdue University

with contributions by
Robert Heinich
Indiana University

Michael Molenda
Indiana University

PEARSON

Merrill
Prentice Hall

Upper Saddle River, New Jersey
Columbus, Ohio

Library of Congress Cataloging in Publication Data

Instructional technology and media for learning / Sharon E. Smaldino . . . [et al.]. — 8th ed.
   p. cm.
   Rev. ed. of: Instructional media and technologies for learning / Robert Heinich . . . [et al.].
  7th ed. c2002.
   ISBN 0-13-113682-8
   1. Educational technology. 2. Audio-visual education. I. Smaldino, Sharon E. II.
   Instructional media and technologies for learning.

   LB1028.3.H45 2005
   371.33—dc22

                                                                    2004044757

Vice President and Executive Publisher: Jeffery W. Johnston
Executive Editor: Debra A. Stollenwerk
Development Assistant: Amy Nelson
Editorial Assistant: Mary Morrill
Production Editor: Mary Harlan
Copy Editor: Robert L. Marcum
Design Coordinator: Diane C. Lorenzo
Text and Cover Design: Kristina D. Holmes
Cover Art: Jason Moore
Illustrations: Carlisle Publishers Services
Production Manager: Pamela D. Bennett
Director of Marketing: Ann Castel Davis
Marketing Manager: Darcy Betts Prybella
Marketing Coordinator: Tyra Poole

This book was set in Galliard by Carlisle Communications, Ltd. It was printed and bound by Courier Kendallville, Inc. The cover was printed by Phoenix Color Corp.

Earlier editions were entitled *Instructional Media and Technologies for Learning,* by Robert Heinich, Michael Molenda, James D. Russell, and Sharon E. Smaldino.

Credits for photos appear on page 391.

Pearson Education Ltd.
Pearson Education Singapore Pte. Ltd.
Pearson Education Canada, Ltd.
Pearson Education—Japan

Pearson Education Australia Pty. Limited
Pearson Education North Asia Ltd.
Pearson Educación de Mexico, S.A. de C.V.
Pearson Education Malaysia Pte. Ltd.

10 9 8 7 6 5 4 3 2
ISBN: 0-13-113682-8

Preface

I *nstructional Technology and Media for Learning,* Eighth Edition, presents a complete range of technology and media formats in terms of how they can be integrated into classroom instruction using the ASSURE model of lesson planning. Written from the viewpoint of the teacher, the text shows specifically and realistically how technology and media fit into the daily life of the classroom. This book is intended for educators at all levels who place a high value on successful learning. Its purpose is to help them incorporate technology and media into their repertoire—to use them as teaching tools and to guide students in using them as learning tools. We draw examples from elementary, secondary, and post-secondary education, as well as corporate training and development, because we know that instructors in these different settings have found previous editions of this book useful in their work.

This new edition is necessitated by the amazing pace of innovation in all aspects of technology, particularly in those related to computers and computer networks, and especially the Internet. In the few years since the seventh edition, the digitization of information has accelerated rapidly and so has school use of new telecommunications resources, such as the Web.

Our Approach

We share a number of convictions that underlie every edition of this textbook. First, we believe in an *eclectic* approach to the design of instruction. Advocates cite an abundance of theories and philosophies in support of different approaches to instruction—behaviorist, cognitivist, constructivist, and so on. We view these contending theoretical positions as differing *perspectives*— different vantage points—from which to examine the complex world of teaching and learning. We value each of them and feel that each is reflected in the guidance we offer.

Second, we have a balanced posture regarding the role of technology in instruction. Because of this perspective we consider each technology in light of its advantages, limitations, and range of applications. No technology can be described solely as being either "good" or "bad," so we strive to give a balanced treatment to the hard and soft technologies, as well as to the simpler and more sophisticated media.

Third, we believe in the possibility of a rapprochement between the humanistic and technological traditions in education. We contend that technology and humanism are two separable dimensions. We demonstrate in Chapter 1 that it's easy to describe instructional arrangements that are high on both dimensions or low on both dimensions, as well as high on one and low on the other. We view them as complementary concepts.

Fourth, we believe that technology can best be integrated into instruction when viewed from the perspective of the teacher rather than that of the technologist. Therefore, throughout the book we attempt to approach technology and media solutions in terms of the day-to-day challenges of teachers and to avoid technical jargon as much as possible. Our examples deal with real, everyday teaching issues, in real content areas, involving real technology and media.

New Conceptual Framework

The first edition of this text introduced the ASSURE model—a procedural guide for incorporating technology and media into instruction. Now, in the eighth edition, in order to fully and clearly illustrate how the ASSURE model can be used in instructional practice, we introduce the **ASSURE Case Framework.** This framework, in

Chapters 4 through 12, shows how technology looks when effectively integrated into instruction; explains chapter content in light of the ASSURE model and effective instructional practice; illustrates how to integrate technology into lessons according to principles of effective instruction; provides clear examples of effective lessons using the ASSURE model; and offers opportunities for you to learn how to create effective lessons using the ASSURE model.

This ASSURE Case Framework consists of the four following key elements:

ASSURE Case Challenge. The Blueprints from the seventh edition have been reorganized to reflect a case-study approach for each of the media chapters. Engaging case scenarios are introduced at the beginning of Chapters 4–12 to illustrate how technology and media can be integrated into learning activities.

ASSURE
Case Challenge

We have developed a case study for this chapter to help you see how computers can be integrated into learning activities. At the end of the chapter you will be challenged to develop your own ASSURE lesson for a case study of your choice using the ASSURE model and incorporating the technology and media described in this chapter. To help you in preparing

your lesson, we have included hints (called "ASSURE Case Connections") throughout the chapter as they relate to the ASSURE Case Challenge.

Dennis Sorge teaches pre-algebra to seventh- and eighth-grade middle school students. They are an average class with a range of abilities in math and reading. They have basic computation skills. Mr. Sorge wants to have his students practice their computation skills while applying them to concepts such as budgeting and making predictions. He wants to engage his students in learning within a real-world situation to make their math experiences more meaningful.

ASSURE Case Connection. This feature provides questions throughout the chapter to encourage readers to connect the chapter content to the ASSURE Case Challenge and classroom practice.

ASSURE Case Connection

Mr. Sorge wants his students to practice their computation skills. He believes he would like to use a computer to keep his students motivated. Would he use the computer as a tool? As an object of instruction? As an instructional device?

ASSURE Case in Practice. An expanded ASSURE Case Challenge, this end-of-chapter feature provides readers with a complete classroom example of technology integration using the ASSURE model.

ASSURE Case in Practice: Mathematics

All of the ASSURE Cases in Practice in this text and an electronic template for creating your own ASSURE Lesson can be found on the enclosed "Classroom Link Portfolio" CD-ROM.

Dennis Sorge's middle school pre-algebra students enjoy competing with classmates while simulating the operation of a hotdog stand. The students practice their math skills while cooperating with one group of peers and competing against other groups.

3. Budget expenses using a budget planning sheet and be able to justify their decisions during a simulation.
4. Make predictions of sales based on previous sales and the weather forecast. The prediction will be within 20 percent of actual sales.
5. Deal with random events that influence outcomes. Students will be able to justify planning for random events before they happen and to justify their strategy for dealing with them after they happen during a simulation.
6. Plan and predict how they should stock a concession

Create Your Own ASSURE Lesson.   After experiencing a full ASSURE Case in Practice, you can create your own lesson plan using the ASSURE model and scenarios provided on the Companion Website at www. prenhall.com/smaldino or your own available classroom situation.

Create Your Own ASSURE Lesson

Using the ASSURE model, design a lesson for a scenario from the table on this book's inside cover or from the Companion Website, or use a scenario of your own design. Use one of the methods described in Chapter 1 and information from this chapter related to incorporating computers and software into your instructional setting. Be sure to include information about the audience, the objectives, and all other elements of the ASSURE model. When completed, reflect on the process you used and what you have learned about matching audience, content, method, and materials.

Also New to This Edition

Not only have we updated the technological information and methodological perspectives, but we have made a number of other changes.

- *New organization.* The text has been reorganized into sections to facilitate understanding of chapter content. The chapters have been clustered, acknowledging the relationship of their themes. Computer-based technology chapters have been moved to an earlier location in the text based on suggestions by a number of users.
- *Skill Builder Exercises/Tutorials.* Located on this text's Companion Website (http://www.prenhall. com/smaldino), these practical tutorial and skill building activities give students a hands-on experience that build students' skills using popular software and hardware applications such as word processing, presentation software, spreadsheets, database applications, desktop publishing, Web page development and design, and bulletin board construction. Activities for these applications allow you to develop actual samples to use in P–12 classrooms.
- *New color photographs and drawings.* More than 300 photographs and drawings are now presented in full color.
- *Updated Classroom Link.* Building on the ASSURE Case Framework in the text, the "Classroom Link Portfolio" CD-ROM that accompanies the text has been significantly updated and expanded with a new, user-friendly design interface with the goal to develop artifacts for an on-going professional portfolio. You have the opportunity to build lesson plans using the ASSURE model, evaluate technology resources using Selection Rubrics that are available on the CD-ROM, and create records of activities as they complete the end-of-chapter portfolio projects. All of these CD-ROM activities are aligned with ISTE/NETS Standards. This CD-ROM is packaged in the back of this book.
- *Classroom examples.* We provide more examples of specific classroom applications of media and technologies across grade levels and subjects.
- *Media specialists' role.* We have made a special effort to draw the connections between the roles of teachers and school media specialists, portraying them as highly complementary and interdependent.
- *Expanded Companion Website.* The Companion Website (CW), at www.prenhall.com/smaldino, has been expanded and is integrated with the text and the CD-ROM to create a complete learning package. Additions include portfolio activities, Web-based activities, and skill builder exercises/tutorials, among other features. See the section titled "CW Resources for the Student" on page x for detailed CW content.

Text Organization

The book begins with a visual introduction—a series of vignettes that depict the many applications of technology and media in enhancing learning—and is divided into five parts organized by themes.

Part 1: Learning Foundations.   This first section contains four chapters devoted to discussion of learning and the design of instruction to enhance learning. Chapter 1 discusses instructional technology, media, and learning. It identifies the purposes served by technology and media and provides theoretical grounding in communications and in the psychology of learning and instruction. Chapter 2 introduces the concept of instructional systems and describes programmed instruction, programmed tutoring, learning centers, cooperative groups, games, and simulations. Chapter 3 presents the ASSURE model for instructional planning. Readers who are already familiar with lesson planning procedures will find the ASSURE model more congenial than the more technical models associated with full-fledged instructional design. This chapter also presents general procedures for appraising, selecting, and using technology and media. Chapter 4 examines principles and procedures of visual design, an important foundation for use of visual media discussed in other chapters.

Part 2: Digital Environments.   The four chapters in this section explore the use of digital environments for learning. Chapters 5 and 6 focus on computer-based technologies, including computer-assisted instruction, integrated learning systems, computers as student tools, multimedia, and hypermedia. Distance education is the focus of Chapter 7, with particular attention paid to online technologies, distance learning issues, broadcast radio and television, as well as audio and video teleconferencing. Chapter 8 focuses on online learning and the use of computer networks, including the Internet, the World Wide Web, intranets, wide area networks (WANs), and local area networks (LANs), to facilitate electronic learning.

Part 3: Traditional Media.   The four chapters in this section focus on those media that have been used in learning settings for many years. Instructional materials and displays are described in Chapter 9. Topics include manipulatives, multimedia kits, field trips, printed materials, free and inexpensive materials, and display surfaces. Chapters 10 through 12 treat the common formats of media. Chapter 10 deals with visual media. Chapter 11 features audio media and the listening process. Video is examined in Chapter 12.

Part 4: Trends in Technology and Media.   In Chapter 13 we consider the possible impacts of current trends in technology, training, and education. We discuss the emerging influences of computer-based media, telecommunications technologies, schools of the future, and workplaces of the future.

Part 5: Classroom Resources.   Section A: "Photography and Visuals" includes information on photography, the parts of a camera, preserving visuals, multi-image presentations, and planning audiovisual presentations. Section B: "Equipment and Setups" provides nuts-and-bolts advice on setting up and handling media hardware, including setups for audio, visual projection, video, and computers. In Section C: "How To . . . Step-by-Step Guides," 30 media production and operation procedures are spelled out with illustrated step-by-step procedures, from "Developing Media Portfolios" and "Creating a *HyperStudio* Stack" to "Developing an Audiovisual Presentation," among others. Troubleshooting suggestions are included as part of these how-to discussions.

Glossary.   The text concludes with a glossary of more than 400 technical terms used in this book and in general discussions of instructional technology and media, followed by a thorough index.

Special Features

See the index of Special Features on p. xxiii, following the Contents.

Advance Organizers.   Each chapter begins with a brief outline and a set of knowledge objectives to provide a more concrete notion of what knowledge and skills are featured in that chapter. Following the objectives is the "Professional Vocabulary," a list of technical terms or terms used in a specialized sense in that chapter. All of these features are intended to give you a strong set of advance organizers, scaffolds for the main content of the chapter.

ASSURE Case in Practice.   As mentioned in preceding paragraphs, this end-of-chapter feature provides readers with a complete classroom example of technology integration using the ASSURE model. (Chapters 3–12)

ASSURE Case in Practice: Mathematics

All of the ASSURE Cases in Practice in this text and an electronic template for creating your own ASSURE Lesson can be found on the enclosed "Classroom Link Portfolio" CD-ROM.

Dennis Sorge's middle school pre-algebra students enjoy competing with classmates while simulating the operation of a hotdog stand. The students practice their math skills while cooperating with one group of peers and competing against other groups.

3. Budget expenses using a budget planning sheet and be able to justify their decisions during a simulation.
4. Make predictions of sales based on previous sales and the weather forecast. The prediction will be within 20 percent of actual sales.
5. Deal with random events that influence outcomes. Students will be able to justify planning for random events before they happen and to justify their strategy for dealing with them after they happen during a simulation.
6. Plan and predict how they should stock a concession

Close-Ups.   These serve as miniature case studies of technology and media applications in a variety of settings. Like the ASSURE Cases in Practice, they show technology and media use *in context*. (All chapters)

Close-Up

NETWORK TERMS

An array of tools and software is used with the Internet and the World Wide Web. Here are brief descriptions of some of them:

- *E-mail*—a method of electronic communication that enables users to send and receive messages from one user to another.
- *FTP (file transfer protocol)*—a protocol (data exchange code standard) that allows users to retrieve files and transfer information from one computer to another over the Internet.
- *IRC (Internet relay chat)*—a text-based program that allows users to chat live across the Internet. (Other examples are AOL Instant Messenger and ICQ [I Seek You].)
- *Java*—an object-oriented programming language used to create interactive applications for Web pages.
- *Lynx*—a text-based Web browser.
- *Search engine*—software that provides key word search capability of registered websites. Common search engines are Google, Yahoo!, Ask Jeeves, and Mootes.
- *Telnet*—a software program that allows users to log onto a re-

Copyright Concerns.   This feature provides students with an integrated discussion of copyright issues linked to specific chapter content. (Chapters 1, 5, 6, 7, 8, 9, 11, 12, 13)

Copyright Concerns

COMPUTER SOFTWARE

Congress amended the Copyright Act to clear up questions of fair use of copyrighted computer programs. The changes defined the term *computer program* for copyright purposes and set forth permissible and nonpermissible use of copyrighted computer software programs. According to the amended law, with a single copy of a program, you may do the following:

- Make multiple copies of a copyrighted program.
- Make additional copies from an archival or backup copy.
- Make copies of copyrighted programs to be sold, leased, loaned, transmitted, or given away.
- Sell a locally produced adaptation of a copyrighted program.
- Make multiple copies of an adaptation of a copyrighted program even for use within a school or school district.
- Put a single copy of a program onto a network without permission or a special site license.

Media Files.   Actual materials in various media formats are highlighted as examples of materials that are commercially available. The materials referred to are meant to be *typical* of a given format, not necessarily as exemplary. No endorsement is implied. (Chapters 2, 5, 6, 9, 11, 12)

Media Files: Computer Software 2

DECISIONS, DECISIONS

Tom Snyder Productions

Simulation

Decisions, Decisions is a series of role-playing software packages designed specifically to generate informed discussion and decision making in the classroom using only one computer. The program has a mode for whole-class discussion with the teacher leading the

lines to create geometric products. "Build It" allows learners to actually construct the products. During "Research It" they refine existing assembly lines to find more efficient ways to create given products. "Ship It" requires students to build their knowledge of geometric attributes as they pack boxes to fill orders. Finally, in "Deliver It" students compete against each other or one of two computer components in a mathematical race to deliver their products.

Selection Rubrics. These new rubrics are related to each of the media formats and make it easy to preview materials systematically and to preserve the information for later reference. Users have permission to photocopy these for personal use. The "Classroom Link Portfolio" CD-ROM computer software allows you to enter your appraisals directly into a template for storage and future use. (Chapters 2, 5, 6, 8, 9, 10, 11, 12, and Section B)

Selection Rubric: Computer Software

Complete an interactive evaluation and add it to your NETS-T portfolio using the Selection Rubric for Computer Software available on the "Classroom Link Portfolio" CD-ROM. A downloadable version of this rubric is available in the Selection Rubrics module of the Companion Website at http://www.prenhall.com/smaldino.

Key Words

_____

_____

_____

Title _____

Series Title (if applicable) _____

Source _____

Format

☐ **Drill-and-practice**

☐ **Game**

Showmanship. These features give specific tips on using technology and media with flair and dramatic effect. (Chapters 3, 9, 10, 12)

Showmanship

CHALKBOARD AND WHITEBOARD

- Put extensive drawing or writing on the board before class. Taking too much time to write or draw creates restlessness and may lead to discipline problems.
- Organize in advance what you plan to write on the board and where you plan to write it.

- Check the visibility of the board from several positions around the room to be sure there is no glare on the surface. In case of glare, move the board (if portable) or pull down the window shades.
- If your printing normally runs "uphill" or "downhill," use water-soluble felt-tip pen markings as temporary guidelines for straighter printing. The guidelines will not be wiped off by a chalk eraser but will wash off when no longer needed.
- Hold the chalk or marker at an angle so that it does not make scratching or squeaking noises.

Technology for Diverse Learners. These new features describe technology that can be used in classrooms for diverse learners. (Chapters 1, 5, 9, 10, 11, 12)

Technology for Diverse Learners

SCREEN READERS

Visually impaired students need to be able to use computer software, e-mail, and the Internet. Adaptive software programs, called screen readers, help these students use computers and to surf the Internet. Using speech synthesizers, the software reads aloud the text and names of icons. Visually impaired learners can navigate using the keyboard, hitting the tab button to move from icon to icon. Nontextual items such as graphics and photos are labeled with alternative textual descriptions, called *alt-tags*, which allow vi-

sually impaired learners to hear descriptions of these items. Among the common screen readers for Windows operating systems is *JAWS* (Job Access With Speech) from Henter-Joyce, Inc. (http://www.hj.com).

There are also devices that convert computer screen content into Braille characteristics for students who are both deaf and blind. These tools translate text to a single line of continually changing Braille. This technique allows these students to use a screen reader system. They don't hear what is on the screen, but they can feel it.

Classroom Link Portfolio Activities. These activities tie together the book, the "Classroom Link Portfolio" CD-ROM, the Companion Website, and the ISTE NETS-T standards. These activities and projects can be found at the end of each chapter and are indicated by an icon combining a CW and a CD-ROM. Students have the opportunity to build lesson plans using the ASSURE model, to evaluate technology resources using the Selection Rubrics, and to create records of activities as they complete the end-of-chapter portfolio activities.

Classroom Link Portfolio Activities

Use the "Classroom Link Portfolio" CD-ROM and the Companion Website as resources in completing these activities. To complete the following activities online go to the Portfolio Activities module in Chapter 5 of the Companion Website (http://www.prenhall.com/smaldino).

1. *Instructional Software Critique.* Select an instructional computer program, load it, and take a brief tour. Record your initial reactions. Critique this program using the "Selection Rubric: Computer

Software" in this chapter (also found on the "Classroom Link Portfolio" CD-ROM), citing sources. Compare and contrast the findings from your initial tour and the Selection Rubric. What will you do the next time you find a new instructional computer program? (ISTE NETS-T 2.B & C; 6.A)

2. *Written Reflection.* Name three ways computers have enhanced your learning. Why were these effective? How might these strategies be used to help students learn in a technology-enhanced environment? (ISTE NETS-T 2.E; 5.B).

Integration Assessments. Each chapter concludes with a set of activities that address real-life skills typically cultivated in courses using this textbook. Activities that can be completed on the Companion Website are indicated with a CW icon. These activities are matched to ISTE NETS-T standards.

Integration Assessments

To complete the specified activities online go to the Integration Assessments module in Chapter 9 of the Companion Website (http://www.prenhall.com/smaldino).

1. Generate two ideas for using learning centers in your own teaching. (ISTE NETS-T 2.A; 3.B)
2. Develop an instructional module for a topic and audience of your choice. (ISTE NETS-T 2.A; 3.B)

describe the types of resources that are available to you. (ISTE NETS-T 2.C)

6. Demonstrate techniques (showmanship tips) for improving your utilization of chalkboards and multipurpose boards. (ISTE NETS-T 2.D; 5.B)
7. Prepare a bulletin board, cloth board, magnetic board, flip chart, or exhibit. Submit the material (or a photograph of the display), a descrip-

Flashbacks. Brief historical vignettes that lend a sense of perspective to today's technologies can be found on the Companion Website.

Supplements for Instructors

Instructor's Guide. Ask your Merrill/Prentice Hall representative or contact the publisher directly for a copy of this comprehensive teaching guide, available to adopters without cost.

Test Bank. Questions for each chapter are available in electronic format. The PC and Macintosh-compatible electronic test bank is available upon request. It allows instructors to create customized exams on a personal computer.

PowerPoint® Presentations. Designed as an instructional tool, the presentations can be used to present and elaborate on chapter material. They are also available on the Companion Website.

Supplements for Students

"Classroom Link Portfolio" CD-ROM. The companion CD-ROM, "Classroom Link Portfolio," will help you create, maintain, and print lesson plans and evaluations of materials based on the ASSURE model. It also helps you develop ISTE standards-aligned artifacts for professional portfolios. The resulting database can be the basis for a teaching portfolio that can grow throughout your career. The portfolio components are connected to the ISTE NETS-T standards. The CD-ROM is fully integrated into the text and the Companion Website with performance-based and reflection-based activities and projects. These activities and projects, found at the end of each chapter, are indicated with a CW/CD-ROM icon. The guide for using the "Classroom Link Portfolio" CD-ROM is located on the Companion Website; the instructions for using this software have been completely revised and simplified.

The Prentice Hall Companion Website

The Companion Website (CW) for this text is located at http://www.prenhall.com/smaldino. A truly integrated Web-based technology resource, the Companion Website for this text builds on and enhances what the textbook already offers. The content is organized by chapter and provides the instructor and student with a variety of meaningful resources. It includes study materials such as knowledge objectives for each chapter, chapter overviews and summaries, interactive practice quizzes with answers, portfolio activities, integration assessments, links to related Web sites, "Flashbacks," a message board to encourage discussion, a chat feature, a library of *PowerPoint* slides, and a detailed guide for using the "Classroom Link Portfolio" CD-ROM.

CW Resources for the Instructor

Syllabus Manager™ provides you, the instructor, with a step-by-step process to create and revise syllabi, with direct links into the Companion Website and other online content without having to learn HTML.

- Your completed syllabus is hosted on our servers, allowing convenient updates from any computer on the Internet. Changes you make to your syllabus are immediately available to your students at their next logon.
- Students may log on to your syllabus at any time. All they need to know is the Web address for the Companion Website and the password you've assigned to your syllabus.
- Clicking on a date, the student is shown the list of activities for that day's assignment. The activities for each assignment are linked directly to text content, saving time for students.
- Adding assignments consists of clicking on the desired due date, then filling in the details of the assignment.
- Links to other activities can be created easily. If the activity is online, a URL can be entered in the space provided, and it will be linked automatically in the final syllabus.
- *PowerPoint*® slides. Designed as an instructional tool, the *PowerPoint* presentations for each chapter can be used to present and elaborate on chapter content.

CW Resources for the Student

The Companion Website provides students with resources and immediate feedback on exercises and other activities linked to the text. In addition, these activities, projects, and resources enhance and extend chapter content to real-world issues and concepts. Each chapter on the CW contains the following modules or sections:

- *Knowledge Objectives*—outlines key concepts
- *True/False Questions*—self-quizzes with automatic grading that provides immediate feedback for students
- *Multiple Choice Questions*— self-quizzes with automatic grading that provides immediate feedback for students
- *Web Links*—links to Internet sites that relate to and enhance chapter content
- *Skill Builder Tutorials*—practical tutorial and skill building activities give students hands-on experiences that build students' skills using popular software

and hardware applications such as word processing, presentation software, spreadsheets, database applications, desktop publishing, Web page development and design, and bulletin board construction. Activities for the above applications allow students to develop actual samples to use in P–12 classrooms.

- *Professional Development Resources*—annotated links to sites that provide resources useful to preservice and in-service teachers, including organizations and standards
- *Portfolio Activities*—performance-based and reflection-based activities and projects that are connected to the ISTE NETS-T standards
- *Integration Assessments*—projects and activities that enhance students' understanding of chapter content as it relates to technology and media
- *Web-based Activities*—meaningful activities that are connected to chapter content and provide Web-based resources for students to use when completing the activities
- *Message Board*—serves as a virtual bulletin board to post—or respond to— questions or comments to and from a national audience
- *Chat*—allows anyone who is using the text anywhere in the country to communicate in a real-time environment—ideal for discussion and study groups, class projects, and so on
- *Other Resources:* In addition, users have access to *PowerPoint* Transparencies, Flashbacks, downloadable classroom resources, and links to dozens of information sources.

Additional Resources for Instructors

Authors' Services.   The authors are eager to assist you in putting together an outstanding course. We offer the following services to instructors who have adopted this book:

- *Telelecture.* Call either of us in advance to arrange a guest lecture in your class via telephone. The only cost to you is for the toll charges. Some instructors use this telelecture as a demonstration of the techniques described in Chapter 7. Our phone numbers, fax numbers, and e-mail addresses are listed in the Instructor's Guide.
- *Workshops.* We have conducted workshops annually since 1982 at the national convention of the Association for Educational Communications and Technology (AECT). This is a forum for exchange of ideas and networking among instructors of courses on technology and media.

If you are an instructor using this text and wish to share your comments, send your name and address to Sharon Smaldino, Northern Illinois University, Gabel Hall 155, College of Education, DeKalb, IL 60115.

ACKNOWLEDGMENTS

Through each of the editions of this book we have been fortunate to have had guidance from the real experts—the people who teach the courses for which this book is designed. In preparing for this edition we surveyed a sample of adopters and other leaders in the field to elicit their advice about content and emphases. We then asked other well-respected colleagues in the field to critique the text. We thank all those who gave their time and talent to help make this the most useful textbook it could be, and in particular those listed here, who reviewed the seventh edition and suggested improvements:

- Joe P. Brasher, Athens State University
- Annette B. Littrell, Tennessee Tech University
- Greer M. Richardson, La Salle University
- Armand Seguin, Emporia State University

We especially thank those who contributed more directly by writing new material, drawing illustrations, taking photographs, and searching for references.

Elizabeth Boling of the School of Education, Indiana University, is responsible for both the outstanding illustrations in Chapter 4 and the accompanying text related to visual design. We are in awe of her phenomenal artistic skill and scholarly mastery of this area. The late Dennis Pett, from his professor emeritus setting in Vermont, carefully reviewed drafts of Chapter 4 and gave generous advice on photography, color, and visual design principles, as well as providing a number of exemplary photographs. Their contributions were so substantial they must be considered co-authors of Chapter 4.

Daniel Callison of the School of Library and Information Science, Indiana University, reviewed the whole book and made many helpful recommendations related to the connections between the teacher and the school library media center and media specialist. The extended ASSURE Case in Chapter 3, which we feel is a significant aid to using the ASSURE model, was developed by Mary Ann Ferkis while a student at Purdue University; it was done as a project in a course using this book.

This book also contains the products of the work of many others who have contributed to past editions; we continue to be indebted to all of them.

The editorial and production staffs of Merrill/ Prentice Hall, particularly Debbie Stollenwerk and Mary Harlan, deserve special commendation. New members of the production team, Valerie Schultz, our photo coordinator, and Kristi Holmes, designer, greatly enhanced the look of this edition. We also want to thank our copy editor, Robert L. Marcum, for his valuable editing contributions and for his assistance with the content related to computers. Molly Lane provided valuable assistance in updating the Suggested Readings. The authors have never had such intense and helpful support from any previous publication team.

We are grateful to our colleagues from our own universities—Indiana, Purdue, Northern Iowa, and Northern Illinois—for their many and valued forms of support over the years.

Finally, we thank our families for all they do to make this project possible.

Sharon E. Smaldino
James D. Russell

About the Authors

Sharon E. Smaldino

Dr. Smaldino is the L. D. and Ruth Morgridge Endowed Chair for Teacher Education in the College of Education at Northern Illinois University. She was a professor of Educational Technology at the University of Northern Iowa for many years prior to moving to NIU. Sharon received her Ph.D. in 1987 from Southern Illinois University, Carbondale. Prior to that she received an M.A. in Elementary Education and served for more than a dozen years as teacher, speech therapist, and special educator in school districts from Florida to Minnesota. At Northern Iowa she taught an introductory educational media course for undergraduates and graduate majors and served as coordinator of the Educational Technology program. Dr. Smaldino also taught graduate courses in Instructional Development, Instructional Computing Design, Desktop Publishing, and Selection and Integration. She has received several awards for her outstanding teaching. In her current role, she is focused in working with faculty and teachers to integrate technology into the learning process. Presenting at state, national, and international conferences, Sharon has become an important voice on applications of technology in the classroom and in distance education. In addition to her teaching and consulting, Dr. Smaldino serves as president of AECT, served on the board of directors of IVLA, and has written articles for state and national journals on her primary research interest, effective technology integration in learning. She worked on a Preparing Tomorrow's Teachers to use Technology (PT3) grant using the Web to deliver information and case studies of teachers using technology in schools. She has also worked on a Teacher Quality Enhancement grant which identified technology as an important aspect of ensuring quality learning environments.

James D. Russell

Dr. Russell is Professor Emeritus of Educational Technology at Purdue University. He still teaches at Purdue during the summer and fall semesters. Jim works part-time for Purdue's Center for Instructional Excellence, where he conducts workshops on teaching techniques and consults on instructional improvement. During spring semesters he is visiting professor of Educational Psychology and Learning Systems at Florida State University. There he also works part-time for the Office of Distributed and Distance Learning. A former high school mathematics and physics teacher, Jim has taught for more than forty years. He has won numerous honors for his teaching at Purdue, including his department's Outstanding Teacher Award and the School of Education's Best Teacher Award. He was also selected as a member of Purdue's teaching academy and inducted into Purdue's Book of Great Teachers. His specialty areas, in which he has achieved national prominence through his writings and presentations, are presentation skills and using media and technology in classrooms. Through his teaching, workshops, consulting, and this textbook, Jim continues to make a significant impact on classroom teaching practice.

Co-authors Through the First Seven Editions

We wish to acknowledge the contributions made by two authors who shared significant roles in the writing of earlier editions of this book. Their ideas and their spirit remain threaded throughout the book.

Robert Heinich

Dr. Heinich is Professor Emeritus in the department of Instructional Systems Technology (IST), Indiana University. He is now retired from active teaching, having served on the faculty since 1969 following completion of his doctorate at University of Southern California and a stint as multimedia editor for Doubleday Publishing. Prior to that he built a nationally prominent media program at the Colorado Springs school district. Bob has been an active leader in the field of educational technology for four decades, serving as president of the Association for Educational Communications and Technology (AECT) from 1971 to 1972 and as president of AECT's foundation from 1972 to 1982. He was editor of AECT's scholarly journal from 1969 to 1983. Indicative of his professional contributions, Dr. Heinich has received the Presidential Citation of the International Society for Performance and Instruction and the Distinguished Service Award of AECT. At Indiana University he served as chairman of the IST department from 1979 to 1984. His many articles and monographs provide some of the major theoretical underpinnings of the field. The University of Northern Colorado honored Bob with their Trail Blazer Award as an outstanding alumnus. He is currently on the board of directors of the Old Colorado City Historical Society in Colorado Springs, where he now lives. He is also on the board of directors of the Colorado Round Dance Association.

Michael Molenda

Dr. Molenda is Associate Professor in Instructional Systems Technology (IST) at Indiana University. He received his Ph.D. from Syracuse University and taught at University of North Carolina at Greensboro before joining Indiana University in 1972. He designs and teaches courses in Media Applications, Instructional Development, Evaluation and Change, and Instructional Technology Foundations. Mike served as chairman of the IST department from 1988 to 1991. He has lectured and consulted extensively on educational technology in Spain, the Netherlands, Indonesia, Korea, Swaziland, and several countries in Latin America and the Middle East. Among his professional distinctions are selection as a Fulbright Lecturer in Peru in 1976, membership on the Board of Directors of AECT, 1988–1991, and presidency of AECT's International Council, 1978–1979. Dr. Molenda's breadth of knowledge of the field of educational technology is indicated by his authorship of articles on educational technology in elementary and secondary education and instructional technology for recent editions of international encyclopedias of education. Since 1997 he has co-authored an annual survey of issues and trends in educational technology for *Educational Media and Technology Yearbook*. Beginning in 2003 Mike served as founding editor of *Asia-Pacific Cybereducation Journal*, an online educational technology journal.

Brief Contents

Contents

Special Features

Selection Rubrics

Showmanship

Technology for Diverse Learners

NOTE: Every effort has been made to provide
accurate and current Internet information in this
book. However, the Internet and information posted
on it are constantly changing, so it is inevitable that
some of the Internet addresses listed in this textbook
will change.

Learning Foundations

The Pervasiveness of Instructional Media

PART 1

THE PERVASIVENESS OF INSTRUCTIONAL MEDIA

The twenty-first century can be characterized as the age of technology and media. As conduits for information and entertainment, technology and the mass media literally surround us daily. Technology, especially in digital formats, permeates our work and play. Technology and media have transformed not only the worlds of work and leisure but the world of education as well. As you think of your future in the world of education, consider these vignettes as samples of the ways technology and media affect the processes of teaching and learning.

1

As Wendi drives to a sales meeting she listens to a new audiotape from the company's training center. It introduces the new products she will be learning more about at the meeting.

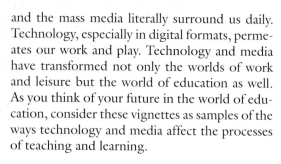

2

In a quiet corner of the office, Jean is guided through a CD-ROM that shows the proper operation of the software she will be using. It will help her complete complex office tasks more efficiently.

3

Second graders Allison and Tiffany use flash cards to practice their subtraction skills. The cards have a problem on one side and an answer on the other; the "repeat" stock grows smaller as Tiffany masters each fact.

4

David and Carl, medical students, use a DVD system in the university's learning center to practice responding to patients in stressful situations. The scenarios present situations they are likely to face in actual practice.

5

Samaritan Club members of junior high school age are studying the meanings of the parables. They compete as teams during the afterschool program at their local church. Matching the facts of the stories with the accepted interpretation is the purpose of the game.

6

Three students eagerly boot (start up) The Great Solar System Rescue disk on one of their school's portable computers. They want to continue where they left off yesterday in a detective story. It challenges their logical reasoning skills in solving the mystery.

7

As he videotapes one of his classmates interviewing a firefighter, Zachary, a high school senior, reflects on what brought him here. He had volunteered to do a video report on urban problems for his social studies class.

8

To learn how to manage her diabetes medications at home, Mary listens to the nurse from her hospital as she explains important procedures. The nurse happily answers Mary's questions.

9

Dinner over, the Lees settle into the family room to watch This Old House. *They are intrigued with the notion of buying and restoring an older house, and this television series provides them with valuable tips.*

In school and after school, at home and at work, children and adults are enjoying the benefits of learning through technology and media. The goal of this book is to help put you into this picture.

Technology, Media, and Learning

Outline

Knowledge Objectives

1. Distinguish between instruction and learning.
2. Describe four psychological perspectives of learning discussed in the text.
3. Define the term *medium*.
4. Name six basic categories of media.
5. Explain the concrete–abstract continuum, indicating how it can be used to aid in the selection of media.
6. Discuss five roles of media in the instructional process, giving an example of media used in each role.
7. Describe 6 of the 10 methods of instruction discussed in this chapter.
8. Discuss technology and distinguish between *instructional technology* and *instructional systems*.

Professional Vocabulary

learning	portfolio
behaviorism	artifact
cognitivism	thematic instruction
constructivism	distance education
social psychology	method
instruction	discussion
medium/media	cooperative learning
text	gaming
audio	simulation
visuals	discovery
motion media	problem solving
manipulative	presentation
people	demonstration
copyright	drill-and-practice
enactive experience	tutorial
iconic representation	technology
symbolic representation	instructional technology
advance organizer	instructional systems

This chapter explores the nature of learning, the various types of media and methods to facilitate learning, and the importance of technology and media within the learning process. The roles of instructor and learner are clearly changing because of the influence of technology in the classroom. No longer are teachers and textbooks the sources of all knowledge. The teacher becomes the facilitator of knowledge acquisition. With a few keystrokes students can explore the world, gaining access to libraries, other teachers and students, and a host of resources to obtain the information they seek.

You can make more effective use of technology and media if you have a basic grasp of our current understanding of how we learn. Instructional technology and media provide you with the tools to engage students in learning. As a teacher, you must be prepared to choose the best tools for your students. Such tools offer powerful possibilities for improving learning. You, however, make the difference in the integration of technology and media into this process.

Learning

Learning is the development of new knowledge, skills, or attitudes as an individual interacts with information and the environment. The *learning environment* includes the physical facilities, the psychological atmosphere, instructional technology, media, and methods. Learning takes place all the time. We learn things by walking down the street, watching TV, surfing the Net, conversing with others, and just by observing what goes on around us. This type of incidental learning is not our major interest as education professionals. Rather, we are concerned primarily with the learning that takes place in response to instructional efforts on the part of students and teachers.

Thus, learning involves the selection, arrangement, and delivery of information in an appropriate environment and the way learners interact with that information. In this chapter we first consider learning, looking at several psychological perspectives and a philosophical perspective. Next we introduce the various types of media, which we will explore in later chapters. We describe various roles of technology and media in learning and present different methods, both student directed and teacher directed. The chapter concludes with a discussion of technology as it relates to learning.

Psychological Perspectives on Learning

How instructors view the role of technology and media in the classroom depends very much on their beliefs about how people learn. Over the past half century there have been several dominant theories of learning. Each has implications for instruction in general and for the use of technology specifically. We will briefly survey each of the major perspectives on learning and discuss their implications. Learning theories and their impact on teaching decisions are discussed in greater detail by Driscoll (2000).

Behaviorist Perspective.   In the 1950s, B. F. Skinner, a psychologist at Harvard University, conducted scientific studies of observable behavior. He was a proponent of **behaviorism.** He was interested in voluntary behavior, such as learning new skills, rather than reflexive behavior, as illustrated by Pavlov's famous salivating dog. He demonstrated that the behavior patterns of an organism could be shaped by reinforcing, or rewarding, the desired responses to the environment. Skinner based his learning theory, known as reinforcement theory, on a series of experiments with pigeons, and he reasoned that the same procedures could be used with humans. The result was the emergence of programmed instruction, a technique of leading a learner through a series of instructional steps to a desired level of per-

formance. Unlike earlier learning research, Skinner's work was very logical and precise, leading directly to improved instructional design.

Behaviorists refuse to speculate on what goes on internally when learning takes place. They rely solely on observable behaviors. As a result, they are more comfortable explaining relatively simple learning tasks. Because of this posture, behaviorism has limited application in designing instruction for higher-level skills. For example, behaviorists are reluctant to make inferences about how learners process information, even when doing so can be helpful in designing instruction that develops problem-solving ability. Behaviorist principles are applied today in computer-based instruction and in Web-based courses.

Cognitivist Perspective.   In the latter half of the twentieth century, cognitivists made new contributions to learning theory and instructional design by creating models of how learners receive, process, and manipulate information. Cognitivism is based on the work of Swiss psychologist Jean Piaget (1977). Cognitive psychologists explore the mental processes individuals use in responding to their environment.

Cognitivism deals with how people think, solve problems, and make decisions. For example, behaviorists simply state that practice strengthens the response to a stimulus. Cognitivists create a mental model of short-term and long-term memory. New information is stored in short-term memory, where it is "rehearsed" until ready to be stored in long-term memory. If the information is not rehearsed, it fades from short-term memory. Learners then combine the information and skills in long-term memory to develop cognitive strategies, or skills for dealing with complex tasks. Cognitivists have a broader perception of learning than that held by behaviorists: Students are less dependent on the guiding hand of the teacher and rely more on their own cognitive strategies in using available learning resources.

Constructivist Perspective.   **Constructivism** is a movement that extends beyond the beliefs of the cognitivist. It considers the engagement of students in meaningful experiences as the essence of experiential learning. The shift is from passive transfer of information to active problem solving and discovery. Constructivists emphasize that learners create their own interpretations of the world of information. They contrast their perspective with those of the behaviorists or cognitivists, who believe that the mind can be "mapped" by the instructor. Constructivists argue that students situate the learning experience within their own experience and that the goal of instruction is not to teach information but to create situations so that students can interpret information for their own understanding. The role of instruction is not to dispense facts but to provide students with ways to assemble knowledge. The constructivist believes that learning occurs most effectively when students are engaged in authentic tasks that relate to meaningful contexts—learning by doing. The ultimate measure of learning is therefore based on the ability of the student to use knowledge to facilitate thinking in real life.

Social-Psychological Perspective. **Social psychology** is another well-established tradition in the study of instruction and learning. Social psychologists look at the effects of the social organization of the classroom on learning. What is the group structure of the classroom—independent study, small groups, or the class as a whole? What is the authority structure—how much control do students have over their own activities? And what is the reward structure—is cooperation rather than competition fostered?

Researchers such as Robert Slavin have taken the position that cooperative learning is both more effective and more socially beneficial than competitive and individualistic learning (Slavin, 1990). Slavin developed a set of cooperative learning techniques that embodies the principles of small-group collaboration, learner-controlled instruction, and rewards based on group achievement. (We discuss these techniques more fully in Chapter 2.)

Approaches to Learning

Instruction is the arrangement of information and the environment to facilitate learning. This may be done by the learner or the instructor. Gagné described instruction as a set of events external to the learner designed to support the internal process of learning (Gagné, 1985). By *environment* we mean not only where instruction takes place but also the technology, methods, and media needed to convey information and guide the learner's study. As implied in the illustrated vignettes on pages 2 and 3 and as detailed later in this chapter, information and environment can change depending on the instructional goal. For example, in Vignette 7, Zachary must have a camera and seek out a location that will fulfill the requirements of the assignment. He will provide the content for his project. In Vignette 4, David and Carl go to a learning center, where they will find the equipment and the media necessary to complete their assignment. The information has been carefully prepared for them.

While behaviorists stress external control over a learner's behavior, cognitivists stress internal, or learner, control over mental processes. This difference in viewpoint influences how media are designed and used.

Behaviorists specify behavioral (performance) objectives, then limit instruction to whatever is necessary to master those objectives. When programmed instruction was introduced, material not directly related to the objectives was carefully screened out. Instructional design and media were highly structured. This approach has been very successful in teaching basic skills and knowledge.

Instructional designs based on cognitive psychology are less structured than those based on behavioral psychology. They allow learners to employ their own cognitive strategies, and they encourage interaction among students. Learning tasks that require problem solving, creative behavior, or cooperative activity lend themselves well to a cognitive instructional approach.

Unlike behaviorists, cognitivists do not limit their definition of learning to observable behavior. They believe that learners learn more than is expressed in immediate behaviors. They may at a later time use knowledge previously learned, but not previously expressed, in building their schemata.

Constructivists, on the other hand, provide a rich learning environment and allow learners to create their own meaning. A rich learning environment can be provided using a variety of media and technology. This is the least structured approach to learning.

Instructors and instructional designers need to develop an eclectic attitude toward competing schools of learning psychology. We are not obliged to swear allegiance to a particular learning theory. We use what works. If we find that a particular learning situation is suited to a behaviorist approach, then we use behaviorist techniques. Conversely, if the situation seems to call for cognitivist or constructivist methods, that is what we use.

Finding a Middle Ground

Throughout this text we recommend an eclectic approach to learning. Inspired by each of the psychological perspectives, designers have developed powerful frameworks for instruction. Indeed, successful instructional practices have features that are supported by virtually all the various perspectives:

- *Active participation*. Effective learning happens when students are actively engaged in meaningful tasks, interacting with the content.
- *Practice*. New learning requires more than one exposure to take root; practice, especially in varying contexts, improves retention rate and the ability to apply the new knowledge, skill, or attitude.
- *Individual differences*. Learners vary in terms of personality, general aptitude, knowledge of a subject, and many other factors; effective methods allow individuals to progress at different rates, cover different materials, and even participate in different activities (Figure 1.1).
- *Feedback*. Learners need to know if their thinking is on track; feedback may be provided by teacher correction of papers, electronic messages from a

Figure 1.1

Technology and media can be designed to provide effective individualized instruction.

computer, the scoring system of a game, or by other means.

- *Realistic contexts.* We are most likely to remember and to apply knowledge that is presented in a real-world context; rote learning leads to "inert knowledge"—we know something but never apply it to real life.
- *Social interaction.* Fellow humans serving as tutors or peer group members can provide a number of pedagogical as well as social supports.

The learning frameworks that we will examine in detail all attempt to incorporate a number of these pedagogical features. Certainly all of them value active participation and interaction. They also encourage learners to use new knowledge, skills, or attitudes by providing for frequent and varied practice. However, they vary in the extent to which they emphasize the other features.

It follows that an eclectic approach is essential when selecting and designing media. Most educators support the cognitivists' emphasis on stimulus-rich materials, confident that students learn more from, say, a video than may be expressed at the time. For example, a high school student may learn about the scientific method during a video of a chemistry experiment even though the objectives for the experiment do not list that topic. A management trainee may learn a great deal about personality differences during a gaming exercise designed to teach an entirely different skill. On the other hand, there are situations, such as teaching basic knowledge (e.g., multiplication tables) or psychomotor skills (e.g.,

keyboarding), which call for the tighter control of behaviorist techniques.

A Philosophical Perspective on Learning

More than a few observers have argued that the widespread use of instructional technology in the classroom leads to treating students as if they were machines rather than human beings—that is, that technology dehumanizes both teaching and learning. Properly used, however, modern instructional technology can individualize and thus humanize this process to a degree previously considered unattainable.

If teachers perceive learners as machines, they will treat them as such, with or without the use of instructional technology and media. If teachers perceive their students as human beings with rights, privileges, and motivations of their own, with or without the aid of technology and media, they will view students as people engaged in learning. In other words, it is the way that technology and media are used, not the technology and media themselves, that tend to mechanize people. Put another way, what is important is not so much what technologies are present in the classroom but rather how the teacher guides students in their use.

Students with a high level of anxiety are prone to make mistakes and to learn less efficiently when under pressure. Many times, stressful learning situations for high-anxiety students make it difficult for them to succeed. Given the same sequence of instruction mediated through technology that will continue only at the command of the students, it may be possible to reduce the pressure. Thus the use of technology can humanize the instruction.

Contrary to what some educators believe, technology and humanism can exist either together or separately in an array of ways. Figure 1.2 suggests four basic combinations of technology and humanism. Here are some examples:

A. A college lecture with little or no interaction between the professor and the students—low in technology and low in humanism.
B. A course consisting of a required series of computer-based lessons, each composed of performance objectives, materials to be used to complete those objectives, and a self-evaluation format—high in technology and low in humanism.
C. Similar to sample B, but students select the topic of study based on their interests and consultation with an instructor. Designed into this instructional system are periodic interactions between student and instructor, discussing the present state of learning and what should be studied next—high in technology and high in humanism.

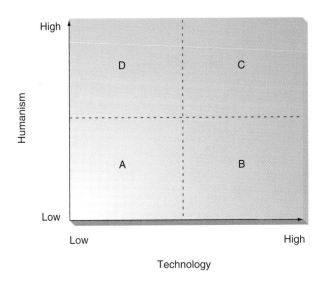

Figure 1.2
Technology and humanism are not opposite ends of a single scale but two different variables, either of which can be high or low.

D. A group meets on a regular basis to discuss common reading assignments—low in technology and high in humanism.

These examples are overly simplified and used only to illustrate the concept, but they serve as a basis for analyzing the relationship between humanism and technology. They illustrate that instruction can be low in both humanism and technology, just as it can be high in both.

Using instructional technology does not preclude a humane teaching/learning environment. On the contrary, instructional media and technologies for learning can help provide a learning atmosphere in which students actively participate. When instructional media and technology are used properly and creatively in the classroom, it is the machines that are turned on and off at will, not the students.

Media

A **medium** (plural, **media**) is a means of communication and source of information. Derived from the Latin word meaning "between," the term refers to anything that carries information between a source and a receiver. Examples include video, television, diagrams, printed materials, computer programs, and instructors. These are considered *instructional media* when they provide messages with an instructional purpose. The purpose of media is to facilitate communication and learning.

For over a hundred years, teachers have used various types of audio and visual aids to help them teach. Recently, teachers have expanded their repertoire of materials and procedures to include the new technologies for learning. The newer learning technologies (products) include the use of computers, compact discs, digital videodiscs (DVDs), satellite communications, and the Internet.

Students are no longer limited to the confines of the classroom. Through the school media center and computer networks such as the Internet and campus intranets, the world becomes each student's classroom.

The media and methods preferred by training directors are often different from those used by teachers. One of the major reasons for this is that schools' curricula are fairly uniform, whereas training programs are often industry specific. Training directors are dealing with adults rather than children and adolescents. Role playing, games, and simulations are used much more frequently in training programs, particularly with management, supervisory, and sales personnel. These people's jobs require a great deal of interaction with people, and the types of training methods that develop relevant skills are given high priority. Trainees will have to call on those skills immediately after the training session and are more likely to become impatient with methods more abstract than the situation demands.

Let's look at six basic types of media used in learning and instruction (Figure 1.3). The most commonly used medium is **text**. Text is alphanumeric characters that may be displayed in any format—book, poster, chalkboard, computer screen, and so on. Another medium commonly used in learning is audio. **Audio** includes anything you can hear—a person's voice, music, mechanical sounds (running car engine), noise, and so on. It may be live or recorded. **Visuals** are regularly used to promote learning. They include diagrams on a poster, drawings on a chalkboard, photographs, graphics in a book, cartoons, and so on. Other types of media are **motion media**. These are media that show motion, including videotape, animation, and so on. One set of material often not considered media are real objects and models. **Manipulatives** are three dimensional and can be touched and handled by students. The sixth and final category of media is **people.** These may be teachers, students, or subject-matter experts. People are critical to learning. Students learn from teachers, other students, and other adults.

When using any media or technology, students and teachers need to be aware of copyright guidelines. See the introduction in "Copyright Concerns: The Copyright Law" (page 11) and the other Copyright Concerns features throughout the text. Suggested readings on copyright appear at the end of this chapter.

The Concrete–Abstract Continuum

Instructional media that incorporate concrete experiences help students integrate prior experience and thus

Text

Audio

Visuals

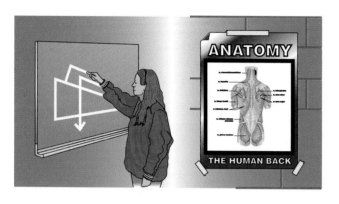

Motion Media

Manipulatives (objects)

People

Figure 1.3
Six basic types of media.

facilitate learning of abstract concepts (Figure 1.4). For example, many students have watched various aspects of the construction of a highway or street. They have seen the machine that lays the asphalt down, they have seen graders at work, and they have seen a number of other stages of road building. However, they need to have all these experiences integrated into a generalized notion of what it means to build a highway. Showing a video that represents all these processes in relation to each other is an ideal way to integrate their various experiences into a meaningful abstraction.

Decisions regarding trade-offs between the concreteness of learning experiences and time constraints have to be made continually by the instructor. In 1946, Edgar Dale developed the "Cone of Experience" (Dale, 1969). In the Cone of Experience we start with the learner as participant in the actual experience, then move to the learner as observer of the actual event, to the learner as observer of an event presented through some medium, and finally to the learner observing symbols that represent an event. Dale contended that learners could make profitable use of more abstract instructional activities to

Copyright Concerns

THE COPYRIGHT LAW

To protect the financial interests of the creators, producers, and distributors of original works of information and art, nations adopt what are referred to as *copyright laws*. **Copyright** refers to the legal rights to an original work. These laws set the conditions under which anyone may copy, in whole or part, original works transmittable in any medium. Without copyright laws, such professionals as writers, artists, and media producers would not "receive the encouragement they need to create the remuneration they fairly deserve for their creations," according to the legislative 1976 Omnibus Copyright Revision Act. The flow of creative work would be reduced to a trickle, and we would all be the losers. For more information, contact your school's library or media specialist or consult references on the subject.

FAIR USE

Fair use is one of the most important exceptions for teachers and students. There are no absolute guidelines for determining what constitutes fair use in an education setting. The law sets forth four basic criteria for determining the principle of fair use:

- The purpose and character of the use, including whether such use is of a commercial nature or is for nonprofit educational purposes (e.g., using a copyrighted work for an educational objective is more likely to be considered fair use than is using it for commercial gain)
- The nature of the copyrighted work (e.g., if the work itself is educational in character, this would tend to support a judgment of fair use)

- The amount and substantiality of the portion used in relation to the copyrighted work as a whole (e.g., using a smaller amount of the total work is more likely to be fair use than using a larger amount)
- The effect of the use on the potential market for or value of the copyrighted work (e.g., if the use negatively impacts potential sales of the original work, this weighs against fair use)

Until the courts decide otherwise, teachers (and media professionals) can use the fair use criteria to decide when to copy materials that would otherwise be protected. Examples follow.

EXAMPLE 1

If the school media center subscribes to a journal or magazine to which you refer students and you make slides of several graphics or photos to help students understand an article, this would be fair use based on the following criteria:

1. The nature of the work is general, and its audience (and market) is not predominantly the educational community.
2. The character of use is nonprofit.
3. The amount copied is minimal.
4. There is no intent to replace the original, only to make it more useful in a class in conjunction with the copyrighted words.

EXAMPLE 2

If you personally subscribe to a journal and include several pictures from it in a presentation in class, it would seem reasonable to do so for the same reasons given in Example 1.

---

the extent that they had built up a stock of more concrete experiences to give meaning to the more abstract representations of reality.

In general, as you move up Dale's Cone of Experience toward the more abstract media, more information can be compressed into a shorter period of time. It takes more time for students to engage in a direct purposeful experience, a contrived experience, or a dramatized experience than it does to present the same information in a videotape, a recording, a series of visual symbols, or a series of verbal symbols.

For example, a field trip can provide a learning experience relatively high in concreteness, but it also takes up a good deal of instructional time, and limited resources in a school district often make it difficult to arrange. A videotape depicting the same experiences as

the field trip will be more abstract, but may be presented to students in a much shorter period of time and with much less effort and money. The greatest amount of information can be presented in the least amount of time through printed or spoken words (the top of the concrete–abstract continuum). But if students do not have the requisite background experience and knowledge to handle these verbal symbols, the time saved in presentation will be time lost in learning.

Psychologist Jerome Bruner, working from a different perspective, devised a descriptive scheme for labeling instructional activities that parallels Dale's. In developing his theory of instruction, Bruner proposed that instruction should proceed from **enactive** (direct) **experience** to **iconic representation** of experience (such as the use of pictures and videotapes) to **symbolic representation**

Figure 1.4

How the instructor integrates technology and media into the lesson is the most important factor in successful learning.

(such as the use of words). He further stated that the sequence in which learners encounter materials has a direct effect on their achieving mastery of the task (Bruner, 1966). Bruner pointed out that this applies to all learners, not just children. When a learning task is presented to adults who have no relevant experiences on which to draw, learning is facilitated when instruction follows a sequence from actual experience to iconic representation to symbolic or abstract representation. As shown in Figure 1.5, Bruner's concepts of enactive, iconic, and symbolic learning may be superimposed on Dale's Cone of Experience.

The Roles of Technology and Media in Learning

Technology and media can serve many roles in learning. The instruction may be dependent on the presence of a teacher (i.e., instructor directed). Even in this situation, media may be heavily used by the teacher. On the other hand, the instruction may not require a teacher. Such student-directed learning is often called *self-instruction*.

Instructor-Directed Learning

A common use of technology and media in an instructional situation is for supplemental support of the "live" in-structor in the classroom (Figure 1.6). Certainly, properly designed instructional media can enhance and promote learning and support teacher-based instruction. But their effectiveness depends on the instructor.

Research has long indicated the importance of the instructor's role in effective use of instructional media. For example, early studies showed that when teachers introduced films, relating them to learning objectives, the amount of information students gained from films increased (Wittich & Fowlkes, 1946).

Later research confirmed and expanded on these original findings. Ausubel (1968), for example, developed the concept of **advance organizers** as an aid to effective instruction. An advance organizer may take the form of an overview of or an introduction to lesson content, a statement of principles contained in the information to be presented, a statement of learning objectives, and so on. Whatever the form, it is intended to create a mindset for reception of instruction.

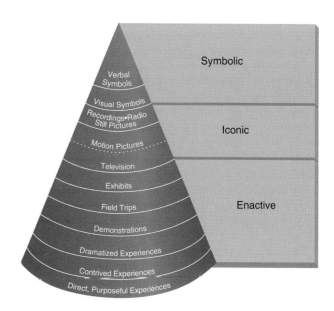

Figure 1.5

Bruner's concepts of enactive, iconic, and symbolic learning may be superimposed on Dale's Cone of Experience.

"The Cone of Experience" from *Audio-Visual Methods in Teaching,* 1st Edition, by Edgar Dale, © 1969. Reprinted with permission of Wadsworth, a division of Thomson Learning. www.thomsonrights.com. Fax 800-730-2215.

Figure 1.6
Instructional media are often used by the classroom teacher to present new information.

Figure 1.7
Carefully designed technology can make independent learning more effective.

Advance organizers can be effective instruments for ensuring that media play their proper role as supplemental supporters of instruction. Many commercially available materials today have built-in advance organizers, which may be used as is or adapted by the instructor. Specific examples from this text include the chapter outline, knowledge objectives, and vocabulary at the beginning of each chapter.

Learner-Directed Learning

Technology and media can also be used effectively in formal education situations where a teacher is not available or is working with other students (Figure 1.7). Media are often "packaged" for this purpose: objectives are listed, guidance in achieving objectives is given, materials are assembled, and self-evaluation guidelines are provided. In informal educational settings, media such as videocassettes and computer courseware can be used by trainees at the worksite or at home. In some instances an instructor may be available for consultation via telephone.

Cooperative learning is closely related to self-instruction. As students work together in groups or in collaboration with the teacher on learning projects, they take more responsibility for learning. Newer technologies such as hypermedia (see Chapter 6) encourage students to rely on their own cognitive strategies in learning. Cooperative learning with hypermedia can lead to stimulating interchanges among students as they go through and discuss their responses to the materials. Hypermedia programs that allow for users to make additions to the information lend themselves particularly well to this type of learning experience. Students report that learning activities with fellow students, as well as with the teacher, help them to gain confidence. This can be a way of building individual responsibility in group work.

The use of learner-directed materials allows teachers to spend more of their time diagnosing and correcting student problems, consulting with individual students, and teaching one on one and in small groups.

How much time the teacher can spend on such activities will depend on the extent of the instructional role assigned to the media. Indeed, under certain circumstances, the entire instructional task can be left to the media. Experimental programs have demonstrated, for example, that an entire course in high school physics can be successfully taught through the use of videotapes and workbooks without direct classroom intervention by the teacher. Successful computer-based courses in calculus have been developed for use by able students whose high schools have no such course.

This is not to say, of course, that instructional technology can or should replace the teacher, but rather that media can help teachers become creative managers of the learning experience instead of merely dispensers of information. Today there are many online resources available to learners and even courses offered through distance learning (see Chapter 7).

Portfolios

A **portfolio** is a collection of student work that illustrates growth over a period of time. Portfolios often include such **artifacts** as student-produced illustrated books, videos, and computer multimedia projects. They usually ask the student to include written reflections on the work. Portfolios might contain the following artifacts:

- Written documents such as poems, stories, or research papers
- Media presentations, such as slide sets or photo essays
- Audio recordings of debates, panel discussions, or oral presentations
- Video recordings of students' athletic, musical, or dancing skills
- Computer multimedia projects incorporating print, data, graphics, and moving images

Students' abilities to prepare mediated presentations that summarize their own understanding of a thematic topic are central to the schooling experience under the concept of portfolios. (See "Developing Media Portfolios" in Classroom Resources, Section C.) Portfolios allow students to do the following:

- Gather, organize, and share information
- Analyze relationships
- Test hypotheses
- Communicate the results effectively
- Record a variety of performances
- Reflect on their learning and activities
- Emphasize their goals, outcomes, and priorities
- Demonstrate their creativity and personality

Educators frustrated with standardized testing and conventional paper-and-pencil assessments are having students demonstrate their achievements by compiling portfolios of their work. Portfolios allow teachers to assess student achievement using samples of student work over time. In addition, portfolios should contain students' reflections about their work. Teachers should select or develop criteria or rubrics for evaluating students' work. These criteria should be distributed prior to the students assembling their portfolios. Many feel that portfolio assessment gives a truer, more rounded view of an individual's strengths and weaknesses. Portfolio assessment is consistent with the constructivist philosophy, which emphasizes that what is important is *the knowledge that students themselves construct*. They claim that the usable residue of years of schooling is rather small, and the small fraction of "school learning" that does remain usable is a conglomeration of information and practical skills that were constructed in the student's own mind through struggle with a meaningful project (Figure 1.8).

The idea of portfolio assessment, then, is to measure students' achievements by their ability to create tangible products exemplifying their accomplishments in terms of analysis, synthesis, and evaluation. Portfolios provide a broad picture of what students know and can do. They

Figure 1.8
Slides, videos, computer-based multimedia, and other student-produced media are included in student portfolios.

can portray both the process and products of student works, as well as demonstrate student growth. Student reflection should be an important component of portfolios. Self-reflection actively involves students in assessing their own learning and actively promotes reflection on their work and abilities.

Electronic portfolios allow students to learn computer skills. You, your students, and their parents can easily compare students' work over several years. Everyone has a more meaningful way of assessing academic performance rather than just using test scores. The use of computer workstations with video and audio digitizing cards, printers, scanners, and digital cameras allows students to produce electronic or digital portfolios. Electronic portfolios are a means of organizing, designing, and viewing traditional styles of portfolios, and are a way of assessing student learning using technology. Physical and social development can be measured as well (Campbell, 1996).

Electronic portfolios have advantages over traditional portfolios in the way they are created and navigated. First, creating electronic portfolios can expand the size of the audience to include other teachers, principals, parents, and students. Online portfolios open the size of the audience to the world. (Be sure to get parental permission before putting any child's materials online. See "Copyright Concerns: Online Materials" in Chapter 8.) Students become more motivated by the larger audience. Photos, video clips, audio recordings, animation, scanned drawings and writings, and hypertext make creating the portfolio more fun and interesting. Students have the opportunity to be creative and exhibit their interests and hobbies. It is easier to satisfy the continual need to add to and update. Storage space is another benefit; rather than file cabinets and shoeboxes, a Zip® disk or CD-ROM can be used to save space. Navigation is another advantage—electronic portfolios are generally better organized and interconnected, allow for multiple paths, are more appealing, and are easily viewed from remote locations (main office, counselor's office, principal's office). Electronic portfolios commonly have a table of contents that make viewing them easier.

Drawbacks are equipment, access, security, and time. To create electronic portfolios with full capabilities hardware is needed: a computer with audio and video capabilities, video camera, digital camera, color scanner, software program, and Internet accessibility. The bare minimum would be a computer and an appropriate software program. Both students and teachers need access to the equipment. Security is a concern when deciding who will have access to the files, such as parents, principals, counselors, teachers, and other students. The project of creating electronic portfolios is time consuming for teachers to learn the program and for teachers and students to input the information. Once the information is in, one has to resize and edit the work to make it presentable.

For some practical tips on assembling and assessing media portfolios, see Kilbane and Milman (2003) or Martin (1999). For additional information on this topic, go to the Web Links module in Chapter 1 of the Companion Website (http://www.prenhall.com/smaldino).

Thematic Instruction

Many teachers are now organizing their instruction around topics or anchors; this is known as **thematic instruction.** Elementary teachers in particular are integrating content and skills from many subjects. At the secondary level, teams of teachers from different content areas are working together to show the overlap of their course content.

These units provide a rich environment or focus within which learning takes place. A good anchor or theme must capture and hold students' attention, provide problem-solving experiences, support interdisciplinary activities, and include a variety of media and technology. Begin the unit with a "shared experience" by having all students read the same book, view a videotape, participate in a simulation, visit a museum, or hear a guest speaker. Then move to "shared expertise," through which students cooperate to gather data and information, analyze their findings, draw conclusions, prepare a group report, and share their results in a mediated presentation. Possible activities include library research, Internet searches, and small-group activities.

Themes used successfully include the Oregon Trail, the Civil War, the Olympics (every four years), the solar system, local history, local industry, travel, holidays (such as Martin Luther King's birthday), and countries.

Distance Education

Distance education is a rapidly developing approach to instruction worldwide. The approach has been widely used by business, industrial, and medical organizations. For many years doctors, veterinarians, pharmacists, engineers, and lawyers have used it to continue their professional education. These individuals are often too busy to participate in classroom-based education. Recently, academic institutions have been using distance education to reach a more diverse and geographically dispersed audience who does not have access to traditional classroom instruction (see Chapter 7 for a full discussion).

The distinguishing characteristic of distance education is the separation of the instructional team and student(s) during learning. As a consequence, the course content must be delivered by instructional media.

The media may be primarily print (books and paper-and-pencil tests), as in traditional correspondence courses. Or, it might involve a variety of technology and media, including audiocassettes, videotapes, videodiscs, and computer courseware sent to individual students. In addition, radio, broadcast television, and teleconferences are utilized for "live" distance education (Figure 1.9). The latter allows for real-time interactive instruction between instructor and students. Computer conferencing enables "conversations" among students who log on at different locations to exchange messages. In addition there are chat rooms, bulletin or discussion boards, and listservs to support distance learning. Computer networks and online courses can be used for distance education (see Chapters 7 and 8).

METHODS

Traditionally, instructional methods have been described as "presentation forms" such as lectures and discussions. In this text, we will differentiate between instructional methods and instructional media. **Methods** are the procedures of instruction selected to help learners achieve the objectives or to internalize the content or message. *Media* then, as already defined, are carriers of information between source and receiver.

We describe in the following paragraphs 10 types of instructional methods. For convenience, we have divided the various methods into two categories. They are those that students control and direct, in which they take the major role, and those in which teachers assume the major role.

Figure 1.9
Students can learn effectively from instructors at a distance via a telecommunications distribution system.

The student-directed methods include discussion, co-operative learning, gaming, simulation, discovery, and problem solving. Teachers usually have a greater responsibility in presentations, demonstrations, drill-and-practice, and tutorials, even though students can do them as well.

Computers can also "take the lead" in many of these methods. Virtually any of the technology and media described throughout this book can be used to implement any of these methods.

Student-Directed Methods

Discussion.   As a method, **discussion** involves the exchange of ideas and opinions among students or among students and teacher. It can be used at any stage of instruction and learning, and in small or large groups. It is a useful way of assessing the knowledge, skills, and attitudes of a group of students before finalizing instructional objectives, particularly if it is a group the instructor has never taught before. In this context, discussion can help the instructor establish the kind of rapport with and within the group that fosters collaborative and cooperative learning.

Discussion can be used to prepare learners for a presentation by arousing their curiosity or by directing their attention to key points. Some media forms are more conducive to discussion during their use than others. For example, viewing a videotape provides a common experience and if it raises appropriate issues gives students something to discuss.

Postpresentation discussions are essential as a forum for questions and answers and for ensuring that all students understand what the instructor intended. They are also critical in helping each learner to internalize the message—to incorporate it into their mental framework. Discussion and student projects are techniques for evaluating the effectiveness of instruction. Although such techniques are useful with all age groups, adult learners in particular welcome the opportunity to participate in sharing experiences with other adults.

Cooperative Learning.   A growing body of research supports the claim that students learn from each other when they work on projects as a team (Slavin, 1989–1990; Harris, 1998). Two or three students at a computer terminal learn more as they carry on discussions while working through the assigned problem. Some computer programs, such as *SimEarth: The Living Planet,* make it possible for several students to work interactively at separate computers.

Many educators have criticized the competitive atmosphere that dominates many classrooms in public schools and higher education. They believe that pitting student against student in the attainment of grades is contrary to the societal requirements of cooperation in life and in most on-the-job situations. Teacher and students often find themselves in a situation where the main emphasis is on test taking and grading. There are other ways to assess student learning, such as the portfolios described earlier in this chapter. Competition in the classroom also interferes with students learning from each other.

Critics of competitive learning urge instead an emphasis on **cooperative learning** as an instructional method. They argue that learners need to develop skills in working and learning together because their eventual workplaces will require teamwork. A common complaint of graduates is that they did not experience working in teams while in school.

Students can learn cooperatively not only by discussing texts and viewing media but also by producing media. For example, the design and production of a video or a slide set as a curriculum project presents an opportunity for cooperative learning. The teacher should be a working partner with the students in such learning situations.

Gaming.   **Gaming** provides a playful environment in which learners follow prescribed rules as they strive to attain a challenging goal. It is a highly motivating tech-

Technology for Diverse Learners

INTRODUCTION

Technology plays an important role in the education of students with exceptionalities. Adapted and specially designed media can contribute enormously to effective instruction of all students and can help them achieve at their highest potential regardless of their innate abilities.

Children with disabilities in particular need special instructional treatment. As a result of inclusion, the number of students with disabilities in the general classroom is increasing. Children with mental retardation need highly structured learning situations because their prior knowledge and ability to incorporate messages into mental constructs is limited. They need to have much more of the message placed within a context with which they are familiar. Students who are hearing or visually impaired require different kinds of learning materials. More emphasis should be placed on audio for students with visual impairments than for other students (Figure 1.10). Adjusting instruction for all exceptional groups requires heavy reliance on media and materials and the appropriate selection of these materials to fit specific purposes. Many teachers have found that many assistive strategies for students with disabilities help all students.

Assistive technologies can be classified as low tech, medium tech, or high tech. For example, a magnifying glass to enlarge printed material for a visually impaired student would be low-tech assistive technology. A mini-booklight to increase illumination would be representative of medium tech. The Kurzweil reader would be an example of high-tech assistive technology.

Diverse learners also include gifted and talented students who, for example, could use videotape and other media to explore topics beyond or in addition to that covered by other students in the class. They can also use the Internet to search for information related to topics being covered in class or for their own personal interests and hobbies. They can be asked to analyze the information

Figure 1.10

The Kurzweil reading machine allows those who are visually impaired to "read" printed material. The device scans the printed page, analyzes letter combinations through a computer, and speaks the words by means of a voice synthesizer.

they locate and to synthesize a class presentation for other students, perhaps using *PowerPoint* and other media and materials.

At the Technology for Education website (http://www.tfeinc.com), teachers and parents can search by category, vendor, or product name for hundreds of assistive tools.

For more information, see the Technology for Diverse Learners features throughout this book, and see Merrill/Prentice Hall's Special Education Resource page. Visit this website through the Web Links module in Chapter 1 of the Companion Website (http://www.prenhall.com/smaldino).

---

nique, especially for tedious and repetitive content. The game may involve one learner or a group of learners (Figure 1.11). Games often require learners to use problem-solving skills or to demonstrate mastery of specific content demanding a high degree of accuracy and efficiency (see Chapter 2).

One common type of instructional game is related to learning about business. Participants form management teams to make decisions regarding a mythical corporation. The team with the highest corporate profits is the winner.

Simulation. **Simulation** involves learners confronting a scaled-down version of a real-life situation. It allows realistic practice without the expense or risks otherwise involved. The simulation may involve participant dialog, manipulation of materials and equipment, or interaction with a computer (see Chapter 2).

Interpersonal skills and laboratory experiments in the physical sciences are popular subjects for simulations. In some simulations learners manipulate mathematical models to determine the effect of changing certain variables, such as controlling a nuclear power

Figure 1.11
Games can be a way for students to be active learners.

plant. Role playing is another common example of the simulation method.

Discovery.   The **discovery** method uses an inductive, or inquiry, approach to learning; it presents problems to be solved through trial and error (Figure 1.12). The aim of the discovery method is to foster a deeper understanding of the content through involvement with it. The rules or procedures that learners discover may be derived from previous experience, based on information in reference books, or stored in a computer database.

Instructional media can help promote discovery or inquiry. For example, videotapes or videodiscs may be used for discovery teaching in the physical sciences. Students view a video to observe the relationships represented in the

visuals and then attempt to discover the principles that explain those relationships. For example, by viewing something as simple as a balloon being weighed before and after being filled with air, students discover that air has weight.

Discovery learning can also assume the form of helping students to seek the information they wish to know about a topic of specific interest to them. Student inquiry, or information research, is a time-consuming but effective method for students to explore knowledge beyond the limits of their textbooks. Such information searches generally lead to the discovery of information that is new to both student and teacher. The library media specialist is an essential ally in guiding students and teachers through their information inquiries, providing assistance on search procedures and guidance in interpreting the information. The library media center provides both content-related materials and media production facilities for students who wish to produce an alternative presentation of what they have learned.

Problem Solving.   Lifelike problems can provide the starting point for learning. In the process of grappling with real-world challenges, students can acquire the knowledge and skills needed after graduation. The technique has evolved from medical education and has moved down through graduate school programs to colleges and now is being used at the high school level and even with elementary students.

Problem solving involves placing students in the active role of being confronted with a novel problem situated in the real world (see "Close-Up: The Ebola Problem"). Students start with limited knowledge, but through peer collaboration and consultation they develop, explain, and defend a solution or position on the problem. It uses reality-based, problem-centered materials that are often presented by media (e.g., written cases, computer-based situations, and videotaped vignettes). As a part of solving the problem, students go to the library media center and/or access computer databases through the Internet.

Learners take more responsibility for their learning as they are placed in the "shoes" (role) of someone facing a real-world problem. The teacher does not present content. Through questioning, the teacher promotes and models practical reasoning and critical thinking. The teacher also facilitates group process and monitors individual learning while being an unobtrusive "guide on the side."

Outcomes include more developed analyzing, problem-framing, problem-solving, and critical-thinking

Figure 1.12
The discovery method involves students in hands-on learning.

Close-Up

THE EBOLA PROBLEM

High school students walked into class recently and found this memo on their desks: You are a United Nations doctor stationed in Brazzaville, Congo. When you arrived at your office this morning a message marked "Urgent" was on your desk from a tribal chieftain in a village 100 miles west of your clinic.

The message read: "Come quickly! This village has been stricken with something no one has seen before. Twenty villagers have terrible fevers, diarrhea, and have become demented. Four have already died a terrible death. The other sixteen sick people have been placed in a hut where we will keep them until you get here. Please help!"

After forming hypotheses about the possible illness that could be affecting the village, the students left their classroom and walked to a darkened classroom, the village hut, where they found fourteen bodies on the floor, cut out of brown wrapping paper. (Yes, the apparent poor arithmetic skills of someone does mean something. An additional death had occurred and a person had left the hut to rejoin the general population.) On each body was a card that listed that person's symptoms. The students had to design a data-gathering plan, establish appropriate precautions for themselves regarding their examination of the afflicted, and organize the data to determine what the villagers might be facing and how far the outbreak had progressed. With help from Tierney's *Current Medical Diagnosis and Treatment* (available in most bookstores), the class decided it was facing an outbreak of ebola and a case of malaria that had been mistakenly grouped with the other sick villagers. The students were then faced with determining what to do for the afflicted and how to prevent the outbreak from spreading.

Source: Consortium for Problem-Based Learning

Figure 1.13
The presentation method allows the teacher to give the same message to all students.

skills. Content knowledge is "learned" so that students can employ it to solve authentic problems. Other outcomes include collaborative learning skills and group skills that are so important in the world of work today.

Teacher-Directed Methods

Presentation. In the **presentation** method, a source tells, dramatizes, or otherwise disseminates information to learners. It is a one-way communication controlled by the source, with no immediate response from or interaction with learners. The source may be a textbook, an audiotape, a videotape, a film, an instructor, and so forth. Reading a book, listening to an audiotape, viewing a videotape, and attending a lecture are examples of the presentation method (Figure 1.13).

Figure 1.14
Demonstrations show a process to be learned or the way something works.

Figure 1.15
Tutorials are one of the most effective instructional methods but one of the most expensive if the tutor's time is included as a cost.

Demonstration.   In this method of instruction, learners view a real or lifelike example of the skill or procedure to be learned (Figure 1.14). **Demonstrations** may be recorded and played back by means of media such as video. If two-way interaction or learner practice with feedback is desired, a live instructor or a tutor is needed.

The objective may be for the learner to imitate a physical performance (such as swinging a golf club or changing the oil in a car) or to adopt the attitudes or values exemplified by someone who serves as a role model. In some cases the point is simply to illustrate how something works, such as the effect of heat on a bimetallic strip. On-the-job training often takes the form of one-on-one demonstration, with the experienced worker showing a new employee how to perform a procedure, such as operating a packaging machine. This arrangement allows questions to be asked and answered so that errors and misperceptions can be resolved.

Drill-and-Practice.   In **drill-and-practice**, learners are led through a series of practice exercises designed to increase fluency in a new skill or to refresh an existing one. Use of the method assumes that learners previously have received some instruction on the concept, principle, or procedure they are to practice. To be effective, the drill and-practice exercises should include feedback to reinforce correct responses and to remediate errors learners might make along the way.

Drill-and-practice is used commonly for such tasks as studying math facts, learning a foreign language, and building a vocabulary. Certain media formats and delivery systems—such as learning laboratory instruction and computer-assisted instruction—lend themselves particularly well to student drill-and-practice exercises. Also, au-

diocassettes can be used effectively for drill-and-practice in spelling, arithmetic, and language instruction.

Tutorial.   In **tutorials,** a *tutor*— in the form of a person, computer software, or special printed materials—presents the content, poses a question or problem, requests a learner's response, analyzes the response, supplies appropriate feedback, and provides practice until the learner demonstrates a predetermined level of competency (Figure 1.15). Tutoring is most often done one on one and is frequently used to teach basic skills, such as reading and arithmetic.

Tutorial arrangements include instructor-to-learner (e.g., Socratic dialog), learner-to-learner (e.g., tutoring or programmed tutoring), computer-to-learner (e.g., computer-assisted tutorial software), and print-to-learner (e.g., branching programmed instruction). These formats are discussed further in Chapters 2, 5 and 6. The computer is especially well suited to play the role of tutor because of its ability to deliver speedily a complex menu of responses to different learner inputs.

TECHNOLOGY

The word **technology** has always had a variety of connotations, ranging from mere hardware to a way of solving problems. The latter is exemplified in the often-quoted definition given by economist John Kenneth Galbraith: "The systematic application of scientific or other organized knowledge to practical tasks" (Galbraith, 1967, p. 12).

The notion of technology being a process is highlighted in the definition of instructional technology given by the leading professional association in that field: "the theory and practice of design, development, utilization, management and evaluation of processes and resources for learning" (Seels & Richey, 1994, p. 9).

Currently when most people hear the word *technology*, they think of products like computers, CD players, and the Space Shuttle. This is one type of technology, which we will refer to as **instructional technology** when it is used for instructional purposes. Examples include computers (see Chapter 5), distance learning hardware (see Chapter 7), and the Internet (see Chapter 8).

When *technology* refers to processes to enhance learning, we will call them **instructional systems**. An instructional system consists of a set of interrelated components that work together, efficiently and reliably, within a particular framework to provide learning activities necessary to accomplish a learning goal. Examples include cooperative learning, simulations, and programmed instruction (see Chapter 2).

The ASSURE model described in Chapter 3 was developed as a planning aid to help ensure that technol-

ogy and media are used to their maximum advantage, not just as interchangeable substitutes for printed or oral messages. The ASSURE model provides a systematic process for creating learning experiences. Contrary to the requirements of research, the requirements of practice demand that the conditions surrounding the use of the materials not be held constant. Indeed, one of the most important roles of technology and media is to serve as a catalyst for change in the whole instructional environment. The effective use of media demands that instructors be better organized in advance, think through their objectives, alter the everyday classroom routine, and evaluate broadly to determine the impact of instruction on mental abilities, feelings, values, interpersonal skills, and motor skills.

Summary: Technology, Media, and Learning

This chapter has introduced you to the foundations that will be important in your study of technology and media as they affect learning. Several perspectives on learning were described. Six basic types of media were introduced. They will be explored in greater detail in later chapters. Likewise, 10 methods for helping learners achieve objectives were presented. The chapter wrapped up with a discussion of technology and the distinction between instructional technologies and instructional systems.

In the next chapter you will learn how to promote the development of new knowledge, skills, or attitudes (learning) through instructional systems. An instructional system is a set of interrelated components that work together to provide learning activities necessary to accomplish a learning goal. The components of all instructional systems include objectives (content to be learned), methods (introduced in this chapter), media (introduced in this chapter), equipment, a learning environment, and people.

Classroom Link Portfolio Activities

Please use the "Classroom Link Portfolio" CD-ROM and the Companion Website as resources in completing these activities. To complete the following activities online go to the Portfolio Activities module in Chapter 1 of the Companion Website (http:// www.prenhall.com/smaldino).

1. *Psychological Analysis of a Lesson.* Select a lesson from the CW, the ASSURE Blueprints on the "Classroom Link Portfolio" CD-ROM, or from the Web. List the elements of the lesson. Indicate how specific portions of the lesson illustrate, if present, the psychological

perspectives addressed in this chapter (behaviorist, cognitivist, constructivist, and social psychology perspectives). Cite the source of the lesson. Reflect on this analysis, providing strengths, weaknesses, and recommendations for teaching this lesson to a specific group of students. (ISTE NETS-T 3.B)

2. *Written Reflection.* Reflect on the four psychological perspectives discussed in the chapter. Give examples of technology lessons based in each from the perspective of a teacher/trainer and as a learner. Which best fits you as a teacher/trainer? As a learner? Why? (ISTE NETS-T 4.B)

Integration Assessments

To complete the specified activities online go to the Integration Assessments module in Chapter 1 of the Companion Website (http:// www. prenhall.com/smaldino).

1. Prepare a report on a topic in the chapter, using references beyond this chapter. The report may be either written or recorded on audiotape. (ISTE NETS-T 5.A)

2. Prepare a 10-minute presentation on your re-action to a topic in the chapter. (ISTE NETS-T 5.C)

3. Analyze an instructional situation (either real or hypothetical) and identify the psychological perspective on learning and the media and methods used. (ISTE NETS-T 5.B)

4. Prepare a short paper on one of the learning theories described in this chapter. Use additional references. (ISTE NETS-T 5.A)

5. Prepare a position paper on the role of humanistic versus technological issues in education. (ISTE NETS-T 5.A)

6. Describe an actual use of instructional technology and/or media in an education or training setting based on your experiences or readings. (ISTE NETS-T 5.C)

References

Ausubel, David. 1968. *Educational psychology*. New York: Holt, Rinehart & Winston.

Bruner, Jerome S. 1966. *Toward a theory of instruction*. Cambridge, MA: Harvard University Press.

Campbell, J. 1996. Electronic portfolios: A five-year history. *Computers and Composition, 13*, 185–194.

Dale, Edgar. 1969. *Audio-visual methods in teaching*, 3rd ed. New York: Holt, Rinehart & Winston.

Driscoll, Marcy P. 2000. *Psychology of learning for instruction*, 2nd ed. Needham Heights, MA: Allyn & Bacon.

Gagné, Robert M. 1985. *The conditions of learning*, 4th ed. New York: Holt, Rinehart, & Winston.

Galbraith, John Kenneth. 1967. *The new industrial state*. Boston: Houghton Mifflin.

Harris, J. 1998. *Virtual architecture*. Eugene, OR: ISTE.

Kilbane, Clare R., and Natalie B. Milman. 2003. *The digital teaching portfolio handbook: A developmental guide for educators*. Boston: Allyn & Bacon.

Martin, Debra B. 1999. *The portfolio planner: Making professional portfolios work for you*. Upper Saddle River, NJ: Merrill/Prentice Hall.

Piaget, Jean. 1977. *The development of thought: Elaboration of cognitive structures*. New York: Viking.

Seels, Barbara B., and Rita C. Richey. 1994. *Instructional technology: The definition and domains of the field*. Washington. DC: Association for Educational Communications and Technology.

Slavin, Robert E. 1989–1990. Research on cooperative learning: Consensus and controversy. *Educational Leadership, 47*(4): 52–54.

———. 1990. *Cooperative learning: Theory, research, and practice*. Upper Saddle River, NJ: Prentice Hall.

Wittich, Walter A., and J. G. Fowlkes. 1946. *Audio-visual paths to learning*. New York: Harper Brothers.

Suggested Readings

Ash, Linda E., and Kay Burke. 2000. *Electronic student portfolios*. Glenview, IL: Pearson Professional Development.

Barron, Ann, and Gary Orwig. 1997. *New technologies for education: A beginner's guide*, 3rd ed. Englewood, CO: Libraries Unlimited.

Bates, T. 2000. Teaching, learning and the impact of multimedia technologies. *Educause Review, 35*(5): 38–43.

Bauer, J. W., E. R. Ellefsen, and A. M. Hall. 1994. A model for using anchored instruction in preservice educational technology classes. In *Technology and teacher education annual*. Charlottesville, VA: AACE.

Becker, Gary H. 1997. *Copyright: A guide to information and resources*, 2nd ed. Lake Mary, FL: Gary H. Becker. (P.O. Box 951870, Lake Mary, FL 32795-1870.)

Bielfefeld, A., and L. Cheeseman. 1997. *Technology and copyright law: A guidebook for the library, research, and teaching professions*. New York: Neal-Schuman.

Botterbush, Hope Roland. 1996. *Copyright in the age of new technology*. Bloomington, IN: Phi Delta Kappa Educational Foundation.

Brown, James M. 2002. Enhancing on-line learning for individuals with disabilities. *New Directions for Teaching and Learning, 91:* 61–68.

Bruwelheide, Janis. 1995. *The copyright primer for librarians and educators*, 2nd ed. Chicago: American Library Association.

Burrill, G. 1997. Algebra for the twenty-first century: A new vision. *NASSP Bulletin, 81* (586): 11–16.

Casey, J. M. 1997. *Early literacy: The empowerment of technology*. Englewood, CO: Libraries Unlimited.

Cole, D. J., C. W. Ryan, F. Kick, and B. K. Mathies. 1999. *Portfolios across the curriculum and beyond*. Thousand Oaks. CA: Corwin.

Eddy, J., J. Brunett, D. Spaulding, and S. Murphy. 1997. Technology assisted education. *Education, 117*(3): 478–480.

Ertmer, P., and T. Newby. 1993. Behaviorism, cognitivism, constructivism: Comparing critical features from an instructional design perspective. *Performance Improvement Quarterly, 6*(4): 50–72.

Goldsby, Dianne, and Minaz Fazal. 2001. Now that your students have created web-based digital portfolios, how do you evaluate them? *Journal of Technology and Teacher Education, 9*(4): 607–616.

Gordon, David T. 2000. *Digital classroom: How technology is changing the way we teach and learn.* Cambridge. MA: Harvard Education Publishing Group.

Hoadley, D., and M. Hoadley. 1993. Copyright: Rights and liabilities of authors and users of multimedia presentations. *Technology and teacher education annual.* Charlottesville, VA: AACE.

Jonassen, David. 1999. Designing constructivist learning environments. In *Instructional-design theories and models.* Vol. 2, edited by Charles M. Reigeluth. Mahwah, NJ: Lawrence Erlbaum Associates.

Jonassen, David H., Jane Howland, Joi Moore, and Rose M. Marra. 2002. *Learning to solve problems with technology: A constructivist perspective,* 2nd ed. Upper Saddle River, NJ: Merrill/Prentice Hall.

Kilbane, C., and N. Milman. 2003. *What every teacher should know about creating digital teaching portfolios.* Boston: Allyn & Bacon.

Lapp, D., J. Flood, and D. Fisher. 1999. Intermediality: How the use of multiple media enhances learning. *The Reading Teacher, 52*(7): 776–780.

Lindaman, C. A., and S. W. Bishop. 1997. Tech labs. *The Science Teacher, 64*(3): 18.

Mahoney, Jim. 2002. *Power and portfolios: Best practices for high school classrooms.* Portsmouth, NH: Heinemann.

Male, Mary. 2002. *Technology for inclusion: Meeting the special needs for all students,* 4th ed. Boston: Allyn & Bacon.

Miller, J. K. 1990. *Using copyrighted videocassettes in classrooms, libraries, and training centers,* 2nd ed. Friday Harbor, VA: Copyright Information Press.

Mundell, Susan B., and Karen DeLario. 1994. *Practical portfolios: Reading, writing, math, and life skills, grades 3–6.* Englewood, CO: Libraries Unlimited.

Olsen, D. G. 1999. Constructivist principles of learning and teaching methods. *Education 120*(2): 347–355.

Purves, A. C. 1996. Electronic portfolios. *Computers and Composition, 13,* 135–146.

Rose, Lane. 1995. *Netlaw: Your rights in the online world.* Berkeley, CA: Osborne McGraw-Hill.

Scherer, Marcia J. 2003. *Connecting to learn: Educational and assistive technology for people with disabilities.* Washington, DC: American Psychological Association.

Schipper, B., and J. Rossi. 1997. *Portfolios in the classroom: Tools for learning and instruction.* York, ME: Stenhouse.

Schramm, Wilbur. 1977. *Big media, little media.* Beverly Hills, CA: Sage.

Schunk, D. H. 2000. *Learning theories: An educational perspective,* 3rd ed. Upper Saddle River, NJ: Merrill/Prentice Hall.

Scott, J. L., and M. Sarkees-Wircenski. 1996. *Overview of vocational and applied technology education.* Homewood, IL: American Technical Publishers.

Simpson, Carol. 2002. Copyright 101. *Educational Leadership, 59*(4): 36–38.

Sinofsky, E. 1994. *A copyright primer for educational and industrial media producers,* 2nd ed. Bloomington, IN: Association for Educational Communications and Technology.

Soloman, K. 1993. Copyright issues and distance learning. *Teleconference, 12*(1): 18–21.

Sunstein. B. S., and J. H. Lovell, eds. 2000. *The portfolio standard: How students can show us what they know and are able to do.* Portsmouth, NH: Heinemann.

Thorson, B. 1998. *Integrating technology into the curriculum.* Westminster, CA: Teacher Created Materials.

User's guide to Folio Live: Electronic portfolio tool. 2003. Boston: McGraw-Hill.

Walmsley, Sean. 1996. Ten ways to improve your theme teaching. *Instructor* (August): 54–60.

Instructional Systems

Outline

Knowledge Objectives

1. Define *instructional systems,* including four components.
2. Describe five characteristics of instructional systems.
3. Relate practice and feedback to instructional systems.
4. Compare and contrast two different types of cooperative learning technologies.
5. Define *game* and *simulation* and properly classify examples of each.
6. Describe programmed instruction and distinguish it from other instructional systems.
7. Generate five guidelines for using programmed instruction in the classroom.
8. Describe programmed tutoring and distinguish it from other instructional systems.
9. Identify two advantages of programmed tutoring that distinguish it from programmed instruction.

Professional Vocabulary

instructional system	simulator
synchronous	role play
asynchronous	simulation game
packaged instruction	cooperative game
cooperative learning	programmed instruction
game	linear programming
frame game	branching programming
simulation	programmed tutoring

Learning doesn't happen by "magic"! There are important decisions that teachers must make to ensure learning. As stated in Chapter 1, *learning* is the development of new knowledge, skills, or attitudes as an individual interacts with information and the environment. We will look at instructional systems (processes) including the media and methods that were discussed in Chapter 1. They are applications of technology to aid learning. As you will see, instructional systems promote learning regardless of the subject matter, the learners, or the learning environment.

We discuss the following instructional systems in this chapter: cooperative learning, games, simulations, simulation games, programmed instruction, and programmed tutoring. The components of all instructional systems include objectives (content to be learned), methods, media, equipment, a learning environment, and people. Each of these components will be described in detail in later chapters. As a result of studying this chapter and others, you will learn to design, implement, and evaluate instructional systems.

INSTRUCTIONAL SYSTEMS

An **instructional system** consists of a set of interrelated components that work together, effectively and reliably, within a particular framework to provide learning activities necessary to accomplish a learning goal.

The many types of instructional systems fall into a number of categories—classroom course (live, face-to-face), broadcast course (television and radio), self-instructional package (self-study), Web-based instruction (intranet/Internet), laboratory activities, workshop, seminar, field trip, computer courseware (computer-based training/desktop multimedia), and teleconferencing. Just as an entertainment system has many interrelated components, so do instructional systems. We examine those components next.

Components of an Instructional System

Just as an entertainment system aims to have a particular effect on a given audience, an instructional system has an objective (knowledge, skills, and attitudes to be taught). The *objective* is what you want to teach and/or what the student wants to learn. The goals and objectives will often indicate the nature of the message and learning activities. Communicating the message and giving learners the opportunity to practice the skills or to construct their own knowledge involves methods, media, and often equipment. There is also an environment (facilities/settings) where the learning takes place. And unless it is a self-instructional activity, people are directly involved, including the student, instructor, teacher, trainer, media specialist, technology coordinator, and others.

Let's look at each of these components in more detail. The following methods were discussed in Chapter 1: discussion, cooperative learning, games, simulation/role play, discovery/inquiry, problem solving, presentation, demonstration, drill-and-practice, and tutorials. These methods lead to specific activities such as case studies, conference (live or electronic chat room), brainstorming, self-study, panels, coaching, reading, projects, lecture, debate, and cooperative learning/collaboration.

To incorporate many of these methods into an instructional system, media are required. In Chapter 1 we discussed audio (person's voice/music/recorded sound), visuals (still pictures/graphics/diagrams/cartoons), motion media (video/animation), manipulatives (real, model, or virtual objects), text (alphanumeric characters), and people (live or telecommunicated). These media are presented via specific materials such as printed materials (e.g., textbooks, manuals, etc.), visual recordings (videotapes, CD-ROM, DVD, etc.), audio recordings (audio-cassettes, CDs, etc.), computer programs, and overhead transparencies.

Many of these materials cannot be used by themselves. They may require equipment such as computers, satellite networks, television receivers, telephone lines, display surfaces (e.g., marker boards, chalkboards, flipchart holders, erasable or electronic whiteboards), projectors (e.g., computer, overhead, film, video), players (e.g., audio cassette recorders/players, VCR, CD player, DVD player), and bulletin boards (actual or electronic). Various types of equipment are dis-

cussed throughout the text, particularly in Classroom Resources, Section B.

Simply stated, the *learning environment* is the setting or physical surroundings in which learning is expected to take place. The environment is sometimes referred to as the *facilities* or *setting*. Learning can take place in a variety of settings in addition to the classroom. It also occurs in the laboratory (computer lab, science lab, or language lab), library, media center, playground, field trip site, theatre, study hall, and at home. Learning environments vary in size, layout, lighting, and seating arrangement, among other things.

A very important component of most instructional systems is people. Unless it is a self-instructional activity, people are directly involved. Even for mediated materials, some professionals consider the producer of the materials to be part of the instructional system. Other personnel might include the teacher in P–12 systems, the professor in postsecondary education, the trainer in business and industrial environments, the media specialist, the technology coordinator, and others. Personnel includes instructional as well as support personnel (Figure 2.1).

Characteristics of an Instructional System

Instructional systems have many characteristics in addition to and different from their components. For example, instruction may be one-way receptive (attending a presentation or reading a book) or two-way interaction (communication with other students and the instructor). In addition, an instructional system may be synchronous or asynchronous. **Synchronous** instruction is when learners must be present for the instruction at the

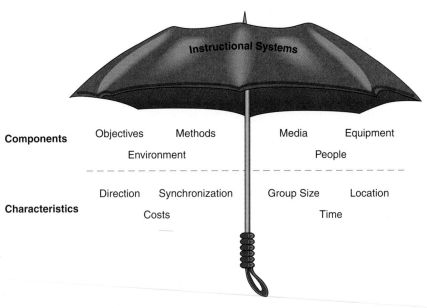

Figure 2.1
The components and characteristics of most instructional systems.

same time. Examples would include a classroom presentation or a live television broadcast (not videotape). Synchronous instruction is of two types. The first is live, face-to-face, as in the classroom example. It occurs at the same time and the same place for all learners. The other type is often referred to as *distance learning* (see Chapter 7). The instruction takes place at the same time, but the learners can be in different places. A live television course can be broadcast around the world by satellite. Unless it is recorded, learners must view it simultaneously regardless of their location.

If the television course is recorded on videotape, then it is asynchronous instruction. **Asynchronous** instruction allows different learners to experience the same content at different times. One of the earliest examples of asynchronous instruction is the book, which also is an example of packaged instruction. (Other examples are instruction delivered by computer courseware and videotape.) **Packaged instruction** lets students control when and sometimes where they choose to learn.

As you are designing an instructional system, you must also consider other characteristics, for example, group size (large, medium, small, individual), time (same time, different time), and location of the learners (same location, different locations). See "Analyzing or Designing an Instructional System," in Classroom Resources, Section C.

Categories of Instructional Systems

Effective instruction derives from well-established principles from instructional psychology. As mentioned in Chapter 1, successful instruction, regardless of the psychological perspective—behaviorist, cognitivist, constructivist, or social psychologist—may incorporate a number of common principles:

- Active participation and interaction
- Practice
- Individualized instruction
- Reinforcement or feedback
- Realistic context
- Cooperative groups

To determine whether a particular attempt to apply such principles in an instructional system actually works, instructional designers try out rough drafts or prototypes with pilot-test groups of learners to find out what works and what needs revising. Revision and testing with various groups determines whether the system is both effective (accomplishes what it claims) and reliable (works with different audiences under different circumstances).

Each of the instructional systems discussed in this chapter has been subjected to extensive testing, both in the form of formal "method A versus method B" experimental comparisons and in the form of qualitative observations. We will discuss the specific research in conjunction with each system. What is notable is that the systems discussed here have demonstrated the most dramatic positive outcomes of any ideas ever studied in educational research. Innovative pedagogical techniques (e.g., text-embedded questions, advance organizers, supplementary media) typically demonstrate an improvement in average student achievement of a few points in percentile rank. But these instructional systems typically show an increase of 15, 20, or more points; that is, the average student scores at the 50th percentile in conventional instruction but scores at or near the 65th percentile in the group taught with one of the instructional systems (Cohen, Kulik, & Kulik, 1982).

Over time, educators have invented a variety of frameworks or templates for instructional systems, from live, self-contained classes to cooperative learning groups and computer-based simulations, among others.

For those familiar with computers, the concept of an operating system (*Windows,* for example) might be a helpful analogy to explain what we mean by a framework or template. An operating system consists of a package of rules and procedures that provides a standardized, consistent pattern for using the computer. Once this template is installed, the user doesn't have to rethink and reinvent procedures for processing data. In a similar way, instructional systems are packages of tested and proven procedures, ready to be "loaded" with some specific content and to lead learners through a particular kind of learning experience.

Each of these instructional systems is designed to overcome one or more of the shortcomings of traditional whole-class instruction. All of them directly address the problem of passivity in that they place the learner in direct, active engagement with the subject matter. The whole point of these instructional systems is to require learner participation. These systems combat boredom by providing a change of pace from lecture and seatwork and by adding motivational features that excite learner interest. They also provide a means for individualizing instruction to a greater degree. Some of the systems discussed in this chapter are specifically designed as independent study methods, allowing individuals to progress at their own pace. Others are designed to be used in small groups; as such, they enlist the energies of students to assist those who need extra explanation, coaching, and practice.

All of these instructional systems center on the provision of ample opportunities for practice, as discussed in Chapter 3. Their creators were guided by different theoretical perspectives, so they have different rationales for doing so. All the systems discussed here emphasize active and continuous practice of relevant knowledge, skills, and attitudes, and all, as part of the total system, provide for rapid, effective feedback. Many of them are driven by the search for ways to build interpersonal feedback into all instruction.

Cooperative Learning

Cooperative learning involves small heterogeneous groups of students working together to achieve a common academic goal or task while working together to learn collaboration and social skills. Group members are *interdependent*—that is, each is dependent on the others for achieving their goal, and all are responsible for each other's learning as well as their own. As an instructional system, cooperative learning involves active participation by all students. Individual differences among students are minimized as they practice the content and social skills. These should be practiced in a realistic, often simulated context while receiving feedback from peers, the teacher, or a computer.

Cooperative learning has gained momentum in both formal and informal education from two converging forces: first, the practical realization that life outside the classroom requires more and more collaborative activity, from the use of teams in the workplace to everyday social life; and second, a growing awareness of the value of social interaction in making learning meaningful.

Advantages

- *Active learning.* Cooperative learning "requires" students to actively interact with others.
- *Social skills.* Students learn to interact with others, developing their interpersonal, communication, leadership, compromise, and collaboration skills.
- *Interdependence.* Positive interdependence and accountability are developed as students interact to reach a common goal.
- *Individual accountability.* When a group's success depends on the input of each individual in it, individuals learn to be accountable for their actions. Cooperative learning systems often utilize a mechanism for assessing both individual students and the group as a whole.

Limitations

- *Student compatibility.* It is sometimes difficult to form groups of students who will work together well. The teacher must know her students well to form groups that will function effectively.
- *Student dependency.* A teacher who allows the best students to "carry" the others may create dependency and defeat the purpose of cooperative learning. The challenge is to devise management systems that require learners to truly collaborate.
- *Time consuming.* Cooperative learning requires more time to cover the same amount of content than do some other methods.
- *Individualists.* Individuals who prefer to work independently do not like cooperative learning.

- *Logistical obstacles.* The teacher must arrange a lot of information, student responsibilities, and assessment activities.

Integration

The notion of students working together in small groups is not new, but ensuring that their efforts are truly collaborative has recently become a point of emphasis. For example, in the past, five students might have been assigned to a project team to prepare a report on Peru. One researched the pre-Columbian Incas, another gathered pictures of llamas, the third prepared a report on the Peru Current and fishing, while the others gathered clothing and food items to give atmosphere to their final presentation. Note that although their efforts were pooled at the end, most of the work was done independently.

Today's notion of cooperative learning entails a deeper level of interaction, based on the principle that articulating and negotiating your ideas with others forces you to process information in a way that improves meaningfulness and retention. We can define this new concept of *cooperative learning* as the instructional use of small groups so that students work together to maximize their own and each other's learning.

Research by David and Roger Johnson (1993) and Robert Slavin (1990) has revealed that not only does cooperative learning yield better acquisition and retention of lesson content, but it also promotes better interpersonal and thinking skills. This research has highlighted the importance of *interdependence* as the key to success in cooperative learning. That is, group members must have a stake in each other's understanding and mastery of the material.

Researchers have devised and validated various specific cooperative learning formats. They are discussed here as instructional systems because they fit the definition: each provides a specific template, expressed in the form of operating rules, procedures, and materials; these templates are structured enough that teachers working in different circumstances can implement them successfully; and they have been validated through field testing.

Students can learn cooperatively not only by being taught with materials but also by producing materials themselves. For example, elementary students can work together to design and produce a videotape or a *PowerPoint* presentation on a topic related to historical content being studied. The students can share their cooperatively developed materials with the rest of the class.

In a science lab, middle school students work together as detectives to determine the nature of an unknown substance. In each group, one student is assigned to search the Internet, another goes to the library for background research, and others design and conduct experiments on the substance. Together they pool their information to come to a combined, cooperative solution.

High school students in an art appreciation course work together in cooperative groups to learn about the different forms of creative art. Each group is composed of three students. One is accomplished at a musical instrument, another has the ability to paint, and a third has the ability to sculpt. The group's task is to learn about the different art forms and their relationships.

Computer-Based Cooperative Learning

Computer assistance can alleviate some of the logistical obstacles to using cooperative learning methods, particularly the tasks of managing information, allocating different individual responsibilities, presenting and monitoring instructional material, analyzing learner responses, administering tests, and scoring and providing remediation for those tests (Figure 2.2).

Mentioned earlier was the critical problem of ensuring that learners recognize their interdependence. Some software programs parcel out different information to different individuals so that they have to constantly check with each other and pool their information to make good decisions. Other programs provide information or give feedback only in displays that are flashed for a limited period of time. Group members are forced to delegate responsibility for watching for certain kinds of messages if they are to succeed. Each member has something different and essential to contribute to the group deliberations.

Group-oriented programs of this sort can also deal with the logistical problems of assisting a number of groups simultaneously, as is necessary in the single-computer classroom. The software manages a rotation of the teams so that there is little time lost waiting in line.

Decisions, Decisions (see "Media Files: Computer Software 2" in Chapter 5) is a series of role-playing software packages by Tom Snyder Productions designed specifically to generate informed discussion and decision making in the classroom using only one computer. The program has a mode for whole-class discussion with the teacher leading the entire group, as in a traditional classroom. In addition, it offers a small-group option for managing a cooperative learning environment.

Online Collaborative Learning

In addition to computer-based collaborative learning, it is also possible to use the Internet for online collaborative learning. The Internet allows students from different schools to work collaboratively.

Such learning can involve students sharing data or collectively creating a report or paper. The students might be able to meet (in person or online) with an expert in the area of study to gain additional information or to share their conclusions. They can share responsibility for preparing the project or report, much like they would do in a face-to-face collaborative activity.

For example, *ThinkQuest* (http://www. thinkquest. org) provides an opportunity for students and teachers to work collaboratively in teams both to learn as they create Web-based learning materials and to teach others. ThinkQuest Inc. is a nonprofit organization that offers programs designed to advance education through the use of technology. It involves participants from around the world who contribute to the success of online collaborative learning programs.

GAMES

The terms *game, simulation,* and *simulation game* are often used interchangeably. But because these terms have different meanings, we will discuss them separately here (Figure 2.3). A **game** is an activity in which participants follow prescribed rules that differ from those of real life as they strive to attain a challenging goal.

The distinction between play and reality is what makes games entertaining. Most people seem to enjoy setting aside the logical rules of everyday life occasionally and entering an artificial environment with different dynamics. For example, in chess the markers each have arbitrarily different movement patterns based roughly on the military potentials of certain societal roles in some ancient time. Players capture each other's markers by observing elaborate rules of play rather than simply reaching across the board to grab the marker.

Attaining the goal usually entails competition—individual against individual, as in chess; group against

Figure 2.2
Increasingly, computer-mediated instruction can be a cooperative learning activity.

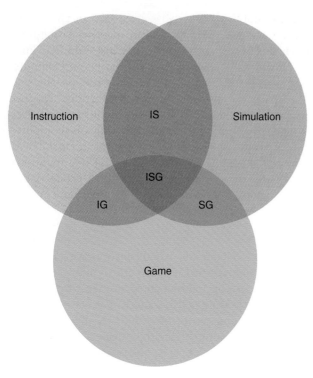

Figure 2.3

Game, simulation, and instruction are separate concepts. However, they do overlap, so a particular activity could be an instructional simulation (IS), an instructional game (IG), a simulation game (SG), or even an instructional simulation game (ISG).

group, as in basketball; or individual against a standard, as in golf (with "par" as the standard). With computer games, players typically are competing against their own previous scores and ultimately against the designer of the game as they approach mastery.

To be challenging, goals should have a probability of achievement of approximately 50 percent. A goal that is always or never attained presents no real challenge; the outcome is too predictable. People exhibit the most interest and motivation when the challenge is in the intermediate range.

On the other hand, striving to attain a challenging goal does not necessarily have to involve competition. Communication games, fantasy games, and encounter games exemplify a whole array of activities in which participants agree to suspend the normal rules of interpersonal communication to pursue such goals as self-awareness, empathy, sensitivity, and leadership development. These activities are considered games but do not entail competition. There is a movement today toward developing cooperative games designed to foster creativity and collaborative decision making. These games combine the elements of cooperative learning with the elements of games. We discuss cooperative simulation games later in this chapter.

Because individuals react differently to competitive environments, the element of competition must be handled very thoughtfully in choosing and using instructional games. Individual-versus-individual competition can be a highly motivating device as long as the contenders are fairly matched and the conflict does not overshadow the educational objective. Group-versus-group competition entails the same cautions, but it has the added attraction of providing practice in cooperation and teamwork. When you carefully organize competitions to ensure fair matches, you can foster highly successful and highly personalized learning.

For instructional purposes, competition involving the individual or team against a given standard is often the safest approach. It allows individualization because different standards can be set for different players. In fact, one of the most effective standards can be the student's own past performance, the goal being to raise the level of aspiration continually.

In any event, in cases in which competition is an element, the scoring system provides a clue as to what type of competition you are fostering. Is one individual or team declared the winner? Or is it possible for all players to attain equally high scores, making everyone a winner? Some instructional games are designed to encourage players to decide among themselves what criteria to apply in determining success.

Games can incorporate the common features of behaviorism, cognitivism, constructivism, and social psychology. Students enjoy actively participating in games. Games provide the opportunity to practice content, such as math facts, vocabulary, and problem-solving skills. Individual differences are accommodated, particularly in team games. Students receive feedback based on the consequences of their actions, answers, and decisions. Games do not necessarily take place in realistic contexts. There is no real-world counterpart to tic-tac-toe or bingo. Games based on realistic contexts are called *simulation games*. Most games provide social interactivity. The exception is solitaire-type games in which players compete against themselves or prescribed standards and do not interact with other players or team members. Games may be paper based or computer based (see "Media Files: Simulations and Games" in this chapter and also see Chapter 5).

Advantages

- *Attractive*. Games provide attractive frameworks for learning activities. They are attractive because they are fun! Children and adults alike tend to react positively to an invitation to play (Figure 2.4).
- *Novel*. As a departure from normal classroom routine, games arouse interest because of their novelty.
- *Atmosphere*. The pleasant, relaxed atmosphere fostered by games can be especially helpful for those (such as low achievers) who avoid other types of structured learning activities.

- *Time on task.* Games can keep learners interested in repetitive tasks, such as memorizing multiplication tables. What would otherwise be tedious drill becomes fun.

Limitations

- *Competition.* Competitive activities can be counterproductive for students who are less interested in competing or who are weak in the content or skill being practiced.
- *Distraction.* Without careful management and debriefing, students can get caught up in the excitement of play and fail to focus on the real objectives.
- *Poor design.* To be instructionally meaningful the game activity must provide actual practice of the intended academic skill. A fatal shortcoming of poorly designed games is that players spend a large

portion of their time waiting for their turn, throwing dice, moving markers around a board, and performing similar trivial actions.

Integration

Instructional games are particularly well suited to the following:

- Attainment of cognitive objectives. Particularly amenable are those involving recognition, discrimination, or memorization, such as grammar, phonics, spelling, arithmetic skills, formulas (in chemistry, physics, logic), basic science concepts, place names, terminology, and so on.
- Adding motivation to topics that ordinarily attract little student interest. Examples are grammar rules, spelling, and math drills.

Close-Up

GAMES IN ELEMENTARY MATHEMATICS

Mathematics Pentathlon is a series of 20 instructional games that motivate the development and practice of mathematics concepts and skills. Designed for grades K–7, the games also promote active problem solving, especially the ability to solve problems that are continually undergoing change.

Classroom use of the program involves students in cooperative communication; in the integration of spatial, logical, and computational reasoning; and in the use of a variety of mathematics manipulatives to foster conceptual understanding.

The program also offers tournament competition. Tournaments are organized into four divisions combining two grade levels in each: Division I, K–1; Division II, 2–3; Division III, 4–5; and Division IV, 6–7. Within each division, individuals or teams compete in five different games; hence the name *pentathlon*. This phase of the program involves the entire educational community and offers students the unique opportunity to balance cooperation with constructive competition.

Mathematics Pentathlon relates to a mathematics curriculum and staff development program known as Mathematics Experience-Based Approach (MEBA). MEBA fosters mathematical understanding by building deliberate connections between physical models, pictures, and symbols and associated concepts and procedures. It also helps learners form and use mental images in solving problems.

MEBA and the associated games are designed to give students practice in nonroutine problem solving—that is, using heuristics to solve problems where known, routine procedures don't work. Ex-

amples of heuristics exercises include building a model or drawing a picture of the problem, finding a simple problem that is analogous to the one being studied, working backwards, and breaking the problem into its subcomponents.

For further information, contact Mary Gilfeather, Pentathlon Institute, Inc., P.O. Box 20590, Indianapolis, IN 46220.

Close-Up

GAMES FOR TEACHING READING

Reading is generally the most emphasized skill at the elementary school level. It is also a subject in which a great deal of practice and a high degree of individualization are necessary. For these reasons, reading teachers find game playing to be an especially valued method.

Featured here are several games involving decoding and comprehension skills. They have been reviewed and recommended by Dixie Lee Spiegel, instructional resources reviewer for *The Reading Teacher.*

DECODING

Road Race (Curriculum Associates) is a board game for two to six players. Players move markers around a track based on the number of words they have made and read. Players roll 10 dice with word parts on them (e.g., *-ight, -ake, -en*) and make words by matching the dice with the letters, digraphs, or blends written on the game board. Players who are waiting their turn can challenge words made by others.

Word Trek (DLM) is a board game for two to four players. In this game, players are dealt eight empty pockets for holding word-family cards. They draw cards containing blends and digraphs and try to form words; if not challenged, they place the words in the pocket until someone completes eight of them. The opportunity to challenge keeps other players involved.

COMPREHENSION

Context Clues (Learning Well) provides practice in determining the meaning of a difficult word encountered in sentence context. The game comes in basic and intermediate versions.

Cause and Effect (Opportunities for Learning, Inc.) provides challenging practice in differentiating between causes and effects. The player reads a paragraph and chooses a cause for a given effect, or vice versa. The game comes in two levels: basic and intermediate.

Spiegel cautions that with many games of this type the teacher must anticipate modifying the materials to make them more instructionally effective. In *Cause and Effect*, players are not required to read at every turn. Because many of the squares on the game board are blank, players can advance without reading. Spiegel simply changed the rules of play so that every square required reading, and the originally designated reading squares were given double value.

Source: Dixie Lee Spiegel, "Instructional Resources: Decoding and Comprehension Games and Manipulatives," The Reading Teacher, 44(3) (November 1990), pp. 258–261.

- Small-group instruction. Games can provide structured activities that students or trainees can conduct by themselves without close instructor supervision.
- Basic skills. Sequence, sense of direction, visual perception, number concepts, and following rules, for example, can be developed by means of card games.
- Vocabulary building. Various commercial games, such as *Boggle, Fluster, Scrabble,* and *Probe,* have been used successfully by teachers to expand spelling and vocabulary skills, although they were designed and are marketed primarily for recreational purposes.

Adapting the Content of Instructional Games

Although most teachers do not design new instructional games from scratch, they often adapt existing games by changing the subject matter while retaining the game's structure. The original game is referred to as a **frame game** because its framework lends itself to multiple adaptations. When one is modifying a frame game, the underlying structure of a familiar game provides the basic procedure of play, or the dynamics of the process. The designer loads the desired content onto a convenient frame (Stolovitch & Thiagarajan, 1980).

Figure 2.4
Game playing appeals to young and old alike.

Familiar games such as *Tic-tac-toe, Rummy, Concentration,* and *Jeopardy,* which were intended for recreation rather than instruction, can serve as potential frameworks for your own instructional content. Some television game shows have been modeled after such parlor games; they can suggest additional frameworks. Here are some sample adaptations:

- *Safety tic-tac-toe.* Use a three-by-three grid; each row represents a place where safety rules pertain to home, school, and street; each column represents the level of question difficulty. Teams take turns selecting and trying to answer safety-related questions, attempting to fill in three squares in a row.
- *Spelling rummy.* Using alphabet cards instead of regular playing cards, players attempt to spell short words following the general rules of rummy.
- *Reading concentration.* This game uses about a dozen matched picture–word pairs of flashcards. Cards are placed face down. On each turn the player turns over two cards, seeking to match a pair. This game exercises both reading ability and memorizing.
- *Word bingo.* Each player's card has a five-by-five grid with a vocabulary word (perhaps in a foreign language) in each square. The leader randomly selects words; players then seek the words on their boards, and if they are found, the square is marked. The winner is the first player with five correctly marked squares in a row.

SIMULATIONS

A **simulation** is an abstraction or simplification of some real-life situation or process. In simulations, participants

usually play a role that involves them in interactions with other people or with elements of the simulated environment. A business management simulation, for example, might put participants into the role of production manager of a mythical corporation, provide them with statistics about business conditions, and direct them to negotiate a new labor contract with the union bargaining team.

Simulations can vary greatly in the extent to which they fully reflect the realities of the situation they are intended to model. A simulation that incorporates too many details of a complex situation might be too complicated and time consuming for the intended audience. On the other hand, if the model is oversimplified, it may fail completely to communicate its intended point. A well-designed simulation provides a faithful model of elements that are most salient to the immediate objective, and it informs the instructor and participants about elements that have been simplified or eliminated.

Simulations are by design active. They are not a "spectator sport." Simulations provide realistic practice with feedback in a realistic context. Most simulations include social interaction. One type of simulation, role play, provides relatively open-ended social interaction between and among individuals. However, there are some simulations, such as flight simulators, in which there is no social interaction. Team simulations allow students to use their individual differences. Some computer-based simulations adjust their difficulty level based on the ability of the "player."

Advantages

- *Realistic.* The prime advantage of simulations is that they allow practice of real-world skills under conditions similar to those in real life.
- *Safe.* Learners can practice risky activities—for example, cardiopulmonary resuscitation—without risking injury to themselves or to others.
- *Simplified.* Simulations are intended to capture the essential features of a situation without dwelling on details that might be distracting or too complex for the learner's current level of understanding.

Limitations

- *Time consuming.* Simulations are often used with problem-based learning methods, allowing learners to immerse themselves in a problematic situation and to experiment with different approaches. Such trial-and-error learning typically requires more time than more expositive methods.

- *Oversimplification.* Constructivists argue that learning should take place in fully realistic situations, with all the complexity of real life. They would be concerned that a simulation might give students a false understanding of the real-life situation.

Integration

Instructional simulations, including role plays, are particularly well suited for the following:

- Training in motor skills, including athletic and mechanical skills, and complex skills that might otherwise be too hazardous or expensive in real-life settings
- Instruction in social interaction and human relations, where displaying empathy and coping with the reactions of other people are major goals
- Development of decision-making skills (e.g., microteaching in teacher education, mock court in law school, management simulations in business administration)

Simulation and Problem-Based Learning

One particular value of simulation is that it implements the problem-based learning method as directly and clearly as possible. In problem-based learning, the learner is led toward understanding principles through grappling with a problem situation. Most simulations attempt to immerse participants in a problem.

Through simulations, we can offer learners a laboratory in areas such as the social sciences and human relations as well as in areas related to the physical sciences, where laboratories have long been taken for granted. It tends to be more time consuming than the straightforward lecture approach, but the payoff is a higher level of comprehension that is likely to be long lasting.

The great advantage of this sort of firsthand immersion in a topic is that students are more likely to be able to apply to real life what they have practiced in simulated circumstances. This raises the issue of the degree of realism captured by a simulation. A common defect in poorly designed simulations is an overemphasis on chance factors in determining outcomes. Much of the reality is spoiled if chance-element cards cause players to gain or lose great quantities of points or other resources regardless of their strategic decisions. An overemphasis on chance or an overly simplified representation of real relationships might end up teaching lessons quite contrary to those intended.

Simulators

Competencies in the motor skill domain require practice under conditions of high feedback, which gives learners the feel of the action. Although it might be ideal to practice such skills under real-life conditions, some (e.g., piloting an airplane or driving a car) can be practiced much more safely and conveniently by means of simulated conditions. The device employed to represent a physical system in a scaled-down form is referred to as a **simulator.**

Simple simulators are in widespread use in applications, such as training workers in a range of manual skills from CPR to welding. One familiar example of a simulator is the flight trainer, a mock-up of the interior of the cockpit complete with controls and gauges. Today the flight crews of most major airlines receive a large portion of their training in flight simulators, which are controlled by computers and offer highly realistic audiovisual effects. Besides eliminating the possibility of loss of life and aircraft, these simulators allow significant savings of energy, in millions of gallons of fuel annually, and other costs. One recent study estimated that in-air training costs about $4,000 per hour, compared with only $400 per hour on the flight simulator, with no loss in effectiveness.

Role Plays

Role play refers to a type of simulation in which the dominant feature is relatively open-ended interaction among people. In essence, a role play asks someone to imagine that she is another person or is in a particular situation; the person then behaves as the other person would or in the way the situation seems to demand. The purpose is to learn something about another kind of person or about the dynamics of an unfamiliar situation. The role descriptions may be very general, leaving participants great latitude. The purpose in many cases is to allow the person's own traits to emerge so that they can be discussed and possibly modified. In other simulations, such as historical recreations, highly detailed roles are described to project the realities of life in that period.

The role-play simulation has proven to be a motivating and effective method of developing social skills, especially empathy (putting oneself in someone else's shoes). Our day-to-day social behavior tends to be governed by our assumptions about who we are, who our peers are, and why they act the way they do. A potent way of challenging, and thereby changing, these assumptions is to experience a slice of life from someone else's perspective.

The sorts of tasks that lend themselves especially well to role playing are counseling, interviewing, sales and customer services, supervision, and management (Figure 2.5). The settings most often simulated are

Figure 2.5
Role playing is an effective method for developing interpersonal skills.

Figure 2.6
A well-designed simulation game stirs emotions and generates classroom dynamics.

committee meetings, negotiation sessions, public meetings, work teams, and one-on-one interviews.

SIMULATION GAMES

A **simulation game** combines the attributes of a simulation (role playing, a model of reality) with the attributes of a game (striving toward a goal, specific rules). Like a simulation, it may be relatively high or low in its modeling of reality. Like a game, it may or may not entail competition.

Because they combine the characteristics of both simulations and games, instructional simulation games have advantages, limitations, and applications in common with both formats, as listed previously. In this regard one of the major reasons for using simulation and gaming methods is that they provide conditions for *holistic learning*. That is, through the modeling of reality and through the players' interactions as they strive to succeed, learners *encounter a whole and dynamic view of the process they are studying*. Conventional instruction tends to segment reality into separate packages (e.g., biology, mathematics, psychology), but that is not how the real world is organized. Through participation in simulation games, players can see the whole process and its dynamic interrelationships in action. In addition, emotions come into play along with the thinking process. Participants commonly experience excitement, elation, disappointment, even anger, as they struggle to succeed (Figure 2.6). This, of course, is how learning takes place in the world outside the classroom.

Integration

Instructional simulation games are found in curriculum applications that require both the repetitive skill practice

associated with games and the reality context associated with simulations. Societal processes, cultural conflicts, historical eras, and ecological systems are popular topics.

In general, teachers frequently use instructional simulation games to provide an overview of a large, dynamic process. The excitement of play stimulates interest in the subject matter, and the holistic treatment of the game gives students a feel for the total process before they approach parts of it in a more linear way.

Cooperative Simulation Games

Traditionally, games—both athletic contests and tabletop board games—have emphasized competition among adversaries. In recent years, sports psychologists and educational psychologists have developed new theories questioning the value and necessity of competition in human development. They contend that if children are nurtured on cooperation, acceptance, and success in a fun-oriented atmosphere they develop strong, positive self-concepts. Out of this new awareness has come the "new games" movement, generating hundreds of **cooperative games** that challenge the body and imagination but that depend on cooperation for success.

Instructional simulation games have been developed that pursue a similar philosophy. *Save the Whales* (see "Media Files: Simulations and Games") demonstrates that these endangered species can be preserved only through human cooperation. In *Mountaineering,* players work as a team to ascend and descend the mountain depicted on the game board, complete with crevasses, avalanches, and blizzards. In *Sky Travelers,* players learn about the earth as they explore it as stranded aliens from outer space; only through teamwork and strategic decision making can they reunite with their mother craft.

The computer has opened up even wider possibilities for simulating problem situations elaborately. A number

Media Files: Simulations and Games

THE GREEN REVOLUTION GAME
Marginal Context Ltd.

Instructional Simulation Game

Content areas: Community development, social studies

Age level: College and adult

The setting of this game is a village in contemporary India. Players attempt to manage their limited resources to provide for their families. Pests, drought, crop failures, shortage of cash and credit, and deaths of family members are among the realistic variables with which each player must contend.

STARPOWER
Simulation Training Systems.

Instructional Simulation

Content areas: Social studies, government

Age level: High school and above

Starpower centers on the trading of tokens that have been distributed randomly at the start of the exercise. During each round, participants try to increase their wealth and move upward in the three-tiered class structure that evolves. Later in play, the rich players make the rules.

WHERE IN THE WORLD IS CARMEN SANDIEGO?
The Learning Company.

Computer-Based Simulation Game

Content areas: History, geography, culture

Age level: Grades 4 through 6

Learners play the role of detective as they follow a trail of clues to track down and apprehend one of the members of Carmen Sandiego's notorious band of thieves. The detective utilizes re-source materials, problem-solving skills, planning methods, and organizational skills to catch the thief. Other variations are available, for example, *Where in the USA . . .*, and *Where in Time. . . .* Each employs different resource materials including an electronic reference database with maps, photos, and video clips. As the detective catches more thieves, the chase becomes more difficult.

SAVE THE WHALES
Animal Town Game Company.

Cooperative Simulation Game

Content areas: Ecology, social development

Age level: Grade 3 through adult

Players learn to act cooperatively as they face oil spills, radioactive waste, and whaling ships in trying to save eight types of whales from extinction. Players earn "survival points" and make group decisions on protecting the whales. This is one of a family of cooperative games distributed by Animal Town Game Company. All aim to encourage cooperation rather than competition.

of development groups have made computer-based simulations that challenge participants to work together to unlock a mystery. The unique feature of these simulations is that they require a group of learners to work synchronously and cooperatively to arrive at a successful conclusion.

To ensure that students have learned the intended lessons from playing a game, it is wise to conduct a debriefing following play. This gives everyone a chance to react and give their opinions, and permits the teacher insight into the game's successful and deficient attributes, as well as into any surprises resulting from playing.

See "Conducting a Debriefing: The Four-D Procedure" in Classroom Resources, Section C.

PROGRAMMED INSTRUCTION

Programmed instruction was chronologically the first instructional system and is an explicit application of principles of learning theory—operant conditioning or reinforcement theory. Since reinforcement theory suggested that people have a tendency to learn behaviors that are followed by reinforcers, psychologist B. F. Skinner wanted to develop a method of instruction whereby students would spend most of their time performing the skills or displaying the knowledge being taught—not just sitting and listening. And each performance must somehow be followed by a reinforcer. Skinner decided that since humans were naturally curious, he could use "knowledge of the correct response" as the reinforcer that would follow the correct performance.

Skinner's initial inventions were elaborate machines that would mechanically present chunks, or "frames," of information; wait for a response to be written or a button to be pressed; then compare the response with the correct answer. If the answer was correct, the machine would display the next frame. Research and practical experience soon indicated, however, that students learned just as well when the sequence—information, question, response, answer—was presented in book form.

The earliest programmed instruction texts arranged the frames across the page in horizontal strips. The student could check the correct response for each question only by turning the page. Later, this method was relaxed, allowing the frames to be arranged vertically, as in conventional printed pages, and became known as **linear programming.** These programmed texts were meant to be read with a piece of paper covering the rest of the page while reading a frame. After writing an answer in the blank on the first frame, for example, the user moved the cover down to see the correct answer printed in the box to the left of the second frame. You will have a better idea of how programmed instruction works if you go through the example in Figure 2.7.

The framework of programmed instruction began with the linear format just described. Early research, however, cast doubt on the necessity or desirability of

	1. Psychologists differ in their explanations of what learning is and precisely how it occurs. The series of statements or "frames" presented here deal with one particular explanation of the process of _____ .
learning	2. We cannot observe learning directly, but we can infer that it has occurred when a person consistently makes a response that he or she previously was unable to make. For example, if a student says "nine" when asked "What is three times three?" she is making a _____ that was probably learned through practice in school.
response	3. If you read "kappa" when asked "What Greek letter is represented by K?" you are making a _____ that you learned through some prior experience.
response	4. The word or picture or other sensory stimulation that causes you to make a response is a stimulus (plural: *stimuli*). Therefore, if "kappa" is your response, "What Greek letter is represented by K?" would be the _____ .
stimulus	5. To the stimulus "good," the student of Spanish responds "bueno"; the student of Arabic responds "gayid." To the stimulus "silver," the student of Spanish records "plata"; the student of Arabic responds "fida." They are responding to English words that are serving as _____ .
stimuli	6. In these frames the written statements are the stimuli to which you are writing _____ in the blanks.
responses	7. We learn to connect certain verbal responses to certain stimuli through the process of forming *associations*. We say that the student associates "nine" with "three times three"; he learns to associate "kappa" with *K;* and he _____ "plata" with "silver."
associates	8. Much verbal learning seems to be based on the formation of associations between _____ and responses.
stimuli	etc.

Figure 2.7

To use this example of programmed instruction, cover all of the page except the first frame with a piece of paper. Write your answer in the blank in the first frame. To verify your answer, slide the cover down to see the correct answer printed to the left of the second frame.

following this rigid format. An early and successful challenge to the linear convention came from Crowder (1963) in the form of "intrinsic programming." The basic method of intrinsic programming was to present a large block of information followed by a multiple-choice question requiring application of the facts or principles presented. Each answer choice directed the reader to a different page. Correct choices allowed the reader to go ahead to new material; incorrect choices led to remedial explanations and more questions.

Because the pattern of frames in intrinsic programming resembled the branches of a tree, it became known as **branching programming** (Figure 2.8). The major advantage of the branching format is that learners who catch on quickly can move through the material much more efficiently, following the "prime path."

Although it has largely been forgotten, programmed instruction played a unique pioneering role in the evolution of computer software. As the computer began to make its way into schools, little software was available. Many developers followed the example of programmed instruction materials and created computer-assisted instruction that would lead users through a series of exercises designed to teach the material.

Early work done by Suppes and Morningstar (1969) focused on using the computer to teach math skills. The lessons followed a drill-and-practice format similar to that found in the paperbound versions of similar materials. Practice and feedback were an integral part of the lesson designs.

These early attempts in using the computer to teach relied on a terminal attached via modem to a mainframe computer. Lessons were delivered to students whenever they logged on. Suppes found that students improved their math skills and enjoyed working on the computer. With the arrival of the microcomputer, the early work of Suppes and others made its way into the classroom. Early microcomputer software emulated these programmed instruction units designed to teach specific subjects. Thus, the computer became a delivery mechanism for programmed instruction.

Programmed instruction thus led to the development of computer-assisted instruction (CAI), and the same principles are currently incorporated in Web-based instruction. All of these formats provide for active learner participation including practice with feedback. The branching programmed instruction format, done so well by computers, was developed by Crowder to provide for individual differences.

Realistic contexts were not a characteristic feature of original programmed instruction or of the first CAI programs. Another limitation of programmed instruction and later CAI was the lack of social interaction. This was overcome with the introduction of programmed tutoring (discussed in the next section).

Programmed instruction usually refers to learning done by an individual using printed materials or a computer. *Programmed tutoring* involves a human tutor working one-on-one with a learner.

Advantages

- *Self-pacing.* Programmed instruction allows individuals to learn at their own pace at a time and place of their choice.
- *Practice and feedback.* It requires learners to participate actively in their learning and provides immediate feedback for each practice attempt.
- *Reliable.* This system provides a reliable form of learning, in that the instructional routine is embodied in print so that it can be mass produced and experienced by many people in exactly the same form.
- *Effective.* Hundreds of research studies compare programmed instruction with conventional instruction. Summaries of these studies indicate slight superiority for programmed instruction.

Limitations

- *Program design.* As with many other media and technologies, the quality of the software varies greatly. Some programmed materials are poorly designed and have little value.
- *Tedious.* The repetition of the same cycle and plowing through an endless series of small steps taxes the attention span and patience of many students. For highly motivated learners with the required reading skills and self-discipline,

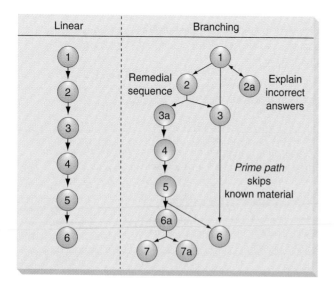

Figure 2.8

Comparison of linear and branching formats of programmed instruction.

programmed instruction can give them a chance to go off on their own and progress as far and as fast as they like. For others, it can be tedious.

- *Lack of social interaction.* Most programmed materials are meant to be used by one individual at a time. Long periods of independent study are inappropriate for younger children. Even older students and adults prefer more social interaction in their learning. Some kinds of skills and understanding are enhanced by the social exchange of group-based instruction. Affective and interpersonal skills are unlikely candidates for programmed instruction.

Integration

Programmed materials have been used successfully from the elementary school through the adult education level and in almost every subject area. By itself or in conjunction with other strategies, a teacher can use a program to teach an entire course or a segment of a course. Many teachers use short programmed units to teach simple principles and terminology. Programmed instruction is particularly useful as an enrichment activity. It can help provide highly motivated students with additional learning experiences that the teacher might ordinarily be unable to provide because of classroom time pressures.

Programmed materials also have proven to be effective in remedial instruction. The program can function as a "tutor" for slow learners in situations where more personalized attention may be virtually impossible (in overcrowded classrooms, for example). Students can even take this particular tutor with them when they leave the classroom! Another reason for the success of programmed materials in remedial instruction is their "failure-proof" design. Because these materials break learning down into small steps and allow students to take as much time as needed for each step, and because the materials are tested, evaluated, and revised carefully prior to publication, they are more likely to provide slower learners with a successful experience.

Like any other instructional material, programmed texts need to be carefully appraised before selection. Also, the success of programmed materials, as with other materials, depends on the skills of the instructor in choosing materials appropriate for the audience and purpose and in integrating them into the instructional program.

PROGRAMMED TUTORING

Programmed tutoring (also referred to as *structured tutoring*) is a type of instructional system that provides one-to-one interaction (Figure 2.9). In programmed tutoring the tutor's responses are programmed in ad-

Figure 2.9

A typical arrangement for a programmed tutoring lesson.

vance in the form of carefully structured printed instructions. In a typical program the tutor and student go through the lesson material together. The tutor's book has the answers to the exercises; the student's book does not. The tutor's role in the program is set forth, step by step, to conform with learner responses to the materials. An excerpt from a typical programmed tutoring tutor's book is shown in Figure 2.10.

Because the tutor goes to the next step on the basis of the learner's last response, programmed tutoring is a form of branching programming. As such, it shares the basic advantage for which branching was originally developed: the fast learner can skip quickly through the material without tedious and unnecessary repetition.

A learner who responds correctly is reinforced and goes on to a new item. If the response is incorrect, a series of increasingly clearer prompts or hints is given. For example, in teaching a beginning reader to follow written instructions, the student's book might say, "Point to your teacher." If the learner does not point to the teacher when first shown the instruction, the tutor might follow this sequence of prompts:

1. "Read it again." (Wait for response.)
2. "What does it say?"
3. "What does it tell you to do?"
4. "Do what it tells you to do."

The sequence of prompts would continue until the learner gives an acceptable response. Then the tutor would provide reinforcement. The idea is to lead the student toward the solution with hints but to avoid actually giving the correct answer.

Advantages

- *Self-pacing.* Programmed tutoring shares with programmed instruction the characteristic of individualized pacing.

STEP 1	Tell the student that this exercise will help him learn to sound out new words.
STEP 2	Point to the first word and ask the student to *sound* it out. a. If the student reads the word correctly, praise him; then go on to the next word. b. If the student is unable to read the word or reads it incorrectly, have him make the individual sounds in the word separately and then assist him in blending the sounds. Example: Word: "THIN" *Tutor:* Place your finger over the last two letters in the word and ask "What sound does the *th* make?" If the student answers correctly, praise him and go to the next sound. If he answers incorrectly or fails to answer, tell him the sound and have him repeat it. Follow the same procedure for each sound in the word, and then show him how to blend the separate sounds.
STEP 3	Follow step 2 for each word on the sheet.
STEP 4	At the end of the session, praise the student.
STEP 5	Fill out your tutor log.

Figure 2.10

The directions given in the tutor's guidebook structure the programmed tutoring lesson.

Source: Grant Von Harrison, *Beginning Reading 1: A Professional Guide for the Lay Tutor* (Provo, UT: Brigham Young University Press, 1972), p. 101. Used by permission of the author.

- *Practice and feedback.* Like programmed instruction, programmed tutoring requires constant learner participation with guidance by the tutor.
- *Social reinforcers.* The use of a live tutor as a mediator adds immensely to the flexibility of the feedback system, and it adds another major advantage over printed self-instructional material by employing social reinforcers in the form of praise ("That's great"; "Oh, what a good answer"; "You're really on the ball today")—a much more powerful reinforcer than just simple knowledge of results.
- *Reliable.* Like programmed instruction, programmed tutoring provides reliable instruction in that the teaching-learning pattern is embodied in a set of written instructions for the tutor. Compared with unstructured tutoring, programmed tutoring has higher reliability because there is a predetermined pattern to the tutor's action. With trained and motivated tutors, this has proven to be one of the most powerful technologies for learning. Administered flexibly and creatively by a live guide, this technology can overcome the monotonous pattern that sometimes results with other programmed formats.
- *Effective.* The effectiveness of programmed tutoring has been well established through the evaluation studies carried out by its originator, Douglas Ellson. The evidence from these was persuasive enough that in the early 1980s the U.S. Department of Education recognized programmed tutoring as one of the half-dozen most effective compensatory education programs. Summaries of research have also found structured tutoring, variously defined, to be among the most effective and cost-effective innovations, with tutees scoring from the 70th to the 79th percentile compared to the 50th percentile for conventional instruction (Levin, Glass, & Meister, 1987).

Limitations

- *Labor intensive.* Programmed tutoring depends on the availability of volunteer tutors. In schools, tutoring is usually done by peers, older students, or parents.
- *Development cost.* The success of programmed tutoring depends on the design of the tutoring guides; their development requires an investment of time and expertise.

Integration

Reading and mathematics have been by far the most popular subjects for tutoring. Being basic skills and highly structured by nature, these subjects lend themselves well to this approach. Remedial instruction is a typical application of tutoring programs.

In using programmed tutoring, keep in mind that research consistently indicates that tutors also learn from tutoring, sometimes more than their tutees! So give everyone a chance to be a tutor. You can do this effectively by using materials that are prestructured to make the tutor's job replicable.

Consider using tutoring to make productive use of high-absence days. Train those who are present to tutor absentees when they return. Tutors will deepen their knowledge; absentees will catch up.

Selection Rubric: Simulations and Games

Complete an interactive evaluation and add it to your NETS-T portfolio using the Selection Rubric for Simulations and Games available on the "Classroom Link Portfolio" CD-ROM. A downloadable version of this rubric is available in the Selection Rubrics module of the Companion Website at http://www.prenhall.com/smaldino.

Key Words

_____

_____

_____

Title _____

Series Title (if applicable) _____

Source _____

Date _____ **Cost** _____

Subject Area _____

Intended Audience _____

Format

☐ Game

☐ Simulation

☐ Simulation game

Brief Description

Objectives

Entry Capabilities Required (e.g., prior knowledge, reading ability, vocabulary level, math ability)

Strong Points

Weak Points

Recommended Action (using criteria on following page)

Name _____ **Date** _____

Rating Area	High Quality	Medium Quality	Low Quality	Rating
Match Curriculum	Curriculum standard addressed and should enhance student learning.	Curriculum standard partially addressed and use might enhance student learning.	Curriculum standard not addressed and use will likely not enhance student learning.	
Accurate & Current	Information correct and does not contain material that is out of date.	Information correct but does contain material that may be out of date.	Information not correct and does contain material that is out of date.	
Clear & Concise Language	Language used is age appropriate and vocabulary is understandable.	Language used is nearly age appropriate and some vocabulary is above/below student age.	Language used is not age appropriate and vocabulary is clearly inappropriate for student age.	
Motivating/ Interesting	Topic presented so that students are likely to be interested and engaged in learning.	Topic presented to interest students most of the time and engage most in learning.	Topic presented so as not to interest students and not engage them in learning.	
Learner Participation	Topic presented so that most students are actively engaged in learning.	Topic presented so that some students are engaged in learning.	Topic presented so that most students are not actively engaged in learning.	
Technical Quality	The material represents best available media.	The material represents media that are good quality, although there are some problems.	The material represents media that are not well prepared and are of very poor quality.	
Effectiveness Rating	There is evidence that use has shown positive impact on student learning.	There is little evidence that use has shown positive impact on student learning.	There is no evidence that use has shown positive impact on student learning.	
Free from Bias	There is no evidence of objectionable bias or advertising.	There is little evidence of bias or advertising.	There is much evidence of bias or advertising.	
User Guide & Documentation	The documentation is excellent resource for use in a lesson. Documentation should help students use the material.	The documentation is good resource for use in a lesson. Documentation may help students use the material.	The documentation is poor resource for use in a lesson. Documentation does not help students use the material.	
Provides Practice of Relevant Skills	Much valuable practice of skills to be learned.	Some practice of skills to be learned.	Little or no practice of skills to be learned.	
Game: Winning Depends on Player Actions Rather Than Chance	The actions of the players determine their success in the game.	Success in the game is determined by both player actions and chance.	Winning or losing the game is determined by chance.	
Simulation: Validity of Simulation; Realistic, Accurate Depiction of Reality	The simulation is an accurate representation of actual situations.	There is some relationship between the simulation and actual situations.	There is little or no correlation between the simulation and actual situations.	
Clear Directions for Play and Debriefing	The directions are clearly stated and easy for users to understand.	The directions are confusing for users at some points.	The directions are poorly stated and difficult for users to understand.	

Summary: Instructional Systems

In this chapter you learned how to promote the development of new knowledge, skills, or attitudes (learning) through instructional systems, sets of interrelated components that work together to provide learning activities necessary to accomplish a learning goal. The components of all instructional systems include objectives (content to be learned), methods, media, equipment, a learning environment, and people. Each of these components will be described in detail in later chapters. Instructional systems discussed in this chapter were cooperative learning, games, simulations, simulation games, programmed instruction, and programmed tutoring.

In the next chapter, you will learn how to design, implement, and evaluate instruction. The ASSURE model is a guide to the major steps in instructional planning. It takes into consideration the audience (your students), the objectives (content), the methods, media, equipment, and the learning environment—all parts of any instructional system.

Classroom Link Portfolio Activities

Please use the "Classroom Link Portfolio" CD-ROM and the Companion Website as resources in completing these activities. These activities are designed to demonstrate your skills and dispositions. To complete the following activities online, go to the Portfolio Activities module in Chapter 2 of the Companion Website (http://www.prenhall.com/smaldino).

1. *Analysis: Instructional Systems.* Locate two examples of instructional systems from the CW, the "Classroom Link Portfolio" CD-ROM, or in your school's media center. Cite and/or describe the sources. Briefly describe each and tell how you would use them. List the strengths and weaknesses as they relate to learning. What recommendations would you make to the developer to improve each one (addressing needs of diverse learners)? Which would you choose to use? Why? (ISTE NETS-T 2.A & C; 6.A & B)

2. *Written Reflection.* Locate a cooperative learning activity lesson from the CW, the "Classroom Link Portfolio" CD-ROM, or on the Web. What do you like and not like about this activity as a teacher/trainer and as a learner? What do you like and not like about cooperative learning as a learner? How does this influence what you need to do as a teacher? (ISTE NETS-T 4.B)

Integration Assessments

To complete the specified activities online, go to the Integration Assessments module in Chapter 2 of the Companion Website (http://www.prenhall.com/smaldino).

1. Observe an actual class session (it may be the course you are taking, one taught where you work, or a class in another setting) and critique it in terms of the characteristics of an instructional system as defined at the beginning of this chapter. (ISTE NETS-T 5.B)

2. Analyze an actual or hypothetical instructional system using "Analyzing or Designing an Instructional System" (see Classroom Resources, Section C). (ISTE NETS-T 5.B)

3. Describe an instructional situation relevant to your own teaching that is appropriate for use of instructional games, simulations, or simulation games. (ISTE NETS-T 3.B)

4. Review a game or simulation related to your own teaching interests and prepare an appraisal report using the "Selection Rubric: Simulations and Games." (ISTE NETS-T 2.C)

5. Prepare a debriefing guide for a lesson utilizing a game or simulation. (ISTE NETS-T 2.E)

6. Think about how you might use a game, simulation, or simulation game in your teaching or training. What would the content and/or objectives be? Would you use a game, simulation, or simulation game? How would you incorporate any of the following features of an instructional system:

   Active participation/interaction
   Practice
   Individual differences
   Reinforcement/feedback
   Realistic context
   Cooperative groups/social interaction

   (ISTE NETS-T 2.A)

7. Describe a real or hypothetical instructional situation in which you believe an instructional

system described in this chapter would be appropriate; justify your recommendation. (ISTE NETS 2.A)

8. Review an example of programmed instruction, computer-assisted instruction, or Web-based instruction. What makes this example an instructional system? (ISTE NETS-T 2.C).

References

Cohen, Peter A., James A. Kulik, and Chen-Lin C. Kulik. 1982. Educational outcomes of tutoring: A meta-analysis of findings. *American Educational Research Journal, 19*(2): 237–248.

Crowder, Norman. 1963. On the differences between linear and intrinsic programming. *Phi Delta Kappan, 44*(6): 250–254.

Johnson, David W., and Roger T. Johnson. 1993. Cooperative learning and feedback in technology-based instruction. In *Interactive instruction and feedback,* edited by J. Dempsey and G. Sales. Englewood Cliffs. NJ: Educational Technology Publications.

Levin, Henry, Gene Glass, and Gail Meister. 1987. Cost-effectiveness of computer-assisted instruction. *Evaluation Review, 11*(1): 50–72.

Slavin, Robert E. 1990. *Cooperative learning: Theory, research, and practice.* Upper Saddle River, NJ: Prentice Hall.

Stolovitch, Harold D., and Sivasailam Thiagarajan. 1980. *Frame games.* Englewood Cliffs. NJ: Educational Technology Publications.

Suppes, Patrick, and M. Morningstar. 1969. Computer-assisted instruction. *Science, 166*(3903): 343–350.

Suggested Readings

Brush, Thomas A. 1998. Embedding cooperative learning into the design of integrated learning systems: Rationale and guidelines. *Educational Technology Research and Development, 46*(3): 5–18.

Buehl, Doug. 2001. *Classroom strategies for interactive learning,* 2nd ed. Newark, DE: International Reading Association.

Campbell, Linda. 2002. *Mindful learning: 101 proven strategies for student and teacher success.* Thousand Oaks, CA: Corwin.

Dempsey, John V., Linda L. Haynes, Barbara A. Lucassen, and Maryann S. Casey. 2002. Forty simple computer games and what they could mean to educators. *Simulation and Gaming, 33*(2): 157–168.

Edens, K. M. 2000. Preparing problem solvers for the 21st century through problem-based learning. *College Teaching, 48*(2): 55–60.

Guskey, Thomas R. 1996. *Implementing mastery learning,* 2nd ed. Belmont, CA: Wadsworth.

Jacobs, George M., Michael A. Power, and Loh Wan Inn. 2002. *The teacher's sourcebook for cooperative learning: Practical techniques, basic principles, and frequently asked questions.* Thousand Oaks, CA: Corwin.

Leigh, Elyssebeth, and Jeff Kinder. 1999. *Learning through fun and games.* New York: McGraw-Hill.

Mazyck, Michael. 2002. Integrated learning systems and student of color: Two decades of use in K–12 education. *TechTrends, 46*(2): 33–39.

Nurrenbern, Susan C., and William R. Robinson. 1997. Cooperative learning: A bibliography. *Journal of Chemical Education, 74*(6): 623.

Putnam, Joanne, Kathryn Markovchick, David W. Johnson, and Roger T. Johnson. 1996. Cooperative learning and peer acceptance of students with learning disabilities. *Journal of Social Psychology, 136*(6): 741.

Ruben, B. D. 1999. Simulations, games, and experience-based learning: The quest for a new paradigm for teaching and learning. *Simulation and Gaming, 30*(4): 498–505.

Scalia, L. M., and B. Scakmary. 1996. Groupware in the classroom: Applications and guidelines. *Computers in the Schools, 12*(4): 39–53.

Sharon, Shlomo. 1999. *Handbook of cooperative learning methods.* Westport, CT: Greenwood.

Shockley, H. Allan. 1992. Turnkey or turkey? Integrating an integrated learning system. *Educational Technology, 32*(9): 22–25.

Slavin, Robert E. 1985. Team-assisted individualization. In *Adapting instruction to individual differences,* edited by M. Wang and H. Walberg. Berkeley, CA: McCutchan.

Snowden, Peggy L., and Linda Garris Christian. 1998. 4 Levels of learning centers for use with young gifted children. *Gifted Child Today, 21*(3): 36–41.

Sugar, Steve, and Kim Kostoroski Sugar. 2002. *Primary games: Experiential learning activities for teaching children K–8.* New York: John Wiley & Sons.

Taylor, Lydotta M., and Joann L. King. 1997. A popcorn project for all students. *Mathematics Teacher, 90*(3): 194.

CHAPTER 3

The ASSURE Model
Creating the
Learning Experience

Outline

Knowledge Objectives

1. Demonstrate your ability to follow the steps involved in systematic planning for learning experiences (the ASSURE model).
2. List five general characteristics of learners and five types of specific competencies.
3. Describe learning style, including four types of traits that affect it.
4. Discuss the rationale for stating objectives for instruction, including purposes or uses of objectives.
5. Write objectives that include the audience, behavior, conditions, and degree of mastery.
6. Demonstrate your ability to follow the basic procedures for selecting, modifying, and designing materials, indicating when each choice is appropriate.
7. Describe ways of modifying materials without actually altering the originals.
8. Create examples of the five basic steps in utilizing instructional materials.
9. Identify general showmanship techniques in reference to planning, practice, and presentation.
10. Describe methods for eliciting student participation during instruction.
11. Justify learner participation when using media and technology.
12. Compare and contrast the techniques for evaluating student achievement, media and methods, and the teacher.

Professional Vocabulary

entry test	affective domain
prerequisite	motor skill domain
learning style	interpersonal domain
motivation	media format
intrinsic motivator	showmanship
extrinsic motivator	feedback
criterion	practice
cognitive domain	authentic assessment

If you are going to use media and technology effectively, you must plan systematically for their use as discussed in the previous chapter. The ASSURE model is a guide to the major steps in this planning. Following the ASSURE model, you begin creating the learning experience by assessing your students' characteristics and the learning objectives to be attained. With these in mind you are in a good position to select the types of media or instructional systems to use and to consider specific materials that you might need.

Students' actual encounter with the media and materials also needs to be planned with care. What will they be doing? The ASSURE model puts a heavy emphasis on *active* student engagement in learning activities.

After instruction, how will you determine whether students have reached the goal? Both the learners and the instructional processes need to be evaluated. Were the materials effective? Were the activities engaging? Answering questions such as these closes the loop and brings you back to the beginning of another cycle.

A Model to Help ASSURE Learning

Analyze Learners

The first step in planning is to identify the learners. Your learners may be, for example, students, trainees, or members of an organization such as a Sunday school, civic club, youth group, or fraternal organization. You must know your students to select the best medium to meet the objectives. The audience can be analyzed in terms of (1) general characteristics, (2) specific entry competencies (knowledge, skills, and attitudes about the topic), and (3) learning style.

State Objectives

The next step is to state the objectives as specifically as possible. The objectives may be derived from a course syllabus, stated in a textbook, taken from a curriculum guide, or developed by the instructor. They should be stated in terms of what the learner will be able to do as a result of instruction. The conditions under which the student or trainee is going to perform and the degree of acceptable performance should be included.

Select Methods, Media, and Materials

Once you have identified your audience and stated your objectives, you have established the beginning points (audience's present knowledge, skills, and attitudes) and ending points (objectives) of instruction. Your task now is to build a bridge between these two points by choosing appropriate methods, technology, and media formats, then deciding on materials to implement these choices. There are three options: (1) select available materials, (2) modify existing materials, or (3) design new materials.

Utilize Media and Materials

Having either selected, modified, or designed your materials, you then must plan how the media, materials, and technology will be used to implement your methods. First, preview the materials and practice the implementation. Next, prepare the class and ready the necessary equipment and facilities. Then conduct the instruction using the utilization techniques described in this and later chapters.

Students may use the media and materials individually, as in self-instruction, or in small groups, as in cooperative learning. They may use printed materials, such as workbooks, or computer-based technology, such as the Internet.

Require Learner Participation

To be effective, instruction should require active mental engagement by learners. There should be activities that allow learners to practice the knowledge or skills and to receive feedback on the appropriateness of their efforts before being formally assessed.

Practice may involve student self-checks, computer-assisted instruction, Internet activities, or group games. Feedback may be provided by the teacher, a computer, other students, or self-evaluation.

Evaluate and Revise

After instruction, it is necessary to evaluate its impact and effectiveness and to assess student learning. To get the total picture, you must evaluate the entire instructional process. Did the learners meet the objectives? Did the methods, media, and technology assist the trainees in reaching the objectives? Could all students use the materials properly?

Wherever there are discrepancies between what you intended and what you attained, you will want to revise the plan for the next time.

THE ASSURE MODEL

All effective instruction requires careful planning. Teaching with instructional media and technology is certainly no exception. This chapter examines how to plan systematically for the effective use of instructional media and technology. We have constructed a procedural model to which we have given the acronym *ASSURE*—it is intended to *assure* effective instruction.

You can think of teaching and learning as progressing through several stages. Gagné (1985) refers to these stages as "events of instruction." Gagné's research revealed that well-designed lessons begin with the arousal of students' interest and then move on to present new material, involve students in practice with feedback, assess their understanding, and go on to followup activities. The ASSURE model incorporates these events of instruction.

The ASSURE model—a procedural guide for planning and conducting instruction that incorporates media and technology—assumes that training or instruction is required. A full-blown process of instructional development would begin with a needs assessment to determine whether instruction is the appropriate solution to a performance problem.

The ASSURE model focuses on planning surrounding the actual classroom use of media and technology. It is less ambitious than models of instructional development, which are intended to guide the entire process of designing instructional systems. Such models include the procedures of the ASSURE model and the processes of needs analysis, subject matter analysis, product design, prototype tryout, system implementation, and the like. These larger-scale instructional development procedures typically involve teams of specialists and require major commitments of time and money. (Further information about instructional design can be found in the References and Suggested Readings at the end of this chapter.) The ASSURE model, on the other hand, is meant for the individual instructor to use when planning classroom use of media and technology.

To illustrate how to use the six steps of the ASSURE model, we will provide an example of a "Case" for each step after it is described. These steps taken together constitute a "Case Sample"—or lesson plan—that describes the instructional planning used by a middle school math teacher who wanted to redesign a unit on statistics. The teacher felt that the mathematics textbook presented statistics (collecting data, interpreting data, and presenting data) very inadequately. One particularly disappointing aspect of textbook material covering this topic was that technology was not incorporated in the teaching. She believed that, considering today's technology-based world, this skill deserved more attention than it traditionally received in schools. Therefore, she chose to develop a unit that addressed some of the basic statistical skills through the use of computer applications.

The "Classroom Link Portfolio" CD-ROM in the back of this book lets you use the ASSURE model to create your own lesson plans. The program presents each step of the model in a flexible format that allows you to develop your own lesson plans by entering them into a computer version of the ASSURE model. Instructions on how to use the "Classroom Link Portfolio" CD-ROM are found online at the Companion Website for this text (http://www.prenhall.com/smaldino), and on the CD-ROM itself.

ANALYZE LEARNERS

If instructional media and technology are to be used effectively, there must be a match between the characteristics of the learner and the content of the methods, media, and materials. The first step in the ASSURE model, therefore, is analysis of your audience.

It is not feasible to analyze every trait of your learners. Several factors, however, are critical for making good methods and media decisions:

- General characteristics
- Specific entry competencies
- Learning styles

General characteristics include broad identifying descriptors such as age, grade level, job or position, and cultural or socioeconomic factors. Specific entry competencies refer to knowledge and skills that learners either possess or lack: prerequisite skills, target skills, and attitudes. The third factor, learning style, refers to the spectrum of psychological traits that affect how we perceive and respond to different stimuli, such as anxiety, aptitude, visual or auditory preference, motivation, and so on.

General Characteristics

Even a superficial analysis of learner characteristics can provide helpful leads in selecting instructional methods and media. For example, students with substandard reading skills may be reached more effectively with nonprint media. If you are dealing with a particular ethnic or cultural subgroup, you might want to give high priority to considerations of ethnic and cultural identity and values in selecting particular materials.

If learner apathy toward the subject matter is a problem, consider using a highly stimulating instructional approach, such as a dramatic videotape, a simulation game, or a technology-based activity.

Learners entering a new conceptual area for the first time may need more direct, concrete kinds of experiences, such as field trips or role-playing exercises (refer to Dale's Cone of Experience in Chapter 1). More advanced learners usually have a sufficient base for using audiovisual or even verbal materials.

Heterogeneous groups, which include learners vary-ing widely in their conceptual sophistication or in the amount of firsthand experience they have with the topic, may profit from an audiovisual experience such as a videotape. Such media presentations provide a com-mon experiential base that can serve as an important point of reference for subsequent group discussion and individual study.

For instructors dealing with a familiar audience, analysis of general characteristics will be something of a given. At times, however, audience analysis may be more difficult. Perhaps your students are new to you, and you have had little time to observe and record their characteristics. Or perhaps they are a more heteroge-neous group than is ordinarily found in the classroom—business trainees, for example, or a civic club, youth group, or fraternal organization—thus making it more difficult to ascertain whether all or even a majority of your learners are ready for the methods and media of in-struction you are considering. In such cases, academic and other records may be helpful, as well as direct ques-tioning of and talking with learners and instructors or other group leaders. Seasoned public speakers—those who regularly address unfamiliar audiences—make it a practice to arrive early and strike up a conversation with audience members. In this way they can pick up valuable clues about the types of people in the audience, their backgrounds, their expectations, and their moods.

Specific Entry Competencies

When you begin to plan any lesson, your first assump-tions are that the learners lack the knowledge or skills you are about to teach and that they possess the knowl-edge or skills needed to understand and learn from the lesson. These assumptions are often mistaken. For ex-ample, a life insurance company used to routinely bring all its new sales associates back to the home office at the end of their first year for a course on setting sales prior-ities. Puzzled by the cool reaction of the agents, the trainer decided to give a pretest, which revealed that a majority of the trainees already knew perfectly well how to set sales priorities. The company shifted to a less ex-pensive and more productive strategy of giving incen-tives to field representatives who sent in acceptable sales plans showing their priorities.

The assumption that learners have the prerequisite knowledge or skill to begin the lesson can seldom be ac-cepted casually in school settings. Teachers of mixed-ability classes routinely anticipate that some students will need remedial help before they are ready to begin a particular unit of instruction. Furthermore, researchers studying the impact of different psychological traits on learning have reached the unexpected conclusion that students' prior knowledge of a particular subject influ-ences how and what they can learn more than does any psychological trait (Dick, Carey, & Carey, 2001). For example, students approaching a subject new to them learn best from structured presentations even if they have a learning style that would otherwise indicate more open-ended, unstructured methods.

These realizations suggest that instructors must verify assumptions about entry competencies through infor-mal means (such as in-class questioning or out-of-class interviews) or more formal means (such as testing with standardized or teacher-made tests). **Entry tests** are as-sessments, both formal and informal, that determine whether students possess the necessary prerequisites. **Prerequisites** are competencies that learners must pos-sess to benefit from the instruction but that you or the media are not going to teach. For example, in teaching an apprentice lathe operator to read blueprints, you might assume that she has the ability to make metric conversions—hence, you would not teach this skill.

Prerequisites (specific entry competencies) should be stated in the same format as are objectives (described in the next section). In the situation involving the appren-tice lathe operator, the prerequisites could be stated as follows: "Apprentice lathe operators are able to convert any given measurement up to one meter from the met-ric system to the English system equivalent or vice versa with 100 percent accuracy." Such previously acquired skills should be assessed before instruction.

Preassessment measures, such as discussions and pretests, are also given before instruction but are used to measure the content to be taught—the target skills. If learners have already mastered what you plan to teach, you are wasting your time and theirs by teaching it.

By analyzing what your audience already knows, you can select appropriate methods and media. For example, if you have a group diverging widely in entry compe-tencies, consider self-instructional materials to allow for self-pacing and other aspects of individualization.

Learning Styles

Learning style refers to a cluster of psychological traits that determine how an individual perceives, interacts with, and responds emotionally to learning environments.

It is clear that certain traits dramatically affect our abil-ity to learn effectively from different methods and media. However, it is not so clear which traits are most impor-tant. Gardner (1999) was dissatisfied with the concept of IQ and its unitary view of intelligence, noting that "not all people have the same abilities; not all of us learn in the same way" (p. 21). He identified nine aspects of intelli-gence: (1) verbal/linguistic (language), (2) logical/mathematical (scientific/quantitative), (3) visual/spatial, (4) musical/rhythmic, (5) bodily/kinesthetic (dancing/athletics), (6) interpersonal (understanding other people), (7) intrapersonal (understanding oneself), (8) naturalist, and (9) existentialist.

Gardner's theory implies that an effective teacher needs to be aware of different learning styles. The best way to do this is to offer variety within a lesson. Teachers, curriculum planners, and media specialists should work together to design curricula in which students have the chance to develop these different aspects of intelligence. It also implies that students vary widely in terms of their strengths and weaknesses in each of these areas. A school adopting this approach would have students engaged in a much greater variety of methods and media than is typical now. Teacher talk and seatwork obviously are not sufficient. Because students have different mixes of strengths and weaknesses, their progress would have to be measured not by conventional grades in conventional subjects but by growth in each type of intelligence. The type of individualized instructional plans and records of progress implied in this approach lend themselves well to the active learning methods, interactive technologies, and information management systems described in later chapters. In fact, experimental schools based on this theory are now in operation.

Learning style variables discussed in the literature can be categorized as perceptual preferences and strengths, information processing habits, motivational factors, and physiological factors.

Perceptual Preferences and Strengths.

Learners vary as to which sensory gateways they prefer using and which they are especially adept at using. The main gateways include auditory, visual, tactile, and kinesthetic. Proponents of the importance of this variable claim that most students do not have a preference or strength for auditory reception, casting doubt on the widespread use of the lecture method. They find that slower learners tend to prefer tactile or kinesthetic experiences; sitting and listening are difficult for them. Dependence on the tactile and kinesthetic modalities decreases with maturity.

Information Processing Habits.

This category includes a range of variables related to how individuals tend to approach the cognitive processing of information.

Gregorc's model of "mind styles," elaborated by Butler (1986), groups learners according to concrete versus abstract and random versus sequential styles. It yields four categories: concrete sequential, concrete random, abstract sequential, and abstract random. Concrete sequential learners prefer direct, hands-on experiences presented in a logical order. They learn best with workbooks, programmed instruction, demonstrations, and structured laboratory exercises. Concrete random learners lean toward a trial-and-error approach, quickly reaching conclusions from exploratory experiences. They prefer methods such as games, simulations, independent study projects, and discovery learning. Abstract sequential learners decode verbal and symbolic messages adeptly, especially when presented in logical sequence. Reading and listening to presentations are preferred methods. Abstract random learners are distinguished by their capacity to draw meaning from human-mediated presentations; they respond to the tone and style of the speaker as well as the message. They do well with group discussion, lectures with question-and-answer periods, videotapes, and television.

Motivational Factors.

Various emotional factors have been found to influence what we pay attention to, how long we pay attention, how much effort we invest in learning, and how feelings may interfere with learning. Anxiety, locus of control (internal/external), degree of structure, achievement motivation, social motivation, cautiousness, and competitiveness are variables frequently cited as critical to learning.

Motivation is an internal state that leads people to choose to work toward or against certain goals and experiences. It defines what people *will* do rather than what they *can* do (Keller, 1987). Motivation influences learning by determining which instructional goals students attend to and which they choose to ignore. It also determines the effort they will expend to reach certain goals.

Motivators can be categorized as either intrinsic or extrinsic. **Intrinsic motivators** are generated by aspects of the experience or task itself, such as challenge or curiosity. A student who has a "short attention span" may spend hours playing computer games, but have trouble spending 10 minutes reading a textbook. **Extrinsic motivators** are generated by factors not directly related to the experience or task, such as grades or recognition. Students may work long and hard to "please" a favorite teacher. Researchers have found that intrinsic motivators are generally more effective. Students who are intrinsically motivated will work harder and learn more because of their personal interest in the material. Whenever possible, it is best to develop a student's intrinsic motivation.

A helpful approach to describing student motivation is Keller's (1987) ARCS model. Keller describes four essential aspects of motivation:

Attention refers to whether students perceive the instruction as interesting and worthy of their consideration.

Relevance refers to whether students perceive the instruction as meeting some personal need or goal.

Confidence refers to whether students expect to succeed based on their own efforts.

Satisfaction refers to the intrinsic and extrinsic rewards students receive from the instruction.

Physiological Factors.   Factors related to gender differences, health, and environmental conditions are among the most obvious influences on the effectiveness of learning. Boys and girls tend to respond differently to various school experiences. For example, boys tend to be more competitive and aggressive than girls and consequently respond better to competitive games. Hunger and illness clearly impede learning. Temperature, noise, lighting, and time of day are everyday phenomena that affect our ability to concentrate and maintain attention. Individuals have different preferences and tolerances regarding these factors.

Dunn and Dunn (1992) have developed standardized instruments to measure the learning styles and environmental preferences of learners that cover these and other physiological factors. They are among the best-known and most widely used instruments in school applications. Teachers who have prescribed individual learning programs based on analysis of these factors feel that they have practical value in improving academic achievement, attitude, and discipline.

The intent in using information about a student's learning style is to adapt instruction to take advantage of a particular style. Many students in a class may have the same or similar learning styles. Using learning styles in teaching can be compared to designing a house for a specific person. The components of houses are basically uniform—kitchen, living room, dining room, bedrooms, baths. However, they can be arranged in an unlimited number of configurations. They may need to be structured to accommodate hobbies, individuals with disabilities, or persons working at home. Furthermore, there are many different styles of architecture, colors, textures, materials, and so on. An architect skillfully selects and arranges all these elements to meet the needs and preferences of the inhabitants—an individual, a couple, a family. In a similar manner, a teacher chooses different methods, media, and materials to meet the needs of students with different learning styles and physiological factors. (See "ASSURE Case Sample: Analyze Learners.")

ASSURE Case Sample

MIDDLE SCHOOL MATHEMATICS

ANALYZE LEARNERS

General Characteristics

The students for whom this lesson is intended are seventh graders enrolled in a general mathematics class geared toward the average learner. The students range in age from 12 to 14 years. Several students have identified learning disabilities, whereas others are on the edge of consideration for the advanced mathematics track. They come from various socioeconomic environments; however, the majority of the students are white, middle-class Americans who live in a rural setting. Generally, the students are well behaved; problems tend to arise, however, when activities are textbook and paper-and-pencil oriented.

Entry Competencies

The seventh grade mathematics students are able to do the following:

- Select, locate, and utilize appropriate reference materials when preparing research projects, using the school library media center
- Locate and identify bar, line, and circle graphs when examining books and other forms of media
- Read and interpret all the statistical or numerical information given to them on a bar, line, or circle graph

- Construct a graph (bar, line, or circle) when given a set of data, colored pencils/pens, a compass, a ruler, and graph paper
- Define and interpret a given example of percentage, mean, median, and mode without aids or references
- Demonstrate standard keyboarding skills, utilizing *AppleWorks* on the *eMac* computer, with an average typing speed of 35 words per minute

Learning Styles

The students dislike the monotony of mathematics textbook assignments. These assignments are usually centered on paper-and-pencil calculation problems. Persistent use of the textbook often results in the students becoming bored and restless. They appear to learn best from activities that incorporate the use of manipulatives. Using the computer and the Internet provides intrinsic motivation. In addition, they like group-oriented learning activities. Regarding testing, many of the students tend to experience difficulty and anxiety during written exams. As a result, the class prefers to be evaluated using methods other than paper-and-pencil tests (e.g., reports, application projects, etc.).

This ASSURE Case Sample was developed by Mary Ann Ferkis, Purdue University.

All of the ASSURE Cases in Practice in this text and an electronic template for creating your own ASSURE Lesson can be found on the enclosed "Classroom Link Portfolio" CD-ROM.

STATE OBJECTIVES

The second step in the ASSURE model is to state the objectives of instruction. What learning outcome is each learner expected to achieve? More precisely, what new capability should learners possess at the completion of instruction? An *objective* is a statement not of what the instructor plans to put into the lesson but of what learners ought to get out of the lesson. An objective is a statement of *what* will be achieved, not *how* it will be achieved.

Your statement of objectives should be as specific as possible. For example, "My students will improve their mathematical skills" is far too general to qualify as a specific lesson objective. It does, however, qualify as a *goal*—a broad statement of purpose. Such a goal might serve as the umbrella for a number of specific objectives, such as, "The second-grade students will be able to solve accurately seven out of eight single-digit addition problems."

Why should you state instructional objectives? First, you must know your objectives in order to make appropriate selection of methods and media. Your objectives will, in a sense, guide your sequence of learning activities and your choice of media. Knowing your objectives will also commit you to create a learning environment in which the objectives can be reached. For example, if the objective of a unit of a driver's training course is "To be able to change a flat tire within 15 minutes," the learning environment must include a car with a flat tire.

Another basic reason for stating your instructional objectives is to help ensure proper evaluation. You won't know whether your learners have achieved an objective unless you are absolutely sure what that objective is.

Without explicit objectives, your students won't know what is expected of them. If objectives are clearly and specifically stated, learning and teaching become objective oriented. Indeed, a statement of objectives may be viewed as a type of contract between teacher and learner: "Here is the objective. My responsibility as the instructor is to provide learning activities suitable for your attaining the objective. Your responsibility as the learner is to participate conscientiously in those learning activities."

The ABCDs of Well-Stated Objectives

A well-stated objective starts by naming the *Audience* for whom the objective is intended. It then specifies the *Behavior* or capability to be demonstrated and the *Conditions* under which the behavior or capability will be observed. Finally, it specifies the *Degree* to which the new skill must be mastered—the standard by which the capability can be judged.

Audience. A major premise of systematic instruction is to focus on what learners are doing, not on what the teacher is doing. Learning is most likely to take place when learners are active, either mentally processing an idea or physically practicing a skill. Because accomplishment of the objective depends on what learners do, the objective begins by stating whose capability is going to be changed—for example, "ninth-grade algebra students" or "newly hired sales representatives." Of course, if you are repeating the objective in material written for student use, the informal "you" is preferable.

Behavior. The heart of the objective is the verb describing the new capability that the audience will have after instruction. This verb is most likely to communicate your intent clearly if it is stated as an observable behavior. What will learners be able to do after completing instruction? Vague terms such as *know, understand,* and *appreciate* do not communicate your aim clearly. Better words include *define, categorize,* and *demonstrate,* which denote observable performance. The Helpful Hundred list in Table 3.1 offers verbs that highlight performance.

The behavior or performance stated in the objective should reflect the real-world capability learners need, not some artificial ability needed for successful performance on a test. As a surgical patient, would you want a surgeon who is "able to select the correct answers on a multiple-choice test on appendectomies"? Or would you want the surgeon to be "able to perform an appendectomy"?

Conditions. A statement of objectives should include the conditions under which the performance is to be observed. For example, are students allowed to use notes in describing the consequences of excessive use of alcohol? If the objective of a particular lesson is for students to be able to identify birds, will identification be made from color representations or black-and-white photographs? What tools or equipment will students be allowed or not allowed to use in demonstrating mastery of the objective? Thus, an objective might state, "Given a political map of Europe, the student will be able to mark the major coal-producing areas." Or it might say, "Without notes, textbook, or any library materials, the student will be able to write a 300-word essay on the relationship of nutrition to learning."

Degree. The final requirement of a well-stated objective is that it indicates the standard, or **criterion,** by which acceptable performance will be judged. What degree of accuracy or proficiency must learners display? Whether the criteria are stated in qualitative or quantitative terms, they should be based on some real-world requirement. For example, how well must the machinist be able to operate a lathe to be a productive employee?

Time and accuracy are meaningful dimensions in many objectives. How quickly must the observable behavior be performed? For example, should students be

Table 3.1
The Helpful Hundred

Suggested Performance Terms					
Add	Compute	Drill	Label	Predict	State
Alphabetize	Conduct	Estimate	Locate	Prepare	Subtract
Analyze	Construct	Evaluate	Make	Present	Suggest
Apply	Contrast	Explain	Manipulate	Produce	Swing
Arrange	Convert	Extrapolate	Match	Pronounce	Tabulate
Assemble	Correct	Fit	Measure	Read	Throw
Attend	Cut	Generate	Modify	Reconstruct	Time
Bisect	Deduce	Graph	Multiply	Reduce	Translate
Build	Defend	Grasp (hold)	Name	Remove	Type
Carve	Define	Grind	Operate	Revise	Underline
Categorize	Demonstrate	Hit	Order	Select	Verbalize
Choose	Derive	Hold	Organize	Sketch	Verify
Classify	Describe	Identify	Outline	Ski	Weave
Color	Design	Illustrate	Pack	Solve	Weigh
Compare	Designate	Indicate	Paint	Sort	Write
Complete	Diagram	Install	Plot	Specify	
Compose	Distinguish	Kick	Position	Square	

able to solve five quadratic equations in 5 minutes, or 10 minutes? How accurate must a measurement be—to the nearest whole number, or within one-sixteenth of an inch, or plus or minus one millimeter?

Quantitative criteria for judging acceptable performance sometimes are difficult to define. For example, how can an English instructor state quantitative criteria for writing an essay or short story? He might stipulate that student work will be scored for development of theme, characterization, originality, or the like. A model story might be used as an example.

The important consideration in appraising your objectives is whether you communicate the intent of the objectives, regardless of their format. If your objectives meet all the criteria in the "Objectives Checklist" on page 55 but still do not communicate accurately your intentions to your colleagues and students, they are inadequate. The final judgment on any objectives must be determined by their usefulness to you and your learners. Guidelines for writing objectives are discussed in Gronlund's (2004) *Writing Instructional Objectives for Teaching and Assessment* and Mager's (1997) *Preparing Instructional Objectives.*

The wording of objectives appearing in instructional materials is often modified. The conditions and degree are often omitted to focus learners' attention on the specific behavior they are to learn. Instructors may specify their own conditions and criteria (degree), ensuring appropriateness for the students and the subject area.

Even though objectives should contain Audience, Behavior, Condition, and Degree, sometimes it is appropriate to leave out one or more of these components. This is done to shorten the objective. The longer the objective, the more difficult it may *appear* to be.

For example, we have not included a statement of Audience for the objectives in this book. You, the reader, are our audience. The instructor selecting the book has determined that it is appropriate for you. When you write objectives for your students, you and they know who the audience is.

The approach just described allows the objective to begin with the action verb, or Behavior. *All* objectives should be stated in observable performance terms.

When writing objectives for this book, we often omit the Conditions because your instructor will determine and should communicate to you the Condition(s) under which the performance is to occur. For your students, it is important that you communicate the Conditions under which they will demonstrate mastery of the specified objective.

Many of the objectives in this book include the Degree; others do not. Your instructor should add those that are missing. Some instructors use different Degrees for different classes, such as an introductory undergraduate course and a graduate course. It is also possible that you may have different students in your class(es). However, in all cases the instructor should communicate all components of the objectives to her students.

Classification of Objectives

Classifying objectives is much more than an academic exercise for educational psychologists. It has practical value because the selection of instructional methods and media, as well as evaluation methods, depends on the types of objectives being pursued.

An objective may be classified according to the primary type of learning outcome at which it is aimed.

OBJECTIVES CHECKLIST

	Appropriately stated	Partly stated	Missing
Audience			
Specifies the learner(s) for whom the objective is intended	❏	❏	❏
Behavior (action verb)			
Describes the capability expected of the learner following instruction	❏	❏	❏

- stated as a learner performance

- stated as observable behavior

- describes a real-world skill (versus mere test performance)

Conditions (materials and/or environment)			
Describes the conditions under which the performance is to be demonstrated	❏	❏	❏

- equipment, tools, aids, or references the learner may or may not use

- special environmental conditions in which the learner has to perform

Degree (criterion)			
States, where applicable, the standard for acceptable performance	❏	❏	❏

- time limit

- range of accuracy

- proportion of correct responses required

- qualitative standards

Although there is a range of opinion on the best way to describe and organize types of learning, three categories (or *domains*), of learning are widely accepted: cognitive skills, affective skills, and motor skills. To these we add a fourth, interpersonal skills, because of the importance of such skills in teamwork.

In the **cognitive domain,** learning involves an array of intellectual capabilities that may be classified either as verbal/visual information or as intellectual skills. Verbal/visual skills require learners to provide a specific response to relatively specific stimuli. They usually involve memorization or recall of facts. Intellectual skills, on the other hand, require thinking and manipulating information.

The **affective domain** involves feelings and values. Affective objectives range from, for example, stimulating interest in a school subject, to encouraging healthy social attitudes, to adopting a set of ethical standards.

In the **motor skill domain,** learning involves athletic, manual, and other such physical skills. Motor skill objectives include capabilities ranging from simple mechanical operations to those entailing sophisticated neuromuscular coordination and strategy, as in competitive sports.

Learning in the **interpersonal domain** involves interaction among people. Interpersonal skills are people-centered skills that require the ability to relate effectively with others. Examples include teamwork, counseling techniques, administrative skills, salesmanship, discussion, and customer relations.

Objectives and Individual Differences

Objectives in any of the domains just discussed may, of course, be adapted to the abilities of individual learners. The stated philosophy of most schools and colleges is to help students fulfill their full potential. In a physical education class with students of mixed ability, for instance, the midsemester goal might be for all students to be able to complete a run of 100 meters outdoors, but the time standards might vary. For some, 12 seconds might be attainable; for many others, 16 seconds; and for some, 20 might be realistic. For a student with physical disabilities, it might be a major victory to move 10 meters in one minute (Figure 3.1).

Objectives are not intended to limit what students learn but rather to provide a minimum level of expected achievement. Serendipitous or incidental learning should be expected to occur (and should be encouraged) as students progress toward an objective. Each learner has different characteristics (as discussed earlier in this chapter). Because of such individual differences, incidental learning takes different forms with different students. Class discussions and other kinds of student

Figure 3.1
When teaching learners who have disabilities, there may be as many different standards for each objective as there are individuals.

involvement in the instructional situation, therefore, should rarely be rigidly limited to a specific objective. Student involvement should allow for incidental learning to be shared and reinforced. Indeed, to foster incidental learning and provide for individual differences, it is sometimes advisable to have students specify some of their own objectives. (See "ASSURE Case Sample: State Objectives.")

SELECT METHODS, MEDIA, AND MATERIALS

A systematic plan for *using* media and technology certainly demands that the methods, media, and materials be *selected* systematically in the first place. The selection process has three steps: (1) deciding on the appropriate method for the given learning tasks, (2) choosing a media format that is suitable for carrying out the method, and (3) selecting, modifying, or designing specific materials within that media format.

Throughout this process, the school library media specialist and/or technology coordinator can be a helpful partner in considering possible methods and media and in sorting through the particular materials available.

Choosing a Method

First, it would be overly simplistic to believe that there is one method that is superior to all others or that serves all learning needs equally well. As mentioned in Chapter 1, any given lesson will probably incorporate two or more methods to serve different purposes at different points in the progression of the lesson. For example, one might

ASSURE Case Sample

MIDDLE SCHOOL MATHEMATICS

STATE OBJECTIVES

The objectives for this lesson are as follows:

1. Given a bar, line, or circle graph, the seventh-grade mathematics student will be able to verbally present all the statistical or numerical information shown on the graph with 100 percent accuracy.
2. Given a set of data, the seventh-grade mathematics student will be able to accurately construct and produce a printout of a graph (bar, line, or circle) using *AppleWorks* software according to established criteria.
3. Working in small groups of three or four, the seventh-grade mathematics students will be able to propose, discuss, and agree on a topic for a group presentation. The presentation topic must incorporate data collection techniques (survey, observation, and/or interview) and the use of graphs (bar, line, and/or circle) to present statistical or numerical information.
4. Using *AppleWorks* software and working in small groups, the seventh-grade mathematics students will be able to write and produce a printout of a written report regarding the data collection techniques associated with the topic of their presentation. Reports will be evaluated based on the quality of the survey, observation sheet, or interview form; the steps taken to collect the data; and the rationale for choosing the specific data collection technique.
5. The seventh-grade mathematics students will be able to present their chosen topic in front of the class. Performance will be evaluated based on general content accuracy, specific use of graphs, and cohesiveness of the presentation.

This ASSURE Case Sample was developed by Mary Ann Ferkis, Purdue University.

All of the ASSURE Cases in Practice in this text and an electronic template for creating your own ASSURE Lesson can be found on the enclosed "Classroom Link Portfolio" CD-ROM.

conduct a simulation activity to gain attention and arouse interest at the beginning of the lesson, then use a demonstration to present new information, and then arrange computer-based drill-and-practice activities to provide practice in the new skill. As indicated earlier in this chapter, teachers often structure assignments to allow students with different preferred learning styles to pursue their individual practice through different methods (e.g., having "abstract random" thinkers use a role-play simulation while "concrete sequential" thinkers use a lab manual for structured problem solving). It is beyond the scope of this book to give detailed guidelines on choosing methods.

Choosing a Media Format

A **media format** is the physical form in which a message is incorporated and displayed. Media formats include, for example, flip charts (still images and text), slides (projected still images), audio (voice and music), video (moving images on a TV screen), and computer multimedia (graphics, text, and moving images on a monitor). Each has different strengths and limitations in terms of the types of messages that can be recorded and displayed. Choosing a media format can be a complex task—considering the vast array of media and technology available, the variety of learners, and the many ob-

jectives to be pursued. Over the years many different formulas have been proposed for simplifying the task. They are referred to as *media selection models,* and they usually take the form of flowcharts or checklists.

Within most media selection models the instructional situation or setting (e.g., large group, small group, or self-instruction), learner variables (e.g., reader, nonreader, or auditory preference), and the nature of the objective (e.g., cognitive, affective, motor skill, or interpersonal) must be considered against the presentational capabilities of each of the media formats (e.g., still visuals, motion visuals, printed words, or spoken words). Some models also take into consideration the capability of each format to give feedback to the learner.

The limitation of such media selection models is their emphasis on simplicity. Reducing the process to a short checklist may lead one to ignore some possibly important considerations.

Our approach in this book is to give you the tools to construct your own schema for selecting appropriate media formats. We accept the desirability of comparing the demands of the setting, learner characteristics, and objectives against the attributes of the various formats. But only you can decide how to weight these considerations: what options you have in terms of setting, which learner characteristics are most critical, and what elements of your objectives are most important in your own situation. You will need to balance simplicity and comprehensiveness in any schema you decide to employ.

Obtaining Specific Materials

Obtaining appropriate materials will generally involve three alternatives: (1) selecting available materials, (2) modifying existing materials, or (3) designing new materials. Obviously, if materials are already available that will allow your students to meet your objectives, by all means use them, thus saving work, time, and money. When the materials available do not completely match your objectives or are not entirely suitable for your audience, an alternative approach is to modify them. If this is not feasible, the final alternative is to design your own materials. Even though this is more expensive and time consuming, it allows you to prepare materials to serve your students and meet your objectives.

Selecting Available Materials

The majority of instructional materials used by teachers and trainers are "off the shelf"—that is, ready-made and available from school, district, or company collections or other easily accessible sources. So, how do you go about making an appropriate choice from available materials?

Involving the Media/Technology Specialist. The media/technology specialist can be an important resource for you. You may need new materials to update the content of a unit. The specialist can tell you about materials housed in a local resource center or school library media center. Identify and discuss your options. As the specialist gains a better idea of your needs, arrangements can be made to contact area media collections (public, academic, or regional) to borrow potentially useful materials. Most school library media centers participate in regional cooperatives, which share materials. If you and the media/technology specialist collaborate with other teachers in your school or district who desire similar materials, you may have an easier time in acquiring materials from national museums or organizations. An appointed group of teachers may review selection and evaluation guides and identify new materials to be purchased for future use. Involving other teachers in previewing also allows you to compare ideas and available materials. Teachers tend to become more critical and selective as they increase their collective knowledge of media and material alternatives.

Surveying the Sources. You might survey some of the published media reference guides or the Internet to get a general idea of what is available. Unfortunately, no single comprehensive guide exists for all audiovisual materials available in all media formats in all subjects; you may have to consult several sources.

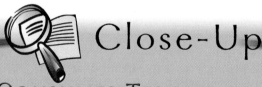

Close-Up

CONSUMER TESTING OF EDUCATIONAL PRODUCTS

As the Consumers Union provides objective evaluative information about household products to general consumers, the Educational Products Information Exchange (EPIE) Institute provides educational software evaluations to the education and training communities.

The EPIE Institute is a nonprofit agency that has been in operation since 1967. Its purpose is to "gather and disseminate descriptive and analytical information—along with empirical information on performance and effects on learners—about instructional materials and systems." P. Kenneth Komoski has been executive director of EPIE since its founding.

EPIE accepts no advertising or commercial sponsorship of any kind. All income is derived from subscriptions, contract services from state and local education agencies, and grants. EPIE offers the following evaluation services to teachers and school systems.

The Education Software Selector (TESS) is a comprehensive database of educational software at every level from preschool to college. Over the years TESS has been available in a variety of formats, most recently on CD-ROM.

Eight major integrated instruction systems (or integrated learning systems) are evaluated in *The EPIE Report on Computer-Based Integrated Systems,* which draws on extensive research by experts in software evaluation and curriculum.

EPIE's Curriculum Analysis Services for Education (CASE) provides schools with a means of analyzing, designing, and aligning their stated curriculum outcomes, textbooks, and other instructional resources. A school's testing program can be compared with state and national programs and curriculum priorities. The service provides grade-by-grade printed reports that are useful for understanding and improving a school's curriculum and instructional program.

To learn more about the institute and its services, contact EPIE Institute, 103-3 W. Montauk Highway, Hampton Bays, NY 11946.

There are three types of guides that can help you select media—comprehensive guides, selective guides, and evaluative guides. Comprehensive guides, such as "A-V Online" and *Bowker's Complete Video Guide,* help you identify the scope of possibilities. However, since they may include items of poor quality and difficult-to-locate titles, you should use these guides only to locate materials for preview. (*Always* preview materials before using them with your students.)

Selective guides, such as *Only the Best Computer Programs, Best Videos for Children and Young Adults,* and *The Elementary School Library Collection,* are compilations of the "best" instructional materials. An advantage of these selective guides is that time has allowed the "best" to surface from a comparison of similar products on the market. A disadvantage is that during the time required for this process to take place, some items may have become outdated and newer items of good quality may not have been included.

Evaluative guides, such as *Booklist, School Library Journal, Choice,* and *Video Rating Guide,* are current and will keep you up to date about new materials. Although they are evaluative, they usually include just one person's opinion; that person's needs and audience may be different from yours.

One of the more comprehensive sources is a set of two indexes published by NICEM (National Information Center for Educational Media): *Film & Video Finder* and *Audiocassette & Compact Disc Finder.* These do not include evaluations. "A-V Online" is a CD-ROM that lists thousands of educational, informational, and documentary materials along with their sources. The disc includes a variety of media formats, such as video, audio, overhead transparencies, and multimedia kits.

In addition to materials themselves that are available on the Internet, listings appear there of materials available elsewhere. Many companies, government agencies, and commercial publishers list materials on the Internet. The majority of vendors now have their catalogs on their websites. Most of these materials are for purchase. Some are free and inexpensive. See Chapter 9 for guidelines about securing and using free and inexpensive materials.

If you are working in elementary or secondary education, you might consult several additional sources that cover a range of media formats, such as *Core Media Collection for Elementary Schools* and *Core Media Collection for Secondary Schools.* These books recommend specific audiovisual titles as core materials for elementary and secondary school media collections.

For general and adult audiences, a major guide is the *Reference List of Audiovisual Materials,* produced by the U.S. government. It describes all the training and educational materials produced by the armed forces and other government agencies that are available for general

purchase. For additional information on this topic, go to the Web Links module in Chapter 3 of the Companion Website (http://www.prenhall.com/smaldino).

Beyond the sources just described, there are more specialized guides and indexes that are limited to specific media formats or specific subjects. These are too many and too diverse to list here, but some are mentioned in the individual chapters dealing with different media formats, and others are gathered under the heading "Specialized Information Sources" on our Companion Website.

Selection Criteria.   The decision about whether to use a particular piece of instructional material depends on several factors. Recent research confirms that certain criteria are critical in the appraisal of materials (McAlpine & Weston, 1994). Among the questions to be asked about each specific piece of media are the following:

- Does it match the curriculum?
- Is it accurate and current?
- Does it contain clear and concise language?
- Will it motivate and maintain interest?
- Does it provide for learner participation?
- Is it of good technical quality?
- Is there evidence of its effectiveness (e.g., field-test results)?
- Is it free from objectionable bias and advertising?
- Is a user guide or other documentation included?

Over the years, scholars have debated about what criteria should be applied in selecting materials. Studies have been conducted to quantify and validate various criteria. The net result is an understanding that different criteria are suitable for different situations. For example, a remedial reading teacher might decide to use a particular computer program primarily because its vocabulary level is just right, regardless of any other qualities. On the other hand, an elementary school teacher with an ethnically diverse class might sort through materials to find those with a special sensitivity to racial and ethnic issues.

Other selection criteria vary with different media formats. Video materials, for example, raise the issue of the pace of presentation, whereas this would not be relevant for overhead transparencies. In examining computer-assisted instruction courseware, one would look for relevant practice and remedial feedback, but these would not be expected in a videotape. To account for these differences, this book provides a separate Selection Rubric for each media format. You will notice that certain criteria appear consistently in each checklist (they are the ones listed here). These are the criteria that we think have the securest basis in research and real-life experience. The Selection Rubrics provide a systematic procedure for judging the qualities of specific materials. But it is up to you to decide which criteria are most important to you in your own instructional setting. The Selection Rubrics appear in the appropriate chapters and are available on our Companion Website (http://www.prenhall.com/smaldino) and on the "Classroom Link Portfolio" CD-ROM.

The Instructor's Personal File. Every instructor should develop a file of media references and appraisals for personal use. An excellent way for you to begin is to develop your own personal file of Selection Rubrics by using the "Classroom Link Portfolio" CD-ROM. Each Selection Rubric in this text has a computer template on the software into which you can enter your own information for future reference.

Modifying Existing Materials

If you cannot locate entirely suitable materials and media off the shelf, you might be able to modify what is available. This can be both challenging and creative. In terms of time and cost, it is a more efficient procedure than designing your own materials, although the type and extent of necessary modification will, of course, vary.

For example, perhaps the only available visual showing a piece of equipment being used in a middle school woodworking class is from a repair manual and contains too much detail and complex terminology. A possible solution to the problem would be to use the picture but modify the caption and simplify or omit some of the labels.

Or let's say there is just one video available that shows a needed visual sequence, but the audio portion of the video is inappropriate because it is at too high or too low a conceptual level or discusses inappropriate points. A simple solution in such a case would be to show the video with the sound turned off and provide the narration yourself. Another modification technique, which many instructors overlook, is to show just a portion of a video, stop the VCR, discuss what has been presented, then continue with another short segment followed by additional discussion. Modification also can be made in the audio portion of foreign-language materials or English-language materials used in a bilingual classroom. Narrations can be changed from one language to another or from a more advanced rendition of a foreign language to a simpler one.

Videocassette recorders provide teachers with the opportunity to modify television programs that previously were available only as shown on the air. You may also record programs off the air for replay later. You may then show them at whatever time best suits the instructional situation and to whatever student group(s) can profit most from viewing them.

One frequently modified media format is a set of slides with an audiotape. If the visuals are appropriate but the language is not, it is possible to change the language. It is also possible to change the emphasis of the narration. For example, an original audiotape might emphasize oceans as part of an ecosystem, whereas you may want to use the slides to show various types of fish found in oceans. By rewriting the narration, you could adapt the material to your purpose while using the same slides. Redoing the tape can also change the level of the presentation. A slide–tape presentation produced to introduce a new product could have three different audiotapes. One tape could be directed toward the customer, another could be prepared for the sales staff, and the third could be used for service personnel.

Some instructional games can be readily modified to meet particular instructional needs. It is possible to use a given game format and change the rules of play to increase or decrease the level of sophistication. Many instructional games require the players to answer questions. It is relatively easy to prepare a new set of questions at a different level of difficulty or even on a new topic.

If you try out modified materials while they are still in more or less rough form, you can then make further modifications in response to student reaction until your materials meet your exact needs.

A word of caution about modifying commercially produced materials (and, indeed, about using commercial products in general): Be sure your handling and use of such materials does not violate copyright laws and restrictions. If in doubt, check with your school administration or legal adviser. Copyright concerns and guidelines are discussed in other chapters. The general guidelines are on page 11.

Designing New Materials

It is easier and less costly to use available materials, with or without modification, than to start from scratch. There is seldom justification for reinventing the wheel. However, there may be times when your only recourse is to design your own materials. As is the case with selecting from available materials, you must consider certain basic elements when designing new materials:

- *Objectives.* What do you want your students to learn?
- *Audience.* What are the characteristics of your learners? Do they have the prerequisite knowledge and skills to use or learn from the materials?
- *Cost.* Is sufficient money available in your budget to meet the cost of supplies (videotapes, audiotapes, etc.) you will need to prepare the materials?
- *Technical Expertise.* Do you have the necessary expertise to design and produce the kind of materials you wish to use? If not, will the necessary technical assistance be available to you? Try to keep your design within the range of your own capabilities. Don't waste time and money trying to produce slick professional materials when simple inexpensive products will get the job done.

ASSURE Case Sample

MIDDLE SCHOOL MATHEMATICS

SELECT METHODS, MEDIA, AND MATERIALS

The teacher first selects a teaching method, followed by materials and equipment that are available at the school. She also modifies and develops other materials. The method she chooses to use is large-group instruction with small groups.

- *Overhead Projector.* The teacher needs to show the class some graphs. She selects the overhead projector to introduce the lesson topic. She will use transparencies with different types of graphs (bar, line, and circle) to review the concept of graphs with students. The overhead projector is available in the classroom, transparencies are easy to prepare, and they may be reused throughout the course of the lesson.
- *eMac Computers.* The school has both PC and *eMac* computers. The teacher needed to choose between the two. Because she was not familiar with the *eMac* computer, she evaluated it using the "Selection Rubric: Computer Hardware," in Classroom Resources, Section B. She also considered the software that is available for each computer system. She selected the *eMac* because it was available to use during her class time and her selected software, *AppleWorks,* would run on it.
- *AppleWorks.* The teacher is familiar with several software packages containing graphing capabilities. She talked with other teachers to get their input regarding a program suitable for her activity. *AppleWorks* was recommended by two of her colleagues. Consequently, she obtained *AppleWorks* installed on an *eMac* from the Instructional Materials Center. She evaluated it using the "Selection Rubric: Computer Software" in Chapter 5. This particular software package meets all the activity needs, whereas others do not have specific necessary features (e.g., pie graphing capability).
- *Video Camera and Tape Recorder.* The teacher has observed that the students enjoy watching/listening to videotapes and audiotapes of their work. They provide a motivational aspect to the assignment. She believes that this assignment lends itself nicely to this application. The video camera and tape recorder were selected to satisfy the objectives and assignment requirements. Additionally, the teacher likes to use the tapes to assist her in evaluating the students and for the students to evaluate themselves.
- *Data Projector.* The teacher needs a way to show students how to make graphs on the computer. In addition, the students need to present their computer-generated graphs. The teacher could make handouts, use an opaque projector to show handouts, or use a document camera. The teacher selected the use of the data projector because the cost of producing about a hundred handouts would be expensive, and using an opaque projector would require a darkened room when the students need to operate computers, whereas all the information could be effectively presented using a data projector.
- *Flip Chart.* The teacher plans to design graphs to present to the class. The graphs will contain titles and labeled axes. In addition, they must be easy to read. She can use the *eMac* and *AppleWorks* to create graphs for the flip chart. She chooses a flip chart with laminated pages so that the students can write on the pages: their marks can be erased and the flip chart pages reused. The flip chart will also provide a change of pace from the overhead projector.
- *Handouts.* Using the *eMac* and *AppleWorks,* the teacher will create a set of handouts that coincide with the flip chart graphs. The instructor chooses to create a set of handouts so that each student will have a set of graphs on which to record notes for future reference. In addition, the handouts will keep all the students involved during the learning activity.

This ASSURE Case Sample was developed by Mary Ann Ferkis, Purdue University.

All of the ASSURE Cases in Practice in this text and an electronic template for creating your own ASSURE Lesson can be found on the enclosed "Classroom Link Portfolio" CD-ROM.

- *Equipment.* Do you have the necessary equipment to produce or use the materials you intend to design?
- *Facilities.* If your design calls for use of special facilities for preparation or use of your materials, are such facilities available?
- *Time.* Can you afford to spend whatever time necessary to design and produce the kind of materials you have in mind?

(See "ASSURE Case Sample: Select Methods, Media, and Materials.")

UTILIZE MEDIA AND MATERIALS

The next step in the ASSURE model is the use of media and materials by the students and teacher. The recommended utilization procedures are based on extensive research. The general principles have remained remarkably constant. The main difference has to do with who is using the materials. The increased availability of media and the philosophical shift from teacher-centered to student-centered learning increases the likelihood that students will be using the materials themselves—as individuals or in small groups—rather than watching as the teacher presents them to a whole class.

The following "5 Ps" apply to either teacher-based or student-centered instruction.

Preview the Materials

You should never use instructional materials without previewing them first. During the selection process you should determine that the materials are appropriate for your audience and objectives. Published reviews, distributor's blurbs, and colleagues' appraisals contribute information about the material; however, you should *insist* on previewing the materials yourself. Only a thorough understanding of the contents will enable you to use the media and materials to their full potential (Figure 3.2).

A recent incident in a Florida high school underscores the importance of previewing materials. A teacher with 32 years of experience showed the videotape *I Spit on Your Grave* to his advanced-placement social studies students. Students, parents, and school administrators were outraged by the sexually explicit content of the video. When questioned about the showing, the teacher said he was unaware that the video contained scenes of a woman being gang-raped and beaten. Obviously, he had not previewed the video!

In other cases, sensitive content may need to be eliminated or at least discussed prior to showing the materials to prevent student embarrassment or upset. In one

case, an elementary teacher and her young students were horrified to find that an unpreviewed and ostensibly unobjectionable film on Canada's fur seals contained a sequence showing baby seals being cold-bloodedly clubbed to death by hunters.

If you do feel that some sensitive material fits with your objectives, then a letter home is in order. By letting parents know about the material in advance you may avoid potential problems. Also, encourage parents to visit with you and discuss the material, or even arrange a special viewing.

Prepare the Materials

Next, you need to prepare the media and materials to support the instructional activities you plan to use. This is true whether you are presenting the materials or your students are using them. The first step is to gather all the materials and equipment that you and the students will need. Determine in what sequence you will use the materials and media. What will you do with them as the presenter? What will the students do as learners? Some teachers keep a list of the materials and equipment needed for each lesson and an outline of the presentation sequence of the activities.

For a teacher-based lesson, you may want to practice using the materials and equipment. For a student-centered lesson, it is important that students have access to all the materials, media, and equipment that they will need. The teacher's role becomes one of facilitator. You should anticipate what materials students will need and be prepared to secure any necessary additional materials.

Prepare the Environment

Wherever the learning is to take place—in the classroom, in a laboratory, at the media center, on the athletic field—the facilities will have to be arranged for proper student use of the materials and media. Certain factors are often taken for granted for any instructional situation—comfortable seating, adequate ventilation, climate control, suitable lighting, and the like. Some media require a darkened room, a convenient power source, and access to light switches. You should check that the equipment is in working order whether it is to be used by you or by your students. Arrange the facilities so that all the students can see and hear properly (Figure 3.3). Arrange the seating so students can see each other if you want them to discuss a topic. (More specific information on audiovisual and computer setups appears in Chapter 5 and in Classroom Resources, Section B.)

Prepare the Learners

Research on learning tells us very clearly that what is learned from an activity depends highly on how learners are prepared for the lesson. We know that in show busi-

Figure 3.2
Preview the materials.

Figure 3.3
Prepare the environment.

Figure 3.5
Provide the learning experience.

ness entertainers are obsessed with having the audience properly warmed up. Preparing learners is just as important when you are providing a learning experience (Figure 3.4).

A proper warmup, from an instructional point of view, may be similar to one of the following:

- An introduction giving a broad overview of the content of the lesson
- A rationale telling how it relates to the topic being studied
- A motivating statement that creates a need to know by telling learners how they will profit from paying attention
- Cues directing attention to specific aspects of the lesson

Several of these functions—directing attention, increasing motivation, providing a rationale—apply whether the lesson is teacher based or student centered.

In some cases you may want to inform students of the objectives. In certain cases, other steps will be needed. For example, you may need to introduce unfamiliar vocabulary or explain special visual effects, such as time-lapse photography. Other preparation steps relevant to particular media will be discussed in later chapters.

Provide the Learning Experience

Now you are ready to provide the instructional experience. If the materials are teacher based, you should present like a professional. One term for this is **showmanship** (see "Showmanship: Classroom Presentation Skills"). Just as an actor or actress must control the attention of an audience, so must an instructor be able to direct attention in the classroom. Later chapters describe showmanship techniques relevant to each specific media format (Figure 3.5).

If the experience is student centered, you must play the role of guide or facilitator, helping students to explore the topic on the Internet, discuss the content, prepare materials for a portfolio, or present information to their classmates. Guidelines in some of the following chapters will assist students in the production of mediated materials. (See "ASSURE Case Sample: Utilize Media and Materials.")

Figure 3.4
Prepare the learners.

Showmanship

CLASSROOM PRESENTATION SKILLS

GETTING READY

Planning

An effective presentation begins with careful and thorough planning. These guidelines apply to classroom instruction as well as to more formal presentations.

1. *Analyze your learners.* What are their needs, values, backgrounds, knowledge levels, and misconceptions?
2. *Specify your objectives.* What should students do? How much time do you have to present? Limit your objectives and content to the time available.
3. *Specify benefits and rationale for the learners.* Why is the message important for them? If you cannot answer this question, perhaps you should not give the presentation.
4. *Identify the key points to cover.* Brainstorm the main ideas. Put them on note cards or stick-on notes. Most presentations will have from five to nine main points.
5. *Identify the subpoints and supporting details.* Again use note cards or stick-on notes. Try to limit yourself to five to nine subpoints for each main point.
6. *Organize the entire presentation in a logical and sequential order.* One organizing strategy is this:

Preview/Overview:	Tell them what you are going to tell them.
Present:	Tell them.
Review:	Tell them what you told them.

Rehearsing

1. Use keyword notes, not a script. Print keywords on an index card. Never read from a script; written language is different from spoken language.
2. Mentally run through the presentation to review each idea in sequence.
3. Do a standup rehearsal of your presentation. Try to practice in the room where you will be presenting or one similar to it.
4. Give a simulated presentation, idea for idea (not word for word), using all media. (Note: This is not usually done for classes but for formal presentations.)
5. Practice answers to questions you anticipate from learners.
6. Videotape (or audiotape) yourself or have a colleague sit in on your rehearsal and give you feedback.

Setting Up

1. Check your equipment in advance of your presentation. Change the arrangements, if necessary, to meet your needs. When the equipment is in place, make sure everything operates properly.
2. For slides and video projection, place the screen front and center (Figure A).
3. Place the overhead projector screen or flip chart at a 45-degree angle and near the corner of the room. Place the overhead screen to your right if you are right handed. Place flip chart to your left if you are right handed. Each should be reversed if you are left handed (Figure B).
4. Position objects being studied in the front and center. Remove them when they are no longer being studied.

PRESENTING

Anxiety

1. Nervousness and excitement are normal before and during a presentation. Some anxiety and concern are important for an enthusiastic and dynamic presentation.
2. Proper planning and preparation should reduce your anxiety.
3. Harness your nervous energy and use it positively with body movement, supporting gestures, and voice projection.

A

B

C

4. Breathe slowly and deeply. Your cardiovascular system will slow down and ease the symptoms of anxiety.

Delivery

1. Stand up when presenting. When you stand, you and your message command more attention.
2. Face the learners. Place your feet 10 to 12 inches apart and distribute your weight equally on both feet. Your knees should be unlocked, with hands out of your pockets and arms at your side. Facing the learners gives you eye contact with them and allows them to see your facial expressions.
3. When using chalkboards or wall charts, don't talk with your back to the learners. In this position you lose eye contact and may not be heard as well. Write on the chalkboard, then talk (Figure C).
4. Stand to one side of the lectern (if you must use one). Stepping to the side or in front of it places you on more personal terms with the learners. It allows you to be seen and to be more natural.
5. Move while you speak. Instructors who stand in one spot and never gesture experience tension. Move and gesture, but don't overdo it.

Voice

1. Use a natural, conversational style. Relate to your learners in a direct and personal manner.
2. Don't read your presentation. Don't read from your overheads or handouts. If part of your presentation is just information transfer, give the students a copy and let them read it.
3. Use vocal variety. A monotone is usually caused by anxiety (rehearsal should help this). Relax with upper and lower body movements.
4. Use a comfortable pace. When you are anxious, your rate of speaking usually increases. Relax and speak in a conversational tone.
5. Speak up so you can be heard in the back of the room. If you speak up, your rate will slow down—solving two problems! Ask people in the back row if your volume is appropriate.
6. A pause (silence) after a key point is an excellent way to emphasize it. The more important the idea, the more important it is for you to pause and let the words sink in before going on to the next idea.

Eye Contact

1. Don't speak until you have established eye contact with your audience. Eye contact will make your presentation similar to a one-on-one conversation.
2. An excellent way to keep your learners' attention is to look eye to eye at each person for at least three seconds. Don't quickly scan the learners or look at the back wall, screen, or notes for long periods of time.

3. Maintain eye contact with your learners. If you must write something on a flip chart, overhead, or chalkboard, stop talking while you write.

Gestures

1. Use natural gestures. Learn to gesture in front of a class as you would if you were having an animated conversation with a friend.
2. Don't put your hands in your pockets. Don't clasp your hands behind your back. Don't wring your hands nervously. Don't play with a pen or other object.

Visuals

1. Visuals help to attract and hold learners' interest. People like to see keywords, diagrams, and drawings.
2. Reinforce and clarify verbal concepts with visuals. A picture is worth a thousand words.
3. Make key points memorable, and help the listener remember your message. Most people remember visuals longer than they remember words and numbers.
4. Visuals lose their effectiveness if overused. A guideline is to use about one visual per minute.
5. In designing visuals:
   • Use headlines only.
   • Eliminate unnecessary words.
   • Write large so words can be read from the back of the room.
   • Use drawings and diagrams whenever possible.
   • Limit to 36 words per visual (6 lines of 6 words each).
6. After using visuals, redirect learners' attention back to you:
   • Shut off the overhead projector when there is a lengthy explanation and there is no need for the audience to see the transparency. Don't turn the machine off and on so frequently that it becomes distracting (30 seconds is a guideline).
   • Turn a flip chart page to a blank one when you are finished referring to it. If the flip chart pages have been prepared in advance, leave blank pages between each prepared sheet so the next prepared page will not show through.
   • Erase any writing on the chalkboard or whiteboard when you no longer need it.
   • Break up slide presentations by inserting a black or translucent slide at points where an explanation is needed or where questions will be asked or answered.
   • Show or demonstrate an object by revealing it when needed and covering it when it is no longer in use. Otherwise, your audience will look at the object and be distracted from your presentation. Avoid passing an object around the audience. Instead, walk around the audience and show the object to everyone briefly and make it available at the end of the presentation.

ASSURE Case Sample

MIDDLE SCHOOL MATHEMATICS

UTILIZE MEDIA AND MATERIALS

Preview the Materials

The teacher previews *Microsoft Works. CricketGraph, AppleWorks,* and some student-produced videotapes.

Prepare the Materials

The teacher makes a set of note cards outlining her lesson. In addition, she prepares the handouts and graphs on flip chart pages using *AppleWorks* and the *eMac.* She also prepares transparencies for use with the overhead projector.

Prepare the Environment

Because the primary portion of the lesson is small-group work, the teacher arranges the student desks in the classroom to form table areas. This will prepare the students for the group work when they come into the room so the lesson will not need to be interrupted. Some of the lesson takes place in the computer lab. Because this activity takes several days to complete, each day may require specific equipment setups. Generally, the overhead projector and flip chart are used for introductory purposes only. The next phase requires the use of a computer lab to teach the students how to use *AppleWorks.* Additionally, an overhead projector, data projector, and demonstration computer will also need to be set up. The regular classroom will be utilized for the students to conduct their small-group planning and for student presentations. There must be an overhead projector, a data projector, and a computer to view student work. In addition, the students will use a VCR with a monitor to play back their tapes for the class. After setting up the equipment, the teacher will also check that it is all in working order.

Prepare the Learners

To prepare the students, the teacher presents the overall plan and objectives for the lesson. Each student receives a handout de-scribing the small-group activity. In addition, the evaluation procedures are given to each student. The teacher presents important aspects of the requirements and evaluation standards using the overhead projector.

Provide the Learning Experience

During the introductory phases of this lesson, the teacher presents materials using the overhead projector, a data projector, computer, flip chart, and VCR. General showmanship techniques and those specific to each of these media are followed:

- *General Techniques.* The only place in the classroom with a screen is front and center. It is used for the overhead projector. When presenting information on the flip chart, the teacher places the chart in the front and to the left of center, since she is right handed. The VCR and monitor are located to the right of the screen.
- *Overhead Projector.* Use an outline to introduce and summarize the material. Turn off the projector when not referring to what is on it. Place notes for each transparency on its frame or cover sheet. Use a pencil as a pointer. Mask unwanted information.
- *Flip Chart.* Use lettering and figures large enough for all to see. Face the class when speaking. Stand out of the students' line of vision. Secure all pages firmly to the flip chart. Provide summary sheets at the end instead of flipping back through the pages.
- *Video.* Check lighting, seating, and volume. List on chalkboard the main points to be covered. Preview new vocabulary. Be a good role model—watch the program yourself. Provide appropriate followup activities and discussion.

This ASSURE Case Sample was developed by Mary Ann Ferkis, Purdue University.

All of the ASSURE Cases in Practice in this text and an electronic template for creating your own ASSURE Lesson can be found on the enclosed "Classroom Link Portfolio" CD-ROM.

REQUIRE LEARNER PARTICIPATION

Educators have long realized that active participation in the learning process enhances learning. In the early 1900s John Dewey urged reorganization of the curriculum and instruction to make student participation central. Later, in the 1950s and 1960s, experiments employing behaviorist approaches demonstrated that instruction providing for constant reinforcement of desired behaviors is more effective than instruction in which responses are not reinforced.

More recently, cognitive theories of learning, which focus on internal mental processes, have also supported the principle that effective learning demands active manipulation of information by learners. Gagné (1985) concluded that there are several necessary conditions for effective learning of each type of objective; the one condition that pertains to all objectives is practice of the desired skill (Figure 3.6)

Figure 3.6
Practicing a desired skill promotes the effectiveness of the learning experience.

The behaviorist perspective proposes that individuals learn what they *do*—that is, learning is a process of trying various behaviors and keeping those that lead to favorable results. If this is so, the instructional designer must find ways to constantly keep the learner *doing* something. Cognitivists propose that learners build up and enrich their mental schemata when their minds are actively engaged in struggling to remember or apply some new concept or principle. The constructivist, like the behaviorist, views learning as an active process. But the emphasis is on active *mental* processing, not physical activity. Knowledge is built on the basis of experience. Student autonomy and initiative are stressed within the context of relevant authentic experiences. The sociopsychological perspective stresses the importance of interpersonal communication as the social basis for knowledge acquisition.

All perspectives also emphasize the importance of **feedback** (productive critical evaluative response):

- Behaviorists, because knowledge of correct response serves as a reinforcer of appropriate behaviors
- Cognitivists, because information about results helps to enrich learners' mental schemata
- Constructivists, because meaning (and knowledge) is enhanced with each personal experience
- Social psychologists, because interpersonal feedback provides both corrective information and emotional support

Feedback can come from oneself (e.g., experiencing the "feel" of swinging a golf club), from print sources (e.g., turning to the back of the book to find the correct answer to a practice exercise), from a device (e.g., the computer gives a corrective statement after you choose an answer to a multiple-choice question), or from other people (e.g., another member of your group agrees with your solution to a problem). Research indicates that the most powerful is interpersonal feedback because face-to-face reactions are more vivid than printed or graphic information, such reactions are more personalized (giving specific performance correction), and group discussion can continue as long as necessary (Johnson & Johnson, 1993).

The implication for designers and instructors is clear. The most effective learning situations are those that require learners to **practice** skills that build toward the objective. The form of the participation may include practicing new spelling or vocabulary words, solving math problems on a worksheet, rehearsing a basketball play, or creating an original product, such as a term paper. Responses may be either observable or unobservable. An example of an *observable* performance is manipulation of task cards illustrating the stages of mitosis. An *unobservable* performance is silent repetition of phrases heard on a French language tape.

In all cases, learners should receive feedback on the correctness of their response. The feedback may come from the teacher, or students may work in small groups and give one another feedback. Feedback may also be achieved through a self-check activity or may come from a computer or mentor. Regardless of the source, the important thing is that students receive helpful feedback (Figure 3.7).

Figure 3.7
Feedback from the learners helps the instructor improve the lesson.

Some media formats lend themselves to participation more than others, at least on the surface. For example, student response to projected still pictures is easier to manage than response to a video. Learners can participate in and respond to the showing of a video. Overt written responses during the showing of a video have been shown to facilitate learning, unless the responses are so involved that students are prevented from watching the video.

Immediate confirmation of a correct response is particularly important when working with students of lower-than-average abilities. For such students, evidence of immediate success can be a strong motivating force for further learning.

Discussions, short quizzes, and application exercises can provide opportunities for practice and feedback during instruction. Followup activities can provide further opportunities. Teacher guides and manuals written to accompany instructional materials often suggest techniques and activities for eliciting and reinforcing student responses.

Research on the internationally renowned television series *Sesame Street* and *Electric Company* demonstrates impressively the importance of following up a media presentation with practice activities. Research on *Sesame Street* showed that frequent viewers not only learned the specific skills presented but also had higher scores on a test of verbal IQ and more positive attitudes about school. Johnston (1987) pointed out, though, that "parental encouragement and supplementary materials were essential to achieving the effects observed" (p. 44). In the case of *Electric Company,* children with low reading ability who watched the programs in school under teacher supervision showed significant reading improvement. Johnston concluded that "learning definitely did occur when viewing was insured, and when teachers supplied additional learning materials and helped the children to rehearse the materials presented on television" (Johnston, 1987, p. 44). (See "ASSURE Case Sample: Require Learner Participation.")

EVALUATE AND REVISE

The final component of the ASSURE model for effective learning is evaluation and revision. Often the most frequently misused aspect of lesson design, evaluation and revision is an essential component to the development of quality instruction. There are many purposes for evaluation. Often the only form seen in education is the paper-and-pencil test, claimed to be used for assessment of student achievement. We will discuss two purposes here: assessing learner achievement and evaluating methods and media.

Although ultimate evaluation must await completion of the instructional unit, evaluation is ongoing. Evaluations are made before, during, and after instruction; for example, before instruction, you would measure learner characteristics to ensure that there is a fit between existing student skills and the methods and materials you intend to use. In addition, materials should be appraised prior to use. During instruction, evaluation may take the form of student practice with feedback, or it may consist of a short quiz or self-evaluation. Evaluation during instruction usually has a diagnostic purpose; that is, it is designed to detect and correct learning/teaching problems and difficulties with the instruction that may interfere with student achievement.

Evaluation is not the end of instruction. It is the starting point of the next and continuing cycle in our systematic ASSURE model for effective use of instructional media. (For a comprehensive general discussion of evaluation and assessment, see the Stiggins reference in this chapter's Suggested Readings.)

Assessment of Learner Achievement

The ultimate question regarding instruction is whether students have learned what they were supposed to learn. Can they display the capabilities specified in the original statement of objectives? The first step in answering this question was taken near the beginning of the ASSURE model, when you formulated your objectives, including a criterion of acceptable performance. When developing assessment tasks, start with your objective and design an activity, which calls for the behavior, stated in the objective. The objective's statement of acceptable performance will help you develop the criteria for evaluating the individual student's or group's performance. If the objective lends itself only to paper-and-pencil evaluation of facts and information, perhaps you need to rewrite it.

The method of assessing achievement depends on the nature of the objective. Some objectives call for relatively simple cognitive skills—for example, recalling Ohm's law, distinguishing adjectives from adverbs, describing a company's absence policy, or summarizing the principles of the Declaration of Independence. Objectives such as these lend themselves to conventional written tests or oral examinations. Other objectives may call for process-type behaviors (e.g., conducting an orchestra, performing a forward roll on a balance beam, operating a metal lathe, or solving quadratic equations), the creation of products (e.g., a sculpture, a written composition, a window display, an account ledger, or a portfolio), or an exhibit of attitudes (e.g., tolerating divergent opinions, appreciating expressionist painting, observing safety procedures on the assembly line, or contributing to community charities).

The assessment procedures should correspond to the objectives stated earlier in the ASSURE model. For example, assume the objective is "Given a diagram of the human trachea, the student nurse will explain a bronchocele, describing the usual cause and the recom-

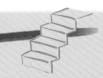

ASSURE Case Sample

MIDDLE SCHOOL MATHEMATICS

REQUIRE LEARNER PARTICIPATION

Large-Group Activities

As a review, introduction, and practice exercise, each student in the class reads and interprets a graph (bar, line, or circle) presented to him/her on the flip chart. Each student writes his/her findings directly on the laminated flip chart page. Using this method the teacher provides practice with feedback to each individual in the class. During the "mini-presentations" the class has handouts that include the same graphs as the flip chart. This enables them to have a record of the exercises for future reference. In addition, it involves the entire class in the learning. The students learn how to utilize the computer lab to practice construction and produce printouts of graphs (bar, line, circle, and others if appropriate) with *AppleWorks*.

Small-Group Activities

Following the large-group activity, the students participate in a small-group activity. Assignments require the students to collect, interpret, and present basic data. Initially, the groups work together to propose, discuss, and agree on a topic for a group presentation. The presentation topic must incorporate data collection techniques (survey, observation, and/or interview) and the use of graphs to present numerical information.

The students collect data in their school for a small-group presentation. The groups choose whether to collect their data through surveys, observations, or personal interviews. Each group uses *AppleWorks* to write and produce a written report regarding the data collection techniques associated with the topic of their presentation.

Survey

The small groups choosing to conduct a survey could use *AppleWorks* to create and write their survey. The group must submit an audiotape of each member administering the survey to a group or individual.

Observation

The small groups electing to use observation techniques use *Apple Works* to create and write an observation sheet to use when they make their observations. The group must submit a videotape of each member conducting an observation.

Personal Interview

The small groups choosing to conduct personal interviews use *AppleWorks* to create and write an interview form to use when they conduct their interviews. The groups must also submit a videotape or an audiotape of each member conducting an interview.

In each case the school media specialist arranges time in the library or in another classroom to help the groups with the audiotapes and videotapes. During the group presentations, the teacher provides the equipment necessary to play back each group's audio- and videotapes.

Reporters from each group present their data on a chart or a graph. The students must accurately construct and produce a printout of a graph (bar, line, or circle) using *AppleWorks*. During the group presentations, the teacher prepares the equipment necessary to view each group's graphs using a data projector. The groups are required to accurately read, interpret, and verbally present all the statistical information shown on their graphs.

This ASSURE Case Sample was developed by Mary Ann Ferkis, Purdue University.

All of the ASSURE Cases in Practice in this text and an electronic template for creating your own ASSURE Lesson can be found on the enclosed "Classroom Link Portfolio" CD-ROM.

---

mended treatment." A possible test question would be "What is a bronchocele? Describe the cause and treatment in your answer."

Assume students are learning to use Boolean logic in their Web searches. The objective might be "Using the *Yahooligans!* search engine on the Internet, the middle school students will locate four references that include two key words provided by the teacher." The assessment could be, "What are four references that discuss 'spiders' and 'poisonous?'" The teacher could provide different key words to each student.

For military training, an objective could be, "With the aid of a topographic map, the officer will call for

field artillery fire using the four essential items of information in prescribed military sequence." An oral test could ask, "Tell me how you would call for artillery fire on point X on the accompanying topographic map."

In schools, rising interest in **authentic assessment** is driven by commitment to competency-based instruction and to constructivist pedagogy. Authentic assessment is usually performance based and requires students to demonstrate what they have learned in a natural context, as opposed to just taking standardized paper-and-pencil tests. Some states have instituted more authentic forms of assessment in their state examination systems; some individual schools have experimented with such means as portfolio assessment (see Chapter 1). Schools and school systems are responding differently to this trend. Although authentic assessment strategies are still far from being the norm, they are increasing in popularity and use.

In educational settings, assessment is often used to measure student learning, to inform students and their parents/guardians of student progress, and to give grades. Authentic assessment is assessment of skills required in the "real world." How many people take paper-and-pencil tests as a part of their occupation? Authentic assessment focuses on the demonstration of mastery and the ability to transfer new knowledge and skills to different situations. Authentic assessment provides students opportunities to display knowledge and skills in a realistic situation, which accurately model the discipline. It is the difference between learning science facts and doing what scientists do.

The authentic assessment task should use processes (psychomotor and/or mental) appropriate to the content and skills being learned. The assessment task should represent the way the discipline is used in the real world. Media and technology can be used as part of authentic assessment, such as producing video productions and developing slide and audiotape presentations and computer-generated reports.

Authentic assessment tasks usually have the following characteristics:

- Have more than one correct approach
- Are thought provoking, not simply requiring recall of memorized facts
- Require decision making, rather than just rote memorization
- Develop thinking in a variety of ways
- Lead to other problems to be solved
- Raise other questions

Types of authentic assessments include the following:

- Student projects such as writing assignments, science projects, and posters
- Performances such as giving speeches, or demonstrating gymnastics or self-defense
- Oral questioning by both teachers and other students
- Discussions of controversial topics and current events
- Portfolios, including examples of student work with summaries and reflections

This trend toward more authentic assessment is important because assessment has long been understood to be the driving force for the rest of the

instructional system, including media, methods, and technology. Authentic assessment focuses on demonstration of mastery and the ability to transfer new knowledge to new situations. This has led to the development of portfolio assessment, which has fueled interest in student production of media, including the compilation of electronic portfolios.

Capabilities of the process, product, or attitude type could be assessed to some extent by means of written or oral tests. But such test results would be indirect and weak evidence of how well learners have mastered the objectives. More direct and stronger evidence would be provided by observing the behavior in action. This implies setting up a situation in which learners can demonstrate the new skill and the instructor can observe and judge it (Figure 3.8).

In the case of process skills, a performance checklist can be an effective, objective way of recording your observations, as shown with the checklist for driving skills (Figure 3.9). Other types of activities that can be properly assessed through performance checklists are sales techniques, telephone-answering skills, and face-to-face customer relations. During instruction these types of activities may need to be evaluated in a simulated situation, with other learners or with the instructor role playing the customer or client.

Attitudes are admittedly difficult to assess. For some attitudinal objectives, long-term observation may be required to determine whether the goal has really been attained. In day-to-day instruction we usually have to rely on what we can observe here and now, however limited that may be. A commonly used technique for making attitudes more visible is the attitude scale (an example regarding biology is shown in Figure 3.10). A number of other suggestions for attitude measurement can be found in Robert Mager's *How to Turn Learners On . . . Without Turning Them Off* (see this chapter's Suggested Readings).

Figure 3.8
A performance-type skill should be judged by observation.

Performance Checklist: Driving Skills

Name_____ Class _____

Indicate yes or no with an X in the appropriate column.

Did the Student   **Yes   No**

1. Fasten seat belt before starting car?   ____   ____
2. Use the ten o'clock and two o'clock hand position on
   steering wheel?   ____   ____
3. Drive with the flow of traffic yet stay within the speed limit?   ____   ____
4. Come to full and complete stops at stop signs?   ____   ____
5. Keep at least a three-second interval behind the vehicle
   ahead?   ____   ____
6. Stay in the proper driving lane—not cross center line?   ____   ____
7. Obey all traffic signs and signals?   ____   ____
8. Negotiate all turns properly (according to driving manual)?   ____   ____
9. Avoid excessive conversation with passengers?   ____   ____
10. Display courtesy to other drivers?   ____   ____

Instructor's Name_____ Date _____

Figure 3.9

A sample performance checklist.

Attitude Scale: Biology

Each of the statements below expresses a feeling toward biology. Please rate each
statement on the extent to which you agree. For each, you may (A) strongly agree,
(B) agree, (C) be undecided, (D) disagree, or (E) strongly disagree.

A	B	C	D	E
Strongly Agree	Agree	Undecided	Disagree	Strongly Disagree

____   1. Biology is very interesting to me.

____   2. I don't like biology, and it scares me to have to take it.

____   3. I am always under a terrible strain in biology class.

____   4. Biology is fascinating and fun.

____   5. Learning biology makes me feel secure.

____   6. Biology makes me feel uncomfortable, restless, irritable, and
          impatient.

____   7. In general, I have a good feeling toward biology.

____   8. When I hear the word *biology*, I have a feeling of dislike.

____   9. I approach biology with a feeling of hesitation.

____ 10. I really like biology.

____ 11. I have always enjoyed studying biology in school.

____ 12. It makes me nervous to even think about doing a biology experiment.

____ 13. I feel at ease in biology and like it very much.

____ 14. I feel a definite positive response to biology; it's enjoyable.

Figure 3.10

A sample attitude scale.

PRODUCT RATING CHECKLIST: Welding

Name _____ Date _____

Rate the welded product by checking the appropriate boxes. Add comments if you wish.

Base metal(s) _____ Filler metal(s) _____

Profile:	Excellent	Very Good	Good	Fair	Poor	Workmanship:	Excellent	Very Good	Good	Fair	Poor
Convexity (max ¹/₃₂″)	☐	☐	☐	☐	☐	Uniform appearance	☐	☐	☐	☐	☐
Fusion on toe	☐	☐	☐	☐	☐	Arc strikes	☐	☐	☐	☐	☐
Overlap	☐	☐	☐	☐	☐	Bead width	☐	☐	☐	☐	☐
Amount of fill	☐	☐	☐	☐	☐	Bead start	☐	☐	☐	☐	☐
						Bead tie-in	☐	☐	☐	☐	☐
Overall Evaluation:						Bead termination	☐	☐	☐	☐	☐
						Penetration	☐	☐	☐	☐	☐
Evaluator Comments:						Amount of spatter	☐	☐	☐	☐	☐

Figure 3.11
A sample product rating checklist.

	Your Reaction
1. I could easily understand the teacher.	☺ 😐 ☹
2. I could always hear the teacher.	☺ 😐 ☹
3. I was not distracted.	☺ 😐 ☹
4. I felt involved.	☺ 😐 ☹
5. The teacher looked at me.	☺ 😐 ☹
6. Overall, I would grade the presentation	A B C D F

Completed forms to be collected by a student.

Figure 3.12
A sample form for students to evaluate their teachers.

For product skills, a product rating checklist can guide your evaluation of critical subskills and make qualitative judgments more objective, as in the accompanying example regarding welding (Figure 3.11). Other types of products that lend themselves to evaluation by a rating scale include pastry from a bakery, compositions in an English course, and computer programs.

Evaluation of Methods and Media

Evaluation also includes assessment of instructional methods and media. Were your instructional materials effective? Could they be improved? Were they cost effective in terms of student achievement? Did your presentation take more time than it was really worth? Particularly after first use, instructional materials need to be evaluated to determine whether future use, with or without modification, is warranted. The results of your evaluation should be entered on a Selection Rubric. Did the media assist the students in meeting the objectives? Were they effective in arousing student interest? Did they provide meaningful student participation?

You may solicit learner input on the effectiveness of specific media, such as a CD or videotape. You may design your own form or use one similar to the "Learner Reaction Form" shown in Figure 3.12.

Class discussions, individual interviews, and observation of student behavior should be used to evaluate instructional media and methods (Figure 3.13). Failure to attain objectives is, of course, a possible indication that something is wrong with the instruction. But analyzing student reaction to your instructional methods can be helpful in more subtle ways. Student–teacher discussion may indicate that your audience would have preferred independent study to your choice of group presentation. Or

Figure 3.13
The ability to create a product should be evaluated by the quality of the product itself.

Figure 3.14
Analysis of student reactions to lessons is an integral part of the instructional process.

perhaps viewers didn't like your selection of overhead transparencies and feel they would have learned more if a videotape had been shown. Your students may let you know, subtly or not so subtly, that your own performance left something to be desired (Figure 3.14).

Conversations with the school media specialist concerning the value of specific media in an instructional unit will help to alert you both to the need for additional instructional materials to improve the lesson in the future.

Evaluation of Instructor

An important component of many instructional systems is the instructor. The instructor should be evaluated along with other components of the system. Many of us fear evaluation, but it is the only way we can improve. Most of us can always improve—or at least confirm we are doing a good job. There are four basic types of instructor evaluation: self, student, peer, and administrator.

For self-evaluation, you can record your presentation on audiotape or videotape, then view it at a later time while using an evaluation form such as the one shown in Figure 3.15.

Students, even in early grades, can provide valuable feedback. The way you design the form and how the students respond will vary with the age of your students (see Figure 3.12).

You may ask a colleague, usually another teacher, to sit in the back of the room and observe your teaching skills. You may ask for an open-ended evaluation (blank sheet of paper) or you may design your own form, including what you want your colleague to observe and what aspect of your teaching you want to improve.

In most schools administrators visit teachers on a scheduled sequence, often annually or semiannually. You may ask an administrator to visit more frequently on an "unofficial" basis. Many schools have a standard form that administrators use to observe teachers and to provide feedback to them. You may also inform your administrator of other characteristics you would like for her to observe.

When designing your own form for self, student, peer, or administrator evaluation, the characteristics in "Showmanship: Classroom Presentation Skills" in this chapter are a good place to start. You may include anxiety, delivery, voice, eye contact, and gestures (see Figure 3.15).

Revision

The final step of the instructional cycle is to sit back and look at the results of your evaluation data gathering. Where are there discrepancies between what you intended to happen and what did happen? Did student achievement fall short on one or more of the objectives? How did students react to your instructional methods and media? Are you satisfied with the value of the materials you selected? You should reflect on the lesson and each component of it. Make notes immediately following completion of the lesson, and refer to them before you implement the lesson again. If your evaluation data indicate shortcomings in any of these areas, now is the time to go back to the faulty part of the plan and revise it. The model works, but only if you constantly use it to upgrade the quality of your instruction. (See "ASSURE Case Sample: Evaluate and Revise.")

Presentation Evaluation Form

Teacher _____ Evaluator _____ Date _____

SA = Strongly Agree   A = Agree   D = Disagree   SD = Strongly Disagree

1. Presenter appeared nervous.   SA   A   D   SD
   Comment _____
   _____

2. Content was delivered well.   SA   A   D   SD
   Comment _____
   _____

3. Movement enhanced presentation.   SA   A   D   SD
   Comment _____
   _____

4. Voice was natural and conversational.   SA   A   D   SD
   Comment _____
   _____

5. Vocal variety was used.   SA   A   D   SD
   Comment _____
   _____

6. Presenter could be easily heard.   SA   A   D   SD
   Comment _____
   _____

7. There were no distracting mannerisms.   SA   A   D   SD
   Comment _____
   _____

8. Eye contact was established and maintained.   SA   A   D   SD
   Comment _____
   _____

9. Natural gestures were used.   SA   A   D   SD
   Comment _____
   _____

10. Overall, presentation was well done.   SA   A   D   SD
    Comment _____
    _____

Strengths of presenter
_____
_____

Weaknesses of presenter
_____
_____

Overall comments
_____
_____
_____

Figure 3.15
A sample instructor evaluation form to be used by peer or administrator.

ASSURE Case Sample

MIDDLE SCHOOL MATHEMATICS

EVALUATE AND REVISE

Assessment of Learner Achievement

The following rating form is used to evaluate students' knowledge of the "Information Statistics" unit. The form is designed for students to complete.

Collecting Data (20 points)

- Did each member of your group collect data at least once and record this on tape?
- Did your group create and write a data collection sheet (survey, observation, or interview)?
- Did your report accurately explain the steps taken to collect your data?
- Did your report state a sound rationale for choosing the specific collection technique?

Presenting the Data (20 points)

- Are your graphs easy to read?
- Do your graphs have appropriate titles?
- Are the components of your graphs labeled correctly?
- Did you provide a printout of your graphs?

Presentation Style (40 points)

- Did your group introduce your presentation topic and tell why you chose it?
- Did you explain your data collection method and give your rationale for its choice?
- Did you play back your data collection tape?
- Did you show your results in the form of graphs?
- Did your group leave time for questions?
- Did your group answer pertinent questions?

Interpretation (20 points)

- Did your group correctly read and interpret the graphs?
- Did your group explain all the statistical information shown on the graphs?

Evaluation of Media and Methods

To successfully evaluate the media and methods utilized, the teacher conducts debriefing activities after teaching the students how to make graphs and after the student presentations. In addition, she talks informally with students during the entire process.

The teacher conducts a debriefing immediately following the graph-making session. She addresses any issues that may have arisen during the instruction. Additionally, she provides time for the students to vent their frustrations and to share their excitement. Then, she reminds them of the purpose of the activity. She also invites comments that address the importance of learning how to make graphs using spreadsheet programs. Specific examples illustrating possible future uses for the skill are also discussed. The primary purpose of this debriefing session is to determine whether the students are comfortable making graphs using the computer.

The teacher conducts a second debriefing session after all the students have made their presentations. She specifically addresses each phase of the instruction: first, the review/introduction phase utilizing the mini-presentation with the flip chart; second, the graph-making session; third, the planning phase of the presentation; fourth, the use of the computer to develop reports; fifth, the student presentations. Student reaction to each of these phases is critical for possible revisions. In addition, evaluation techniques for learner achievement are discussed. To complete the debriefing exercise, the teacher asks students to write the purpose of the project. In addition, they are asked to write whether they liked the activities, and to state why or why not.

Evaluation of Overall Instruction

The students and teacher complete a teacher-developed form for an overall evaluation of learner achievement, media, and methods. The student average is compared with the teacher's *perceptions*. For items that appear discrepant, the teacher will address the need for revision in her choice of learning activities, media selections, methods, and evaluation materials.

This ASSURE Case Sample was developed by Mary Ann Ferkis, Purdue University.

All of the ASSURE Cases in Practice in this text and an electronic template for creating your own ASSURE Lesson can be found on the enclosed "Classroom Link Portfolio" CD-ROM.

Summary: Using the ASSURE Model

This chapter has introduced you to the AS-SURE model, which you will use in the following chapters. More importantly, the model can be used when you design lessons or any presentation, whether for a group of students, a church group, social or fraternal organization, or club. The model incorporates the most important parts of instructional planning:

Who is your audience?

What are your objectives?

Which methods, media, and materials will you and your learners use?

How can you and your learners make best use of the materials?

How will you get your learners involved in learning?

How will you evaluate both the learners and your instruction?

What should you revise if you do the presentation again?

Classroom Link Portfolio Activities

Please use the "Classroom Link Portfolio" CD-ROM and the Companion Website as resources in completing these activities. To complete the following activities online go to the Portfolio Activities module in Chapter 3 of the Companion Website (http://www.prenhall.com/smaldino).

1. *Planning for Instruction.* Select a content area standard or topic you might like to teach. Use the Les-

son Planning function on the "Classroom Link Portfolio" CD-ROM to create a lesson to address this topic and/or standard, addressing issues of diverse learners. (ISTE NETS-T 2.A & C; 3.A & B; 6.C & E)

2. *Written Reflection.* Briefly describe lesson planning using the ASSURE model. What do you see as the benefits and drawbacks of using this model? What works best for you? Why? (ISTE NETS-T 2.B)

Integration Assessments

To complete the specified activities online go to the Integration Assessments module in Chapter 3 of the Companion Website (http://www.prenhall.com/smaldino).

1. Plan a presentation using the procedures described in this chapter. Your description must follow the "ASSURE Template" in this chapter. (ISTE NETS-T 5.C)

2. Write at least five objectives for a lesson you might teach. Choose a topic that allows you to write objectives in more than one domain.

3. Select a chapter from a textbook of interest to you and derive a set of at least five objectives that you feel the author intended.

4. Plan, prepare, and present a brief lesson incorporating two or more media. Have your audience (one person or more) give you feedback on your presentation skills. (ISTE NETS-T 2.A)

5. Select a lesson you might teach, such as a chapter from a textbook, and develop a set of evaluation instruments (not necessarily all paper-and-pencil test items).

6. Locate a lesson plan on the Internet and evaluate it using the ASSURE model as a guideline. (ISTE NETS-T 2.C)

7. Identify a group of learners (students or trainees) with which you are familiar. Describe the general characteristics and their specific entry competencies for a topic of your choice. Discuss their learning styles in terms of their perceptual preferences/strengths, information processing habits, motivational factors, and physiological factors.

8. Locate a set of objectives on the Internet, classify them, and critique them using the "Objectives Checklist" in this chapter. (ISTE NETS-T 2.C)

9. Search the Internet and find some materials you could use in a lesson. Design a lesson around the materials using the "Classroom Link Portfolio" CD-ROM. (ISTE NETS 2.A & 2.C)

10. Locate a lesson, perhaps using the Internet, which does *not* provide learner practice and feedback. Design activities for that lesson that do provide practice and feedback.

11. Using the Internet, locate an article on authentic assessment or a constructivist view of student evaluation. Write a one- to two-page summary and one to two pages describing your reflection on or reaction to the article. (ISTE NETS-T 2.B, 5.B)

ASSURE Case Template

A TEMPLATE FOR PLANNING

This is a description of the instructional situation.

ANALYZE LEARNERS

General Characteristics

This is a description of the class as a whole (e.g., age, grade, etc.).

Entry Competencies

This is a description of the types of knowledge expected of the learners.

Learning Styles

This is a description of the learning stylistic preferences of individual members of the class.

STATE OBJECTIVES

Objectives are descriptions of the learning outcomes and are written using the ABCD format.

SELECT METHODS, MEDIA, AND MATERIALS

Include all the methods, media, and materials that are essential to the lesson.

Rationale

It is important to consider why certain media have been selected.

Evaluation of Commercial Materials

Selection Rubrics are valuable when selecting commercial materials.

UTILIZE MATERIALS

Preview Materials

It is essential to know the materials prior to teaching with them.

Prepare the Materials

Experience using the materials is important.

Prepare the Environment

Setting up the instructional environment helps to make the learning experience valuable.

Prepare the Learners

Knowing what is expected of them helps learners be involved in the learning.

Provide the Learning Experience

The actual presentation needs to be considered.

REQUIRE LEARNER PARTICIPATION

A description of the activities designed to provide practice with feedback for the learners.

EVALUATE AND REVISE

Assessment of Learner Achievement

How will the objectives be "tested"?

Evaluation of Instruction (including media and methods)

To ensure quality instruction, it is important to evaluate the experience for future planning.

All of the ASSURE Cases in Practice in this text and an electronic template for creating your own ASSURE Lesson can be found on the enclosed "Classroom Link Portfolio" CD-ROM.

References

Butler, Kathleen A. 1986. *Learning and teaching style: In theory and in practice,* 2nd ed. Columbia, CT: Learner's Dimension.

Dick, Walter, Lou Carey, and Jim Carey. 2001. *The systematic design of instruction,* 5th ed. New York: Longman.

Dunn, Rita, and Kenneth Dunn. 1992. *Teaching elementary students through their individual learning styles: Practical applications for grades 3–6.* Boston: Allyn & Bacon.

Gagné, Robert M. 1985. *The conditions of learning,* 4th ed. New York: Holt, Rinehart & Winston.

Gardner, Howard. 1999. *Intelligence reframed: Multiple intelligences for the 21st century.* New York: Basic Books.

Gronlund, Norman E. 2004. *Writing instructional objectives for teaching and assessment,* 7th ed. Upper Saddle River. NJ: Merrill/Prentice Hall.

Johnson, David W., and Roger T. Johnson. 1993. Cooperative learning and feedback in technology-based instruction. In *Interactive instruction and feedback*, edited by J. Dempsey and G. Sales. Englewood Cliffs, NJ: Educational Technology Publications.

Johnston, Jerome. 1987. *Electronic learning: From audiotape to videotape*. Hillsdale, NJ: Lawrence Erlbaum Associates.

Keller, John. 1987. The systematic process of motivational design. *Performance and Instruction, 26*(9): 1–8.

Mager, Robert F. 1997. *Preparing instructional objectives*, 3rd ed. Atlanta, GA: Center for Effective Performance.

McAlpine, Lynn, and Cynthia Weston. 1994. The attributes of instructional materials. *Performance Improvement Quarterly, 7*(1): 19–30.

Suggested Readings

General References

Kafai, Yasmin, and Mitchel Resnick. 1996. *Constructivism in practice: Designing, thinking, and learning in a digital world*. Mahwah, NJ: Lawrence Erlbaum Associates.

Messerer, J. 1997. Adaptive technology: Unleashing the power of technology for all students. *Learning and Leading with Technology, 24*(5): 50–53.

Prestidge-Glaser, L. K. 2000. Authentic assessment: Employing appropriate tools for evaluating students' work in the 21st century. *Intervention in School and Clinic, 35*(3): 178–182.

Stiggins, Richard J. 2005. *Student-involved classroom assessment*, 4th ed. Upper Saddle River. NJ: Merrill/Prentice Hall.

Waddeck, J. 1997. Physical considerations in the development of a computer learning environment. *British Journal of Educational Technology, 28*(1): 69–71.

Media Selection and Use

Arredondo, Lani. 1991. *How to present like a pro*. New York: McGraw-Hill.

Hybert, Peter R. 2000. Choosing training delivery media. *Performance Improvement, 39*(5): 18–25.

Kang, S. H. 1996–1997. The effects of using an advance organizer on students' learning in a computer simulation environment. *Journal of Educational Technology Systems, 25*(1): 57–65.

Mager, Robert F. 1997a. *How to turn learners on . . . without turning them off,* 3rd ed. Atlanta, GA: Center for Effective Performance.

———. 1997b. *Making instruction work,* 2nd ed. Atlanta, GA: Center for Effective Performance.

———. 1997c. *Measuring instructional results,* 3rd ed. Atlanta, GA: Center for Effective Performance.

Vaccare, Carmel, and Greg Sherman. 2001. A pragmatic model for instructional technology selection. *Educational Media and Technology Yearbook, 26:* 16–23.

Instructional Design

Boyle, T. 1997. *Design for multimedia learning*. Upper Saddle River, NJ: Merrill/Prentice Hall.

Jonassen, D. H. 1997. Instructional design models for well-structured and ill-structured problem-solving learning outcomes. *Educational Technology Research and Development, 45*(1): 65–94.

Morrison, Gary R., Steven M. Ross, and Jerrold E. Kemp. 2004. *Designing effective instruction*, 4th ed. New York: John Wiley & Sons.

Reiser, Robert A., and Walter Dick. 1995. *Instructional planning: A guide for teachers,* 2nd ed. Boston: Allyn & Bacon.

Smith, Patricia L., and Tillman J. Ragan, 1999. *Instructional design*, 2nd ed. New York: John Wiley & Sons.

Sugrue, Brenda. 2002. Performance-based instructional design for e-learning. *Performance Improvement, 41*(7): 45–51.

Learning Styles

Armstrong, Thomas. 1994. *Multiple intelligences in the classroom*. Alexandria, VA: ASCD.

Beck, Charles R. 2001. Matching teaching strategies to learning style preferences. *Teacher Educator, 37*(1): 1–15.

Delahoussaye, Martin. 2002. The perfect learner: An expert debate on learning styles. *Training, 39*(5): 28–36.

Fritz, Margaret. 2002. Using learning styles inventories to promote active learning. *Journal of College Reading and Learning, 32*(2): 183–88.

Gardner, Howard. 1993. *Multiple intelligences: The theory in practice*. New York: Basic Books.

Keller, J. M. 1987. Development and use of the ARCS model of instructional design. *Journal of Instructional Development, 10*(3): 2–10.

———. 1999. Using the ARCS motivational process in computer-based instruction and distance education. *New Directions for Teaching and Learning, 78:* 39–47.

Love, Patrick. 1995. Enhancing student learning: Intellectual, social, and emotional integration. Washington, DC: ERIC Clearinghouse on Higher Education (Report no. 4).

Melora, G. E. 1996. Investigating learning styles on different hypertext environments: Hierarchical-like and network-like structures. *Journal of Educational Computing Research, 14*(4): 313–328.

Sansone, C., and J. Harackiewicz, eds. 2000. *Intrinsic and extrinsic motivation: The search for optimal motivation and performance*. San Diego: Academic Press.

Tobias, C. U. 1996. *Every child can succeed: Making the most of your child's learning style*. Colorado Springs, CO: Focus on the Family.

Tobias, Sigmund, 1987. Learner characteristics. In *Instructional technology: Foundations*, edited by Robert M. Gagné. Hillsdale, NJ: Lawrence Erlbaum Associates.

Visual Principles

Outline

Knowledge Objectives

1. Describe the roles that visuals play in instruction.
2. Define *visual literacy* in your own words.
3. Identify two general methods that you may use to teach visual literacy.
4. Describe the factors that influence students' decoding of visuals.
5. Describe the factors that influence students' encoding of visuals.
6. State in your own words the goals that good visual design aims to achieve.
7. Regarding the visual design process, characterize the qualities that a designer would look for in the individual visual and verbal elements of the design, including elements that add appeal.
8. Describe the factors that a designer would manipulate in establishing an underlying pattern to the design.
9. Describe the factors that a designer would manipulate in arranging the visual and verbal elements to achieve clear communication, reduce effort in interpreting, increase active engagement, and focus viewer attention.
10. List various roles that color can play in enhancing the impact of visual displays.

Professional Vocabulary

referent	proximity
iconic	directional
visual literacy	figure–ground contrast
sans serif	storyboarding
optical spacing	digital camera
alignment	scanner
rule of thirds	charge-coupled device (CCD)
complementary colors	photo CD
analogous colors	

Because so much learning involves visual imagery, the design and use of visuals in instruction is worthy of separate consideration. Most of the media discussed in this text—transparencies, slides, video programs, computer courseware, multimedia—have a visual component. The rapidly increasing visual capabilities of computers and digital telecommunications can only heighten the importance of visuals in education. Unfortunately, in the past teachers and materials designers have too often used this valuable visual capability primarily to show pictures of . . . WORDS! (See Figure 4.1.) The overemphasis on words has contributed to the failure of formal education to reach its ideal of universal success. We know that some students learn more readily through visual imagery, and even those who are verbal learners need visual supports to grasp certain types of concepts.

This chapter examines the functions and characteristics of visuals and visual literacy; it presents guidelines for designing and using visuals effectively. We suggest specific applications for teacher-made materials such as bulletin board displays and computer screens.

Significant contributions to this chapter were made by Elizabeth Boling, MFA, and Dennis Pett, EdD, both of Indiana University.

ASSURE
Case Challenge

We have developed a case study for this chapter to help you see how visuals can be integrated into learning activities. At the end of the chapter you will be challenged to develop your own ASSURE lesson for a case study of your choice using the AS-SURE model and incorporating the technology and media described in this chapter. To help you prepare your lesson, we have included hints (called "ASSURE Case Connections") throughout the chapter as they relate to the ASSURE Case Challenge.

Ms. Herr wants to improve her sixth-grade students' skills in using visuals to communicate along with their oral and written communication skills. She is interested in having her students work in pairs to support each other in learning how to use visuals as part of their presentations in class.

The students in this class are culturally diverse. Most work below grade level in their reading abilities. Many have difficulty with organizing their thoughts and do not do well with written work. They benefit from instruction that is connected to real-world experiences.

THE ROLES OF VISUALS IN INSTRUCTION

Attempts to make broad generalizations about the role of visuals in learning invariably fail to yield simple answers. For example, a major synthesis of research studies comparing visual-based lessons (those using photographs, overhead transparencies, video, and the like) with conventional instruction indicated a small overall superiority in achievement for students who experienced the visual treatment (Cohen, Ebeling, & Kulik, 1981). However, on closer examination it was found that the degree of superiority depended on many factors, including the subject matter and the utilization practices of the teacher. As discussed in Chapter 3, individual students vary in terms of their visual "intelligence" and in the way they process and use visual information.

One role that visuals definitely play is to provide a concrete **referent** for ideas. Words don't (usually) look or sound like the thing they stand for, but visuals are **iconic**—that is, they have some resemblance to the thing they represent (see Dale's Cone of Experience in Chapter 1). As such, they serve as a more easily remembered link to the original idea (Figure 4.2). Visuals can also motivate learners by attracting their attention, holding their attention, and generating emotional responses.

Parts of a Letter

- **Return Address**
- **Inside Address**
- **Salutation**
- **Body**
- **Closing**
- **Signature**

Figure 4.1
Too often, visual media are used to show only verbal messages.

Figure 4.2
A color photograph can be a highly iconic visual, capturing much of the reality of the original referent.

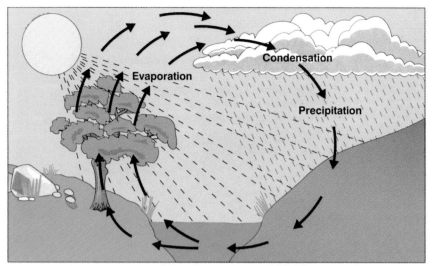

Figure 4.3
A complex process can be simplified visually and therefore made easier to understand and remember.

Visuals can simplify information that is difficult to understand (Figure 4.3). Diagrams can make it easy to store and retrieve such information. They can also serve an organizing function by illustrating the relationships among elements, as in a flowchart or timeline.

Finally, visuals provide a redundant channel; that is, when accompanying spoken or written verbal information they present that information in a different modality, giving some learners a chance to comprehend visually what they might miss verbally.

VISUAL LITERACY

Consider the sorts of visuals that are used every day for important communication purposes, such as the emergency information cards in airplanes (Figure 4.4) or highway signs that warn of dangerous curves or obstructions. They work only to the extent that you are "literate" in the conventions of that medium. Whereas the term *literacy* once was used only to refer to reading and writing of verbal information, today we use the term **visual literacy** to refer to the learned ability to interpret visual messages accurately and to create such messages. Research on visual literacy examines the influence of the visual processing system on the acquisition of knowledge, skills, and attitudes. Interest in visual literacy has grown to the point that it has become a professional interest area. The International Visual Literacy Association (IVLA), which conducts formal meetings and publishes its own periodical, is an organization established for professionals involved in visual literacy.

The critical role of visuals in education was recognized forcefully a century ago by John Dewey (1897), probably the most influential American philosopher of education:

> I believe much of the time and attention now given to the preparation and presentation of lessons might be more wisely and profitably expended in training the student's power of imagery and in seeing to it that he is continually forming definite, vivid, and growing images of the various subjects with which he comes in contact in his experience. (p. 80)

Visual literacy can be developed through two major approaches:

- *Input strategies.* Helping learners to *decode*, or "read," visuals proficiently by practicing visual analysis skills (e.g., through picture analysis and discussion of multimedia and video programs).

Figure 4.4
Well-designed visuals communicate clearly across boundaries of language and culture.
Source: Copyright Aero Safety Graphics, Inc. Used by permission..

Close-Up

VISUAL LITERACY EDUCATION

Visual literacy education programs have been developed throughout the United States and in many other countries to introduce students to the concepts and skills related to interpreting visuals and communicating visually. These programs are designed for children from preschool through high school and encompass both encoding and decoding visual information in all media. Visual literacy has now become well accepted as an important aspect of the curriculum at all levels of education.

One such program in the Minneapolis public schools involves students in many viewing skills activities and media production projects with the aim of developing critical viewing and thinking skills. Students examine all media with a focus on how elements such as color, camera angle, and pacing can affect the impact of visual messages. "Visual Education," the district's curriculum guide, encourages teachers to consider visual learning styles and emphasizes the importance of visuals in developing creativity and critical thinking skills. In many media centers around the district, students create poster campaigns, design new products and advertising, examine their television viewing habits, and analyze commercial messages. They produce videos using camcorders, and they design projects in video, photography, and other media.

In programs such as this all over the country, teachers are encouraged to think visually and to focus students' attention on the visual aspects of textbooks and storybooks while reading. Visuals inundate today's students, so their ability to read, understand, create, and analyze the persuasiveness of visuals has become more

important than ever. Media production, computer design, and critical thinking skills can enhance students' abilities to work and succeed in an increasingly visual world.

Elementary teachers have discovered the appeal of visual tools such as tangrams, visual searchers, and three-dimensional shapes. The concepts of sequencing, patterning, visual analogies, visual perception, visual attributes, and categorization are enhanced by other visual teaching tools, such as Venn diagrams, hidden pictures, drawings, memory games, and video clips. Students work alone or together on visual learning activities and develop communication, organization, and reporting skills in the process.

Source: Rhonda S. Robinson, Northern Illinois University.

- *Output strategies.* Helping learners to *encode,* or "write," visuals—to express themselves and communicate with others (e.g., through planning and producing photo and video presentations). These input and output strategies are shown in Figures 4.5 through 4.8.

Decoding: Interpreting Visuals

Seeing a visual does not automatically ensure that one will learn from it. Learners must be guided toward correct decoding of visuals (see Figure 4.4). One aspect of visual literacy, then, is the skill of interpreting and creating meaning from surrounding stimuli.

Figure 4.5
Reading is the "decoding" activity of print literacy.

Figure 4.6
Writing is the "encoding" activity of print literacy.

Figure 4.7
Interpreting a video program is the "decoding" activity of visual literacy.

Figure 4.8
Creating a video program is the "encoding" activity of visual literacy.

Figure 4.9
What story do you think this picture is telling? Do you think a 5-year-old would see the same story?

Developmental Effects.　Many variables affect how a learner decodes a visual. Prior to the age of 12, children tend to interpret visuals section by section rather than as a whole. In reporting what they see in a picture, they are likely to single out specific elements within the scene. Students who are older, however, tend to summarize the whole scene and report a conclusion about the meaning of the picture (Figure 4.9).

Hence, abstract symbols or a series of still pictures whose relationship is not clearly spelled out may fail to communicate as intended with younger viewers (Figure 4.10). On the other hand, highly realistic visuals may distract younger children. However, as Dwyer (1978, p. 33) notes, "As a child gets older, he becomes more capable of attending selectively to those features of an instructional presentation that have the greatest potential for enhancing his learning of desired information."

Cultural Effects.　In teaching, we must keep in mind that the act of decoding visuals may be affected by the viewer's cultural background. Different cultural groups

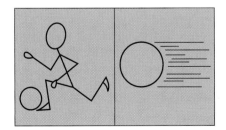

Figure 4.10
An active posture, as in the drawing on the left, communicates movement more reliably than arbitrary graphic conventions such as speed lines, as in the drawing on the right.

BUFFALO BILL'S WILD WEST
AND CONGRESS OF ROUGH RIDERS OF THE WORLD.

A CONGRESS OF AMERICAN INDIANS, REPRESENTING VARIOUS TRIBES, CHARACTERS AND PECULIARITIES OF THE WILY DUSKY WARRIORS IN SCENES FROM ACTUAL LIFE GIVING THEIR WEIRD WAR DANCES AND PICTURESQUE STYLE OF HORSEMANSHIP.

COL. W. F. CODY,
BUFFALO BILL
WILL APPEAR
AT EVERY PERFORMANCE

Figure 4.11
The cultural biases of a communicator, although unspoken, may be perceived vividly by viewers having a different cultural background.

municate better (e.g., drawings can eliminate distracting pictorial elements and highlight the important details). Even though many learners prefer very realistic visuals over abstract representations, teachers must strike a balance between the two to achieve their instructional purposes. Even though young learners prefer simple visuals and older students prefer more complex ones, simpler visuals are usually more effective, whatever the age group.

Regardless of their different starting points and differences in bias, students develop their visual abilities by *using* them. They can practice by viewing and critiquing visual displays, such as magazine ads, and by thinking critically about and discussing television programs. This chapter begins the exploration of these possibilities.

may perceive visual materials in different ways. For example, let's say your instruction includes visuals depicting scenes typical of the home life and street life of inner-city children. It is almost certain that students who live in such an area will decode these visuals differently than will students whose cultural (and socioeconomic) backgrounds do not include firsthand knowledge of inner-city living. Similarly, scenes depicting life in the Old West might be interpreted quite differently by a Native American child than they would be by an African American, Caucasian, or Mexican American child (Figure 4.11).

Visual Preferences.   In selecting visuals, teachers have to make appropriate choices between the sorts of visuals that are preferred and those that are most effective. People do not necessarily learn best from the kinds of pictures they prefer to look at. For instance, research on picture preferences indicates that children in upper elementary grades tend to prefer color to black and white and to choose photographs over drawings; younger children tend to prefer simple illustrations, whereas older children tend to prefer moderately complex illustrations (Myatt & Carter, 1979).

Most learners prefer colored visuals over black-and-white visuals. However, there is no significant difference in the amount of learning except when color is related to the content to be learned (e.g., when workers must learn to assemble electrical components with different-colored wires, the presence of color is essential). Most learners also prefer photographs over line drawings, even though in many situations line drawings may com-

Encoding: Creating Visuals

Another route to visual literacy is through student creation of visual presentations. Just as writing can spur reading, producing media can be a highly effective way of understanding media.

Most older students have access to a camera. For example, you could encourage students to present reports to the class by carefully selecting sets of 35mm slides, which can help them to develop their aesthetic talents. The video camcorder is another convenient tool for students to practice creating and presenting ideas and events pictorially (Figure 4.12). Or students can scan photos or drawings into a computer-generated presentation using software such as *PowerPoint*.

One skill nearly always included in visual education curricula is that of sequencing. Reading specialists have long known that the ability to *sequence*—that is, to arrange ideas in logical order—is an extremely important factor in verbal literacy, especially in the ability to communicate in writing.

Children who have grown up constantly exposed to movies and television may expect the visuals they encounter in school to be similarly packaged and sequenced. They may need practice in arranging visuals into logical sequence, which is a learned skill, like the verbal sequencing in reading and writing. For this reason, many visual education programs, especially for primary school children, emphasize creative activities that call for arranging and making visuals.

Figure 4.12
The camcorder is a handy tool for creating visual reports.

This chapter emphasizes the principles that define effective visuals. The main purpose is to help you increase your own critical ability with visuals. But we also want to provide you with additional tools for teaching others these skills. This chapter focuses on understanding visual design and doing visual displays—creative activities that are certainly appropriate for students. Teachers use the storyboarding techniques discussed later in this chapter not only for their own planning but as a learning tool for their students; it helps them practice inferencing, sequencing information, and so on. Chapter 10 discusses slides and multi-image presentations, and Chapter 12 explores the possibilities of local video production. These skills are not just for you—you should pass them on to your students as well.

GOALS OF VISUAL DESIGN

What does a professional visual designer think about when facing a visual design problem? The considerations are too numerous and complex to be spelled out fully here. However, there are a few fundamental principles of visual design that even novices may pursue. For purposes of information and instruction, good visual design tries to achieve at least four basic goals in terms of improving communication:

- Ensure legibility.
- Reduce the effort required to interpret the message.

- Increase the viewer's active engagement with the message.
- Focus attention on the most important parts of the message.

Ensure Legibility

A visual cannot even begin to do its job unless all viewers can see the words and images. It's surprising how often this simple rule is broken. Think of how many times you have heard a presenter say, "You may not be able to see what's on this transparency [or slide], so let me read it to you." The goal of good visual design is to remove as many obstacles as possible that might impede transmission of your message (specific guidelines on, for example, the size of letters appear later in this chapter).

Reduce Effort

As a designer you want to convey your message in such a way that viewers expend little effort making sense out of what they are seeing and are free to use most of their mental effort for understanding the message itself. You may use several simple processes to help reduce the effort required to interpret your visuals. Later in this chapter you will see how establishing an underlying pattern (alignment, shape, balance), putting like things together (proximity), and following a regular pattern in your treatment (consistency) contribute to this goal. Using harmonious color combinations and figures that contrast with their backgrounds also play roles.

Increase Active Engagement

Your message doesn't stand a chance unless people pay attention to it. So a major goal is to make your design as appealing as possible—to get viewers' attention and to entice them into thinking about your message. Ideas elaborated later in this chapter include using novelty to grab attention and using textures and interactive features to get viewers actively engaged with your message. Choosing a style appropriate for your audience and using appealing color schemes also will help you gain and hold your audience.

Focus Attention

Having enticed viewers into your display, you then face the challenge of directing their attention to the most important parts of your message. The overall design pattern plus specific directional guides (woven into the design and color cues) are your means for achieving the goal of focusing attention.

ASSURE Case Connection

Ms. Herr understands how important it is to prepare visuals to ensure they will facilitate learning. How should she begin to teach her students about interpreting visuals? How can she capitalize on their diversity to help her explain *visual literacy* to them?

Processes of Visual Design

This section outlines a set of procedures for carrying out visual design so as to enhance these goals. Throughout this chapter are specific examples of these procedures and explanations of how these decisions contribute to reaching the four basic goals of visual design. In Classroom Resources, Section C, see "Using Color in Instructional Materials," "Designing Computer Screens," "Designing Text," "Designing Bulletin Boards," and "Designing Overhead Transparencies."

Teachers, designers, and others who create visual and verbal/visual displays face a series of design decisions about how to arrange the elements to achieve their goals. We will group these decisions into three sets:

1. *Elements:* Selecting and assembling the verbal/visual elements to incorporate into the display
2. *Pattern:* Choosing an underlying pattern for the elements of the display
3. *Arrangement:* Arranging the individual elements within the underlying pattern

As a final step, check your decisions against the goals and revise as needed.

Elements

Designing a visual display begins with gathering or producing the individual pictorial and text elements that you expect to use in the display. This assumes, of course, that you have already determined students' needs and interests regarding the topic and decided what objective you might achieve through the visual you are planning—be it a bulletin board, an overhead transparency, printed handouts, or computer screen display.

In selecting or producing the pictorial and text elements, you will want to make your choices based on achieving the visual design goals—ensuring legibility, helping viewers to quickly see your message, getting viewers actively engaged with your message, and focusing attention on key points. We have grouped the following design suggestions according to the various elements or components of the display: the visual elements (choosing the type of visual), the verbal elements (lettering style and location), and the elements that add appeal (surprise, texture, interaction).

Visual Elements. The type of visual selected for a particular situation depends on the learning task. Visual symbols, one classification of learning resources in Dale's Cone of Experience (discussed in Chapter 1), can be subdivided into three categories: realistic, analogic, and organizational (Houghton & Willows, 1987).

Realistic visuals show the actual object under study. For example, the color photograph of a covered wagon in Figure 4.13 is a realistic visual. Using realistic colors

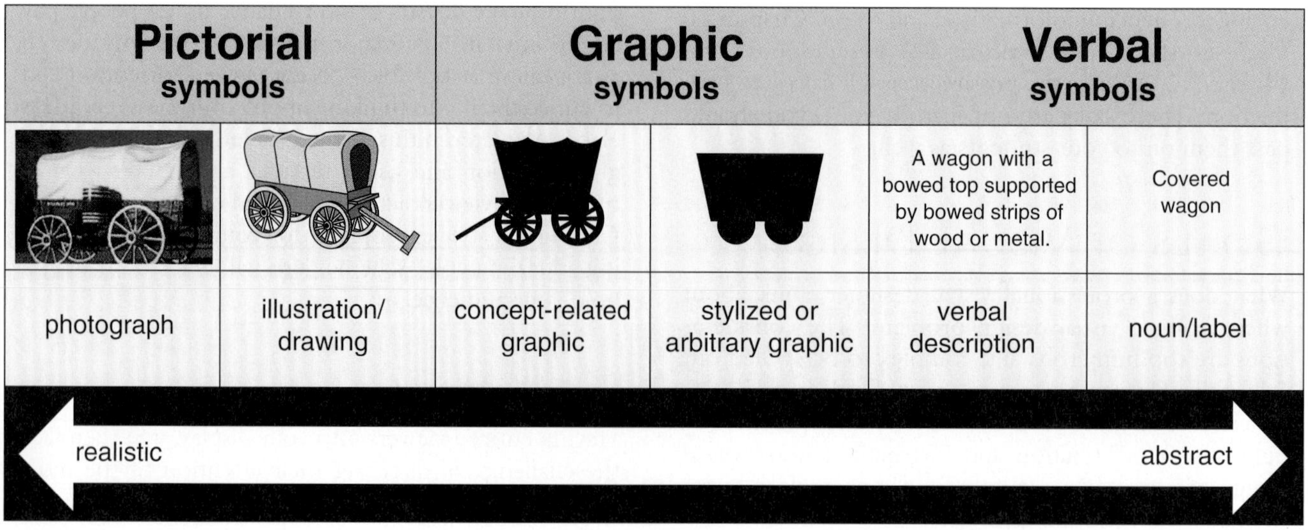
Pictorial symbols
Graphic symbols
Verbal symbols
A wagon with a bowed top supported by bowed strips of wood or metal.
Covered wagon
photograph
illustration/ drawing
concept-related graphic
stylized or arbitrary graphic
verbal description
noun/label
realistic
abstract

Figure 4.13
Photographs, illustrations, graphics, and words represent a continuum of realism for different kinds of symbols.

can heighten the degree of realism; this is one of the major instructional purposes that color serves. No representation, of course, is totally realistic. The real object or event will always have aspects that cannot be captured pictorially, even in a three-dimensional color motion picture. The various visual forms themselves range in representation from highly realistic to highly abstract.

One might be inclined to conclude that effective communication is always best served by the most realistic visual available. After all, the more realistic a visual is, the closer it is to the original. This, however, is not necessarily so. There is ample research to show that under certain circumstances, realism can actually interfere with communication and learning. For example, the ability to sort out the relevant from the irrelevant in a pictorial representation grows with age and experience. So, for younger children and for older learners who are encountering an idea for the first time, the wealth of detail found in a realistic visual may increase the likelihood that the learner will be distracted by irrelevant elements of the visual.

As Dwyer (1978, p. 33) notes in his review of visual research, "The arbitrary addition of stimuli in visuals makes it difficult for learners to identify the essential learning cues from among the more realistic background stimuli." Dwyer concludes that rather than being a simple yes-or-no issue, the amount of realism desired has a curvilinear relationship to learning: either too much or too little realism may affect achievement adversely (Figure 4.14).

Analogic visuals convey a concept or topic by showing something else and implying a similarity. Teaching about electricity flow by showing water flowing in series and parallel pipes is an example of using analogic visuals. An analogy for white blood cells fighting off infection might be an army attacking a stronghold. Later in this chapter, we use the color wheel as an analogy to help you visualize the relationships among the colors of the visible spectrum. Such visuals help learners interpret new information in light of prior knowledge and thereby facilitate learning (Figure 4.15).

Organizational visuals include flowcharts, graphs, maps, schematics, and classification charts. (See Chapter 10 for details on types of charts and graphs.) These graphic organizers can show relationships among the main points or concepts in textual material. This type of visual (such as the one in Figure 4.16) helps communicate the organization of the content.

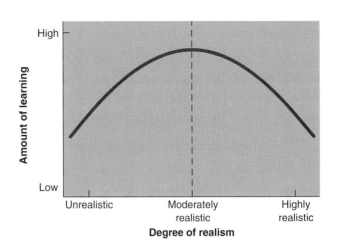

Figure 4.14

Visuals tend to become less useful as they approach the extremes of very abstract or very realistic.

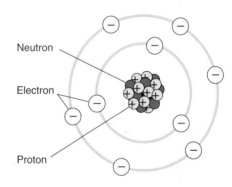

Figure 4.15

The solar system is often used as a visual analogy to explain the composition of an atom.

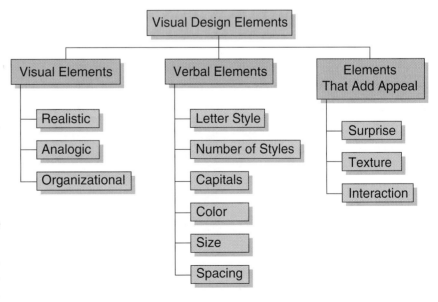

Figure 4.16

An organizational chart, such as this one representing a section of this chapter, can help show relationships among concepts.

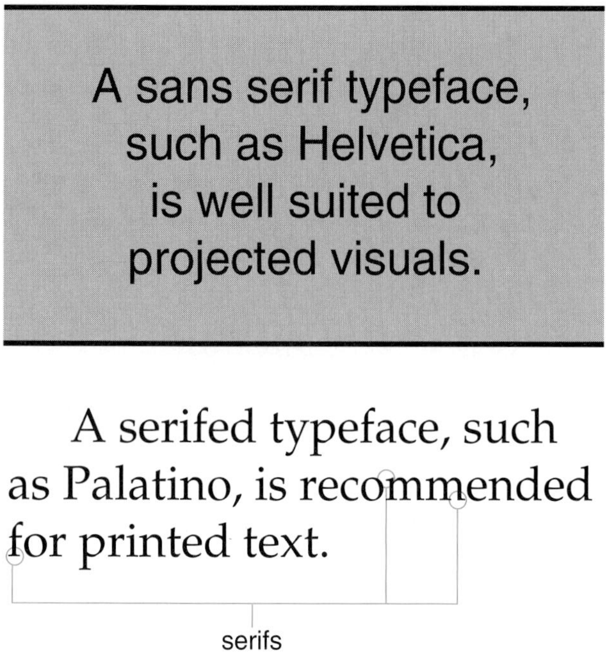

A sans serif typeface,
such as Helvetica,
is well suited to
projected visuals.

A serifed typeface, such
as Palatino, is recommended
for printed text.

serifs

Figure 4.17
Styles of type should be selected to suit their purpose.

Verbal Elements. Most displays incorporate some type of verbal information in addition to visuals. In evaluating a display for its instructional potential or in preparing your own display, you need to consider the lettering as carefully as you consider the pictorial elements, for it can communicate powerfully, too. At a minimum, you have to be sure that the lettering is legible in terms of size and spacing and of a style that is consistent with your intended message.

Letter Style.   The style of the lettering should be consistent and should harmonize with the other elements of the visual. For straightforward informational or instructional purposes, a plain (i.e., not decorative) lettering style is recommended. You may choose a **sans serif** style, such as Helvetica, or a simple serif style, such as Palatino, for either projected visuals or bulletin boards. As illustrated in Figure 4.17, it is recommended that you use sans serif typefaces for projected visuals and displays and serif typefaces for printed materials such as handouts (Faiola, 2000).

Number of Lettering Styles.   A display—or a series of related visuals,

such as a slide series—should use no more than two different type styles, and these should harmonize with each other. When preparing text on a computer it is tempting to use many variations of a typeface, but for good communication it is best to limit the number of variations (e.g., bold, italic, underline, size changes) to a maximum of four. That is, you could use two different type sizes plus some italics and some underlining, or three different type sizes plus bold for emphasis.

Capitals.   For best legibility, use lowercase letters, adding capitals only where normally required. Short headlines may appear in all capitals, but phrases of more than three words and full sentences should follow the rule of lowercase lettering.

Color of Lettering.   As discussed later in the section "Figure–Ground Contrast," the color of the lettering should contrast with the background color both for the sake of simple legibility and for the sake of emphasis in cases where you want to call particular attention to the verbal message. You also must remember that some of your learners may be color blind. Legibility depends mainly on contrast between the lettering color and the background color.

Size of Lettering.   Displays such as bulletin boards and posters are often meant to be viewed by people situated at a distance of 30 or 40 feet or more. In these cases the size of the lettering is crucial for legibility. A common rule of thumb is to make lowercase letters ½ inch high for each 10 feet of viewer distance. This means, for example, that to be legible to a student seated in the last seat of a 30-foot-long classroom the lettering would have to be at least 1½ inches in height. Figure 4.18 illustrates these minimum specifications for lettering height.

Spacing Between Letters.   The distance between the letters of the individual words must be judged by experi-

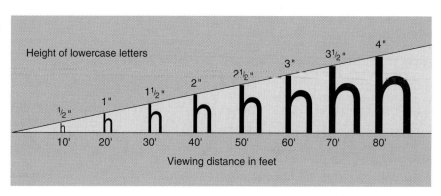

Figure 4.18
These are the minimum heights of boldface lowercase letters for visibility at increasing distances.

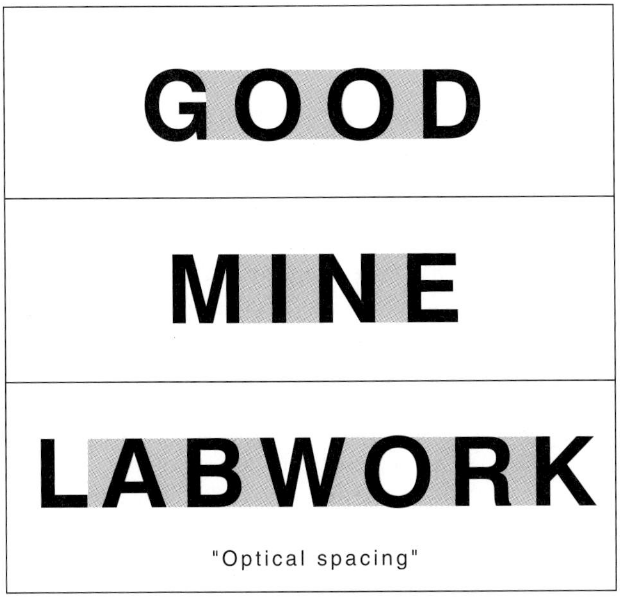

GOOD

MINE

LABWORK

"Optical spacing"

Figure 4.19
Optical spacing means estimating approximately equal amounts of white space between letters.

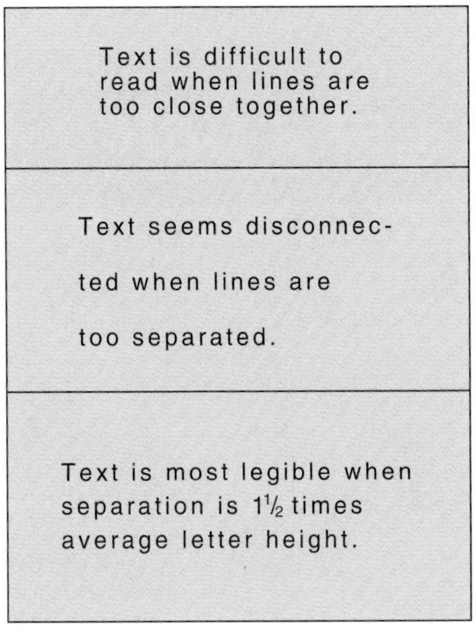

Text is difficult to
read when lines are
too close together.

Text seems disconnec-

ted when lines are

too separated.

Text is most legible when
separation is 1½ times
average letter height.

Figure 4.20
Lines of text should not be too cramped or too widely spaced.

ence rather than on a mechanical basis. This is because some letters (e.g., capital *A, I, K,* and *W*) are quite irregular in shape compared with rectangular letters (e.g., capital *H, M, N,* and *S*) and circular letters (e.g., capital *C, G, O,* and *Q*). When rectangular letters or circular letters are combined with each other at equal spacing, rather regular patterns of white space occur between letters. But when irregular letters are combined with others in this way, the patterns of white space can be very uneven. The only way to overcome this potentially distracting unevenness is to space all your letters by **optical spacing**—that is, by what *appears* even to the eye (Figure 4.19).

Spacing Between Lines. The vertical spacing between lines of printed material is also important for legibility. If the lines are too close together, they will tend to blur at a distance; if they are too far apart, they will seem disjointed (i.e., not part of the same unit). For a happy medium, the vertical space between the lines should be slightly less than the average height of the lowercase letters. To achieve this, use a ruler to draw lines lightly on your blank layout. Separate baselines by about one and a half times the height of the lowercase letters. Lettering on these lines will then result in text with the correct spacing (Figure 4.20).

Elements That Add Appeal. Your visual has no chance of having an effect unless it captures and holds the viewer's attention. Let's look at three devices for making displays more appealing: surprise, texture, and interaction.

Surprise. What grabs attention? The unexpected, primarily. Think of an unusual metaphor, an incongruous combination of word and picture, an abrupt infusion of color, a dramatic change of size. People pay attention as long as they are getting novel stimuli or new information. They tune out when the message becomes monotonous.

Texture. Most visuals are two dimensional. However, you can add a third dimension by using texture or actual materials. Texture is a characteristic of three-dimensional objects and materials. It can convey a clearer idea of the subject to the viewer by involving the sense of touch—for example, touching samples of different cereal grains. Or texture can simply invite involvement—for example, using cotton balls to represent clouds or showing book jackets to entice students to read a new book. Company products can be incorporated into a display. Components of equipment can be shown with drawings and captions.

Interaction. The R of the ASSURE model ("*Require learner participation*") applies to all forms of media. Viewers can be asked to respond to visual displays by manipulating materials on a display, perhaps to answer questions raised in the display. Students can move answer cards to math facts into the correct position. Answers to geography questions can be hidden under movable flaps. The teacher or learners can move dials on a weather display to indicate the forecast for the day or the actual weather outside the classroom. One example of an interactive format is shown in Figure 4.21.

Figure 4.21
Encouraging interaction adds greatly to the appeal of a display.

Pattern

Having made tentative decisions about what elements to include in your visual display, you are ready to consider its overall "look." The idea is to establish an underlying pattern—to decide how the viewer's eye will flow across your display. The major factors that affect the overall look are alignment of elements, shape, balance, style, color scheme, and color appeal.

Alignment. When you position the primary elements within a display so that they have a clear visual relationship to each other, viewers expend little effort making sense out of what they are seeing and are free to concentrate on understanding the message being conveyed. The most effective way to establish such visual relationships is to use **alignment.** Viewers will perceive elements to be aligned when the edges of those elements are aligned on the same imaginary horizontal or vertical line, as shown in Figure 4.22. These imaginary lines should be parallel to the edges of the display. For an irregularly shaped element, surround it mentally with a rectangle and

align that rectangle, as shown in Figure 4.23.

Shape. Another way to arrange the visual and verbal elements is to put them into a shape that is already familiar to the viewer. Your aim should be to use a pattern that attracts and focuses attention as effortlessly as possible. A simple geometric figure, such as a circle, triangle, or rectangle, provides a convenient framework because its shape is predictable to most viewers (Figure 4.24). Shapes that approximate certain letters of the alphabet have the same virtue. The letters *Z, L, T,* and *U* are frequently used as underlying patterns in display layouts (Figure 4.25). Of course, the words used in the layout, as well as the pictures, form part of the shape.

Another principle that can guide the placement of visual elements is the **rule of thirds.** That is, elements arranged along any of the one-third dividing lines take on importance and liveliness. The most dominant and dynamic position is at any of the intersections of the horizontal and vertical one-third dividing lines, especially the upper

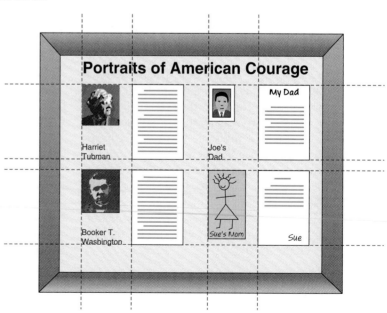

Figure 4.22
Pictorial elements should be aligned with reference to the edges of the display.

Figure 4.23
An irregularly shaped element can be aligned by mentally surrounding it with a rectangle.

left intersection (Figure 4.26). The most stable and least interesting point on the grid is dead center. Items placed in the corners or at the edges tend to be ignored or to make the arrangement unbalanced.

Balance. A psychological sense of equilibrium, or *balance*, is achieved when the "weight" of the elements in a display is equally distributed on each side of an axis, either horizontally or vertically or both. When the design is repeated on both sides, the balance is symmetrical, or formal.

In most cases, though, for visuals that will catch the eye and serve an informational purpose you should aim to achieve an asymmetrical, or informal, balance. With asymmetrical balance there is rough equivalence of weight, but with different elements on each side (e.g., one large open square on one side, three small dark circles on the other). Informal balance is preferred because

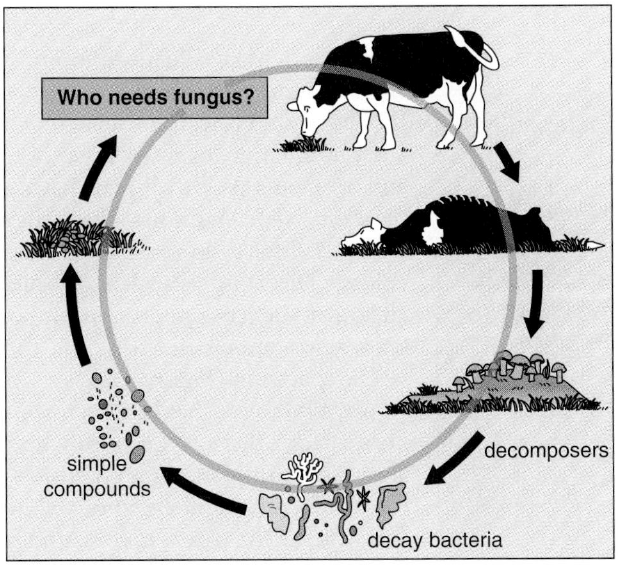

Figure 4.24
Arrangement of elements in a familiar geometric pattern, such as a circle, makes a display easier to decode.

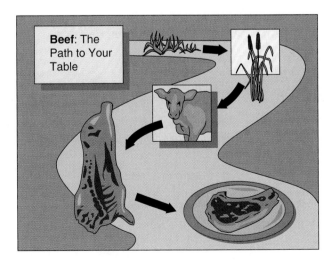

Figure 4.25
Arrangement in the shape of the letter Z leads the viewer's eye from upper left to lower right.

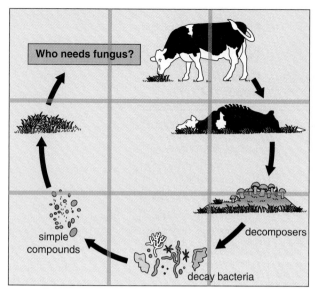

Figure 4.26
According to the "rule of thirds," the most important elements should appear near the intersections of the lines dividing the visual into thirds.

Figure 4.28
A slide set intended for an adult, professional audience should have a different style than one intended for elementary school–age children.

it is more dynamic and more interesting than formal balance (Figure 4.27). In general, try to avoid *imbalance*—using a distinctly disproportionate weight distribution—because it tends to be jarring.

Style.   Different audiences and different settings call for different design styles. Think about the simple, uncluttered, primary-color "look" of the *Barney and Friends* television show compared with the complex imagery, busy scenes, and realistic color of an adult action

drama. Likewise, you would not use the same stylistic treatment for a first-grade bulletin board (see, for example, Figure 4.21) as you would for a slide set made to show at a teachers' professional development conference (Figure 4.28). Your choice of lettering and type of pictures should be consistent with each other and with the preferences of the audience.

Color Scheme.   When choosing a color scheme for a display, consider the harmoniousness of the colors. Viewers are more likely to linger over and to remember a display having pleasant color harmony than they would a display done with clashing colors. The color wheel is a visual analogy to help us understand the relationships among the colors of the visible spectrum (Figure 4.29).

Any two colors that lie directly opposite each other on the color wheel are called **complementary colors**—for example, red and green or yellow and violet. (The latter combination is one of the most popular ones for colored overhead transparencies—yellow-orange lettering on a blue-violet background.) Complementary colors often harmonize well

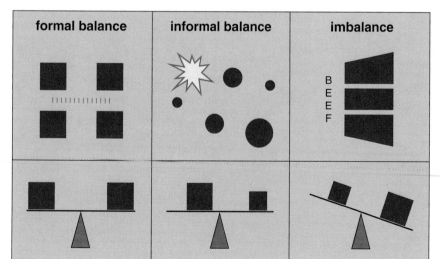

Figure 4.27
The analogy of a balance scale, shown in the bottom row, represents the three different types of balance.

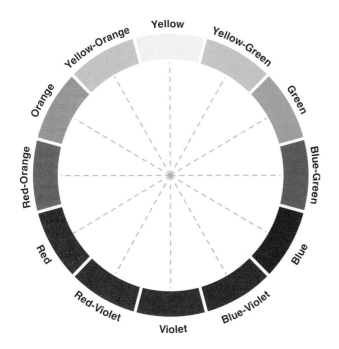

Figure 4.29
The traditional color wheel helps one visualize complementary colors.

each other the eye cannot focus on both at the same time, so you get an unpleasant vibrating effect. (See "Using Color in Instructional Materials" in Classroom Resources, Section C.)

Colors that lie next to each other on the color wheel are called **analogous colors**—for example, blue-green, blue, and blue-violet. Analogous colors may also form pleasing combinations when used together in a display.

When thinking about a color scheme for a display or a computer screen, it may be helpful to think in terms of a background color, a color for the images or text appearing against that background, and a color for highlights. Colors that work well together are shown in Table 4.1.

Please view these suggestions about color schemes as general guidelines, not as absolute rules, because in any situation there are many factors that will have an impact on whether particular colors will work well together. Keep in mind that these generalizations also assume normal color vision on the part of viewers. We know that 8 percent of all men and less than 1 percent of all women are color blind. Most color-blind people confuse reds with greens and see mainly in shades of blue and yellow. That is, for color-blind viewers, red lettering on a green background might be difficult to distinguish. You can alleviate this problem by making sure that the colors vary in darkness, for example, by using dark red letters on a light green background.

Colors on a computer screen may not be the same from one computer to another. Projected colors may also be different. Colors that look good on your computer may look different when projected. It is a good idea to practice your presentation to determine if the projected colors are acceptable to you. Some colors may fade in brightness.

in terms of an overall color scheme (Figure 4.30). However, try not to directly juxtapose two complementary colors (e.g., placing green letters on a red background). There are two reasons for this. First, if the colors are of equal value, or darkness, the letters will not have good figure–ground contrast. Second, when saturated (intense) complementary colors are placed directly next to

Color Appeal. Artists have long appreciated that blue, green, and violet are considered "cool" colors, whereas red and orange are considered "warm" colors. Research has shown that this is a learned phenomenon. When choosing colors for instructional materials, consider the emotional response you are seeking—an active, dynamic, warm feeling or a more contemplative, thoughtful, cool feeling. Also, saturated reds and oranges appear to approach the viewer, whereas cool colors tend to recede. Take advantage of this effect by highlighting important cues in red or orange, helping them leap out at the viewer the way a red STOP sign stands out even in a cluttered urban landscape.

Figure 4.30
Complementary colors, such as violet and yellow, can make pleasing combinations.

Table 4.1
Effective combinations of colors for background and images for displays and computer screens

BACKGROUND	FOREGROUND IMAGES AND TEXT	HIGHLIGHTS
white	dark blue	red, orange
light gray	blue, green, black	red
blue	light yellow, white	yellow, red
light blue	dark blue, dark green	red-orange
light yellow	violet, brown	red

Based on recommendations in "Color in Instructional Communication," by Judy Loosmore, Performance and Instruction *33 (November–December 1994): 36–38.*

By the same reasoning, use cool colors for backgrounds (Figures 4.31 and 4.32).

Response to warm and cool colors seems to be related to age. In general, children seem to prefer warm colors (particularly red, pink, yellow, and orange). Children also prefer brighter colors and combinations of intense colors more than do adults. With maturity tends to come a changing preference toward cooler colors and subtler combinations.

There is also a cultural basis to color response. These responses are often deep seated and unconscious. For example, in North America certain colors are associated with certain holidays: red for Christmas and Valentine's Day, green for St. Patrick's Day, yellow and purple for Easter, orange and black for Halloween. Such symbolism can vary dramatically across cultures. For example, in Western countries black is the color of mourning, whereas in China and Japan white is the color of mourning.

ASSURE Case Connection

Ms. Herr recognizes that her students may know something about how visuals enhance their learning because they have had experience using posters, books, and bulletin boards in class. She is not certain they understand how the uses of visuals affect the way people interpret information. How can she introduce this concept in a way that will make it both interesting and informative to her students? Which elements (visual, verbal, appeal) would be most important for her to emphasize? Why?

Arrangement

Proximity. Once you have established the overall shape of your display, you will want to arrange the items within that pattern. Viewers assume that elements close to each other are related and those that are far apart are unrelated. You can use this principle of **proximity** by putting related elements close together and moving unrelated elements apart. Figure 4.33 shows how confusing it can be when this rule is broken. If a display includes verbal labels for the picture elements, connect the related words and pictures clearly (Figure 4.34).

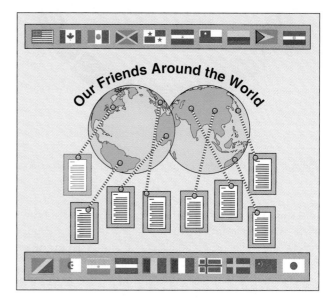

Figure 4.31
In this bulletin board display, warm colors fit with the friendly motif.

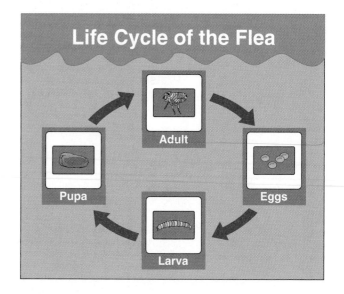

Figure 4.32
Here cool colors predominate, consistent with a more scientific atmosphere.

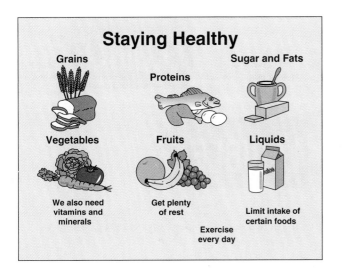

Figure 4.33
Here it is difficult to be sure which labels go with which images.

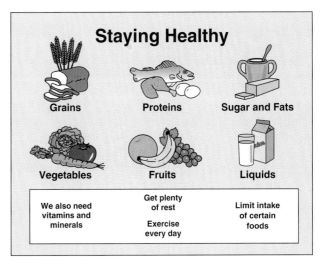

Figure 4.34
This display communicates clearly because the principle of proximity is observed.

Directionals. Viewers scan a display, with their attention moving from one part to another. The underlying pattern of the elements of the display will be the main determinant of the eye movement pattern. But if you want viewers to "read" the display in a particular sequence or focus on some particular element, you can use various other devices, called **directionals,** to direct attention. An arrow (as in Figure 4.32) is an obvious device for directing the viewer's attention. For verbal material, you may emphasize key words by bold type, and use bullets to indicate items in a list (as shown in Figure 4.1).

Colored elements—whether words or images—in a monochrome display will also draw the eye. Notice how the "hot" arrows in Figure 4.32 stand out from the cool background. Throughout this book we use colored text on "monochrome" pages as a way to call attention to topical headings and special features. Further, a color repeated in different parts of a display tends to show a relationship between or among those parts. For example, if only two symbols in a display are shown in cherry red, they will appear to be related to each other, and the viewer's gaze will go back and forth between them. The more extreme the color is (e.g., red or blue, at the opposite ends of the color spectrum), the more likely it will attract attention.

Figure–Ground Contrast. Important elements, especially wording, should stand out in good contrast to the background. The simple rule of **figure–ground contrast** is that dark figures show up best on light grounds and light figures show up best on dark grounds (Figure 4.35).

Different color combinations provide different figure–ground contrasts. When lettering or graphic symbols are the "figures," they will show up more clearly on certain backgrounds. As indicated in Figure 4.36, black on yellow is the most legible combination (Birren, 1963). Obviously, a combination of dark figures on a

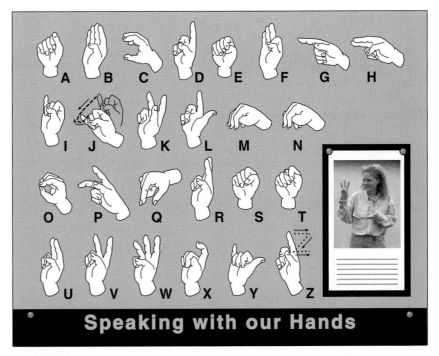

Figure 4.35
Sharp figure–ground contrast helps the important elements stand out.

 **(a)** Black on yellow

 **(b)** Green, red, or blue on white (clear film)

 **(c)** White (clear film) on blue

 **(d)** Black on white (clear film)

 **(e)** Yellow on black

Figure 4.36
Black lettering on a yellow background (a) is the most legible; the other combinations are shown in descending order of legibility.

 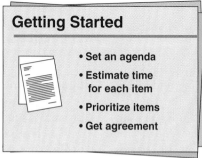 

Figure 4.37
Consistency in the placement of elements, color, and text treatment adds greatly to the readability of a series of visuals.

dark background will be even less legible than the combinations shown.

Consistency.   If you are planning a series of displays, such as a set of overhead transparencies, a multipage handout, or a series of computer screens, you should be consistent in your arrangement of the elements. As viewers go through the series of images they begin unconsciously to form a set of rules about where information will appear in your display. The more often the arrangement conforms to these rules (or exhibits *consistency*) the more viewers trust the rules. Every time the arrangement breaks the rules, viewers have to expend mental energy deciding whether this is a deliberate exception or whether they need to revise the rules. You enhance consistency when you place similar elements in similar locations, use the same text treatment for headlines, and use the same color scheme throughout the series of displays (Figure 4.37).

VISUAL PLANNING TOOLS

This chapter emphasizes the design decisions that you must make, not the technical steps involved in the production processes. For those encountering visual design

for the first time, don't expect the process to be quick or easy, especially at the beginning. These skills grow with practice, and with practice you will find yourself thinking visually more often as you grapple with instructional problems.

Storyboard

If you are designing a *series* of visuals—such as for several related overhead transparencies, a slide set, a video sequence, or a series of computer screens—**storyboarding** is a handy method of planning. This technique, borrowed from film and video production, allows you to creatively arrange and rearrange a whole sequence of thumbnail sketches. In storyboarding, you place on a card or piece of paper a sketch or some other simple representation of the visual you plan to use along with the narration and production notes that link the visuals to the narration. After developing a series of such cards, place them in rough sequence on a flat surface or on a storyboard holder (see Figure A.4 in Classroom Resources, Section A).

Index cards are commonly used for storyboarding because they are durable, inexpensive, and available in a variety of colors and sizes. You also may use small pieces of paper. Self-sticking removable notes have become popu-

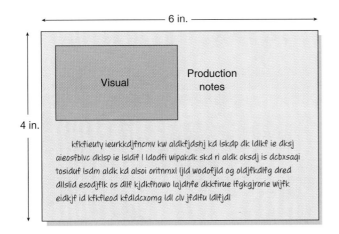

Figure 4.38

The storyboard card contains places for the visual, production notes, and the narration.

lar because they will stick to almost anything—cardboard, desks, walls, chalkboards, bulletin boards, and so on.

Divide the individual storyboard cards into areas to accommodate the visual, the narration, and the production notes (Figure 4.38). The exact format of the storyboard card should fit your needs and purposes. Design a card that facilitates your work if the existing or recommended format is not suitable. You can make a simple sketch or write a short description of the desired visual on the card, or use Polaroid pictures or visuals cut from magazines.

You may streamline your storyboarding by using computer software designed for this purpose, such as *StoryBoard Artist*. Such software allows you to draw pictures with the mouse, import graphics from files, and manipulate images (enlarging, reducing, and so on). You may couple these images with text and store them as cards, arranging them in different sequences on the screen according to your needs. (Storyboarding is discussed at greater length in Classroom Resources, Section A.)

Another software product, *Inspiration* (see "Media File: Computer Software 1" in Chapter 5), while not designed for storyboarding, may be used to help students organize their thoughts. They can use the software to help them map out their ideas, using notations to help with some of the details. *Inspiration* does limit students in their ability to couple the images with the text, but it allows them to move their ideas around the computer screen easily and makes it possible for them to get their information organized.

Types of Letters

A variety of lettering techniques for visuals exists. The simplest is freehand lettering with markers and felt-tip pens, which come in an array of colors and sizes.

You also may cut letters from construction paper or other materials. Precut letters are available in stationery and office supply stores. The letters are easy to use because most come with an adhesive backing; however, they are rather expensive.

Some media centers and graphic production units in business and industry use mechanical lettering devices (however, desktop publishing has almost entirely taken their place). With such devices, the style and size of the letters are determined by interchangeable large plastic wheels. The letters are "printed" on strips of clear plastic or colored film. Once the backing has been removed, the letters will adhere to most surfaces. You also may use an available desktop publishing system to prepare lettering in various styles and sizes. The lettering ranges from a fraction of an inch in height for overhead transparencies to over a foot high for banners.

Drawing, Sketching, and Cartooning

As we will describe in Chapter 10, drawings, sketches, and cartoons are visuals that can enhance learning. There are many sources of these in magazines, textbooks, and advertisements. One often overlooked source is *you*. You don't have to be an artist to draw. There are some basic guidelines and many how-to books that can help you communicate effectively using these graphic media.

With a little practice, you may be surprised by how well you can draw. Simple drawings can enhance chalkboard presentations, class handouts, bulletin boards, and overhead transparencies. For ideas on getting started, see "Sketching" in Classroom Resources, Section C, and the Suggested Readings at the end of this chapter.

DIGITAL IMAGES

As computer technologies advance, creating visual images has moved into the digital world. Students may use digital cameras to create originals or may transfer images into digital formats using scanners.

Digital imaging allows users to capture, edit, display, share, and network still and video images. The technology makes the process very easy for both teachers and students. Users may send images to other digital devices, store them in computers, or share them through the Internet. Digital images are another example of *nonlinear media*. The picture and video quality can provide equally clear details and often richer colors than their analog counterparts.

These technologies provide students with the tools to create visual images, including drawings and photographs, and to integrate them into computer-based materials such as desktop published documents, hypermedia projects, World Wide Web pages, and e-mail messages. Students may import digital images into their documents as they are or enhance or change them by using special software, and can quickly make their documents more exciting by using pictures as part of their message.

Digital Cameras

Digital cameras are small and lightweight with fewer moving parts than traditional cameras. Instead of squinting through a tiny optical viewfinder, most digital cameras permit you to see a large image displayed on the back of the camera before you take the "picture." They capture the images directly onto a special memory card instead of film. Consequently there is no waiting for film processing. The "photo" can be viewed immediately using a screen on the back of the camera. You can delete images you don't want and reshoot on the spot until you get exactly what you want.

Printing the digital images is quick and easy with a color printer or "photo printer." You can insert the memory card into your computer to place the image in a document or report. You can use your computer to print the images. It is possible to make copies of the "photo" without using a computer. "Photo printers" make copies directly from the data on the memory card. Copies of digital photos can be made without degradation in quality and the colors resist fading over time (Figure 4.39).

Scanners

Scanners work with computers to transfer existing visual images, such as drawings or photographs, into digitized computer graphic files. As with digital photographs, students may quickly incorporate scanned images into a word processing file or enhance or change them using software.

The *flatbed* scanner looks like the top of a photocopy machine and is connected to the computer with special cables. The user lifts the lid of the scanner and places the image face down on the glass surface. Special software on the computer operates the scanner. Inside the scanner is a lens or mirror system to focus the light reflected from

Figure 4.40
Scanning images is a simple task.

the original into a **charge-coupled device (CCD).** This device changes the optical image into electrical charges, which in turn are converted into a digital form acceptable by a computer (Figure 4.40).

Photo CDs

An alternative for digital images that is less expensive and that uses equipment that might already be in schools is the **photo CD.** Students may use a regular camera and film to take photographs. Then, when having the film developed, instead of getting glossy prints, they can have their photographs stored on a CD-ROM. One CD can store 100 to 150 images. A unique feature of this technology is that additional pictures can be added to the CD at a later date.

A photo CD can be read by a CD-ROM player connected to the computer. Students may then incorporate into their documents the images displayed on the screen. It is an inexpensive way to capture a large number of images in a small space.

Caution When Editing Images

It is important to recognize the need for caution when digitally editing or changing images, as there arises the possibility of misrepresentation. With the advanced capabilities of computer tools, a computer user could alter an image in a way that might distort reality and present a false message to the reader or that might violate a copyright holder's rights in regard to the original image (see "Copyright Concerns" in Chapter 1).

ASSURE Case Connection

Ms. Herr has access to a computer lab with scanners attached to several of the computers. She can check out several digital cameras from the school media center. How might she encourage her students to use digital images in their preparation of their visuals?

Figure 4.39
Digital cameras make it easy to take photos to use in computer-based programs or on a website.

VISUAL DESIGN CHECKLIST

KEY WORDS: _____ , _____ , _____

Material being evaluated _____

Evaluator _____ **Date** _____

	Exemplary	Acceptable	Poor	Comments
Overall Pattern				
Alignment	❑	❑	❑	
Shape	❑	❑	❑	
Balance	❑	❑	❑	
Style	❑	❑	❑	
Color scheme	❑	❑	❑	
Color appeal	❑	❑	❑	
Arrangement				
Proximity	❑	❑	❑	
Directionals	❑	❑	❑	
Figure-ground contrast	❑	❑	❑	
Consistency	❑	❑	❑	
Verbal Elements				
Lettering style	❑	❑	❑	
Letter size and spacing	❑	❑	❑	
Appeal				
Surprise	❑	❑	❑	
Texture	❑	❑	❑	
Interaction	❑	❑	❑	

Summary: Using the ASSURE Model for Visual Principles

As with other media and technology, the ASSURE model introduced in Chapter 3 is helpful in preparing lessons incorporating the use of visual principles.

Analyze Learners

Lesson development begins by identifying your students' unique attributes and learning characteristics.

State Objectives

Before stating specific objectives, you may wish to explore how to use visual principles in support of student learning. Sometimes it is more appropriate to state specific objectives after you have identified the direction you will take with the content and what materials you will use.

Select Methods, Media, and Materials

Use the visual principles discussed in this chapter as the basis for selecting, modifying, or designing your materials. Adjust the specific application of each principle to suit the specific nature of your topic and objectives.

You should preview and appraise both commercially and locally produced materials before using them with your students. You may wish to use the "Visual Design Checklist" to guide your selection decisions.

Utilize Media and Materials

Follow the visual principles discussed in this chapter to facilitate your students' learning, modifying the material's use to fit your needs. Remember, the same basic presentation rules apply regardless of visual medium.

Require Learner Participation

Introduce and explain the visual principles involved in your specific objective. Have the students do specific activities that rely on their ability to interpret visuals. Students will find more value in the materials if they are able to understand the visual principles that those materials embody.

Evaluate and Revise

It is important to consider how materials that rely on visual principles help students to interpret information. As with all media- and technology-based lessons, you may choose to revise your selection of materials after you have determined how well they have worked. In addition, you want to be certain that all materials used have been cleared of any potential copyright issues.

ASSURE Case in Practice: Visual Literacy and Writing

All of the ASSURE Cases in Practice in this text and an electronic template for creating your own ASSURE Lesson can be found on the enclosed "Classroom Link Portfolio" CD-ROM.

Ms. Herr wants to improve student skills in using visuals to communicate along with oral and written communication skills. Students work in pairs to help and support each other.

Analyze Learners

General Characteristics

The sixth-grade class at St. Matthew School has 33 students who come from diverse cultural and language backgrounds; in this school in Brooklyn, New York, 85 percent of the students are Hispanic, 10 percent are African American, and 5 percent are Asian American. According to standardized tests, almost all the students in this class are achieving well below grade level in reading.

Entry Competencies

Because Ms. Herr is focusing on reading and writing skills, she administers a standardized rating scale to evaluate compositional ability. Her students are writing at about 50 percent competency for content and mechanics compared with other sixth-grade populations in the United States.

Ms. Herr has discovered that her students have difficulty organizing their writing because they lack a sense of sentence and paragraph structure. She also realizes that they have difficulty retaining information when it is presented in a way that is disconnected from their experience.

Learning Styles

The students are already visually oriented because they have grown up in the MTV generation. However, even though they prefer visual communication, they lack skills in this area just as they do in oral communication. The school has learning style data on file for most of these students, who tend to be concrete random. The desire to please the teacher is a strong motivator for many of these sixth graders. The school routinely addresses many of the possible physiological factors that might interfere with learning. There is a "breakfast before school" program for those who qualify and a school nurse is available to assist those students who are not feeling well.

State Objectives

The main objective for this unit is as follows: Given themes developed by student pairs, sixth-grade students will be able to compose visual essays in sequential and descriptive styles that exhibit composition skills appropriate to their grade level.

A supporting objective includes the following: In pairs, students will exhibit active listening skills so that they will successfully reach consensus, be able to express themselves orally, and make oral presentations of their photo essay storyboards using coherent standard English.

Select Methods, Media, and Materials

Ms. Herr prefers to follow the whole-language approach, integrating listening, speaking, reading, and writing activities together in one unit. She decides to use a visual literacy approach implemented through cooperative learning pairs and discovery methods to provide concrete experiences that might help fill gaps in students' mental schemata. She wants to improve both language ability and motivation by providing meaningful connections between the students' real-world experiences and their language activities in school. This means that the students, rather than the teacher, would be the main performers.

First, Ms. Herr prepares materials for a schematic mapping activity the whole class will do. She visually models the process of building a map of ideas by using the overhead projector in the front of the room.

Next, she organizes student pairs to create photo essays. There is a logistical hurdle: getting enough cameras to allow all students to have hands-on experiences taking pictures. Fortunately, the library media specialist is able to help her obtain 20 cameras from the district media center.

Finally, she decides the students need to learn to use the computer program, *Inspiration,* to help them develop storyboards to organize their photo essays. Students will each write an essay based on their pair's photo story.

Utilize Media and Materials

The two-week unit begins with Ms. Herr conducting a large-group brainstorming session, using the overhead projector, to develop schematic maps. They start with the general theme of "Brooklyn's Amazing History" and break that down into subtopics, such as "The Role of the Subway." These subtopics constitute the content for the photo shooting that follows.

Students, working in pairs, use the computer program, *Inspiration,* brainstorming their ideas to develop storyboards of their photo stories.

Require Learner Participation

Following these planning sessions, the pairs of students go out into their neighborhoods to shoot the photographs they had visualized in their schematic maps.

When the finished photos are available, the pairs use storyboarding techniques to organize their pictures and prepare captions. Each pair presents their storyboard to the rest of the class. The unit culminates with each student writing an essay on the photo story created by the pair.

This procedure is repeated once, for a total of four weeks of planning, photographing, storyboarding, and writing.

Evaluate and Revise

Ms. Herr analyzes the essays, again using a standardized rating scale. The typical score for each of the essays is in the 70 percent range. The structure of the essays is improved compared with those written earlier, although there are still obvious deficiencies in spelling and grammar.

Ms. Herr also uses simple rating forms for class members to give feedback on each oral presentation; she notes that students make fewer negative and more positive comments about the second attempts.

The teacher also keeps an informal journal of instances of nonstandard English use in students' everyday classroom speaking. She notices that a number of students are improving their ability to speak standard English.

In class discussion after completing the two projects, students agree that they prefer this approach to conventional writing approaches.

This ASSURE Case in Practice is adapted from an actual case report by Richard Sinatra, Jeffrey S. Beaudry, Josephine Stahl-Bemake, and E. Francine Guastello, "Combining Visual Literacy, Text Understanding, and Writing for Culturally Diverse Students," Journal of Reading *(May 1990), pp. 612–617.*

Create Your Own ASSURE Lesson

Using the ASSURE model, design a lesson for a scenario from the table on this book's inside cover or from the Companion Website, or use a scenario of your own design. Use one of the methods described in Chapter 1 and information from this chapter related to incorporating visuals into your instructional setting. Be sure to include information about the audience, the objectives, and all other elements of the ASSURE model. When completed, reflect on the process you used and what you have learned about matching audience, content, method, and materials.

Classroom Link Portfolio Activities

Use the "Classroom Link Portfolio" CD-ROM and the Companion Website as resources in completing these activities. To complete the following activities online go to the Portfolio Activities module in Chapter 4 of the Companion Website (http://www.prenhall.com/smaldino).

1. *Planning Lessons to Improve Visual Literacy Skills.* Plan a set of learning activities to improve the visual literacy skills of a present or future learner you might work with, focusing on a standard or topic of interest. What activities can students do to improve their skills in (1) interpreting visuals, and (2) creating visuals? How does this activity fit with content standards? (ISTE NETS-T 2.A; 3.A)

2. *Written Reflection.* Reflect on a recent learning experience in which you were the learner. How valuable were each of the following for you? For a visually impaired learner? For a hearing-impaired student? (ISTE NETS-T 4.B; 6.B)

   - When you had to read something
   - When you had to write something
   - When you had to interpret visuals
   - When you had to create visuals

Integration Assessments

To complete the specified activities online go to the Integration Assessments module in Chapter 5 of the Companion Website (http://www. prenhall.com/ smaldino).

1. Critique a bulletin board or other display using the "Visual Design Checklist" in this chapter. Attach a description of audience, objectives, and the features of the display that help achieve the goals of visual design. (ISTE NETS-T 2.C)
2. Locate a visual (not a photograph) on a website and evaluate it using the guidelines/principles in this chapter. (ISTE NETS-T 2.C)
3. Design a series of computer screens related to an instructional purpose exemplifying the principles given in "Designing Computer Screens" in Classroom Resources, Section C. Attach a description of audience, objectives, and features that help achieve the goals of visual design. (ISTE NETS-T 2.A)
4. Design a visual using computer graphics and describe which guidelines and principles you used. (ISTE NETS-T 2.A)
5. Critique either a display or a computer lesson using the criteria described in the "Visual Design Checklist" and in "Designing Computer Screens" in Classroom Resources, Section C. (ISTE NETS-T 2.C)
6. Develop a storyboard for a visual presentation, such as a *PowerPoint* presentation. Incorporate at least six visuals. You may develop it either on a computer using software such as *Inspiration*, or using paper and pencil. (ISTE NETS-T 2.A)

References

Birren, Faber. 1963. *Color: A survey in words and pictures.* New Hyde Park, NY: University Books.

Cohen, Peter A., Barbara J. Ebeling, and James A. Kulik. 1981. A meta-analysis of outcome studies of visual-based instruction. *Educational Communications and Technology Journal,* 29(1): 26–36.

Dewey, John. 1897. My pedagogic is creed, Article 4, the nature of method. *School Journal* (January): 77–80.

Dwyer, Francis M. 1978. *Strategies for improving visual learning.* State College, PA: Learning Services.

Faiola, Anthony. 2000. *Typography primer.* Pittsburgh, PA: GATF.

Houghton, H. A., and D. M. Willows, eds. 1987. *The psychology of illustration.* Vol. 2. New York: Verlag.

Myatt, Barbara, and Juliet Mason Carter. 1979. Picture preferences of children and young adults. *Educational Communication and Technology Journal, 27*(1): 45–53.

Suggested Readings

Adams, Dennis, and Mary Hamm. 2000. Literacy, learning, and media. *TECHNOS, 9*(4): 22–27.

Allen, Rodney. 1993. Snapshot geography: Using travel photographs to learn geography in upper elementary schools. *Canadian Social Studies, 27*(2): 63–66.

Aso, Kazutoshi. 2001. Visual images as educational materials in mathematics. *Community College Journal of Research and Practice, 25*(5–6): 355–360.

Bailey, Gerald D., and Marie Blythe. 1998. Outlining, diagramming, & storyboarding: Or how to create great educational web sites. *Learning and Leading with Technology, 25*(8): 6–11.

Begoray, Deborah L. 2000. Seventy plus ideas for viewing and representing (and they're not just for language arts!). *English Quarterly, 32*(1–2): 30–39.

Bevlin, Marjorie Elliot. 1994. *Design through discovery: An introduction to art and design.* Fort Worth, TX: Harcourt Brace.

Boyle, Tim. 1997. *Design for multimedia learning.* London: Prentice Hall.

Davidson, Hall. 1999. The educators' lean and mean no fat guide to fair use. *Technology & Learning, 20*(2): 58–62.

Dwyer, Francis M. 1987. *Enhancing visualized instruction.* State College, PA: Learning Services.

Edwards, Carolyn Pope, and Linda Mayo Willis. 2000. Integrating visual and verbal literacies in the early childhood classroom. *Early Childhood Education Journal, 27*(4): 259–265.

Glasgow, Jacqueline N. 1994. Teaching visual literacy for the 21st century. *Journal of Reading, 37*(6): 494–500.

Hyerle, David. 2000. *Field guide to using visual tools.* Alexandria, VA: Association for Supervision & Curriculum Development.

Lauer, David A., and Stephen Pentak. 1995. *Design basics.* Fort Worth, TX: Harcourt Brace.

Lohr, Linda L. 2002. *Creating graphics for learning and performance: Lessons in visual literacy.* Upper Saddle River, NJ: Prentice Hall.

Luckner, John, Sandra Bowen, and Kathy Carter. 2001. Visual teaching strategies for students who are deaf or hard of hearing. *Teaching Exceptional Children, 33*(3): 38–44.

MacGregor, S. Kim. 2002. The computer paint program: A palette for facilitating visual and verbal literacy. *Computers in the Schools, 19*(1–2): 163–178.

Margulies, Nancy. 2002. *Mapping inner space: Learning and teaching visual mapping,* 2nd ed. Tucson, AZ: Zephyr.

Moore, David M., and Francis M. Dwyer, eds. 1994. *Visual literacy: A spectrum of visual learning.* Englewood Cliffs, NJ: Educational Technology Publications.

Oehring, Sandra. 1993. Teaching with technology: Hands-on: On camera—and in the computer. *Instructor, 102*(9): 76.

Oring, Stuart A. 2000. A call for visual literacy. *School Arts, 99*(8): 58–60.

Payne, Bill. 1993. A word is worth a thousand pictures: Teaching students to think critically in a culture of images. *Social Studies Review, 32*(3): 38–43.

Rakes, Glenda C. 1999. Teaching visual literacy in a multimedia age. *TechTrends, 43*(4): 14–18.

Salomon, G. 1997. Of mind and media: How cultures' symbolic forms affect learning and thinking. *Phi Delta Kappan, 78*(5): 375–380.

Wilde, Richard, and Judith Wilde. 2000. *Visual literacy: A conceptual approach to graphic problem solving.* New York: Watson-Guptill.

Wileman, Ralph E. 1993. *Visual communicating.* Englewood Cliffs. NJ: Educational Technology Publications.

Digital Environments

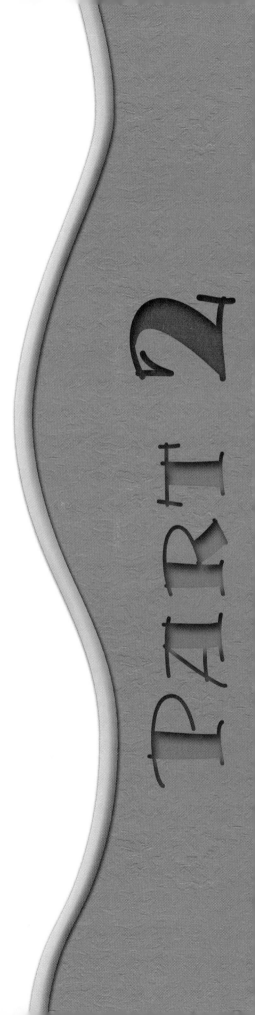

PART 2

CHAPTER 5

Computers

Outline

Knowledge Objectives

1. Distinguish between *computer-assisted instruction (CAI)* and *computer-managed instruction (CMI)*.
2. Create examples of the role of the computer as an object of instruction, as a tool, as an instructional device, as a means of teaching logical thinking, as a media center resource, and as a performance support.
3. Discuss the advantages and limitations of the use of computers in learning.
4. Describe techniques for and examples of integrating computers into the curriculum.
5. Compare and contrast the six types of computer-assisted instruction in terms of the role of the computer and the role of the learner, including a specific example of courseware for each.
6. Describe two applications, two advantages, and two limitations of integrated learning systems.
7. Outline the process and materials needed for selecting and integrating computer-based programs.
8. Identify five criteria besides cost that are important considerations in purchasing a computer for instructional purposes.
9. Discuss the difference among a one-computer classroom, a multiple-computer classroom, and computer laboratories in terms of setups and uses.

Professional Vocabulary

computer-assisted instruction (CAI)	byte
computer-managed instruction (CMI)	bit
software	kilobyte (Kb)
database	megabyte (Mb)
alt-tag	gigabyte (Gb)
performance support system	terabyte (Tb)
lab pack	removable-storage device
site license	CD-ROM (compact disc–read-only
integrated learning system (ILS)	memory)
hardware	computer classroom
read-only memory (ROM)	computer laboratory
random-access memory (RAM)	

Since the advent of the personal computer in the mid 1980s, computers have rapidly become one of the key instructional technologies used in both formal and informal education. Teachers can use the computer as an aid to managing classroom activities; it has a multitude of roles to play in the curriculum, ranging from tutor to student tool. To make informed choices, you need to be familiar with the various computer applications—games, simulations, tutorials, problem-solving programs, word processing, graphic tools, and integrated learning systems.

It is extremely important to develop critical skills in appraising instructional software because there are so many available programs. The hardware, too, becomes much less intimidating when you know some of the basic technology. Whether you teach with a single computer in the classroom or a room full of them, these basic guidelines will help you make optimal use of them.

ASSURE
Case Challenge

We have developed a case study for this chapter to help you see how computers can be integrated into learning activities. At the end of the chapter you will be challenged to develop your own ASSURE lesson for a case study of your choice using the ASSURE model and incorporating the technology and media described in this chapter. To help you in preparing your lesson, we have included hints (called "ASSURE Case Connections") throughout the chapter as they relate to the ASSURE Case Challenge.

Dennis Sorge teaches pre-algebra to seventh- and eighth-grade middle school students. They are an average class with a range of abilities in math and reading. They have basic computation skills. Mr. Sorge wants to have his students practice their computation skills while applying them to concepts such as budgeting and making predictions. He wants to engage his students in learning within a real-world situation to make their math experiences more meaningful.

ROLES OF COMPUTERS IN LEARNING

The computer provides virtually instantaneous response to student input, has extensive capacity to store and manipulate information, and is unmatched in its ability to serve many students simultaneously. It has become a tool of choice in instruction. The computer's role has changed because of its ability to provide rich learning experiences for students, giving them the power to influence the depth and direction of their learning. It has the ability to control and integrate a variety of media—still and motion pictures, graphics, and sounds, as well as printed information. The computer can also record, analyze, and react to student responses typed on a keyboard or selected with a mouse (Figure 5.1).

There are two major applications of computers in instruction: **computer-assisted instruction (CAI)** and **computer-managed instruction (CMI).** In CAI students interact directly with the computer as part of the instructional activity. This may be in the form of material presented by the computer in a controlled sequence, such as a drill-and-practice program, or as a student-initiated creative activity, like a desktop-published book of student poems. In CMI the computer helps both instructor and students in maintaining information about students and in guiding instruction. That is, the computer can organize and store easily retrievable information about each student and about relevant instructional materials. Learners may take tests on the computer or input information into a personal portfolio. Further, the computer can diagnose the learning needs of students and prescribe optimal sequences of instruction for them.

Continual advances in microprocessor technology have allowed today's devices to greatly surpass their predecessors in speed, flexibility, and raw computational power (Figures 5.2 and 5.3). The potential uses of computers in educational settings go far beyond direct instruction. One function is administrative—keeping school records, scheduling classes, doing payroll, and managing student assessment data. Another is service oriented, as when guidance programs use computers to deliver career planning assistance. In the domain of instruction there are four broad classes of computer applications:

- As an object of instruction
- As a tool
- As an instructional device
- As a means of teaching logical thinking

Figure 5.1

Computers have become pervasive in education and training. Most learners have access to and are influenced by computer-based instruction.

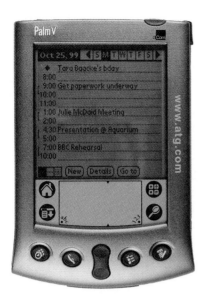

Figure 5.2
Innovative computer systems such as Palm V have helped popularize the use of microcomputers in business and at home.

Figure 5.3
The mainframe computer with its massive components was the norm before the advent of the microcomputer.

Within each of these categories, the role of the computer is varied and extensive.

Object of Instruction

The computer may itself be the object of instruction. For example, in computer literacy courses students can learn about how computers are used in society, and in vocational courses students learn to use computers on the job for data processing and analysis purposes. In this role, the computer is treated like any other machine one is learning to use.

When a learner is studying computer programming, the computer and the associated **software** (programs and applications) are the objects of instruction. The various programming languages and the techniques for constructing a program using these languages are beyond the scope of this book.

Tool

In its role as a tool, the computer assists both teachers and students. Some of the roles of the computer are relatively simple, such as a sophisticated calculator and typewriter. Other roles are more advanced, such as multimedia composer, presentation aid, communication device, and data retrieval source. Whatever the reason for using the computer, as a tool it has become indispensable (Figure 5.4).

Traditionally, computers were used for reinforcing traditional instruction. The software was designed to provide direct instruction or practice to students, often programmed to branch to other segments of the lesson based on student responses. Many of these types of programs are still in use today.

In an effort to recognize the constructive nature of learning, current methods are based on engaging students in learning in such ways that allow them to develop, or construct, their own mental structure (schemata) in a particular area of study (Figure 5.5). To engage students in this type of learning, the environment must provide them with materials that allow them to explore. Papert's "microworlds"—environments that permit students to freely experiment, test, and invent—allow students to focus on a problem area and to create solutions that are meaningful to them (Papert, 1982, 1993).

Jonassen, Howland, Moore, and Marra (2003) have expanded this idea by suggesting that technology

Figure 5.4
Laptop computers have changed the way people use computers. Combined with wireless technology, they have made computing truly portable.

Figure 5.5
As a tool, the computer can be useful to students as they search for new information.

becomes an "intellectual partner" with students by engaging and supporting them in their learning. Students learn with technology; technology is the environment that engages students to use cognitive learning strategies and critical thinking skills. When students use technology, they are controlling how and when the technology provides them with the information they need.

Many computer software packages are available to create such learning environments and assist students in constructing their schemata. Programs such as *Inspiration* (see "Media Files: Computer Software 1"), a cognitive mapping program, provide students with the means to relate the information to their lives and to alter those relationships as they continue to explore. Other programs, such as *HyperStudio,* permit students to develop files of data that are related in meaningful ways.

Writing. Computers are being used widely for word processing and desktop publishing. Most students have access to word processing programs with which they complete term papers and assignments. Some students create multimedia term papers, integrating such media as graphics, sound, and motion for a more complete presentation. Presentation software, which incorporates the computer with video projection, can be used for student presentations. Computers also allow students to communicate with others around the world via e-mail (electronic mail, discussed in Chapter 8).

Calculating. The computer can also serve as a tool during instruction. Learners can use them to solve complex mathematical calculations, as a pocket calculator is used, but with increased power and speed. Any computer can analyze data, perform repeated calculations, or even gather data when hooked up to laboratory equipment.

Retrieving Information. Today's students need to learn to manage information—to retrieve, sort, and organize it—and to evaluate their findings. For inquiry and research, students can use a **database,** a collection of related information organized for quick access to specific items. Whereas a telephone book is a printed database, databases can also be stored in a computer (e.g., a computer database can include a list of telephone numbers by name or company). A database is a versatile and easy-to-learn computer tool. It can be thought of as an electronic file cabinet (Figure 5.6).

There are two types of databases. Classroom databases are created by students. For example, students can design information sheets and questionnaires, collect data, input relevant facts, and then retrieve data in a variety of ways. The facts selected might include student information, book reports, or sample math problems. Having constructed databases as part of their research, students are in a position to engage in higher-level thinking skills as they analyze and interpret the data.

Another type of database is the commercial database. These are either purchased on CD-ROMs or accessed via an Internet connection. For example, *Fifty States,* a database on disc, contains information such as population, capital, area, major rivers, and state bird, flower, and tree for all the states in the United States. Several companies have developed database materials for use in

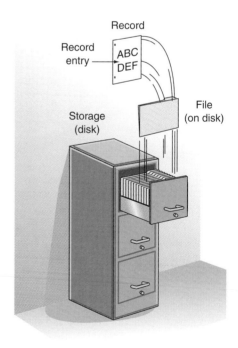

Figure 5.6
A database is used to organize information so the user can easily sort, rank, calculate, and store it.

the classroom. Other larger computer databases are available online and may contain medical information, historical data, census figures, and the like.

Instructional Device

Computer-assisted instruction (CAI) helps students learn specific skills. For example, *Math Blaster Plus* assists students in learning math facts (addition, subtraction, multiplication, and division) through drill-and-practice using an arcade game format. Software is capable of providing students with complex tasks to engage them in real-world problems. Programs such as *National Inspirer* ask students to engage in activities related to geography. Video technologies can easily be incorporated, focusing attention on tangible examples. Word processing, graphics, and a host of computer software help students organize and communicate their ideas.

Summaries of research with students at various levels—elementary, secondary, college, and adult education—show that computer-based instruction generally has positive effects on student achievement. One set of summaries by James Kulik and his colleagues (1986) concluded that, on the average, computer-based instruction assisted students in raising their achievement scores by 10 to 18 percentage points compared with conventional instruction.

Teaching Logical Thinking

Seymour Papert, in his 1982 book, *Mindstorms*, and again in his 1993 book, *The Children's Machine*, suggests that the computer should be an "object to think with," not a dispenser of information. Using Logo, a procedural language that was designed for learners, students can learn about the complexity of mathematics within their daily lives. Children can build and test theories about mathematics. Beyond the nature of the computer language itself, there is an underlying educational philosophy based on the concept that learners need to manipulate their environment to understand the concepts they are exploring. They begin to explore mathematics, seeing relationships between it and other daily activities. Papert suggests that when students have the opportunity to use programs such as Logo, they begin to develop "powerful ideas" and in doing so, begin to develop a sense of mastery over their learning environment.

Because Logo is very easy to learn, many believe that it is a children's computer language. Yet it is a very sophisticated language, capable of engaging even the expert computer programmer. Logo is attractive even to younger learners because they find the problem-solving activities to be challenging.

David Jonassen and his colleagues (2003) argue that many potential computer applications can be used to provide the type of learning environment Papert offered with Logo. Jonassen proposes eleven kinds of problem-solving scenarios: (1) logical problems; (2) algorithmic problems; (3) story problems; (4) rule-using problems; (5) decision-making problems; (6) troubleshooting problems; (7) diagnosis-solution problems; (8) tactical/strategic performance; (9) case/systems analysis problems; (10) design problems; and (11) dilemmas. He suggests technology applications available to support learners in each type of situation. He believes that technology plays an important part in helping learners with the problems they are challenged to solve. They can use the technology to seek information, find models, make decisions, and design solutions. He notes that there are many resources available to facilitate student learning.

Technology for Diverse Learners

DESIGN GUIDELINES

Follow these guidelines when designing screens for the visually impaired and other disabled users:

- Use alternative textual descriptions (**alt-tags**) to provide brief descriptions of graphics or images. For example, include the text *cat* along with the image of the feline.
- Avoid using complex multicolumn tables. Assistive technologies read one entire line at a time across multiple columns instead of reading each column separately.

- Include meaningful hypertext links. A nondescriptive "click here" link tells the visually impaired learner nothing about that link.

For more guidelines, visit the website of the World Wide Web Consortium (W3C) Accessibility Initiative at http://www.w3.org/wai

You can test any site's accessibility using the program *Bobby* (http://www.cast.org/bobby) created by the Center for Applied Special Technology (CAST). *Bobby* analyzes Web pages for their accessibility to people with disabilities.

Close-Up

IT ALL STARTED WITH A BAD SMELL

A school in Ann Arbor, Michigan, had a small park with a stream next to its property. A distinct odor was rising from the stream and people were beginning to complain. A trio of science teachers decided to integrate their classes and present their students with the problem of the smelly stream. They introduced students to the scientific inquiry model and provided them with an array of technologies that could help them analyze and hypothesize. Soon, as groups of students worked together, solutions to the problem of the bad odor began to materialize. Further, the students began to investigate the source of the problem and initiated community action to alleviate it. The success ensuing from this reorganization of the science classes and integration of technologies demonstrated to the administration that problem-based learning is a constructive and beneficial way for students to learn.

Source: Hi-C Research Group, University of Michigan
(http://oi.eecs.umich.edu/highc/)

ASSURE Case Connection

Mr. Sorge wants his students to practice their computation skills. He believes he would like to use a computer to keep his students motivated. Would he use the computer as a tool? As an object of instruction? As an instructional device?

Computers in the School Library Media Center. There are many types of applications of computers in schools today. Nearly all school library media centers have at least one station that is designated for database searches using CD-ROMs and the Internet. Among the types of materials available are encyclopedias and research databases.

CD-ROM encyclopedias can be complete and unabridged. These appear to be similar to the bound-book format. The advantage of the CD-ROM encyclopedia is that it allows options within the search process. For example, when a student wants to search for information about Queen Elizabeth I, the encyclopedia is a natural place for the student to begin the search. In the traditional book-bound format, the student might choose the "E" volume and look up "Elizabeth, Queen" and that might be the extent of the search. However, with the CD-ROM version of the encyclopedia, when the student types in "Elizabeth," a large

menu of choices is displayed on the screen, including "Shakespeare," "Spanish Armada," "Philip II of Spain," and "England's colonial empire." Kenilworth might even be shown because of its retelling of the legend of Sir Walter Raleigh. Also, each of these options is linked not only with "Queen Elizabeth I" but also with each other. The student is thus encouraged to explore the interrelationships among people, places, and events.

Most CD-ROM encyclopedias include color photographs, animations, and sound (Figure 5.7). Thus, a student searching for information about lions would not only be able to find text-based information, but also could view a photograph or short video clip about lions and hear a lion's roar. These encyclopedias tend to be abridged because of the large memory requirements of graphics and video (CD-ROM seems to have limitless capacity, but visuals and audio use a large amount of memory).

Computers in the Classroom. In addition to encyclopedias, other types of books are being produced on CD-ROM, such as the Arthur series from Living Books. Discis Books was one of the earliest companies to produce such classics as Beatrix Potter's *Peter Rabbit* and Edgar Allan Poe's *The Tell-Tale Heart* on CD-ROM discs. These books not only appear as text with pictures but are also interactive. The student who is having difficulty with a particular word on a page can point and

Figure 5.7
Multimedia software features a point-and-click approach, allowing the user to move around within an information database such as an encyclopedia.

click on that word and get it pronounced or even defined. Further, if the student's reading skills are weak, the whole story can be read by the computer. A child's voice reads many of the stories; for others, a pleasant adult voice reads the story. In the case of *The Tell-Tale Heart,* the student can experience two different readers' interpretations, thus gaining even further insight into Poe's short story. Background music or other sounds enhance the pleasure of reading. Many of the discs come with two audio tracks—one in English and the other in a designated language, such as French.

These CD-ROM books provide additional help to you as a teacher. A list can be maintained of all the words that a student identified while reading. You can quickly glance at the list and determine the vocabulary words for which that student might need assistance. Further, comprehension and reading analysis questions are presented to students for independent study of the story. Along with the questions are suggestions for the types of responses they might consider. You might use these as aids to inspire students to explore other answers to those or similar questions (Figure 5.8).

In the classroom, you might find that CD-ROM books are essential to use with students who are having difficulty with the assigned reading. Another possible application would be to provide students with CD-ROM books to supplement their reading and writing. Using a CD-ROM story such as *Just Grandma and Me,* you may have students write their own version of the story. Or, without finishing the story in class, the students could try to write their own endings. Think of the potential vocabulary development and creative writing experiences these might provide for your students.

As a teacher you are expected to maintain records on your students' academic progress. You can use the computer to keep records on each of your students that you can use to help you make decisions about their studies

Close-Up

A RURAL COMMUNITY BUILDS ITS FUTURE

Teachers in the Traer, Iowa, school district collaborated to provide the students in this rural community with many educational advantages. They carefully examined the school curriculum and looked closely at its articulation. Starting with nothing, they purchased technology and integrated it into the curriculum where appropriate. Together, teachers and students conducted community fundraisers and attended school board meetings to bring about change and to increase the amount of technology available to students in the school. Today, students have ready access to the school's rich array of resources through a schoolwide network and several computer labs, as well as access to resources outside the school walls through America Online™. Now students can use these technology-rich resources to enhance their learning by using online databases and word processing to complete assignments.

Technology for Diverse Learners

SCREEN READERS

Visually impaired students need to be able to use computer software, e-mail, and the Internet. Adaptive software programs, called screen readers, help these students use computers and to surf the Internet. Using speech synthesizers, the software reads aloud the text and names of icons. Visually impaired learners can navigate using the keyboard, hitting the tab button to move from icon to icon. Nontextual items such as graphics and photos are labeled with alternative textual descriptions, called *alt-tags,* which allow vi-

sually impaired learners to hear descriptions of these items. Among the common screen readers for Windows operating systems is *JAWS* (Job Access With Speech) from Henter-Joyce, Inc. (http://www.hj.com).

There are also devices that convert computer screen content into Braille characteristics for students who are both deaf and blind. These tools translate text to a single line of continually changing Braille. This technique allows these students to use a screen reader system. They don't hear what is on the screen, but they can feel it.

and to use when conferring with parents and school officials. This type of information is critical to ensuring that you provide your students with opportunities to learn (Figure 5.9).

As instructional activities employ a wider variety of media and printed materials (other than regular textbooks), the task of keeping track of the ever-increasing supply of materials becomes more demanding. Many courses of instruction use booklets and worksheets. The computer can keep a record of the number of such items on hand and signal you when additional copies are necessary. In some cases you can store the text of the booklets and worksheets in the computer and print copies on demand.

You can use the computer to access lists of materials available in your media center. Using the Internet, you also can access other databases, including materials available in nearby public and university libraries.

With increased concern for efficient allocation of limited funds and other resources, the computer is a handy tool for developing budgets and keeping records of expenditures. Many instructors store in their computer a list of desired materials and equipment for future purchase. As funds become available, they may quickly generate a request for these materials, along with necessary purchasing information.

Performance Support Systems. In the world of work, an educational and training concept borrowed from Japanese manufacturing is *kanban,* or "just-in-time training." Rather than teaching people skills and knowledge that they might use in the future, just-in-

Figure 5.8
Students can enjoy books on CD-ROM.

Figure 5.9
Computerized gradebooks are an easy and convenient way for teachers to manage student information.

time training delivers knowledge and expertise when workers need it. At the heart of this type of training is the use of performance support systems on the job.

A **performance support system** uses a variety of online aids both to improve current job performance and to plan further career development. Computer-based systems allow access to specific reference documents when they are needed and may even advise workers if they are having difficulties on the job. The consequence of just-in-time training is that it changes the role of formal education from teaching content to having students learn how to learn. Raybould (1990) describes an electronic performance support system that improves worker productivity by providing on-the-job access to integrated information advice and learning experiences.

In the introduction to their book, *Future Work,* Winslow and Bramer (1994) discuss the emergence of Integrated Performance Support (IPS) systems. They believe that, "above all, Integrated Performance Support anticipates the next phase of the world economy: the movement from an information economy to a knowledge economy. Here, the basic economic resource will not be capital, not labor, nor natural resources, but rather knowledge" (p. 4). IPS systems support worker performance with knowledge whenever and wherever a worker needs support. They may include advice, tools, reference, and training provided to workers at their work location at the moment of need. Using performance support systems, workers will take a fraction of the time to reach basic proficiency levels. Employees will be able to meet customer expectations because the knowledge they need to respond to a customer's request is right there at their fingertips. The result will be more satisfied customers. Future workers; while they are still in school, will need to learn how to effectively and efficiently use performance support systems.

Advantages

- *Learner control.* Computer-based instruction allows students some control over the rate and sequence of their learning (individualization). High-speed personalized responses to learner actions yield a high rate of reinforcement.
- *Special needs.* Computer-assisted instruction is effective with special learners—at-risk students, student with diverse ethnic backgrounds, and students with disabilities. Their special needs can be accommodated and instruction proceeds at an appropriate pace.
- *Record keeping.* The record-keeping ability of the computer makes individualized instruction feasible; teachers can prepare individual lessons for all students (particularly mainstreamed special students) and monitor their progress.

- *Information management.* Computers can cover a growing knowledge base associated with the information explosion. They can manage all types of information: graphic, text, audio, and video. More information is put easily at the instructor's and student's disposal.
- *Diverse experiences.* Computers provide diverse learning experiences. These can employ a variety of instructional methods and can be at the level of basic instruction, remediation, or enrichment.
- *Communication precision.* One serendipitous effect of working with computers is that they literally force us to communicate with them in an orderly and logical way. The computer user must learn to communicate with explicit, exact instructions and responses.

Limitations

- *Copyright.* The ease with which software can be duplicated without permission has inhibited some commercial publishers and private entrepreneurs from producing and marketing high-quality instructional software (see "Copyright Concerns: Computer Software," p. 119).
- *High expectations.* Users, both learners and teachers, may have unrealistic expectations for computer-based instruction. Many view computers as magical and expect learning to happen with little or no effort, but in reality (and as with all other learning tools) users derive benefits proportional to their investments.
- *Limited range of objectives.* Currently, computers are used to teach only a limited range of objectives. Most computer-based instruction does not teach effectively in the affective, motor, and interpersonal skills domains. Even in the cognitive domain, current programs tend to teach at the lower levels of knowledge and comprehension.
- *Controlled environment.* Creativity may be stifled in computerized instruction. The computer is slavish in its adherence to its program. Creative or original learner responses will be ignored or even rebuked if the program's designer has not anticipated such possibilities.
- *Lack of social interaction.* Computer-based instruction often lacks social interaction. Learners tend to work on their own at a computer, and there may be little if any face-to-face interaction with teachers or other learners.
- *Novelty effect.* The novelty associated with CAI in its earlier days has decreased. As learners have become more familiar with computers in the home and in the workplace, the newness of the computer experience has worn off and may now have less motivational value.

Integrating the Computer into the Curriculum

Putting computers in classrooms is only part of the task. The ultimate value of technology in education and training depends on how fully computers are integrated into the curriculum. Instructors need a framework for using computer technology that covers a variety of learning styles and accommodates varied teaching methods (Figure 5.10). Most important, results need to be measurable against a clear set of goals and objectives—the second step in the ASSURE model. In classrooms where computer technology is integrated successfully, students use it with the same ease with which they use books, maps, pencils, and pens. In technology-rich classrooms students and teachers engage in problem solving, cultivate creativity, collaborate globally, and discover the value of lifelong learning. (See "Integrating Computers into the Curriculum," in Classroom Resources, Section C.)

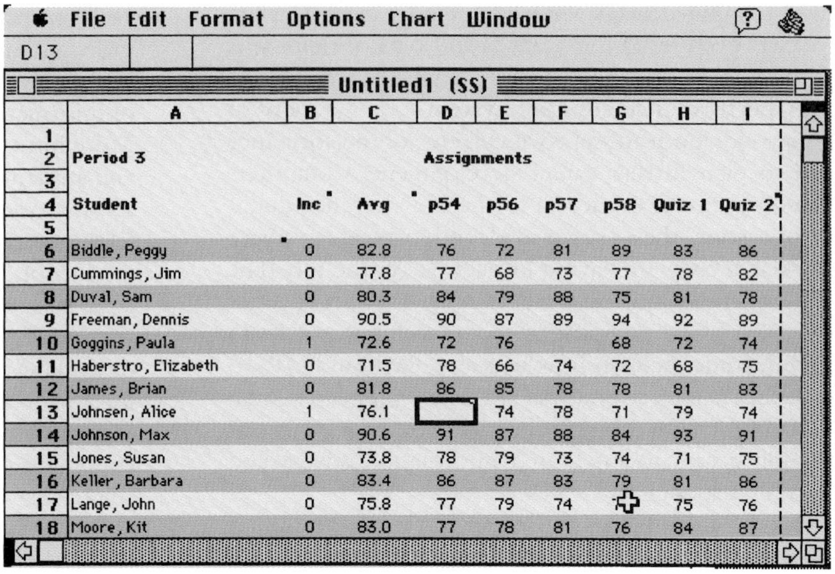

	A	B	C	D	E	F	G	H	I
1									
2	Period 3				Assignments				
3									
4	Student	Inc	Avg	p54	p56	p57	p58	Quiz 1	Quiz 2
5									
6	Biddle, Peggy	0	82.8	76	72	81	89	83	86
7	Cummings, Jim	0	77.8	77	68	73	77	78	82
8	Duval, Sam	0	80.3	84	79	88	75	81	78
9	Freeman, Dennis	0	90.5	90	87	89	94	92	89
10	Goggins, Paula	1	72.6	72	76		68	72	74
11	Haberstro, Elizabeth	0	71.5	78	66	74	72	68	75
12	James, Brian	0	81.8	86	85	78	78	81	83
13	Johnsen, Alice	1	76.1		74	78	71	79	74
14	Johnson, Max	0	90.6	91	87	88	84	93	91
15	Jones, Susan	0	73.8	78	79	73	74	71	75
16	Keller, Barbara	0	83.4	86	87	83	79	81	86
17	Lange, John	0	75.8	77	79	74	[illegible]	75	76
18	Moore, Kit	0	83.0	77	78	81	76	84	87

Figure 5.11
A spreadsheet is a page of rows and columns that displays word, numeric, and formula entries. A spreadsheet can be used to record, average, and manipulate data.

More emphasis is placed on providing opportunities for problem solving and cooperative learning methods.

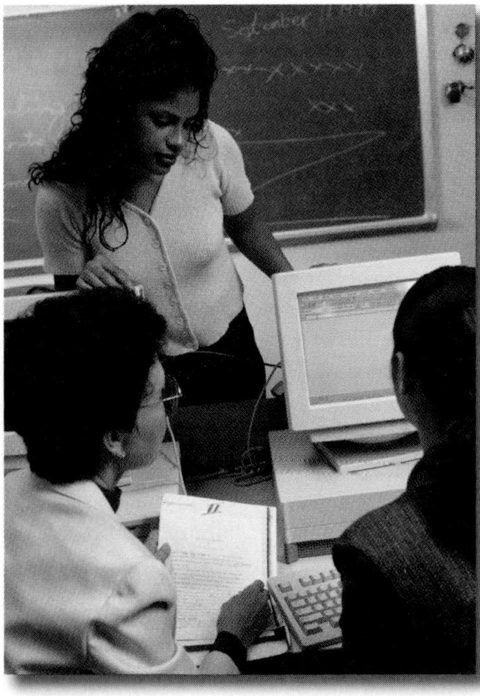

Figure 5.10
To ensure good utilization of computers in the curriculum, teachers need continued inservice training.

With increasing ease of use, the computer is becoming a more natural tool to use in these types of learning situations. Software is now available to provide students with experiences in working together to solve complex problems. Often students incorporate several different types of applications to explore a problem situation. For example, when assigned to prepare a report on ecology, a group of students used computer databases to search for resources they could use in their report. They sent e-mail messages to people in several locations requesting information. They used database and spreadsheet programs to store and sort their information (Figure 5.11). For their report they used a word processor and a hypermedia program to prepare written material and used a data projector to display for their classmates the information they had collected about the topic.

The procedure for educating students has shifted from providing them with information to opening doors for them to explore topics and to create meaningful learning experiences for themselves. Computer technology has been avidly incorporated into this process. The implication is that educators are moving away from the idea of school as a place to get knowledge to the view that *school is a place to learn how to learn*. The example of students working on an ecology report is not new within the school curriculum, but the approach certainly is. The challenge for you as a teacher is to provide opportunities for all students to use technology in meaningful ways to accomplish learning tasks. This may mean that you select specific software for individual students—for example, to practice math skills or to search online databases.

You should be a model user of computer software for your students. Students will quickly notice if the teacher makes illegal copies of programs and doesn't follow copyright guidelines. Remember, actions speak louder than words (see "Copyright Concerns: Computer Software"). Also, check with your technology coordinator, library media specialist, and/or principal for specific guidelines for your school. In general, you or your school may make *one* archival or backup copy of a copyrighted computer program. The backup may be used *only* to make another copy if the original is damaged or lost. This also applies to loading software onto a hard drive. Only *one* copy may be made, the original disk or CD-ROM is stored unless needed to reload the software if the software malfunctions. Only one copy may be used at a time. You may *not* make multiple copies of a copyrighted program without permission of the copyright holder. Some programs, depending on licensing, may be used on a computer network within your school. Be sure to check the licensing arrangements for each piece of software. If in doubt, ask! Ignorance is no excuse!

Most pieces of software list the rights and limitations of their use on the container or in documentation that accompanies the program. A program may not be put on multiple computers in a classroom or laboratory unless specifically licensed to do so. Most software may only be used on one machine at a time. Your school usually pays more for software that may be used on multiple computers simultaneously. A **lab pack** specifies the number of simultaneous uses of the software, usually 5 or 10. A **site license** allows a school or a school district to make unlimited copies of the program or to put the software on a server for multiple uses by students and teachers. A site license costs more but provides greater flexibility in software use.

Computer systems can deliver instruction directly to students by allowing them to interact with lessons designed especially for the assigned task. As mentioned earlier, this type of teaching tool is referred to as *computer-assisted instruction (CAI)*. The possibilities can be discussed in terms of the various types of available software and the instructional methods used. These types of software have been changing over time, allowing for more flexibility and complexity while giving students more freedom to learn. The basic premise of these types of software follows the instructional methods presented in Chapter 1.

Concept Processing

When engaged in thinking, students explore the possible connections between related ideas. Often they employ a technique referred to as *concept mapping*. Ideas about a topic are linked, forming a complex web of interrelated thoughts. Software packages such as *Inspiration* are designed to facilitate this process (see "Media Files: Computer Software 1"). Students map their ideas in boxes on

Copyright Concerns

COMPUTER SOFTWARE

Congress amended the Copyright Act to clear up questions of fair use of copyrighted computer programs. The changes defined the term *computer program* for copyright purposes and set forth permissible and nonpermissible use of copyrighted computer software programs. According to the amended law, with a single copy of a program, you may do the following:

- Make one backup or archival copy of a computer program; also, you may use a "locksmith" program to bypass the copy-prevention code on the original to make the archival copy.
- Install one copy of the program onto a computer hard drive.
- Adapt a computer program from one language to another if the program is not available in that language.
- Add features to a copyrighted program to make better use of the program.
- Adapt a copyrighted program to meet local needs.

Without the copyright owner's permission, you may *not* do the following with a single copy:

- Make multiple copies of a copyrighted program.
- Make additional copies from an archival or backup copy.
- Make copies of copyrighted programs to be sold, leased, loaned, transmitted, or given away.
- Sell a locally produced adaptation of a copyrighted program.
- Make multiple copies of an adaptation of a copyrighted program even for use within a school or school district.
- Put a single copy of a program onto a network without permission or a special site license.
- Duplicate the printed copyrighted software documentation unless allowed by the copyrighted program.

These guidelines seem to be reasonable while still protecting the proprietary rights of copyright holders. In fact, the guidelines are more liberal than those affecting the use of audiovisual materials.

For general information on copyright, see the Copyright Concerns on page 11 in Chapter 1. Suggested readings on copyright appear at the end of Chapter 1.

Media Files: Computer Software 1

INSPIRATION

Inspiration Software, Inc.

Concept-Processing Program

Inspiration is a software package that facilitates brainstorming, concept mapping, and planning. It creates a visual diagram of the ideas generated by an individual or group. Use the program to create overviews, presentation visuals, and flow charts. It is designed to help younger students develop skills in concept mapping. Once their thoughts have been visualized, *Inspiration* easily converts the concept map into a word processing outline.

MAVIS BEACON TEACHES TYPING

Software Toolworks: Mindscape

Tutorial Program

Mavis Beacon Teaches Typing teaches the learner to keyboard. Included are carefully guided instructions at each level, as well as practice opportunities to improve speed and accuracy, Graphics, charts, and appearances by Mavis herself encourage novice typists to continue to work on their skills. Progress records are maintained for each learner, providing the teacher with information and allowing the learner to resume following an interruption in the instruction.

LOGICAL JOURNEY OF THE ZOOMBINIS

Broderbund, Inc.

Game

Logical Journey of the Zoombinis is a fascinating and challenging game designed to help students explore and apply fundamental principles of logic, problem solving, and data analysis. It contains 12 puzzles, with levels of difficulty, to support growth in mathematical concepts and thinking skills. Because the game engages students in creative and divergent thinking, they are able to solve many of the puzzles in a nonlinear, intuitive manner, which is one valued problem-solving approach.

the computer screen—moving the idea boxes, connecting them, matching them with other ideas, and ultimately creating a graphic representation of their ideas. The program allows students to weigh the importance of each of the concepts mapped. Further, *Inspiration* will convert the concept map into a formal outline to help students in their writing.

Drill-and-Practice

Drill-and-practice programs lead learners through a series of examples to increase dexterity and fluency in a skill. The computer does not display impatience and goes ahead only when mastery is shown. Drill-and-practice is used predominantly for math drills, foreign language translation, vocabulary building, and the like. For example, the program *Sentences* lets learners practice sentence construction.

Drill-and-practice programs provide a variety of questions with varied formats. The student is usually allowed several tries before the computer presents the correct answer. Several levels of difficulty can be available within the same program, which also gives correction, remediation, or encouragement as appropriate.

Tutorial

In the tutorial role, the computer acts as the teacher. All interaction is between the computer and the learner. An example is *Mavis Beacon Teaches Typing*, which guides students to learn touch-typing skills (see "Media Files: Computer Software 1").

In this method, the pattern followed is basically that of branching programmed instruction (explained in Chapter 2); information is presented in small units followed by a question or task. The computer analyzes the student's responses (compared with responses supplied by the designer) and gives appropriate feedback. A complicated network of pathways, or branches, can be programmed. The more alternatives available to the computer, the more adaptive the tutorial can be to individual differences. The extent to which a skilled, live tutor can be approximated depends on the creativity of the software designer.

Games

In Chapter 2 we discussed the distinction between gaming and simulation. A game activity may or may not entail simulation elements. Likewise, a game may or may not be instructional. It depends on whether the skill practiced in the game is an academic one—that is, related to a specific instructional objective or a workplace skill.

Recreational games can serve a useful purpose in building computer literacy in an enjoyable, nonthreatening manner. But, the ultimate goal of useful learning must be kept in mind. Instructors experienced in computer utilization recommend rationing purely recreational game use, using it as a reward for completing other assignments. Games range from those with specific learning outcomes, such as *Logical Journey of the Zoombinis* (see "Media Files: Computer Software 1"), to those that emphasize entertainment while teaching problem-solving strategies, such as *King Arthur's Magic Castle*.

Simulation

The simulation method of instruction is described in Chapter 2. In this method, learners confront an approximation of a real-life situation. It allows realistic practice without the expense or risks otherwise involved.

The computer-based simulation *SimCity* puts the user in charge of a growing city. Students can build a city from the ground up or choose to manage one of several well-known cities around the world. They control the city budget, construction, and location of city services. Their decisions affect pollution, crime, and traffic. Students learn the consequences of actions in a complex environment.

In military and industrial settings, training for operation and maintenance of complex equipment—aircraft, weapons systems, nuclear power plants, oil rigs, and the like—is often given on computer-based simulators. As discussed in Chapter 2, these large-scale simulators allow trainees to experience lifelike situations without the danger and expense involved in practice with the actual equipment.

Discovery

Discovery is a general term to describe activities using an inductive approach to learning; that is, presenting problems that students solve through trial and error or systematic approaches. It approximates laboratory learning outside the classroom.

Using the discovery method in CAI, learners employ an information retrieval strategy to get information from a database. For example, a salesperson interested in learning about competitors' products can select from a set of critical product features, display them on the computer, and draw conclusions about the comparisons of the products. Some discovery lessons analyze large databases of election information, populations statistics, or other user-built databases.

Problem Solving

In problem solving, learners use previously mastered skills to resolve a challenging problem. Students must examine the data or information presented, clearly define the problem, perhaps state hypotheses, perform experiments, then reexamine the data and generate a solution. The computer may present the problem, process the data, maintain a database, and provide feedback when appropriate.

One commercially available problem-solving program is *Memory: A First Step in Problem Solving*. It provides students in kindergarten through sixth grade with opportunities to practice the skill and strategies involved in problem solving. The program introduces a generic approach to problem solving across all subject areas as well as in common lifelike situations. The goal is not to present a fixed problem-solving model but to promote the use of an individualized, systematic approach in which students establish a model that is appropriate to a specific problem, using strategies from their personal repertoire. The multimedia kit includes a chart showing a problem-solving matrix, classroom lessons, software summary sheets, program descriptions for each computer disk, computer disks, and a hand puppet for use with younger students.

Another problem-solving program, *The Factory Deluxe*, challenges learners to "manufacture" products according to specifications provided by the computer. There are hundreds of different patterns to be duplicated at nine levels of difficulty. The sequence in which the four types of machines, rotator, puncher, striper, and cutter, are used is another critical factor. Of course, there are numerous ways to solve each challenging problem presented by the program (see "Media Files: Computer Software 2").

During problem-solving activities students not only learn about the content under study but also develop higher-level thinking skills. These higher-level cognitive processes include reasoning skills and logical and critical

Media Files: Computer Software 2

DECISIONS, DECISIONS
Tom Snyder Productions

Simulation

Decisions, Decisions is a series of role-playing software packages designed specifically to generate informed discussion and decision making in the classroom using only one computer. The program has a mode for whole-class discussion with the teacher leading the entire group, as in a traditional classroom. In addition, it offers a small-group option for managing a cooperative learning environment. Up to six small groups of students move through the simulation independently directed by the computer. Titles include *Substance Abuse, Violence in Media, Immigration, The Environment,* and *Town Government.* Additional multimedia sets include *Rainforest Researchers* and *The Great Ocean Rescue.*

EXPLORER SERIES
LOGAL® Software, Inc.

Discovery Program

Every classroom is filled with students of varying abilities and learning styles. This innovative series of programs focuses on the everyday experiences students are most likely to have in common and uses them as a springboard for helping them to learn abstract scientific concepts. The three programs in this series are *Biology Explorer, Chemistry Explorer,* and *Physics Explorer.* Each program includes a series of guided activities that engage learners, incorporating a learning model that leads students from simple to more complex concepts.

THE FACTORY DELUXE
Sunburst (www.Sunburst.com)

Problem-Solving Program

The Factory Deluxe focuses on several strategies used in problem solving: working backward, analyzing a process, determining a sequence, and applying creativity. Learners are given a square on the computer and four types of machines. The "rotator" machine can be programmed to rotate the square 30, 45, 60, 90, 120, 135, 150, or 180 degrees. The "puncher" machine can punch square or triangular holes in the product as it passes through the machine. The "striper" machine paints thin, medium, or thick stripes of various colors. And the "cutter" cuts off and discards part of the product.

The program has five types of activities. In "Try It" students experiment with one to ten machines as they put together assembly lines to create geometric products. "Build It" allows learners to actually construct the products. During "Research It" they refine existing assembly lines to find more efficient ways to create given products. "Ship It" requires students to build their knowledge of geometric attributes as they pack boxes to fill orders. Finally, in "Deliver It" students compete against each other or one of two computer components in a mathematical race to deliver their products.

INSPIRER GEOGRAPHY SERIES
Tom Snyder Productions

Computer-Based Cooperative Learning

The *Inspirer* Geography Series is a collection of exciting scavenger hunt software that inspires students to learn geography. Teams of students travel throughout an area of the world in search of important resources and commodities. Working in teams, students interpret maps, share information, and plan strategies. They have an opportunity to learn about and appreciate the diverse resources and geography of a specific region of the world. Titles include *National Inspirer, International Inspirer, Europe Inspirer, Africa Inspirer,* and *Asia Inspirer.*

thinking. The primary reason for teaching elementary computer languages, such as Logo, is not for students to learn programming itself but to enable them to use the computer for problem solving.

Table 5.1 presents an organized overview of the computer-assisted instruction methods discussed in this section.

Assure Case Connection

Mr. Sorge is comfortable with several different software packages which might help his students with their computation skills. He is considering the possibility of using a drill-and-practice program. He is also considering using a mathematics game package. Which of the methods might Mr. Sorge consider for integrating the computer into his instruction?

Table 5.1
Utilization of CAI methods

Methods	Description	Role of Teacher	Role of Computer	Role of Student	Applications/ Examples
Drill-and-Practice	Content already taught Reviews basic facts and terminology Variety of questions in varied formats Question-answer drills repeated as necessary	Arranges for prior instruction Selects material Matches drill to student Checks progress	Asks questions "Evaluates" student response Provides immediate feedback Records student progress	Provides feedback Practices content already taught Responds to questions Receives confirmation or correction Chooses content and difficulty level	Parts of a microscope Completing balance sheets Vocabulary building Math facts Product knowledge
Tutorial	Presentation of new information Teaches concepts and principles Provides remedial instruction	Selects material Adapts instruction Monitors	Presents information Asks questions Monitors responses Provides remedial feedback Summarizes key points Keeps records	Interacts with computer Sees results Answers questions Asks questions	Clerical training Bank teller training Science Medical procedures Bible study
Games	Competitive Drill-and-practice in a motivational format Individual or small group	Sets limits Directs process Monitors results	Acts as competitor, judge, and scorekeeper	Learns facts, strategies, skills Evaluates choices Competes with computer	Fraction games Counting games Spelling games Typing (arcade-type) games
Simulation	Approximates real-life situations Based on realistic models Individual or small group	Introduces subject Presents background Guides "debriefing"	Plays role(s) Delivers results of decisions Maintains the model and its database	Practices decision making Makes choices Receives results of decisions Evaluates decisions	Troubleshooting History Medical diagnosis Simulators (pilot, driver) Business management Laboratory experiments
Discovery	Inquiry into database Inductive approach Trial and error Tests hypotheses	Presents basic problem Monitors student progress	Presents student with source of information Stores data Permits search procedures	Makes hypotheses Tests guesses Develops principles or rules	Social science Science Food-intake analysis Career choices
Problem Solving	Defines problem States hypothesis Examines data Generates solution	Assigns problems Assists students Checks results	Presents problem Manipulates data Maintains database	Defines the problem Sets up the solution Manipulates variables Conducts trial and error	Business Creativity Troubleshooting Mathematics Computer programming

Information Tools

As students begin to work with information, they find the computer tools available to them help make the process easier and fun. Using a word processing program for writing makes it easy for students to edit their work. Once they have gathered their ideas into concept maps, they then begin to work those ideas into connected text. The word processor makes it possible for students to work with their ideas and to quickly make changes as they explore various ways to present them. Spelling and grammar checking are available to students. A thesaurus makes it easier for them to find the right word for a specific situation. And editing, a process children are not prone to enjoy, suddenly becomes easier. Students are more willing to make changes when editing is simplified.

Students enjoy putting their ideas onto the page. They especially enjoy seeing their work in finished copy. Desktop publishing allows students to not only print a nice copy of their work, but also to design layouts that are creative and a pleasure to see (Figure 5.12). Using a desktop publishing program, students can add graphics to their pages. They can see how their pages will look before they print them. Students of all ages like to produce their writings in formal documents, such as small books and newsletters. Class newsletters are very popular, with students working together to produce a document that they are proud to share with family and friends.

As students work with large amounts of information, it is essential that they learn how to cluster it. A database allows students to store information in ways that make it easy for them to retrieve it. By learning how to develop databases, students begin to organize their knowledge and understand ways they can group their information.

Figure 5.12

Desktop publishing software allows students to produce their own written materials with minimal time and little computer expertise.

A database allows students to quickly get the specific information they are seeking. Computer catalogs and onsite/online databases allow students to search for information. The amount of information available today is constantly growing. When students understand how information is organized and what the process is for retrieving it, they can gather vast amounts quickly and easily.

Graphics Tools

Drawing and creating graphics is a fun activity for students. Computer software such as *KidPix* can make drawing even more pleasurable. This software allows children to use, for example, a "rubber stamp" that makes noise as it marks on the screen, to erase a picture to find a hidden one behind it, and to use a "drippy" paintbrush. Computer technology thus changes the dynamics of art for children.

As students gain skill in using drawing software, they can learn to use more complex drawing and drafting programs. High school students can use computer-aided design (CAD) and graphics programs to prepare complex visuals. Many of the skills associated with these types of software are easy for students to learn. For example, an art program such as *Photo Deluxe* allows students to develop complex projects using an array of tools, ranging from basic drawing tools for lines and shapes to advanced drawing tools for editing and redesigning. They may create their own pictures, or may begin by using commercially designed clip art, available from many suppliers (Figure 5.13). A simple picture can be developed into a very artistic piece with only a few keystrokes.

Further, presentation software has become a very popular format for teachers and students alike. With the computer connected to a data projector, it is possible to create colorful and animated overheads. Supervise carefully, though; using a program such as Microsoft's *PowerPoint*, individuals sometimes spend more time deciding the color scheme or the font style than they do actually preparing the content of the presentation. (See Chapter 4 for further discussion on this topic.)

INTEGRATED LEARNING SYSTEMS

In many schools a viable form of computer use is the **integrated learning system (ILS),** referring to a networked set of computer workstations equipped with software that provides a particular set of sequential lessons. Students work through these lessons as prescribed by the built-in management system, which tracks individual student progress. These systems are "integrated"

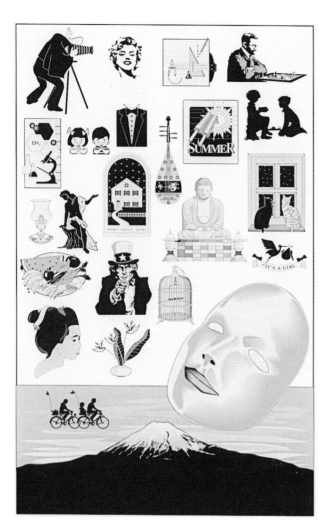

Figure 5.13

Examples of computer clip art.

Source: Used by permission of C.A.R., Inc., 7009 Kingsbury, St. Louis, MO 63130. These illustrations taken from the Clipables® EPS Graphics Library. Clipables is a registered trademark of C.A.R., Inc. All rights reserved.

in the sense that each lesson is connected with the next, all lessons are correlated with a set of objectives, and all tests are matched to the lessons and objectives. Further, the software typically is customized to match the content, objectives, and chapter sequence of the textbook used.

An ILS installation might, for example, provide four networked computer workstations in each classroom in a school building. The menu might include hundreds of carefully sequenced lessons throughout several grade levels and subjects. The teacher can decide which students will use the system for which lessons. Students work individually at the workstations for about 45 minutes per day. When they finish one lesson they are tested and directed to the next appropriate lesson. The management software gathers and stores all information about student progress and supplies reports to the teacher and administrators.

Advantages

- *Self-pacing.* Students can move through the material at their own pace, being tested and branched at frequent intervals.
- *Total package.* A major advantage from the administrative standpoint is having a total integrated package of hardware and software; there is no need to try to piece together your own network or to shop for and evaluate courseware.
- *Validated.* The learning programs can be tested and validated before distribution; with a large base of clients, the vendors can afford to invest in curriculum research and development. Vendors revise and update software on a regular basis. Some vendors even provide "money-back guarantees" of student success.

Limitations

- *Courseware quality.* The quality of the courseware is variable; some of it is low-level, uninspiring drill-and-practice material. The instructional strategies used in computer-assisted programs may be contrary to your own teaching philosophy. A frequent criticism is overemphasis on low-level knowledge and skills. These criticisms are not necessarily inherent in truly integrated learning systems, but they do apply to many commercial packages.
- *Evidence of effectiveness.* There is little objective research to indicate the effectiveness of these materials; most of the existing studies have been commissioned by one of the vendors and have been conducted with less than acceptable rigor.
- *Loss of flexibility.* One of the trade-offs made in adopting an integrated learning system is flexibility. Teachers and students are limited to using the same hardware and software in the same way. Some argue that the real potential of computers is achieved when users have control and can take off in their own directions. The standardization imposed by the typical ILS is contrary to the impulses of most teachers to maintain autonomy in terms of content and methods.
- *Reports.* The individual progress reports given to teachers are often hard to interpret.
- *Curricular integration.* Perhaps the most serious risk of the ILS is, ironically, its lack of integration with the curriculum. The components of the computer system are integrated with each other, but the system may not be integrated with the rest of the school curriculum. One of the most frequent criticisms of curricula is that of fractionation—fragments of facts and skills taught in isolation, not coalescing into a whole.

Integration

ILSs are used most commonly for basic mathematics and language arts instruction. Often, low-achieving or special needs students leave their regular classrooms to use the ILS in a cubicle within a computer lab environment. Homebound students can be linked to the network as well. Some systems specialize in software for remediation of basic skills; others offer broad curricula encompassing virtually all the standard school subjects. Some systems use the networking capability to make databases, such as encyclopedias and libraries of video clips, available to all users.

Attractive applications in the future are likely to be ones in which the ILS lessons are one component of an overall school program that combines team teaching, thematic units, student and parent involvement in goal setting, and customization to the prescriptions of the local teaching staff. An ILS not comprehensively integrated into the curriculum will not help students achieve desired educational outcomes.

SOFTWARE SELECTION

Selection Criteria

There are several factors associated with selecting software (see "Selection Rubric: Computer Software," p. 133). Foremost is to examine the software within the context of the learning outcomes. Other factors that should be considered include content, format, ease of operation, design, and completeness of the package.

In addition, software programs, also called *applications,* are written to run on specific operating systems. An *operating system,* such as *Mac OS, Windows,* or *Unix,* is software that functions as the computer's interface with the user. It determines precisely how user, computer, and application interact to produce the desired results. The software you select must be designed to run on your available operating system and must function properly with your specific hardware configuration (see next section).

Accuracy. When looking at software, you need to consider the content in terms of its accuracy. If the software is older, some of the information may be out of date. Also, it is important to consider the sequencing of the information. Information should be presented in a clear and logical manner. Finally, you need to examine the intent of the lesson and its relation to your intended student goals.

Feedback. It is important that software follow sound educational techniques and principles. In a drill-and-practice program it is important that students have frequent informative feedback.

Learner Control. Another important criterion is the amount of learner control given to the student. Students should be able to control the pacing and direction of their learning. Software should provide students with opportunities to select topics within areas of study. Also, students need to be able to control how quickly they progress through material. Finally, the information needs to be presented in a manner designed to maintain student interest and involvement in the tasks.

Prerequisites. Practical examples that relate to students' own experiences are more valuable to learning. Prerequisite skills need to be identified if they are essential for successful use of the software. Information needs to be presented at a level appropriate for students.

Ease of Use. Software needs to be easy to use. Software is *user friendly* if it makes the computer transparent in the learning process. When students must focus more on operating the software than on understanding the content, then the computer is interfering with, rather than assisting, learning.

Special Features. Sometimes software has special effects or features that may be essential for effective learning. Often, however, these are only window dressing and add no value to the learning. In fact, they may interfere with learning. Color, graphics, animation, and sound should be a part of quality software only if they contribute to student learning. As discussed in Chapter 4, text should be presented in a consistent manner, using size, color, and location to reduce the cognitive burden of deciphering meaning. Keystroking and mousing techniques should be intuitive for students. The manner in which students interact with software needs to be transparent, allowing them to focus on content.

ASSURE Case Connection

Mr. Sorge needs to examine the mathematics software available. He is considering using a simulation software program. What important aspects of the program does he need to consider?

COMPUTER HARDWARE

Basic Components

Regardless of the size of the computer or complexity of the system, computers have a number of standard components. The physical equipment that makes up the computer is referred to as the **hardware.** A computer's specific combination of hardware components is referred to as its *configuration.* The basic hardware components are diagrammed in Figure 5.14.

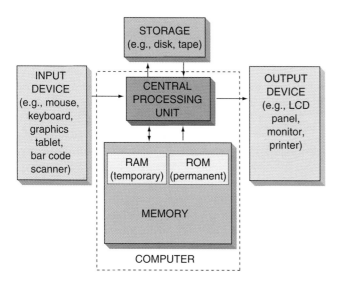

Figure 5.14

Basic elements of a desktop or laptop computer.

Input Device. Input devices transmit information into the computer. The most commonly used input device is the keyboard. Others include the mouse, trackball, joystick, graphics tablet, and even voice. Both students and teachers can use graphics tablets to incorporate drawings into their programs. Science laboratory monitoring devices can also be connected directly to a personal computer with the proper interface device.

Central Processing Unit. The central processing unit (CPU) is the core element, or "brain," that carries out all the calculations and controls the total system. In a personal computer the CPU is one (or more) of the tiny chips (microprocessors) inside the machine (Figure 5.15).

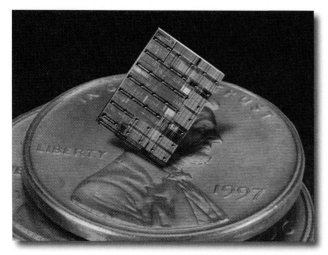

Figure 5.15

The tiny microprocessor fostered the microcomputer revolution. Chips like this one are used in home appliances, automobiles, toys, and hundreds of other devices, giving each a "brain" of its own.

Memory. Memory stores information for manipulation by the CPU. The memory contains the *control function*—that is, the programs written to tell the CPU what to do in what order. In computers, control instructions and sets of data are stored in two types of memory:

- **Read-only memory (ROM).** This consists of the control instructions that have been "wired" permanently into the memory and which the computer will need constantly, such as programming languages and internal monitoring functions.
- **Random access memory (RAM).** This is the flexible part of the memory. The particular program or set of data being manipulated by the user is temporarily stored in RAM, then erased to make way for the next program.

A computer's memory size is usually described in terms of how many bytes it can store at one time. A **byte** is the number of bits required to represent and store one character (letter or number) of text. A **bit** is a single unit of data, coded in binary form as either 0 (off) or 1 (on). A byte is most commonly made up of 8 or 16 (sometimes 32 or 64) bits of various combinations of 0s and 1s (Figure 5.16).

A **kilobyte (Kb)** refers to approximately 1,000 bytes (1,024 to be exact), a **megabyte (Mb or "meg")** indicates 1,000 Kb or approximately a million bytes, and a **gigabyte (Gb or "gig")** is equal to 1,000 Mb or approximately one billion bytes. A megabyte is the unit used to measure the RAM storage capacity of a computer. Thus, if a computer can store 1,024,000 bytes, it is said to have 1 "meg" of memory capacity. We now talk about storage in terms of **terabytes (Tb),** which is a million megabytes or a trillion bytes. The more powerful machines are capable of processing more bytes simultaneously, thus increasing their processing capacity.

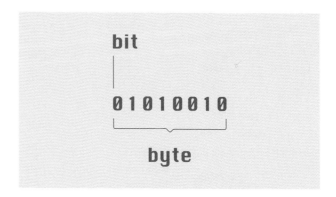

Figure 5.16

Representation of the letter A in ASCII (American Standard Code for Information Interchange) code when 8 bits represent 1 byte.

A computer's memory is one of its limiting factors. You need to be sure that the computer has enough memory to run the software you will be using. If you plan to use more than one application at a time, it is recommended you have a minimum of 128 Mb of RAM; 256 to 512 Mb is preferable. One megabyte of memory can hold approximately 2,000 single-spaced pages of text, but many graphics and animations may themselves require several megabytes to display properly.

Storage.   The computer's operating system, application programs, and data files are stored outside its CPU when not in use. The most common storage mechanism is the magnetic disk. Recordable CD-ROMs are common, with recordable DVDs becoming available on most machines. Storage capacity (measured in Mb or Gb) has expanded to keep pace with the rapidly growing memory demands of today's software and the ever-increasing size of graphics- and animation-laden multimedia data files.

Magnetic disk devices may be built into the computer or are available as stand-alone ("external") devices. The disk is made of thin plastic, coated with a magnetic recording surface, and encased in a protective shell.

In general, fixed media devices are called *hard disks,* although removable hard disks are also available. This disk is a rigid device with a magnetic recording surface. Current hard disk capacities range from several hundred megabytes to multiple gigabytes (Table 5.2).

Low-capacity removable media devices are called *floppy disks.* They were originally 5¼ inch diameter plastic disks encased in a stiff yet flexible paper or plastic shell (hence the name "floppy" disk). The size of the disk was reduced to 3½ inches in diameter and encased in a rigid plastic shell. The storage capacity ranges from 800 Kb to

Table 5.2
Disk types

Type	Size	Physical Characteristics	Storage Capacity	Machines Using
Removable storage disk	Varies—usually 3¾ in. or 5½ in. diameter	Thin flexible plastic disk in a stiff plastic case	High density, 100 megabytes to 4.6 gigabytes	Used with an external drive or special internal drive. Available for both Macintosh and PC
Hard disks	Varies—usually 5¼ in. or 3½ in. diameter	Metal or metal-coated platters Internal or external to the computer	240 megabytes to one gigabyte most common; up to several gigabytes available for some machines	Available for all computers
Compact discs (CD-ROM, CD-B, CD-RW, DVD, DVD-R, DVD-RW)	4¾ in. diameter	Metalicized disc coated with clear plastic	650 megabytes or more	Commonly used with Macs and PCs
USB (Universal Serial Bus) Minidrive	Varies—usually about 1 in. wide by 3 in. in length	Hard outer surface with USB connection; some have removable storage chips.	Range from 8 meg to 1 gig	Commonly used with Macs and PCs

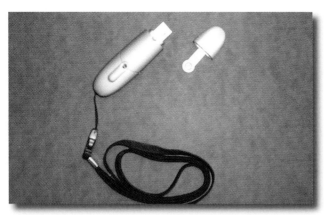

Figure 5.17
The USB Minidrive is a convenient way to transfer information from one computer to another.

1.6 Mb. Floppy disks have gradually been replaced by removable media devices.

High-capacity removable media devices, a kind of hybrid of hard and floppy disks, are replacing floppy disks as the portable storage format of choice. Generally termed **removable-storage devices,** they are small, portable, and used primarily for backing up and archiving computer files. One of the more popular formats for this type of storage device is the Zip® disk, with the appropriate disk drive. Approximately the same size and construction as floppy disks, these devices come in 100 and 250 Mb. Other brands are available in larger capacities, but they are not as commonly used. More recently, a USB minidrive is a form of removable hard disk that relies on a USB technology, a connection format that allows the user to connect a device without having to restart the computer (Figure 5.17). This type of hard disk can range from a few megabytes to a gigabyte or more. Some minidrives, also referred to as "keys," have removable flash memory cards, which allows the user to increase the memory capacity of the minidrive by changing the memory chip. This same memory chip might also fit into a digital camera or a hand-held computer device, thus making the interchange of visual and text information very flexible. The USB minidrive does not require any special wiring and can fit into your pocket. One additional feature of the minidrive is the ability to use the same device on either a PC or a Macintosh computer.

Applications of removable-storage devices include the following:

- Archiving old files that you don't use anymore but may want to access someday
- Storing unusually large files, such as graphic images that you need infrequently
- Exchanging large files with someone
- Moving your files from one computer to another, perhaps from your desktop to your laptop computer

- Keeping certain files separate from files on your hard disk (e.g., old test files)

The compact disc, used for digitally storing and reproducing music and verbal narration, is also used to store and retrieve text and graphics. A **CD-ROM (compact disc–read-only memory)** drive can read data from a compact disc in much the same way as from a floppy or hard disk. CD-ROM has the advantage of storing more data—approximately 250,000 pages of text or the equivalent of several hundred floppy disks. An entire encyclopedia can be stored on a single CD-ROM with room to spare. A computer can find and list all page references to any topic in that encyclopedia within seconds.

Nearly all computers now have CD-ROM read/write drives built into them. This makes it possible for the computer to not only read what is on a CD-ROM, but also to be able to copy data to a blank CD-ROM disc. Most computers are now available with DVD devices to play DVD media. As the technology advances, DVD-R (recordable DVD) will become the standard. DVD devices are capable of reading both DVD and CD-ROM discs. The DVD can store up to 5.2 gigabytes of data at a cost of less than a penny per megabyte of storage.

Its vast storage capacity makes the DVD an extremely attractive medium for reference materials, multimedia applications, simulation games, virtual reality experiences, and complex problem-solving exercises.

Output Device.   Output devices display the results of your program. A television-type monitor, referred to as a CRT (cathode-ray tube), is one type of output device. Liquid-crystal (LCD) and other display types provide a very clear and precise visual display. The monitor may be built into the computer package or may be a separate component.

Computers also commonly provide output in the form of data printed on paper sheets (hardcopy). Printers are available in a range of prices and quality (Figure 5.18). Quality of text and graphics correlates with cost. Printers are being combined with scanners and photocopiers to make them "all-in-one" devices. Some types of printers also include fax capabilities.

COMPUTER FACILITIES

There are a variety of facilities for computer use. They range from the computer classroom (one or more computers in a single classroom) to the computer laboratory.

The One-Computer Classroom

In some schools access to computers is still limited. Often there is a single computer lab where a teacher can take a whole class of students to work on computers as part of a lesson. However, increased interest by many teachers in incorporating the computer into their lessons

Technology for Diverse Learners

SPEECH FACILITATOR

Speech boards couple images with vocal output. One such device is Pathfinder, which features a static keyboard, a color dynamic display using vocabulary, pictures, complete keyboard emulation, and infrared controls. Pathfinder is produced by Prentke Romich (http://www.prentrom.com).

Figure 5.18
A typical printer for use with a computer.

limits the number of times per week that any one teacher can use the computer lab. One solution has been to have a computer placed in each classroom. This single computer is therefore available to the teacher and students to use throughout the day.

It is possible for a teacher to use a single computer in creative ways with a whole class of students. Some software lends itself to being used by single students who need to work on specific tasks; other software is designed for group activities. For example, with the series of programs *Decisions, Decisions,* groups of students interact with the computer to get specific information before they can proceed with their group activity (see "Media Files: Computer Software 2"). The students do not need to work on the computer during the entire lesson. While one group interacts with the computer, the remaining groups are working at their desks.

The one-computer classroom, then, can be viewed as a place where you may use the computer in many ways:

- *Large group.* With a data projector you can demonstrate to a whole class how to use a particular software program or how to manage a particular set of data.
- *Small group.* A small group of students can work together with the computer. Students can interact with a program in groups, then return to their seats, allowing others to have some time on the computer. Each group has a turn using the software to gather or present data.
- *Learning center.* Individual students or small groups can go to a learning center that has at its core a

Technology for Diverse Learners

PHYSICAL DISABILITIES

Switch-accessible software is available for students who have difficulty operating a mouse or keyboard. When a student is unable to control small motor movements, the switch makes it possible to move the arrow or to use special keys on the keyboard to interact with the computer. The switch is generally large enough for students who are unable to grasp a small device, such as a joystick. One manufacturer is Simtech Publications (http://www.hsj.com).

 Close-Up

CLASSROOM USE OF A SINGLE COMPUTER

A high school economics teacher uses a single computer with a class of 24 students. A computer coupled with a video data projector allows all students to see what is on the monitor. The teacher uses prepared computer graphics instead of overhead transparencies for key points and illustrative graphs. She can advance from one visual to the next as needed and can also reveal key words from the presentation with the touch of a key.

The biggest advantage of the computer in a large-group instructional situation is its usefulness in presenting "what if" results. For example, while presenting the concepts of supply and demand, students can discuss the effect of an increase in availability of a product on its cost. Following the discussion the teacher can project the results. The teacher can also put student-suggested values into the computer, and the class can see the results immediately. Economics comes alive in the classroom when years of data can be manipulated within minutes for all to see.

computer. Integrating a specific software program into the center, you create another type of interactive learning center.
- *Personal secretary.* Every teacher is responsible for maintaining grades, communicating with parents, and preparing instructional materials. The computer can assist you with these types of tasks.

The Multiple-Computer Classroom

A **computer classroom** is useful when the teacher wants to present to all students simultaneously. The arrangement is helpful when the instructor is teaching students to use the same software simultaneously (Figures 5.19 through 5.22). Networked computers with monitors recessed in the tables for both students and teachers allow eye contact and facilitate communication. Students can work in groups of two or three and share one computer. The teacher should have a projection device to display information for all students on one screen. In some networks the teacher can control and monitor what is shown on each student computer.

The Computer Laboratory

When a teacher wants each student to be working on a computer during a lesson, it is necessary for the whole

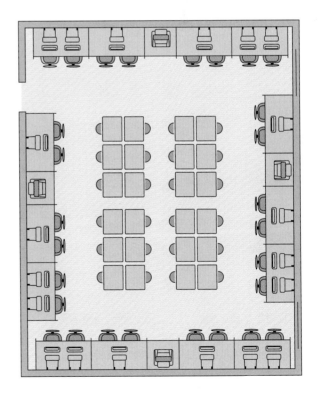

Figure 5.19
Computers around the wall in a laboratory allow one teacher to monitor all student activity.

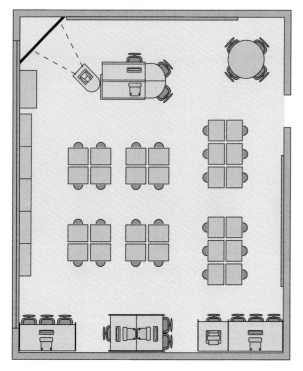

Figure 5.20

An elementary classroom with four computers (bottom) used for individual and small-group study. (Plan developed by Interactive Learning Systems, Inc., Cincinnati, OH.)

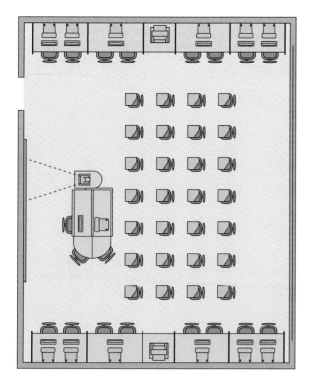

Figure 5.21

A high school classroom with 12 computers and 2 printers (along both side walls) used individually. (Plan developed by Interactive Learning Systems, Inc., Cincinnati, OH.)

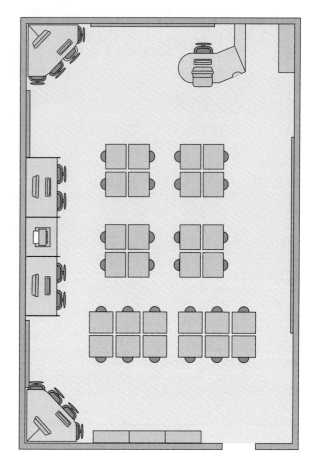

Figure 5.22

A middle school classroom with chairs arranged at computers for collaborative learning. (Plan developed by Interactive Learning Systems, Inc., Cincinnati, OH.)

class to have access to computers simultaneously. Schools often place 15 to 20 computers together in a single room called a **computer laboratory.** The computer laboratory is appropriate if you want students to be working independently or in small groups on different programs and different activities. To monitor student activity, to keep them on task, and to prevent them from viewing inappropriate or irrelevant material, the computers can be placed around the walls of the laboratory with the monitors facing the center of the room (see Figure 5.19). You can quickly see what each student is doing and respond to student questions individually.

We believe that the trend is toward the multiple-computer classroom. In the early days when schools had a limited number of computers, they assembled them in a laboratory. As more computers became available single computers were assigned to individual classrooms. Teachers soon discovered how they could successfully use multiple computers in their classrooms. Some schools have done away with their computer laboratories, distributing those computers to individual class-

Selection Rubric: Computer Software

Complete an interactive evaluation and add it to your NETS-T portfolio using the Selection Rubric for Computer Software available on the "Classroom Link Portfolio" CD-ROM. A downloadable version of this rubric is available in the Selection Rubrics module of the Companion Website at http://www.prenhall.com/smaldino.

Key Words

_____

_____

_____

Title _____

Series Title (if applicable) _____

Source _____

Date _____ Cost _____ Length _____ minutes

Subject Area _____

Intended Audience _____

Format

☐ Drill-and-practice

☐ Game

☐ Simulation

☐ Discovery program

☐ Problem solving

Brief Description

Objectives

Entry Capabilities Required (e.g., prior knowledge, reading ability, vocabulary level, math ability)

Strong Points

Weak Points

Recommended Action (using criteria on the following page)

Name _____ Date _____

Rating Area	High Quality	Medium Quality	Low Quality	Rating
Match Curriculum	Curriculum standard addressed and use of software should enhance student learning.	Curriculum standard partially addressed and use of software may enhance student learning.	Curriculum standard not addressed and use of software will likely not enhance student learning.	
Accurate & Current	Information correct and does not contain material that is out of date.	Information correct but does contain material that is out of date.	Information is not correct and does contain material that is out of date.	
Clear & Concise Language	Language used is age appropriate and vocabulary is understandable.	Language used is nearly age appropriate and some vocabulary is above/below student age.	Language used is not age appropriate and vocabulary is clearly inappropriate for student age.	
Motivating/ Interesting	Topic presented so that students are likely to be interested and engaged in learning.	Topic presented to interest students most of the time and engage most in learning.	Topic presented so as not to interest students and not engage them in learning.	
Learner Participation	Topic presented so that most students are actively engaged in learning.	Topic presented so that some students are engaged in learning.	Topic presented so that most students are not actively engaged in learning.	
Technical Quality	The material represents best available media.	The material represents media that are good quality, although there are some problems.	The material represents media that are not well prepared and are of very poor quality.	
Effectiveness Rating	There is evidence that use of these media has shown positive impact on student learning.	There is little evidence that use of these media has shown positive impact on student learning.	There is no evidence that use of these media has shown positive impact on student learning.	
Free from Bias	There is no evidence of objectionable bias or advertising.	There is little evidence of bias or advertising.	There is much evidence of bias or advertising.	
User Guide & Documentation	The documentation is excellent resource for use in a lesson. Documentation should help students use the software.	The documentation is good resource for use in a lesson. Documentation may help students use the software.	The documentation is poor resource for use in a lesson. Documentation does not help students use the software.	
Clear Directions	The material is presented so most students can follow and achieve the outcome.	The material is presented so some students can follow and achieve the outcome.	The material is presented so most students cannot follow and achieve the outcome.	
Stimulates Creativity	Most students can use the software to create original pieces that represent their learning.	Some students can use the software to start original pieces that begin to show their learning.	Most students cannot use the software to create original pieces that represent their learning.	

rooms. Consequently, many classrooms that had just one computer now have several.

There are advantages to using a computer lab. A group of students can be taught the same lesson simultaneously, which might be more efficient for the teacher. Also, software can be located in one place conveniently. Supervision and security are often easier when all the computers are located in a single room.

The foremost limitation with the computer lab is access. If there are no other computers available to students outside the computer lab, then students may have a problem. If a class is scheduled to use the lab, students will have to wait until the lab is not scheduled to use the facilities. Also, because of scheduling problems, some classes may not have access to the lab at all.

Labs are often structured to facilitate ease of use by using networks, which make it easy to use the available software. Another solution would be to place comput-ers throughout the school building. Thus, students can access computers in the computer lab, their classrooms, and the media center.

Assure Case Connection

Mr. Sorge has two computers in his classroom. He can reserve the nearby computer lab, which has 25 computers. He wants to have his students use the computer to practice their computation skills, but he also wants them to recognize the practical application of those skills. So, he wants to use a simulation software program that will give them practice in their skills while using them in a meaningful way. Should he have his students work in groups using the two computers in his classroom? Or should he take his class to the computer lab?

Summary: Using the ASSURE Model for Computers

As with other media and technology, the AS-SURE model introduced in Chapter 3 is helpful in preparing lessons incorporating the use of computers.

Analyze Learners

Lesson development begins by identifying your students' unique attributes and learning characteristics. You also will wish to determine their various levels of experience with using computers.

State Objectives

Before stating specific objectives, you may wish to explore how to use computers and software in support of student learning. Sometimes it is more appropriate to state specific objectives after you have identified the direction you will take with the content and what materials you will use.

Select Methods, Media, and Materials

Use the information on computers and software discussed in this chapter as the basis for selecting, modifying, or designing your materials. Adjust the specific applications to suit the specific nature of your topic and objectives.

When selecting software, first determine what is available locally, consulting with your school media specialist about what software you may access through the school. If nothing acceptable to your needs is available, consider using software such as *HyperStudio* to produce your own materials.

You should preview and appraise both commercially and locally produced materials before using them with your students. You may wish to use the "Selection Rubric: Computer Software" to guide your selection decisions.

Utilize Media and Materials

Follow the suggestions discussed in this chapter to facilitate your students' learning, modifying each computer and software use to fit your needs. The number of computers you have access to at one time, as well as their location, will determine how you schedule your students' learning experiences, as discussed in the chapter.

Require Learner Participation

Introduce and explain the software involved in your specific objective. Have the students do specific activities that rely on their ability to use the computer. Students will find more value in the materials if they are able to connect what they are doing to what they are learning. Have them create and save their own special files, or have them design simple files, such as databases or *HyperStudio* stacks, that they can then share with other students.

Evaluate and Revise

It is important to consider how materials that students themselves create help them to interpret information. You may choose to assess students on both the content and quality of their finished product. As with all media- and technology-based lessons, you may choose to revise your selection of materials after you have determined how well they have worked. In addition, you want to be certain that all materials used have been cleared of any potential copyright issues.

ASSURE Case in Practice: Mathematics

All of the ASSURE Cases in Practice in this text and an electronic template for creating your own ASSURE Lesson can be found on the enclosed "Classroom Link Portfolio" CD-ROM.

Dennis Sorge's middle school pre-algebra students enjoy competing with classmates while simulating the operation of a hotdog stand. The students practice their math skills while cooperating with one group of peers and competing against other groups.

Analyze Learners

General Characteristics

Mr. Sorge's class is made up of 20 general math students in grades 7 and 8, representing a range of abilities. Some students have minor physical handicaps and others have learning disabilities. The school is located in a rural area of the Midwest. The majority of the students have attended high school football games and most have purchased hotdogs, soft drinks, and chips while at a game.

Entry Competencies

Approximately 80 percent of the students are able to do the following:
1. Add and subtract five-digit numbers with decimals (money amounts).
2. Multiply amounts up to one hundred dollars by double-digit quantities.

Learning Styles

Most students, especially those with low verbal skills, prefer visual learning. Most students enjoy both interacting and competing with their peers. The majority is motivated by using a computer. About half of the students enjoy learning and most are motivated by the class and the study of mathematics.

State Objectives

Mr. Sorge wanted his students to practice real-world applications of math skills while having a good time. The specific objectives of the lesson were that, on completion, the general math students would be able to do the following:
1. Solve five-digit addition and subtraction problems at 90 percent accuracy without the use of a calculator.
2. Calculate the income and expenses of a hotdog stand with 100 percent accuracy in a group situation without the use of a calculator.

3. Budget expenses using a budget planning sheet and be able to justify their decisions during a simulation.
4. Make predictions of sales based on previous sales and the weather forecast. The prediction will be within 20 percent of actual sales.
5. Deal with random events that influence outcomes. Students will be able to justify planning for random events before they happen and to justify their strategy for dealing with them after they happen during a simulation.
6. Plan and predict how they should stock a concession stand given the type of event, the weather forecast, records of past sales, and so on during a simulation.
7. Demonstrate team-building skills in a competition situation.
8. Prepare a report that accurately reflects the team's expenses and income and that is properly written (spelling, punctuation, and sentence structure).

Select Methods, Media, and Materials

Mr. Sorge wanted his students to experience the application of math skills in a lifelike situation. Therefore, he chose to use a simulation. He also wanted to capitalize on his students' love of competition while building team skills such as cooperation. Therefore, he chose to incorporate a game format within the simulation. Because he didn't have time to design such an activity, he decided the only way to carry it out would be through a computer simulation. He searched through catalogs in the school media center and found a program called *Hotdog Stand: The Works*, distributed by Sunburst Communications.

Utilize Media and Materials

The 20 students in his class were randomly divided into four teams of five. Each team worked in a cooperative manner to achieve the highest possible end-of-season profit. As an incentive, the team earning the most profit received a picnic with the teacher during an upcoming lunch period. Mr. Sorge demonstrated to students how to use the software and explained the goals of the simulation game. He kept his introduction brief so the students could get into *Hotdog Stand: The Works* quickly. He explained specific details as questions arose. His philosophy was to not give them answers for which they had no questions.

Require Learner Participation

During the lesson the students participated in discussions and had to justify their decisions to their peers. The teacher then divided the class into small groups to make specific decisions for specific events. The activity provided practice and feedback as students discussed and decided the data to enter into the computer program. Feedback was provided by the computer, peers, and Mr. Sorge. While participating in the simulation game, students began to understand how certain variables, such as weather conditions, crowd size, product quality, and product price, influence sales. How they dealt with these factors ultimately affected their success as a team. Students were motivated by the simulation game to become actively involved in developing a variety of mathematical and practical skills.

Evaluate and Revise

Mr. Sorge gave a written test following the use of *Hotdog Stand: The Works* to evaluate Objectives 1 and 2; he decided not to evaluate Objectives 3 though 6. To evaluate

Objective 7, Mr. Sorge observed students during the simulation game to see if they demonstrated appropriate interpersonal skills. Students were evaluated on journals (written as "Annual Reports" for their concession stand operation). The students were asked to justify their decisions. They were evaluated on these justifications, *not* on the decisions they made or their outcome.

Reports were collected from each student and evaluated by Mr. Sorge and the school's English teacher to measure Objective 8 and to give students feedback on their writing and mathematical skills.

The effectiveness of implementation was determined by several techniques. Mr. Sorge observed students as they participated in the simulation. Did the students' decisions improve as they participated in the simulation? He also listened for student comments that indicated their strategies and decision-making skills.

Create Your Own ASSURE Lesson

Using the ASSURE model, design a lesson for a scenario from the table on this book's inside cover or from the Companion Website, or use a scenario of your own design. Use one of the methods described in Chapter 1 and information from this chapter related to incorporating computers and software into your instructional setting. Be sure to include information about the audience, the objectives, and all other elements of the ASSURE model. When completed, reflect on the process you used and what you have learned about matching audience, content, method, and materials.

Classroom Link Portfolio Activities

Use the "Classroom Link Portfolio" CD-ROM and the Companion Website as resources in completing these activities. To complete the following activities online go to the Portfolio Activities module in Chapter 5 of the Companion Website (http://www.prenhall.com/smaldino).

1. *Instructional Software Critique.* Select an instructional computer program, load it, and take a brief tour. Record your initial reactions. Critique this program using the "Selection Rubric: Computer Software" in this chapter (also found on the "Classroom Link Portfolio" CD-ROM), citing sources. Compare and contrast the findings from your initial tour and the Selection Rubric. What will you do the next time you find a new instructional computer program? (ISTE NETS-T 2.B & C; 6.A)

2. *Written Reflection.* Name three ways computers have enhanced your learning. Why were these effective? How might these strategies be used to help students learn in a technology-enhanced environment? (ISTE NETS-T 2.E; 5.B).

Integration Assessments

To complete the specific activities online go to the Integration Assessments module in Chapter 5 on the Companion Website (http://www.prenhall.com/smaldino).

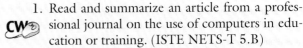

1. Read and summarize an article from a professional journal on the use of computers in education or training. (ISTE NETS-T 5.B)

2. Interview a student or instructor who has used computers for instruction. Report on how the computer was used, including the user's perceptions of its strengths and limitations. (ISTE NETS-T 5.B)

3. Create a list of topics you would include if you were to conduct a one-day computer implementation workshop for teachers or trainers in your content area. (ISTE NETS-T 5.B)

4. Describe how you could use a computer as an object of instruction or as a tool during instruction within your field. (ISTE NETS-T 2.B)

5. Create a situation in which you could use computer-based materials. Include a description of the audience, the objectives, the role of the computer, and the expected outcomes of using the computer. (ISTE NETS-T 2.A)

6. Locate at least five computer programs suitable for your content area using the information sources available to you. (ISTE NETS-T 2.C)

References

Jonassen, David H., J. Howland, J. Moore, and Rose M. Marra. 2003. *Learning to solve problems with technology: A constructivist perspective.* Upper Saddle River, NJ: Merrill/Prentice Hall.

Kulik, C.-L., J. A. Kulik, and B. J. Schwalb. 1986. The effectiveness of computer-based adult education: A meta-analysis. *Journal of Educational Computing Research,* 2(2): 235–252.

Papert, Seymour. 1982. *Mindstorms: Children, computers, and powerful ideas.* New York: Basic Books.

———. 1993. *The children's machine: Rethinking school in the age of the computer.* New York: Basic Books.

Raybould, B. 1990. Solving human performance problems with computers. *Performance & Instruction* 4(14): 4.

Winslow, C. D., and W. L. Bramer. 1994. *Future work.* New York: Free Press.

Suggested Readings

Armstrong, D. 1996. Technology integration at the middle and high school levels: A model for staff development. *NASSP Bulletin, 80*(October): 81–88.

Bauer, Anne M., and Mary E. Ulrich. 2002. "I've got a palm in my pocket": Using handheld computers in an inclusive classroom. *Teaching Exceptional Children, 35*(2): 18–22.

Brunner, Cornelia, and William Tally. 1999. *The new media literacy handbook: An educator's guide to bringing new media into the classroom.* Thousand Oaks, CA: Corwin.

Cooper, J., and J. Stone. 1996. Gender, computer-assisted learning, and anxiety: With a little help from a friend. *Journal of Educational Computing Research, 15*(1): 67–91.

Davis C., and D. D. Shade. 1997. Integrating computers into the early childhood curriculum. *Principal, 76*(May): 34–35.

Dockterman, David A. 1997. *Great teaching in the one computer classroom,* 4th ed. Cambridge, MA: Tom Snyder Productions.

Doti Ryan, Concetta, and Scott Bricher (illustrator). 1999. *Making the most of the one-computer classroom.* Torrance, CA: Frank Schaffer.

German, M. 1997. Computer literacy: Teaching for the real world. *Principal, 76*(4): 46–47.

Ivers, Karen S. 2003. *A teacher's guide to using technology in the classroom.* Westport, CT: Greenwood.

Lewis, Ann. 1999. Integrated learning systems and pupils with low attainments in reading. *British Journal of Special Education, 26*(3): 153–157.

Lockard, James, and Peter Abrams. 2003. *Computers for twenty-first century educators,* 5th ed. Upper Saddle River, NJ: Pearson Education.

Pereus, Steven C. 2002. Selecting software. *American School Board Journal, 189*(10): 32–35.

Poole, Bernard J. 1997. *Education for an information age: Teaching in the computerized classroom,* 2nd ed. New York: McGraw-Hill.

Pownell, David, and Gerald D. Bailey. 2001. Getting a handle on handhelds: What to consider before you introduce handheld computers in your schools. *American School Board Journal, 188*(6): 18–21.

Roblyer, M. D. 2003. *Integrating educational technology into teaching,* 3rd ed. Upper Saddle River, NJ: Merrill/Prentice Hall.

Ruthven, Kenneth, and Sara Hennessy. 2002. A practitioner model of the use of computer-based tools and resources to support mathematics teaching and learning. *Educational Studies in Mathematics, 49*(1): 47–88.

Scott, R. C., and S. C. Rockwell. 1997. The effect of communication, writing, and technology apprehension on likelihood of use of new communication technologies. *Communication in Education, 46*(1): 44–62.

Secules, T. 1997. Creating schools for thought. *Educational Leadership, 54*(March): 56–60.

Straesser, Rudolf. 2001. Cabri-Geometre: Does dynamic geometry software (DGS) change geometry and its teaching and learning? *International Journal of Computers for Mathematical Learning, 6*(3): 319–333.

Sy, Leith. 1999. Practice tests as formative assessment improve student performance on computer-managed learning assignments. *Assessment & Evaluation in Higher Education, 24*(3): 330–343.

Tiene, Drew, and Pamela Luft. 2001. Teaching in a technology-rich classroom. *Educational Technology, 41*(4): 23–31.

Wiest, Lynda R. 2001. The role of computers in mathematics teaching and learning. *Computers in the Schools, 17*(1–2): 41–55.

Winer, Laura R., and Jeremy Cooperstock. 2002. The "intelligent classroom": Changing teaching and learning with an evolving technological environment. *Computers and Education, 38*(1–3): 253–266.

Multimedia

CHAPTER 6

Outline

Multimedia Kits
Hypermedia
Interactive Media
Virtual Reality
Expert Systems

Knowledge Objectives

1. Define *multimedia* and describe five instructional examples.
2. Describe instructional applications that are especially appropriate for multimedia kits.
3. Define *hypermedia* and describe three instructional applications.
4. Describe an instructional situation in which you could use hypermedia materials. Include the setting, topic, audience, objectives, content of the interactive video materials, and rationale for using this media format.
5. Diagram and briefly describe the components of an interactive media system.
6. Define *virtual reality* and describe how it might be used in education.
7. Describe instructional applications that are especially appropriate for virtual reality.
8. Describe an instructional situation in which you might use an expert system. Include the setting, topic, audience, objectives, content of the system, and rationale for using this media format.

Professional Vocabulary

multimedia	script
multimedia kit	button
hypertext	navigate
hypermedia	interactive media
browse	virtual reality (VR)
link	expert system
author	

Chapters throughout this book focus on various individual audio media, visual media, and computers. This chapter discusses combinations of these media. The generic term **multimedia** refers to the sequential or simultaneous use of a variety of media formats in a given presentation or self-study program.

Multimedia systems may consist of traditional media in combination or they may incorporate the computer as a display device for text, pictures, graphics, sound, and video. The term *multimedia* goes back to the 1950s and describes early attempts to combine various still and motion media for heightened educational effect. Multimedia involves more than simply integrating these formats into a structured program in which each element complements the others so that the whole is greater than the sum of the parts. Today examples of multimedia in education and training include slides with synchronized audiotapes, videotapes, CD-ROMs, DVD, the World Wide Web, and virtual reality.

The goal of multimedia in education and training is to immerse the learner in a multisensory experience to promote learning. One can read about walking on a beach. Someone describing the experience orally along with the recorded sounds of the waves enhances the "experience." The addition of motion video lets one "see" the sights. Running one's hands or feet through a box of sand and handling sea shells lets the "experience" become more real. Multimedia makes one's experience as realistic as possible without actually being there.

In the past the predominant mode of providing instructional experiences was the written and spoken word through textbooks and the lecture. As shown in Dale's Cone of Experience (see Chapter 1), "verbal symbols" are the most abstract. A newer form of media, virtual reality, is near the bottom (more concrete) of Dale's Cone. Virtual reality is very effective and efficient in recreating reality and approaches "direct purposeful experiences"—the most tangible mode of learning.

ASSURE
Case Challenge

We have developed a case study for this chapter to help you see how multimedia can be integrated into learning activities. At the end of the chapter you will be challenged to develop your own ASSURE lesson for a case study of your choice using the ASSURE model and incorporating the technology and media described in this chapter. To help you in preparing your lesson, we have included hints (called "ASSURE Case Connections") throughout the chapter as they relate to the ASSURE Case Challenge.

Mr. Winters hopes to interest his 11th-grade students in the events that led up to King John's signing of the Magna Carta. He knows that when they are actively engaged in learning, his students tend to do well in their studies. He also knows that they like to be creative and use their imaginations.

Instructional designers understand that individual learners respond differently to various information sources and instructional methods, so chances of reaching an individual are increased when a variety of media are used. Multimedia also attempts to simulate more closely the conditions of real-world learning, a world of multisensory, all-at-once experiences.

Multimedia addresses different learning styles (see Chapter 3). Auditory learners, visual learners, and tactile learners all benefit from multimedia's varied presentation forms. The redundancy of print, sound, visuals, and motion media allows learners to choose for themselves the most meaningful sensory mode. When you, the instructor, have a clear sense of objectives and the necessary student practice, you can decide what media will best facilitate the learning and how best to deliver it.

This chapter will explore the following types of multimedia:

- *Multimedia kits*—a collection of materials involving more than one type of medium and organized around a single topic
- *Hypermedia*—media that allow the composition and display of nonsequential materials
- *Interactive media*—media that require learners to practice skills and receive feedback
- *Virtual reality*—media in which users experience multisensory immersions and interact with phenomena as they would in the physical world
- *Expert systems*—software packages that teach learners how to solve a complex problem by applying the collective wisdom of experts in a given field

MULTIMEDIA KITS

A **multimedia kit** is a collection of teaching/learning materials involving more than one type of medium and organized around a single topic. Kits may include CD-ROMs, slides, audiotapes, videotapes, still pictures, study prints, overhead transparencies, maps, worksheets, charts, graphs, booklets, real objects, and models (Figure 6.1).

Some multimedia kits are designed for the teacher to use in classroom presentations. Others are designed for use by individual students or by small groups.

Commercial multimedia kits are available for a variety of educational subjects. These learning kits may include videotapes, audiocassettes, floor games, board games, posters, full-color photographs, activity cards, murals, wall charts, geometric shapes, flash cards, laboratory materials for science experiments, and even puppets to act out stories. They also normally include student worksheets and a teacher's manual.

Teachers or media specialists can also prepare multimedia kits. The main purpose of a kit is to give learners a chance at firsthand learning—to touch, to observe, to experiment, to wonder, to decide.

Availability and cost of materials are obviously important considerations. Will there be one kit for all students to share, or can the kit be duplicated for all? If so, where will students find the necessary equipment? Can the kit be used in a variety of instructional situations?

Advantages

- *Interest*. Multimedia kits arouse interest because they are multisensory. Everyone likes to touch and manipulate real objects—to inspect unusual specimens up close.

- *Cooperation.* Kits can be an ideal mechanism for stimulating small-group project work. Cooperative learning activities can revolve around experiments, problem solving, role playing, or other types of hands-on practice.
- *Logistics.* Kits have an obvious logistical advantage. Being packaged, they can be transported and used outside the classroom, such as in the media center or at home.

Figure 6.1
Multimedia kits provide varied sensory experiences. They give the concrete referents needed to build a strong foundation for more abstract mental abilities.

Limitations

- *Expense.* Learning with multimedia kits can be more expensive than with other, more conventional methods.
- *Time consuming.* It can be time consuming to produce and maintain the materials.
- *Replacement.* Lost components can make the kit frustrating to use.

Integration

Multimedia kits are particularly well suited to content for which discovery learning is preferred. You can pose questions to guide learners' exploration and arrival at conclusions. Science topics are well suited to this approach. For

Close-Up

TEACHER-MADE MULTIMEDIA KITS

An elementary teacher developed a series of separate multimedia kits on science topics for use with her third-grade class. She incorporated real objects, such as musical instruments, magnets, small motors, rocks, harmless chemicals, and insect specimens in the kits. She also gathered pictures associated with each topic from magazines and old textbooks. A study guide, prepared for each unit, required students to inquire about the topic, make hypotheses, and conduct investigations. References were included for books and other nonprint sources on the topic. Audiotapes were prepared for use at school and at home for students who had access to audiocassette players.

For a unit on sound, the teacher prepared a multimedia kit that included several musical instruments, cassette recordings of common noises for listeners to identify, anatomical models of the human ear, books about how humans hear, and educational videos explaining how animals like bats, dogs, and dolphins hear and use sound.

The students enjoyed taking the kits home to work on the experiments. The response from parents was very positive. Several

parents reported that they, too, learned by working through the activities with their children. Students often preferred to stay in at recess and work on the multimedia kits in the science corner.

example, a kit on magnetism might include several types of magnets, iron filings, and metal objects that may or may not be attracted to magnets. In mathematics, a kit on measurement might include a folding meter stick and directions for measuring various objects and dimensions around the home or in school.

ASSURE Case Connection

Mr. Winters considers creating a learning center with a variety of materials about King John, the Magna Carta, and England in the Middle Ages. He could incorporate maps, charts, documents, and other types of materials. Could he consider using computer-based materials? Would audio or video be a possibility?

HYPERMEDIA

The term **hypertext** was coined by Nelson in 1974 to describe "nonsequential documents" composed of text, audio, and visual information stored in a computer, with the computer being used to link and annotate related chunks of information (nodes) into larger networks, or webs (Nelson, 1974a & b). The goal of hypertext is to immerse users in a richly textured information environment, one in which words, sounds, and still and motion images can be connected in diverse ways. Enthusiasts feel that the characteristics of hypertext parallel the associative properties of the mind, thereby making the construction of one's own web a creative educational activity.

Media Files: Computer Software

UNDERSTANDING TAXES
Internal Revenue Service
Multimedia Resource Package

The *Teacher Resource Package*, available from the IRS, serves as an introduction to taxes for high school students. The content enhances teaching about the history, politics, and economics of the U.S. tax system. Activities include preparation of Forms W-4, 1040EZ, and 1040A. Media included in the large 3-ring, loose-leaf binder include a CD, a videotape, overhead transparencies, handout masters, lesson plans, and a user's guide for the computer software supplement. A website (www.irs.treas.gov/taxi) provides online learning centers developed for high school students and teachers. (TAXI stands for Tax Interactive). The resource package is available free to teachers and is updated with annual mailings.

RAINFOREST RESEARCHERS
Tom Snyder Productions
CD-ROM and Videotape

This combination of CD-ROM, videotape, and printed materials virtually puts your students in the middle of the Indonesian rainforest. They work as teams of scientists and through collaborative problem solving explore the diverse and mysterious web of life in this rich ecosystem. Students work in cooperative teams of four, each taking on the role of a chemist, ethnobotanist, taxonomist, or ecologist. Teams watch a videotape and use onscreen displays to guide them in analyzing information, collaborating, and making decisions. This innovate package was selected as Best Curriculum Software for Middle Schools by the Software Publishers Association.

ENVIRONMENTS MODULE
Encyclopedia Britannica Educational Corp.
Commercial Multimedia Kit

Barley, bugs, beetles, and brine shrimp are just a few of the living organisms the students work with in this multimedia kit. Relating what they see in the experiments with what they see in the interactive videos, students come to appreciate that living things are dependent on the conditions of their environments.

Among other things, this commercial multimedia kit includes videocassettes and/or videodiscs in both English and Spanish, bilingual computer software, scientific equipment, and coupons to secure live organisms. There is also a teacher guide and teacher preparation video.

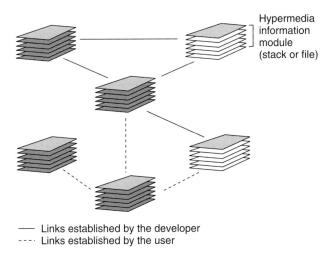

— Links established by the developer
---- Links established by the user

Figure 6.2
Hypermedia organization.

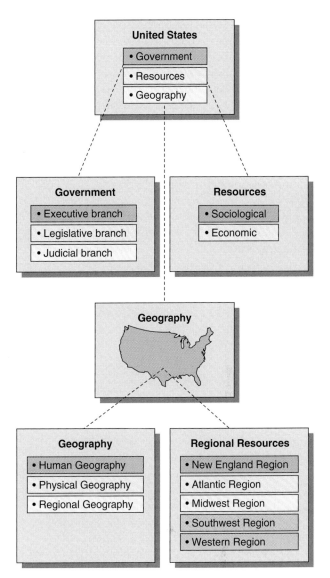

Figure 6.3
Sample stack.

Hypermedia refers to computer software that uses elements of text, graphics, video, and audio connected in such a way that the user can easily move within the information. Users choose the pathway that is unique to their own style of thinking and processing information. According to its very nature, it provides a learning environment that is interactive and exploratory (Figure 6.2).

Hypermedia is based on cognitive theories of how people structure knowledge and how they learn. It is designed to resemble the way people organize information with concepts and their relationships. These relationships, or links, are associations between ideas—for example, when thinking about bicycles, one creates a link between ideas about transportation and recreation. With hypermedia, one can link asynchronous data sources directly to compose and display nonsequential information that may include text, audio, and visual information. There is no continuous flow of text, as in a textbook or novel. Rather, the information is broken into small units that the author or user associates in a variety of ways. Using the bicycle example, the learner can connect the word "bicycle" with a photo of a girl riding a bicycle in a field and a video clip of a Hong Kong boy carrying a duck to market on the back of a bicycle.

The intent of hypermedia is to enable the user to move about within a particular set of information without necessarily using a predetermined structure or sequence. The chunks of information are analogous to notes on a collection of cards. Each card contains a bit of information. Subsequent cards or sets of cards (often referred to as *stacks*) may contain extensions of the information from the initial card or other relevant or related information (Figure 6.3). Hypermedia programs are usually set up so that each computer screen display is equivalent to what is displayed on one of the cards.

Computer hypermedia systems can be used for several different purposes:

- *Browsing.* Users **browse**, or navigate through the information by choosing routes that are of interest. You can explore features in detail as it suits your personal learning style.
- *Linking.* Users can create their own special connections, or **links**, within the information.
- *Authoring.* Users can **author**, or create, their own unique collections of information, adding or linking text, graphics, and audio as they wish. They can use this creation for their own individual use, to share with others, or to prepare a report or presentation.

Hypermedia materials can be created easily (see "Creating a *HyperStudio* Stack" in Classroom Resources, Section C). The user can write a **script** using a special scripting language that is more like spoken language than earlier programming codes (such as those used for BASIC and Pascal). Any object can become "hyper" through scripting. For example, a word can become "hot," thus allowing the user to connect to a glossary or to other concepts associated with that particular term. Graphics and buttons can also be scripted as links to other information. The user, with the aid of a mouse, points to a word or button and clicks the mouse. A **button** is an icon that might be a picture or graphic or might look like a button one might press on any electric device. The button is used to move around in the hypermedia environment. In a hypermedia environment, then, you activate the link and make the connection between pieces of information. The linking interface lets you **navigate**, or move about, more quickly and precisely within a hypermedia environment. The interactive nature of hypermedia is the essence of its advantages. Hypermedia engages learners to make choices about moving within the material in meaningful ways, thus fulfilling the requirement of learner participation (the R of the ASSURE model).

Advantages

- *Engrossing.* The opportunity for deep involvement can capture and hold student interest.
- *Multisensory.* The incorporation of sounds and images along with text expands the channels to the mind.
- *Connections.* By using "hot buttons" students can connect ideas from different media sources, for example, connecting the sound of a foghorn with the word "lighthouse."
- *Individualized.* Web structure allows users to navigate through the information according to their interests and to build their own unique mental structures based on their exploration.
- *Teacher and student creation.* Software allows teachers and students to easily create their own hypermedia files; student projects can become opportunities for collaborative work.

Limitations

- *Getting lost.* Users can get confused, or "lost in cyberspace," when using hypermedia programs because of limited clues as to where they are in the material.
- *Lack of structure.* Students whose learning style requires more structured guidance may become frustrated. Students may also make poor decisions about how much information they need to explore.
- *Noninteractive.* Programs can be simply one-way presentations of information with no specific opportunities for interactive practice with feedback.

- *Complex.* More advanced programs may be difficult to use, especially for student production because they require the ability to use a scripting language.
- *Time consuming.* Because they are nonlinear and invite exploration, hypermedia programs tend to require more time for students to reach prespecified objectives. Because they are more complex than conventional instructional materials, hypermedia systems require time for both teachers and students to learn to use.

Integration

Hypermedia can be developed and used on the same computer systems that are commonly found in schools. They are applied in all areas of the curriculum, for any learning goals that are suited to individual or small-group exploration of a body of information. Hypermedia programs are available as off-the-shelf courseware; teachers can create them to fit unique local needs; or students can create them as a way of organizing and synthesizing their research on a topic of interest.

Ready-made hypermedia instructional courseware is available for teachers to use in their classrooms. Many titles have been developed for use in all areas of study. For example, *Digestion* is designed to be used by secondary science students; with complex and accurate diagrams, students can learn about the process of digestion. This program is available as a complete package; you do not have to do anything to the software. However, you will need to consider how to best introduce the application into the curriculum and what types of followup are appropriate.

Connie Courbat, a third-grade teacher, developed *HyperStudio* stacks to use with her students for their study of the Oregon Trail and the westward movement. Her academically challenged students used an instructional stack and reported on the information they learned. With her more advanced students, she developed a shell for stacks that her students could use to create their own stacks. These stacks were created to help the rest of the class learn more about the westward movement. All the students had an opportunity to utilize hypermedia in a manner appropriate to their learning levels, and everyone enjoyed their learning experiences.

Teachers can either adapt existing materials or create new materials to fill a need of their own students. When you and your students are creating any multimedia materials, be certain to follow copyright guidelines (see "Copyright Concerns: Multimedia Materials"). Because hypermedia software—for example, *HyperStudio*—provides an easy-to-use authoring language, many teachers have learned to successfully develop their own hypermedia materials. (See "Creating a *HyperStudio* Stack," in Classroom Resources, Section C, for directions on using

Copyright Concerns

MULTIMEDIA MATERIALS

The advent of new technologies, such as the Internet, the World Wide Web, CD-ROM, and videodisc, have made it necessary to re-examine the copyright laws in view of multimedia capabilities. In September 1996, a U.S. House of Representatives Subcommittee on Courts and Intellectual Property adopted a set of fair use guidelines for the production and use of multimedia in educational settings. These guidelines include the following allowances:

- When creating multimedia programs, students and teachers may legally use the following copyrighted materials:
  Text: up to 10% or 1,000 words, whichever is less
  Audio: up to 10%, but not more than 30 seconds
  Images: not more than five images by the same artist or photographer
  Video: up to 10% or three minutes, whichever is less
  Numerical data: up to 10% or 2500 fields or cell entries, whichever is less
- Educators may use their multimedia projects and materials for educational purposes for a period of up to two years after the first instructional use in class. Beyond that period they must acquire permission of the holders of each copyrighted portion.

- Students and educators may retain multimedia projects for personal portfolios to be used later for assessment of learning or for tenure review and job interviews.
- Educators and students are advised to include at the opening of their multimedia project and in any accompanying print material a notice that certain materials are included under the fair use exemption of the U.S. copyright law. It is always best to give credit for the sources of any materials used. For information concerning usage guidelines for online information and data, see the following Internet sites:
  Copyright and fair use: http://fairuse.stanford.edu/
  Cyberspace law for nonlawyers: http://www.counsel.com/cyberspace/
  U.S. Copyright Office: http://lcweb.loc.gov/copyright/
  U.S. House of Representatives Internet Law Library—intellectual property; copyright: http://law.house.gov/325.htm

For additional information on this topic and to visit these websites, go to the Web Links module in Chapter 10 of the Companion Website (http://www.prenhall.com/smaldino). For general information on copyright, see the Copyright Concerns on page 11 in Chapter 1. Suggested readings on copyright appear at the end of Chapter 1.

---

one popular authoring system.) One caution: don't think that ability to use the authoring tool automatically bestows expertise either in instructional design or visual design. These skills are usually developed through special study and lots of practice. Some advice on screen design is provided in "Designing Computer Screens," in Classroom Resources, Section C.

Hypermedia can shift the roles of teacher and learners in the classroom. Because hypermedia materials are so easy to develop, it is feasible for students to create their own programs and thus gain the benefits of creative learning. Given instruction, students can create hypermedia materials that revolve around a particular topic of study. Your role becomes that of resource person for the students. Digital video and audio can be added to hypermedia files with little effort. Most computer systems have the capabilities of adding digitized "video clips" without any additional software or hardware. For example, *QuickTime* color "movies" can be imported into *HyperStudio* stacks with ease. In addition, *QuickTime* movies can be added to other types of files, such as word processing documents.

It is beyond the scope of this chapter to describe in detail the various techniques for developing hyperme-

dia. Resources on hypermedia development are listed in the Suggested Readings at the end of the chapter.

Assure Case Connection

Mr. Winters could create a set of *HyperStudio* stacks with a variety of information about the topics related to the signing of the Magna Carta. He could incorporate maps, charts, documents, and audio and video clips. Could he consider creating only a shell so his students can investigate the topics and create their own *HyperStudio* materials?

INTERACTIVE MEDIA

Computer-based **interactive media** creates a multimedia learning environment that capitalizes on the features of both video and computer-assisted instruction. It is an instructional delivery system in which recorded visuals, sound, and video materials are presented under computer control to viewers who not only see and hear the pictures and sounds but also make active responses, with those responses affecting the pace and sequence of the presentation.

The video portion of interactive media is provided through CD-ROM, DVD, or the Web. Because CD-ROM discs can store many types of digital information, including text, graphics, photographs, animation, and audio, they are popular in school settings, library media centers, and classrooms of all sorts. Anything that can be stored on a computer disk can be stored on a CD-ROM (Figure 6.4). Multimedia CD-ROM products are commonly found in school library media centers, primarily in the form of encyclopedias or other reference databases. The application of multimedia and hypermedia to core curriculum is increasing with the advent of improved quality of available resources. In higher education there is large-scale experimentation with locally produced multimedia and hypermedia, but such applications have been limited to specific content areas, such as modern languages, communications, and technology studies.

The images can be presented in slow motion, fast motion, or frame-by-frame (as in a slide show). The audio portion may occupy two separate audio channels, making possible two different narrations for each motion sequence.

The interactive aspect of interactive video is provided through computers, which have powerful decision-making abilities. Combining computers and video allows the strengths of each to compensate for the limitations of the other to provide a rich educational environment for the learner. Interactive media is a powerful, practical method for individualizing and personalizing instruction.

With the introduction of hypermedia, it has become easier to prepare teacher-developed and student-developed interactive multimedia. Students are discov-

ering an innovative way to activate their learning through simple-to-prepare hypermedia stacks.

The heart of an interactive media system is the computer, which provides the "intelligence" and interactivity required. The computer can command the system to present audio or video information, wait for the learner's response, and branch to the appropriate point in the instructional program from that response.

The learner communicates with the instructional program by responding to audio, visual, or verbal stimuli displayed on the monitor. Input devices provide the means for these responses. These devices include such items as a keyboard, keypad, light pen, barcode reader, touch-sensitive screen, and mouse.

A monitor displays the picture and emits the sound from the video source. It can also display the output from the computer software, which may have text, graphics, or sound effects. In most systems the computer output can be superimposed over the video image.

Advantages

- *Multiple media.* Text, audio, graphics, still pictures, and motion pictures can all be combined in one easy-to-use system.
- *Learner participation.* The R of the ASSURE model is achieved with interactive video materials because they require that learners engage in activities. These materials help to maintain students' attention, and they allow greater participation than does video viewing alone.
- *Individualization.* Individualization is provided for because branching allows instruction on remedial as well as enrichment levels.
- *Flexibility.* The learner may choose what to study from the menu, selecting those areas that seem interesting, that seem most logically to answer a question, or that present the greatest challenge.
- *Simulations.* Interactive video may be used to provide simulation experiences in such areas as medicine, machine operations, and especially interpersonal skills. The development of skills in working with children in a classroom, which otherwise would require role playing or live interactions, can be provided as an individual, self-paced simulation exercise.

Limitations

- *Cost.* The most significant limitation to interactive video is the cost, although the prices of ready-made discs and hardware are decreasing.
- *Production expense.* It can be expensive to produce commercial CD-ROM and DVD discs, which may not meet local needs.

Figure 6.4
CD-ROM discs are popular for storing interactive media programs.

- *Rigidity.* Commercial discs cannot be changed once they have been made; therefore, material may become outdated.

Integration

Interactive media systems are valuable for tasks that must be shown rather than simply told. Some instruction cannot be adequately presented by printed materials. If the learner needs to interact with the instruction, interactive media is an appropriate choice.

Interactive media systems are currently being used in a variety of instructional applications, from teaching scientific phenomena to teaching special education students to tell time. The programs can challenge a small group of gifted students or provide remedial instruction for students who might be having difficulty with particular concepts.

Individuals as well as small groups can use interactive media programs. There is a growing trend, particularly in elementary education, toward small-group applications, providing opportunities for students to engage in cooperative and collaborative problem-solving activities.

Interactive media may also be used for large-group instruction. The teacher alone may use the instructional program, with large-screen projection or an LCD projector for presentation to the whole class. The teacher can then move through the material in a sequence that will promote learning—stopping where appropriate for discussion, jumping ahead to new material, or reviewing when necessary. The pause-and-discuss method might work well when reviewing a topic.

Although interactive media is readily available in the schools, it has actually been used in training since the early 1980s by many corporations and the military. The use of packaged programs originally was more than twice as common as the use of custom-designed programs. Such areas as medicine, auto mechanics, electronic ignition systems, and communication skills were incorporated into interactive media materials.

Interactive multimedia formats have gained a foothold in corporate training, primarily delivering basic courses across multiple sites. Organizations routinely incorporate multimedia courseware into their training programs; thus the supply of less expensive off-the-shelf materials has increased as demand has risen.

Assure Case Connection

Mr. Winters might try to locate interactive media that could be used by his students to investigate aspects of the period or the particular events leading up to the actual signing of the Magna Carta. Or he could consider showing students materials in a large-group setting. What types of interactive media might he consider using?

Virtual Reality

Virtual reality (VR) is one of the newest applications of computer-based technologies. There are actually several levels of virtual reality, from complex, meaning you are completely immersed inside the virtual environment, to augmented, or partially immersed, to desktop level, meaning you are using your computer to look into a virtual "window."

At the complex level, virtual reality is a computer-generated, three-dimensional environment where the user can operate as an active participant. The user wears a special headpiece that contains a three-dimensional liquid crystal video display and headphones. The user participates within the three-dimensional world by manipulating a joystick or a special data glove worn on one hand. The data glove may be used to point, handle, and move objects and to direct the user's movements within the virtual world (Figure 6.5). Or the environment can be a chamber or room where the images are projected on the walls, ceiling, and floor. The "CAVE" at the University of Illinois was the first such environment where the user stepped inside the chamber to experience a virtual world.

At the augmented level, the virtual world is created inside a simulated setting, such as a flight simulator. Users interact with this type of virtual reality using real-world artifacts such as joysticks or special equipment. This type of technology has been used by the military for many years for training.

Desktop virtual reality (desktop VR) is most commonly found in education. The computer desktop is

Figure 6.5
Virtual reality puts the user "into" a multisensory experience.

used to create the setting to view the virtual world without placing users into that environment. They are free to navigate around the virtual setting using standard computer interfaces. Often what is available is a 360-degree view of an object or an environment, where users can view it from any angle and get a perspective that would simulate seeing the actual item or setting.

The essence of virtual reality is the expansion of experiences. Because virtual reality places users into the virtual environment, it provides them an opportunity to interact with that environment in a unique way, giving them the "ultimate" chance to grasp new ideas. For example, students can take a virtual field trip to a city without leaving their classroom.

Advantages

- *Safety.* Virtual reality creates a realistic world without subjecting viewers to actual or imagined danger or hazards.
- *Expansive.* It provides students with opportunities to explore places not feasible in the real world (e.g., outer space or inside an active volcano).
- *Opportunities to explore.* Virtual reality allows students to experiment with simulated environments.

Limitations

- *Cost.* The equipment is extremely expensive for the complex environments.
- *Complexity.* The technology is very complex and does not lend itself to most classroom uses, with the exception of desktop VR.
- *Limited titles.* There are limited software "realities" available at this time, although the number is growing almost daily.

Integration

Computer-controlled environments allow users to experience multisensory immersion and to interact with certain phenomena as they would in the physical world. Several applications of virtual reality have been demonstrated to be highly effective. One such application is in the area of space exploration. Because virtual reality can simulate the outer space environment, the user can practice exploring space safely and efficiently. Without this type of technology, such an experience would be impossible for all of us.

The most visible applications of VR have been high-fidelity simulators for airplane and Space Shuttle flight training and tank warfare training. VR also allows people to experience things not possible in the physical world. They can take a virtual ride through the human circulatory system or can tour an ancient Mayan civilization. VR has also found successful applications in health care, architecture, interior design, city planning, product design, and all sorts of activities involving visualization (McLellan, 1996). One application found at the school level is the "virtual field trip." Adaptive technologies for special education are also being developed and tested.

Virtual reality is showing great promise in education because of the availability of software to create the virtual worlds. *QuickTime VR* utilizes several tools that allow students to create unique realities using simple tools. A digital camera on a special tripod attachment lets the student take photographs of an environment in a 360-degree perspective. Computer software "stitches" the digital pictures together and creates a special movie. When viewing the movie, the user can, with a simple movement of the mouse, move the picture in any direction. This gives the user the feeling of standing in a spot and turning around, looking in any direction.

Virtual reality has shown great promise in the area of medicine. The virtual hospital provides training and updating for medical professionals throughout the country. Given that most hospital staff cannot leave their assigned duties for any length of time, a training climate that simulates the hospital environment while helping staff to upgrade their skills is ideal. The virtual hospital also provides information on new techniques and resources that might prove valuable in particular settings.

Some virtual reality applications are appropriate for schools. One example is a math program that lets students explore solutions to problems by actually manipulating the variables. Students experience algebraic concepts by moving numbered cubes in space, thus developing a unique understanding of the concepts.

Beyond simply manipulating the numbers to solve problems, this math program lets the teacher decide if it should correct the students when they make an error. The teacher may decide to let the computer program ignore only certain types of errors to let the students discover the mathematical relationships for themselves.

The three-dimensional rooms, or *caves,* where the user actually stands within the virtual environment, experiencing it from a total three-dimensional perspective, are often used for scientific study. Such applications as neurobiology and pharmacology have capitalized on this technology. Now scientists can enter a cell and manipulate or insert molecules and then observe the results of these actions.

Selection Rubric: Multimedia

Complete an interactive evaluation and add it to your NETS-T portfolio using the Selection Rubric for Multimedia available on the "Classroom Link Portfolio" CD-ROM. A downloadable version of this rubric is available in the Selection Rubrics module of the Companion Website at http://www.prenhall.com/smaldino.

Key Words

_____

_____

_____

Title _____

Series Title (if applicable) _____

Source _____

Date _____ Cost _____ Length _____ minutes

Subject Area _____

Intended Audience _____

Format

☐ Hypermedia

☐ Interactive video

☐ CD-ROM

☐ Virtual reality

Brief Description

Objectives

Entry Capabilities Required (e.g., prior knowledge, reading ability, vocabulary level, math ability)

Strong Points

Weak Points

Recommended Action (using criteria on the following page)

Name _____ Date _____

Rating Area	High Quality	Medium Quality	Low Quality	Rating
Match Curriculum	Curriculum standard addressed and use of multimedia should enhance student learning.	Curriculum standard partially addressed and use of multimedia may enhance student learning.	Curriculum standard not addressed and use of multimedia will likely not enhance student learning.	
Accurate & Current	Information correct and does not contain material that is out of date.	Information correct but does contain material that is out of date.	Information is not correct and does contain material that is out of date.	
Clear & Concise Language	Language used is age appropriate and vocabulary is understandable.	Language used is nearly age appropriate and some vocabulary is above/below student age.	Language used is not age appropriate and vocabulary is clearly inappropriate for student age.	
Motivating/ Interesting	Topic presented so that students are likely to be interested and engaged in learning.	Topic presented to interest students most of the time and engage most in learning.	Topic presented so as not to interest students and not engage them in learning.	
Learner Participation	Topic presented so that most students are actively engaged in learning.	Topic presented so that some students are engaged in learning.	Topic presented so that most students are not actively engaged in learning.	
Technical Quality	The material represents best available media.	The material represents media that are good quality, although there are some problems.	The material represents media that are not well prepared and are of very poor quality.	
Effectiveness Rating	There is evidence that use of these media has shown positive impact on student learning.	There is little evidence that use of these media has shown positive impact on student learning.	There is no evidence that use of these media has shown positive impact on student learning.	
Free from Bias	There is no evidence of objectionable bias or advertising.	There is little evidence of bias or advertising.	There is much evidence of bias or advertising.	
User Guide & Documentation	The documentation is excellent resource for use in a lesson. Documentation should help students use the material.	The documentation is good resource for use in a lesson. Documentation may help students use the material.	The documentation is poor resource for use in a lesson. Documentation does not help students use the material.	
Clear Directions	The material is presented so most students can understand how to use the software.	The material is presented so some students can understand how to use the software.	The material is presented so most students cannot understand how to use the software.	
Stimulates Creativity	Most students can use the software to create new ways of interfacing with the material.	Some students can use the software to create some new ways of interfacing with portions of the material.	Most students cannot use the software or cannot create new ways of interfacing with the material.	

erences and strengths tend to be auditory. The "mind styles" of these students are predominantly concrete sequential and abstract sequential. In general, they prefer a high degree of structure and are motivated to achieve because most desire to go on to postsecondary education. Other than the special-needs students, there appear to be no significant physiological factors the teacher, Rod Winters, needs to consider when he designs the lesson.

State Objectives

On completion of the lesson, the students will be able to do the following:

1. Describe the governance of England in the years just prior to 1215.
2. Identify the groups that were vying for political power in England at this period.
3. Paraphrase the main ideas contained in the Magna Carta.
4. Relate the main ideas of the Magna Carta to the interests of the contending groups.
5. Find ideas in today's world parallel to those of the Magna Carta.

Select Methods, Media, and Materials

Mr. Winters felt that his students did not have a high level of interest in this topic and saw little relevance to their own lives. However, he also knew that they enjoyed working in small groups, especially if they could choose their own teammates and topics. So he decided to approach this topic through the discovery method by forming the students into project groups, each selecting a different question to pursue.

Mr. Winters knew that some of the students were learning to create *HyperStudio* stacks in their computer skills class. He felt that they would be excited about using this tool to prepare their reports, so he engaged the computer science teacher, Philip Hibbard, to be a consultant to the students as they developed *HyperStudio* reports.

Because a wealth of materials was available he worked with other teachers to make these materials accessible to his students. Mr. Winters worked with the school library media specialist to place some books on reserve in the library, along with some videos, maps, and other materials. He also arranged for one member of each team to have a special account number for the local university's online database service. The media specialist helped him plan a field trip to the museum that included a visit with a historian from the university.

Utilize Media and Materials

The groups were scheduled to meet with Mr. Winters during the first and second weeks of the project. These meetings were to provide Mr. Winters with information about students' progress on their topic. In addition, he was able to help each group with further ideas about sources of information. The meetings helped to ensure a coordinated effort on the part of each group.

The computer science teacher worked with the students to develop a *HyperStudio* stack shell that would be used by all the groups. The students extended their knowledge of *HyperStudio* and how to design stacks. They also learned how to help their group members when working with *HyperStudio*.

During the third week of study, Mr. Winters and Mr. Hibbard worked together during class time and during other nonscheduled computer lab times to help the groups prepare their stacks.

Require Learner Participation

Each group met with Mr. Winters several times during the two-week period. They presented information about their activities and the ways they were working together as a group. These meetings assured Mr. Winters that each student in the group was participating in the activities.

The groups worked together in the computer lab during class time. Although this made for crowded conditions, the students did not seem to mind. Mr. Hibbard insisted that each member of the group have equal opportunity to work on the *HyperStudio* stack.

When all the stacks were ready, the group leaders met and developed a stack that would provide the user with access to the whole set of stacks. This stack included cards for the title, names of the group members, and a menu of choices to access the various stacks.

Evaluate and Revise

The students were delighted with the results of their activities and requested that they share their stack with the eighth-grade social studies class. They had learned that these students were learning about English history and thought that their stacks might be of interest to them. They also asked the eighth graders what they liked about the stacks.

Students were given an opportunity to study the information from the class project in preparation for a written test on the objectives. Mr. Winters prepared a short-answer test that focused on each of the topic areas in the *HyperStudio* stacks. For students with reading difficulties, Mr. Winters arranged time to meet with them to discuss each of the topic areas, thus checking their knowledge of the events.

Create Your Own ASSURE Lesson

Using the ASSURE model, design a lesson for a scenario from the table on this book's inside cover or from the Companion Website, or use a scenario of your own design. Use one of the methods described in Chapter 1 and information from this chapter related to incorporating multimedia into your instructional setting. Be sure to include information about the audience, the objectives, and all other elements of the ASSURE model. When completed, reflect on the process you used and what you have learned about matching audience, content, method, and materials.

Classroom Link Portfolio Activities

Use the "Classroom Link Portfolio" CD-ROM and the Companion Website as resources in completing these activities. To complete the following activities online go to the Portfolio Activities module in Chapter 6 of the Companion Website (http://www.prenhall.com/smaldino).

1. *Using Multimedia Technology in Learning.* Select a topic or standard. Describe three ways to use multimedia technology as described in this chapter to address the diverse learning needs of students and three to develop students' higher-order skills and creativity. (ISTE NETS-T 3.A, B, & C; 6.B & E)

2. *Written Reflection.* Identify at least three techniques that develop students' higher-order skills and creativity using multimedia technology. Now compare these techniques with other kind of media (of your choice). Which do you determine works best? (ISTE NETS-T 3.C)

Integration Assessments

To complete the specified activities online go to the Integration Assessments module in Chapter 6 of the Companion Website (http://www.prenhall.com/smaldino).

1. Plan a lesson in which you use commercial interactive video materials. Use the "ASSURE Case" template format provided in Chapter 3 or on the "Classroom Link Portfolio" CD-ROM. (ISTE NETS-T 2.A & E; 3.A, B, & C; 6.B)

2. Plan a simple hypermedia presentation using the storyboarding techniques suggested in Chapter 4. (ISTE NETS-T 2.A)

3. Locate and examine several CD-ROM materials that you might use in a classroom. Prepare either a written or an oral report on the possible applications and relative merits of these materials. (ISTE NETS-T 2.C)

4. Locate and examine an interactive video or hypermedia program. Prepare either a written or an oral report on the possible applications and relative merits of these materials. (ISTE NETS-T 2.C)

5. Plan a lesson in which you utilize computer multimedia materials. Describe the audience, the objectives, and the materials to be incorporated. Explain the roles of the students and of the instructor using these materials. Use the "ASSURE Case" template format provided in Chapter 3 or on the "Classroom Link Portfolio" CD-ROM. (ISTE NETS-T 2.A & E; 3.A, B, & C; 6.B)

6. Plan a lesson in which you have your students prepare their own hypermedia materials. Describe the audience, the objectives, and the materials to be incorporated. Explain how the students will prepare their hypermedia materials. Use the "ASSURE Case" template format provided in Chapter 3 or on the "Classroom Link Portfolio" CD-ROM (ISTE NETS-T 2.A & E; 3.A, B, & C; 6.B)

References

McClellan, Hilary. 1996. Virtual realities. In *Handbook of research for educational communications and technology,* edited by D. Jonassen. New York: Simon & Schuster.

Nelson, Theodor H. 1974a. *Computer lib: You can and must understand computers.* Chicago: Nelson.

———. 1974b. *Dream machines.* South Bend, IN: The Distributors.

Suggested Readings

Brewer, Sally, Donna Baumbach, and Mary Bird. 2000. CD-ROMs . . . Millions of ideas for millions of learners. *Educational Media International, 30*(1): 14–17.

Brush, Thomas, and John Saye. 2001. The use of embedded scaffolds with hypermedia-supported student-centered learning. *Journal of Educational Multimedia and Hypermedia, 10*(4): 333–356.

Carr, Tracy, and Asha K. Jitendra. 2000. Using hypermedia and multimedia to promote project-based learning of at-risk high school students. *Intervention in School and Clinic, 36*(1): 40–44.

Clemons, Stephanie. 2000. Developing multimedia courseware: Another technology teaching tool. *Technology Teacher, 60*(2): 9–14.

Counts, Edward L. 2003. *Multimedia design and production: Projects for students and teachers.* Upper Saddle River, NJ: Pearson Education.

Eder, Peter F. 1997. The emerging interactive society. *Futurist, 31*(3): 43–46.

Grabowski, B.L., and R.V. Small. 1997. Information, instruction, and learning: A hypermedia perspective. *Performance Improvement Quarterly 10*(1): 156–166.

Green, Timothy D., and Abbie Brown. 2002. *Multimedia projects in the classroom: A guide to development and evaluation.* Thousand Oaks, CA: Sage.

Hannafin, M. J. 1997. Student-centered learning and interactive multimedia: Status, issues and implications. *Contemporary Education, 68*(2): 94–99.

Hoffman, S. 1997. Elaboration theory and hypermedia: Is there a link? *Educational Technology 37*(1): 57–64.

Howarth, M. 1997. Visual elements and container metaphors for multi-media. *British Journal of Educational Technology, 28*(2): 125–133.

Ivers, Karen S., and Ann E. Barron. 2002. *Multimedia projects in education: Designing, producing, and assessing.* Westport, CT: Greenwood.

Koehler, Matthew J. 2002. Designing case-based hypermedia for developing understanding of children's mathematical reasoning. *Cognition and Instruction, 20*(2): 151–195.

Lifter, Marsha, and Marian E. Adams. 1998. *Kid Pix simple projects.* Westminster, CA: Teacher Created Materials.

Lloyd, Gwendolyn M., and Melvin Wilson. 2001. Offering prospective teachers tools to connect theory and practice: Hypermedia in mathematics teacher education. *Journal of Technology and Teacher Education, 9*(4): 497–518.

McDonald, Jacqueline. 1996. The great solar system rescue. *School Science and Mathematics, 96*(6): 329.

Nelson, Wayne A., Kathleen A. Bueno, and Steven Huffstutler. 1999. If you build it, they will come. But how will they use it? *Journal of Research on Computing in Education, 32*(2): 270–286.

Nichols, Paul. 1996. Digital versatile disc: The holy grail? *Computers in Libraries, 16*(5): 61.

Power on! New tools for teaching and learning. 1988. Washington, DC: U.S. Congress, Office of Technology Assessment.

Reinking, David, and Janet Watkins. 2000. A formative experiment investigating the use of multimedia book reviews to increase elementary students' independent reading. *Reading Research Quarterly, 35*(3): 384–419.

Simkins, Michael, Barbara Means, Karen Cole, Fern Tavalin, and Cole Karen. 2002. *Increasing student learning through multimedia projects.* Alexandria, VA: Association for Supervision and Curriculum Development.

Thrush, Emily Austin, and Michael Bodary. 2000. Virtual reality, combat, and communication. *Journal of Business and Technical Communication, 14*(3): 315–327.

Warren, James R., Johannes N. van Dijk, and Marcel J. Jobing. 1997. Human factors in the simulation of information systems. *Simulation & Gaming, 28*(1): 65–87.

Distance Education

Outline

Knowledge Objectives

1. Define *distance education*.
2. State a rationale for the educational use of telecommunications at the elementary, secondary, postsecondary, and informal education levels.
3. Compare and contrast telecommunication systems and describe how they facilitate distance learning.
4. Compare the advantages and limitations of each of the types of telecommunications systems described in this chapter.
5. Distinguish between the delivery systems for one-way and two-way television on the basis of their communication capabilities.
6. Create an example of an educational application that incorporates two or more telecommunication delivery systems.
7. Describe an instructional application that would be appropriate for teleconferencing in elementary, secondary, postsecondary, or informal education.
8. Describe the functions performed by a classroom teacher in a distance education setting.

Professional Vocabulary

distance education

telecommunications

Star Schools

origination classroom

distance site

audio teleconference

audiographic teleconference

instructional television fixed service (ITFS)

closed-circuit television (CCTV)

compressed video

One of the greatest advantages offered by modern electronic technology is the ability to instruct without the teacher's direct presence. That is, we can "time-shift" instruction—experience it at some time after the live lesson—and "place-shift" instruction—experience it at some place away from the live teacher. Of course, the book was the first invention that made it possible to time-shift and place-shift instruction, and it continues in that use today.

For a century people in all parts of the world have been able to participate in guided independent study through correspondence courses via the traditional mail system. Learners receive printed lessons, do written assignments, and get feedback from the remote instructor. But the proliferation of newer electronic technologies now makes it possible to experience place-shifted instruction with a stunning array of additional auditory and visual stimuli, far more rapidly, and with a far richer range of interaction, not only with the instructor but also with other learners. This chapter introduces the concepts of distance education and distance learning as well as providing information about audio and video telecommunication delivery systems. Chapter 8, "Online Learning," will focus on computer-based distance education.

DISTANCE EDUCATION

Distance education has become the popular term to describe learning via telecommunications. In this chapter the term **telecommunications** embraces a variety of media configurations, including radio, telephone, and television (broadcast, wired, and satellite). What they all have in common is implied in the Greek root word *tele,* which means "at a distance"

ASSURE
Case Challenge

We have developed a case study for this chapter to help you see how computers can be integrated into learning activities. At the end of the chapter you will be challenged to develop your own ASSURE lesson for a case study of your choice using the ASSURE model and incorporating the technology and media described in this chapter. To help you in preparing your lesson, we have included hints (called "ASSURE Case Connections") throughout the chapter as they relate to the ASSURE Case Challenge.

Three high school science teachers have decided to work collaboratively in teaching a unit on space exploration. They wish to expand the learning opportunities for their students by having them work together collaboratively at a distance.

The schools are located in similar communities, although they are too far apart to bring the students together except by using a telecommunications system. There are many similarities among the high schools and the students. Neither the students nor the teachers have had much experience using telecommunications prior to this unit, but are eager to learn. They hope that a successful demonstration with this unit will open the door to expanded collaborative learning opportunities in the future.

or "far off"; that is, they are systems for communicating over a distance. We will examine in Chapter 8 the role of computers in distance education.

More formally defined, *distance learning* is a form of education characterized by the following:

- Physical separation of learners from the teacher
- Organized instructional program
- Telecommunications media
- Two-way communication

As the examples in this chapter will make clear, the converging of electronic technologies has fostered a rich hybridization of media configurations. We seldom see an instructional telecommunication system that is of one pure type. Typically, programs are distributed by a combination of broadcast, wired, or satellite-relayed transmissions, and students respond through some combination of mail, fax, telephone, or computer transmissions (Figure 7.1).

Familiarity with these alternative pathways to learning is essential to today's educators. As early as 1989 the U.S. Office of Technology Assessment recognized that advances in technology will affect education.

Technologies for learning at a distance, while reaching a small but growing number of teachers today, will clearly affect the teaching force of tomorrow. Some will teach on these systems, others will use them to provide additional resources in their classrooms, and many will receive professional education and training over them. Few will be unaffected (U.S. Congress, Office of Technology Assessment, 1989).

Elementary Education

At the elementary school level, teachers tend to use prerecorded videocassettes more often than live broadcast television programs. Still, several broadcast series are frequently used: at the early elementary level, *Sesame Street* and *Clifford;* at the intermediate levels, *Reading Rainbow, Between the Lions, Arthur,* and *ZOOM.* These programs are used mainly as enrichment rather than as the core of instruction (Figure 7.2). Teachers who use educational television programming tend to use more

Figure 7.1

The proliferation of telecommunications makes information accessible at more and more locations, such as libraries.

Figure 7.2
Big Bird is a main character on Sesame Street, *which after more than 30 years is still the most recognized educational program for children.*

than one program (usually two or three), but not a whole series (Children's Television Workshop, 1990).

Secondary Education

At the secondary level, television is used mainly to expand the curricular offerings of a specific high school. Rural schools are able to offer a full core curriculum. In advanced or specialized subjects for which there are not

enough students in one school to justify hiring a teacher, school administrations frequently use television to connect several schools, thus creating a large enough "class" to be affordable. For example, the StarNet network, a satellite network based in Texas, reaches high school students across the United States via satellite. StarNet offers such courses as foreign languages (Spanish, French, German, Latin, and Japanese), calculus, physics, psychology, and art history. These live, interactive classes, which use telephone talkback, are scheduled throughout the school day on two channels. As opposed to the elementary school pattern, these programs tend to be used in their entirety and provide core instruction.

Distance learning at the P–12 level in the United States gained impetus in the late 1980s from the **Star Schools** program, initiated by the U.S. Department of Education. This program provided multimillion-dollar grants for regional consortia to develop instructional networks that reach elementary and secondary students in rural, disadvantaged, and small schools. StarNet's collaboration with schools throughout the country is an example of the type of network that is providing students with educational opportunities that would otherwise be difficult or impossible to obtain. Star School projects also included single statewide networks that link schools within a state.

Projects such as the Iowa Distance Education Alliance (IDEA) have trained teachers, provided courses or students, and expanded the nature of distance education at the state level. For example, students who were studying manned space flight via distance education became engaged in dialogues with James VanAllen, of the University of Iowa, and NASA space scientists. The Iowa project uses a statewide fiber optic telecommunication system that connects elementary, secondary, and postsecondary educational facilities in all 99 counties.

Close-Up

SATELLITE SERVES RURAL HIGH SCHOOL

Eddyville (Oregon) High School is a small, rural high school serving a logging community located on the Pacific Ocean. It is part of a sparsely populated school district covering 1,800 square miles. The school, like many others in similar situations, has difficulty offering a broad enough curriculum to meet the diverse needs of the students. In this case, the interactive television programs delivered by satellite from StarNet network in San Antonio, Texas, helped to fill the gaps. Eddyville High School was about to elimi-

nate classes in French and Spanish because the teacher of those subjects moved away. By subscribing to StarNet the school enabled its students to take not only those language courses but also psychology, sociology, and art appreciation.

The video lessons are broadcast on a regular schedule, and the students participate along with students at many other sites around the country. At each site there is a telephone to allow question-and-answer (one-way video, two-way audio) sessions. Students, teachers, and parents appreciate the chance to have an enriched curriculum at a cost even a small school can afford.

Source: StarNet Information (StarNet Network, 1999), www.starnet.org

The opportunities offered through such projects as StarNet and IDEA continue to expand the educational horizons for many students. Whole courses and special events provide students with the means to expand their educational opportunities, especially in rural areas.

Postsecondary Education

At the postsecondary level, telecommunication systems are used extensively for both on-campus and off-campus education. Hundreds of community colleges, technical schools, colleges, and universities in North America use telecommunications as part of their regular instructional programs. The purpose generally is to expand the number of students who can be reached by one instructor in a given course. For example, closed-circuit television is often used to connect classrooms of students in different buildings, or even in different cities, to a professor speaking from a studio or camera-equipped classroom.

The fastest growing application, though, is for reaching off-campus audiences with college or university courses. An early large-scale distance education program in the United States was begun in the mid 1950s with *TV College*, an extension of the City Colleges of Chicago, using the broadcasting facilities of WTTW-TV, a public television station.

More recently, government-sponsored distance education programs throughout the world have emulated the idea of the British Open University, which began with an enrollment of 40,000 in 1971 and grew to 200,000 by 2000. In Canada, Thailand, Indonesia, and dozens of other countries, these types of programs provide access to postsecondary education in situations where conventional universities simply cannot handle the demand for further education. In each case, radio, television, the Internet (see Chapter 8), and other telecommunication systems play a significant role in providing part of the instructional program. However, printed materials and various sorts of face-to-face instruction remain a component of these and most other distance education programs. Virtual campuses, like the University of Phoenix, allow students to enroll in programs of study without having to attend classes on a centralized campus setting.

Informal Education

As pervasive as telecommunications have become in formal education, there is an equally formidable range of applications outside the confines of degree-granting educational institutions. Hospitals, government agencies, businesses, engineering and architectural firms, and corporations of all sorts use telecommunications to fill part of their need for constant training and upgrading of their personnel. Here the rationale is clearly economic—to provide cost-effective training to large numbers of people who may be distributed across numerous sites. In many cases, such as with multinational corporations, it is often vitally important that the training be standardized. For example, the marketing strategy for a line of garden tractors or a new type of insurance policy demands that all the sales representatives emphasize the same points in their sales presentations. A packaged training course delivered by television can provide the fast, mass-distributed, simultaneous, standardized training needed.

A telecommunications application that combines formal education and on-site corporate training is a program offered by National Technological University (NTU). This graduate degree–granting program serves on-the-job engineers with televised and online courses leading to masters degrees (see "Close-up: The University Without a Campus").

DISTANCE EDUCATION ROLES

Role of the Student

Students need to understand their roles in a distance education experience. Early attempts at this type of instruction tended to involve an instructor who only lectured with students passively sitting in the distance sites, often not attending to the instructor's "talking head." With technological advances, interactions among students and between sites is feasible. Students can become more engaged in their learning. It remains the teacher's responsibility, however, to organize the lessons to encourage interactivity and to guide students on how to interact appropriately.

Students need to know how to use the technology to communicate with the teacher and with each other. When students want to ask questions, or want to add to the discussion, they must be able to use the technology to interact. Students not only need to know how to operate the microphone or how to post to a bulletin board discussion, they also need to understand communication etiquette. A student's "right to interrupt" becomes an important concept when working with multiple video or audio sites in a course. If the teacher does not give equal time to all sites, or if the student has a question that needs to be addressed, it may be necessary for the student to interrupt the teacher's instruction.

Role of the Teacher

When we begin to talk about the teacher in the distance education classroom, it is necessary to think about the setting in a new light. The classroom is now a *series* of "rooms," connected electronically. In a television environment the **origination classroom** is the one where the teacher is present. **Distance sites** or remote classrooms

Close-Up

THE UNIVERSITY WITHOUT A CAMPUS

In the fast-paced world of high technology, a corporation's knowledge base can become obsolete overnight. How can a nation keep its engineering talent up to date? In the United States, instructional television lessons delivered by satellite are one answer. The National Technological University (NTU) was formed in 1984 through the collaboration of more than a dozen large corporations, two dozen universities, and the federal government. It now operates as a private nonprofit university offering its own master's degrees in computer engineering, manufacturing systems, and other fields.

The students at NTU are engineers employed at cooperating businesses and government agencies. Each organization maintains classrooms and a satellite downlink. The employee students choose from among dozens of courses, which are broadcast 20 hours a day, six days a week, on two channels. Most of these classes are videotaped and broadcast one way via satellite, but about 30 percent are live and interactive, with two-way audio feedback from the receiving sites.

Through NTU, engineers can stay current in their fields and advance toward a master's degree without leaving their jobs or commuting long distances. Because this school without a campus

involves many of the leading engineering universities in the nation, students have access to the top specialists in their fields of study. NTU demonstrates vividly how technology can be harnessed to promote productivity.

Source: National Technological University, P.O. Box 700, Fort Collins, CO 80522.

---

are the locations connected by the telecommunications system. At the distance sites, there may be only one or two students, or there may be a full class. Additionally, there may be a distance-site facilitator, an adult whose responsibility it is to work with the teacher. The facilitator may be another teacher or a classroom aide. The duties of the facilitator vary depending on the course content and the origination classroom teacher's needs.

Experience has shown that in P–12 education, student success increases when the teacher and the distance-site facilitator work as a team. Students learn more in cases where the distance-site facilitator does the following:

- Watch and participate actively in all programs with the students
- Encourage interaction with the teacher and other students
- Answer questions at that site
- Solve immediate problems
- Provide additional quizzes and worksheets
- Take responsibility for operating and troubleshooting the equipment

To play an active, facilitating role requires advance planning and training. Ideally, the distance teacher and

facilitator meet before the course starts to discuss goals for the class and instructional strategies. For example, they may agree to allow students in receiving classrooms to discuss and explain points to each other during class with talkback microphones off. Such peer cooperation can greatly enhance the learning atmosphere in what might otherwise be a stilted, restrictive environment.

In an online environment, the teacher's role may shift to that of facilitator of the learning rather than directly leading the class. With online education, the teacher must ensure that all students clearly understand their responsibilities and how to conduct themselves in the class. Further, the teacher must keep a "watchful eye" on the class to be sure no one is falling behind. So, in addition to facilitating the learning, the teacher becomes the classroom monitor as well. Many teachers will tell you that teaching online is not easier; it is often perceived as much more time consuming.

Role of Technology

With technologies for distance learning that rely on television, the teacher may need to change existing teaching materials (Figure 7.3). Students benefit from visuals

Figure 7.3
Videoconferencing systems can be designed so that the teacher can select the image to be shown with a single mouse click.

that are included in the instructional experience. Visuals used in other types of instructional settings may need to be adapted to use in a distance education classroom. The document camera is a valuable teaching tool for showing students visuals and for demonstrating specific tasks. Although teachers may be able to use classroom materials such as overhead transparencies, these materials tend to be in a format not easily visible on the monitors. Television has a horizontal, or "landscape," orientation, which means that materials prepared in a vertical orientation will not be as easily seen. It may be necessary to redo materials. One suggestion is to have all classroom materials prepared so they can be used in either a regular or a television classroom setting.

Color, size, and design are important considerations. Television is not a very good medium for quality color transmission or for showing fine detail. So, for example, a science teacher who is demonstrating a chemical reaction that relies on color change may find that students at the distance sites do not see the desired outcomes. Although it is possible to zoom a document camera in for close-up of a page, definition and quality may be lost. Also, some graphics may be too "busy" for television, creating distractions for students. Contrast is an issue when trying to display detail.

In an online environment, visuals can be brought into documents as well as provided by links to certain pages or sites. Scanned images, digital photos, and other types of digitized visuals can become an integral part of the materials students use in their learning experience (Figure 7.4).

INSTRUCTIONAL COMMUNICATION FUNCTIONS

Regardless of the technology used, from live teacher to computer conferencing, an instructional telecommunication system must perform certain functions to be effective (Figure 7.5):

- *Information presentation.* A standard element in any lesson is the presentation of some sort of information to the learner. Common examples include the following:
  - Teacher lecture and demonstration
  - Printed text and illustrations (e.g., textbooks, handouts, correspondence study materials)
  - Live or recorded voice, music, and other sounds
  - Full-motion images (video, CD-ROM)
- *Student–teacher interaction.* We know that most learning takes place when learners are participating actively—mentally processing the material. Teachers attempt to induce activity in various ways, such as the following:
  - Question-and-answer sessions (carried out during or after the lesson)
  - Practice with feedback (carried out as drill-and-practice or discussion activities during the class or as homework)
  - Testing
- *Student–student interaction.* For many educational objectives, student interaction with other students, in pairs or small groups, can be extremely effective. Some common ways of structuring student interaction are the following:
  - Discussion groups (in or out of class)
  - Structured group activities (e.g., role playing or games)
  - Group projects
  - Peer tutoring
- *Access to learning resources.* Lessons and courses are usually structured with the assumption that learners will spend time outside of class working individually with the material, doing homework, projects, papers, and the like. The external learning resources may take the following forms:
  - Printed materials (e.g., textbooks, supplementary readings, worksheets)
  - Audiovisual materials (e.g., audio- or videocassettes, multimedia systems, CD-ROM)
  - Computer databases (e.g., for online searches)

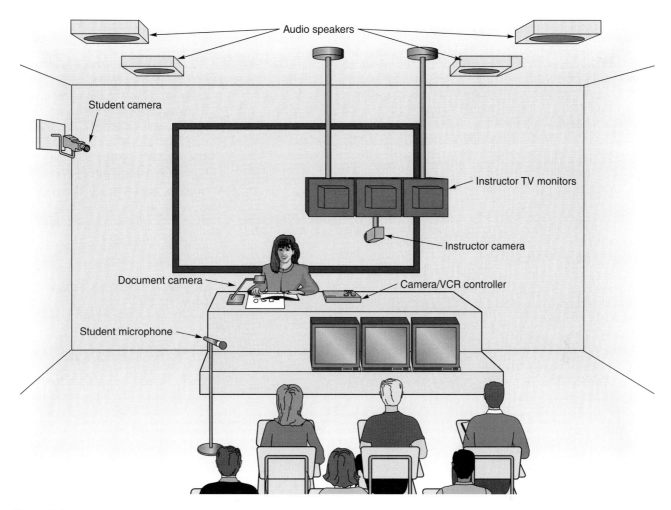

Figure 7.4

Classroom setup for interactive TV. At the originating classroom, both teacher and students must have camera(s), microphone(s), and monitor(s) to communicate with students in remote classrooms.

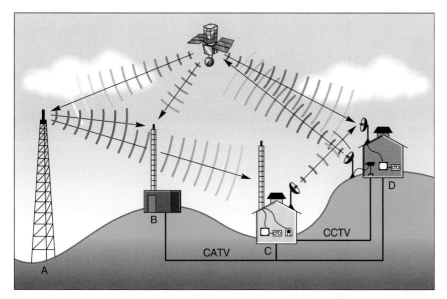

Figure 7.5

A hypothetical instructional telecommunications system. You should be able to trace and name at least a half dozen different pathways a radio, TV, or computer message could follow to reach one of the school buildings. This would make a good self-test after reading the chapter.

Table 7.1
Telecommunication systems

System	Presentation	Interaction
Radio, broadcast	Voice, music	Homework, tests by mail
Audio teleconference	Voice, music (live)	Question-and-answer with live feedback Homework, tests by mail
Audiographic teleconference	Voice, music (live) Still pictures, graphics	Question-and-answer with live feedback Still pictures, graphics Homework, tests by mail or fax
Computer conference	Electronic text, data, graphs (time-shifted)	Written (typed) exchange with other students Written (typed) exchange with teacher
Television, one-way video, one-way audio	Voice, music Still pictures, graphics Motion images	Homework, tests by mail
Television, one-way video, two-way audio (video teleconference)	Voice, music (live) Still pictures, graphics Motion images	Vocal question-and-answer with teacher Vocal exchange with other students Homework, tests by mail
Television, two-way video, two-way audio (two-way video teleconference)	Voice, music (live) Still pictures, graphics Motion images	Vocal and visual question-and-answer with teacher Vocal and visual exchange with other students Homework, tests by mail

- Kits (e.g., for laboratory experiments or to examine specimens of real objects)
- Library materials (e.g., original source documents)

Each of the various telecommunication systems has strengths and limitations in these areas. The characteristics of the systems are summarized in Table 7.1 and discussed at greater length in the following sections of this chapter.

BROADCAST RADIO

When we listen to radio, we hear electronic signals that are *broadcast*, or transmitted through the air, over regular AM or FM radio frequencies. Broadcast radio can be adapted to educational use, as shown in Figure 7.6. Although such radio is basically a format for one-way lectures or dramatic presentations, some de-

gree of interactivity can be added by using printed materials to accompany the programs and requiring listeners to send responses back to the instructor. Some programs provide a telephone number for the students to contact the instructor.

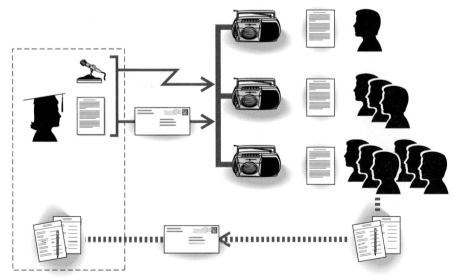

Figure 7.6

Broadcast radio. A degree of interaction can be added by sending print materials to students through the mail; they can, in turn, send written work back to the teacher for correction and evaluation.

Advantages

- *Cost*. Radio is a less expensive broadcast medium than is television. It is still used in developing countries and in other localities where there are geographic or economic constraints on the technologies they can employ.
- *Range*. Radio programs can reach a large, geographically dispersed population with a single message.
- *Flexibility*. The audio medium is extremely flexible and can have a powerful, dramatic effect, particularly for conveying music, discussion, and storytelling.
- *Imagination stimulator*. Because radio is an audio-only medium, listeners are free to use their imaginations to create the image.

Limitations

- *Schedule*. Broadcast radio is being displaced by prerecorded material. Instructors resist using media that must be used according to a rigid schedule.
- *Operation expense*. It is difficult to justify the expense of operating broadcast facilities when prerecorded materials are readily available.

Integration

Radio was the first telecommunication system adapted to educational purposes in North America. Much of the early technical experimentation with radio broadcasting was carried out at stations operated by colleges and universities.

During that pretelevision period in the United States, many school and college stations linked themselves into networks, usually of statewide scope devoted to providing in-school educational programs at the P–12 level. Ohio started a *School of the Air* in the early 1930s, and others followed in the Midwest, New York, and Texas. Although some of these efforts lasted well into the television era, most languished when television became widely available in their area. In Canada, the Canadian Broadcasting Corporation (CBC) organized educational programming on a national scale.

In developing countries, where large populations still reside in isolated villages, millions of children attend schools where the learning resources begin and end with the teacher and chalkboard. In their search for a low-cost technology that could provide stimulating resources to schools scattered over vast geographic regions, educators have rediscovered broadcast radio (Figure 7.7). A project in the late 1970s in Nicaragua demonstrated success in providing mathematics lessons over the radio. Lessons were designed with embedded questions and prerecorded feedback to learners' re-

Figure 7.7

In Kenya, "interactive" radio has proved to be a cost-effective method for teaching.

sponses. The key to success was the novel format requiring fast-paced responses by the students to questions or other cues given in the broadcast program. Because of its great success in Nicaragua and in other field trials, "interactive" radio has expanded to other countries, including Honduras, Bolivia, and Kenya. English has become a popular subject for educational radio, with lessons in listening, speaking, reading, and writing. Mathematics, health, agriculture, and economics are also taught by radio.

ASSURE Case Connection

Radio is a viable option for a one-way delivery of information. Since the science teachers wish to have their students engage in interaction, they will have to consider how to arrange for the interactions. Could they use the radio option to deliver portions of the instruction and rely on telephone connections to have the students work together?

AUDIO TELECONFERENCE

The **audio teleconference** is an extension of a simple telephone call. Advances in telephone technology now allow individuals or groups of people at two or more locations to hear and be heard clearly and easily (Figure 7.8).

An audio teleconference—a live, two-way conversation using telephone lines or satellites—connects people at different locations. For example, a class can chat with the author of a book they have recently read. They only need to have a speakerphone connection in their classroom. The author needs only a telephone. For connecting two or more groups, a special microphone-amplifier

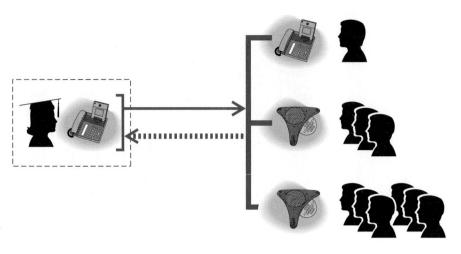

Figure 7.8
Audio teleconference. Interaction takes place through the telephone system; groups of listeners use speakerphones.

device, preferably voice activated, is needed at each location. This device assures that the voices are picked up faithfully and amplified clearly at the listening end. In the middle is a "bridge," an electronic system that joins the calls from all participating locations, equalizes the sound levels, filters out extraneous noises, and takes care of disconnections. The bridge may be either supplied by the telephone company or rented for the occasion from a commercial company.

Advantages

- *Cost effective.* Schools can invite an expert into the classroom to engage in a dialog with students. The audio teleconference is often seen as a cost-effective way to hold a meeting or training session without the expense of time and money involved in travel.
- *Easy to use.* It is the most easily accessible form of telecommunications because it uses telephone service. Commercial phone companies have made it easy to set up audio teleconferences from any phone.
- *Interactive.* All participants get the same message—and interactivity. They can talk to the instructor or to the other learners.

Limitations

- *Lack of visual information.* The lack of a visual dimension poses limitations. This can be offset by arranging to have material at the sites in advance.
- *Poor audio.* To have acceptable audio quality, each receiving site needs to have special microphone-amplifier devices.
- *Intimidating.* Lack of experience with this type of communication technology may make some

learners less willing to participate.

Integration

This system is frequently used at the secondary and postsecondary levels to connect students at two or more sites with an author to discuss his or her writing or with a public official to discuss current legislation. It has been used heavily in Alaska to bring inservice training to teachers. Audio teleconferencing is popular in corporate and professional education for training—for example, to discuss the features of a new service, to teach sales representatives the latest selling techniques, to update accountants on changes in the tax laws, and so on. It is not unusual to connect 10, 20, or 30 sites for one audio teleconference.

AUDIOGRAPHIC TELECONFERENCE

An **audiographic teleconference** adds still picture transmission to an audio teleconference (Figure 7.9). Several different devices can be used to send pictures and graphics over the same telephone lines as the voice signal: slow-scan (single frame) analog video, facsimile (fax) paper copies, or an electronic graphics tablet. The common denominator in these devices is a method of converting the image to digital form for transmission. (See Chapter 8 for information regarding using computers for audio and image transmission.)

Advantages

- *Visual.* The big advantage of audiographic systems over other audio formats is the addition of the visual element.
- *Cost.* Unless full-motion images are needed, audiographics can provide an audiovisual experience at a fraction of the cost of television.

Limitations

- *Availability.* Hardware and software audiographic technologies are not readily available.
- *Time factor.* It can take nearly a full minute to transmit a still image via fax or slow-scan technologies.

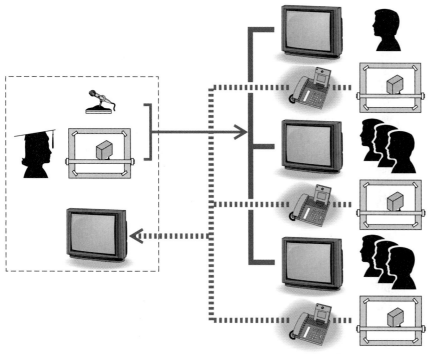

synchronous discussion using any of these technologies? Will the students be able to work together so they could share their notes and other visual information quickly and easily?

Television in Distance Education

One-Way Video, One-Way Audio

Of all the uses of television in education, the viewing of prerecorded videocassettes is the most common (we discuss this application in Chapter 12). Here we will consider the next most common form of television use—live viewing of programs without direct feedback to the presenter.

We use the term *one-way television* to refer to all the television delivery systems in which programs are transmitted to students without an interactive connection with the teacher (Figure 7.10). This includes five principal types of delivery systems: broadcast, satellite, microwave, closed-circuit, and cable or fiber optics.

Figure 7.9

Audiographic teleconference. In addition to hearing each other, participants can see visuals sent to a TV set one frame at a time via a graphics tablet or slow-scan video.

Integration

Many schools and colleges use audiographic teleconferencing to connect students in a number of isolated locales with a teacher. This is especially the case in rural areas where there may not be enough students in one school to justify hiring a teacher for a particular subject, even if it is a required subject. Through audiographics a teacher at any one location can teach students at all the other sites. At Utah State University, for example, graduate classes are made available to sites scattered throughout Utah plus sites in Idaho and Wyoming even when there is just one student at a particular site. Corporations in the telephone business, such as AT&T, have been especially aggressive in using audiographics as a major tool for employee training. Online electronic whiteboards are quickly replacing the audiographic format.

Assure Case Connection

Would a teleconferencing option be reasonable for the science teachers to consider? Can the instruction be delivered using audio and visuals, along with having

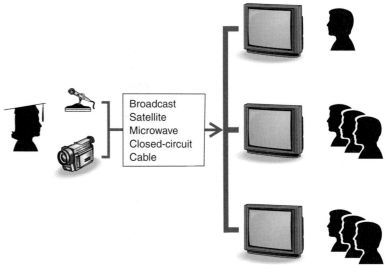

Figure 7.10

Television—one-way video, one-way audio. One-way television, such as broadcast, has no provision for immediate feedback to the source.

Broadcast Transmission. Broadcasting, the transmission of powerful electromagnetic waves through the air, is the delivery system that made television a popular home entertainment medium. Broadcast television signals, using the very-high and ultra-high frequencies (VHF and UHF), radiate outward to the horizon from the transmitting antenna (Figure 7.11). Relay stations carry those signals around obstacles, such as mountains, and to outlying communities beyond the prime coverage area. Any standard TV set can freely receive these signals. Broadcasting is a common format for both commercial and public television programs.

In the United States, most public television stations serve as outlets for the network programming of the Public Broadcasting Service (PBS). Their evening schedules feature PBS offerings and other programs aimed at home viewers in general, while during the daytime hours these stations typically carry instructional programs designed for specific school or college audiences.

Public television attempts to offer an alternative type of programming for viewers who are not well served by the mass audience programs of commercial broadcasting. In reaching out to selected subgroups, public television programming does not usually attract viewers on a scale comparable to that of the commercial networks. However, well-produced programs such as *NOW*, *Masterpiece Theatre*, and *NOVA* have won critical acclaim and loyal audiences that in recent years have grown as large as those for many commercial programs.

The types of programs carried on public television—documentaries, dramas, public affairs features, musical performances, science programs, and the like—are often useful as adjuncts to instruction in schools and colleges. Programs for direct classroom use to reach specific curriculum objectives—instructional television (ITV)—are a mainstay of most public television stations' daytime schedules (Figure 7.12).

ITV programs tend to be about 15 minutes (at the earlier grade levels) to 30 minutes long, and a single program is often repeated at different hours throughout the week to allow for flexibility in classroom scheduling. Contrary to the popular image, broadcast ITV programs usually do not present core instruction in basic subject areas. One leading researcher (Rockman, 1976) described ITV's role this way:

- To assist classroom teachers in subjects in which they often have the most difficulty (e.g., art, music, mathematics, science, and health)
- To supplement classroom instruction in subject areas in which limited classroom resources may prevent full examination of historical or international events
- To bring outside stimulation to subject areas, such as literature, where teachers have difficulty exciting and motivating students

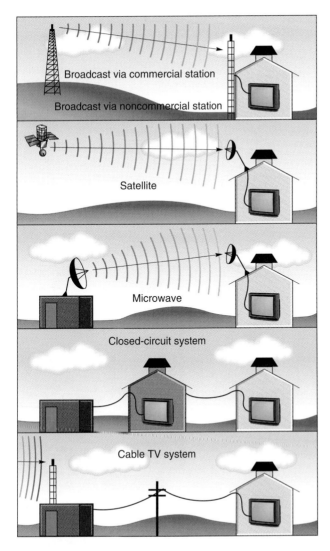

Figure 7.11
One-way video distribution systems.

Figure 7.12
Although in-classroom playback of videocassettes is the primary delivery system for instructional television, off-air reception from public TV stations is still common.

Figure 7.13
Satellite dishes bring signals directly to any setting, no matter how remote.

Satellite Transmission. Satellite communication refers to an orbiting device in space that receives signals from stations on earth and retransmits them to distant locations (Figure 7.13). Today's satellites are *geosynchronous*, meaning that their orbits are synchronized with the earth's own rotation so that they appear to be positioned over the same spot on earth, serving, in effect, as a transmitting tower 23,000 miles high. At that altitude, a satellite's coverage area could include nearly half of the earth's surface. This, of course, is a far larger area than for any other transmission method.

Satellites now carry most international telephone calls as well as most network television transmissions.

The trend in recent years has been to build larger and more powerful satellites, allowing the ground reception equipment to become smaller and simpler. We now have satellites that allow home reception with dish receivers no more than 18 inches across. There has been a great proliferation of receiving systems for the home, workplace, and school.

Several programming services broadcast to schools directly via satellite, including Channel One and the Discovery Channel. Channel One programs are broadcast at night via satellite and are picked up and recorded at individual schools on timer-activated video recorders (see "Close-Up: News for Schools"). Both Channel One and Discovery have resources on the Web for students and for teachers. Similarly, many public broadcast programs have Web resources.

Microwave Transmission. Television signals broadcast in the microwave spectrum (above 2,000 MHz) are referred to as *microwave* transmission. As with other forms of telecommunications, a license is required to transmit with microwave, and in the United States a specific part of the microwave spectrum has been reserved for educational institutions—the 2500–2690 band, called **instructional television fixed service (ITFS).**

ITFS (and other microwave transmissions) have one major technical limitation: signals broadcast at these high microwave frequencies travel in a line-of-sight pattern. Consequently, the coverage of ITFS is limited to areas in direct sightline of the transmission tower. More than 100 educational licensees operate

Close-Up

NEWS FOR SCHOOLS

Elementary and secondary school students have daily access to a specially produced 15-minute news program through *CNN Newsroom*. Each program contains current news presented with scripting and graphics that give students a context for understanding the news they hear.

Participating schools can tape the programs off cable or satellite without charge and can receive free teacher's guides to accompany the programs.

There is evidence that even this brief daily exposure to real-world events can have a beneficial effect on students. In the early days of *CNN Newsroom*, one enthusiastic fourth-grade teacher reported that his class scored at the 88th percentile on standardized tests in both science and social studies after a year of watching and

discussing *CNN Newsroom*. These scores translate to an equivalent of ninth grade in social studies and seventh grade in science; they were more than 10 points above the average for the rest of the school's fourth graders, who don't have access to the program.[1]

CNN Newsroom originated as a rival to Channel One, a secondary school news service of Whittle Communications. Channel One provides a daily 12-minute news program that includes two minutes of commercials. In exchange for promising that students watch the programs (including the commercials), the schools receive video reception, recording, and playback equipment. The inclusion of commercials has made Channel One controversial in many locations.

[1] "CNN Newsroom Improves Science and Social Studies Test Scores," Advisory Group Briefing. Turner Educational Services, Inc. (December 1991), pp. 4–5.

several hundred channels in the ITFS spectrum. Even though reception is limited to a line-of-sight radius, this is large enough to cover some school districts. Within higher education, ITFS is used primarily for graduate and professional school distance education—for example, connecting engineering or medical schools with professionals in the field who desire a refresher course.

Closed-Circuit Television. The term **closed-circuit television (CCTV)** refers to a private distribution system connected by wire. This wire may be regular copper wire that carries electrical impulses or thin glass optical fiber that carries impulses in the form of light. CCTV signals cannot be received outside the private network. A major advantage of CCTV is that such systems do not require government licensing and can be set up freely by any institution that desires to do so. Closed circuit is used mainly to connect the buildings on an individual school or college campus and gives a private, multichannel capability within those confines. The cost of distribution rises as the network expands (unlike with broadcast TV), so CCTV is not generally used for reaching a large geographic area. However, many states, such as Indiana, Iowa, and South Dakota, have CCTV networks connecting schools and colleges hundreds of miles apart.

It is difficult to characterize the applications of CCTV because, being unregulated, it has no central information source. Also, CCTV systems can be as simple as a camera connected to a monitor in the same room (e.g., for image magnification of a science demonstration) or as complex as a campuswide wired distributed system (e.g., for distribution of video programs from a central library to any classroom). Because the cost of building a CCTV system increases with larger geographic areas, it is not widely used to interconnect buildings spread out over a school district. However, it is frequently used to connect buildings on a college or university campus.

Cable Television. The cable concept of television program delivery was first applied commercially in the 1950s in an isolated town where, due to interference from a mountain overshadowing the town, people were unable to receive a viewable signal from the nearest TV station. Local businesspeople developed the idea of building a master antenna atop the mountain. There the weak signals were amplified and fed into a coaxial cable that ran down the mountain into the town (Figure 7.14). By paying an installation charge and a monthly subscription fee, customers could have their homes connected to the cable. This idea of having a single tall antenna to serve a

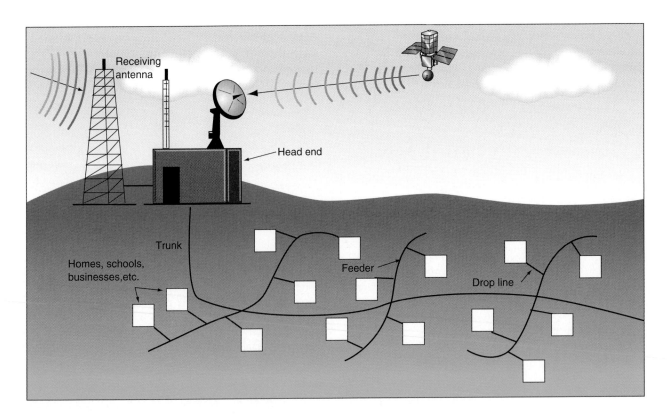

Figure 7.14
Cable television distribution system. Multiple program sources are combined at the "head end" and distributed through trunks, feeders, and drop lines to individual homes, schools, and businesses.

whole community gave the process the name *community antenna television,* or *CATV,* now more commonly known as cable television. Many schools and most post-secondary institutions are now connected to commercial cable systems, often without monthly charges. Educational institutions are often invited to use one of the cable channels for their own purposes.

The availability of multiple channels with cable facilitates a number of special services:

- Transmission of several programs simultaneously and repetition of programs at different hours for more flexibility with classroom schedules
- *Narrowcasting,* or aiming specialized programs at small subgroups (e.g., those speaking foreign languages or having sight or hearing impairments)
- Retrieval of remotely stored libraries of video materials, allowing teachers or individual students access to materials on demand without the logistic struggle often associated with instructional media use

Furthermore, many cable operators provide schools with special programming, teachers' guides, and even special computer services. Many program sources available via cable are not retransmitted from broadcasts but are sent out only on cable. A number of these offer high-quality programming suitable for school use. The Discovery Channel, the Learning Channel, Cable News Network, and C-Span are a few examples, all of which offer program guides for teachers. The school library media specialist may already have these available for teachers or can assist in obtaining them.

Fiber Optics.   Fiber optics is a fascinating and newer example of links in telecommunications systems. Optical fibers retain the physical link of phone lines but are only a fraction of the diameter of wire (Figure 7.15). All homes, schools, libraries, and offices in a city can be interconnected and tied into state, national, and international networks. An optical fiber carries digital, rather than analog, signals as pulses of light generated by a laser device no bigger than a grain of salt. The millions of pulses per second emitted by the laser make it possible to carry many more messages than copper wires or coaxial cables. For example, two optical fibers can handle 6,000 telephone conversations at one time, a task that would take 250 copper wires. The use of fiber optics also helps to save scarce resources. Silicon, used to make the optical fibers, is the second most abundant element on the earth, whereas copper reserves are dwindling.

The digital code can transmit print, audio, and images either separately or simultaneously. The digital signal is also devoid of background noise and is much less vulnerable to distortion caused by external sources such as magnetic fields and electrical storms.

Education networks have become prime users of the technology of fiber optics. New facilities are using optical fibers in place of cable, and older facilities are replacing cables with space-saving optical fibers. Hooking up computers with cables or over phone wires limits what can be transferred from one computer to another. Phone lines are too slow and operate on too narrow a *bandwidth* (total available frequency range) to handle multimedia applications, such as video, sound, and animation. Wireless networks promise to provide easier and better transmission of multimedia materials. Schools are finding it practical to build networks combining wireless and fiber optic cable technologies. The emergence of wireless and high-speed networking augments the usefulness of collaborative software packages and makes them less expensive, as well as more accessible to students.

One-Way Video, Two-Way Audio.   Virtually all the television modes mentioned so far can be converted into a two-way communication system by using a device for sending audio feedback to the presenter. In the case of broadcast, satellite, and microwave transmissions, the talkback capability is usually added by means of a telephone for calling the originating studio. In the case of closed-circuit and cable systems, the talkback channel may be incorporated in the CCTV or CATV wiring itself (Figure 7.16).

Two-Way Video, Two-Way Audio

Fully interactive television with two-way communication of both audio and video, or two-way television, is achieved by equipping both the sending and receiving sites with camera and microphone and interconnecting them by some means capable of two-way transmission. This may be fiber optics, cable, microwave, satellite, or a combination of these. A school or other organization may

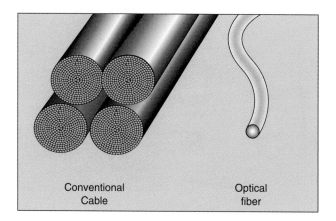

Figure 7.15

A single optical fiber can transmit as many messages as more than one hundred copper wires.

Conventional Cable

Optical fiber

operate its own video teleconference facilities or lease them as needed for particular occasions.

Many two-way video, two-way audio systems rely on full-motion video pictures (Figure 7.17). Technically, it is much more difficult and expensive to transmit a full-motion video image than a still picture. The full-motion image requires a signal channel as broad as that used by broadcast TV stations, whereas a still picture uses a narrow signal and can be sent over a telephone line. **Compressed video** removes redundant information, transmitting only the frames in which there is some motion. In this way the video information can be "squeezed" through a telephone line. This compression is important because it costs only about one-tenth as much to transmit through a phone line as through a broadband channel. There is a

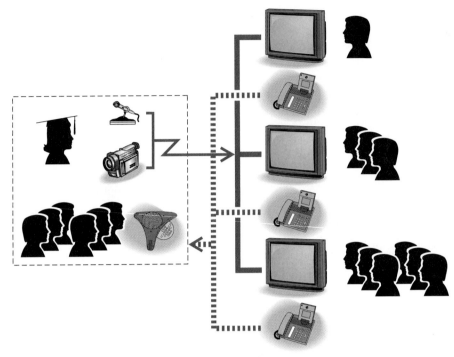

Figure 7.16

Television—one-way video, two-way audio. This is probably the most widely used and most economical means of adding immediate interactivity to instructional TV.

perceptible difference in the fluidity of the motion depicted, but participants easily adapt to this. Compressed

video is gaining popularity rapidly wherever two-way television is being used. (See "Close-Up: School–University Co-

Close-Up

SHARING TEACHERS VIA VIDEOCONFERENCING

How can small rural schools offer advanced courses in mathematics, foreign languages, and science when no single school has a large enough enrollment to justify its own teacher? Four school districts in Carroll County, Illinois, have been experimenting with a simplified two-way videoconferencing system as an answer to this question. Each participating school has set up one classroom as a teleconference room, equipped with cameras, microphones, video recorder, monitors, and a special effects generator/switcher. Classes are taught live at the school in which there is a qualified teacher; students in any of the other three schools may participate.

Students in the receiving schools watch and listen to the class. They can also be heard and seen by activating the camera and microphone in their own classroom. A camera mounted above the teacher's desk gives close-up views of visual materials.

Lessons can be videotaped for review by absent students. They can also be videotaped in advance when the instructor must be absent during usual class times.

Data source: Rhondo S. Robinson, professor, Northern Illinois University, De Kalb, IL.

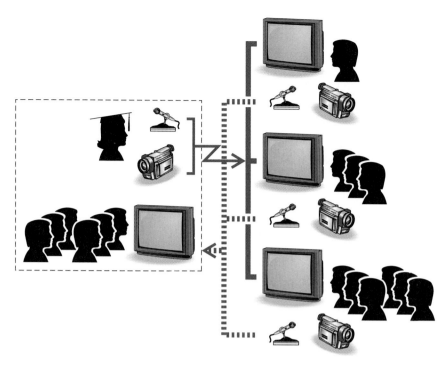

Figure 7.17

Television—two-way video, two-way audio. Full auditory and visual interactivity requires a camera and microphone at each reception site.

operation Through Compressed Video.") Compressed video is also used for computer desktop video (see Chapter 8).

ONLINE TECHNOLOGIES

Online technologies (those that rely on computer-based systems) have opened up an array of distance learning op-

portunities. Where once students had to drive a short distance to attend a class conveyed by a video or audio connection, computer-based systems let them remain in their home or workplace to participate in learning activities. Software programs, cameras, and an array of resources can give students distance learning experiences similar to those that used the older distance education systems. Students can attend class at a designated time, can participate in an audio or text-based chat, can post to bulletin board discussions, and can access information related to coursework right from the computer. (This type of learning experience is the subject of Chapter 8.)

Accessing Resources at a Distance

One element often overlooked in a distance learning situation is the access students have to resource materials. If a teacher wishes to have students engage in research or certain types of activities, it is critical that they have access to related materials. A teacher may need to change particular types of activities or to make special arrangements for materials to be sent to the distance-site classrooms. Students at a distance site should not be at a learning disadvantage because of limited resources. It is the teacher's responsibility, often

---

Close-Up

SCHOOL–UNIVERSITY COOPERATION THROUGH COMPRESSED VIDEO

The Wyoming Centers for Teaching and Learning Network (WCTLN) is a cooperative venture among school districts and the School of Education at the University of Wyoming. This network uses compressed video and other technologies to connect schools in nine districts with each other and with the university.

The telecommunication network was set up to deal with the problem of small populations spread over a vast geographic area. Many teachers work in small, isolated schools with limited curriculum offerings. Because of the relatively low cost of building and operating a compressed video system (compared with regular

broadband video), it is now possible for students in one locale to participate in live, two-way audio and video exchanges with students and teachers at other schools.

Besides being used to enrich the curricula at K–12 schools, the system is used by teachers and administrators for electronic inservice meetings, saving them from driving hundreds of miles to meet face to face. The School of Education uses the system to enable teacher trainees to observe real classrooms. The system also allows student teachers to be observed by their School of Education supervisors while they are working in the field. Considering that some of these school sites are a seven-hour drive from the university, the video system yields tremendous savings in time and effort.

Source: Landra Rezabek and Barbara Hakes, College of Education, University of Wyoming.

Close-Up

FREE CLEARINGHOUSE ON DISTANCE LEARNING

The National Distance Learning Center (NDLC) is a centralized online database containing detailed program listings for distance-learning courses, including credit and noncredit courses, teleconferences, seminars, and inservice training courses. The listings pertain to all audiences—primary, secondary, and continuing education. NDLC provides program information on courses available in all distance-learning formats, including satellite broadcast, audio- and videocassette, and print.

There is no charge to access the system or to scan the database, and access requires only a computer and modem; communications software for the modem will even be sent without charge if needed.

For more information, contact the National Distance Learning Center, Owensboro Community College, 4800 Hartford Road, Owensboro, KY 42303. The college's Web address is http://www.occ.uky.edu; you can access the NDLC database directly using Telnet at telnet://ndlc.occ.uky.edu. Visit these websites through the Web Links module in Chapter 7 of the Companion Website (http://www.prenhall.com/smaldino).

working closely with the school library media specialist, to ensure that all students have equal access to the materials essential for learning. While the World Wide Web has eased this concern a bit, there are still some courses where the resources for the students are not readily available on the Web, or copyright issues do not allow using the Web to provide those resources. Your school library media specialist will be aware of the copyright issues and will be able to help you provide easy access to materials.

Advantages

- *Cost efficiency.* All forms of broadcasting share the attribute of reaching geographically dispersed audiences in a cost-efficient way.
- *Audiovisual capacity.* All television systems allow the transmission of motion images and sound over a distance.
- *Two-way possibilities.* When learners can communicate with the instructor and other students via telephone or two-way video you can approximate a live classroom interaction.
- *Online possibilities.* When possible, online technologies can provide access to resources and to instruction that might not be otherwise possible.

Limitations

- *Cost for two-way.* Adding the capacity for two-way communication may require costly hardware installation, including a bridge if multiple sites are connected at once. If using telephones, there may be toll charges for the calls.
- *Facilities for two-way.* The special setups needed for two-way video require that a classroom be dedicated to this use, thus making it difficult to use the room for other purposes.

- *Isolation.* Learners who participate in broadcast lessons without talkback capabilities can feel like "second-class citizens" having little rapport with the rest of the group.
- *Technical problems.* Technical problems may interrupt the instruction and may create confusion and frustration for the instructor and students.
- *Inexperience.* Instructors may not feel comfortable teaching in this type of setting.
- *Reluctance.* Students may be reluctant to assume greater responsibility for their own learning.
- *Connectivity.* Students may have difficulty accessing certain types of online connections due to their access to the Internet.

ASSURE Case Connection

A statewide interactive television system is available and the science teachers can schedule it at times that are compatible with their classes. Options for delivering visuals include faxing and the Internet. Will the use of such a system make it possible for the teachers to work collaboratively to develop and deliver the instruction? Will the students be able to work together on their assignments?

Integration

Commercial and noncommercial stations are providing programming for use in educational settings. In fact, one-quarter of the programs used by teachers in schools originate from commercial stations. These include dramas, dance and music performances, documentaries, and news and public affairs programs. Popular television programs can also be used to spark discussions of social issues.

Copyright Concerns

DISTANCE LEARNING AND THE COPYRIGHT LAW

The electronic delivery of instruction has created new concerns related to copyright law. For the most part, fair use applies. However, certain specific considerations have been recognized in distance learning:

1. Off-air recordings for nonprofit educational institutions are to be retained no more than 45 days.
2. Off-air recordings may not be altered from their original content. This includes combining or merging, physically or electronically, to constitute teaching anthologies or compilations.
3. Broadcasting of copyrighted materials is allowed if the following terms are met:

- The broadcast is part of a systematic, ongoing instructional activity.
- It is directly related and of material assistance to the teaching of content.
- Transmission is received in classrooms only, or in similar settings normally devoted to instruction.
- The broadcast is aimed at regularly enrolled students and conducted by a recognized educational institution.

If the class is being recorded, it is a definite copyright infringement if prior approval for material presentation is not obtained.

For general information on copyright, see the Copyright Concerns in Chapter 1. Suggested readings on copyright appear at the end of Chapter 1.

Summary: Using the ASSURE Model for Distance Education

As with other media and technology, the ASSURE model introduced in Chapter 3 is helpful in preparing lessons incorporating the use of distance education.

Analyze Learners

Lesson development begins by identifying your students' unique attributes and learning characteristics. You also will wish to determine their various levels of experience with using distance learning.

State Objectives

Before stating specific objectives, you may wish to explore how you want students to achieve their learning in a distance education setting. It is important to state specific objectives after you have identified the scope of the technologies you will be able to use in distance education.

Select Methods, Media, and Materials

Selecting your method will depend on a number of issues, including your students, how much experience they have had with the topic, expected outcomes, and so on. Once you have chosen your method, you move to selecting the appropriate media to help your students learn.

The materials you select will depend on students' ages, experience, expectations, and, more importantly, their access to these resources at a distance.

Utilize Media and Materials

Access to types of media will affect how you use them. If you have access to media that is available to the class, it might be easier for you to use those resources. If you have access to limited equipment or resources, you might rely on the resources at the different distance settings.

Require Learner Participation

Have students do specific activities in their distance settings. Students will find more value in the learning experience if they are able to be actively engaged in their learning. Have students make presentations using *PowerPoint* instead of sitting passively. Or, students could use the technology to create learning experiences for their peers.

Evaluate and Revise

Student work is integral to the distance learning environment. Students can be assessed on the quality of their interactions and on how well they have presented their learning. It is important to consider how materials that rely on distance education help students to interpret information. As with all media- and technology-based lessons, you may choose to revise your selection of materials after you have determined how well they have worked. In addition, you want to be certain that all materials used have been cleared of any potential copyright issues.

ASSURE Case in Practice: Exploring New Worlds

All of the ASSURE Cases in Practice in this text and an electronic template for creating your own ASSURE Lesson can be found on the enclosed "Classroom Link Portfolio" CD-ROM.

Three science teachers in different communities around the state decided to work together on a unit about space exploration. They wanted to expand the resources available to their students by using the statewide community college interactive instructional television system.

Analyze Learners

General Characteristics

The students in the three classes are all 17 to 18 years old and reside in rural communities that are miles apart. They are a homogeneous group, both in terms of their socioeconomic background and in their general learning abilities. Class size ranges from 18 to 22 students.

Entry Competencies

The students have engaged in hands-on science in each of their classes. They have not worked with teachers or students from other schools prior to this experience. They have never used the interactive television system. The students have had little experience talking with experts in the field of science other than their teachers.

Learning Styles

The majority of the students prefer to work in small groups with their peers. They do not like to be at the front of the classroom presenting information. They have not experienced seeing themselves on television before and it is anticipated they will appear shy and unwilling to talk in this class.

State Objectives

The students will be able to do the following:
1. Using the interactive television system, students will engage in a dialog with experts in space exploration, with each student preparing a question in advance of the session.
2. After the interviews and gathering additional data, students will prepare a statement on their views of space exploration.
3. Using the interactive television system, students will discuss their divergent views with the experts by preparing presentations and transmitting them between sites.

Select Methods, Media, and Materials

The teachers, working together, decided to begin the space exploration unit by posing the question, "Is manned space exploration an appropriate way to extend our knowledge of outer space?" Each teacher will conduct a discussion with students prior to connecting them via the statewide television system.

Experts who favor both manned and unmanned space exploration will be invited, via the television system, to present their views on the subject. Students at their schools, using the school media centers and the Internet, will prepare a position paper on their views of manned versus unmanned space exploration.

Students will also present their views to all three classes using the interactive television system. After the presentations, the teachers will group the students to prepare their presentations for the experts. Groups of students will present their views on this topic to the experts at a third interactive television session.

Utilize Media and Materials

The students were taught how to use the interactive television equipment in stages. First they were taught how to use the microphones to ask questions of each expert presenter. Next they were taught how to use the cameras for displaying their documents and showing themselves or others during both their own presentations and the later dialog with the experts.

As students were preparing their position papers they worked with the library media specialist to access resources on the Internet. Many of them used the World Wide Web to locate sites around the world.

Require Learner Participation

The active engagement of students in this project was monitored to ensure that all students had a question for each of the invited experts. Further, each student had to prepare a presentation using the interactive television system. Finally, working in groups, the students had to prepare a presentation to engage in dialog with the experts.

Evaluate and Revise

At the end of the unit, the teachers conducted a debriefing with each of their classes to determine if the students found this to be a valuable experience. By listing the students' responses, the three teachers could decide if they wished to engage in a similar activity in the future. The teachers also contacted the invited experts for their reactions to the experience and to see what the teachers might do to improve the exchange of information.

From these data, the teachers learned that the students valued the opportunity to meet with the experts. They liked hearing what the experts had to say. They found writing their position papers to be challenging, especially knowing they had to share them with everyone else. Some expressed concern they were not able to do a good job with this part. Also, students expressed concern with having to work with others in the groups to prepare their presentations for the experts. They found this to be very different from anything they had done before.

The experts stated they enjoyed the experience because not only did they get to work with high school students, but they also had the chance to hear divergent views from young people. They were willing to engage in this type of activity in the future.

After discussing the unit and agreeing on some procedural changes, the teachers and the school media specialists all agreed that they would like to work on this type of activity again.

Create Your Own ASSURE Lesson

Using the ASSURE model, design a lesson for a scenario from the Companion Website or use a scenario of your own design. Use one of the methods described in Chapter 1 and information from this chapter related to incorporating distance education into your instructional setting. Be sure to include information about the audience, the objectives, and all other elements of the ASSURE model. When completed, reflect on the process you used and what you have learned about matching audience, content, method, and materials.

Classroom Link Portfolio Activities

Use the "Classroom Link Portfolio" CD-ROM and the Companion Website as resources in completing these activities. To complete the following activities online go to the Portfolio Activities module in Chapter 7 of the Companion Website (http://www.prenhall.com/smaldino).

1. *Planning Distance Instruction.* Locate a lesson on the "Classroom Link Portfolio" CD-ROM or the Internet on a topic or curriculum standard of your choice. First, note the activities and media incorporated into the lesson. Second, note the changes needed to provide that learning experience at a distance. Third, identify the reasons for the change. Then, describe the assessment strategy you would use. Cite the source. (ISTE NETS-T 2.B & C; 3.B; 6.A)

2. *Written Reflection.* Reflect on your prior learning experiences. When have you engaged in distance learning, either formally or informally? Describe that experience. What occurred in the distance-learning experience that helped you learn? What would you have liked to have had included as part of that experience? What does this mean for you as a teacher? (ISTE NETS-T 5.A & 5.B; 6.E)

Integration Assessments

To complete the specified activities online go to the Integration Assessments module in Chapter 7 of the Companion Website (http://www.prenhall.com/smaldino).

1. Investigate the use of radio for instructional purposes in a local school or college. Check with a local public radio station to see if it supports any specific instructional activities. (ISTE NETS-T 1.A)

2. Interview a teacher who regularly uses broadcast television programs in the classroom. Prepare a brief written or recorded report addressing the objectives covered, techniques utilized, and

problems encountered. An example might be elementary students using a two-way audio/video system to investigate a community issue. (ISTE NETS-T 5.B)

 3. Generate a list of interesting uses of teleconferencing telecommunications for a course you are currently enrolled in. Whom might you and your classmates communicate with? For what purposes? (ISTE NETS-T 2.C)

4. Prepare an abstract of a report of a research or demonstration project related to instructional telecommunications (e.g., two schools sharing one teacher by means of interactive instructional television). (ISTE NETS-T 1.B, 4.B, 5.B)

5. Observe a class taught at a distance. Describe how the teacher and students interact with each other. Also, describe the types and uses of media within the lesson. (ISTE NETS-T 5.B)

Organizations

Visit these websites through the Web Links module in Chapter 7 of the Companion Website (http://www.prenhall.com/smaldino).

Agency for Instructional Technology (AIT)
P.O. Box A
1800 N. Stonelake Drive
Bloomington, IN 47402-0120
http://www.ait.net

Produces television programs and computer courseware as the coordinating agency of a consortium that includes most of the United States and the Canadian provinces. It also serves as a national distribution center. It publishes a newsletter and an annual catalog listing dozens of series incorporating several hundred separate programs. Emphasis is on the elementary and secondary levels.

Association for Educational Communications and Technology (AECT)
1800 N. Stonelake Drive
Suite 2
Bloomington, IN 47404
http://www.aect.org

Holds conferences, publishes journals and books related to instructional uses of media (including TV), and represents the educational communication/technology profession. Its Division of Telecommunications addresses the concerns of members who work in instructional TV and radio.

The Cable Center
2327 E. Evans
Denver, CO 80208
http://www.cablecenter.org

Serves as a source for information about cable telecommunications. It provides comprehensive and educational perspectives on the industry. The center engages in research on the use of cable television.

Sesame Workshop (formerly Children's Television Workshop)
1 Lincoln Plaza
New York, NY 10023
http://www.sesameworkshop.org

Corporation for Public Broadcasting (CPB)
901 E Street, NW
Washington, DC 20004-2006
http://www.cpb.org

Nonprofit, private corporation established and funded in part by the federal government. It performs a broad coordinating function for the nation's public radio and television stations and supports the interests of public broadcasting in general. CPB carries out research on the educational applications of television and coordinates the Annenberg Project, aimed at providing programming for higher education.

Media Communications Association–International (formerly International Television Association)
7600 Terrace Avenue
Suite 203
Middleton, WI 53562
http://www.mca-i.org

Organization of nonbroadcast television professionals in 14 countries, primarily in North America. It supports the use of television in the private sector—training, communications, and public relations—and sponsors regional and national conferences and an awards program.

Satellite Educational Resources Consortium (SERC)
PO Box 50,008
Columbia, SC 29250
http://www.serc.org

References

Children's Television Workshop. 1990. *A study of the role of educational television programming in elementary schools.* New York: Author.

Rockman, Saul. 1976. Instructional television is alive and well. In *The future of public broadcasting,* edited by Douglass Cater and Michael J. Nyhan. New York: Praeger.

U.S. Congress, Office of Technology Assessment. 1989. *Linking for learning: A new course for education.* Washington, DC: U.S. Government Printing Office.

Suggested Readings

Bansal, Kiron, and Sohanvir S. Chaudhary. 1999. Interactive radio for supporting distance education: An evaluation study. *Indian Journal of Open Learning,* 8(1): 61–71.

Blubaugh, Donelle. 1999. Bringing cable into the classroom. *Educational Leadership,* 56(5): 61–65.

Burns, John T. 2002. Evaluation of staff development and training models to support implementation of videoconferencing technology for teaching and learning in a distributed university. *Quarterly Review of Distance Education,* 3(3): 327–340.

Chaudhary, Sohanvir S., and Kiron Bansal. 2000. Interactive radio counseling in Indira Gandhi National Open University: A study. *Journal of Distance Education,* 15(2): 37–51.

Cheney, Christine O., Michael M. Warner, and Diann N. Laing. 2001. Developing a web-enhanced, televised distance education course: Practices, problems, and potential. *Computers in the Schools,* 17(3–4): 171–188.

Cyrs, Thomas E., and Frank A. Smith. 1990. *Teleclass teaching: A research guide,* 2nd ed. Las Cruces, NM: Center for Educational Development, New Mexico State University.

Fulford, Catherine P., and Greg Sakaguchi. 2001. Developing a taxonomy of interaction strategies for two-way interactive distance education television. *International Journal of Instructional Media,* 28(4): 375–396.

Keegan, Desmond. 1990. *Foundations of distance education,* 2nd ed. New York, Routledge.

MacIntosh, Judith. 2001. Learner concerns and teaching strategies for video-conferencing. *Journal of Continuing Education in Nursing,* 32(6): 260–265.

Mantyla, Karen. 2001. *The 2000/2001 distance learning yearbook.* New York: McGraw-Hill.

McGowan, Andrew Scott. 1995. Reaching the public through cable and educational television. *Phi Delta Kappan,* 77(2): 182.

McLoughlin, Catherine. 1999. Providing enrichment and acceleration in the electronic classroom: A case study of audiographic conferencing. *Journal of Special Education Technology,* 14(2): 54–69.

Petracchi, Helen E. 2000. Distance education: What do our students tell us? *Research on Social Work,* 10(3): 362–376.

Roblyer, M. D. 1999. Is choice important in distance learning? A study of student motives for taking Internet-based courses in high school and community college levels. *Journal of Research on Computing in Education,* 32(1): 157–171.

Ryan-Nicholls, Kimberly D. 2001. Interactive instructional television (IITV) classroom system design. *Quarterly Review of Distance Education,* 2(3): 265–274.

Schwalb, Edward M. 2003. *ITV handbook: Technologies and standards.* Upper Saddle River, NJ: Prentice Hall.

Simonson, M., Smaldino, S., Albright, M. & Zvacek, S. 2003. *Teaching and learning at a distance: Foundations of distance education,* 2nd ed. Upper Saddle River, NJ: Merrill-Prentice Hall.

Soloman, K. 1993. Copyright issues and distance learning. *Teleconference,* 12(1): 18–21.

Thoms, Karen Jarrett. 1999. Teaching via ITV: Taking instructional design to the next level. *T.H.E. Journal,* 26(9): 60–66.

U.S. Agency for International Development. 1990. *Interactive radio instruction: Confronting a crisis in basic education.* Washington, DC: Author, Educational Development Center.

CHAPTER 8

Online Learning

Outline

Online Learning
 Networks
  Issues

Knowledge Objectives

1. Compare and contrast *online learning* and *distance education*.
2. Discuss the advantages, limitations, and integration of electronic learning.
3. Describe the characteristics of local area networks (LANs), wide area networks (WANs), and wireless networks.
4. Describe the characteristics of the Internet, including its advantages, limitations, and instructional applications.
5. Select a grade level you are interested in teaching. Discuss the pros and cons of the amount of access and supervision students at this level should have when using the Internet.
6. Describe the characteristics of intranets, including their advantages, limitations, and instructional applications.
7. Compare and contrast the characteristics, advantages, and limitations of local area networks, wide area networks, wireless networks, and intranets from an educational or training perspective.
8. Discuss appropriate etiquette when using the Internet. Include 10 guidelines for users.
9. Select an example from a "Copyright Concerns" or create another example and prepare a presentation for your class that reflects your opinion on the issue.

Professional Vocabulary

online learning
electronic learning (e-learning)
blended learning
hybrid learning
WebQuest
network
electronic mail (e-mail)
attachment
newsgroup
listserv
download
chat room
Internet
local area network (LAN)
file server
wide area network (WAN)
computer conferencing
desktop video conferencing
wireless network

Internet service provider (ISP)
Integrated Services Digital Network (ISDN)
Digital Subscriber Line (DSL)
cable modem
gateway
portal
search engine
World Wide Web (the Web)
hypertext transfer protocol (HTTP)
Web page
website
uniform resource locator (URL)
intranet
computer platform
firewall
acceptable use policy (AUP)
netiquette
emoticon

Online learning (also called **electronic learning,** or **e-learning**) is the result of instruction that is delivered electronically using computers and computer-based media. The materials are often accessed through a network. Sources include websites, the Internet, intranets, CD-ROMs, and DVDs. In addition to delivering instruction, e-learning can monitor learner performance and report learner progress. E-learning is not just accessing information (e.g., Web pages), but guiding learners to specific outcomes (e.g., objectives).

ASSURE
Case Challenge

We have developed a case study for this chapter to help you see how online learning technology can be integrated into learning activities. At the end of the chapter you will be challenged to develop your own ASSURE lesson for a case study of your choice using the ASSURE model and incorporating the technology and media described in this chapter. To help you prepare your lesson, we have included hints

(called "ASSURE Case Connections") throughout the chapter as they relate to the ASSURE Case Challenge.

High school social studies teacher Mr. Plosnik wants to develop a lesson for his students to study the Holocaust and its implications for their lives today and in the future. He wants to dispel misinformation his students may have about the Holocaust. One question he wants to address is, "Could the Holocaust happen again?"

The students are juniors and seniors with a range of experiences and abilities. Assume that whatever technology and media you might want to use is available in Mr. Plosnik's school.

Often e-learning is combined with live, face-to-face instruction and called **blended learning,** or **hybrid learning**. In this chapter we will explore learning using e-mail, the Internet, intranets, networks, and the issues associated with their use. CD-ROMs and DVDs are discussed in Chapters 10 and 12.

As teachers, you need to be aware of the variety of options for both distance education (Chapter 7) and online learning. You need to be able to select the best technology and media to help your students learn.

Because online electronic learning is essentially a subset of distance learning, the distinctions between them can be confusing. There is a lot of overlap. See Table 8.1 for a comparison, with distinctions noted.

ONLINE LEARNING

The potential for educational applications of online learning is growing. Students no longer only have access to textbooks, but to content materials located far beyond the walls of the school building. You and your students can obtain information housed in multiple, distant, and inaccessible libraries around the world! Resources once beyond the dreams of all but the most affluent are potentially available to everyone. Thus, increasing numbers of schools are getting "wired" with networking services such as AOL and EduCom.

Students and teachers can enhance classroom learning by accessing information from an array of sources (databases, libraries, special interest groups), communicating via computer with other students or with experts in a particular field of study, and exchanging data. Activities such as those conducted by National Geographic make it possible for students and teachers alike to reap the benefits of connecting into a national network of students, teachers, and scientists to investigate a variety of topics (Figure 8.1).

Teachers and their students can access electronic documents to enrich their study. Students can actively participate because online learning provides an interactive learning environment. Students can link electronic information to their papers and projects, making them

Table 8.1
Comparison of Distance Education and Online Learning

Distance Education (Chapter 7)	**Online Learning (Chapter 8)**
Learning via telecommunications media— radio, telephone, television	Instruction delivered by computer, often using networks
Communication is often one way	Communication is usually two way
Similarities = Both can be used as part of organized instructional program.	
Both can be used at all levels (P–20).	
Both can be used in both formal and informal education.	
Both can be used for all subject-matter disciplines.	
Both done with physical separation of learners and teacher.	

Figure 8.1
Wireless networks allow students to connect to the Internet from any setting.

"living" documents wired with hypertext buttons. (See Chapter 6 for a discussion of hypermedia.)

Because computers have the ability to deliver information in any media (including print, video, and recordings of voice and music) the computer has become a boundless library. As students are able to communicate instantly with text, picture, voice, data, and two-way video, the resulting interactions are changing the roles of students and teachers. Teachers can now be separated geographically from their students, and students can learn from other students in classrooms all over the world.

Advantages

- *Variety of media.* The Internet is a versatile means of delivering information to learners around the world. Internet sites may contain a variety of media, including text, audio, graphics, animation, video, and downloadable software.
- *Up-to-date information.* Until recently, educators were limited to the resources in their classrooms or school buildings. Now, with the ability to connect to resources in the community and throughout the world, new vistas on teaching and learning have opened up. Students can access libraries and databases well beyond local limits; this expands the horizons for smaller and rural schools as well as for individuals participating in home schooling.
- *Navigation.* A primary advantage of the Internet is the ability to move easily within and among documents. With the push of a button or the click of a mouse, users can search a variety of documents in multiple locations without moving from their computers.

- *Idea exchange.* Students can engage in "conversation" with experts in specific fields of study. Further, they can participate in activities that allow them to exchange ideas with other students, even those living in other countries.
- *Convenient communication.* E-mail allows people in various locations to share ideas, just as they do now on the telephone, but without playing "telephone tag" so common among busy people. Users can "speak" to each other at different times and respond at their own convenience. Records are kept of their exchanges.
- *Low cost.* The costs of hardware, software, telephone time, and telecommunication services are nominal and are decreasing.

Limitations

- *Age-inappropriate material.* One concern is that some of the topics discussed on computer networks, especially on the Internet, are not appropriate for younger students. Tobacco and alcohol ads are on the Internet along with games and music kids enjoy. Students can find their way, innocently enough, into topics that might be too advanced for their understanding or too adult for their viewing. Close supervision is essential. There is no organization or agency controlling activity on some computer networks. Control is in the hands of individuals; consequently, students may access questionable materials. Software, such as *NetNanny,* is available to prohibit access to topics specified by the teacher or parent, and is now required in libraries that receive federal funds.
- *Copyright.* Because information is so easily accessible, it is also very simple for an individual to quickly download a file and, with a few changes, illegally appropriate it. Thus, students may turn in a paper or project that is not their own work.
- *Unprecedented growth.* It is estimated that several thousand new websites are added to the Internet every day. This growth makes finding information extremely difficult. To assist in information retrieval, several commercial companies and universities provide search engines that follow Web links and return results matching your query.
- *Support.* Good technical support needs to be readily available. Without such support and thoughtful management, a computer network may die quickly. Problems on a network can disable a lab or even shut down an entire school or corporation. Technical supervisors are needed to set up and maintain networks.
- *Access.* Whether by means of a hardwired or wireless system or a modem, all users must have a way of connecting to the network.

- *Access speed*. Another limitation is the speed at which users can access information. Lengthy wait times can be prevented through prudent Web page design. Web pages designed for modem users should contain text and no individual graphic larger than 50K. Another way to reduce wait time is to install Integrated Services Digital Network (ISDN) digital communication lines capable of transmitting information at speeds of 128 kilobytes per second (kbps) or more.
- *Lack of quality control*. Users need to be critical thinkers and readers who know how to evaluate information. Everything posted on the Internet is not "gospel." Anybody can post anything on the Web, including unsubstantiated, erroneous, or untruthful information.

Integration

Whole courses and programs of study are available through online learning. Students can access courses that might not be available to them at their school. Students can take advanced placement classes from other high schools or from colleges and universities anywhere in the world. It is possible to obtain a high school or college diploma without ever having set foot in a classroom. There are many software applications (e.g., *WebCT, Blackboard*) that provide both ease of access to the instruction and resources for the instructor and students for successful study online.

There are issues that need to be addressed by anyone wishing to venture into this area of academic study. First is the credentials of the institution offering the degree. Another is the issue of the quality and rigor of the courses. Finally, there are issues related to costs associated with online courses, such as the equipment requirements, online charges, and tuition.

E-mail can be integrated into lessons and used by students to gather information from, and ask questions of, individuals beyond the school walls (e.g., other students and experts). For example, during a unit on weather, students can gather weather data (temperatures, rainfall, and wind direction) from students in other geographic areas. They can also request weather maps from the local TV meteorologist, which can be sent as attachments to e-mail. Experts from the National Weather Service can be contacted for the answers to specific questions. Of course, as the teacher, you should always make any necessary arrangement in advance.

Students can also use e-mail to gather information for individual projects. For example, middle school students selecting careers to investigate can contact individuals in those professions for answers to student-generated questions. The products of the students' investigation can be "job reports," to be shared with the class either as an oral presentation or a written document.

Although students can access a rich array of information on the Web, their searches often use random or low-level thinking skills. Teachers can use a **"WebQuest"** to help their students use the Web effectively in gathering information in student-centered learning activities (Dodge, 1999). Developed by Bernie Dodge at San Diego State University, WebQuests infuse the Internet into the school's curriculum. A WebQuest is an inquiry-oriented activity in which some or all of the information that students interact with comes from resources on the Internet. Students follow a series of steps to gather information meaningful to the task. Teachers design a WebQuest with specific learning outcomes in mind. There are specific steps for the students in a quest:

1. *Introduction*—A scenario points to key issues or concepts to prepare the students to ask questions.
2. *Task*—Students identify issues or problems and form questions for the quest.
3. *Process*—In groups, students assume roles and begin to identify the procedures they will follow to gather information to answer their questions.
4. *Sources*—Resources are identified by the teacher and students to investigate in their quest. This is one area where the teacher helps to provide the links to websites and to provide access to print-based materials in the classroom or school library.
5. *Conclusion*—This is the end of the quest, but it invites students to continue to investigate issues or problems. Quests often end with an evaluation of the process students used along with benchmarks for achievement.

WebQuests can be applied to the following types of lessons and information sources, among others:

- Monitoring current events for social studies
- Science activities such as tracking weather and studying space probes on other planets (e.g., NASA at http://www.nasa.gov)
- Sharing instructional ideas and techniques with other teachers (e.g., Kathy Schrock's Guide at http://school.discovery.com/schrockguide)
- Databases of teaching methods, instructional strategies, and lesson plans
- Teacher training workshops, tutorials, and courses available online
- Teacher discussion groups with online exchange of advice and information
- Teacher information on curriculum topics (e.g., T.H.E. *Journal*'s Education Resource for Teachers at http://www.eduhound.com)
- Job banks and résumé services

One growing use of electronic learning at the P–12 level promotes writing skills by connecting students with "electronic pen pals" or "key pals." For example, one teacher recently connected her elementary students with students in a language arts methods class at a university across the state (see "Close-Up: Key Pals"). The students exchange e-mail, with the university students helping the younger ones with their writing. Both groups benefit from this experience. The younger students learn ways to improve their writing, and the college students learn about working with children.

Systems have also been set up that allow students from different countries, even those speaking different languages, to learn about each other's cultures through computer-mediated communications.

In addition, mentors can be linked with students to help them learn about a variety of topics. Students can participate in projects conducted with other classes in other locations, allowing students to plan and produce projects collaboratively. Examples include sharing local history with students in other geographic locations and collaborating with students in different classes to solve complex mathematical problems.

Communications with parents can be enhanced for those homes with e-mail access. General information can be sent to all parents or specific information or questions can be addressed to an individual student's parents or guardians. For those parents without e-mail, teachers will need to employ written correspondence or the telephone.

Teachers can also use e-mail to share ideas with other teachers. Lesson plans can be sent as attachments. Questions can be asked of an individual teacher or a group of teachers (e.g., all physics teachers in a state).

Electronic communities provide their members with access to information. A number of cities have created websites that involve a broad cross-section of their community, including schools, businesses, local government, and social agencies. The artificial wall between the classroom and the world beyond is dissolving, making it possible for students and teachers to access information and people from every imaginable source.

Many museums are creating online exhibits or tours of their collections. An increasing number of online journals and magazines are being published, either as supplements to existing print versions or as entirely new efforts. Most major publishers have put their catalogs on the Web, making it easy to locate and order books, software, and other products. Many publishers are willing to make their actual products available online. They provide a trial package, one that "dissolves" within a certain period of time—usually 30 days. However, there is still the issue of illegal copying and distribution of materials, which makes some publishers wary of complete and unlimited access to software and files.

Currently many *Fortune* 500 companies are using online learning for training applications. Providing training modules (whether or not computer based) over a corporate intranet (discussed later in this chapter) helps to reduce costs and to decrease the time required to provide employees with the latest version of materials. Updating training materials to reflect changes in the company's policies or products is relatively easy. In the past, revisions often required shipping printed materials and/or computer disks to all training sites. Electronic learning provides flexibility to employees as well because they may study materials at any time and at any location. Trainees can submit answers to tests through the intranet. Once

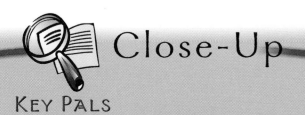

Close-Up

KEY PALS

Rick Traw, professor at the University of Northern Iowa, wanted to expand the methods experiences of his elementary education students in the area of language arts. Because of scheduling difficulties, it was impossible for him to have his students go to a school to work on writing skills with a group of elementary children. With the aid of the university's expanded computer network system, it was possible for the students at the elementary school to be connected to the university students. The elementary students met their university pen pals (or "key pals") and began to exchange letters. The children had a new and exciting audience for their writing, and the university students had an opportunity to learn about children's writing firsthand. Traw and the classroom teacher provided guidance to the college students in techniques for assisting children with their writing.

the answers are in the database, they are scored and the results made available immediately to trainees and the course administrator, even if they are thousands of miles apart. Online learning is very useful for training when the audience is large and geographically dispersed and when the instruction is updated frequently (see "Close-Up: Deere & Company Delivers Training over Its Intranet").

For additional information on this topic, or to visit these websites, go to the Web Links module in Chapter 8 of the Companion Website (http://www.prenhall.com/smaldinio).

ASSURE Case Connection

What might Mr. Plosnik's objectives be for this lesson? How may he and his students find media and materials electronically? How could students use the network—for communication, for information retrieval, for information publishing? For more than one purpose?

NETWORKS

With improvements in technology and telecommunication systems, it is possible to use computers to connect students to people and resources outside of the class-room. Once you connect computers in ways that enable people to communicate and share information, you have a **network**. Networks connect schools, homes, libraries, educational institutions, organizations, and businesses so that students, families, and professionals can access or share information and instruction instantly in several ways.

One of the most common uses of the Internet in education is **electronic mail (e-mail)**. Students (and you) can communicate via e-mail with other students, teachers, and experts anywhere in the world. The sender can include **attachments**, which are separate files (e.g., documents and graphics), in addition to the e-mail message.

Internet users can communicate with one another by participating in discussion groups, which are of two types: **newsgroups** (sometimes called *chat groups* or *conferences*) and mailing lists (also called **listservs**). Both newsgroups and mailing lists are typically dedicated to a single subject, and allow you to read comments, questions, and answers of others on the same subject and to post comments, questions, and answers of your own.

You and your students can receive, or **download,** information (retrieving files, documents, data, computer programs, or images from other computer systems). This information can be used for individual assignments

Close-Up

DEERE & COMPANY DELIVERS TRAINING OVER ITS INTRANET

Deere & Company, manufacturer of a range of equipment under the John Deere name, uses its intranet to deliver self-study training courses to technicians. Its training consists of computer hardware–related courses for its field technicians located around the world. The courses are designed as updates to provide trainees with supplemental information on new equipment. Trainees register for the three- to four-hour courses, receive a password, log on to the firewall-protected intranet, choose the module they wish to take, and work on the course as time permits—often at home. On completion, trainees take an online test, which is sent to the training department for grading. Results are e-mailed to the trainee, the trainee's manager, and the human resources department. Consequently trainees receive feedback on their performance much faster than in mailed correspondence courses in the past. Other advantages include savings in postage, printing, travel, and employee time away from the job.

Source: Deere & Company.

and group projects. There is a wealth of information available beyond the classroom or the school's library and media center.

Students and teachers may engage in one-on-one communication in real time in a written conversation, using specially designed text entry windows called **chat rooms.** Multiple users can communicate simultaneously using text rather than voice. For example, teachers can conduct small group instruction and discussions regardless of where the students are physically—in another classroom, in another building, or at home. Students can also communicate in real time with each other. Unfortunately, students may "chat" when they should be attending to classroom activities.

The value of a network is that any individual can communicate with anyone else on the network. Additionally, all individuals can access information on the network regardless of the type of computer each one has. Computer networks come in many sizes and are used for many types of applications. The most widely known and used network is the **Internet.** Actually, the

Internet is an international collection of computer networks, a colossal network of networks!

Local Area Network (LAN)

The simplest of all networks is a **local area network (LAN).** A LAN connects computers within a limited area, normally a building, office, or laboratory. These networks connect individual computers to one another to permit exchange of files and other resources (Figure 8.2).

A LAN relies on a centralized computer called a **file server** that "serves" all other computers connected to it via special wiring. A computer lab is often itself a LAN because all the computers in the lab are connected to a single file server, usually tucked away in a closet or other out-of-the-way space. Whole buildings can also be connected to a local area network. A single computer, generally located in the office or media center, can serve as an entire school's file server. Through a LAN, all of the classrooms in a school can have access to the school's collection of software.

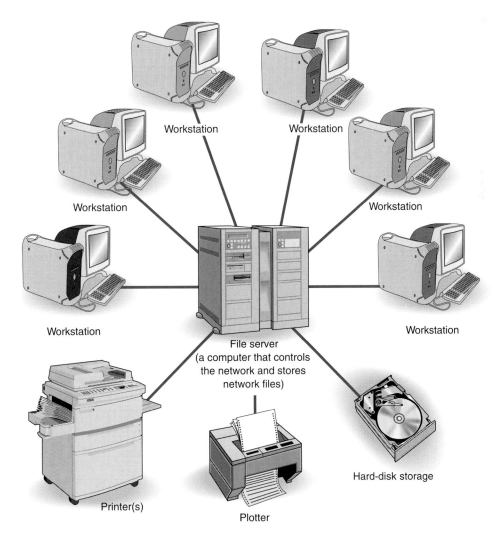

Figure 8.2

A typical local area network (LAN) for a computer lab.

Figure 8.3
Students can use a WAN to interact with other students and teachers throughout the district.

Wide Area Network (WAN)

Networks that extend beyond the walls of a room or building are called **wide area networks (WANs).** Some WANs use a hardwired configuration; a campuswide network connecting all buildings via a cable or fiber system is one such example. In this arrangement, the buildings are linked to a centralized computer that serves as the host for all the software used in common.

Even though a WAN can connect computers over a wide geographic area (across a city or state or even a country, for example), it often connects the buildings within a school system or on a college campus (Figure 8.3).

Computer conferencing connects two or more computers together for textual and graphical information exchange. In the past, this type of technology was very expensive, so educators were not able to afford it. Now the classroom computer can be connected with people and resources well beyond the limits of the school building.

Desktop video conferencing is real-time (synchronous) person-to-person or group conferencing on the Internet. With special software and a video camera, you can experience audio and full-color video "chats" on the computer. Everyone can participate in the "live" discussion. A group can interactively share documents and information and have access to such features as a whiteboard and chat windows.

Within a school, LANs can also reduce a technology coordinator's workload, which might otherwise include installing software, inventorying software, and other such tasks. Coordinators can then spend more time working with teachers and students rather than with machines and software. For example, the media center can store its catalog of materials on the file server. Teachers and students then have easy access to the information available on a certain topic.

Wireless Network

As the name implies, a **wireless network** connects computers without wire. Instead it uses radio frequency, microwave, or infrared technology that relies on a base station for connection to the network. Such networks use transmitters placed inside the room, throughout the building, or across campus and operate in the same manner as hardwired networks. Some cities are installing wireless networks in their downtown areas. Wireless networks omit the need for cabling, which can be costly to install, particularly in older buildings. Computers are also no longer bound to workstations. Laptops may be used anywhere within the room, building, or campus.

The Internet

The Internet is a worldwide system for linking smaller computer networks together. It is a network of networks with a frequently changing collection of millions of computer networks serving tens of millions of people around the world (Figure 8.4). Any individual on the Internet can communicate with anyone else on the Internet. Users can access any information, regardless of the type of computer they have, because of standard *protocols* that allow all computers to communicate with each other. Most information is shared without charge except for whatever access fee is required to maintain an account with an **Internet service provider (ISP)** such as America Online (AOL), Yahoo!, or any of the many local or community ISPs. Many businesses and most colleges and universities provide Internet accounts to their employees, faculty, and students at no charge.

Both telephone companies and television cable companies provide high-speed access to the Internet. **Integrated Services Digital Network (ISDN)** lines provide speeds up to 5 times that of regular analog phone lines. A **Digital Subscriber Line (DSL)** provides even faster access—up to 30 times that of a standard phone line. TV cable companies offer a comparable high-speed service through a **cable modem.** All of these access services are popular with the home consumer.

Special communication software connects the computer to a telecommunication service. When you make a connection to the Internet you enlist the help of four communication services: your computer, the ISP, the server (host computer), and the telecommunications network (communication software and a modem and phone or cable modem). Your computer (the *client*) runs communications software. Your modem and communications software provide an open path between your computer and your ISP. The ISP provides you a link to the Internet.

Many educational and commercial networks are developing ways to connect to the Internet. These connections, referred to as **gateways** or **portals,** are designed to

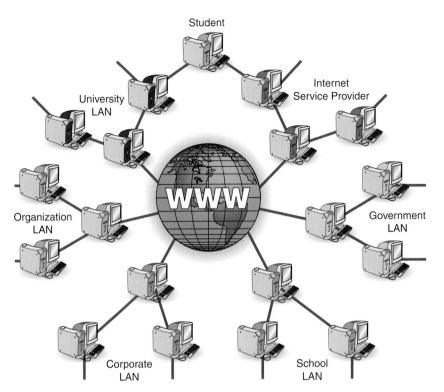

Figure 8.4
The Internet is a collection of computer networks. A student, for example, might access the Internet from her home computer either through the University LAN or through an Internet service provider.

der copyright. Unless a document indicates that you have the right to reproduce it (many Internet postings do just that), you must obtain permission to make more than a single copy for personal use (see "Copyright Concerns" in this chapter and in Chapter 1).

Internet Services. The Internet connects thousands of computer networks worldwide. It provides users with several basic types of connection services:

- Electronic mail (e-mail) for person-to-person communication
- A type of electronic, public bulletin board enabling a person to connect with a group interested in the same topic
- Information search capabilities for accessing libraries and databases of information throughout the world
- Access to highly specialized computer programs not readily available to individuals

provide access to many different services. The capabilities of any one service are thus expanded. The attraction is that the maze of connections is largely "transparent" to the user. Users just *log on* (enter the computer system, often with a special password for privacy) to their computer, connect to their networking service or ISP, and begin to exchange information (Figure 8.5).

Complicating information retrieval is the fact that the Internet does not operate hierarchically. There are no comprehensive directory trees or indexes for Internet resources. There is no Library of Congress cataloging scheme or Dewey Decimal system. You can consider the Internet as a library where every shelf is labeled "Miscellaneous." Finding one interesting service or item of information is no guarantee that you're on the right track to others. In fact, most of the Internet's resources are in little cul-de-sacs on the network, not linked in any predictable way to other, similar resources. You find information on the Internet using **search engines,** programs that identify websites containing user-entered keywords or phrases (see "Searching the Internet," in Classroom Resources, Section C).

When searching the Internet it is important to respect copyright laws and the intellectual property of others, the same as when doing research using traditional methods. Materials on the Internet and items downloaded from commercial services are generally un-

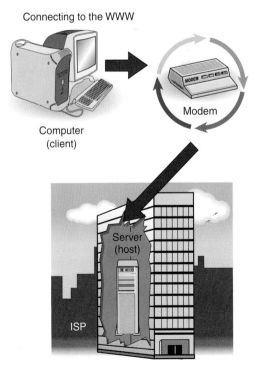

Figure 8.5
You can connect to the World Wide Web from your home or classroom through an Internet service provider (ISP).

Close-Up

NETWORK TERMS

An array of tools and software is used with the Internet and the World Wide Web. Here are brief descriptions of some of them:

- *E-mail*—a method of electronic communication that enables users to send and receive messages from one user to another.
- *FTP (file transfer protocol)*—a protocol (data exchange code standard) that allows users to retrieve files and transfer information from one computer to another over the Internet.
- *HTML (hypertext markup language)*—the programming language that defines the format of a World Wide Web page. This relatively simple code can be purchased as software to streamline the creation of Web pages.
- *HTTP (hypertext transfer protocol)*—the Web protocol that ensures compatibility before transferring information.
- *Hypertext*—a way of organizing information using layered connections that link information through nonlinear, related nodes.
- *Hytelnet*—a collection of sites and services available through Telnet.
- *Internet*—a worldwide system linking computer networks.

- *IRC (Internet relay chat)*—a text-based program that allows users to chat live across the Internet. (Other examples are AOL Instant Messenger and ICQ [I Seek You].)
- *Java*—an object-oriented programming language used to create interactive applications for Web pages.
- *Lynx*—a text-based Web browser.
- *Search engine*—software that provides key word search capability of registered websites. Common search engines are Google, Yahoo!, Ask Jeeves, and Mootes.
- *Telnet*—a software program that allows users to log onto a remote computer such as a library or database or to log into your "home" server to check your own e-mail.
- *URL (uniform resource locator)*—the address for a Web page containing the protocol type, domain, directory, and name of the page.
- *Usenet newsgroups*—a protocol that allows users to search and read discussion topics on the Internet.
- *Web browser*—software, such as Microsoft *Internet Explorer* and Apple's *Safari*, used to search the World Wide Web and to access multimedia information (text, graphics, audio, digital video) on the Internet.

- "Live" communication, allowing individuals on the Internet to "chat" or "talk" in real time, as quickly as they can type their messages
- Audio communication, allowing individuals with appropriate software to literally talk with each other as they would do over the telephone
- Video-based communication, through software such as iChat, AOL Instant Messenger, ICQ, MSN Messenger, and Yahoo! Messenger, letting individuals or small groups see and hear each other and show objects in real time.

Internet Addresses. Each individual Internet user has a unique address. An Internet address contains three parts: the person's name or *username* (pseudonym), the computer network where he or she can be reached, and the type of organization he or she is part of. For example, the following is the e-mail address for one of this book's authors:

jrussell@purdue.edu

name organization type of network

Organization Abbreviations

commercial	com
educational	edu
government (U.S.)	gov
military (U.S.)	mil
service networks	net
nonprofit organization	org
business	biz
cooperative businesses	coop
open to anyone	info
museum	museum
personal registrations	name
licensed professionals	pro
air transportation	aero

International Abbreviations. Each country outside the United States has its own two-letter abbreviation that appears in place of the organization, as in the following examples:

Australia	au
Canada	ca
Italy	it
Mexico	mx
Netherlands	nl

The World Wide Web

The **World Wide Web (the Web)** is a network of networks that allows you to access, view, and maintain documents that can include text, data, sound, and video. It is not separate from the Internet. Instead it rides on top of it, in the same way that an application such as *PowerPoint* runs on top of an operating system such as *Windows.*

The Web is a series of communications protocols between client and server. These protocols present information in documents that can be linked to other documents and stored on computers throughout the Internet. The Web protocol, called **hypertext transfer protocol (HTTP),** ensures compatibility before transferring information. The Web is comprised of documents called **Web pages.** Each individual collection of pages is called a **website.** Users access a website by entering its address or **uniform resource locator (URL)** into their browser (see the list of sample websites at the end of this chapter). The URL contains the name of the host computer (server), the name of the domain, the directory on the server, and the name of the Web page (actual filename) (Figure 8.6). Navigation within and among Web pages relies on hypertext links that, when selected, move users to another location on the same page, another website on the same host computer, or to a different computer on the Web.

To use the Web for online learning, Web pages have to be designed and written, and a host computer must be identified to house them. Universities and large companies are usually directly connected to the Internet and run the necessary Web hosting (server) software.

Intranets

A special type of network, called an **intranet,** is not used by the general public, but by corporations and large organizations. It is a proprietary or closed network that connects multiple sites across the country or around the world. Systems connected to an intranet are private and accessible only by individuals within a given organization or corporation.

Intranets provide internal networks for companies or schools. Intranets are a way of increasing communication, collaboration, and information dissemination within companies or schools where divisions, departments, and workgroups each use a different **computer platform** (hardware and/or operating system), or where users work in geographically distant locations. Users access the intranet either directly or by dialing into the network. Even though an intranet may be connected to a larger network (the Internet, for example), a software

---

http://www.ncrel.org/tandl/homepg.htm

| format protocol | name of server | domain name | directory on server | actual filename |

Figure 8.6
Sample Web address or uniform resource locator (URL).

Close-Up

GLOBE—NETWORK TECHNOLOGY IN THE CURRICULUM

The GLOBE program uses technology to promote scientific inquiry and environmentalism. To participate, students use the Internet to send atmospheric data they collect to a GLOBE (Global Learning and Observations to Benefit the Environment) processing facility in Boulder, Colorado. In return, the class receives environmental images vividly depicting their observations along with observations sent in by students from around the world. Professionals from many disciplines participate in and use GLOBE. For example, scientists use the valuable student-collected data to research global change. There are opportunities for students to chat with scientists and astronauts. Students benefit too, learning about data collection, scientific protocols, and databases.

For additional information on this topic, go to the Web Links module in Chapter 8 of the Companion Website (http://www.prenhall.com/smaldino).

Intranet   Firewall   Internet

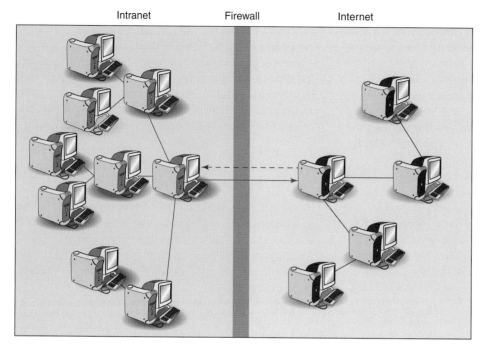

Figure 8.7

A firewall protects an internal network (intranet) from external users but allows internal users to access external networks (Internet).

package called a **firewall** prevents external users from accessing the internal network, while allowing internal users to access external networks (Figure 8.7).

Advantages of Networks

- *Ease of communication.* A network allows people to communicate with each other by leaving messages on the network system.
- *Sharing hardware.* Many users, for example, may access a single printer.
- *Centralization.* Information resides in a central database accessible by all employees or students at any time.
- *Consistency.* Because of the central location of information, all interested parties view the same copy of educational materials.
- *Currency.* A network allows for easy, low-cost, timely updates of materials, removing the need to constantly replace multiple copies of obsolete materials. Everyone has access to the most current version of the material.

Limitations of Networks

- *Cost.* It is expensive to establish a buildingwide network. The file server must be a large-capacity computer and the entire building must be wired to connect the computers. Wireless networks are even more expensive. If the system is to be effective, each room or office must have computers to allow everyone access.

- *Requires special network-compatible software.* This software generally is costly, although not as expensive as purchasing individual software for each computer.
- *Limited number of users.* Without extra equipment, users may have to wait their turn to gain access.
- *Unreliable remote connections.* An employee or learner dialing in from home may occasionally encounter line problems or a broken connection. This can be particularly frustrating if the person is downloading information from the network.
- *Speed of response.* Currently, response time can be very slow for sending or downloading graphics, photos, animation, audio, or video. Video and audio streaming technologies show promise in eliminating some of the problems associated with speed for downloading visual and audio information. The problem with this technology is that the information does not reside on the user's computer in the end.

Integration of Networks

One example of online learning using a network is in a computer lab, with 15 to 20 computers connected together. When a teacher wants each student to be working on a computer during a lesson, the lab makes it possible for the whole class to have access to computers simultaneously. Software and data files for a network can be located in one convenient place. Supervision and security are easier when all computers are located in a single room. Another application when teaching in a computer lab is that teachers can freeze students' screens and/or their keyboards to capture students' attention (Figure 8.8).

Students and teachers can access services and information both in and out of the classroom (Figure 8.9). Materials such as documents, government information, databases, online bibliographies, articles, publications, and computer software are available. Other applications include science experiments that involve sharing data among many locations (e.g., National Geographic at http://www.nationalgeographic.com or NOAA at http://www.NOAA.gov).

Figure 8.8
With a LAN a teacher can provide common instruction for all students in a lab.

Figure 8.9
The Web is a very effective tool for accessing material and information outside the classroom.

Most colleges and universities, as well as major corporations, government agencies, and school systems, have established websites as information centers and include information about programs of study, products, services, events, facilities, and materials available. Classroom Connect (http://www.classroom.net) is a good source of information about Web applications in P–12 settings. The Center for Networked Information Discovery and Retrieval site (http://k12.cnidr.org) is devoted to issues having to do with the use of information technology for school reform. Included on this site are resources for teachers and ideas for using technology in learning. Visit these websites through the Web Links module in Chapter 8 of the Companion Website (http://www.prenhall.com/smaldino).

ASSURE Case Connection

Mr. Plosnik could use a computer network to allow his students to access information. What type(s) of network could he use? Which type would you recommend? Why?

ISSUES

There are many important issues associated with electronic learning, especially when using the Internet. They include security, monitoring student use, acceptable use policies, and etiquette.

Close-Up

COMPUTERS FOR YOUTH: SPREADING THE NET

Computers for Youth (CFY) is trying to bridge the digital divide by training low-income children, as well as their parents and teachers, to use the Internet. The organization spends an entire school year at each school, showing students and their families how to surf the Web. Students who attend a three-and-a-half-hour course are provided with used computers contributed by local firms and three months of free Internet and e-mail access. Although some nonprofits advocate public technology centers where children can go online in libraries or recreation centers, CFY believes that students need computers in the home to really learn the skills they need. This allows students to spend as much time as they need learning the technology, and also enables students and their parents to communicate more freely with teachers outside of school. Currently, CFY is working with Kipp Academy, a New York City public middle school attended mostly by low-income African American and Hispanic students. Beyond nonprofits, corporations are also working to solve the problem of digital divide—many companies are looking to secure a future workforce with solid technology skills. The government is contributing to computer training efforts as well.

Source: Industry Standard, April 3, 2000.

Copyright Concerns

ONLINE MATERIALS

On October 28, 1998, President Clinton signed the Digital Millennium Copyright Act, a bill providing new guidelines for dealing with online copyrighted materials. Basically, it says that existing guidelines for printed material apply to the Internet. One cannot reproduce or distribute or transmit electronically other people's materials without their permission. In addition, you cannot link your website to something within someone else's site without permission. You can link to their homepage. Users must be aware that they are being transferred from your site to another site. You should request permission even to link to someone else's home page.

You and your students may legally look at materials on the Internet or a website, just as you may read a book in the library. However, you may *not* legally upload or download copyrighted works without the copyright holder's permission because doing so involves copying that work. Exceptions are those that fall within fair use—just as with any published materials. Remember, publishing materials on a website is no different than publishing them in a book.

Frequently, unauthorized copies of copyrighted works are posted on a website without the knowledge of the copyright owner. Recently a student of one of the authors found the AS-SURE Model on a website without attribution as to its source. The causal observer would assume it was developed by the university on whose website it was found. Not the case, and a serious violation of copyright law!

Example 1.

You find useful instructional materials on another teacher's website. There is no copyright notice anywhere on the materials. Can you legally distribute the materials to your student for educational purposes? Contrary to popular opinion, *all* material on the Internet is copyrighted unless stated otherwise. It is copyrighted even if it does *not* display the copyright symbol.

Example 2.

You download an article from a large city newspaper's website and then make copies to distribute to your students prior to a class discussion on the topic. Can you do this without violating copyright? Yes, this would be permissible for most of the newspaper following the current photocopying guidelines, which establish precedent for making multiple copies for classroom use. The exception would be individually bylined, copyrighted articles, such as Jack Anderson's column. Such articles *cannot* be copied legally for class distribution (adapted from Becker, 1997).

Example 3.

Students in your class write poems and some are very creative. You decide to post the better ones on the school website. Can you legally do this? No, unless you have permission of the students and their parent or guardian.

Example 4.

You receive a personal e-mail message from a fellow teacher. Because the content is so helpful, you forward the message on to other teachers. Have you violated any copyright laws? Probably, because many people regard e-mail messages as copyrighted items. It is definitely a "gray area" with a strong possibility that a claim of copyright violation may be made. As far as we know this type of case has not been tried in a court of law. However, in this case you have violated the Privacy Act. It is recommended that you not forward any e-mail, without permission, in consideration of both copyright and the Privacy Act. You may quote excerpts and report the gist of the message. If the teacher had sent you an original poem, which is automatically copyrighted, then you have definitely violated *both* copyright law and the Privacy Act (adapted from Becker, 1997).

Educators should use copyrighted materials from and over the Internet the same way they use them in print formats. The following guidelines are based on what the authors have read in the literature and online. These guidelines do *not* reflect a legal opinion.

1. Assume all materials are copyrighted unless otherwise stated. Almost everything created privately after April 1989 is copyrighted and protected whether or not it has a copyright notice.
2. You *cannot* even give away copyrighted material for educational purposes except under fair use guidelines.
3. Follow fair use precedents and guidelines set in current copyright law. Fair use should be a short excerpt and must be attributed to the original author and copyright holder.
4. All materials posted on the Internet are copyrighted. They can legally be read, but *not* legally forwarded or copied for instructional purposes, except under fair use. You can make one copy for your personal use.
5. A few words and ideas cannot be copyrighted. However, individual words and brand names, such as "Apple" applied to computers, can be trademarked.

Because the copyright law is still muddled, the best guideline is to always obtain permission. It is usually not that difficult. When in doubt, ask!

For general information on copyright, see the Copyright Concerns in Chapter 1. Suggested readings on copyright appear at the end of Chapter 1.

Selection Rubric: Web Resources

Complete an interactive evaluation and add it to your NETS-T portfolio using the Selection Rubric for Web Resources available on the "Classroom Link Portfolio" CD-ROM. A downloadable version of this rubric is available in the Selection Rubrics module of the Companion Website at http://www.prenhall.com/smaldino.

Key Words

_____

_____

_____

Title _____

Series Title (if applicable) _____

Source _____

Date _____ Cost _____ Length _____

Subject Area _____

Intended Audience _____

Format

☐ WebQuest

☐ Website

☐ Web Page

☐ Web Browser

☐ Web Authoring

Brief Description

Objectives

Entry Capabilities Required (e.g., prior knowledge, reading ability, vocabulary level, math ability)

Strong Points

Weak Points

Recommended Action (using criteria on the following page)

Name _____ Date _____

Rating Area	High Quality	Medium Quality	Low Quality	Rating
Match Curriculum	Curriculum standard addressed and use of web resource should enhance student learning.	Curriculum standard partially addressed and use of web resource may enhance student learning.	Curriculum standard not addressed and use of web resource will likely not enhance student learning.	
Accurate & Current	Information correct and does not contain material that is out of date.	Information correct but does contain material that is out of date.	Information is not correct and does not contain material that is out of date.	
Clear & Concise Language	Language used is age appropriate and vocabulary is understandable.	Language used is nearly age appropriate and some vocabulary is above/below student age.	Language used is not age appropriate and vocabulary is clearly inappropriate for student age.	
Motivating/ Interesting	Topic presented so that students are likely to be interested and engaged in learning.	Topic presented to interest students most of the time and engage most in learning.	Topic presented so as not to interest students and not engage them in learning.	
Learner Participation	Topic presented so that most students are actively engaged in learning.	Topic presented so that some students are engaged in learning.	Topic presented so that most students are not actively engaged in learning.	
Technical Quality	The material represents best available media.	The material represents media that are good quality, although there are some problems.	The material represents media that are not well prepared and are of very poor quality.	
Effectiveness Rating	There is evidence that use of these media has shown positive impact on student learning.	There is little evidence that use of these media has shown positive impact on student learning.	There is no evidence that use of these media has shown positive impact on student learning.	
Free from Bias	There is no evidence of objectionable bias or advertising.	There is little evidence of bias or advertising.	There is much evidence of bias or advertising.	
User Guide & Documentation	The documentation is excellent resource for use in a lesson. Documentation should help students use the Web resource.	The documentation is good resource for use in a lesson. Documentation may help students use the Web resource.	The documentation is poor resource for use in a lesson. Documentation does not help students use the Web resource.	
Clear Directions	Navigation is logical and pages are well organized.	Navigation is logical for main use, but can be confusing.	Navigation is not logical and pages are not well organized.	
Stimulates Creativity	Use of Web resource gives students many opportunities to engage in new learning experiences.	Use of Web resource gives students some opportunities to engage in new learning experiences.	Use of Web resource gives students no opportunities to engage in new learning experiences.	
Visual Design	The Web resource is designed with appropriate use of graphics and text to ensure student understanding.	The Web resource is designed with graphics and text that are of average quality.	The Web resource is designed with graphics and text that are of poor quality and distract students from understanding.	
Quality of Links	The Web resource links facilitate navigating the material and finding additional information.	The Web resource links are not easy to navigate and make it difficult to find additional information.	The Web resource links make it very difficult to navigate the material and to find additional information.	
Site Map	The Site Map is available and useful for students to navigate and access information.	The Site Map is available and somewhat useful for students to navigate and access information.	The Site Map is not available or not useful for students to navigate and access information.	

Security

Students should be instructed not to give out personal information such as their phone numbers, addresses, and other personal information over the Internet. Students have been contacted and even harmed by unscrupulous individuals. It may be wise for students to give their school's address for correspondence. Also, as an educator, you must have parental permission to post children's photos on the Web.

The Center for Education and Research in Information Assurance and Security (CERIAS) focuses on multidisciplinary research and education in the areas of information security. The organization is concerned with supporting educators in issues of privacy, ethics, and management of information. Issues such as confidentiality of student records, privacy of information, and protection of students while they work online are important considerations. This organization provides guidelines for educators to establish policies within their schools to protect students, teachers, and the school community (contact them at http://www.cerias.org).

Monitoring Student Use

Teachers and parents must monitor students when using the Internet to ensure that their behavior is appropriate and to discourage them from exploring inappropriate material either deliberately or accidentally. The amount and level of monitoring is often based on the age of the students—younger students *may* need more monitoring than older students. Your final decisions about monitoring should be made in conjunction with parents and school administrators. Also, if a student encounters information or visuals that are inappropriate, that student should feel comfortable letting the teacher know about that source. There are software packages available to allow the teacher to prevent students from going to sites that are "off limits." They allow the teacher to "wack" the site and save it on the local computer hard drive. In this case students simulate visiting the Web while they are not actually connected.

Acceptable Use Policies

Acceptable use policies (AUPs) are agreements among students, parents/guardians, and the school administration outlining what is considered proper use of the Internet by all parties involved. Many schools have developed acceptable use policies. Check to see if your school has such a policy.

The policies usually include that the school will do what it can to control access to inappropriate information, that students will accept responsibility for not accessing such information, and that parents understand that there are possibilities that their children may access such information in spite of the school's efforts. All parties sign the document agreeing that they have read and will abide by the policy. Most states' Departments of Education have generated resources to assist educators in developing an AUP to use in their schools. For additional information on this topic, go to the Web Links module in Chapter 8 of the Companion Website (http://www.prenhall.com/smaldino).

Etiquette

There are informal rules for appropriate behavior on the Internet. Using the analogy of the Internet as the information superhighway, these are the "rules of the road." Referred to as **netiquette,** they apply to e-mail and to other interactions on the Web:

- Keep your message short and simple. Try to limit your message to *one* screen. Think before you write. Make it brief, descriptive, and to the point.
- Identify yourself as the sender somewhere in the communication; include your name and school address. Not all Internet addresses clearly identify the sender.
- Double check the address or URL before sending a message.
- When replying to a message, include the pertinent portions of the original message.
- Don't write anything you would not want somebody other than the receiver to read. E-mail can be intercepted and/or forwarded.
- Check spelling, grammar, and punctuation. Use lowercase letters except for proper names and beginnings of sentences.
- Be sensitive to others. Treat other people with respect and courtesy, especially in reference to social, cultural, and ethnic differences.
- Don't use sarcasm. It often falls flat and doesn't come across as you intended.
- Be careful with humor. It is a two-edged sword. The reader doesn't have the benefit of your facial expression, body language, or tone of voice. You can use **emoticons** or "e-mail body language" such as ;) for a wink or :(for a frown, but it doesn't communicate as well as being there.
- Cooperate and share. Consider yourself a guest on the system just as if you were a guest in someone's home. Be willing to share information with others on the Internet. In exchange for help and information you receive, be willing to answer questions and to share your resources.
- Carefully consider copyright. Just because something can be copied electronically doesn't mean it should be distributed without permission. Unless stated otherwise, *all material* on the

Internet is copyrighted (see "Copyright Concerns" in this chapter and in Chapter 1).

- Be alert for obscenity. Laws governing obscenity apply to messages on the Internet. However, material that is not deemed legally obscene may still be inappropriate for schoolage children!

ASSURE Case Connection

What precautions should Mr. Plosnik take regarding security, monitoring student use, acceptable use policies, and netiquette?

Summary: Using the ASSURE Model for Online Learning

As with other media and technology, the ASSURE model introduced in Chapter 3 is helpful in preparing lessons incorporating the use of computer networks, especially the Internet.

Analyze Learners

Lesson development begins by identifying the audience. In most cases the audience will be the students in your class(es). You also will wish to determine their various levels of experience using online resources.

State Objectives

Before stating specific objectives, you may wish to explore how you want students to use the network (to access information? to communicate with other students, professionals, or content experts?). You will also want to consider the content available on the network your students will be using. Sometimes it is more appropriate to state specific objectives after you have identified potential materials and resources.

Select Methods, Media, and Materials

Selecting materials often begins by "surfing" the Web. You can locate websites on a specific subject matter by using a search engine such as *Google, Ask Jeeves, Mootes,* or *Yahoo!* You should use more than one search engine because different engines will locate different information and sources; no one engine looks at everything. You should not base your lesson on data obtained from a single source—even a source as rich as the Internet. Don't forget to explore books, magazine articles, and other media (slides, videotapes, etc.). The media specialist in your school can be a valuable team member in the search for materials. You and/or the media specialist can, ironically enough, identify many of these materials through online searches.

Utilize Media and Materials

When you assign students to use computer networks, you may wish to provide them the e-mail addresses of individuals they may want to contact, a list of selected websites, and a brief guide to using their browser (such as the *Quick Reference Guide for Netscape Navigator*). You may want to expand learning opportunities outside formal classroom time. The length of the lesson will depend on the scope of materials available, manner of presentation, and available time. When using the Internet, provide time for students to search for relevant materials. If the computers are not in your classroom, allocate additional time for students to get to the computers housed in the computer lab, media center, or multimedia classroom, and to return to the classroom.

Require Learner Participation

Get the students involved in finding the necessary information and materials and/or making contact with individuals. Don't tell them exactly where to find the resources or individuals. The *process* of searching may be one of their most important outcomes, especially for early lessons using computer networks. Ask students to document (log) their search strategies, progress, and outcomes and either present their results to the class or turn in a report to you.

Evaluate and Revise

If you require students to log their search strategies, progress, and outcomes, you may use this documentation for assessment along with presentations, reports, and other assessment procedures. As with all media- and technology-based lessons, you may choose to revise your lesson plan after you have determined how well it worked. In addition, computer networks and sites change frequently, so you may be forced to change your lesson before offering it again. Be sure to check the most important sites and access procedures just prior to presenting your lesson. In addition, you want to be certain that all online materials used have been cleared of any potential copyright issues.

ASSURE Case in Practice: Using the Web to Learn About the Holocaust

All of the ASSURE Cases in Practice in this text and an electronic template for creating your own ASSURE Lesson can be found on the enclosed "Classroom Link Portfolio" CD-ROM.

Secondary Social Studies

The purposes of this lesson were to study the Holocaust and its implications for our lives today and to dispel misinformation students may have had prior to studying the Holocaust. It also raised the question, "Could the Holocaust happen again?"

Analyze Learners

General Characteristics

Mr. Plosnik's students are juniors and seniors in high school. They represent a range of experiences and grade-point averages. The college preparatory curriculum of the school could be considered above average.

Entry Competencies

The students have read about and discussed the historical events surrounding Germany's role in World War II. They have studied printed and televised news reports pertaining to social crises in other countries that may relate to the events of the Holocaust of the 1940s.

Learning Styles

Students in the class exhibit a variety of learning styles. The majority of the students prefer to search for materials on their own and then discuss their findings with their classmates and teacher.

State Objectives

Not all of the project's objectives appear in this ASSURE Case in Practice. Sample cognitive objectives for the lesson include the following:

1. After locating a given World Wide Web site related to the class study of the Holocaust, students will review the information and answer the questions in the workbook. Answers will contain information quoted and referenced from the website and be prepared in a grammatically correct document.
2. Using Internet search engines, students will locate at least three additional sites relating to the Holocaust and select images, sound files, and video clips of personal interest.

Sample affective objectives for the lesson include the following:

1. During class discussion and in their writings, students will espouse the position that just because the Holocaust happened, it was not inevitable.
2. Students will avoid stereotypical descriptions.

Sample technology-related objectives for the lesson include the following:

1. During further exploration of topics, students will use the Internet and its wealth of educational materials as a resource tool.
2. Students will navigate the World Wide Web to locate specific websites and search for sites using one of the Web search engines.

Select Methods, Media, and Materials

Because the students lacked direct experience with the Holocaust, the teacher, Tim Plosnik, and a college professor, Lawrence A. Tomei, sought to provide experiences that could help students better understand the complexity of the subject. They wanted to help students make connections between their own lives and the experiences of those who suffered the Holocaust.

While preparing the lesson, Dr. Tomei conducted the initial exploration of the Internet, locating over 240 websites related to the Holocaust. On these sites students would be able to view photos of the prison camps, listen to prisoners' songs, view video clips of the atrocities, and download these files to classroom computers. Virtual tours of the Anne Frank House in Amsterdam and the Holocaust Memorial Museum in Washington, DC, were also located.

Mr. Plosnik synthesized the wealth of material into the session objectives. He decided what material was appropriate for his students and which sites could contribute to the objectives of his class. Together, the teacher and the professor were able to construct a lesson that combined the strengths of technology with the pedagogy of sound classroom objectives.

The teacher and facilitator wanted students to use the computer and its link to the Internet to encounter a range of human experience. They also found materials in the school library and media center. The resources appeared almost unlimited.

Given the amount of materials available, they decided to use a discovery method with a teacher-created student workbook as a guide.

Utilize Media and Materials

Preview the Materials

As noted, Mr. Plosnik and Dr. Tomei previewed many materials as part of their selection process.

Prepare the Materials

They developed a student workbook to guide students' learning with questions, suggested activities, and lists of resources. Dr. Tomei also developed a *PowerPoint* presentation as an overview and introduction to the topic.

Prepare the Environment

The teacher arranged to increase class time in a computer laboratory with Internet connections. The facilities were scheduled and the Internet hookups checked prior to the lesson.

Prepare the Learners

Mr. Plosnik prepared students to participate actively in the lesson. He indicated to students that their ideas and opinions matter and that history has multiple ramifications for them both as individuals and as members of society.

He instructed students to review the information and to seek answers to questions just as historians do. Questions included: "Why did the Holocaust happen?" and "What were the world events that permitted such an atrocity?" Their responses were to contain information quoted and referenced from the Internet and other sources. The results had to be grammatically correct.

Provide the Learning Experience

The teacher took on the role of facilitator in this discovery learning environment.

Require Learner Participation

The students completed the teacher-prepared workbook, which posed the following questions to guide learning:

- What was the Holocaust?
- Who were the Nazis and why did they rise to power?
- Why did the Nazis want to kill large numbers of people?
- How did the Nazis carry out their policy of genocide?
- How did the world respond to the Holocaust?

The questions focused students' attention to basic knowledge and information. Self-exploration of learning materials was followed by cooperative learning sessions and discussion. Many of the Web locations stimulated considerable discussion.

During a virtual tour of the Anne Frank House in Amsterdam, students learned the stories of the other individuals who hid with the Frank family. The virtual tour of the U.S. Holocaust Memorial Museum allowed students to review the museum's educational resources.

Students selected a specific image (or two) and explained how that image represents the Holocaust and why they selected it.

Evaluate and Revise

Evaluation of Learners

Students were guided on their exploration by the student workbook, which contained a description of each website to be visited, along with specific questions to ensure they found the information that the teacher was addressing. Unstructured time was also allowed for student self-exploration.

Assessment of the completed workbook provided one criterion by which Mr. Plosnik evaluated student performance. He used quizzes to evaluate the lesson objectives.

Mr. Plosnik also encouraged students to connect the Holocaust to other historical and contemporary events. Students reflected on what they learned and considered what the Holocaust meant to them personally as citizens of a democracy.

Evaluation of Instruction (Including Media and Materials)

Mr. Plosnik asked students to provide their own evaluation of the learning outcomes of the lesson, based on the information discovered and its value as a source of additional material from the perspective of the lesson objectives. In addition to reviewing these student outcomes, he prepared an evaluation of the lesson and the value of the Internet exploration method of learning.

Students completed a formal evaluation (questionnaire) focusing on the delivery method used for the class sessions. In addition, Mr. Plosnik provided Dr. Tomei with a detailed report concerning the application of technology for this lesson.

Revise

Based on student input, Mr. Plosnik revised the workbook and student guidelines before using the lesson again.

Adapted from a lesson by Dr. Lawrence A. Tomei, Duquesne University.

Create Your Own ASSURE Lesson

Using the ASSURE model, design a lesson for a scenario from the Companion Website or use a scenario of your own design. Use one of the methods described in Chapter 1 and information from this chapter related to incorporating online learning into your instructional setting. Be sure to include information about the audience, the objectives, and all other elements of the ASSURE model. When the lesson is completed, reflect on the process you used and what you have learned about matching audience, content, method, and materials.

Classroom Link Portfolio Activities

Use the "Classroom Link Portfolio" CD-ROM and the Companion Website as resources in completing these activities. To complete the following activities online go to the Portfolio Activities module in Chapter 8 of the Companion Website (http://www. prenhall.com/smaldino).

1. *Lesson Planning Using WebQuests.* Develop a lesson incorporating a WebQuest to engage learners. *Written Reflection.* How does the WebQuest change the manner in which you accomplish the lesson? What changes did you need to make in the design of the lesson to incorporate the WebQuest?

What Internet safety issues have to be addressed? What learner skills and assessment considerations do you need to address when including a WebQuest? (ISTE NETS-T 1.A; 2.A & C; 3.A; 6.D)

2. *Creating Websites.* Create a website to meet a content standard or a topic of interest to you. *Written Reflection.* Describe the process, the frustrations, the successes. How would you teach your students how to create a website? What considerations do you need to address when designing the lesson? What resources might you include to enhance their learning experience? How will you assess their learning? (ISTE NETS-T 2.A; 2.C; 4.A & C)

Integration Assessments

To complete the specified activities online go to the Integration Assessments module in Chapter 8 of the Companion Website (http://www.prenhall. com/smaldino).

1. Create your own webpage following the guidelines in "Creating a Web Page" in Classroom Resources, Section C. (ISTE NETS-T 2.A & B)
2. Develop an Internet acceptable use policy for your school (either where you attended or where you teach). (ISTE NETS-T 3.D; 6.D)

3. Search the Internet for sites relating to a topic of your choice. Document your search strategy and submit the results of your search. (ISTE NETS-T 2.C; 5.B)
4. Develop a lesson incorporating the Internet following the ASSURE model. (ISTE NETS-T 2.A)
5. Prepare a position paper on the use of the World Wide Web for education and training now and in the future. (ISTE NETS-T 5.A & B)

Sample Websites for Teachers and Students

The Adventures of Cyberbee™
http://www.cyberbee.com/

A site filled with helpful ideas and activities for using the Internet in education.

Classroom Connect
http://www.classroom.net

A valuable site for P–12 teachers and students, including classroom links, materials for educators, addresses of other educators online, and products to bring the Internet into the classroom.

CNN Interactive
http://www.cnn.com

An up-to-the-minute source of news, weather, sports, science and technical information, show business, and health.

Animal Planet
http://www.discovery.com/?channel-APL

Features a collection of articles from the Discovery Channel as well as news stories about animals from around the world.

Crayola
http://www.crayola.com/educators/

A colorful site with activities, stories, and games for young people.

Kathy Schrock's Guide for Educators
http://school.discovery.com/schrockguide/

Includes a list of Internet sites found to be useful for enhancing curriculum and teacher professional growth.

Maps and References—Odden's Bookmarks
http://oddens.geo.vv.nl/index.html

A listing of maps, atlases, geographic references, and other resources.

San Diego Zoo and Wild Animal Park

http://www.sandiegozoo.org/

Provides a virtual tour of the San Diego Zoo and includes information about the zoo, its inhabitants, and endangered species.

Visit the Yuckiest Site on the Internet
http://www.yucky.kids.discovery.com/

This site provides information teachers and students want to know about the world of science—and the focus is on "yucky things" like worms and cockroaches and other gross things!

References

Becker, G. H. 1997. *Copyright: A guide to information and resources,* 2nd ed. Lake Mary, FL: Author. (P.O. Box 951870, Lake Mary, FL 32795-1870.)

Dodge, B. 1999. *The WebQuest page.* Accessed online at http://edweb.sdsu.edu/webquest/webquest.html

Suggested Readings

Bannan-Ritland, Brenda, Douglas M. Harvey, and William D. Milheim. 1998. A general framework for web-based instruction. *Educational Media International, 35*(2): 77–81.

Barrie, J. M., and D. E. Presti. 1996. The World Wide Web as an instructional tool. *Science, 274*(5286): 371.

Collis, B. 1996. *Tele-learning in a digital world: The future of distance learning.* London: International Thompson Computer Press.

Cotton, E. G. 1996. *The online classroom: Teaching with the Internet.* Bloomington, IN: ERIC Clearinghouse on Reading, English, and Communication.

Craver, Kathleen W. 2002. *Creating cyber libraries: An instructional guide for school library media specialists.* Westport, CT: Greenwood.

Gardner, P. 1996. *Internet for teachers & parents.* Westminster, CA: Teacher Created Materials.

Great teaching with the Internet: Resource guide. 1998. Watertown, MA: Tom Snyder Productions.

Hasler-Waters, Lisa, and Wallace Napier. 2002. Building and supporting student team collaboration in the virtual classroom. *Quarterly Review of Distance Education, 3*(3): 345–352.

Hopey, C. E., and L. Ginsberg. 1996. Distance learning and new technologies: You can't predict the future, but you can plan for it. *Adult Learning, 8*(1): 22.

Hopper, Keith B. 2001. Is the Internet a classroom? *TechTrends, 45*(5): 35–43.

Horton, William, and Katherine Horton. 2003. *E-learning tools and techniques: A consumer's guide for trainers, teachers, educators, and instructional designers.* New York: John Wiley & Sons.

Jasinski, Marie, and Sivasailam Thiagarajan. 2000. Virtual games for real learning: Learning online with serious fun. *Educational Technology, 40*(4): 61–63.

Jukes, Ian, Bruce MacDonald, and Anita Dosaj. 2002. *Netsavvy: Building information literacy in the classroom.* Thousand Oaks, CA: Corwin.

Kearsley, G. 2000. *Online education: Learning and teaching in cyberspace.* Belmont, CA: Wadsworth.

Kehoe, B., and V. Mixon. 1997. *Children and the Internet.* Upper Saddle River, NJ: Prentice Hall.

Kelly, Rebecca. 2000. Working with WebQuests. *Teaching Exceptional Children, 32*(6): 4–13.

Lamb, Annette, and Larry Johnson, 1997. *Cruisin' the information highway: Internet in the K–12 classroom,* 2nd ed. Emporia, KS: Vision to Action.

Lamb, A., and W. Smith. 2000. Ten facts of life for distance learning. *TechTrends, 44*(1): 12–15.

Lamb, A., N. Smith, and L. Johnson. 1996. *Surfin' the Internet: Practical ideas from A to Z.* Emporia, KS: Vision to Action.

Levin, J. 1999. Multiplicity in learning and teaching: A framework for developing innovative online education. *Journal of Research on Computing in Education, 32*(2): 256–269.

Mioduser, David, Raft Nachmias, Orly Lahav, and Avigail Oren. 2000. Web-based learning environments: Current pedagogical and technological state. *Journal of Research on Computing in Education, 33*(1): 55–76.

Palloff, Rena M., and H. Keith Pratt. 1999. *Building learning communities in cyberspace: Effective strategies for the online classroom.* San Francisco: Jossey-Bass.

———. 2001. *Lessons from the cyberspace classroom.* New York: John Wiley & Sons.

Piskurich, George M. 2003. *The AMA handbook of e-learning: Effective design, implementation, and technology solutions.* New York: American Management Association.

Rivard, J. D. 1998. *Quick guide to the Internet for educators.* Boston: Allyn & Bacon.

Roblyer, M. D. 2001. *Ten first steps on the Internet.* Upper Saddle River, NJ: Prentice Hall.

———. 2002. *Starting out on the Internet: A learning journey for teachers,* 2nd ed. Upper Saddle River, NJ: Prentice Hall.

Ryder, R. J., and T. Hughes. 2000. *Internet for educators,* 3rd ed. Upper Saddle River, NJ: Prentice Hall.

Sales, Gregory C. 2002. *A quick guide to e-learning.* Andover, MN: Expert.

Seal, Kala Chand, and Zbigniew H. Przasnyski. 2001. Using the World Wide Web for teaching improvement. *Computers and Education, 36*(1): 33–40.

Serim, F., and M. Koch. 1996. *NetLearning: Teachers use the Internet.* Sebastopol, CA: Songline Studios.

Simmons, Bryan, Bill Havice, and Clint Isbell. 1999. Electronic field trip: Incorporating desktop videoconferencing in the elementary school classroom. *Technology and Children, 3*(4): 3–5.

Stull, A., and R. J. Ryder. 1999. *Education on the Internet: A student's guide.* Upper Saddle River, NJ: Prentice Hall.

Wresch, W. 1997. *A teacher's guide to the information highway.* Upper Saddle River, NJ: Prentice Hall.

Yaworski, JoAnn. 2002. How to build a web site in six easy steps. *Journal of College Reading and Learning, 32*(2): 148–153.

Traditional Media

PART 3

CHAPTER 9

Instructional Materials and Displays

Outline

Knowledge Objectives

1. Discuss four types of learning centers, and give one specific example of each.
2. Describe five essential components of an instructional module.
3. Describe instructional applications that are especially appropriate for manipulatives.
4. Discuss the advantages, limitations, and applications of printed materials in instruction.
5. Demonstrate your ability to follow the proper procedures for locating, obtaining, appraising, and using free and inexpensive materials.
6. Compare the advantages and limitations of various types of display surfaces.
7. Justify the use of a field trip for a particular instructional purpose of interest to you and describe how you might introduce it and follow it up.
8. Explain why a virtual field trip might be an alternative to a regular field trip and describe how you might introduce it and follow it up.
9. Describe instructional applications that are especially appropriate for exhibits, displays, and dioramas.

Professional Vocabulary

learning center

instructional module

manipulative

real object

model

mock-up

chalkboard

whiteboard

electronic whiteboard

bulletin board

cloth board

magnetic board

flip chart

exhibit

field trip

virtual field trip

display

diorama

Not all media plug into an electrical outlet. A variety of media can make your students' learning more realistic and engaging. Instructional materials include learning centers, printed materials, and free and inexpensive materials. Objects and models bring "the real thing" into the classroom. In addition, many computer software packages include manipulatives and workbooks for students to use as part of their learning experience. Students often construct such displays themselves as part of group projects.

Many of the media and materials discussed in this chapter are so common that instructors are inclined to underestimate their instructional value. You need to be able to use chalkboards, whiteboards, flip charts, bulletin boards, and other display formats confidently. Materials don't have to be digital or expensive to be useful. Small can indeed be beautiful, and inexpensive can be effective (Figure 9.1)!

LEARNING CENTERS

A combination of instructional materials and a display, the **learning center** is a self-contained environment designed to promote individual or small-group learning around a specific task. A learning center may be as simple as a table and some chairs around which students discuss, or it may be as sophisticated as several networked computers used by a group for collaborative research and problem solving.

An individual teacher may use one learning center within a classroom as a way of breaking the class into small groups to perform hands-on activities (e.g., in a science class with a laboratory-type learning center). Or a whole school may be organized to incorporate

ASSURE
Case Challenge

We have developed a case study for this chapter to help you see how instructional materials and displays can be integrated into learning activities. At the end of the chapter you will be challenged to develop your own ASSURE lesson for a case study of your choice using the ASSURE model and incorpo-

rating the technology and media described in this chapter. To help you in preparing your lesson, we have included hints (called "ASSURE Case Connections") throughout the chapter as they relate to the ASSURE Case Challenge.

Jan Smith, the chief welding instructor at Summit VoTech College, wants to teach her students basic welding skills. Her students are very diverse—ranging in age from 18 to 68 and with a variety of reading levels from 6th grade to 14th grade. Most of them are highly motivated to learn to weld for their personal use or to get a better job.

Figure 9.1
Nonprojected visuals are widely used media.

learning centers into the daily mix of activities, as in the Project CHILD schools (see "Close-Up: Project CHILD").

Learning centers should encourage active participation rather than having students simply sit and read a book. Most learning centers provide student practice with feedback through individualized activities. They tend to be designed for use by individuals; however, they can be designed for pairs or triads.

Learning centers may be set up in any suitable and available classroom space. They are also commonly found in school library media centers. Learning centers with many stations are found in business, industry, medical facilities, and the armed forces.

Learning center materials may include practically any or all of the media and technology mentioned in this text. Teachers or media specialists may purchase center materials and software from commercial producers or may create them themselves.

Although students may perform simple learning center activities at their desks or at some other open space, it is advisable that learning centers be confined to a clearly identifiable area and that they be at least partially enclosed to reduce distractions. Learning carrels, or booths, which may be purchased from commercial sources or made locally, provide a clearly defined enclosure. You can make carrels by placing simple cardboard dividers on classroom tables.

Carrels are often referred to as being either "dry" or "wet." A *dry carrel* provides private space for study or other learning activities but contains no electrical equipment. The typical library carrel is a dry carrel. A *wet carrel*, on the other hand, is equipped with outlets for audiovisual devices such as cassette recorders, television monitors, or computer terminals (Figure 9.2). An extensive exploration of the possibilities of computer-based learning centers is found in Riedl (1995).

Advantages

- *Self-pacing.* Centers encourage students to take responsibility for their own learning and allow them to learn at their own pace, thus minimizing the possibility of failure and maximizing the likelihood of success.
- *Active learning.* Learning centers provide for student participation in the learning experience, for student response, and for immediate feedback to student response.

Close-Up

PROJECT CHILD

In Project CHILD (Changing How Instruction for Learning is Delivered),[1] clusters of classrooms become learning resource rooms, each focused on one of the core subject areas: reading, writing, and mathematics. Children spend 60 to 90 minutes in each of the cluster classrooms working at a variety of learning stations. Each CHILD classroom has six learning stations:

- *Computer Station* for learning with instructional software
- *Teacher Station* for small-group tutorials
- *Textbook Station* for written work
- *Challenge Station* for learning in a gamelike format
- *Exploration Station* for hands-on activities and projects
- *Imagination Station* for creative expression

Students stay with the same team of teachers for three years in cross-grade clusters (P–2) or (3–5). All teachers have special training to use technology and cooperative learning techniques in their designated specialty area. Required curriculum content is covered in six-week thematic units coordinated across curricular areas and across grade levels.

For example, reading and writing are integrated through literature themes (fantasy, biographies, modern fiction, etc.). Students learn reading strategies in whole-class and small groups. Teachers plan reading lessons to include an array of materials, including newspapers, library books, songbooks, magazines, games, charts, reference books, and material written by students in the writing classroom. Students use computers to read for information, to write original compositions, and to practice specific language skills.

The computer activities are based on a range of software from many different sources, including Web-based systems.

More than 10 years of evaluations have shown that CHILD students have made the following gains:

- Significantly higher performance on standardized tests
- Fewer discipline problems
- Higher rates of attendance

For additional information on this topic, go to http://www.ifsi.org/CHILD and to the Web Links module in Chapter 9 of the Companion Website (http://www.prenhall.com/smaldino).

Source: Sarah M. Butzin, "Project CHILD: The Perfect Fit for Multimedia Elementary Schools," Multimedia Schools, Nov.–Dec. 2002, pp. 14–16.

---

[1]Project CHILD was formerly called "Computers Helping Instruction and Learning Development."

Figure 9.2
This "wet" carrel is equipped with media hardware.

- *Teacher role.* Learning centers allow the teacher to play more of a coaching role, moving around the classroom and providing individual help to students when they need it (Figure 9.3).

Limitations

- *Cost.* A great deal of time must be spent in planning and setting up centers and in collecting and arranging for center materials. The equipment and materials used in the center, too, entail costs.
- *Management.* Teachers who use learning centers must be very good at classroom organization and management.
- *Student responsibility.* Any form of independent study will be successful only insofar as students are

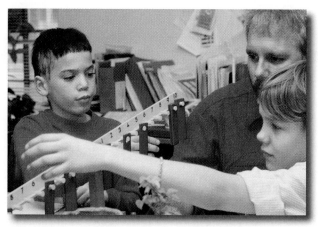

Figure 9.3
Learning centers offer opportunities for informal teacher–student interaction.

able and willing to accept some responsibility for their own learning.

- *Student isolation.* Learning centers need not be limited to individual student use; small groups can be assigned to work together. If students do work alone, you must make other provisions to provide for the social dimensions of learning.

Integration

You can use learning centers for a number of specialized purposes (Figure 9.4). We describe here some of the specialized types of centers.

Skill Centers.   These can provide students with an opportunity to do additional practice, typically to reinforce a lesson previously taught through other media or methods. Basic skills that are built up through drill-and-practice lend themselves to the skill center approach. For example, you might design a skill center to give practice in using prefixes for students who are learning to write.

Interest Centers.   Interest centers can stimulate new interests and encourage creativity. For example, you might set up a get-acquainted center on insect life in the classroom before actually beginning a unit on specific insects.

Remedial Centers.   Remedial centers can help students who need additional assistance with a particular concept or skill. A student who has difficulty determining the least common denominator of a group of fractions, for example, could receive the needed help in a remedial learning center.

Enrichment Centers.   Enrichment centers can provide stimulating additional learning experiences for students who have completed other classroom activities. You might, for example, allow students who have completed their assigned math activities to go to a center that features computer-based math games.

INSTRUCTIONAL MODULES

An **instructional module** is any self-contained instructional unit designed for use by a single learner or a small group of learners without a teacher's presence. Since the whole purpose of modules is to facilitate learning without constant supervision, all the elements of a lesson a teacher usually provides have to be built into a set of printed, audiovisual, or computer-based materials (or a combination of all of these). The module must gain the student's attention, introduce the topic, present new content, provide practice-and-feedback activities, test for mastery, and assign followup remediation or enrichment. The main difference between a module and just a simple book, video, or computer lesson is that all of the instructional management procedures have to be provided. These are often called *wraparounds*.

Components of Modules

Instructional modules may have many different components, but certain ones are essential:

Figure 9.4
Learning centers can develop skills, generate interest, provide remediation, and add enrichment.

Close-Up

MATH MANIACS LEARNING CENTER

A middle school teacher capitalizes on her students' enthusiasm for solving mathematics problems by designing a learning center based on a recent school play's theme of becoming a "maniac" for doing good deeds. Center materials include a variety of problems that students might encounter in trying to do a good deed in the community. All the problems involve applying math knowledge and skills the students have been learning. Students work collaboratively in teams to develop solutions to the math problems. Each team complete worksheets and then posts its solutions for the other teams to see and discuss. The problems are planned so there can be more than one way to resolve the issue and so that several different math approaches could be used. The center is designed so that all students can eventually master their math knowledge and skills.

- *Rationale.* Provide an overview of the content of the module and an explanation of why the learner should study it.
- *Objectives.* State in performance terms what the learner is expected to gain from studying the module.
- *Entry test.* Determine whether the learner has mastered the prerequisite skills needed to enter the module.
- *Multimedia materials.* Use a variety of media to involve learners actively and to utilize a number of their senses. Most media formats lend themselves to use in modules.
- *Learning activities.* All the methods described in Chapter 1 may be incorporated into modules. Having a variety of methods and media increases student interest and meets student needs.
- *Self-test.* Give students a chance to review and check their own progress.
- *Posttest.* Assess whether students have mastered the objectives of the module.

Designing Modules

A module should include an introduction to the topic, preferably in the form of a question or a problem that will stimulate curiosity. It also must provide instructions or suggestions about how students are to use the com-

ponents of the module. In most cases, a printed guide serves as the pathfinder through the various activities of the module. The printed guide may also contain questions and space for answers. (See "Designing Text," in Classroom Resources, Section C.)

Some teachers prefer to put their "user's guide" on audiotape, which can be helpful for those with reading problems. (See "Recording Audiocassettes," in Classroom Resources, Section C.)

When individuals or small groups are using modules on their own, the teacher needs a plan for monitoring their progress. Ideally, after finishing a module, the individual or small group meets with the teacher to discuss the content they were pursuing, their outcomes, and their understandings. They also report any difficulties they might have had in using the module. Such discussions, in addition to or instead of more conventional tests, provide valuable feedback about student progress and about the strengths and weaknesses of the module.

ASSURE Case Connection

How might Jan Smith use learning centers to teach welding? As a part of learning centers or separately, how might she use instructional modules to teach welding? If you were the instructor, which approach would you choose? Why?

MANIPULATIVES

Manipulatives are objects that can be viewed and handled in a learning setting. They are often included in learning centers and instructional modules (discussed earlier in this chapter). Field trips, displays, and dioramas (discussed later in this chapter) usually include manipulatives. They attract student attention and promote learning because students can handle and inspect them. There are three types of manipulatives: real objects, models, and mock-ups.

Real Objects

Real objects—such as coins, tools, artifacts, plants, and animals—are some of the most accessible, intriguing, and involving materials in educational use (Figure 9.5).

The gerbils that draw a crowd in kindergarten, the terrarium that introduces middle schoolers to the concept of ecology, the collection of Colonial-era coins, the frogs dissected in the college biology laboratory, the real, live baby being bathed in the parenting class—these are just a few examples of the potential of real objects to elucidate the obscure and to stimulate the imagination.

Being concrete, real objects fit near the bottom of Dale's Cone of Experience (see Chapter 1), meaning that they are especially appropriate for learners who are encountering a subject about which they have had little direct experience in their daily lives. Going back in time, at least to Comenius in the seventeenth century (see the Flashbacks feature on the Companion Website at http://www.prenhall. com/smaldino for more information), educators have understood the dangers of plunging into abstract concepts and principles without building a foundation in concrete experience. *Verbalism* is a term that refers to parroting words without meaningful understanding. To build schemata that have meaning and relevance in their lives, learners need a base in concrete experience, and bringing real objects into the classroom can help in this.

Real objects may be used as is, or you may modify them to enhance instruction. Examples of modification include the following:

- *Cutaways:* Devices such as machines with one side cut away to allow close observation of the inner workings (Figure 9.6).
- *Specimens:* Actual plants, animals, or parts thereof preserved for convenient inspection
- *Exhibits:* Collections of artifacts, often of a scientific or historical nature, brought together with printed information to illustrate a point (Figure 9.7)

Besides their obvious virtues as a means of presenting information, raising questions, and providing hands-on learning experiences, real objects can also play a valuable role in the evaluation phase of instruction. They can be displayed in a central location. Learners can identify them, classify them, describe their functioning, discuss their utility, or compare and contrast them. Such a testing situation emphasizes the real-world application of the topic of study, aids transfer of training, and helps transcend the merely verbal level of learning.

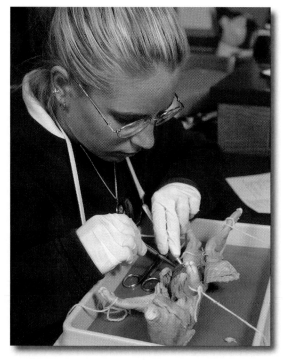

Figure 9.5

There is no substitute for the real thing when learning some content.

Figure 9.6

A cutaway of an engine reveals its hidden components.

Figure 9.7
Cultural artifacts come to life when presented in a well-designed exhibit.

Figure 9.9
Artifacts and models provide hands-on experiences.

Models

Models are three-dimensional representations of real objects. A model may be larger, smaller, or the same size as the object it represents. It may be complete in detail or simplified for instructional purposes. Indeed, models can provide learning experiences that real things cannot provide (Figure 9.8). For example, important details can be accented with color. Some models can be disassembled to provide interior views not possible with the real thing.

Models of almost anything—from airplanes to zebras—can be purchased for classroom use. Providing collections of models is a standard service of most media centers. School district and regional media centers and museums often loan artifacts and models, usually as part of multimedia kits (we described such kits in Chapter 6).

A variety of model kits is also available for you or your students to assemble. Assembly itself can be instructional. Classroom construction of model kits appeals to children of all ages (and, indeed, to adults) and can stimulate inquiry and discovery (Figure 9.9). Assembly activities help sharpen both cognitive and psychomotor skills.

Mock-Ups

Mock-ups, simplified representations of complex devices, are prevalent in industrial training. By highlighting essential elements and eliminating distracting details, mock-ups clarify the complex. They are sometimes constructed as working models to illustrate the basic operations of a real device (Figure 9.10). These allow individuals or small groups to manipulate the mock-up at their convenience, working with the subject matter until they comprehend it. For example, a mock-up of a laptop computer might have the internal components spread out on a large board with the components labeled and the circuit diagrams printed on the board. The most sophisticated type of mock-up, the simulator, is a device that allows learners to experience the important aspects of a real-life activity without the risks (simulators were discussed in detail in Chapter 2).

Manipulatives are the recommended media when realism is essential for learning. They provide concepts that involve three dimensions; tasks that require identification by size, shape, or color; and hands-on or laboratory practice.

Figure 9.8
An anatomical model, being three-dimensional, is a more concrete referent than a photograph, drawing, or even a videotape.

Showmanship

MANIPULATIVES

- Familiarize yourself with the object or model before using it in classroom instruction.
- Practice your presentation. If your object or model is a working one, be sure you know how it works and what might go wrong.

- Be sure your audience does not get the wrong impression of the size, shape, or color of the real object, if the model differs from it in these respects.
- Whenever feasible, encourage students to handle and manipulate the objects and models under study.
- Store objects out of sight when not using them for instruction. Left standing around, they are likely to take students' attention away from other classroom activities.

Figure 9.10
A mock-up of an electrical system provides the learner with a working model from which distracting details have been deleted.

Computer Programs and Manipulatives

The recent addition of manipulatives and student hands-on materials included with computer software packages is an example of how traditional instructional materials are being incorporated into software programs to provide powerful learning experiences. Students learn about a problem from the software, use the manipulatives included in the package to experiment with possible answers, and then when they feel they have resolved it, they enter the information into the computer to see if they have the right answer to the problem. This seems to be the best of both worlds, efficient use of a computer and authentic learning experiences for students.

ASSURE Case Connection

What types of manipulatives could be incorporated into Jan Smith's lesson on welding? What items would you choose, assuming that they are available? Why?

PRINTED MATERIALS

Printed materials include textbooks, fiction and nonfiction books, booklets, pamphlets, study guides, manuals, and worksheets, as well as word processed documents prepared by students and teachers. Textbooks have long been the foundation of classroom instruction. The other forms of media discussed in this textbook are frequently used in conjunction with and as supplements to printed materials.

Advantages

- *Availability.* Printed materials are readily available on a variety of topics and in many different formats.
- *Flexibility.* They are adaptable to many purposes and may be used in any lighted environment.
- *Portability.* They are easily carried from place to place and do not require any equipment or electricity.
- *User friendly.* Properly designed printed materials are easy to use, not requiring special effort to "navigate" through.
- *Economical.* Printed materials are relatively inexpensive to produce or purchase and can be reused. In fact, some may be obtained free, as described in the next section.

Limitations

- *Reading level.* The major limitation of printed materials is that they are written at a certain reading level. Some students are nonreaders or lack adequate literacy skills; some printed materials are above their reading level.
- *Prior knowledge.* Even though textbooks are generally written to be considerate of the reader, with clear language and simple sentence structures, readers who lack some prerequisite knowledge may struggle to comprehend the text.
- *Memorization.* Some teachers require students to memorize many facts and definitions. This practice diminishes printed materials to mere memorization aids.

Copyright Concerns

PRINT MEDIA

For educational use, a teacher may make a single copy of a chapter from a book; an article from a periodical or newspaper; a short story, short essay, or short poem, whether or not from a collective work; an illustration from a book, periodical, or newspaper. The context in which the term *teacher* is used seems to be broad enough to include support personnel working with teachers and trainers.

The guidelines further stipulate the amount of material that may fairly be copied and the special circumstances that permit multiple copies. *Fair use* is defined as one illustration per book or periodical, 250 words from a textbook, two lines from a poem, or 10 percent of a prose work up to 1,000 words. Multiple copies cannot exceed the number of students in a class, nor can there be more than two excerpts or one short poem, article, story, or essay copied from the same author. These limitations (e.g., nine instances of multiple copying; two excerpts or one short item) do not apply to current news periodicals, newspapers, and current news sections of other periodicals.

However, multiple copies must meet the "spontaneity" test. The copying must be initiated by the individual teacher, not directed or suggested by any other authority. The decision to use the work and the "inspiration" for its use must be close enough to the moment of use to preclude waiting for permission from the copyright holder. This means, of course, that the same "inspiration" cannot occur the same time next term.

The last guideline, concerning market value, means, that copying must not substitute for purchasing the original or creating or replacing an anthology or compilation of works protected by copyright. It also prohibits copying works intended to be consumable (e.g., workbooks and standardized tests).

If a work is out of print (e.g., no longer available from the copyright holder), you are not affecting the market value of the work by copying it. The market value guideline can act in favor of the user, as we will see from the examples presented in the Copyright Concerns features throughout this text.

The term, or period of time, of the copyright has been changed by the Sonny Bono Copyright Term Extension Act of 1998. For an individual author, the copyright term continues for his or her life and for 70 years after his or her death. If a work is made for hire (i.e., by an employee or by someone commissioned to do the work), the term is 100 years from the year of creation or 75 years from the year of first publication or distribution, whichever comes first. Works copyrighted prior to January 1, 1978, are protected for 28 years and then may have their copyright renewed. The renewal will protect them for a term of 75 years after their original copyright date.

For general information on copyright, see the Copyright Concerns in Chapter 1. Suggested readings on copyright appear at the end of Chapter 1.

- *Vocabulary.* Some texts introduce a large number of vocabulary terms and concepts in a short amount of space. This practice places a heavy cognitive burden on students, which may be overwhelming for some.
- *One-way presentation.* Since most printed materials are not interactive, they tend to be used in a passive way, often without comprehension.
- *Curriculum determination.* Sometimes textbooks dictate the curriculum rather than being used to support the curriculum. Textbooks are often written to accommodate the curriculum guidelines of particular states or provinces. Consequently, the preferences of these authorities disproportionately influence textbook content and its treatment.
- *Cursory appraisal.* Selection committees might not examine textbooks carefully. Sometimes textbooks are chosen by the "five-minute thumb test"— whatever catches the reviewer's eye while thumbing through the textbook.

Integration

The most common application of printed materials is presenting information. Students are given reading assignments and are held accountable for the material during class discussions and on tests. Teacher-made handouts can also complement a teacher's presentation, or students may use them as they study independently. (See "Designing Text," in Classroom Resources, Section C.)

Students may also use printed materials to augment either teacher-presented information or other forms of media. Students frequently refer to supplementary printed materials (such as books and magazines from the media center) to locate information on a specific topic not covered in their textbook.

Printed materials are used in all subject areas and with students of all ages once they learn to read. The media center is a source of a variety of printed materials on countless topics and in almost every conceivable format (Figure 9.11).

Figure 9.11
Children's books and other printed materials can be used anytime and anywhere.

Utilization

When using printed materials for instruction, one of the main roles of the teacher is to get learners actively involved with the material. One technique is to have students use the "SQ3R" method: Survey, Question, Read, Recite, and Review. *Survey* requires students to skim through the printed material and to read the overview and/or summary. In the *Question* step they write a list of questions to answer while reading. In the *Read* stage students are encouraged to look for the organization of the material, put brackets around the main ideas, underline supporting details, and answer the questions written in the previous step. *Recite* requires them to test themselves while reading and to put the content into their own words. *Review* suggests that the students look over the material immediately after reading it, the next day, a week later, and so on (Robinson, 1946).

Other utilization techniques for printed materials include directing student reading with objectives or questions and providing a worksheet if one is not included

Technology for Diverse Learners

TEXT READERS AND BOOKS ON CD

Students who are poor readers because of dyslexia and other learning disabilities find that their reading is slow, inaccurate, and boring. They frequently have to reread passages, struggle to decode unfamiliar words, and suffer from fatigue and stress.

Students with visual impairments or severe learning disabilities have access to thousands of books recorded on CD from Recording for the Blind and Dyslexic (http://www.rfbd.org). A collection of over 6,000 digitally recorded educational titles, including books from the "Harry Potter" series, have been added to the nonprofit organization's collection of 91,000 accessible textbooks.

The books allow instant access to any page, chapter, or subheading with the touch of a button. To listen, students need a portable CD player equipped to play the books, or a multimedia computer with a CD-ROM drive and specialized software.

Kurzweil 3000, a text-to-speech program, provides them with a multisensory approach by presenting printed or electronic text with additional visual and audible cues. It can "read" the Internet. Advantages of Kurzweil 3000 include:

- The Real Speak "voice" is a more lifelike rendition of speech rather than the cognitive dissonance of most "electronic voices."
- Student productivity and the ability to work independently increase.

- The system has a voice notes feature for students with short-term memory issues.
- In addition to having the text read to them, students have the opportunity to read with the program.
- Students can import their own writing into Kurzweil 3000 to ease the challenges of the editing process.
- Language tools include a dictionary, a syllabication feature, and a thesaurus.

A student uses an older model Kurzweil that "voices" scanned text.

in the materials. You should emphasize the use of visuals in printed materials and teach students to read visuals. You need to instruct students on the appropriate use of printed materials.

FREE AND INEXPENSIVE MATERIALS

With the ever-increasing costs of instructional materials, teachers and trainers should be aware of the variety of materials they may obtain for classroom use at little or no cost (Figure 9.12). These free and inexpensive materials can supplement instruction in many subjects; they can be the main source of instruction on certain topics. For example, many videotapes are available for loan without a rental fee; the only expense is the return postage. By definition, any material that you can borrow or acquire permanently for instructional purposes without a significant cost, usually less than a couple of dollars, can be referred to as free or inexpensive.

The types of free and inexpensive materials are almost endless. The more commonly available items include posters, games, pamphlets, brochures, reports, charts, maps, books, audiotapes, videotapes, multimedia kits, and real objects. The more costly items, such as videotapes, are usually sent only on a free-loan basis and must be returned to the supplier after use. In some instances, single copies of audiocassettes, computer software, and videocassettes will be donated to your organization or school media center to be shared among many users.

Another resource that has become very important for obtaining free and inexpensive materials is the Internet (see Chapter 8). By connecting to websites around the world, teachers and students can acquire materials, photographs, and other educational resources. In addition, many teachers are placing their ideas for teaching an array of subjects, along with media and materials, on the Web.

Free and inexpensive materials include all the types of media discussed in this textbook—visuals, real objects, models, overhead transparencies, slides, audiotapes, CDs, videotapes, photographs, and even computer programs (called *shareware* or *freeware*). The applications of this variety of materials are described in detail in the chapters of this book related to specific types of media (see the Contents).

Advantages

- *Up to date.* Free and inexpensive materials can provide up-to-date information that is not contained in textbooks or other commercially available media.
- *In-depth treatment.* Such materials often provide in-depth treatment of a topic. If classroom quantities are available, students can read and discuss printed materials as they would textbook material. If quantities are limited, you can place them in a learning center for independent or small-group study.
- *Variety of uses.* These materials lend themselves to your own classroom presentations. Individual students who want to explore a subject of interest can use the audiovisual materials for self-study or for presentation to the class. Posters, charts, and maps can be combined to create topical displays. These can be motivational (as in the case of a safety poster) or used for direct instruction (as in studying the solar system). Materials that you do not have to return can be modified and adapted for various instructional or display purposes.
- *Student manipulation.* Materials that are expendable have the extra advantage of allowing learners to get actively involved with them. For example, students can cut out pictures for notebooks and displays. They can assemble printed information and visuals in scrapbooks as reports of individual and group projects.

Limitations

- *Bias or advertising.* Many free and inexpensive materials are described as *sponsored* materials because their production and distribution are sponsored by particular organizations. These organizations— whether private corporations, nonprofit associations, or government agencies—often have a message to

Figure 9.12
Free and inexpensive materials are available from a variety of sources.

convey. You might consider covering or removing the advertisement, but that, too, raises ethical questions in view of the effort and expense that the sponsor has incurred in providing the materials to you.

- *Special interests.* What may be even more troublesome is sponsored material that does not contain outright advertising but promotes some special interest in a less obvious way. Propagandistic or more subtly biased materials can thus enter the curriculum through the back door. Preview carefully and exercise caution when you consider sponsored materials. If possible, solicit informational materials on the same subject from several points of view. Thereby, students are afforded a balance and diversity of opinions.
- *Limited quantities.* With the increasing expense of producing both printed and mediated materials, your supplier may have to impose limits on the quantities of items available at one time. You may not be able to obtain a copy of the material for every student in the class.

Sources

There are local, state, national, and international sources of free and inexpensive materials, and many of these are now available as websites. Many local government agencies, community groups, and private businesses provide informational materials on free loan. Public libraries often make videotapes, prints, and computer software available. Even libraries in small communities may have access to materials through a statewide network. These materials usually can be loaned to schools and other organizations. Other state and federal government agencies—such as cooperative extension services, public health departments, and parks departments—make materials available for use in schools, churches, hospitals, and companies.

Community organizations such as the American Red Cross, the League of Women Voters, and medical societies welcome opportunities to spread information about their special interests. Videotapes, printed material, and guest speakers are frequently offered.

Among business organizations, utilities (telephone, electric, gas, and water companies) are most likely to employ education specialists who can inform you about the instructional services they offer. Chambers of commerce often can suggest private corporations that might supply materials of interest to you.

Nationally, one of the most prolific sources of free and inexpensive materials is the federal government. In the United States, two federal agencies offer special access to materials—the U.S. Government Printing Office (http://www.gpoaccess.gov) and the former National Audiovisual Center, now called the National Technical Information Services (http://www.ntis.gov). Your key to the tremendous wealth of posters, charts, brochures, books, and other printed government documents available to the general public is *Selected U.S. Government Publications.* Their websites offer an array of free materials for classroom teachers. Visit these websites through the Web Links module in Chapter 9 of the Companion Website (http://www.prenhall.com/smaldino).

Trade and professional associations, such as the American Dental Association and the National Association of Broadcasters, also aim to acquaint the general public with their fields of interest and the causes they promote. Private corporations, such as automobile manufacturers, communication companies, and food producers, that operate on a national or even international level, often offer sponsored materials.

Most foreign governments disseminate information about their countries to promote trade, tourism, and international understanding. They typically offer free posters, maps, and informational booklets plus videotapes on a free-loan basis. To find out what is available for any particular country, write to or e-mail the embassy of that country. International organizations such as the Organization of American States (OAS), the United Nations (UN), and the North Atlantic Treaty Organization (NATO) also operate information offices and websites. Airline and cruise ship companies are popular sources of posters of foreign countries. Consult a local travel agent for possible materials and addresses.

Obtaining Materials

When you have determined what you can use and where you can obtain it, write or e-mail the supplier; some agencies will not supply free and inexpensive materials unless you write on school or company letterhead. For classroom quantities (when they are available), send just one letter. Do not have each student write individually. If a single student is requesting one copy of something for a class project, the student can write the letter, but you should also sign it. We recommend that you request a preview copy of the material before requesting multiple copies. Don't send a request for "anything you have"! Be specific and specify at least the subject area and the grade level. Ask for only what you need. Don't stockpile materials or take unfair advantage of a free offer. Somebody is paying for those materials, so don't waste them. Follow up with a thank-you note to the supplier; mention how you used the materials and what the students' reactions were. Be courteous, but be honest! Many suppliers attempt to improve free and inexpensive materials on the basis of user comments.

Appraising Materials

As with any other types of material, appraise the educational value of free and inexpensive materials critically. Some are very slick (technically well presented) but not educationally sound. Use the appropriate "Selection Rubric" for the type of media (printed material, videotape, etc.) you are appraising. All the "Selection Rubrics" in this book have the rating criterion "Free from bias." Use it judiciously when reviewing free and inexpensive materials.

For additional information on this topic, go to the Web Links module in Chapter 9 of the Companion Website (http://www.prenhall.com/smaldino).

ASSURE Case Connection

What types of printed materials including free and inexpensive ones could Jan Smith use in presenting her welding instruction? What precautions should she consider if using free and inexpensive materials?

DISPLAY SURFACES

If you are going to use visuals such as photographs, drawings, charts, graphs, or posters, you need a way to display them. Visuals may be displayed in the classroom in a variety of ways, ranging from simply holding up a single visual in your hand to constructing elaborate exhibits for permanent display. Classroom surfaces commonly used for display of visuals include chalkboards, whiteboards, electronic whiteboards, bulletin boards, cloth boards, magnetic boards, and flip charts. Exhibits provide a display format incorporating a variety of materials such as real objects and models along with visuals; we discuss these in the next section. How you display your visuals will depend on a number of factors, including the nature of your audience, the nature of your visuals, the instructional setting, and, of course, the availability of the various display surfaces.

Chalkboards and Whiteboards

The most common display surface in the classroom is, of course, the **chalkboard** (Figure 9.13). Once called *blackboards,* they now come in a variety of colors, as does chalk. Although the chalkboard is most commonly used to support verbal communication, you can use it as a surface on which to draw visuals (or pictures can be fastened to the molding above the chalkboard, taped to the board with masking tape, or placed in the chalk tray) to help illustrate instructional units. You may draw graphics, such as sketches and diagrams or charts and graphs, on the chalkboard for display to the class.

Chalkboards are slowly being replaced by **whiteboards** in schools (Figure 9.14). These are also called *multipurpose boards* and *marker boards.* Most new and remodeled schools use whiteboards. Teachers with allergies and those who don't like chalk on their hands and clothes are delighted. In addition chalk dust is the "enemy" of computers—potentially doing costly damage.

Figure 9.13
The chalkboard is universally recognized as a flexible and economical display surface.

Figure 9.14
Whiteboards are replacing chalkboards in business and industrial training classrooms and in some educational institutions.

A chalkboard or whiteboard is such a common classroom item that instructors often neglect to give them the attention and respect they deserve as instructional devices. Using a chalkboard or whiteboard effectively requires conscious effort (See "Showmanship: Chalkboard and Whiteboard").

Whiteboards require a special erasable marker rather than chalk. Do not use permanent felt-tip markers. These markers may permanently damage the surface.

The white surface is also suitable for projection of video, *PowerPoint* frames, slides, and overhead transparencies. Materials cut from thin plastic, such as figures and letters, will adhere to the surface when rubbed in place. Some of these boards have a steel backing and can be used as a magnetic board (see later in this section).

In addition to their variety of uses, whiteboards have the advantage of being able to display bright, colorful lines. At least eight different colors of markers are currently available.

Showmanship

CHALKBOARD AND WHITEBOARD

- Put extensive drawing or writing on the board before class. Taking too much time to write or draw creates restlessness and may lead to discipline problems.
- Organize in advance what you plan to write on the board and where you plan to write it.
- Cover material such as a test or extensive lesson materials with wrapping paper, newspaper, or a pull-down map until you are ready to use it.
- Eye contact with students is important! Face the class when you are talking. Do not talk to the board. Do not turn your back to the class unless it is absolutely necessary.
- Vary your presentation techniques. Do not overuse or rely entirely on the board. Use handouts, the overhead projector, flip charts, and other media during instruction when appropriate.
- Print neatly rather than using script. For a 32-foot-long classroom, the letters should be 1½–2 inches high and the line forming the letters should be ¼ inch thick.

- Check the visibility of the board from several positions around the room to be sure there is no glare on the surface. In case of glare, move the board (if portable) or pull down the window shades.
- If your printing normally runs "uphill" or "downhill," use water-soluble felt-tip pen markings as temporary guidelines for straighter printing. The guidelines will not be wiped off by a chalk eraser but will wash off when no longer needed.
- Hold the chalk or marker at an angle so that it does not make scratching or squeaking noises.
- Use color for emphasis, but don't overuse it. Two or three different colors work best.
- Move around so you do not block what you have written on the board. Do not stand in front of what you have written.
- Use drawing aids such as rulers, stencils, and templates (patterns) to save time and improve the quality of your drawings.
- For frequently drawn shapes, use a template cut from wood or heavy cardboard. A dresser drawer knob or empty thread spool mounted on the template makes it easier to hold in position while tracing around it.
- Outline your drawings with barely visible lines before class and then fill them in with bold lines in front of the class. Your audience will think you are an artist!

A whiteboard will provide many years of use if cared for properly. Completely erase it after each use; it can be erased like a chalkboard using a felt eraser. Do not let the marks remain on the board overnight. The longer the marks remain on the board, the more difficult they are to erase. You can erase old marks by tracing over them with a black erasable marker and erasing immediately.

For general cleaning, simply wipe the board clean with a soft, damp cloth. If further cleaning is necessary, use a commercial mild spray cleaner. You can also apply a soapy detergent solution and rub briskly with a soft, clean cloth. Always rinse thoroughly with clean water and dry with a soft towel after cleaning.

The special erasable markers also require some special care. They have a solvent base that dries quickly, which is the key to their erasability. Keep the markers tightly capped and store them in a horizontal position with the cap tight when not in use to prevent them from drying out. If a marker dries out, cap it, turn it upside down, and shake it vigorously for 20 seconds. Leaving the marker stored overnight with the tip end down may also help.

Electronic Whiteboards

Electronic whiteboards allow you to "capture" digitally anything written on them. You can write on the electronic whiteboard using any erasable marker. If you make a mistake, erase your error as you would on any multipurpose board. Electronic whiteboards work in conjunction with a desktop computer into which frames are fed and from which the frames can be edited, printed, faxed, or e-mailed.

You can make as many copies of each frame as you like. By copying the information almost instantaneously, you are free to erase the board and continue without losing valuable time or ideas.

Many electronic whiteboards contain multiple screens or frames that can be scrolled forward and backward. You can prepare content beforehand on any or all of the screens. During your presentation you can reveal the frames one at a time, and add new information as desired. You can move the writing surface forward or backward to the desired frame quickly and easily.

The electronic whiteboard is especially valuable for brainstorming sessions and for summarizing group discussions. Copies could be particularly helpful for students who miss class. You can include complex drawings without having students hand copy them. Workers can take the notes into the field, laboratory, or assembly plant for immediate use. Some of these boards can directly transmit a video signal to a monitor in the same room or to a distant location.

There are two types of electronic whiteboards—standard and interactive (Figure 9.15).

Standard models let you send written information as an image file to an attached computer or printer. You can

Figure 9.15
Diagrams and words on an electronic whiteboard can be reproduced on paper with the push of a button.

Figure 9.16
Bulletin boards, long a standard in elementary classrooms, can be primarily decorative, motivational, or instructional.

e-mail or store on a computer network any "captured" frames. With more complex (and expensive) models, you can send the material to a network, such as the Internet, or project the image using an LCD projector.

With interactive electronic whiteboards, the computer and electronic whiteboard configuration lets you open and run software programs, surf the Web, review documents, and toggle between items as you would on a desktop computer. Interactive whiteboards allow data and information sharing during a videoconference. They can also be used as an electronic "chalkboard" during distance learning.

Because of the high cost of current models, the electronic whiteboard is not commonly found in P–12 settings. They are being used in postsecondary and corporate settings.

Bulletin Boards

The term **bulletin board** implies a surface on which bulletins—brief news announcements of urgent interest—are posted for public notice. This was the original purpose of bulletin boards, but it does not describe the variety of uses of these display spaces today. A bulletin board is a surface of variable size and shape made of a material that holds pins, thumbtacks, and other sharp fasteners without damage to the board (Figure 9.16). In practice, bulletin board displays tend to serve three broad purposes: decorative, motivational, or instructional.

The decorative bulletin board is probably the most common, certainly in schools. Its function is to lend visual stimulation to the environment. You might have a bulletin board that displays the colors and designs asso-

ciated with a special holiday or a season. Or, you might have one showing books that students might be interested in reading for pleasure.

Displaying student work exemplifies the motivational use of bulletin boards. The public recognition offered by such displays can play an important role in the life of the classroom. It fosters pride in achievement, reinforcing students' efforts to do a good job. It is also relatively easy for you to create a display of student work.

The third broad purpose of bulletin boards is instructional, complementing the educational or training objectives of the formal curriculum. Rather than merely presenting static informational messages, you may design displays that actively invite participation. Such displays ask questions and give viewers some means of manipulating parts of the display to verify their answers, such as flaps, pockets, dials, or movable parts.

Another form of learner participation is in taking part in the actual construction of the display. For example, to introduce a unit on animals, an elementary teacher might ask each student to bring in a picture of a favorite animal. The students would then make a bulletin board incorporating all the pictures. Or a geometry teacher might divide the class into five groups and assign each group a different geometric shape. As the class studies each shape, the appropriate group would construct a bulletin board on that shape. A discussion leader in a book club might prepare a portable bulletin board to stimulate discussion of the book everyone has read for the monthly meeting.

Preparing an effective bulletin board display, whether done by teacher or students, requires some thought and planning. As with any instructional activity, the objective is primary. A display should focus on one main topic or objective. One way to attract attention to your display and to prompt the viewer's thinking about your topic is to lead off with a catchy headline, one that communicates the main theme, perhaps with a question, a challenge, or a humorous phrase.

Once you have decided on an approach and have assembled some materials, you can refer to "Designing Bulletin Boards" in Classroom Resources, Section C for tips on arranging the elements into a display that will send its message clearly and attractively (Figure 9.17).

Criteria for Evaluating Your Bulletin Boards.

- *Emphatic.* Conveys message quickly and clearly
- *Attractive.* Color and arrangement catch and hold interest
- *Balanced.* Formal or informal
- *Unified.* Repeated shapes or colors or use of borders hold display together visually
- *Interactive.* Involves the viewer
- *Legible.* Lettering and visuals can be read across the room
- *Lettered properly.* Spelled correctly, plain typeface, use of lowercase except where capitals needed
- *Relative.* Correlated with lesson objectives
- *Durable.* Well constructed physically, items securely attached
- *Neat.* A clean, neat appearance makes the display more attractive, shows that the designer has regard for the audience, and provides a proper role model for student work

Materials for production of bulletin boards may be available through the school media center. Most schools have work rooms with large tables where you may construct items for your bulletin board and consider various layouts.

Figure 9.18
The Ellison Prestige™ die-cutter quickly cuts out large letters or decorative shapes for bulletin boards

A popular letter cutting device is the Ellison Prestige™ die cutter (Figure 9.18). This allows for neat, large letters or other shapes to be cut quickly from construction paper.

The media center may also store the components for bulletin board displays so that teachers can share materials and have easy access to them.

Bulletin boards need not always be attached permanently to the wall. You may choose to set portable boards on an easel for temporary display. Beware of having too many bulletin boards, though. Too many competing visual displays in one place can lessen their individual impact.

Cloth Boards

Cloth boards are constructed of cloth stretched over a sturdy backing material such as plywood, Masonite, or heavy cardboard (Figure 9.19). The cloth used for the board may be of various types, including flannel, felt, or hook-and-loop material.

Pieces of flannel stick together when gentle pressure is applied. You can draw with felt-tip markers on visuals cut from flannel and put them on a flannel board. You can back still pictures and graphics with pieces of flannel. Coarse sandpaper also works to attach visuals to a cloth board. Pipe cleaners, available in a variety of colors, and fuzzy yarns stick to the flannel, and you can use them for drawing lines and letters. If adhesion is less than desired, slant the board slightly back at the top to prevent materials from slipping.

The most expensive cloth board is made from hook-and-loop material (such as Velcro®). The hook-

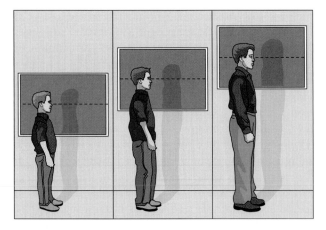

Figure 9.17
The placement of a display should vary according to the average height of the intended viewers. A useful rule of thumb is to align the middle of the display with the viewer's eye level.

Figure 9.19
Cloth boards are often used to involve students in storytelling.

and-loop board has a fine but fuzzy surface composed of tiny, strong nylon loops. The material used for backing visuals and other items to be attached to the board has a coarse, hooklike texture. When pressed together, the two surfaces stick firmly. You can purchase the hooklike material in rolls or strips. One great advantage of the hook-and-loop board is that it can support large and heavy visuals, even books and other three-dimensional objects. One square inch of the cloth can support up to 10 pounds of properly backed visual material.

Teachers of reading and other creative activities often use the cloth board to illustrate stories, poems, and other reading materials. For example, they may place on the board visuals depicting characters and scenes in a story and move them around as the story unfolds. If you use this approach, you may encourage your students' creativity by allowing them to manipulate cloth-board materials. Shy children may particularly profit from this kind of activity. It encourages them to speak through the visual representations of story characters as they move the illustrations on the board.

Be sure you have proper storage space for your cloth board and cloth-board visuals when not in use. Proper storage will help keep them clean and prevent them from being bent or torn. If possible, store your materials on a flat surface rather than stacking them up against a wall. If you use

sandpaper backing on your visuals, put paper between them during storage, as sandpaper can scratch the surface of visuals.

Magnetic Boards

Magnetic boards serve much the same purpose as cloth boards. Visuals are backed with magnets and then placed on the metal surface of the board (Figure 9.20). Magnetic boards, magnets, and flexible strips of magnetic materials for use in backing are available commercially. Plastic lettering with magnetic backing is available from teacher supply stores and can be used for captioning visuals.

Any metal surface in the classroom to which you can attach a magnet can serve as a magnetic board. For example, some chalkboards and whiteboards are backed with steel and thus attract magnet-backed visuals. Use chalk or markers for captioning or to depict lines of association between visuals. You can also use steel cabinets and metal walls and doors as magnetic boards.

You can make your own magnetic board from a thin sheet of galvanized iron, a cookie sheet, a lap tray, or any similar thin sheet of metal. Paint the metal in the color of your choice with paint designed for use on metal surfaces or cover it with adhesive-backed paper. Unpainted surfaces may be unattractive and cause glare. Another alternative is to fasten steel screening to a nonmetal surface, such as plywood, and cover it with cloth.

Figure 9.20
Magnetic boards allow quick manipulation of letters and other materials.

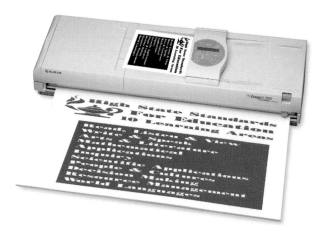

Figure 9.21

The PosterPrinter can convert a notebook-size original into a poster or banner that is many times larger.

The major advantage of magnetic boards is that maneuvering visuals is easier and quicker than with cloth boards. For example, physical education instructors often use them to demonstrate rapid changes in player positions. Magnetic boards also have greater adhesive quality. Visuals displayed on a magnetic board are not likely to slip or fall. They move only when you move them.

Flip Charts

A **flip chart** is a pad of large paper fastened together at the top and mounted to an easel. The individual sheets each hold a limited verbal/visual message and usually are arranged for sequential presentation to a small group. You may write messages extemporaneously while talking or you can prepare them in advance to be revealed one at a time. You can use poster makers, such as the *PosterPrinter*, to produce flip chart pages (Figure 9.21). Commercially produced materials are also available in this format; they are especially prevalent in reading and science instruction and military training. Prepared visual sequences are especially useful for instruction involving sequential steps in a process. The diagrams or words can serve as cues, reminding you of the next point in your presentation.

The most common use of flip charts, though, is for the extemporaneous drawing of key illustrations and key words to supplement a standup presentation. The flip chart is an extremely versatile, convenient, and inexpensive media format. It requires no

electrical power, has no moving parts to wear out, can be used in a range of lighting conditions, is portable, and requires only a marking pen as peripheral equipment. Next to the chalkboard, it is the most user-friendly media tool. But don't let the flip chart's simplicity fool you. Using it professionally takes some practice.

Audience members seem to regard the flip chart in friendly terms. It seems casual and comfortable, a pleasing change of pace in an increasingly high-technology world. It is an exceptionally valuable aid to any group discussion. You may record ideas contributed by group members in a way visible to all participants, make any desired comments or corrections, and preserve the results. If you wish, tear the finished sheets off the pad and tape them to walls or windows for later reference. Flip charts are available in a variety of sizes for large-group use; others, often referred to as *travel easels*, are designed for portability (Figure 9.22).

Flip-chart-size Post-it® easel pads are available from 3M. These 25-by-30-inch self-sticking easel sheets come in white or with a blue grid on white. The easel pads have a built-in handle, a sturdy backing, and a cover flap to protect the sheets from damage or flapping while in transit. The universal slots on the backing attach to most easel stands. Each sheet peels off for quick posting or can be flipped over the top of the pad.

EXHIBITS

Exhibits are collections of various objects and visuals designed to form an integrated whole for instructional purposes (Figure 9.23). Any of the visuals discussed in Chapter 10 as well as real objects, models, and mockups can be included in an exhibit, and any of the display

Figure 9.22

Flip charts, a standard in business and industrial training, are also used in schools.

Showmanship

FLIP CHARTS

- Position the flip chart at an angle so everyone can see it. Place it in the left front corner (as you face the audience) if you are right handed and in the right front corner if you are left handed.
- Be sure the easel is properly assembled and the pages are securely fastened so the flip chart will not fall apart during your presentation.
- Prepare lettering and visuals in advance or outline their shape using a light-blue pencil; then trace them during your presentation.
- For group-generated responses, draw lettering guidelines with a blue pencil.
- Keep lettering and visuals simple but large enough for everyone to see.

- Use more than one color, but not more than four.
- Use broad-tip marking pens that provide contrast but will not bleed through to the next sheet.
- Print rather than use cursive writing.
- Keep words short or use well-understood abbreviations.
- Include simple drawings, symbols, and charts.
- Talk to the audience, not to the flip chart.
- Avoid blocking the audience's view of the flip chart.
- Be sure your materials are in proper sequence.
- Have a blank sheet exposed when not referring to the flip chart.
- Reveal pages only when you are ready to discuss them, not before.
- Put summary points on the last sheet rather than paging back as you make your summary.

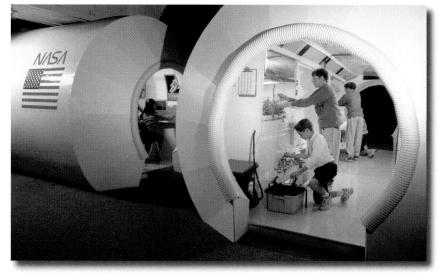

Figure 9.23
A complex exhibit such as this one brings together real objects, still pictures, and other visuals with verbal information.

surfaces discussed in this chapter can contribute to an exhibit. Exhibits can generally be used for the same instructional purposes and in the same ways as their individual components are used.

Exhibit locations are readily available in most classrooms. You can set up simple exhibits on a table, shelf, or desk. More complex exhibits may require considerable floor space and special structures (a booth or bookshelf, for example).

The school media center is a convenient location for exhibits, displays, and dioramas. Often area museums or historical societies will lend these items. The media cen-

ter may also provide space for display of student-produced exhibits.

There are three types of exhibits—field trips, displays, and dioramas. Field trips are an exhibit of real things in their natural environment. A display is a collection of materials, whereas a diorama shows a three-dimensional scene.

Field Trips

The **field trip,** an excursion outside the classroom to study real processes, people, and objects, often grows out of students' need for firsthand experiences. It makes it possible for students to encounter phenomena that cannot be brought into the classroom for observation and study.

Examples of field trips include a trip of a few minutes into the schoolyard to observe a tree, a trek across the street to see construction work, or a longer trip of several days to tour historical locations. Popular field trip sites include zoos, museums, public buildings, and parks. Dale's Cone of Experience (see Chapter 1) places field trips toward the middle of the cone because, although the experience is "real," students typically are only seeing and hearing the phenomena, not directly manipulating them.

The school media specialist can increase the chances for a successful field trip experience by maintaining a local resource file. This file includes lists of possible sites to visit. Usually the file record includes the name, address, and phone number of the person to contact. A good resource file will also include notes regarding the value of previous trips. Some district media centers and public libraries maintain a local resource file as part of their electronic catalog.

Virtual field trips are an extension of actual field trips. Often the expense or the time to travel to a particular interesting location is not possible. But, with the World Wide Web, children may experience the sights and sounds of a faraway location from their home or school. For example, if you are studying Paris, France, it would be nearly impossible for the whole class to go there. However, with a few simple clicks of a mouse, the whole class can see and hear the sights of the city. Although it is not exactly the same as being there, it certainly makes it possible to learn about a location with some authenticity to the experience. (See "Media Files: Instructional Material.")

In addition to taking virtual field trips using the World Wide Web, videoconferencing can also be used. Teachers with videoconferencing receiving can take their students to any location with videoconference-sending capabilities. Some of these trips are offered at predetermined dates and times and are available on a first-come, first-served basis. The only charge is for network time—no transportation or other fees.

The Cincinnati Zoo (http://www. cincyzoo.org) offers virtual field trips. Students get to interact live with zookeepers. Their program "Nobody Likes Me," for example, introduces students to frogs, toads, bats, bugs, and snakes.

For any field trip to be justified, it should grow out of and be directly related to the regular course of study. (See "Conducting a Field Trip" in Classroom Resources, Section C, and Figure 9.24.) You should devise lead-in as well as followup (including evaluation) activities. The lead-in prepares the students for the field trip; the followup helps them reflect on the experience and integrate it into their own schemata.

The followup is a vital aspect of a field trip. If the purpose for making the trip is to get additional factual information, the evaluation will be more formal. If the objectives are the formation

Figure 9.24
Field trips provide students with opportunities for firsthand observation and participation, as in this trip to an aquarium.

of attitudes and appreciation, followup activities might include discussion, role playing, or creative art projects. Whatever form it takes, followup activity should assess the success of the trip. Students and teachers should address content as well as possible ways to improve future trips.

Displays

A **display** is an array of objects, visuals, and printed materials (e.g., labels and descriptions). Most displays include descriptive information about the objects or visuals shown. Instructional displays are used in the classroom (Figure 9.25), in museums, and in many other settings.

Figure 9.25
Books related to a topic of study can enhance student observation skills.

Student assembly of a display can be a motivating learning experience. It can foster retention of subject matter and sharpen visual skills. For a lesson on transportation, one sixth-grade teacher had each student bring in a replica of a vehicle. Some students made their own vehicles from construction paper. Others brought in toys from home or contributed vehicles assembled from hobby kits (e.g., boats, cars, trucks, trains, space ships). The teacher placed tables and other classroom furniture along a wall to provide the children with a shelf on which to arrange their three-dimensional objects. On the wall above the display surface, the teacher placed a long sheet of paper containing a timeline. The timeline illustrated forms of transportation from the past (humans and beasts), through the present (trains, cars, planes), and into the future (space vehicles). The display was a great success!

Dioramas

Dioramas are static displays consisting of a three-dimensional foreground and a flat background to create a realistic scene. The foreground is usually a landscape of some sort with models of people, animals, vehicles, equipment, or buildings. The naturalistic background may be a photograph, drawing, or painting. The diorama is usually contained within a box, with the sides of the box providing a backdrop. The rear corners or the entire back may be rounded to provide an illusion of depth, and lights can be added for a special effect.

Dioramas are usually designed to reproduce past or present scenes and events or to depict future ones. Examples in museums are often life size, whereas those used in classrooms are usually on a smaller scale (Figure 9.26). In industry, dioramas often are constructed to show company products in use.

You may construct dioramas to illustrate your lessons or to introduce new topics. You may ask students to design their own dioramas as a followup activity to instruction (see "Media Files: Instructional Material"). Scenes from history, particularly battles, are often portrayed with model figures. Animals can be shown in their natural habitats for a biology class. Scenes including towns and landscapes from various parts of the world make stimulating dioramas for geography instruction. Prehistoric landscapes and geologic formations are also popular topics for dioramas.

Figure 9.26
Calvin and Hobbes © 1990 Watterson. Reprinted with permission of Universal Press Syndicate. All rights reserved.

Media Files: Instructional Material

DIORAMA DESIGNER™
Tom Snyder Productions
Diorama Graphics Program

It is easy for students to create dioramas on the computer using the *Diorama Designer*™ program. They can design original dioramas, print them in color, and assemble them to demonstrate understanding of historical periods for interdisciplinary units in social studies, language arts, or other classes. Students can select from a variety of backgrounds and decorative elements. People and furniture can be printed separately as 3-D elements to place inside the diorama. Dioramas can be printed in different sizes, from small enough to fit in a shoebox to a puppet-sized stage. Options include making posters, puppets, and masks.

A variation of this is *Rainforest Designer®*, which lets students design, build, and print 3-D rainforest habitats.

For additional information, visit the Tom Snyder Productions website (www.tomsnyder.com).

SCIENCE COURT® EXPLORATIONS
Tom Snyder Productions
CD-ROM Series

An exciting science CD-ROM series that combines the power of technology with the effectiveness of hands-on manipulatives is available in an all-in-one easy-to-use kit. *Science Court Explorations,* designed for grades 2–4, is an extension of Tom Snyder Production's award-winning *Science Court®* series.

Science Court Explorations comes with a hybrid Mac/Win CD-ROM, a class set of manipulatives (enough for six cooperative learning teams), and a comprehensive teacher's guide with reproducible worksheets and take-home activities.

Science Court Explorations introduces and reinforces the scientific method and fundamental science concepts for young students. A funny and compelling animated story on CD-ROM introduces a scientific question. The CD-ROM then walks students step by step through the scientific process and illustrates how to set up the hands-on experiment. Working in teams, students use the experiment to test hypotheses and answer the question.

Titles include "Pendulums," "Rockets," "Flight," "Heat Absorption," "Magnets," and "Friction."

For additional information, visit the Tom Snyder Productions website (www.tomsnyder.com).

QUEST INTERACTIVE EXPEDITIONS
Classroom Connect
Interactive Internet Activity

Classroom Connect is the innovator of the *Quest Interactive Expeditions* concept—using the Internet to provide collaborative and experiential virtual field trips to P–12 school participants and general onlookers from around the world. Classroom Connect has guided students in many online Quests, including *AfricaQuest, GalapagosQuest, AsiaQuest, AmericaQuest, IslandQuest,* and *AustraliaQuest.* During *AmericaQuest,* approximately 6,000 classrooms registered to participate, with 240,000 school students involved and hundreds of thousands of additional onlookers logged in from around the world to follow the Quest team's journey.

Each Quest involves a team of 8 to 10 people riding mountain bikes through sometimes harsh and rugged environments—always with the goal to unravel some of the greatest mysteries of all time. This is a place where students can participate in online adventures around the world.

Quests allow students and teachers to explore math, science, language arts, social studies, geography, and much more. Students interact with other students and learn more about different cultures along the way. For example, in conjunction with *AustraliaQuest,* a special Aboriginal team was asked to connect the Quest team with Aboriginal culture in Australia. Through the knowledge and experience of this group, students and teachers were introduced to Aboriginal history and culture.

Selection Rubric: Printed Materials

Complete an interactive evaluation and add it to your NETS-T portfolio using the Selection Rubric for Printed Materials available on the "Classroom Link Portfolio" CD-ROM. A downloadable version of this rubric is available in the Selection Rubrics module of the Companion Website at http://www.prenhall.com/smaldino.

Key Words

_____

_____

_____

Title _____

Series Title (if applicable) _____

Source _____

Date _____ Cost _____ Length _____

Subject Area _____

Intended Audience _____

Format

☐ Textbook

☐ Fiction

☐ Nonfiction

☐ Pamphlet

☐ Manual

Brief Description

Objectives

Entry Capabilities Required (e.g., prior knowledge, reading ability, vocabulary level, math ability)

Strong Points

Weak Points

Recommended Action (using criteria on the following page)

Name _____ Date _____

Rating Area	High Quality	Medium Quality	Low Quality	Rating
Match Curriculum	Curriculum standard addressed and use of print should enhance student learning.	Curriculum standard partially addressed and use of print may enhance student learning.	Curriculum standard not addressed and use of print will likely not enhance student learning.	
Accurate & Current	Information correct and does not contain material that is out of date.	Information correct but does contain material that is out of date.	Information is not correct and does contain material that is out of date.	
Clear & Concise Language	Language used is age appropriate and vocabulary is understandable.	Language used is nearly age appropriate and some vocabulary is above/below student age.	Language used is not age appropriate and vocabulary is clearly inappropriate for student age.	
Motivating/ Interesting	Topic presented so that students are likely to be interested and engaged in learning.	Topic presented to interest students most of the time and engage most in learning.	Topic presented so as not to interest students and not engage them in learning.	
Learner Participation	Topic presented so that most students are actively engaged in learning.	Topic presented so that some students are engaged in learning.	Topic presented so that most students are not actively engaged in learning.	
Technical Quality	The material represents best available media.	The material represents media that are good quality, although there are some problems.	The material represents media that are not well prepared and are of very poor quality.	
Effectiveness Rating	There is evidence that use of these media has shown positive impact on student learning.	There is little evidence that use of these media has shown positive impact on student learning.	There is no evidence that use of these media has shown positive impact on student learning.	
Free from Bias	There is no evidence of objectionable bias or advertising.	There is little evidence of bias or advertising.	There is much evidence of bias or advertising.	
User Guide & Documentation	The documentation is excellent resource for use in a lesson. Documentation should help students use the materials.	The documentation is good resource for use in a lesson. Documentation may help students use the materials.	The documentation is poor resource for use in a lesson. Documentation does not help students use the materials.	
Reading Level	The material is presented at an appropriate reading level so most students can understand the information.	The material is presented at a reading level so that students can understand most of the information.	The material is presented at a reading level so most students cannot understand the information.	
Clarity of Organization	The material is presented in such a way that students are able to use the information.	The material is presented in such a way that students are able to use most of the information.	The material is presented in such a way that students are unable to use the information.	
Table of Contents/Index	The Table of Contents and Index are useful for students to access information.	The Table of Contents and Index are moderately useful for students to access information.	The Table of Contents and Index are not useful for students to access information.	

Summary: Using the ASSURE Model with Instructional Materials and Displays

As with other media and technology, the AS-SURE model introduced in Chapter 3 is helpful in preparing lessons incorporating learning centers, instructional modules, manipulatives, printed materials, free and inexpensive materials, and displays and exhibits.

Analyze Learners

Lesson development begins by identifying your students' unique attributes and learning characteristics. You also will wish to determine their various levels of experience with using instructional materials, manipulatives, displays, and exhibits.

State Objectives

Before stating specific objectives, you may wish to explore how you want students to use the materials (in a learning center, as an individual or with a group?) You will also want to consider the materials available in your classroom and at your school's media center. Would a real or virtual field trip offer students the best learning experience? Sometimes it is more appropriate to state specific objectives after you have identified potential materials and resources.

Select Methods, Media, and Materials

Use the information on instructional materials, manipulatives, displays, and exhibits discussed in this chapter as the basis for selecting, modifying, or designing your materials. Adjust the specific applications to suit the specific nature of your topic and objectives.

You should preview and appraise both commercially and locally produced materials before using them with your students. For printed materials use "Selection Rubric: Printed Materials." If you are considering free and inexpensive materials that are in videocassette format, use "Selection Rubric: Video" in Chapter 12. For a listing of all the Selection Rubrics in the book, see the Special Features list at the end of the Contents. Choose the one that will meet your needs.

Utilize Media and Materials

Just as you used the appropriate Selection Rubric for the type of media under consideration, use the appropriate Showmanship or Classroom Resource "How to . . . " for the media and materials that you select to utilize. Within this chapter there are Showmanship guidelines for manipulatives, chalkboards and whiteboards, and flip charts. "How to . . . " guidelines for preparing text, designing bulletin boards, and conducting field trips appear in Classroom Resources, Section C. For a complete listing of the Showmanship guidelines in the book, see the appropriate list at the end of the Contents.

Require Learner Participation

Get the students involved in learning activities. Learning centers require student participation. Instructional modules also require involvement. When at all possible allow students to handle manipulatives. When using printed materials, supplement them with objectives or questions that encourage students to find the answers rather than just reading passively. Remember SQ3R! If you are having the students participate in a real or virtual field trip, find ways to actively involve them before, during, and after the experience.

Evaluate and Revise

As with all technology and media, evaluate the materials, the student learning, and your use of the instructional materials and display surfaces. Refer back to your objectives when deciding how you will assess student learning. The students themselves can give you valuable feedback on the value of the learning center, instructional module, or field trip. As with all media- and technology-based lessons, you may choose to revise your selection of materials after you have determined how well they have worked. In addition, you want to be certain that all materials used have been cleared of any potential copyright issues.

ASSURE Case in Practice: Vocational Technical College Welding Class

All of the ASSURE Cases in Practice in this text and an electronic template for creating your own ASSURE Lesson can be found on the enclosed "Classroom Link Portfolio" CD-ROM.

Analyze Learners

General Characteristics

The students at the Summit VoTech College range in age from 18 to 68 and include both men and women. All are high school graduates or have earned their GED, but most have low reading abilities (the average is 9th grade, with a range from 6th to 14th).

Most students are highly motivated to learn how to weld. With this skill they can get a high-paying job at a local manufacturing company. These jobs are some of the highest-paying ones in the area for high school graduates.

Entry Competencies

The chief requirements are the ability to follow instructions (which may be committed to memory after several weeks on the job) and to demonstrate good manual dexterity.

Students who are "coming back to school" while working are highly motivated to be successful. This is especially true of the "older" workers (25 years or older). The younger students sometimes just want to get by with as little effort as possible.

Learning Styles

The students display a range of learning styles. Most of them have limited language skills, low math ability, good visual and spatial skills, and excellent kinesthetic ability.

State Objectives

On completion of the welding unit, the students will be able to do the following:

- Weld two pieces of metal according to specifications in the Product Rating Checklist (see Chapter 3, Figure 3.11) within seven minutes when given the necessary components and appropriate tools.

Subobjectives include the following:

- Adjust welding machine to proper settings for type of materials to be welded without reference to the manual and within 10 percent of the suggested settings.
- Demonstrate a proper weld using the materials and equipment provided. The bead must meet the criteria in the Product Rating Checklist and must be completed within seven minutes.

There are several other subobjectives as well as this affective objective:

- Wear safety helmet and work gloves during the entire welding process. (The students know they should do this, but they don't always do so.)

Select Methods, Media, and Materials

After checking through catalogs of industrial training materials and talking with curriculum directors from other vocational technical schools, Jan Smith, the chief welding instructor, decided to develop a set of drawings and photographs to be incorporated into a small (9-by-12-inch) flip chart for students to use. Jan wanted her students to learn to weld with the actual materials in front of them. Therefore, she rejected the idea of using one of the many videotapes on welding. The videotapes required viewing in a classroom and then going to the lab to practice the skills. Because of the need for hands-on practice and training, Jan developed a self-instructional unit incorporating actual welding materials, the flip chart, and an audiotape. She used humor to enhance motivation for those students who are not motivated.

Utilize the Materials

The students will be allowed to use the set of drawings and photographs incorporated into the small flip chart and practice actual welding as many times as necessary in the laboratory. An instructor will be available to answer questions and to evaluate the completed welds.

Require Learner Participation

The students will practice the skill and an instructor will provide constructive feedback. When the instructor is satisfied that a student has mastered the task, that student will do three test welds with different metals. The instructor will evaluate these test welds using the Product Rating Checklist. If all criteria are met the student receives a mastery score.

Evaluate and Revise

Jan will evaluate the students and the instruction based on a number of factors. The number of defective welds identified by the instructors during competency testing is one criterion. The instructors also will constantly observe the students for safety procedures (gloves and helmet) and welding sequence.

Create Your Own ASSURE Lesson

Using the ASSURE model, design a lesson for a scenario from the Companion Website or use a scenario of your own design. Use one of the methods described in Chapter 1 and information from this chapter related to incorporating instructional materials and displays into your instructional setting. Be sure to include information about the audience, the objectives, and all other elements of the ASSURE model. When completed, reflect on the process you used and what you have learned about matching audience, content, method, and materials.

Classroom Link Portfolio Activities

Use the "Classroom Link Portfolio" CD-ROM and the Companion Website as resources in completing these activities. To complete the following activities online go to the Portfolio Activities module in Chapter 9 of the Companion Website (http://www. prenhall.com/smaldino).

1. *Planning Lessons Using Media Resources:* Locate a lesson or unit of study and identify all the various media resources that are included in the design of the lesson. Cite sources. What activities are identified in the lesson? How do the media you identified enhance the learning activities presented? What might you add to make it better? (ISTE NETS-T 2.C; 6.A)

2. *Written Reflection.* Examine and reflect on the copyright guidelines given in this chapter. How might a teacher use media to enhance student learning and expand their access to resources within the guidelines? (ISTE NETS-T 6.A & D)

Integration Assessments

To complete the specified activities online go to the Integration Assessments module in Chapter 9 of the Companion Website (http://www.prenhall. com/smaldino).

1. Generate two ideas for using learning centers in your own teaching. (ISTE NETS-T 2.A; 3.B)
2. Develop an instructional module for a topic and audience of your choice. (ISTE NETS-T 2.A; 3.B)
3. Obtain an example of a manipulative(s) that you could use for instruction. Submit the manipulative(s) and a description of how you would use them, including an objective. (ISTE NETS-T 2.C; 3.B)
4. Use the "Selection Rubric: Print Materials" to evaluate a textbook, fiction book, nonfiction book, pamphlet, or manual. (ISTE NETS-T 2.C)
5. Use the World Wide Web to locate free or inexpensive materials. Identify the website and describe the types of resources that are available to you. (ISTE NETS-T 2.C)
6. Demonstrate techniques (showmanship tips) for improving your utilization of chalkboards and multipurpose boards. (ISTE NETS-T 2.D; 5.B)
7. Prepare a bulletin board, cloth board, magnetic board, flip chart, or exhibit. Submit the material (or a photograph of the display), a description of the intended audience, the objectives, how you will use it, and how you will evaluate it. (ISTE NETS-T 2.A)
8. Demonstrate techniques (showmanship tips) to enhance learning from flip charts. (ISTE NETS-T 2.D; 5.B)
9. Plan a lesson that would include a field trip. Locate at least one site on the World Wide Web that could be a place to visit as a virtual field trip in your lesson. (ISTE NETS-T 2.A)

References

Riedl, Joan. 1995. *The integrated technology classroom.* Des Moines, IA: Longwood/Allyn & Bacon.

Robinson, F. P. 1946. *Effective study.* New York: Harper & Row.

Suggested Readings

Alvarado, Amy Edmonds, and Patricia R. Herr. 2003. *Inquiry-based learning using everyday objects: Hands-on instructional strategies that promote active learning in grades 3–8.* Thousand Oaks, CA: Sage.

Austin, Janet. 1996. Artful teaching in artful classrooms. *Primary Educator, 2*(5): 12.

Blenz-Clucas, Beth. 1993. Bring the museum to the media center. *School Library Journal, 39*(9): 150–153.

Burn, Bonnie E. 1996. *Flip chart power.* San Diego: Pfeiffer.

Cooper, Gail, and Garry Cooper. 2001. *New virtual field trips.* Englewood, CO: Libraries Unlimited/Teacher Ideas Press.

Davis, Douglas. 2002. *Scala guide to art on the Internet.* New York: iBooks.

Elementary teachers guide to free curriculum materials, 60th ed. 2003. Randolph, WI: Educators Progress Service.

Fail, J. 1995. Teaching ecology in urban environments. *The American Biology Teacher, 57*(8): 522–525.

Free stuff for everyone. 1996. Highland Park, IL: Prime.

Gravois, Michael. 1999. *25 totally awesome and totally easy bulletin boards: Reproducible templates and how-tos for interactive bulletin boards that make learning fun.* New York: Scholastic.

Holleman, Curt. 2000. Electronic resources: Are basic criteria for the selection of materials changing? *Library Trends, 48*(4): 694–710.

Karnes, Frances A., and Suzanne M. Bean. 2001. *Methods and materials for teaching the gifted.* Waco, TX: Prufrock.

Leach, B. 1997. A street scene: Building a bustling playdough street scene. *Child Education, 74*(January): 42.

Lindroth, Linda. 1999. How to find free resources on the Internet. *Teaching PreK–8, 29*(8): 22–23.

Lucas, Robert William. 1999. *The big book of flip charts: A comprehensive guide for presenters, trainers, and facilitators.* New York: McGraw-Hill.

Middle school teachers guide to free curriculum materials, 5th ed. 2002. Randolph, WI: Educators Progress Service.

Orion, N., A. Hofstein, P. Tamir, and G. Giddings. 1997. Developing and validation of an instrument for assessing the learning environment of outdoor science activities. *Science Education, 81*(2): 161–171.

Scott, Kristin S. 1993. Multisensory mathematics for children with mild disabilities. *Exceptionality: A Research Journal, 4*(2): 125–129.

Secondary teachers guide to free curriculum materials, 112th ed. 2003. Randolph, WI: Educators Progress Service.

Stainfield, John, Peter Fisher, Bob Ford, and Michael Solem. 2000. International virtual field trips: A new direction? *Journal of Geography in Higher Education, 24*(2): 255–262.

Visuals

Outline

Knowledge Objectives

1. Identify six types of visuals and compare their advantages and limitations.
2. Describe specific situations in which the document camera would be especially useful.
3. Describe the characteristics and operation of overhead transparency projection.
4. Describe specific applications of overheads to your teaching field.
5. Outline the procedures for creating transparencies by each of these methods: direct drawing, electrostatic film process, and computer generation.
6. Identify examples of digital images that exhibit the guidelines for the design of effective visuals.
7. Describe the advantages, limitations, and integration of digital image formats.
8. Discuss the advantages and limitations of using the data projector for image projection.

Professional Vocabulary

nonprojected visuals

visuals

study prints

projected visuals

document camera

overhead projection

fresnel lens

transparency

acetate

overlay

keystone effect

electrostatic film (xerography)

presentation graphics software

slide

liquid crystal display (LCD)

Not all media plug into an electrical outlet. There is a variety of nonprojected media that can make your instruction more realistic and engaging. Pictures, charts, graphs, posters, and cartoons—including those that students themselves produce—can provide powerful visual support to abstract ideas. These nonprojected media can be displayed in a variety of ways. Projected media, such as overhead transparencies and *PowerPoint* slides, can enhance a presentation made by students or teachers.

In this chapter we examine the variety of visual materials that you can use to enhance learning. By using visuals you, the instructor, can find ways of helping students understand complex ideas. Visuals can engage learners in their quest for knowledge. You can display nonprojected visuals in the classroom or use them as part of a group learning activity. Projected visuals can present information to the whole group.

NONPROJECTED VISUALS

Nonprojected visuals can translate abstract ideas into a more realistic format (Figure 10.1). They allow instruction to move down from the level of verbal symbols in Dale's Cone of Experience (see Chapter 1) to a more concrete level.

Nonprojected visuals are easy to use because they do not require any equipment. They are relatively inexpensive. Many can be obtained at little or no cost. They can be used in many ways at all levels of instruction and in all disciplines. You may also use them to stimulate creative expression, such as telling or writing stories or composing poetry.

You may use all types of nonprojected visuals in testing and evaluation. They are particularly helpful with objectives requiring identification of people, places, or things.

Some nonprojected visuals are simply too small to use before a group. It is possible to enlarge any visual photographically, but that can be expensive. A document camera (discussed later in this chapter) can show an enlarged image before a group.

ASSURE Case Challenge

We have developed a case study for this chapter to help you see how visuals can be integrated into learning activities. At the end of the chapter you will be challenged to develop your own ASSURE lesson for a case study of your choice using the ASSURE model and incorporating the technology and media described in this chapter. To help you prepare your lesson, we have included hints (called "ASSURE Case Connections")

throughout the chapter as they relate to the ASSURE Case Challenge.

Mr. Donalds is a general sales manager for a regional company. The company sales have been at a plateau for several years. Mr. Donalds believes he has a strategy for improving the situation. He needs to convince the management and marketing divisions to approve of the plan.

Mr. Donalds knows the members of his potential audience. They have been with the company for various lengths of time, from 2 to 10 years. Each has an opinion of the issues related to the sales issues. In general, these people will need to be convinced that there is a need for a new strategy.

Mr. Donalds hopes that at the end of his presentation to the group they will adopt his marketing strategy.

Some nonprojected visuals demand special caution. Because the images are visually symbolic rather than fully representational, they leave more room for viewers to misinterpret the intended meaning. (We discussed this phenomenon in Chapter 4.) For example, when newspaper readers interpret editorial cartoons they may draw conclusions that are opposite of what the artist intended. Psychologists find that people tend to project their own hopes, fears, and preconceptions onto images or verbal messages that are ambiguous.

Next we will explore six types of **visuals** commonly found in the classroom situation: still pictures, drawings (including sketches and diagrams), charts, graphs, posters, and cartoons.

See Classroom Resources, Section C for information and techniques to preserve nonprojected visuals, including mounting (rubber cement and dry mounting), laminating, filing, and storing.

Still Pictures

Still pictures are photographic (or photographlike) representations of people, places, and things. The still pictures most commonly used in instruction are photographs; postcards; illustrations from books, periodicals, and catalogs; and **study prints** (oversized illustrations commercially prepared to accompany specific instructional units).

Still pictures are readily available in books (including textbooks), magazines, newspapers, catalogs, and calendars. In addition, you can purchase large photographs from educational supply companies to use with groups of students, or you can obtain them from your media center or library.

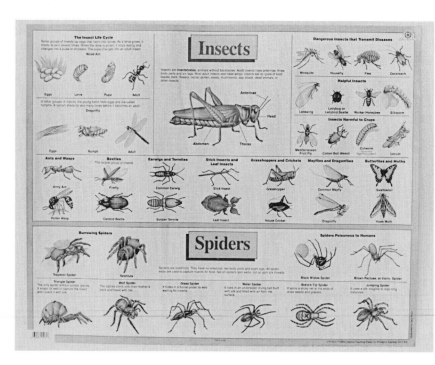

Figure 10.1

Visuals carry the main message in a well-designed chart.

Close-Up

USING NONPROJECTED VISUALS

Students of all ages can use visuals. These elementary school students examine images and texts related to their study of Spanish. The teacher assigns small groups of students to study different Spanish-speaking countries. Each small group works collaboratively to prepare a report, with drawings and charts, to share with the class. Following each group's presentation the teacher facilitates a discussion of the topic and summarizes key points. They use pictures to help present their information to the class.

An eighth grade health class is studying about the need for a healthy diet to support their growing bodies. One unit focuses on the relationship between nutrition and a healthy heart. Some posters and other visual materials were obtained by their teacher from local sources. The students put together a display of foods, along with additional visual materials to explain the significance of the foods that were selected. The display and written materials will be shared with other classes.

Still pictures are two dimensional. You can compensate for the lack of three-dimensionality by providing a group of pictures showing the same object or scene from several different angles or positions. Also, a series of sequential still pictures can suggest motion.

You may use photographs in a variety of ways. Teacher-made or student-made photographs may illustrate and help teach specific lesson topics. Photographs of local architecture, for example, can illustrate a unit on architectural styles. (In this case, you could reinforce the students' skill in "reading" a visual by pointing out that merely looking at the buildings in our environment is not the same as really "seeing" them.) Photographs taken on field trips can be valuable for classroom followup activities.

You may include skill in decoding textbook pictures in instructional objectives to motivate learners to use them for study purposes. The quality and quantity of illustrations are, of course, important factors in textbook choice. You may use pictures from newspapers and periodicals in similar ways.

Students should understand that textbook pictures are not decorations but are intended to be study aids and should be used as such. Encourage students to give attention to them.

Photographic study prints—enlargements printed in a durable form for individuals to use or for display—also have many applications in the instructional setting. They are especially helpful in the study of processes—the production of iron or paper, for example, or the operation of the internal combustion engine. They are also very useful in teaching the social sciences. In geography they may help illustrate relationships between people and their environment that, because of space limitations, could not be depicted easily in textbook pictures.

Drawings

Drawings, sketches, and diagrams employ the graphic arrangement of lines to represent persons, places, things, and concepts. Drawings are, in general, more finished and representational than sketches (e.g., stick figure compositions), which are likely to lack detail. Diagrams are usually intended to show relationships or to help explain processes, such as how something works or is constructed (Figure 10.2).

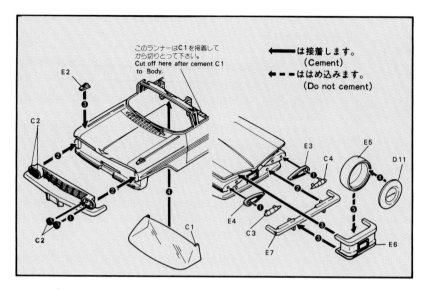

は接着します。
(Cement)

は はめ込みます。
(Do not cement)

このランナーはC1を接着して
から切りとって下さい。
Cut off here after cement C1
to Body.

Figure 10.2

The use of visual symbols greatly reduces the need for words in this multilingual diagram for assembling a plastic scale model of an automobile.

Drawings are readily found in textbooks and other classroom materials. You can use them in all phases of instruction, from introduction of the topic through evaluation. Because they are likely to be less detailed and more to the instructional point than photographic materials, students of all ages understand them easily.

Teacher-made drawings can be effective aids to learning. You can sketch on a chalkboard or whiteboard (or some other appropriate surface) to coincide with specific aspects of your instructional unit. For example, you may quickly and easily draw stick figures to show motion in an otherwise static representation.

Charts

Charts are visual representations of abstract relationships such as chronologies, quantities, and hierarchies. They appear frequently in textbooks and training manuals as tables and flowcharts. They are also published as wall charts for group viewing in the form of organization charts, classification charts (e.g., the periodic table), and timelines (see "Types of Charts").

A chart should have a clear, well-defined instructional purpose. In general (especially for younger students), it should express only one major concept or configuration of concepts. If you are developing your own charts, be sure they contain the minimum of visual and verbal information needed for understanding. A cluttered chart is a confusing chart. If you have a lot of information to convey, develop a series of simple charts rather than a single complex one. Use the KISS principle—Keep It Simple for Students!

A well-designed chart should communicate its message primarily through the visual channel. The verbal material should supplement the visual, not the reverse.

Graphs

Graphs provide a visual representation of numerical data. They also illustrate relationships among units of the data and trends in the data. Many tabular charts can be converted into graphs, as shown in Figure 10.3.

Data can be interpreted more quickly in graph form than in tabular form. Graphs are also more visually interesting than tables. There are four major types of graphs: bar, pictorial, circle, and line (see "Types of Graphs"). The type you choose will depend largely on the complexity of the information you wish to present and the graph-interpretation skills of your audience. Numerous computer software programs now make it easy to produce professional-looking charts, graphs, and other visuals. Type your data into the computer, and the computer will create the type of chart or graph you wish. When you see the preliminary result on the computer monitor, you can change parameters (axes, size, orientation, etc.). Some programs even provide output in a variety of colors.

Most spreadsheet programs, such as *AppleWorks* and *Excel*, have a chart and graph option. Spreadsheet programs are easy-to-use tools for creating graphs from numerical data.

You and your students can use drawing programs for layout and design, as well as for drawing and illustrating. Most computer graphics programs come with hundreds or even thousands of typefaces and clip-art images and can manipulate visuals in every imaginable way. Examples of these programs are *AppleWorks*, *Photoshop*, and *Adobe Illustrator*.

Posters

Posters incorporate visual combinations of images, lines, color, and words. They are intended to catch and hold the viewer's attention at least long enough to communicate a brief message, usually a persuasive one. To be effective, posters must be colorful and dynamic. They must grab attention and communicate their message quickly. One drawback in using posters is that their message is quickly blunted by familiarity. Consequently, they should not be left on display for too long. Commercial billboards are an example of posters on a very large scale.

Types of Charts

Organization charts show the structure or chain of command in an organization such as a company, corporation, civic group, or government department. Usually they deal with the interrelationship of personnel or departments.

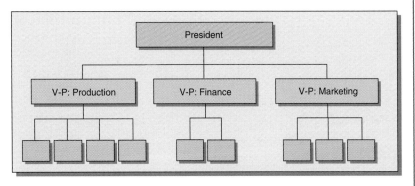

Classification charts are similar to organization charts but are used chiefly to classify or categorize objects, events, or species. A common type of classification chart is one showing the taxonomy of animals and plants according to natural characteristics. Dale's Cone of Experience classifies media from concrete to abstract.

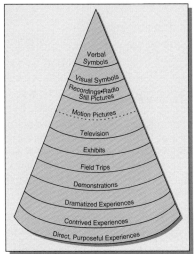

Time lines illustrate chronological relationships between events. They are most often used to show historical events in sequence or the relationship of famous people and these events. Pictures or drawings can be added to the time line to illustrate important concepts. Time lines are very helpful for summarizing a series of events.

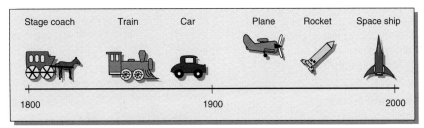

Tabular charts, or tables, contain numerical information, or data. They are also convenient for showing time information when the data are presented in columns, as in timetables for railroads and airlines.

Import Percentages				
	Wheat	Cotton	Steel	Oil
USA	0	0	20	35
England	65	95	35	10
France	15	95	30	90
Japan	85	15	0	95
Brazil	0	0	20	70

Flowcharts, or process charts, show a sequence, a procedure, or, as the name implies, the flow of a process. Flowcharts show how different activities, ingredients, or procedures are interrelated.

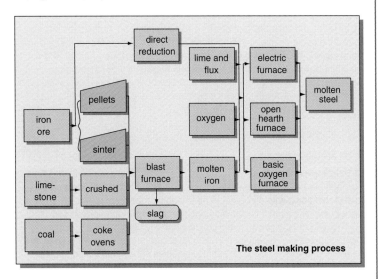

The steel making process

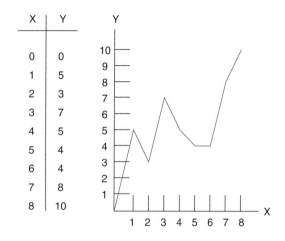

X	Y
0	0
1	5
2	3
3	7
4	5
5	4
6	4
7	8
8	10

Figure 10.3

A line graph can make a table of data much easier to interpret.

Posters can be effective in numerous learning situations. They can stimulate interest in a new topic, a special class, or a school event. They may be employed for motivation—luring students to a school meeting or to the media center, for example, or encouraging them to read more. In industrial education courses, science laboratories, and other situations where danger may be involved, posters can remind people of safety tips. Posters can also promote good health practices such as not using drugs. An effective learning technique is to have students design posters as part of a class project, during fire prevention week or dental health month, for example (Figure 10.4).

You may obtain posters from a variety of sources, including commercial companies, airlines, travel agencies, and government departments. You can make your own

Types of Graphs

Bar graphs are easy to read and can be used with elementary age students. The height of the bar is the measure of the quantity being represented. The width of all bars should be the same to avoid confusion. A single bar can be divided to show parts of a whole. It is best to limit the quantities being compared to eight or less; otherwise the graph becomes cluttered and confusing. The bar graph, a one-scale graph, is particularly appropriate for comparing similar items at different times or different items at the same time; for example, the height of one plant over time or the heights of several students at any given time. The bar graph shows variation in only one dimension.

Pictorial graphs are an alternate form of the bar graph in which numerical units are represented by a simple drawing. Pictorial graphs are visually interesting and appeal to a wide audience, especially young students. However, they are slightly more difficult to read than bar graphs. Since pictorial symbols are used to represent a specific quantity, partial symbols are used to depict fractional quantities. To help avoid confusion in such cases, print values below or to the right of each line of figures.

Circle (or pie) graphs are relatively easy to interpret. In this type of graph, a circle or "pie" is divided into segments, each representing a part or percentage of the whole. One typical use of the circle graph is to depict tax-dollar allocations. The combined segments of a circle graph should, of course, equal 100 percent. Areas of special interest can be highlighted by illustrating a piece of pie separately from the whole.

Line graphs are the most precise and complex of all graphs. Line graphs are based on two scales at right angles. Each point has a value on the vertical scale and a value on the horizontal scale. Lines (or curves) are drawn to connect the points. Line graphs show variations in two dimensions, or how two or more factors change over time. For example, a graph can show the relation between pressure and temperature when the volume of a gas is held constant. Because line graphs are precise, they are very useful in plotting trends. They can also help simplify a mass of complex information.

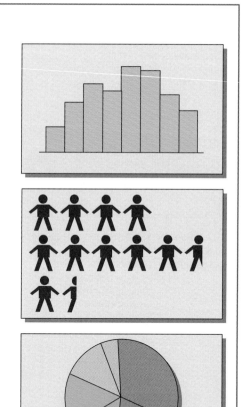

Figure 10.4
Posters catch the eye to convey a single, simple message.

posters with colored markers, computer printouts, and devices that print poster-sized pages. If you draw your own posters, follow the visual design guidelines in Chapter 4 and refer to "Sketching" in Classroom Resources, Section C. You can make computer-generated posters and banners by taping together standard-size printer paper. Software, such as *Print Shop Deluxe,* can facilitate poster design and production.

Cartoons

Cartoons (line drawings that are rough caricatures of real people and events) are perhaps the most popular and familiar visual format. They appear in a variety of print media—newspapers, periodicals, textbooks—and range from comic strips intended primarily to entertain to drawings intended to make important social or political comments. Humor and satire are mainstays of the cartoonist's skill.

Cartoons are easily and quickly read and appeal to children and adults alike. The best of them contain wisdom as well as wit. You can often use them to make or reinforce a point of instruction. Appreciation and interpretation, however, may depend on the experience and sophistication of the viewer. Be sure the cartoons you use for instructional purposes are within the experiential and intellectual range of your students.

ASSURE Case Connection

Mr. Donalds could consider using one or more types of nonprojected visuals for his presentation. Which type of nonprojected visuals might serve him well in presenting sales information? How can he be certain that the members of his audience will be able to see the materials?

PROJECTED VISUALS

Because an illuminated screen in a darkened room tends to rivet the attention of viewers, projected visuals have long been popular as a medium of instruction as well as entertainment. The lighted screen is a silent shout—a shout even the most reluctant learners are likely to heed.

Some of this attraction may be due to the aura of magic that seems to surround such presentations. The room lights are dimmed, the viewers grow quiet in expectation,

Showmanship

NONPROJECTED VISUALS

- Use large visuals that everyone can see simultaneously. (If visuals are not large enough for all to see, use one of the projection techniques described in this chapter.)
- Use visuals that are not cluttered with illegible details.
- Cover irrelevant material with plain paper.
- Hold visuals steady when showing them to a group by resting them against a desk or table or putting them on an easel.
- Limit the number of visuals used in a given period of time. It is better to use a few visuals well than to overwhelm your audience with an abundance of underexplained visuals.

- Use just one visual at a time, except for purposes of comparison. Lay one visual flat before going on to the next.
- Keep your audience's attention and help them learn from a visual by asking direct questions about it.
- Teach your audience to interpret visuals (see Chapter 4).
- Display pertinent questions alongside each visual. Cover the answers with flaps of paper. Have students immediately check their own responses for accuracy.
- Provide written or verbal cues to highlight important information contained in the visuals.

you throw a switch, and (presto!) a large, bright image appears on the screen. You have the attention of your audience, who is ready to receive the message. Exploit this readiness by selecting materials that will maintain viewers' attention and by using them in a way that involves viewers actively in learning.

Projected visuals are defined here as media formats in which still images are enlarged and displayed on a screen. Such projection may be achieved by passing a strong light through transparent film (as in overhead transparencies), magnifying the image through a series of lenses, and casting this image onto a reflective surface. Or the image can be displayed on a monitor using a document camera. Newer techniques include storing the images electronically and projecting them in a digital or analog format. Digital storage mechanisms include CD-ROM, the photo CD, digital cameras, DVD, and the scanner. The most common analog storage medium for visuals is CD-ROM, with DVD becoming a very popular digital alternative. Many visual images are available on videodisc.

Integration

Projected visuals are suitable for use at all grade levels and for instruction in all curriculum areas. Many high-quality commercial visuals are available. Tens of thousands of titles are available either in school media center collections or directly from the producers. In general, the fine arts, geography, and the sciences are especially well represented with commercially distributed visuals.

Following are some typical subjects among the myriad possibilities for visual presentations:

- Provide a tour for new employees of a local business without walking through the plant.
- Make a visual history of your community, school, or organization.
- Illustrate lectures about art history or art technique.
- Document student activities, products of student work, or community problems (e.g., crime and pollution).
- Present a preoperative explanation of a surgical procedure tailored to a specific surgeon's patients.
- Show people at work in various jobs, for career awareness.
- Illustrate the uses of a company's products throughout the world.
- Teach a step-by-step process with close-ups of each operation.
- Simulate a field trip.
- Promote public understanding of your school or organization.

The focus of the rest of this chapter is on the characteristics and applications of document cameras, overhead transparencies, slides, digital images, and digital

and analog image projection systems—the most widely used means of projecting visuals in education and training settings.

DOCUMENT CAMERAS

The **document camera** is a video camera mounted on a copy stand, pointed downward at documents, flat pictures, or graphics and small objects (such as coins). The image may be projected onto a large screen within the room or it may be transmitted to distant sites via telecommunications. You may place any sort of visual on the stage, and you can manipulate the material or write on it, as you would on overhead transparencies. With backlighting you can show overheads or slides.

Some document cameras can be folded into portable units and moved into classrooms. Connecting the camera to television monitors or data projectors in the classroom for a demonstration can mean that all students will have an equal view of some small items being displayed, or can view the same action simultaneously without having to crowd around. The camera can be focused very closely on the object, providing a close-up image that allows everyone a detailed view. Because most of the cameras are color, the images are presented accurately.

One alternative to the copy stand version of a document camera is the computer flex camera, which is often used for telecommunications. This camera can be connected to the television monitor or data projector and used in the same way as the document camera. The advantage to using this type of camera in this setting is that it is smaller and less expensive. A limitation is that the quality of the image may be compromised. (See "Operating a Document Camera" in Classroom Resources, Section C.)

Advantages

- *No production required.* A document camera allows on-the-spot projection of readily available classroom materials, such as diagrams, newspapers, and illustrations from books and magazines. Three-dimensional objects (especially relatively flat ones such as coins, plant leaves, and insect specimens) can be magnified for close-up inspection.
- *All students have equal view.* This type of projection permits everyone to have an equal opportunity to view the same material easily.
- *Allows group viewing of student work.* This type of projection permits group viewing and discussion of student work, such as drawings, student compositions, solutions to math problems, and the like.

- *Requires normal room lighting.* Because of the type of image projection, the room does not require dimming as might be necessary for other types of projected visuals.

Limitations

- *Bulky hardware.* Even though the document camera can be moved easily, it requires a monitor, which is bulky, heavy, and cumbersome to move without a cart, or a video projector, which requires a screen on which to project. Using a data projector helps to eliminate this concern.
- *Monitor or projector required.* You cannot use it without a monitor or video projector.
- *Additional lighting.* Document cameras need additional lights for a good image. Some cameras come with lights, but they are more expensive than those without.

Integration

The document camera is useful for small groups, classroom-size groups, or even distant audiences that need to view printed or visual material together. Applications may be found in all curriculum areas at all grade levels. Here are just a few typical examples:

- *All subjects:* Group critique of student work and review of test items
- *Art:* Group discussion of reproductions of paintings and architectural details; study of advertising layouts
- *Business:* Group work on business and accounting forms or close-up viewing of such documents as organization charts, sales territory maps, and parts of a product
- *Home Economics:* Group viewing of sewing patterns, textiles, recipes; close-up views of fabrics and weaving styles
- *Industry:* Projection of blueprints for group study; description of assembly line flow with production diagrams
- *Language Arts:* Group critique of student compositions, picture books, or reference books
- *Medicine:* Group study of anatomical drawings; discussion of diabetic diets and food exchange charts
- *Military:* Review of maps and official documents; illustration of flight plans
- *Music:* Group reading of musical scores
- *Religion:* Religious story illustrations; group examination of religious documents
- *Science:* Magnification of specimens; group study of maps and tables
- *Social Studies:* Map study; viewing of artifacts from other cultures, postcards, and atlas illustrations

ASSURE Case Connection

Can Mr. Donalds use a document camera for displaying company reports to his audience? How might this enhance his presentation?

OVERHEAD PROJECTION

Because of its many virtues, the **overhead projection** system (Figure 10.5) has become the most widely used audiovisual device in North American classrooms and training sites.

The typical overhead projector is a simple device (Figure 10.6). Basically, it is a box with a large aperture, or "stage," on the top surface. Light from a powerful lamp inside the box is condensed by a special type of lens, known as a **fresnel lens**, and passes through a transparency (approximately 8 by 10 inches) placed on the stage. A lens-and-mirror system mounted on a bracket above the box turns the light beam 90 degrees and projects the image back over the shoulder of the presenter. This type of projector, in which the light passes *through* the transparency, is referred to as a *transmissive* type. (See "Operating an Overhead Projector" in Classroom Resources, Section C.)

Because of the widespread familiarity of overhead projection, the general term **transparency** has taken on, in the instructional setting, the specific meaning of the large-format 8-by-10-inch film used with the overhead projector. Transparencies may be composed of photographic film, clear **acetate**, or any of a number of other transparent materials capable of being imprinted with an

Figure 10.5
With the overhead projector, the presenter maintains eye contact with viewers.

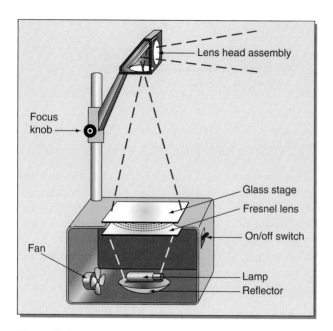

Figure 10.6

The transmissive type of overhead projector; the light from the lamp is transmitted through the glass stage and transparency.

image by means of chemical or heat processes. The individual sheets of transparent film are called "acetates" in reference to the chemical composition of the standard type of film.

You may use transparencies individually or make them into a series of images consisting of a base visual with one or more overlays attached to the base with hinges. **Overlays** are sheets of transparent film, each containing additional information, that are laid over the base transparency. You may then explain complex topics step by step by flipping a series of overlays one at a time, adding additional features to a diagram (Figure 10.7).

Advantages

- *Brightness.* Its bright lamp and efficient optical system generate so much light on the screen that the overhead can be used with normal room lighting.
- *Eye contact.* You operate the projector from the front of the room while facing the audience, allowing you to maintain direct eye contact.
- *Ease of use.* Most overhead projectors are lightweight and portable. All are simple to operate.
- *Abundance of materials.* The machine can project a variety of materials, including cutout silhouettes, small opaque objects, and many types of transparencies.
- *Manipulable.* You can manipulate projected materials. You can point to important items, highlight them with colored pens, add details

Showmanship

PROJECTED VISUALS

In addition to the general guidelines for media utilization discussed in Chapter 3, here are several specific practices that can add professionalism to your presentations using projected visuals:

- *Use visual variety.* Mix the types of visuals, using verbal titles to help break the presentation into segments. Use visuals that are not cluttered with illegible details. Teach your audience to interpret visuals (see Chapter 4).
- *Rehearse.* Plan and rehearse your narration to accompany projected visuals (e.g., slides or *PowerPoint*) if it is not already recorded on tape or other audio medium.
- *Doublecheck slides.* Make certain your slides are in sequential order and are right side up. Disarrangement can be embarrassing to you and annoying to your audience.
- *Use remote control.* Use a remote control device; this will allow you to stand at the side of the room. From this position you can keep an eye on the visuals while maintaining some eye contact with the audience.
- *Maintain reading light.* Prepare a way to light up your script after dimming the room lights; a penlight or flashlight will serve this purpose.

- *Keep it moving.* Limit your discussion of each visual. Even a minute of narration can seem long to your audience unless there is a complex visual to examine at the same time.
- *Use mood music.* Consider adding a musical accompaniment to your live or recorded narration. This can help to establish the desired mood and keep your audience attentive. But do not have music playing in the background when actually narrating.
- *Pause for discussion.* Get students actively involved by asking relevant questions during your visual presentation. You may want to ask students to take turns reading the captions (if any) aloud; this is a useful reading activity for early elementary students. Provide written or verbal cues to highlight important information contained in the visuals.
- *Avoid irrelevant images.* If there is a "talky" section in the middle of your presentation, use a gray or black visual or turn off the projector rather than hold an irrelevant visual on the screen. Cover irrelevant material until ready for students to view it.
- *Test visually.* Since the visual presentation presumably is providing critical visual information, consider using visuals to test the mastery of visual concepts. You can, for instance, use specific visuals and ask individual students to identify or describe the object or process shown. If visuals are not large enough for all to see, use one of the projection techniques described in this chapter.

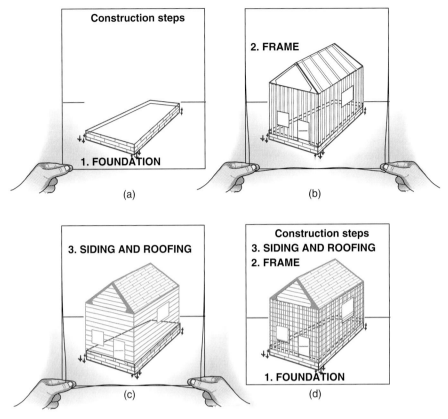

Construction steps

1. FOUNDATION

(a)

2. FRAME

(b)

3. SIDING AND ROOFING

(c)

Construction steps
3. SIDING AND ROOFING
2. FRAME

1. FOUNDATION

(d)

Figure 10.7
By means of overlays, the presenter can build up complex visuals step by step. Part (d) shows the result of combining overlays (a), (b), and (c).

The study produced the following findings (Wharton Applied Research Center, 1981):

- More individuals decided to act on the recommendations of presenters who used overheads than on the recommendation of presenters who did not.
- Presenters who used overheads were perceived as better prepared, more professional, more persuasive, more credible, and more interesting.
- Groups in which presenters used overheads were more likely to reach consensus on their decisions than groups where no overheads were employed.
- *Organization and discussion.* Another study suggests that teachers who use the overhead projector tend to be more organized than teachers who rely on notes or printed outlines. Students in this study participated more frequently in discussions in the classes where the overhead was used (Cabeceiras, 1972).

(notes, diagrams, etc.) during the lesson by marking on the transparency with a marking pen, or cover part of the message and progressively reveal information. As noted previously, you can present complex visuals in a series of overlays.

- *Availability of materials.* Commercially produced transparencies and transparency masters cover a range of curriculum areas.
- *Self-prepared materials.* You can easily prepare your own transparencies (we describe several common methods of production later in this section).
- *Advance preparation.* Information that might otherwise have to be placed on a chalkboard during a class session (e.g., lesson outlines) may be prepared in advance for presentation at the proper time. Research indicates that retention of main points improves significantly when outlines are presented.
- *Impact on attitudes.* The use of overhead transparencies also has positive effects on attitude in business meetings. In one study, candidates for master's degrees in business administration participated in a business simulation that involved group meetings to decide whether to introduce a new product.

Limitations

- *Not preprogrammed.* The effectiveness of overhead projection presentations is totally dependent on the presenter. The overhead projector cannot be programmed to display visual sequences by itself, nor is an audio accompaniment provided.
- *Not self-instructional.* The overhead system does not lend itself to independent study. It is designed for large-group presentation. Of course, an individual student could look at a transparency by holding it up to the light, but because captions and audio tracks are not a part of this format, the material would ordinarily not be self-instructional.
- *Production process required.* Printed materials and other nontransparent items, such as magazine illustrations, cannot be projected immediately, as is possible with the document camera. To use the overhead system such materials have to be made into transparencies by means of some production process.
- *Keystone effect.* Distortion of images is more prevalent with the overhead than with other projection systems. The projector is commonly placed at desktop level to facilitate the instructor's writing on transparencies. The screen, on the other hand, needs to be placed on a higher level for

unobstructed audience sightlines. This discrepancy in levels causes a distortion referred to as the **keystone effect.** (This problem and its solution are discussed in "Eliminating the Keystone Effect" in Classroom Resources, Section C.)

Integration

Because the image is large and you can manipulate or add to it while projecting, the overhead projector is extraordinarily versatile. It has been used to communicate visually in every subject in the curriculum. Here are a few ideas:

- *Art:* Use strips of colored acetate to demonstrate the composition of primary and secondary colors by overlapping red, yellow, and blue.
- *Drama:* Put a floor plan on the base cell and add overlays to show acting circles and how areas are lit.
- *Language Arts:* Use different colored pens to highlight nouns, verbs, and other parts of speech.
- *Literature:* Visually compare different forms of poetry (e.g., haiku, sonnet) and compare meter patterns.
- *Music:* Show a staff with notes arranged in three-part harmony, with different colored notes for each part.
- *Mathematics:* Use circles and squares that are cut into pieces to illustrate different fractions. Many such transparent manipulatives are distributed by publishers as adjuncts to math textbooks.
- *Library Skills:* Show a floor plan of the layout of the school media center as part of library orientation.
- *Consumer Science:* Make thermal transparencies of blank checks and balance sheets; demonstrate how to make out a check and balance the check register.
- *Geography:* Use a clear plastic ruler over a transparency of a map; demonstrate how to measure the distance between any two points.
- *Science:* Show how iron filings align to poles of a magnet placed on an overhead projector stage.

ASSURE Case Connection

Why might Mr. Donalds consider using transparencies for his presentation? Should he prepare them using a word processor or use other software, such as *PowerPoint*? Could the company sales reports be made into transparencies for easier viewing by the members of the audience?

Creating Overhead Transparencies

As previously noted, a major advantage of the overhead system is that instructors (and students!) can easily prepare their own transparencies. One of the first methods involved simple hand drawing on clear acetate sheets; numerous other methods of preparing transparencies have evolved over the years. We will look closely at the processes most commonly used in the classroom—direct drawing, electrostatic film process (xerography), and computer printing.

Direct Drawing Method. The most obvious way of quickly preparing a transparency is simply to draw directly on a transparent sheet with a marking pen (Figure 10.8). Clear acetate of 5–10 mils (.005–.010 inches) is recommended. Other types of plastic can be used. Although some of these alternatives may be a great deal cheaper than the thicker acetate, some impose limitations in terms of durability, ease of handling, and ability to accept different inks (e.g., some disintegrate completely under alcohol-based inks). Blue-tinted acetate is preferred because it reduces the glare of the projected image.

Although the glass stage of the overhead projector generally measures about 10 by 10 inches, your drawing and lettering should be restricted to a rectangular "message area" of about 7½ by 9½ inches. This fits the dimensions of acetate sheets, which are commonly cut into rectangles of 8 by 10 inches or 8½ by 11 inches (Figure 10.9).

If you are doing freehand lettering, keep in mind that neatness counts, as does legibility. Your imperfections will be magnified to the size of the projection screen. Viewers can't learn from what they can't decipher. Note the guidelines given in "Designing Overhead Transparencies" in Classroom Resources, Section C.

Figure 10.8
Many overhead projector users draw directly on the transparency.

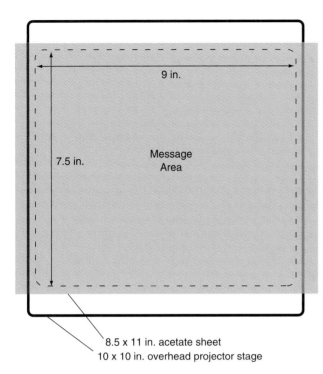

Figure 10.9
Comparative dimensions of an overhead transparency and the projector stage.

Some overhead projectors come equipped with a pair of roller attachments made to carry long rolls of plastic that can be advanced or reversed by a small hand crank. This assures a steady supply of transparency material for extemporaneous use. It also allows you to prepare in advance a series of images in proper sequence.

In addition to the transparency, you will need a writing instrument. Felt-tip marking pens are the handiest for this purpose. They come in two general types—water soluble and permanent ink. However, not all are suitable for overhead transparencies. Here are some cautions to keep in mind:

- Ordinary felt-tip pens with water-soluble ink generally will not adhere well to acetate; the ink tends to bead up and evaporate. Look for a label saying, "overhead projector pen"; this indicates it will adhere to acetate and project color. You can erase such special ink with a damp tissue or wash the transparency completely clean and reuse it.
- Virtually any permanent-ink felt-tip pen will adhere to acetate, but only those marked "overhead projector pen" are made to project in color. Other types may project only in black and may even damage the transparency film. Most users choose a permanent ink for hand-drawn transparencies prepared in advance, especially if they are going to be reused, because water-based ink is likely to smear as you work on the different areas of the transparency or as you handle it during use.

- Permanent ink markings can be erased with special plastic erasers or with correction markers containing alcohol-based solvents (Figure 10.10), but it is not practical to clean and reuse transparencies that have extensive permanent ink markings.
- During a presentation, you may use highlighter pens made especially for overhead projection to draw attention to critical information. This can add a dramatic touch, but be careful—they are permanent. Put a clear acetate sheet on top of your finished transparency to protect it.
- Least commonly used are wax-based pencils. Most will project only in black. They can be erased with a soft, dry cloth.

Electrostatic Film Process (Xerography). All plain-paper copiers that operate by the **electrostatic film (xerography)** process can be used to make black-and-white transparencies. Generally the single-sheet paper guide rather than the paper tray is used when copying the information from a printed page onto the transparent acetate. Some models can also produce high-quality full-color transparencies from paper originals or slides. These are most often found at commercial copying services.

Electrostatic copying requires a paper master and specially treated film. The film is electrically charged and light sensitive. Any source that yields good opaque markings can be used (e.g., computer printer output, clippings from printed material, drawings made by ball-point pen or dark felt-tip marker).

Overheads Created by Computer. Computers have eased the task of creating overhead transparencies and similar types of visuals. With any word processing software you can prepare simple verbal overheads—sentences, lists, visuals, and the like. You can print each screen on plain paper and use it as a master to make electrostatic transparencies.

Figure 10.10
Plastic erasers will remove permanent ink, at least that of the same manufacturer.

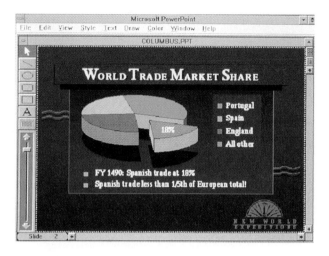

Figure 10.11
Presentation graphics software enables you to compose overhead transparencies with ease. Powerpoint *screen shot reprinted by permission from Microsoft Corporation.*

With **presentation graphics software**, such as Microsoft's *PowerPoint,* even users without specialized graphics training can create attractive graphic displays in a form suitable for professional presentation. You select a visual style from a menu, specify the desired type of graphic (e.g., outline, bulleted list, graph, map, or combination), then just type in your message where directed by the program (Figure 10.11). The program automatically selects legible type fonts and sizes and organizes the pictures and text into a clean visual layout. The visual can be printed directly onto transparency film or onto a paper copy, which you may then use as a master to make xerographic transparencies. Among the types of graphics software available are the following:

- *Presentation programs*—special software that simplifies creation of slides or transparencies of graphics that combine text, data, and visuals
- *Drawing and paint programs*—allow the user to draw geometric shapes and figures; can also incorporate text
- *Charting programs*—especially suited to making charts, graphs, and reports from spreadsheet data
- *Photo-enhancement programs*—allow the manipulation of color and use of special effects to alter photographs and slides
- *Desktop publishing programs*—combine features of many other methods to create sophisticated products such as newsletters and books

There are several technical processes for producing transparencies directly with a computer printer. You need to select the proper type of transparency film for your printer:

- Laser printers print images directly onto special film.
- Ink-jet printers spray droplets of ink onto specially coated ink-jet film.

- Pen plotters draw with pens directly onto specially coated film.
- Impact printers press the ink from ribbons onto impact film.

SLIDES

The term **slide** refers to a small-format photographic transparency individually mounted for one-at-a-time projection. The standard size of slides is 2 by 2 inches (5 by 5 centimeters) measured by the outer dimensions of the slide mount. When 35mm and other popular types of slide film are sent out to be processed, they are mounted in 2-by-2-inch frames. The actual dimensions of the image itself will vary with the type of film and camera.

Advantages

- *Sequencing.* Because you can arrange slides into many different sequences, they are more flexible than fixed-sequence materials.
- *Automatic cameras.* As photographic equipment is continually refined and simplified, even amateurs are now able to produce their own high-quality slides. Automatic exposure controls, easy focusing, and high-speed color film have contributed to this trend.
- *Automatic projectors.* The assembly of slide programs is facilitated by today's projectors, which hold sets of slides in trays and feed them into view in sequence. Most projectors also offer the convenience of remote control advancing of slides, allowing you to remain at the front of the room or off to one side while advancing the slides via a pushbutton unit connected by wire to the projector. Wireless remote control is also available. Certain models can be preset to advance automatically. This feature allows continuous showing in exhibits, display cases, and other automated situations.
- *Collection building.* General availability and ease of handling make it relatively easy to build up permanent collections of slides for specific instructional purposes. You and your fellow instructors may collect and store your own collections, or the slides may be compiled and kept in a learning resource center. Such collections enable you to assemble presentations partially or wholly from existing images, thus reducing the expense required for new production.
- *Individualized instruction.* You may integrate slides into individualized instruction programs. Although slides have been developed primarily as a large-group medium, recent hardware innovations have made slides feasible for small-group and independent study as well.

Limitations

- *Disorganization.* Because slides come as individual units, they can easily become disorganized. Even when they are stored in trays, if the locking ring is loosened, the slides can spill out.
- *Jamming.* Slide mounts come in cardboard, plastic, and glass of varying thicknesses. This lack of standardization can lead to jamming of slides in the slide-changing mechanism: cardboard becomes dogeared and the frayed edges get caught in the mechanism; plastic mounts swell or warp in the heat of the lamp; glass mounts thicker than the aperture chamber fail to drop into showing position.
- *Susceptible to damage.* Slides can easily accumulate dust and fingerprints; careless storage or handling can lead to permanent damage.

Integration

Slides are suitable for use at all grade levels and in all curriculum areas. Many high-quality commercial slides are available. Most commonly used slides are those produced by the instructor or students using a simple-to-use camera with special film.

Following are some typical ways slides can be used for presentations:

- Provide an overview of what students will see on a field trip.
- Use slides to help students recall what they saw on a field trip.
- Make a slide show of your community, school, or organization.
- Use slides to illustrate art as part of a presentation.
- Document student activities.
- Show people at work in various jobs, for career awareness.
- Illustrate the uses of a company's products throughout the world.
- Teach a step-by-step process with close-ups of each operation.

ASSURE Case Connection

Mr. Donalds can prepare slides as visuals for his presentation. What types of information can he put on the slides? Since the room will need to be darkened when the slides are being shown, will the members of the audience benefit from viewing the information using this format?

Teacher- and Student-Produced Slides

A major advantage of slides as an instructional medium is the ease with which both teachers and students can produce them. Modern cameras are so simple to operate that even the most amateur of photographers can

Figure 10.12
Teacher or students can prepare slide sets showing local events or landmarks.

expect good results. General guidelines for photography appear in Classroom Resources, Sections A and C. To make slides you follow the same procedures but substitute slide film for print film. As with other locally produced materials, slides made by teachers or students have an immediacy, relevance, and credibility lacking in more generic materials (Figure 10.12).

Producing "Slide Shows" by Digital Photography. When digital camera systems were first introduced, they were considered replacements for conventional film photography. However, limitations of image resolution initially discouraged users from giving up their film cameras in favor of digital cameras for everyday picture taking—for either prints or slides. But the new megapixel digital cameras have found their place in popular picture taking and in the computer realm. They are widely used to capture images to incorporate into documents produced by presentation software or desktop publishing. The images made with this technology can be arranged in a sequence and shown on the computer screen as a kind of slide show.

Producing Slides with a Computer. Traditionally, slides have been made by shooting photographs of people, places, things, or images drawn by graphic artists. Computers now offer the capability of generating graphic images that can become slides. There are presentation graphics software programs especially adapted to producing output in the slide format. They are capable of producing images of very high resolution—as sharp and clearly defined as those of photos.

Their high quality, ease of production, and flexibility of use have made computer-produced slides popular. They can be used to prepare self-instructional units or modules. Sound–slide modules have been found to provide as much of an impact as a video at a fraction of the production cost.

Technology for Diverse Learners

POWERPOINT™

Teachers can do several things to make *PowerPoint*-based presentations more accessible to visually impaired students, including converting *PowerPoint* text to Braille. However, it may be better to increase the interaction between teacher and students during and immediately after the presentation. Increasing verbalization and descriptions of the text and images increases the odds of visually impaired students' comprehension and retention. (This really applies to all students!)

PowerPoint presentation software is easy to use and makes colorful projected presentations. Students, as well as instructors, can make slide shows with *PowerPoint* with little training on the software itself. Each slide (the term used to describe the individual projected image) can have a variety of styles. There are templates that provide a set color scheme and font choice. Many of these are very bright and easy to read. Or the user can decide to select a different color scheme. This is relatively easy to do. Graphics are provided within the program, or visual images can be imported onto the slides. These special digital images customize the presentation. In addition to using the existing templates for presentations, it is possible to create original backgrounds and color schemes.

Finally, *PowerPoint* allows the user to include music and animation. There are times when the presenter does not need to speak about the topic; easily attached audio files can enhance a presentation by providing a musical interlude when there are a set of slides where the visuals or text are all that is necessary. It also is possible to add hyperlinked buttons to other programs, such as a Web browser, to demonstrate a particular point within a presentation. Digital video files can be integrated into a presentation as well.

DIGITAL IMAGES

It is possible to store images in a digital (or analog) form and show them on a computer or television monitor or project them before a group. Available digital storage media include CD-ROM, photo CD, DVD-ROM, and computer disks. (See, for example, "Close-Up: How a Compact Disc Works," in Chapter 11.)

CD-ROM

CD-ROM (compact disc–read-only memory) has the capacity to handle not only quality sound but also large quantities of text and visuals. CD-ROM is a storage system that utilizes a compact, rugged, and lightweight disc only 12 centimeters (4.72 inches) in diameter. It is an optical storage medium that uses a tiny laser beam to retrieve the information on the disc. CD-ROM discs are "read only," which means that the user cannot change or modify the information on the disc. Recordable and rewriteable compact discs are available. Students can create their own CD-ROMs. One suggestion might be for students to produce their portfolio materials on a CD-ROM because the storage capacity and ease of access to the information makes this a very valuable way for students to store that information.

Because CD-ROM discs can store many types of digital information, including text, graphics, photographs, animation, and audio, they are popular in school settings, library media centers, and classrooms of all sorts. Anything that can be stored on a computer disk can be stored on a CD-ROM.

CD-ROM discs require their own special player; the audio CD player attached to your stereo system will not play them. However, most computer CD-ROM players can also play audio CDs. The CD-ROM player must be connected to a computer with an interface cable. Most computers come equipped with a CD-ROM player built into the system. A computer monitor displays the data from the CD-ROM disc. You interact with the information in the same way you would interact with other computer-based multimedia materials.

Many schools and colleges have slide libraries as resources for teaching subjects, such as art history and biology, which require great numbers of visual images. In some schools these visual libraries are being replaced by CD-ROM or DVD discs, which can hold a whole subject area library on one disc. A single disc is less expensive to purchase and far easier to store and maintain.

Photo CD

The photo CD (photographic compact disc) utilizes digital technology as described to store photographic images. For only a few dollars you can have your photographs, from a regular camera, developed and placed on a compact disc. You can show the photographs on the photo CD using a special photo CD player and display them on a television set, or using your computer you can project them for a group as described later in this chapter. You can alter the sequence of visuals and create a slide show effect with your photographs.

DVD-ROM

Similar to the CD-ROM, DVD-ROM (Digital Versatile Disc–Read-Only Memory) is also a digital storage format, but with greater capacity for storage. DVD-ROM is an ideal medium for text, visuals, animation, motion video, and audio formats that have large storage requirements. Like CD-ROM, DVD-ROM is a storage system that utilizes a compact, rugged, and lightweight disc only 12 centimeters (4.72 inches) in diameter. It is an optical storage medium that uses a tiny laser beam to retrieve the information on the disc. DVD-ROM discs are "read only," which means that the user cannot change or modify the information on the disc. Recordable and rewriteable DVD discs are available but can be expensive. In time, because of the ability to hold extensive quantities of data, DVD-ROM will replace CD-ROM. Many models of computers are now being produced with DVD/CD-ROM drives (Figure 10.13).

The advantages of DVD as a video format are that the viewer can decide how to interact with the material from a menu of choices. One limitation in education with DVD is the limited, but constantly increasing, number of titles available outside of full-feature films. This is changing as digital moviemaking and DVD authoring software, such as Apple's *iMovie, iDVD,* and *Final Cut,* become more available to developers of educational materials (*iMovie* and *iDVD* now come installed on all new Apple Computers).

Digital Camera

Instead of storing the visuals on photographic film, some digital cameras connect directly to the computer to place the images onto the hard drive. Others store the images directly onto a a small digital film card, or "smart card," inside the camera. These smart cards have increased storage capacities, often megabytes of capacity, allowing you to store hundreds of images on one card. Once the picture is taken, it is easy to connect the camera or use the smart card (which does require a special input device) to put the image onto the computer (Figure 10.14).

These images can be used in many different ways. You can connect the computer to show the visuals on the monitor, and may in turn connect the computer to a data projector (discussed earlier) for group viewing. You can use the images as part of other documents, such as newsletters or word processed papers. These images can also be incorporated into Web pages. Because they are digital, the images are easy to place into these types of files.

Advantages.

- *Images are digital.* The great advantage of the digital camera is that it enables you to store pictures as digital images so you do not have to have them developed or use any additional devices to capture them from traditional cameras.
- *Vast capacity.* The digital camera, especially the one that uses a smart card, can store a great number of visuals.
- *Zoom capability.* Many models of digital cameras have zoom and macro options, which makes it possible for "close-up" photographs.
- *Ease of use.* Most digital cameras are very easy to use. Even young children can take pictures with digital cameras.

Limitations.

- *Expense.* Digital cameras are more expensive to purchase, but they do not require any additional expenditures for films, like traditional cameras.

Figure 10.13
Computers have built-in CD-RW or DVD drives for displaying CD or DVD material.

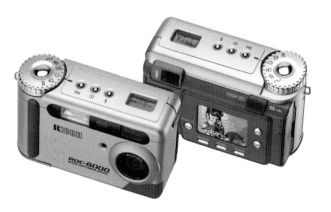

Figure 10.14
Pictures taken with a digital camera can be incorporated immediately into a computer presentation.

- *Fragile.* Digital cameras can be a bit more fragile to handle than some traditional cameras. Some of the controls are smaller than on traditional cameras.

Digital Scanner

Instead of creating new pictures for each event, it is possible to use existing photographs. A scanner that has been connected directly to the computer can let you turn a photograph into a digital image. You first need to place the image onto the scanner, then using a scanning software program on the computer, you can convert that image into digital form. The image can be saved to the computer hard drive or onto a floppy or Zip® disk. These images can be used in the same ways you can use digital images from a digital camera, such as in newsletters, word processed papers, or Web pages.

It is also possible to use software programs, such as *Photoshop*, to alter the digital images in ways that enhance or improve the quality or the very nature of the image. Images can be edited to eliminate portions of the photo that are unimportant. One word of caution here: It also is possible to alter or distort the image in such a way as to change it from the original. Students need to learn the importance of ethical use of images to convey messages and issues related to respecting copyright.

Advantages

- *Random access.* Digital images stored on discs can be rapidly and randomly accessed, often in fractions of a second, even with 54,000 images to choose from on a disc. You can predetermine a random sequence of visuals before a presentation or select visuals based on questions from students.
- *Durability.* The discs are very durable. Fingerprints do not interfere with the quality of the projected visual as is the case with slides. The discs are almost impossible to break unless they are deliberately abused.
- *Storage capacity.* All the discs store thousands of colorful images at your fingertips.
- *High-quality visuals.* The quality of digital still images is better than the photographic image on slides and does not fade with time as photographic images do.
- *Portable.* Digital discs are extremely portable. While you may carry digital discs without protection, it is best to keep CDs in their jewel cases and videodiscs in their cardboard jackets.
- *Less storage space.* It would require 675 80-slide trays to store the 54,000 still images on a single digital disc. The digitized images are also less sensitive to extreme heat, cold, and humidity.

Limitations

- *Expensive to produce.* Digital images on commercial discs are time consuming and expensive to produce.

Digital cameras and "frame grabbers" allow individuals to produce their own visuals, but this equipment is more expensive than photographic equipment and may be beyond your school's budget.
- *Requires player and projector.* As with slides, viewing digital images requires a projector or viewer. However, compared to slide projectors, digital equipment tends to be more complex, more expensive, and more difficult to operate.

Integration

Projected digital visuals are suitable for most of the same applications where you would use overhead transparencies or slides. Common applications of digital media involve individual students viewing on computers images stored on a CD-ROM or computer disk.

- Third-grade students view animals of the world from a CD-ROM as they prepare to present a play for the PTA depicting endangered species.
- A seventh-grade history student prepares an individual report on early American inventors using clip-art visuals from a computer disk.
- A tenth-grade literature class views a DVD film version of a book they have just completed. The teacher stops the movie at key moments and keeps the images on the monitor for discussion in class.
- Five vocational technical students use a digital camera to document the variety of work activities during a visit to a discount department store. They will prepare a class presentation on opportunities for graduates of their school.
- A college biology instructor has thousands of visuals from a DVD available at her fingertips, which she can use to illustrate her lectures.
- Using a standard camera, a corporate trainer takes individual photos of each student in his training classes. When he sends the film away for processing, he requests a photo CD. Before each future class, the trainer accesses the photo CD to refresh his memory so he can call the students by name when he sees them again.

ASSURE Case Connection

Would it help Mr. Donalds to prepare the information in advance and distribute a CD-ROM or DVD for the members of his audience? How could this save time during his presentation?

DIGITAL IMAGE PROJECTION

Digital (and analog) images can be shown to individuals using a computer monitor (Figure 10.15). For showing digital images to a group, you can use a large television monitor (see Classroom Resources, Section B, for size guidelines) or a data projector (discussed earlier).

Selection Rubric: Visuals

Complete an interactive evaluation and add it to your NETS-T portfolio using the Selection Rubric for Visuals available on the "Classroom Link Portfolio" CD-ROM. A downloadable version of this rubric is available in the Selection Rubrics module of the Companion Website at http://www.prenhall.com/smaldino.

Key Words:

_____

_____

_____

Title _____

Series Title (if applicable) _____

Source _____

Date _____ Cost _____

Subject Area _____

Intended Audience _____

Brief Description

Format

☐ Still Picture

☐ Drawing/Cartoon

☐ Chart/Graph

☐ Poster

☐ Overhead Transparency

☐ Computer Image

☐ Sound/Slide

Objectives

Entry Capabilities Required (e.g., prior knowledge, reading ability, vocabulary level, math ability)

Strong Points

Weak Points

Recommended Action (using criteria on the following page)

Name _____ Date _____

Rating Area	High Quality	Medium Quality	Low Quality	Rating
Match Curriculum	Curriculum standard addressed and use of visual should enhance student learning.	Curriculum standard partially addressed and use of visual might enhance student learning.	Curriculum standard not addressed and use will likely not enhance student learning.	
Accurate & Current	Information correct and does not contain material that is out of date.	Information correct but does contain material that is out of date.	Information not correct and does contain material that is out of date.	
Clear & Concise Language	Language used is age appropriate and vocabulary is understandable.	Language used is nearly age appropriate and some vocabulary is above/below student age.	Language used is not age appropriate and vocabulary is clearly inappropriate for student age.	
Motivating/ Interesting	Topic presented so that students are likely to be interested and engaged in learning.	Topic presented to interest students most of the time and engage most in learning.	Topic presented so as not to interest students and not engage them in learning.	
Learner Participation	Topic presented so that most students are actively engaged in learning.	Topic presented so that some students are engaged in learning.	Topic presented so that most students are not actively engaged in learning.	
Technical Quality	The material represents best available media.	The material represents media that are good quality, although there are some problems.	The material represents media that are not well prepared and are of very poor quality.	
Effectiveness Rating	There is evidence that use of these media has shown positive impact on student learning.	There is little evidence that use of these media has shown positive impact on student learning.	There is no evidence that use of these media has shown positive impact on student learning.	
Free from Bias	There is no evidence of objectionable bias or advertising.	There is little evidence of bias or advertising.	There is much evidence of bias or advertising.	
User Guide & Documentation	The documentation is excellent resource for use in a lesson. Documentation should help students use the material.	The documentation is good resource for use in a lesson. Documentation may help students use the material.	The documentation is poor resource for use in a lesson. Documentation does not help students use the material.	
Legibility for Use (Size and Clarity)	The visual material is presented so that most students can see and understand the information.	The visual material is presented so that some students can see and start to understand some information.	The visual material is presented so that most students cannot see or understand most of the information.	
Simplicity (Clear, Unified Design)	The visual material is well organized; students should be able to understand the information.	The visual material is fairly well organized; students might be able to understand the information.	The visual material is poorly organized; most students are unable to understand the information.	
Appropriate Use of Color	Colors fit the nature of the subject and enhance the learning potential.	Colors marginally fit the nature of the subject and may enhance the learning potential.	Colors do not fit the nature of the subject and do not enhance the learning potential.	
Communicates Clearly and Effectively	The information is presented visually to ensure learning.	The information is presented visually in a way that may lead to learning.	The information is presented visually in a way that may not lead to learning.	
Appealing Visuals	The visuals should attract the attention of most learners.	The visuals may attract the attention of some learners.	The visuals may not attract the attention of many learners.	

Designed for use with presentation graphics software, **liquid crystal display (LCD)** data projectors are separate, freestanding units. The light source is built into the projector (Figure 10.16). Data projectors have audio capabilities in addition to the visual output. With a data projector, images can be projected from a computer, a video player (either videotape or DVD), or a television signal. The advantage the projector brings is the ability to show full-motion video signals in addition to the still images of a traditional presentation software package. (See "Operating a Data Projector" in Classroom Resources, Section C.)

Figure 10.15
LCD projectors allow computer images to be shown to a group.

Figure 10.16
Computer data or images, as well as videos, can be projected by desktop projectors.

Advantages

- *Image choices.* The great advantage of the data projector is that it enables you to project anything that appears on your computer monitor—text, data, or visual—onto a large screen.
- *Vast capacity.* The computer can store a seemingly infinite number of visuals, which you may summon by pressing a key.
- *Interactivity.* You can change the display just before or even during a showing, so data projectors are ideal for "what-if" displays of spreadsheet data or graphs or brainstorming activities using such software as *Inspiration*. This becomes an interactive medium when viewers' decisions or ideas are fed into the program and the outcome is displayed on the screen.

Limitations

- *Legibility.* Low resolution can make presentations best suited to small or medium-size groups (up to about 50 people) in which no one is seated more than four screen widths from the screen. A solution for larger groups is to enlarge the display options within the software package.
- *Expense.* Data projectors have a higher price tag; however, this is changing over time.

Integration

The extra expense and logistical arrangements required by data projection would be difficult to justify for simple, static presentations. Where it yields real benefits, though, is in providing dynamic or interactive presentations, such as in the following:

- Demonstrating computer software functions to a group of students
- Searching an electronic encyclopedia (on CD-ROM) or website with a whole class following along
- Conducting a brainstorming session, capturing all suggestions on the computer display (and then printing them out at the conclusion)
- Presenting color animation sequences or viewing a digital video
- Teaching math or statistics formulas by changing the inputs and watching the output change on the screen graphically

ASSURE Case Connection

Mr. Donalds could prepare *PowerPoint* slides to use with his presentation. What could he do to impress the audience, especially management, if he used *PowerPoint?* What considerations should he take into account when he is producing digital visual images for his presentation?

Summary: Using the ASSURE Model for Visuals

As with other media and technology, the AS-SURE model introduced in Chapter 3 is helpful in preparing lessons incorporating the use of visuals.

Analyze Learners

Lesson development begins by identifying your students' unique attributes and learning characteristics. You also will wish to determine their various levels of experience with using visuals.

State Objectives

Before stating specific objectives, you may wish to explore how to use visuals in support of student learning. Sometimes it is more appropriate to state specific objectives after you have identified the direction you will take with the content and what materials you will use.

Select Methods, Media, and Materials

Use the information on visuals discussed in this chapter as the basis for selecting, modifying, or designing your materials. Adjust the specific applications to suit the specific nature of your topic and objectives.

You should preview and appraise both commercially and locally produced materials before using them with your students. You may wish to use the "Selection Rubric: Visuals" to guide your selection decisions.

Utilize Media and Materials

Follow the suggestions discussed in this chapter to facilitate your students' learning, modifying each material's use to fit your needs. The equipment you have access to, as well as its location, will determine how you schedule your students' learning experiences, as discussed in the chapter. If you have access to a data projector, you may plan for all students viewing images together. For print-based visuals you may consider setting up a learning center.

Require Learner Participation

Introduce and explain the visuals involved in your specific objective. Have the students do specific activities that rely on their ability to use visuals. Students will find more value in the materials if they are able to connect what they are doing to what they are learning. Have them make slide shows with *PowerPoint* using images from a CD you have prepared. Or have students make a collage or illustrate a short story or theme paper they have written, using a combination of found photographic prints and pictures they take themselves.

Evaluate and Revise

It is important to consider how materials that rely on nonprojected and projected visuals help students to interpret information. You may assess students on the quality of their produced images, or on how well they incorporated them into their other work. As with all media- and technology-based lessons, you may choose to revise your selection of materials after you have determined how well they have worked. In addition, you want to be certain that all materials used have been cleared of any potential copyright issues.

ASSURE Case in Practice: A Presentation to Management

All of the ASSURE Cases in Practice in this text and an electronic template for creating your own ASSURE Lesson can be found on the enclosed "Classroom Link Portfolio" CD-ROM.

Company sales have been on a plateau for three years, and the general sales manager, Mr. Donalds, has devised a strategy to expand existing markets and open new ones. His goal is to convince management and the marketing division to adopt this new marketing strategy.

Analyze Learners

General Characteristics

The audience consists of the chief executive officer (CEO), the marketing vice president, the financial vice president, and three regional sales managers. The financial vice president joined the company 2 years ago, but the others have been with the company at least 10 years. The financial vice president believes a sharp increase in profits would firmly secure her job. The marketing members of the audience feel somewhat threatened by the implication that their efforts have been ineffective; they are apprehensive about the difficulties involved in restructuring the sales force. The CEO is concerned about a board of directors disgruntled over stagnant sales. He wants to be convinced, but not at the expense of creating a hostile sales group.

Entry Competencies

Each member of the audience has successful business experience, but in different areas. The financial vice president appraises all company activities strictly by the balance sheet. The marketing vice president wants to show an interest in overall company performance but looks at proposals from the point of view of the marketing division. The regional sales managers believe they have developed loyal and effective sales forces. All have demonstrated the ability to grasp quickly the ramifications of new ideas.

Learning Styles

The members display a range of learning styles. Most of them have good visual and spatial skills and excellent math ability.

State Objectives

Objectives include the following:

- The CEO will endorse the proposal by agreeing to present it to the board of directors.
- The financial vice president will estimate the impact of the proposal on the profit margin of the company.
- The marketing vice president will demonstrate support by suggesting a plan to restructure the sales procedures.
- The regional sales managers will indicate how the sales representatives can benefit from an expanded market.
- The marketing vice president and the regional sales managers will agree to meet with the general sales manager to develop an implementation strategy, including a training program for sales representatives.

Select Methods, Media, and Materials

Mr. Donalds is well aware that he has a tough audience to convince. A well-organized and illustrated presentation is a must. Equally important is the need to maintain constant interaction with the audience during the presentation, so he chooses to adopt the discussion method. He consults with the company training director on the media to use. The company training director suggests *PowerPoint* slides as the heart of the presentation, with a flip chart available for spontaneous notes and reactions. Together they go to a local graphics design shop to work out the sketches for the slides. The graphics are designed on computers and, when ap-

proved, the slides are generated. Several color photographs are part of the presentation: these are made into *PowerPoint* slides using the color digital images from the company website.

Utilize Media and Materials

Mr. Donalds has selected a meeting room best suited for data projection and has prepared for the meeting by arranging for pads, pencils, and beverages. He reviews past accomplishments of the company, paying particular attention to the important contributions of the people in the room. He stresses how the company has responded successfully to similar challenges in the past. He then starts to unfold his plan, inviting comments as he goes along. On the flip chart, he notes comments to be discussed more fully.

Require Learner Participation

Because Mr. Donalds invites comments, members of the audience become collaborators rather than spectators. As he answers questions indicating misgivings, the audience gradually begins adding to his presentation. The presentation ends more like a conference than a sales pitch. Instead of thinking about the plan later, the group talks about it now.

The CEO enthusiastically asks Mr. Donalds to present the proposal to the board. The financial vice president volunteers to work up the sales projections into a financial statement. The marketing personnel set a time and place to put together an implementation strategy.

Evaluate and Revise

The objectives have been achieved, but now Mr. Donalds must adapt the presentation to a new audience, the board of directors. He particularly reviews the questions and comments of the CEO as guides to the approach to use with the board. He also wants to work closely with the financial vice president on the presentation of the fiscal projections of the marketing strategy.

He is eager to talk with his former associates on the sales force to prepare himself better for the meeting with the marketing vice president and the regional sales managers.

Create Your Own ASSURE Lesson

Using the ASSURE model, design a lesson for a scenario from the Companion Website or use a scenario of your own design. Use one of the methods described in Chapter 1 and information from this chapter related to incorporating visuals into your instructional setting. Be sure to include information about the audience, the objectives, and all other elements of the ASSURE model. When completed, reflect on the process you used and what you have learned about matching audience, content, method, and materials.

Classroom Link Portfolio Activities

Use the "Classroom Link Portfolio" CD-ROM and the Companion Website as resources in completing these activities. To complete the following activities online go to the Portfolio Activities module in Chapter 10 of the Companion Website (http://www.prenhall.com/smaldino).

1. *Planning Lessons Requiring Visuals.* Plan a lesson in which students will be developing reports or presentations about a topic of study, suggesting strategies they might consider in selecting appropriate print and nonprint visuals. What do you need to do to help them select and plan for the use of visuals? (ISTE NETS 2.D; 3.D; 5.B)

2. *Written Reflection.* Reflect on a recent lesson in one of the following settings: (1) lecture; (2) small-group activity; (3) independent learning experience. What visuals were used? How did they enhance your learning experience? How could other visuals have improved your experience? If you had designed that lesson, what visuals would you select and why? (ISTE NETS 4.C; 6.B)

Integration Assessments

To complete the specified activities online go to the Integration Assessments module in Chapter 10 of the Companion Website (http://www.prenhall.com/smaldino).

1. Examine a major selection source for visuals (such as "A-V Online") and report on the sorts of materials that you believe would be useful in your own teaching. (ISTE NETS 2.C)

2. Create one graph (line, bar, circle, or pictorial) and one chart (organization, classification, timeline, tabular, or flow) for a topic you might teach. Use the "Selection Rubric: Visuals" as a guideline. (ISTE NETS 3.C)

3. Make a list of 10 possible posters students could make to depict aspects of your teaching area. Prepare one yourself to serve as a model or motivational device. (ISTE NETS 3.C)

4. Prepare a set of transparencies for a topic you might teach. Use at least two of the following production methods: direct drawing by hand, electrostatic (xerography) process, computer generation of presentation graphics. (ISTE NETS-T 2.A)

5. Create an original example of an instructional situation in which you might use a set of teacher- or student-made slides. (ISTE NETS 2.A)

6. Produce a set of slides for a topic you might teach. Use a regular film camera, a digital camera, or computer images presented on a data projector. Describe the intended audience and purpose, and state specifically how you would use the slides. (Alternative: Describe a project for student-produced slides; include audience, purpose, and plan for guiding students.) (ISTE NETS 2.A)

7. Prepare a *PowerPoint* presentation and evaluate it using "Selection Rubric: Visuals." (ISTE NETS 2.A)

8. Plan a lesson where you might have the students use a digital camera to prepare a visual display. What issues do you need to address? What concerns would you have? What skills will your students need? (ISTE NETS 2.E)

9. Plan a lesson where your students will prepare a presentation using digital technologies. What types of technologies will you require them to use? What skills will your students need? (ISTE NETS 2.E)

10. Prepare a storyboard for a silent, sound, or multi-image slide presentation. (ISTE NETS-T 2.A)

11. Describe how you might utilize a data projector in a particular instructional situation. (ISTE NETS 3.B, C, D)

References

Cabeceiras, James. 1972. Observed differences in teacher verbal behavior when using and not using the overhead projector. *AV Communication Review* (fall): 271–280.

Wharton Applied Research Center. 1981. *A study of the effects of the use of overhead transparencies on business meetings.* Philadelphia: University of Pennsylvania. Wharton School.

Suggested Readings

Alper, M. V. 1996. Visual literature/aesthetic development research: museum–public school cooperation. *Visual Arts Research, 22*(spring): 62–78.

Costa, Manuel Joao. 2001. Using the separation of poster handouts into sections to develop student skills. *Biochemistry and Molecular Biology Education, 29*(3): 98–100.

DeCorte, Erik, ed. 1993. Comprehension of graphics in text. *Learning and Instruction* (3): 3, 151–249.

Educators guide to free films, filmstrips, and slides, 62nd ed. 2002. Randolph, WI: Educators Progress Service.

Eshel, A. 1997. A visual aid for teaching basic concepts of soil–water physics. *American Biology Teacher, 59*(4): n.p.

Feicht, Louis. 1999. Making charts: Do your students really understand the data? *Mathematics Teaching in the Middle School, 5*(1): 16–18.

Gros, B. 1997. Instructional design and the authoring of multimedia and hypermedia systems: Does a marriage make sense? *Educational Technology, 37*(January–February): 48–56.

Hay, Iain, and Susan M. Thomas. 1999. Making sense with posters in biological science education. *Journal of Biological Education, 33*(4): 209–214.

Kelly, Janet. 1999. Improving problem solving through drawings. *Teaching Children Mathematics, 6*(1): 48–51.

Lai, Shu-Ling. 2000. Influence of audio-visual presentations on learning abstract concepts. *International Journal of Instructional Media, 27*(2): 199–206.

Mills, David A., Kevin Kelley, and Michael Jones. 2001. Use of a digital camera to document student observations in a microbiology laboratory class. *American Biology Teacher, 63*(2): 119–123.

Mitchell, Cindi. 2000. *Math skills made fun: Great graph art decimals and fractions.* New York: Scholastic.

Romance, Nancy R., and Michael R. Vitale. 1999. Concept mapping as a tool for learning: Broadening the framework for student-centered instruction. *College Teaching, 47*(2): 74–79.

Rose, S. A., and P. M. Fernlund. 1997. Using technology for powerful social studies learning. *Social Education, 61*(March): 160–166.

Saloman, G. 1997. Of mind and media: How culture's symbolic forms affect learning and thinking. *Phi Delta Kappan, 78*(January): 375–380.

Scanlan, Stephen J., and Seth L. Feinberg. 2000. The cartoon society: Using "The Simpsons" to teach and learn sociology. *Teaching Sociology, 28*(2): 127–139.

Seamon, Mary Ploski, and Eric J. Levitt. 2003. *Digital cameras in the classroom.* Worthington, OH: Linworth.

Stephenson, Philip, and Paul Warwick. 2002. Using concept cartoons to support progression in students' understanding of light. *Physics Education, 37*(2): 135–141.

Van der Molen, J. H. W., and T. H. A. van der Voort. 1997. Children's recall of television and print news: A media comparison study. *Journal of Educational Psychology, 89*(March): 82–91.

Zevenbergen, Robyn. 2001. Peer assessment of student constructed posters: Assessment alternatives in preservice mathematics education. *Journal of Mathematics Teacher Education, 4*(2): 95–113.

CHAPTER 11

Audio

Outline

Knowledge Objectives

1. Distinguish between *hearing* and *listening*.
2. Identify four areas of breakdown in audio communication and specify the causes of such breakdowns.
3. Describe four techniques for improving listening skills.
4. Describe the two types of audio media most often used for instruction. Include distinguishing characteristics and limitations of each type.
5. Compare the advantages and limitations of audio media.
6. Describe one possible use of audio media in your teaching field. Include the subject area, audience, objective(s), role of the student, and evaluation techniques to be used.
7. Describe one procedure for editing audiotapes.
8. Identify five criteria for appraising and selecting audio materials.
9. Demonstrate your ability to follow the proper procedures for utilizing audio materials.

Professional Vocabulary

hearing
listening
auditory fatigue

digital recording
MP3 (MPEG Audio Layer 3)
oral history

If you were asked which learning activities consume the major portion of a student's classroom time, would you say reading instructional materials, answering questions, reciting what one has learned, or taking tests? Actually, typical elementary and secondary students spend about 50 percent of their school time just listening (Figure 11.1). College students are likely to spend nearly 90 percent of their time in class listening to lectures and seminar discussions (Figure 11.2). The importance, then, of audio experiences in the classroom should not be underestimated. This chapter discusses various means—referred to as *audio media*—for recording and transmitting the human voice and other sounds for instructional purposes.

Figure 11.1
Elementary and secondary students spend about half of their in-school time listening to others.

ASSURE
Case Challenge

We have developed a case study for this chapter to help you see how audio can be integrated into learning activities. At the end of the chapter you will be challenged to develop your own ASSURE lesson for a case study of your choice using the ASSURE model and incorporating the technology and media described in this chapter. To help you prepare your lesson, we have included hints (called "ASSURE Case Connections") throughout the chapter as they relate to the ASSURE Case Challenge.

A contemporary American literature class in a community college in the Pacific Northwest is studying regional fiction. The instructor has decided on Eudora Welty to represent Southern fiction. She has chosen her short story "Why I live at the P.O." as the story to represent this type of regional fiction. Her students are highly motivated because they are taking the class to transfer to a four-year college. Most are recent high school graduates, but some of the women in the class are using the community college to resume educations interrupted by other events in their lives. Reading abilities range from 8th-grade to 11th-grade levels. The instructor has discovered that they have little familiarity with contemporary literature. Most of the students are verbal learners. They enjoy discussing content rather than writing about it.

Before discussing audio formats in particular and audio media in general, let's examine the hearing–listening process itself and the development of listening skills.

HEARING AND LISTENING

Hearing and listening are not the same thing, although they are, of course, interrelated. At the risk of oversimplification, we might say that hearing is a physiological process, whereas listening is a psychological process.

Physiologically, **hearing** is a process in which sound waves entering the outer ear are transmitted to the eardrum, converted into mechanical vibrations in the middle ear, and changed in the inner ear into electrical impulses that travel to the brain.

The psychological process of **listening** begins with someone's awareness of and attention to sounds or speech patterns (receiving), proceeds through identification and recognition of specific auditory signals (decoding), and ends in comprehension (understanding).

Hearing and listening are also communication and learning processes. As with visual communication and learning, a message is encoded by a sender and decoded by a receiver. The quality of the encoded message is affected by the ability of the sender to express the message clearly and logically. The understandability of the decoded message is affected by the ability of the receiver to comprehend the message.

The efficiency of communication is also affected as the message passes from sender to receiver. Breakdowns in audio communications can occur at any point in the process: encoding, hearing, listening, or decoding, as illustrated in Figure 11.3.

Appropriate encoding of the message depends on the sender's skill in organizing and presenting it. For example, the vocabulary level of the message must be within the vocabulary level of the receiver.

Transmission and reception might be inhibited by a number of obstacles. First, the volume of the sound might be too low or too high. If too low, we have trouble picking up the meaning with any accuracy. If too high, we try to shield our ears, shutting out the offending sounds.

Figure 11.2
At the college level, about 90 percent of class time is spent listening.

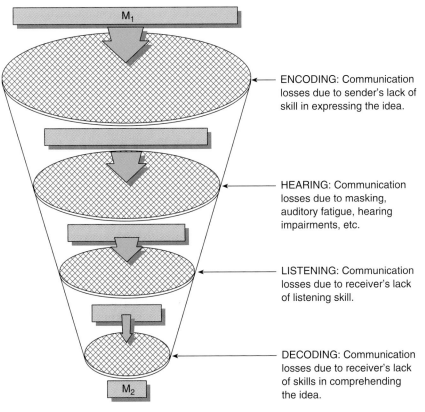

ENCODING: Communication losses due to sender's lack of skill in expressing the idea.

HEARING: Communication losses due to masking, auditory fatigue, hearing impairments, etc.

LISTENING: Communication losses due to receiver's lack of listening skill.

DECODING: Communication losses due to receiver's lack of skills in comprehending the idea.

Figure 11.3

In the hearing–listening process, impediments at each step act like filters, reducing the perceived meaning to a small fraction of the intended meaning. M_1 = meaning originally intended by the sender. M_2 = meaning as received and comprehended by the receiver.

entirely until it stops, and then you notice the cessation. This is an example of auditory fatigue, the process of gradually "tuning out" or losing consciousness of a sound source—a process that is physiological as well as psychological. That is, the neural mechanisms transmitting the sound to the brain literally become fatigued from "carrying the same load" over and over. In addition, your conscious awareness of the noise is diminished because it is "old news" and no longer of interest. The brain has a remarkable capacity for filtering out sounds it doesn't want or need to attend to.

Third, an individual's ability to hear may be physically impaired. When students have a cold, it is possible that their ability to hear in a noisy classroom is reduced. Even a small difference in acuity can cause students to have difficulty discriminating between words and phrases—thus the potential for confusion. And, with the trend toward including students with significant loss of hearing acuity in regular hearing classrooms, teachers may need to be certain that they make special considerations to provide special visual cues to ensure that these students clearly understand the information.

Second, a sound that is sustained monotonously, such as the droning voice of a teacher, may trigger **auditory fatigue.** You have probably had the experience of hearing an annoying sound—for example, a noisy muffler on the car you are riding in. But after a while you hardly notice the sound at all. You might stop thinking about it

The message can also be affected by the receiver's listening skills or lack of them. Receivers must be able to direct and sustain concentration on a given series of sounds (the message). They must have the skill to think

Technology for Diverse Learners

HEARING-IMPAIRED LEARNERS

The most familiar technique is closed-captioning for television and video programs. Multimedia presentations and audio materials on the Web need this feature as well.

One option is coding audio files with a form of markup language called Synchronized Multimedia Integration Language (SMIL, pro-

nounced "smile"; http://www.w3.org/audiovisual). Microsoft Corporation has its own captioning system, called Synchronized Accessible Media Interchange (SAMI, http://www.microsoft.com/enable/SAMI), which also provides multimedia captioning.

This technology is also useful for students who are learning a second language, those listening to content in a noisy environment, and students learning to read who need additional practice.

ahead while receiving the message (we think faster than we hear, just as we think faster than we read or write) and use this time differential to organize and internalize the information so they can comprehend it.

Finally, communication can break down because the receiver lacks the experiential background to internalize and thus comprehend the message.

DEVELOPING LISTENING SKILLS

Until recently, much attention in formal education was given to reading and writing, a little was given to speaking, and essentially none was given to listening. Now, however, educators recognize listening as a skill that, like all skills, one can improve with practice (Figure 11.4).

Hearing is the foundation of listening. Therefore, you should first determine whether all of your students can hear normally. Most school systems regularly use speech and hearing therapists to administer audiometric hearing tests to provide the data you need. Standardized tests also measure students' listening abilities. These tests are often administered by the school district, so check on the availability of listening test scores.

You can use a number of techniques to improve student listening abilities:

- *Guide listening.* To guide their listening, give students some objectives or questions beforehand. Start with short passages and one or two objectives. Then gradually increase the length of the passage and the number and complexity of the objectives or questions.
- *Give directions.* Give students directions individually or as a group on audiotape. You can then evaluate their ability to follow these instructions. With audio instructions, you can examine worksheets or

products of the activity. When giving directions orally, observe the "say it only once" rule so that students place value on both your and their time and their incentive to listen is reinforced.

- *Ask students to listen for main ideas, details, or inferences.* Keeping the age level of your students in mind, you can present an oral passage. You can read a story and ask primary students to draw what is happening. Ask students to listen for the main idea and then write it down. Use this technique, too, when you want students to draw details and inferences from the passage.
- *Use context in listening.* Younger students can learn to distinguish meanings in an auditory context by listening to sentences with words missing and then supplying the appropriate words.
- *Analyze the structure of a presentation.* Ask students to outline (analyze and organize) an oral presentation. You can then determine how well they were able to discern the main ideas and to identify the subtopics.
- *Distinguish between relevant and irrelevant information.* After listening to an oral presentation of information, ask students to identify the main idea and then rate (from most to least relevant) all other presented ideas. A simpler technique for elementary students is to have them identify irrelevant words in sentences or irrelevant sentences in paragraphs.

AUDIO FORMATS

Let's examine the comparative strengths and limitations of the audio formats most often used for instructional purposes—cassette tapes and compact discs. The differences between these media are summarized in Table 11.1.

Audiotapes

The major advantages of audiotape are that you can record your own tapes easily and economically, and when the content becomes outdated or no longer useful, you can erase the magnetic signal on the tape and reuse it. Tapes are not easily damaged, and they store easily. Unlike discs, broken tapes can be repaired, but not easily.

Of course, there are some limitations to magnetic tape recordings. Background noises or a mechanical hum may sometimes be recorded along with the intended material. Even a relatively low-level noise can ruin an otherwise good recording.

Figure 11.4
Listening skills are an important component of oral communication.

Table 11.1
Common audio formats

Format		Speed	Advantages	Limitations	Uses
Cassette audiotape	Size: 2½ by 4 by ½ in.	1⅞ ips[1]	Very portable (small and light) Durable Easy to use (no threading) Can prevent accidental erasing Requires little storage space	Tape sometimes sticks or tangles Noise and hiss Poor fidelity with inexpensive players Broken tapes not easy to repair Difficult to edit	Listening "in the field" using battery power Student-made recordings Extended discussions Individual listening Assessment tool (e.g., reading)
	Tape ⅛ in. wide				
Compact disc	Size: 4.72 in.	Variable high speed	Very durable High fidelity No background noise Random search	Impractical to prepare locally Initial expense of equipment	Music Drama

[1] ips = inches per second.

The audio device most commonly found in the classroom is the cassette tape recorder. Cassette tapes are identified according to the amount of recording time they contain. For example, a C-60 cassette can record 60 minutes of sound using both sides (i.e., 30 minutes on each side). A C-90 can record 45 minutes on each side. Cassettes are available in various lengths. The size of the plastic cassette containing the tape is the same in all cases, and all can be played on any cassette machine.

The cassette is durable; it is virtually immune to shock and abrasion. It can be snapped into and out of a recorder in seconds. It is not necessary to rewind the tape before removing it from the machine.

There are a few drawbacks to cassettes. For instance, longer tapes, particularly C-120s, sometimes become stuck or tangled in the recorder because of the thinness of the tape. If this happens, and unless the content on the tape is unique and of considerable value, you are best advised to throw the tape away. If it sticks or gets tangled in the machine once, it is likely to do so again.

The frequency response and overall quality (fidelity) of cassette playback units are not as good as those of compact disc (CD) players because of the small speakers in most portable cassette playback units. However, for most instructional uses the quality is more than adequate.

It is very easy to copy favorite music from CD discs to an audiotape, creating an individual assortment of music from a variety of sources. It is important to check the copyright restrictions as they apply in this circumstance (see "Copyright Concerns: Music").

Copyright Concerns

MUSIC

For academic uses other than performances, teachers and students may make copies of up to 10 percent of a musical work provided the excerpt does not comprise a part of the whole that would constitute a performable unit such as a section, movement, or aria. The number of copies should not exceed one copy per student.

Example: From experience you know that recordings of literary works put out by major record labels may disappear from their catalogs in a few years. For example, RCA Victor once made available a recording of Shakespeare's *Midsummer Night's Dream* with Mendelssohn's incidental music inserted appropriately. It is no longer available. If you taped the CDs, put the tapes on the shelf as a contingency, and used the CDs in class, you would at least have the tape available if your CDs were damaged. You would not have intended to deprive anyone of income; you would simply have used the technology to guarantee availability to yourself.

For general information on copyright, see the Copyright Concerns in Chapter 1. Suggested readings on copyright appear at the end of Chapter 1.

Compact Discs

Physically, the compact disc (CD) looks like a small, silver platter. The music or other sounds are stored as digitized bits of information (see "Close-Up: How a Compact Disc Works"). The disc is only 12 centimeters (4.75 inches) in diameter, yet it stores an incredible amount of information. Current CDs contain as much as 80 minutes of music.

The technology of the CD makes it an attractive addition to education programs. Users can quickly locate selections on the disc and can program them to play in any desired sequence. Information can be selectively retrieved by learners or programmed by the instructor. A major advantage of the CD is its resistance to damage. Stains can be washed off, and ordinary scratches do not affect playback. If there is a scratch that can affect the quality of the audio signal, a resin is now available to repair the disc.

Compact disc technology has been accepted rapidly for use in the home, and the CD's advantages, especially its resistance to damage, have made it a standard format in education.

When talking about audio CD, we are in essence talking about the same technology used in CD-ROM. CD-ROM utilizes more of the capacity of the optical technology by adding text and graphics to the disc. We discuss CD-ROM in more depth in Chapter 6. A similar technology, DVD, provides more storage capacity than does CD-ROM. This means that large files, such as audio files, can be stored with little concern for space,

Close-Up

HOW A COMPACT DISC WORKS

Until the compact disc was developed, all retail audio recordings were analog recordings; that is, they retained the essential waveform of the sound, whether as grooves in a phonograph record or as patterns of magnetized particles on audiotape. CDs are made using digital recording. In **digital recording,** analog information (whether in the form of music, speech, or print) is transformed into *binary* information—a series of 1s and 0s, the same mathematical code used in computers. A powerful laser burns a microscopic pit into the plastic master for each 1 in the digital code. A blank space corresponds to 0. The laser moves in an ever-widening spiral from the center of the master to the edge, leaving on the disc hundreds of thousands of binary bits. As a low-power laser beam in the playback unit picks up the pattern of pits and blank spaces, the beam is reflected back into the laser mechanism, and the digital code is transformed into the original analog sound. The laser mechanism does not come in direct physical contact with the CD and can move independently of the disc, unlike the stylus in a record groove or a tape head. This means that the laser beam can scan the CD and quickly locate desired information. In other words, the CD can be programmed so the user can quickly access any part of the disc. CD players can indicate what track is playing, the sequence in which tracks will be played, how many more tracks are on the disc, and the remaining playing time. Another characteristic of digital recording is the complete absence of background noise.

The compact disc, shown approximately one-half its actual size, is a three-layer sandwich. The digital code in the form of pits is on the top side of a clear, tough plastic very much like Plexiglas. A reflective coating of aluminum is placed on top of the pitted plastic surface. A protective coating of acrylic resin is applied on the top of the reflective surface. Label information is printed on top of the resin. This arrangement protects the program information from both the top and bottom surfaces of the disc. The laser beam reads the code through the clear plastic, and it is reflected back by the aluminum layer.

Unlike phonograph records, the recording on a CD begins near the center and ends at the outer rim. Also unlike records, the CD does not rotate at a constant speed as the laser reads the data. The speed varies from 500 rpm at the innermost track to 200 rpm at the outer edge.

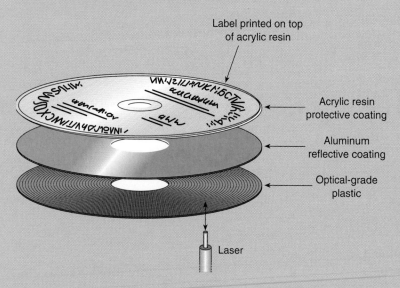

Label printed on top of acrylic resin

Acrylic resin protective coating

Aluminum reflective coating

Optical-grade plastic

Laser

The layers of a compact disc.

while ensuring quality sound reproduction. The equipment to create, or "burn," CD-ROM and DVD audio discs has become very affordable for the average audiophile, which makes it easy for an individual to prepare CD and DVD discs that contain "favorite" music on them. Copyright needs to be checked when doing this (see "Copyright Concerns: Music").

CDs have been eagerly accepted by consumers as a preferred audio format, but for audiophiles on the go (walking, jogging, or driving) they have one serious drawback: the size of the portable playback equipment. One additional problem has been the tendency to be sensitive to movement, like the impact when a person is jogging. This problem has been resolved by newer equipment. To reduce the effects of skipping, the playback head repositions itself after a bump, and a memory chip holds three to seven seconds of sound that might have been lost. Portable players of MP3 files (discussed next) such as the Rio and the iPod, eliminate this problem altogether.

ASSURE Case Connection

Would the students benefit most from listening to the story or from reading it? How easily do you think the instructor will find a recording of the author reading the short story? It might be easier to locate audiotapes; access to a CD version might be more expensive and it might be more difficult to locate this particular short story. Many popular fiction novels and short stories collections are being prepared for consumer use. What issues are important to consider when selecting an audio format?

MP3/WAVE File Formats

A new direction for audio is the ability to use your computer and the Internet to obtain audio files. **MP3 (MPEG Audio Layer 3)** is an audio compression format that makes large audio files available by shrinking them into smaller files that can quickly and easily be captured on the Internet. These files are sometimes available as *streamed audio,* which means they are sent in packets to the user, giving the user an opportunity to listen to portions of the file while waiting for additional portions of the file to be downloaded. MP3 is an "open" standard, which means it is available to anyone who has access to the Internet. The software your computer needs to use MP3 audio files is often free to the user. Many audio files are also free or available for download at low cost at many subscription-based websites or at pay-as-you-go sites such as Apple Computer's iTunes Music Store.

MP3 is a way for audiophiles to enjoy their favorite pieces of music, and to obtain the newest versions of a particular artist's songs. Some Internet sites let the users customize their selections so they can create unique "albums." On the downside, a word of caution related to copyright. Not all Internet sites make legal copies of music available. It is the responsibility of the user to respect the copyright laws related to audio (see "Copyright Concerns: The Internet and Music").

WAVE audio files are another common way to store and use audio data. This Windows-based digital format for audio relies on sampling frequencies, multiple channels, and compression algorithms to create the

Copyright Concerns

THE INTERNET AND MUSIC

United States copyright law grants the owner of a copyrighted musical work the exclusive right to perform it publicly, which means such performances require the copyright owner's permission. This includes website transmissions of music. Just as you pay for use of other forms of music (e.g., CDs), you must also pay for the use of music you download from the Internet. The copyright owners of sound recordings have rights set forth in the Digital Performance Right in Sound Recordings Act of 1995 and the Digital Millennium Copyright Act of 1998. These laws give sound recording copyright owners rights to online performances of their recordings.

Internet transmissions involve the reproduction and distribution of musical works and the copying of a copyrighted musical work or sound recording onto your server or hard drive (as when you load the file containing the work). Unauthorized copying constitutes exploitation of the reproduction rights. You must contact the copyright owner of the sound recording (usually the record label) for authorization to copy the sound recording onto your server or hard drive. Some Internet sites advertise music free from copyright. You are wise to check out sites that offer music files, as it is better to ask than to be caught with illegal copies of music.

For general information on copyright, see the Copyright Concerns in Chapter 1. Suggested readings on copyright appear at the end of Chapter 1.

files. Advantages to using the WAVE file format include the high quality of the audio files and the use of multiple channels for the sound. One limitation of using WAVE file format is that the standard is still being established, thus creating some confusion and complications among users of this audio format. WAVE files also tend to be very large files.

Advantages

- *Inexpensive*. In the case of audiotape, once the tapes and equipment have been purchased, there is no additional cost because the tape is erasable and reusable. Individual audiocassettes are inexpensive. In the case of MP3 files, many are available on the Internet for free or at low cost.
- *Readily available and simple to use*. Most students have been using audiocassette recorders since they were very young. Audio equipment is easy to operate.
- *Reproducible*. You can easily duplicate audiotapes in whatever quantities you need, for use in the classroom, in the media center, and at home. Remember to observe copyright guidelines.
- *Provides verbal message for nonreaders*. Students who cannot read can learn from audio media, which provide basic language experiences. Students can listen and follow along with visual and text material.
- *Ideal for teaching foreign languages*. Cassettes and CDs are excellent media for teaching foreign languages. They allow students to hear words pronounced by native speakers. Students can play back chosen sequences as often as necessary and, with CDs, may use the format's random-access capacity to construct their own sequences. Students may use cassettes to record their own pronunciations for comparison.
- *Stimulating*. Audio media can provide a stimulating alternative to reading and listening to the teacher. Audio can present verbal messages more dramatically than text can. With a little imagination on your part, audio can be very versatile.
- *Repeatable*. Users can replay portions of the program as often as needed to understand it.
- *Portable*. Audiocassette recorders are portable and can even be used "in the field" with battery power. Cassette recorders are ideal for home study; many students already have their own cassette machines.
- *Ease of lesson preparation*. Instructors can record their own audiotaped lessons easily and economically, erasing and recording over material that has become outdated or is no longer useful.
- *Selections easy to locate*. In the case of CDs, teachers and students can quickly locate selections on the compact discs and program the machine to play in any desired sequence.

- *Resistance to damage*. Cassette tapes are enclosed in a damage-resistant plastic cassette. In the case of CDs, there is no tape to tangle and break. Stains can be washed off, and ordinary scratches do not affect playback. MP3 files can be stored on a computer hard drive or on disks.

Limitations

- *Fixed sequence*. Audiotapes fix the sequence of a presentation even though it is possible to rewind the tape and hear a recorded segment again or advance the tape to an upcoming portion. It is difficult to scan audio materials as you would printed text materials. CDs do not share this limitation, which is why this format now plays a significant role in instruction. MP3 gives the user an opportunity to customize the audio format, which might lead to copyright violations.
- *Doesn't monitor attention*. Some students have difficulty studying independently, so when they listen to audiocassettes their attention tends to wander. They may hear the recorded message but not listen attentively and comprehend. Teachers can readily detect when students are drifting away from a lecture, but a cassette recorder cannot do this.
- *Difficulty in pacing*. Determining the appropriate pace for presenting information can be difficult if your students have a range of attention spans and experiential backgrounds.
- *Difficulty in locating segment*. It is sometimes difficult to locate a specific segment on an audiotape. Counters on the recorders assist retrieval, but they are not very accurate. CDs give much easier accessibility to specific selections.
- *Potential for accidental erasure*. Audiotapes can be erased easily, which can be problematic. Just as they can be quickly and easily erased when no longer needed, they can be accidentally erased when they should be saved. Be sure to remove the record lockout tab of any cassette you wish to safeguard. Because they are magnetic, audiotapes must be kept away from magnets, which can cause erasure.

Integration

The uses of audio media are limited only by the imagination of you and your students. You can use audio media in all phases of instruction—from introduction of a topic to evaluation of student learning. Perhaps the most rapidly growing general use of audio media today is in the area of self-paced instruction. The slower student can go back and repeat segments of instruction as often as necessary because the recorder-playback machine is a very patient tutor. The accelerated student can skip ahead or increase the pace of her instruction.

Prerecorded audio materials are available in a variety of subjects. For music classes, tapes and CDs can be used to introduce new material or to provide musical accompaniment. The sounds of various musical instruments can be presented individually or in combinations. In preschool and primary grades, tapes and CDs can be used for developing rhythm, telling stories, playing games, and acting out stories or songs. In social studies, the tape recorder can bring the voices of persons who have made history into the classroom. The sounds of current events can also be presented.

A common application of audio media is in learning centers. Sometimes these are even referred to as "listening centers" because of their use of audio-based materials. (We describe learning centers in more detail in Chapter 9.)

As another example, a middle school teacher inserts a cassette into the sound system of her car for the 20-minute daily commute to her school. After a few seconds of music, the song fades as the narrator says, "What's new in classroom management techniques? Today we are going to explore together three techniques

Media Files: Audio

A Jug Band Peter and the Wolf
Alacazam!
Cassette/CD

Here is a fun version of Prokofiev's *Peter and the Wolf* arranged for a band of folk instruments (and a few standard instruments played in folk style). The instruments include fiddle, mandolin, guitar, banjo, kazoo, whistle, mouth harp, jug, washtub bass, and clarinet. The accompanying booklet explains how the music was transcribed to retain the spirit of the original. Though the instruments are different, the story line is the same. This is not recommended as a replacement of the original but should be used as an interesting adaptation. Dave Van Ronk, a folksinger, does the narration. He also sings a group of folk songs that should appeal to children.

Audio Theatre Production Kit
Balance Publishing
CD

Students can create their own audio theatre productions. The kit contains two versions of a script, one with altered vocabulary to meet the needs of below-grade readers, the second for grade-level and above-grade-level readers. In addition, there is a CD with background music and sound effects. Students, working together, record their production to be shared with others. They develop technical skills, as well as working collaboratively in the production. It is a motivating way to help students with their reading and vocabulary competencies.

Self-Esteem for Women
Career Track
Cassette Tapes and Workbook

These tapes and workbook describe how women can increase their self-worth and life satisfaction. The program helps them feel good about themselves just as they are. It gives them skills they need to grow into the persons they want to become, in both their personal and professional lives. Topics include why eliminating negative self-talk is more powerful than increasing positive self-talk, how to open your mind to new possibilities, and how to recognize and measure your own growth and success.

A Kid's-Eye View of the Environment
Mish Mash Music
CD/Cassette

Michael Mish based this series of songs on his many visits to schools in southern California to talk to children about the environment. He found them to be more aware and concerned about environmental problems than he expected. Mish took the topics that the children were most concerned about (e.g., recycling, water and air pollution, and the greenhouse effect) and put them to music. The songs are engaging, with sing-along choruses. The messages should get primary-age children talking about making this a safer, cleaner world.

Technology for Diverse Learners

SPEECH-IMPAIRED STUDENTS AND TEACHERS

Technology has come to the aid of speech-impaired students and teachers. These include those who have had surgery on or near their vocal cords or who have been affected by cerebral palsy, Parkinson's disease, stroke, or ALS (Lou Gehrig's disease).

Voice processors and speech enhancers use the latest technology to turn unclear or slurred speech into vocalizations that can be readily understood.

Individuals with speech impairments can speak into a small microphone connected to a device that uses the latest in voice-processing technology. The device adds volume, level of articulation, and clarity to the voice without making it sound robotic. Other students and teachers have an easier time understanding the speaker. One manufacturer is Electronic Speech Enhancement (http://www.speechenhancer.com).

---

that will enhance your classroom skills. . . ." The cassette turns the automobile into a learning environment, thereby making use of otherwise unproductive time.

Audiotapes can be prepared by students to use in presentations to the class. Students can prepare the tapes with special sound effects or elements of music to enhance a portion of their speech. Students also could use an audiotape of an interview with a special individual as a part of their presentation.

Audiotapes are an excellent way in which to record student speaking and reading-aloud skills for a portfolio. The student can prepare specific passages or read certain materials to add to a taped collection to demonstrate progress.

Many self-help and skills-training materials are available on audiotape for adults. Audiotapes to teach a person to use a specific computer program provide the step-by-step procedures necessary. Personnel departments often provide materials on tape for their employees to listen to while traveling. This way an individual can learn about the new policies or procedures within the company without having to read many pages of text.

One special application of prerecorded audio media is "talking books" for blind or visually impaired students. More recently, this service has been expanded to meet the needs of students who are nonreaders because of a learning disability such as dyslexia. The National Library Service for the Blind and Physically Handicapped (NLS), Library of Congress administers a free library program of braille and recorded materials circulated to eligible borrowers through a network of cooperating libraries. At present, over 325,000 braille and recorded book titles and 70 magazine titles are available. The service is a cooperative effort of the Library of Congress and 57 regional and 81 subregional libraries in the

United States. Audiocassettes are the standard format. Many textbooks are now being offered through this service. There is an effort to move toward digital mastering of the materials to ensure the quality of the audio and the longevity of the materials.

PRODUCING MATERIALS ON CASSETTE TAPES

Students and teachers can easily prepare their own cassette tapes (see "Recording Audiocassettes" in Classroom Resources, Section C). Students can use cassette tapes for gathering oral histories and preparing oral book reports (Figure 11.5). Teachers can prepare tapes for use in direct instruction; for example, a vocational-technical school instructor can create audiotapes with directions for students to follow. Skills practice, such as pronunciation of a foreign language, can also be provided by audiocassette.

A popular project in 12th-grade social studies classes is the recording of **oral histories.** The students interview local senior citizens regarding the history of their community. Only one student interviews each senior citizen, but the interviewing task is rotated among the students, and the entire class assists in determining which questions to ask. In preparation for this project, students study both national and local history. All the tapes prepared during the interviews are kept in the school media center. Excerpts are duplicated and edited into programs for use with other social studies classes and for broadcast by the local radio station. This audiotape project serves the dual purpose of informing students and local residents about local history and collecting and preserving information that might otherwise be lost.

Selection Rubric: Audio Materials

Complete an interactive evaluation and add it to your NETS-T portfolio using the Selection Rubric for Audio materials available on the "Classroom Link Portfolio" CD-ROM. A downloadable version of this rubric is available in the Selection Rubrics module of the Companion Website at http://www.prenhall.com/smaldino.

Key Words

_____

_____

_____

Title _____

Series Title (if applicable) _____

Source _____

Date _____ Cost _____ Length _____ minutes

Subject Area _____

Intended Audience _____

Format

☐ Cassette

☐ Compact disc

Brief Description

Objectives

Entry Capabilities Required (e.g., prior knowledge, reading ability, vocabulary level, math ability)

Strong Points

Weak Points

Recommended Action (using criteria on the following page)

Name _____ Date _____

Rating Area	High Quality	Medium Quality	Low Quality	Rating
Match Curriculum	Curriculum standard addressed and use of audio should enhance student learning.	Curriculum standard partially addressed and use of audio may enhance student learning.	Curriculum standard not addressed and use of audio will likely not enhance student learning.	
Accurate & Current	Information correct and does not contain material that is out of date.	Information correct but does contain material that is out of date.	Information is not correct and does contain material that is out of date.	
Clear & Concise Language	Language used is age appropriate and vocabulary is understandable.	Language used is nearly age appropriate and some vocabulary is above/below student age.	Language used is not age appropriate and vocabulary is clearly inappropriate for student age.	
Motivating/ Interesting	Topic presented so that students are likely to be interested and engaged in learning.	Topic presented to interest students most of the time and engage most in learning.	Topic presented so as not to interest students and not engage them in learning.	
Learner Participation	Topic presented so that most students are actively engaged in learning.	Topic presented so that some students are engaged in learning.	Topic presented so that most students are not actively engaged in learning.	
Technical Quality	The material represents best available media.	The material represents media that are good quality, although there are some problems.	The material represents media that are not well prepared and are of very poor quality.	
Effectiveness Rating	There is evidence that use of these media has shown positive impact on student learning.	There is little evidence that use of these media has shown positive impact on student learning.	There is no evidence that use of these media has shown positive impact on student learning.	
Free from Bias	There is no evidence of objectionable bias or advertising.	There is little evidence of bias or advertising.	There is much evidence of bias or advertising.	
User Guide & Documentation	The documentation is excellent resource for use in a lesson. Documentation should help students use the material.	The documentation is good resource for use in a lesson. Documentation may help students use the material.	The documentation is poor resource for use in a lesson. Documentation does not help students use the material.	
Pacing Appropriate	The audio material is presented so most students can understand and process the information.	The audio material is presented so some students start to understand and process the information.	The audio material is presented so most students cannot understand and process the information.	
Clarity of Organization	The audio material is well organized so most students can understand the information.	The audio material is fairly well organized so students might understand the information.	The audio material is not well organized so most students cannot understand the information.	

From Smaldino, Russell, Heinich, and Molenda, *Instructional Technology and Media for Learning*, 8th ed. Copyright ©2005 by Pearson Education, Inc. All rights reserved.

Figure 11.5
Students and teachers can easily create their own audiotapes.

The cassette recorder can be used for presenting book reports. Students may record their book reports during study time in the media center or at home. You can evaluate the reports and keep the best ones on file in the media center. Encourage other students to listen to them before selecting books to read. Limit reports to three minutes, and require students to extract the main ideas from the book and to organize their thoughts carefully. During the taping, they practice their speaking skills. Encourage them to make the report as exciting as possible to interest other students in reading the book.

Tape recorders can be used to record information gleaned from a field trip. On returning to the classroom, students can play back the tape for discussion and review. Many museums, observatories, and other public exhibit areas now supply visitors with prerecorded messages about various items on display, which may (with permission) be rerecorded for playback in the classroom.

Students can also record themselves reciting, presenting a speech, performing music, and so on. They can then listen to the tape privately or have the performance critiqued by the teacher or other students. Initial efforts can be kept for comparison with later performances and for reinforcement of learning. Many small-group projects can include recorded reports students present to the rest of the class. These recordings can become part of each student's portfolio. Media portfolios are discussed in Chapter 1.

In a vocational-technical school, dental laboratory technology students are instructed on the procedures for constructing prosthetic devices such as partial plates and bridges by listening to an audiotape prepared by their instructor. To be efficient and effective in their work, these students must have both hands free and their eyes must be on their work, not on a textbook or manual. Audiotapes allow the students to move at their own pace, and the instructor is free to circulate around the laboratory and discuss each student's work individually.

A teacher of ninth-grade students with learning difficulties (but average intelligence) provides instruction on how to listen to lectures, speeches, and other oral presentations. The students practice their listening skills with tapes of recorded stories, poetry, and instructions. The teacher also uses commercially available tapes of speeches and narration. After the students have practiced their listening skills under teacher direction, they are evaluated using a tape they have not heard before. The students listen to the five-minute tape without taking notes; the teacher then gives them a series of questions dealing with important content from the passage.

An often overlooked use of audio materials is for evaluating student attainment of lesson objectives. For example, you may prerecord test questions for members of the class to use individually. You may ask students to identify sounds in a recording (e.g., to name the solo instrument being played in a particular musical movement) or to identify the composer of a particular piece of music. Students in social studies classes could be asked to identify the historical person most likely to have made excerpted passages from famous speeches, or to identify the time period of excerpted passages based on their content. Testing and evaluating in the audio mode is especially appropriate when teaching and learning have also been in that particular mode.

USING AUDIO FILES IN MULTIMEDIA

One way to enhance multimedia files such as *PowerPoint* (see Chapter 10) or *HyperStudio* (see Chapter 6) is to add audio files. Using audio within a multimedia presentation can enhance the interest or focus of the topic being presented. In addition, audio files can compensate for possible reading or learning problems that students might have. For example, when doing a presentation of great composers, a teacher can add short samples of the composers' work by inserting a link to an audio file stored on the hard drive. This can provide the students with a better understanding of that particular piece of music. Or, a *HyperStudio* stack designed for readers can be used by nonreaders with the addition of teacher-prepared scripts that actually read the text to the student using software such as *Blabbermouth*.

To accomplish this is relatively easy if you have the right equipment and enough memory on the computer as audio files can be quite large unless compacted. Both

PowerPoint and *HyperStudio* have audio files included in their software packages. Or, using a CD or audiotape, audio files can be created using a program such as *SoundEdit*. The digital audio file can then be added to the presentation. Or, using a microphone and *SoundEdit*, the teacher or student can create original audio to enhance the information presented. The process for creating a digital audio file is similar to that of creating an audiotape. (See "Recording Audiocassettes" in Classroom Resources, Section C.)

Summary: Using the ASSURE Model for Audio

As with other media and technology, the ASSURE model introduced in Chapter 3 is helpful in preparing lessons incorporating the use of audio.

Analyze Learners

Lesson development begins by identifying your students' unique attributes and learning characteristics. You also will wish to determine their various levels of experience with using audio.

State Objectives

Before stating specific objectives, you may wish to explore how to use audio in support of student learning. Sometimes it is more appropriate to state specific objectives after you have identified the direction you will take with the content and what materials you will use.

Select Methods, Media, and Materials

Use the information on audio discussed in this chapter as the basis for selecting, modifying, or designing your materials. Adjust the specific applications to suit the specific nature of your topic and objectives.

In selecting audio materials to use in your instruction, first consult with your school media specialist to determine what is available at your media center. For materials that are unavailable, consult the appropriate directory: For general audio sources see the *Schwann Record and Tape Guide;* for music CDs see *Best Rated CDs: Classical,* and *Best Rated CDs: Jazz and Pop.*

You should preview and appraise both commercially and locally produced materials before using them with your students. You may wish to use the "Selection Rubric: Audio Materials" to guide your selection decisions.

Utilize Media and Materials

Follow the suggestions discussed in this chapter to facilitate your students' learning, modifying each of the materials you use to fit your needs. The audio equipment and source materials you have access to, as well as its location, will determine how you schedule your students' learning experiences, as discussed in the chapter. If you have access to an audio playback system for the classroom, you may want all students to listen simultaneously. If you have limited access to equipment and audio source materials, you may consider creating a learning center.

Require Learner Participation

Introduce and explain the audio involved in your specific objective. Have the students do specific activities that rely on their ability to use audio. Students will find more value in the materials if they are able to connect what they are doing to what they are learning. Have them create slide shows with synchronized sound using *PowerPoint* and audio files either downloaded from the Internet or from sources you prepare, that they can then share with other students. Or, have them record a soundtrack to accompany an oral presentation.

Evaluate and Revise

It is important to consider how materials that rely on audio help students to interpret information. You can assess students on the quality of their created audio materials, and on how well they integrated them into their other learning. As with all media- and technology-based lessons, you may choose to revise your selection of materials after you have determined how well they have worked. In addition, you want to be certain that all materials used have been cleared of any potential copyright issues.

ASSURE Case in Practice: An Author Reads Her Short Story

All of the ASSURE Cases in Practice in this text and an electronic template for creating your own ASSURE Lesson can be found on the enclosed "Classroom Link Portfolio" CD-ROM.

This is a class in contemporary American literature in a community college in the Pacific Northwest. The instructor has decided on Eudora Welty to represent Southern fiction. She has chosen her short story "Why I Live at the P.O." and plans to include a recording of Miss Welty reading the story.

Analyze Learners

General Characteristics

All the students are taking the class because they plan to transfer to a four-year educational institution. Most are recent high school graduates, but some of the women in the class are using the community college to resume educations interrupted by other events in their lives. Reading abilities range from 8th-grade to 11th-grade levels.

Entry Competencies

The students are fairly well motivated, but the instructor has discovered that they have little familiarity with contemporary literature. Most can locate Mississippi on a map, but very few of the students have been to the Deep South, so Miss Welty's Mississippi accent may be difficult for them to understand. Because the story deals with family squabbles, the instructor is counting on the experiences of the older women in the class to give an important dimension to the class discussions.

Learning Styles

The learning styles of the students vary greatly. Because the class is elective, most students who enroll are verbal learners, although their reading levels tend to be low for college students. However, as a result of growing up with television and audio recordings, they are good listeners and prefer to hear material rather than to read it. They also enjoy discussing content rather than writing about it.

State Objectives

After listening to the recording, the students will be able to do the following:
1. State the main theme of the story.
2. Discuss the motivations of the main characters.
3. Identify the relationships among the main characters.
4. Compare the behaviors of the characters with those of people they know.

Select Methods, Media, and Materials

The instructor selected "Why I Live at the P.O." because she knew about the recording by the author. She believes that hearing as well as reading the short story will help the slower readers. She knows that Miss Welty is an amateur photographer and that a book of her photographs of people and scenes in her native Jackson, Mississippi, has been published. After securing permission from the publisher, the instructor asks the media center to make a series of slides from selected photographs from her copy of the book to give the students the flavor of the environment of the story. The instructor asks the Southern wife of a faculty member to read the narration she has written to accompany the set of slides. This will give the students some practice listening to a Southern accent before hearing Miss Welty.

Utilize Media and Materials

The classroom is acoustically suitable for hearing the tape, but the instructor realizes that a playback unit with better speakers than those on her portable machine will be necessary. She arranges with the media center to obtain a good playback unit. She has also requested a slide projector and screen and has arranged the slides in the tray.

The reading assignment included material on the influence of the South on Southern writers. On the day before the oral reading, the instructor hands out a sheet listing colloquialisms from the story with explanations.

On the day of the reading, the instructor introduces the woman who will read the narration for the slides and proceeds to present the slide set. The slide presentation elicits a number of questions about life in the South. The instructor then introduces the recording, closing with the warning that contrary to what they may have heard about languorous Southern speech, Eudora Welty speaks very rapidly.

Require Learner Participation

The students are encouraged to ask questions during and following the slide presentation. They take notes while the story is being read. After the recording, the class discusses the short story. The older women in the class give their insights into the problems of family relations.

As a culminating exercise, the instructor asks the students to write a short essay comparing the characters in the story with people they know.

Evaluate and Revise

From the discussion in class, the instructor determines that the recording added to the understanding of the theme and the motivations of the characters. On the basis of the response to the slide presentation, the instructor decides to use the technique in other units of the course.

The essays demonstrate that the students gave a good deal of thought to the way behavior patterns are influenced by where people live. The instructor gives the class a brief multiple-choice test on the people in the story to determine how well the students understood the interactions among the characters.

Create Your Own ASSURE Lesson

Using the ASSURE model, design a lesson for a scenario from the table on this book's inside cover or from the Companion Website, or use a scenario of your own design. Use one of the methods described in Chapter 1 and information from this chapter related to incorporating audio into your instructional setting. Be sure to include information about the audience, the objectives, and all other elements of the ASSURE model. When completed, reflect on the process you used and what you have learned about matching audience, content, method, and materials.

Classroom Link Portfolio Activities

Use the "Classroom Link Portfolio" CD-ROM and the Companion Website as resources in completing these activities. To complete the following activities online go to the Portfolio Activities module in Chapter 11 of the Companion Website (http://www. prenhall.com/smaldino).

1. *Planning Lessons Using Audio Input.* Prepare an independent learning module, such as a learning center. Include an audiotape to help learners use the resources in that learning center to accomplish the task(s) you have identified. What do you need to do to prepare an audiotape? What will your learners do to ensure they use the tape to their benefit? What modifications are needed for different students? (ISTE NETS-T 3.A & B; 6.B & E)

2. *Written Reflection.* Use an audiotape to collect your thoughts and ideas about what it means to use technology in your teaching. Listen to your tape after a few entries. What have you learned about your ideas? How does keeping your ideas on audiotape impact your collection of reflections? Would you consider your audiotape to be a variation of a journal? Why or why not? (ISTE NETS-T 4.B; 5.B)

Integration Assessments

To complete the specified activities online go to the Integration Assessments module in Chapter 11 of the Companion Website (http://www.prenhall. com/smaldino).

1. Create a lesson in which audio is an important media component. As you finalize the lesson for entry into your portfolio, consider the following questions: A. How does using audio connect to the content standard you've selected? B. How does the use of audio support student learning in this lesson? C. What have you learned about student learning by preparing this lesson? (ISTE NETS-T 2.A; 5.B)

2. Prepare an audiotape that features your voice and some music. Have your class evaluate it using the criteria in the Checklist for Student/Teacher-Prepared Audiocassettes in "Recording Audiocassettes" (Classroom Resources, Section C). Include a brief description of each step from the ASSURE model. (ISTE NETS-T 3.C)

3. Obtain any commercially prepared audio materials and appraise them using a given set of criteria (such as that given in "Selection Rubric: Audio Materials"). (ISTE NETS-T 2.A)

4. Develop a short oral history of your school or organization by interviewing people associated with it for a long time. Edit your interviews into a five-minute presentation. (ISTE NETS-T 3.C)

5. Select the best audio format for a given instructional situation and justify the selection of that format, stating advantages and limitations. (ISTE NETS-T 2.C)

6. Prepare an outline for a short oral presentation. Deliver your presentation as if you were addressing the intended audience, and record it. Critique your presentation for style as well as content. Revise and present again. (ISTE NETS-T 5.C)

7. Plan a brief audio-based lesson on a basic skill (e.g., spelling or arithmetic), or prepare a performance aid (e.g., how to make out a bank check or how to fill out an application form). Design the lesson with paper and pencil first, then record it on tape. (ISTE NETS-T 2.D)

Suggested Readings

Brown, Jean E. 2002. Audio books in the classroom: Bridging between language arts and social studies. *ALAN Review, 29*(3): 58–59.

Crandell, C., Joseph J. Smaldino, and Carol Flexer. 1995. *Sound-field amplification: Theory and practical applications.* San Diego, CA: Singular.

Egbert, Joy. 1992. Talk to me: An exploratory study of audiotaped dialogue journals. *Journal of Intensive English Studies* (Fall): 91–100.

Frey, Barbara, and Karen Overfield. 2002. Audio professional development workshops: Less glamorous, more cost effective. *New Horizons in Adult Education, 16*(2): n.p.

Hagopian, Patrick. 2000. Voices from Vietnam: Veterans' oral histories in the classroom. *Journal of American History, 87*(2): 593–601.

Isbell, Rebecca T. 2002. Telling and retelling stories: Learning language and literacy. Supporting language learning. *Young Children, 57*(2): 26–30.

Jalongo, M. R. 1995. Promoting active listening in the classroom. *Childhood Education, 72*(1): n.p.

Kersten, Fred. 1993. A/V alternatives for interesting homework. *Music Educators Journal* (January): 33–35.

Koskinen, Patricia S., Irene H. Blum, Stephanie A. Bisson, Stephanie M. Phillips, Terry S. Creamer, and Tara Kelley Baker. 1999. Shared reading, books, and audiotapes: Supporting diverse students in school and at home. *Reading Teacher, 52*(5): 430–444.

LaLone, Mary B. 1999. Preserving Appalachian heritage: A model for oral history research and teaching. *Journal of Appalachian Studies, 5*(1): 115–122.

Mason, Harriett. 1996. *Power of storytelling: A step-by-step guide to dramatic learning in K–12.* Thousand Oaks, CA: Sage.

McDrury, Janice, and Maxine Alterio. 2003. *Learning through storytelling: Using reflection and experience to improve learning.* London: Kogan Page.

Mody, M., M. Studdert-Kennedy, and S. Brady. 1997. Speech perception deficits in poor readers: Auditory processing or phonological coding? *Journal of Experimental Child Psychology, 64*(2): n.p.

Petress, Kenneth C. 1999. Listening: A vital skill. *Journal of Instructional Psychology, 26*(4): 261–262.

Ratcliff, Nancy J. 2002. Using authentic assessment to document the emerging literacy skills of young children. *Childhood Education, 78*(2): 66–69.

Rea-Dickins, Pauline. 2001. Mirror, mirror on the wall: Identifying processes of classroom assessment. *Language Testing, 18*(4): 429–462.

Roy, Loriene. 1993. Planning an oral history project. *Journal of Youth Services in Libraries, 6*(4): 409–413.

Schmeidler, Emilie, and Corinne Kirchner. 2001. Adding audio description: Does it make a difference? *Journal of Visual Impairment and Blindness, 95*(4): 197–212.

Tucker, Judith Cook. 1992. Let their voices be heard! Building a multicultural audio collection. *Multicultural Review* (April): 16–21.

Woods, Robert, and Jack Keeler. 2001. The effect of instructor's use of audio e-mail messages on student participation in and perceptions of online learning: A preliminary case study. *Open Learning, 16*(3): 263–278.

Video

Outline

Knowledge Objectives

1. Identify four common video formats and compare the characteristics, advantages, and limitations of the various formats.
2. Describe five attributes of video.
3. Compare the advantages and limitations of video.
4. Create original examples of applications of video in each instructional domain—cognitive, affective, motor, and interpersonal.
5. Describe techniques for video design and production by students and teachers.
6. Characterize the acceptance of video in education and in corporate settings.
7. Outline the process for selecting video, including at least five appraisal criteria.
8. Describe instructional applications that are especially appropriate for video.
9. Describe the ideal physical arrangements for class viewing of video. Your description must include seating, monitor placement, lighting, and volume, along with the minimum and maximum viewing distances and angles.

Professional Vocabulary

video

television

DVD

digital video

streaming video

time lapse

slow motion

animation

persistence of vision

documentary

charge-coupled device (CCD)

in-house video

digital video editing

Originally, the concept of video was synonymous with that of broadcast television, but the concept has expanded dramatically in recent years. In this text we use the term **video** to refer to electronic storage of moving images (videotapes, DVD, etc.). **Television** is the transmission of live moving images electronically, either through air or through wires or cables. New technologies connected to television sets have proliferated, such as home computers, videocassette recorders, DVD players, video games, and specialized cable TV services. Other hybrids are still emerging. These new services continue to multiply because it tends to be cheaper and more efficient to transmit information electronically than to transport information, goods, and people physically.

The Latin word *video* means "I see." Any electronic media format that employs "motion pictures" to present a message can be referred to as video. Thus, we have videocassettes, DVD, interactive CD-ROM, video games, and so on. This chapter will present information on the various types of video technologies that are available to the instructor.

VIDEO FORMATS

Video versions of the moving image are recorded on tape or disc, each packaged in forms that vary in size, shape, speed, recording method, and playback mechanism. The most common video formats are summarized in Table 12.1.

ASSURE
Case Challenge

We have developed a case study for this chapter to help you see how video can be integrated into learning activities. At the end of the chapter you will be challenged to develop your own ASSURE lesson for a case study of your choice using the AS-SURE model and incorporating the technology and media described in this chapter. To help you prepare your lesson, we have included hints (called "ASSURE Case Connections") throughout the chapter as they relate to the ASSURE Case Challenge.

Brad Strucker plans to teach his elementary students about the Panama Canal. The majority of his students are unfamiliar with it, although they do know what a local barge canal looks like. Few of his students have traveled outside their home state.

The classroom is located in an urban setting, with the majority of his students being from lower-middle socioeconomic status families. Nearly half of the students come from single-parent homes. Mr. Strucker finds these students to be a challenge to motivate to learn.

Mr. Strucker is concerned that his students need to know this information to be able to pass an end-of-year standardized test that contains questions about Central America, including questions on the Panama Canal. He wants his students to do well on the test.

Table 12.1
Common video formats

Format	Speed	Advantages	Limitations
Videocassette VHS	1.31 ips[1] (120 min at standard speed)	Self-contained and self-threading Abundant software available Easy local production	Video quality low; not broadcast quality Quality deteriorates with use
Tape width: ½ in.			
Videocassette (Hi 8)	1.31 ips[1] (120 min at standard speed)	Most compact format Full compatibility among all makes and models Easy local production	Video quality lower Limited acceptance in education; little software available
Tape width: 8 mm (about ¼ in.)			
Compact disc (DVD)	Variable high speed	Easy to use Low-cost hardware and software Worldwide standard Self-contained hardware	Limited educational software
Diameter: 4.72 in.			

[1] ips = inches per second.

Videotape

The VHS ½-inch format is the preferred medium for commercial distribution of moving images. Virtually all of us have rented a VHS version of a movie, and most of us have recorded a TV program on VHS for later or repeated viewing. (Be aware of copyright issues when recording broadcast programs for educational use. See "Copyright Concerns: Off-Air Videotaping.") Time-shifting the TV schedule has become a major sport in many homes. VHS is also the current preferred format for amateur and nonstudio production of recorded moving images in education.

Digital Video

One attractive attribute of digital video is the quality of the image. It is the highest quality of image available, relying on 500 lines of resolution, double that of analog video. The cameras to record digital video are usually smaller and more compact than analog cameras. Thus, they are easier to carry and can be used by children. Another advantage of digital video is that editing can be done on a computer using software that makes it easy to manipulate the sequence of images. The quality of the video image will not degrade during editing and copying, as happens to analog video quality. Finally, it is quick and easy to transfer video to the computer using a high-speed connection such as FireWire. FireWire moves large video files without requiring compression, which ensures that image quality will be retained during the transfers.

DVD

DVD (digital videodisc) is a medium offering digital storage and playback of full-motion video. Just as audio can be digitized (as described in Chapter 11),

Copyright Concerns

OFF-AIR VIDEOTAPING

The Copyright Act of 1976 did not cover educational uses of videotaped copies of copyrighted broadcasts. A negotiating committee composed of representatives from industry, education, and government agreed on a set of guidelines for video recording of broadcasts for educational use. According to these guidelines, you may do the following:

- Ask a media center to record the program for you if you cannot do so or if you lack the equipment.
- Retain a videotaped copy of a broadcast (including cable transmission) for a period of 45 calendar days, after which you must erase the program.
- Use the program in class once during the first 10 school days of the 45 calendar days, and a second time if instruction needs to be reinforced.
- Have professional staff view the program several times for evaluation purposes during the full 45-day period.
- Make a limited number of copies to meet legitimate needs, but you must erase these copies when erasing the original videotape.
- Use only a part of the program if instructional needs warrant.
- Enter into a licensing agreement with the copyright holder to continue use of the program.

You (and media centers) may *not* do the following:

- Videotape premium cable services such as HBO without express permission.

- Alter the original content of the program.
- Exclude the copyright notice on the program.
- Record a program in anticipation of a request for use; the request to record must come from an instructor.
- Retain the program, and any copies, after 45 days.

Remember that these guidelines are not part of the copyright act but are rather a "gentleman's agreement" between producers and educators. You should accept them as guidelines in good faith.

Example: Suppose a video you frequently use drops out of the distributor's catalog; it is now "out of print." To protect the print you now have, it would seem reasonable, after unsuccessful attempts to reach the copyright owner to get permission, to copy the video and use the copy in class. If, at a later date, the title is put back on the market by the same or another distributor, you must go back to using your original copy. This is not uncommon. For example, *Pacific 231*, an effective film to demonstrate editing, was originally distributed by Young America Films. After Young America Films was purchased by another company, *Pacific 231* was dropped from the catalog. It was not available for almost 20 years. Then, Pyramid Films secured the distribution rights, and it is now available for purchase. During the period of unavailability, it would have been reasonable to use a videotaped copy.

For general information on copyright, see the Copyright Concerns in Chapter 1. Suggested readings on copyright appear at the end of Chapter 1.

video images can be converted into a digital format. **Digital video** images can be manipulated (e.g., content, size, and color can be changed), stored, duplicated, and replayed without loss of quality. With digital video stored on DVDs or in a computer, you and your students can edit the content and sequence of the moving images.

The disc is the same physical size as an audio CD or a CD-ROM but can hold enough data for four full-length feature films (almost nine hours of video) with high-quality soundtracks. Like CDs and CD-ROMs, DVD has instant random access and is highly durable. There is no distortion when you watch a DVD in slow motion. DVD discs provide far superior sound and picture quality compared to standard VHS videotapes. Unlike videotape, DVD discs do not deteriorate over time. They are doing for movies (films and videotapes) what the CD did for music.

Video-based courses with multiple soundtracks can be aimed at different types of students. Text can be displayed in multiple languages and used to subtitle or annotate video content. Some discs offer the ability to view an object from different angles selected by the student: up to nine different camera angles selected in real time during playback. Discs offer index searching of title, chapter, track, or time-code for instant navigation—random access. Barcodes can be added to text materials to access the video on the DVD, adding to the instructional value. A single-layer DVD can store over two hours of high-quality, digital video including eight separate high-quality audio tracks for multiple languages, different grade or learning levels, or special video descriptions for blind or visually impaired students. Digital videodisc-recordable (DVD-R) is available to allow people to record their own DVDs as they do with videotapes.

All DVD discs can be played on all DVD players. The devices also play audio CDs. Many computers have built-in DVD players (which often also record), replacing the CD-ROM drive as the digital drive format.

Internet Video

Video also can be delivered via the Internet, usually using **streaming video.** The same technique can also be used with sound alone. *Streaming* means that the file doesn't have to be completely downloaded before it starts playing. Instead, as soon as the user clicks on a link that contains streaming video (or audio), the content begins to play. The video content is actually downloading to the user's computer in a series of small information packets that arrive shortly before the viewer sees (or hears) the material. Any video (or audio) materials can be delivered over the Internet using the streaming technique. The content is not stored on your computer. It "flows" into your active memory, is displayed (or played), and then is erased.

ASSURE Case Connection

Mr. Strucker could consider using videotapes about the Panama Canal. The school's centralized media resource center has a list of 10 videotapes about Central America, and 3 of them highlight the Panama Canal. All are available to check out in the time frame of the unit. The only DVD with information on the Panama Canal is the encyclopedia DVD in the school media center.

SPECIAL ATTRIBUTES

Because most of us are inclined to think of video as media designed to produce a realistic image of the world around us, we tend to forget that a basic attribute of motion media is the ability to manipulate temporal and spatial perspectives. Manipulation of time and space not only serves dramatic and creative ends; it also has important implications for instruction.

Manipulation of Time

Video permits us to increase or decrease the amount of time required to observe an event. For example, it would take an impossibly long time for students to actually witness a highway being constructed, but a carefully edited videotape of the different activities that go into building a highway can recreate the essentials of such an event in a few minutes.

We can also take out pieces of time. For example, you are familiar with the type of sequence in which a scene fades out and then fades in the next day. Time has been taken out of the sequence, but we accept that the night has passed even though we did not experience it in real time.

Compression of Time.   Video can compress the time it takes to observe an event. A flower can appear to open before our eyes, or stars can streak across the nighttime sky. (Figure 12.1). This technique, known as **time lapse,** has important instructional uses. For example, the process of a chrysalis turning into a butterfly is too slow for easy classroom observation. However, through time-lapse videography, the butterfly can emerge from the chrysalis in a matter of minutes.

Expansion of Time.   Time can also be expanded in motion media through a technique called **slow motion.** Some events occur too fast to be seen by the naked eye. By photographing such events at extremely high speeds and then projecting the image at normal speed, we can observe what is happening (Figure 12.2). For example, a chameleon catches an insect too rapidly for the naked eye to observe; high-speed videography can slow down the motion so that we can observe the process.

Figure 12.1

In time lapse, a slow event is condensed into a short screen time by allowing several seconds to elapse between shooting each frame of video.

Figure 12.2

In slow motion, a fast event is expanded into a longer screen time by shooting video at a speed greater than 24 frames per second.

Manipulation of Space

Motion media permit us to view phenomena in microcosm and macrocosm—that is, at extremely close range or from a vast distance. Your students can view the earth from the space shuttle (macro view). At the other extreme, they can observe cell division under a microscope (micro view).

Video and live television allow us and our students to observe two events occurring simultaneously but many miles apart using split screen. This technique is often viewed in sports events such as the Olympics where a

view of the current participant is matched to that of a previous contestant.

Animation

Time and space can also be manipulated by **animation.** This is a technique in which the producer takes advantage of **persistence of vision** to give motion to otherwise inanimate objects. There are various and more or less sophisticated techniques for achieving animation, but basically animation is made up of a series of photographs or drawings of small displacements of objects or images. If such an object is photographed on a single film frame, then moved a very short distance and rephotographed, moved again, rephotographed, and so on, the object when projected will look as though it has been continuously moving through space.

With the continuing evolution of computer programs that can manipulate visual images, we are experiencing a rediscovery of the art of animation through the video display format. Computer-generated animation sequences are being used more and more in instructional video programs to depict complex or rapid processes in simplified form.

Understanding Video Conventions

The devices and techniques used in video to manipulate time and space employ what are for most of us readily accepted conventions. We understand that the athlete whose jump is stopped in midair is not actually frozen in space, that the flashback is not an actual reversal of our normal time continuum, that the light bulb does not really disintegrate slowly enough for us to see that it implodes rather than explodes. Teachers, however, must keep in mind that the ability to make sense out of video conventions is an acquired skill. When do children learn to handle flashbacks, dissolves, jump cuts, and so on? Unfortunately, we know very little about when and how children learn to make sense of manipulation of reality, and much research on the matter remains to be done.

Video is not alone in its reliance on accepted conventions for interpretation and appreciation. Flashback techniques are regularly used in literature and usually accepted by readers. The theatrical convention of the aside is readily accepted by playgoers. The following anecdote about Picasso illustrates how a new artistic convention may seem to the uninitiated as merely a distortion of reality rather than, as intended, a particular and valid view of reality. It also illustrates how a convention (in this case a convention of photography) can become so readily accepted and commonplace that we are amusingly surprised at being reminded it exists.

Picasso showed an American soldier through his villa one day, and on completion of the tour the young man felt compelled to confess that he didn't dig Picasso's

Technology for Diverse Learners

HEARING-IMPAIRED LEARNERS

For many years captioned video was only available on films through a specific company. More recently, captioning has become more readily available on televisions and other video formats. *Captioning* consists of a box of text at the bottom of the viewing area. The text provides viewers with hearing difficulties the opportunity to read what others are hearing through the audio channel of the video.

---

weird way of painting, because nothing on the canvas looked the way it really is. Picasso turned the conversation to more acceptable matters by asking the soldier if he had a girl back in the States. The boy proudly pulled out a wallet photograph. As Picasso handed it back, he said: "She's an attractive girl, but isn't she awfully small?" (Forsdale & Forsdale, 1966, p. 609).

ASSURE Case Connection

Videotapes made using accepted video conventions might help the elementary students understand how the Panama Canal helps ships travel between the Atlantic and Pacific oceans. Would Mr. Strucker need to consider the age of his students and some of the special attributes of video, such as the use of time lapse or animation? What attributes might be inappropriate for his students?

Advantages

- *Motion.* Moving images have an obvious advantage over still visuals in portraying concepts in which motion is essential to mastery (such as psychomotor skills).
- *Processes.* Operations, such as assembly line steps or science experiments, in which sequential movement is critical can be shown more effectively.
- *Risk-free observation.* Video allows learners to observe phenomena that might be dangerous to view directly, such as an eclipse of the sun, a volcanic eruption, or warfare.
- *Dramatization.* Dramatic recreations can bring historical events and personalities to life. They allow students to observe and analyze human interactions.
- *Skill learning.* Research indicates that mastery of physical skills requires repeated observation and practice. Through video, students can view a performance over and over again for emulation. They can observe video of their own performance for feedback and improvement.

- *Affective learning.* Because of its great potential for emotional impact, video can be useful in shaping personal and social attitudes. Documentary and propaganda video and films have often been found to have a measurable impact on audience attitudes.
- *Problem solving.* Open-ended dramatizations are frequently used to present unresolved situations, leaving it to the viewers to discuss various ways of dealing with the problem.
- *Cultural understanding.* We can develop a deep appreciation for other cultures by seeing depictions of everyday life in other societies. The whole genre of ethnographic video can serve this purpose. Feature-length ethnographic videos available include *The Hunters, The Tribe That Hides from Man, The Nuer,* and *River of Sand.*
- *Establishing commonality.* By viewing video programs together, a disparate group of people can build up a common base of experience to discuss an issue effectively.

Limitations

- *Fixed pace.* Although videos can be stopped for discussion, this is not usually done in group showings. Because the program runs at a fixed pace, some viewers may fall behind while others are waiting impatiently for the next point.
- *Talking head.* Many videos, especially in-house productions, consist mostly of close-ups of people talking. Video is not a great oral medium—it is a visual medium! Use audiotapes for verbal messages.
- *Still phenomena.* Although video is advantageous for concepts that involve motion, it may be unsuitable for other topics where detailed study of a single visual is involved (e.g., a map, a wiring diagram, or an organization chart).
- *Misinterpretation.* Documentaries and dramatizations often present a complex or sophisticated treatment of an issue. A scene

Technology for Diverse Learners

VISUALLY IMPAIRED LEARNERS

A technique called "Descriptive Video" is available to those who have visual impairments. A soft-spoken voice describes the scenes that are on the video. The visually impaired individual then is able to hear the description and grasp the idea of what is being presented visually. This service is available in many television programs. More recently, rentable video also has provided this option.

intended as satire might be taken literally by a young or naive viewer. The thoughts of a main character may be interpreted as the attitudes and values of the producer.

- *Abstract, nonvisual instruction.* Video is poor at presenting abstract, nonvisual information. The preferred medium for words alone is text. Philosophy and mathematics do not lend themselves well to video unless the specific concepts discussed lend themselves to illustration using historical footage, graphic representation, or stylized imagery.
- *Logistics.* In schools, videos tend to be stored in the media center rather than in the classroom. Consequently the appropriate video and equipment must be ordered in advance. Training programs usually rent videos from a distributor or from corporate headquarters. This again means that

videos have to be ordered well in advance of their intended use. Arrangements have to be made so that the correct title arrives at the right place at the right time and that the proper equipment is available and in good condition. The complexity of these arrangements may discourage many instructors.

INTEGRATION

Videos are available on almost any topic and for all types of learners in all the domains of instruction—cognitive, affective, motor skill, and interpersonal. As noted previously, video can manipulate both time and space. It can take the learner almost anywhere and extend students' interests beyond the walls of the classroom. Objects too large to bring into the classroom can be studied as well as those too small to see with the naked eye. Events too

Showmanship

VIDEO

The following generic tips apply to the enhancement of video presentations:

- *Sightlines.* Check lighting, seating, and volume control to be sure that everyone can see and hear the presentation.
- *Mental set.* Get students mentally prepared by briefly reviewing previous related study and evoking questions about the current topic.
- *Advance organizer.* List on the chalkboard the main points to be covered in the presentation.
- *Vocabulary.* Preview any new vocabulary.
- *Short segments.* Show only 8 to 12 minutes of a video at any one time (even shorter for younger students). Rather than showing a 30-minute video from start to finish, increase viewer learning and retention by using the following technique: Intro-

duce the first segment and show about 10 minutes of the video, stopping at a logical breaking point. Discuss the segment and then introduce the second segment, tying it to the first. Show the second 10-minute segment and repeat the procedure. Of course, you may choose to show only part of a video. You do not have to show it all.

- *Role model.* Most important, get involved in the program yourself. Watch attentively and respond when the presenter asks for a response. Highlight major points by adding them to the chalkboard during the lesson.
- *Followup.* Reinforce the presentation with meaningful followup activities.
- *Light control.* When using video projection with videotape or DVD, dim the light. Turn lights off if dimming is not available. If you are using a video monitor (TV), you can use normal room lighting. Dim the lights above and behind the monitor if possible.

dangerous to observe, such as an eclipse of the sun, can be studied safely. The time and expense of a field trip can be avoided. Many companies and national parks provide video tours to observe assembly lines, services, and the features of nature.

Certain special effects, such as slow motion, can be obtained with DVD presentations. Videocassette recorders (VCRs) can be remotely controlled, meaning the instructor (or operator) does not have to stay close to the machine. Because of the ease of operating the equipment,

Media Files: Video

MATH . . . WHO NEEDS IT?
FASE Productions
Video

This videocassette is aimed at parents and their kids. It gives a perspective on the rewards and opportunities open to anyone with good math skills. It challenges myths about math, pokes fun at society's misconceptions of the subject, and provokes viewers to think and talk about math in a more positive way.

RECYCLING IS FUN
Bullfrog Films
Video

Three captivating young children explore the three *R*s of recycling—reduce, recycle, and reuse. To educate themselves, they visit a landfill, a recycling center, and their local supermarket to find out what they can do to help with our solid waste crisis. They discover their own power to recycle and choose what they buy, for the benefit of their world. A study guide is provided for the teacher and students.

PLANNING YOUR APPROACH TO READING
Agency for Instructional Technology
Video

Four members of a rock band use reading strategies to help them organize their group, acquire costumes, find an engagement, and play at a dance. Other readers use strategies to carry out research on pilgrims in a library and to read a wrestling magazine. Rappers explain how to preview, and a magician's assistant skims and scans to save the magician from a falling ax.

EVERYDAY CREATIVITY
CRM Learning
Video

Famed National Geographic photographer Dewitt Jones uses memorable stories and his own inspirational photos to show that everyone can be more creative in everything from problem solving to dealing with others.

ONE WOMAN, ONE VOTE
PBS Video
Video

Witness the 70-year struggle for women's suffrage, from fledgling alliances to a sophisticated mass movement. This video documents the history of the women's suffrage movement from the Seneca Falls Convention in 1848, when Elizabeth Cady Stanton demanded the right for women to vote, to the last battle for passage of the 19th Amendment in 1920.

ARE YOU ADDICTED?
Human Relations Media
Video

An awardwinning video directed toward adolescents focuses on three young people dealing with addictions. Two medical experts provide a definition of addiction and guide students through the signs and symptoms that can lead to an addiction. The end of the video emphasizes recovery.

video lends itself to individual study. All of this means that video can be incorporated easily into a variety of pedagogical methods. It is possible to alter the motion sequence, preprogram that sequence, and operate the video equipment by remote control. A VCR and TV set are easy to use.

You can use video to provide baseline knowledge for all learners. The packaged media can serve as an alternative to lectures. You can give students a viewing assignment before coming to class. Class time is then available for hands-on experiences, discussion, or applications of knowledge.

Cognitive Skills

In the cognitive domain, learners can observe dramatic recreations of historical events and actual recordings of more recent events. Color, sound, and motion make personalities come to life. The textbook can be enhanced by showing processes, relationships, and techniques. Students can read books in conjunction with viewing videotapes. You may have students read before viewing as an introduction to the topic, or use the program to interest students in reading about the topic.

Demonstrations

Video is great for showing how things work. For example, there is a short educational video called *Colonial Cooper.* Made at Colonial Williamsburg, it shows how an eighteenth-century artisan made a barrel. Demonstrations of motor skills can be more easily seen through media than in real life. If you are teaching a step-by-step process, you can show it in real time, sped up to give an overview, or slowed down to show specific details. With DVD you can even stop the action for careful study or move forward one frame at a time. Recording student performances on videotape can provide practice with feedback. Learners can observe their own performances and also receive feedback from colleagues and the instructor.

Virtual Field Trips

Videos can take students to places they might not be able to go otherwise. You can take your students to the Amazon rainforest, the jungles of New Guinea, or the tundra of the frozen Artic. Most of us will never take a safari to Africa or spend sev-

eral months in the Alaskan bush to observe the behavior of animals in the wild. We can go to these places and many others on video.

Documentary

Video is the primary medium for documenting actual events and bringing them into the classroom. The **documentary** deals with fact, not fiction or fictionalized versions of fact (Figure 12.3). It attempts to depict essentially true stories about real situations and people. The commercial networks (broadcast and cable) and the Public Broadcasting System regularly produce significant documentaries. Special programs, such as *The Second Russian Revolution,* present in-depth analyses of recent events and issues. The miniseries *The Civil War* is an example of a documentary presentation of a critical period in U.S. history. Programs such as *NOVA* and the National Geographic specials offer outstanding documentaries in science, culture, and nature. Virtually all television documentaries are available for purchase as videos.

Dramatization

Video has the power to hold your students spellbound as a human drama unfolds before their eyes. For example, television programs such as *ER* can take them into an emergency room to observe what goes on there. Reenactments of many important events in history are available on video. Feature films on videotape and DVD offer teachers and students hundreds of choices.

Figure 12.3

Documentaries bring real-world experiences into the classroom.

Discussion Basics

By viewing a video program together, a diverse group of learners can build a common base of experience as a catalyst for discussion. When students are learning interpersonal skills, such as dealing with conflict resolution, counseling, sales techniques, and peer relationships, they can observe others on video for demonstration and analysis. They can then practice their interpersonal skills before a camera, watch themselves, and receive feedback from peers and instructors. Role-play vignettes can be analyzed to determine what happened and to ask the learners what they should do next. Open-ended dramatizations can present unresolved confrontations, leaving it to the viewers to discuss various ways of dealing with the problem.

Attitude Development

Most educational presentations target recipients' cognitive or psychomotor domains of learning. However, when there is an element of emotion or the desire for affective learning, video usually works well. Attitudes can be influenced by role models and dramatic messages on video. Because of their great potential for emotional impact, video and film can be useful in shaping personal and social attitudes. Documentary programs have often been found to have a measurable impact on audience attitudes. Documentaries made during the Great Depression, for example, bring the hardships of that era to students who have never known hard times. Cultural understanding can be developed through viewing video depicting people from all parts of the globe.

Reports and Portfolios

Students can use excerpts from videos as part of oral reports, turning the sound off and using their own narration. Student-produced videotapes and video segments on computers are being used for evaluation. Student portfolios with a multimedia approach are being used instead of word processed term papers. Students can research a topic using books, databases, videotapes, CD-ROMs, and other media. Relevant content can be "captured" on video, edited, and displayed for classmates, parents, and the teacher.

Training

Video is the second most frequently used training media used by businesses. According to *Training* magazine ("Industry Report," 2003), videotapes are used by 88 percent of U.S. organizations with 100 or more employees. The amount of videotape use is exceeded only by workbooks and manuals (used in 93% of these organizations).

In addition to the advantages already cited, production of video is much easier to handle within the organization. With internal production, all phases of the production can be managed at fairly low cost. While educational institutions have relatively similar curricular needs and therefore can rely primarily on commercially produced materials, training needs for the most part are situation specific, making in-house production of video a necessity (see "Producing Video" later in this chapter).

In addition to customization, there is the factor of rapid change. Increasing competition and technological change dictate an instructional medium that can turn out updated and modified programs rapidly.

Corporate use of video therefore contrasts sharply with school use in terms of the amount of locally produced material used. Most large corporate users maintain professional-quality production studios and equipment for in-the-field location shooting. Of course, many corporate skills are generic in nature—such as supervisory skills, management of meetings, and stress management. These lend themselves to off-the-shelf, or commercially produced, media.

Many organizations use video for the following:

- Orientation of new employees
- Training in job-related skills
- Development of interpersonal abilities for management
- Introduction of new products, policies, or markets
- Customer training
- Standardization of training among dispersed offices

Portability and ease of use are advantages in all these uses of video. For example, a life insurance company can send a video to its sales representatives for them to study at their local office or at home. Also, each representative can take the video to a potential client's home knowing a VCR will probably be available. Video is so common and easy to use that many companies now distribute tapes to potential customers to promote products and series. Many manufacturers are including videotapes as part of their instructional materials instead of instruction manuals to ensure owners will understand how to use the product.

Classroom Access

School-owned video collections are increasing in size—more than doubling, on average, every few years. School library media centers are becoming equipped with computer-controlled media distribution systems. These allow teachers to schedule video showings and have them sent to the classroom by cable or fiber optics when activated by controls in the classroom. Equipment and materials do not have to be moved around the school. Because of these distribution systems and the ability to receive and record educational and news cable channels, and the growing availability of streaming video delivery directly over the Internet, the classroom of the future will have access to a variety of instructional video materials within the school.

SELECTING VIDEO

Locating Materials

Program guides and directories can help keep you abreast of available materials in your areas of interest and guide you toward selection of materials best suited to your particular teaching needs. Librarians, media specialists, and teachers working as partners should communicate constantly concerning the resources needed for instruction. A basic resource for you, then, is a collection of catalogs of rental agencies you are most likely to use. To be more thorough in your search you will want *The Educational Film/Video Locator,* a comprehensive list of the videotapes available in various college and university rental collections. The most comprehensive list of current educational video is "A-V Online," which is in CD-ROM format. Other broad listings are *Bowker's Complete Video Directory* and *Video Source Book.* Additional information may be found on the Companion Website (http://www.prenhall.com/smaldino).

Appraising Videos

After you have located some potentially useful videos, you will want to preview and appraise them (Figure 12.4). Some schools and organizations have standard appraisal forms ready to use. Some of these are meticulously detailed, covering every possible factor; others are much more perfunctory. A good appraisal form will be brief enough not to be intimidating but complete enough to help individuals choose materials that may be useful for current and future applications. It should also stand as a public record that you can use to justify the purchase or rental of specific titles. The "Selection Rubric: Video" includes the most commonly used criteria, particularly those that research indicates really do make a difference.

Appraising and previewing also give you the opportunity to make notes for class discussion of the video, and to note key points in the program to explain or emphasize to students (Figures 12.5 and 12.6).

Sponsored Videos

Private companies, associations, and government agencies sponsor videos for a variety of reasons. Private companies may make them to promote their products or to

Figure 12.5
Class discussion can be used before and after viewing material.

Figure 12.4
Previewing the material allows the teacher to properly introduce and follow up the material.

Figure 12.6
Video materials can be stopped to explain key points.

Close-Up

HOW A VIDEO CAMERA WORKS

Light enters a video camera through the lens. In a portable camera (camcorder), the light is focused onto a light-sensitive electronic assembly called a **charge-coupled device (CCD),** which changes the wavelengths into electrical charges. A filter connected to the CCD separates the charges by color. These video signals are amplified and sent to the recording mechanism in the camera. The audio is picked up by a microphone attached to the camera (or by a detached microphone) and recorded on one edge of the videotape.

Before the development of the CCD, the video camera had to house three tubes, one for each primary color. A system of dichroic mirrors sent each color to its respective tube. This made the camera so bulky that the signals had to be sent to a separate videotape recorder. The CCD made it possible to include the recording mechanism in the camera, thus creating the portable units so much in favor for nonstudio videotaping. Because of its superior quality, the dichroic mirror system is still preferred for studio production.

The recorded videotape can be played back through the camera itself or through a videotape player. A video signal is so complex that the videotape speed must be much greater than that for an audio recording. This is achieved by rotating the record/playback head, called the drum, at high speed while the tape moves across it in a helical path. The video signal occupies the greater part of the tape while the edges carry the audio and the signals that frame the image on the screen.

The magnetic signals on the tape are converted to electrical impulses that are decoded into the primary colors of light: blue, red, and green. These signals are amplified and projected onto the screen by an electronic gun. The screen surface is covered with more than 300,000 phosphor dots arranged in groups of three for the three colors. A metal perforated mask behind the screen keeps each electron beam in line with its own color dots and away from the other colors. The electronic gun scans the picture tube 30 times a second. Persistence of vision converts these scans into a moving image.

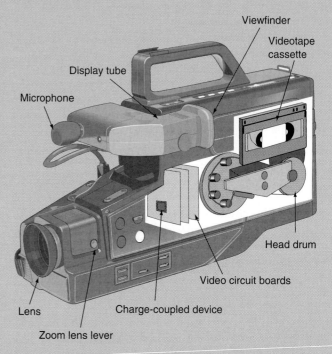

Parts of a video camera

enhance their public image. Associations and government agencies sponsor videos to promote causes, such as better health habits, conservation of natural resources, and proper use of park and recreation areas. Many of these sponsored videos make worthwhile instructional materials. They also have the considerable advantage of being free.

A certain amount of caution, however, is called for in using sponsored programs for instructional purposes. Some privately produced materials may be too flagrantly self-serving. Or they may deal with products not very suitable for certain instructional settings, for example, the manufacturing of alcoholic beverages or cigarettes. Some association and government materials may contain a sizable dose of propaganda or special pleading for pet causes along with their content. You must *always* preview sponsored materials.

When properly selected, many sponsored materials can be valuable additions to classroom instruction. Modern Talking Picture Service is one of the major distributors of sponsored videos. The best single source of information on sponsored films is *Free Videotapes*. Additional information may be found on the Companion Website (http://www.prenhall.com/smaldino).

PRODUCING VIDEO

In-house video refers to videos produced within one's own classroom or company. With in-house video production, students and instructors are not limited to off-the-shelf materials but can with reasonable ease prepare custom materials (see Clendenin, 1998). This feature sets video apart from some of the other media. Do-it-yourself video has become commonplace since the popularization of the battery-operated portable video recording systems.

The development of the camcorder (camera and recorder built into a single book-size unit) has increased the ease and portability of video recording. It allows video production to be taken into the field, wherever

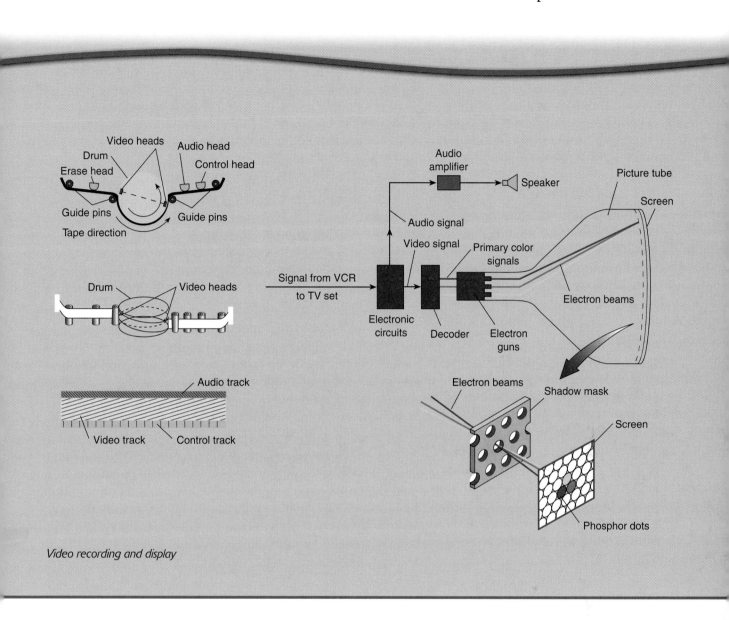

Video recording and display

that might be: the science laboratory, the classroom, the counseling office, the athletic field, the factory assembly line, the hospital, the neighborhood, and even the home. Equally important, the simplicity of the system has made it feasible for nonprofessionals, instructors, and students alike to create their own video materials.

Locally produced video can be used for virtually any of the purposes described earlier. Its unique capability is to capture sight and sound for immediate playback. This medium thus works well with activities that are enhanced by immediate feedback: group dynamics sessions, athletic practice, skills training, and interpersonal techniques.

Other applications that emphasize the local aspect of video production include the following:

- Dramatization of student stories, songs, and poems
- Student documentaries of school or neighborhood issues
- Preservation of local folklore

- Demonstrations of science experiments and safety drills
- Replays of field trips for in-class followup
- Career information on local businesses

Growing numbers of school library media centers are now adding to their environments a small video studio for student productions. Many students come to school with home experiences in using portable cameras. Student production will increase as equipment continues to become less expensive, more light sensitive, and easier to use. Elementary and secondary students can be involved in scripting, recording, editing, and revising their own video productions.

As with all media production, preproduction planning is necessary. Storyboarding (see Chapter 4) can be used by students of all ages to facilitate planning and production of video. Storyboarding is particularly helpful when a group of students is cooperatively involved in designing a video.

Analog Video Production

Video production requires a camera, a recorder, a microphone, and perhaps editing equipment. Most cameras are of the viewfinder type. The viewfinder camera is so named because it has built into it a small TV set that allows the operator to monitor the image being received by the pickup tube. Even small hand-held cameras typically contain built-in viewfinders with one-inch screens (see "Close-Up: How a Video Camera Works").

Hand-held cameras usually come with a microphone built into the front of the camera. This microphone has an automatic level control, a feature that automatically adjusts the volume to keep the sound at an audible level. The camera "hears" as well as "sees." The problem is that these microphones amplify all sounds within their range, including shuffling feet, coughing, street noises, and equipment noise, along with the sounds you want. You may therefore want to bypass the built-in microphone by plugging in a separate microphone better suited to your particular purpose.

The *lavaliere*, or neck mike, is a good choice when recording a single speaker. It can be clipped to a tie or dress, hung around the neck, or even hidden under lightweight clothing. A desk stand may be used to hold a microphone for a speaker or several discussants seated at a table. For situations in which there is unwanted background noise or the speaker is moving, a highly directional microphone is best. For practical tips on video production, see "Setting Up a Single-Camera Video Production" in Classroom Resources, Section C.

Standard video editing equipment is very expensive. However, you and your students can do your own video editing with two VCRs, connecting them by a patch cord or cable to record from one tape to another. It is also possible to record from a videodisc to videotape using a similar setup. In all cases be sure to follow the copyright guidelines in Chapter 1 and in "Copyright Concerns: Off-Air Videotaping" in this chapter.

Digital Video Editing

Digital video editing refers to the means by which video can be taken apart and put back together using a computer and appropriate software. It is also called *nonlinear editing*. Digital video camcorders are smaller than analog video cameras and are simple to operate. With some digital camcorders there is no videotape, while others use specialized videotape to record in a digital mode.

After shooting video, you can watch it on the camera's built-in LCD monitor. You can also connect the camcorder to the television monitor, or you can transfer the images to the computer. Many camcorders allow you to edit right in the camera.

Using a special video transfer cable or FireWire connection, you can connect the camcorder, either analog or digital, to the computer to copy the video images directly to the computer hard drive. You and your students can then edit the video within the computer, without using the videotape equipment. You can also use the computer as a display device; using a digitizing camera for motion media, moving images from any of the analog sources can be displayed on the screen without being stored.

There are several methods for storing video on a computer. One format is *QuickTime,* for use with *Mac OS,* and *Windows* operating systems. Many applications, such as *Compton's Multimedia Encyclopedia,* incorporate *QuickTime* "movies." Students can produce their own to add visuals, graphics, and text to their portfolios or projects.

By doing your own video productions, you can target your video to a specific audience with specific content. The productions can be readily and easily updated. Once the equipment (cameras, computers, and software) has been purchased, the production of in-house video is very inexpensive. Software for in-house production includes Apple's *iMovie 4* and Avid Technology's *Cinema* and *VideoShop.* These types of software are readily available, inexpensive (*iMovie 4* comes preloaded on new Apple computers), and easy to use. Very young children can learn to use software and video cameras quickly. Remember, you and your students must follow copyright guidelines (see the "Copyright Concerns" in this chapter and in Chapter 1).

Selection Rubric: Video

Complete an interactive evaluation and add it to your NETS-T portfolio using the Selection Rubric for Video available on the "Classroom Link Portfolio" CD-ROM. A downloadable version of this rubric is available in the Selection Rubrics module of the Companion Website at http://www.prenhall.com/smaldino.

Key Words

_____

_____

_____

Title _____

Series Title (if applicable) _____

Source _____

Date _____ Cost _____ Length _____ minutes

Subject Area _____

Intended Audience _____

Format

☐ VHS

☐ DVD

☐ Internet Video

Brief Description

Objectives

Entry Capabilities Required (e.g., prior knowledge, reading ability, vocabulary level, math ability)

Strong Points

Weak Points

Recommended Action (using criteria on the following page)

Rating Area	High Quality	Medium Quality	Low Quality	Rating
Match Curriculum	Curriculum standard addressed and use of video should enhance student learning.	Curriculum standard partially addressed and use of video may enhance student learning.	Curriculum standard not addressed and use of video will likely not enhance student learning.	
Accurate & Current	Information correct and does not contain material that is out of date.	Information correct but does contain material that is out of date.	Information is not correct and does contain material that is out of date.	
Clear & Concise Language	Language used is age appropriate and vocabulary is understandable.	Language used is nearly age appropriate and some vocabulary is above/below student age.	Language used is not age appropriate and vocabulary is clearly inappropriate for student age.	
Motivating/ Interesting	Topic presented so that students are likely to be interested and engaged in learning.	Topic presented to interest students most of the time and engage most in learning.	Topic presented so as not to interest students and not engage them in learning.	
Learner Participation	Topic presented so that most students are actively engaged in learning.	Topic presented so that some students are engaged in learning.	Topic presented so that most students are not actively engaged in learning.	
Technical Quality	The material represents best available media.	The material represents media that are good quality, although there are some problems.	The material represents media that are not well prepared and are of very poor quality.	
Effectiveness Rating	There is evidence that use of these media has shown positive impact on student learning.	There is little evidence that use of these media has shown positive impact on student learning.	There is no evidence that use of these media has shown positive impact on student learning.	
Free from Bias	There is no evidence of objectionable bias or advertising.	There is little evidence of bias or advertising.	There is much evidence of bias or advertising.	
User Guide & Documentation	The documentation is excellent resource for use in a lesson. Documentation should help students use the material.	The documentation is good resource for use in a lesson. Documentation may help students use the material.	The documentation is poor resource for use in a lesson. Documentation does not help students use the material.	
Pacing Appropriate	The video material is presented so most students can understand and process the information.	The video material is presented so some students start to understand and process the information.	The video material is presented so most students cannot understand and process the information.	
Use of Cognitive Learning Aids (Overviews, Cues, Summary)	The video material is well organized and uses cognitive learning aids.	The video material is fairly well organized and uses some cognitive learning aids.	The video material is not well organized and does not use cognitive learning aids.	

Summary: Using the ASSURE Model for Video

As with other media and technology, the ASSURE model introduced in Chapter 3 is helpful in preparing lessons incorporating the use of video.

Analyze Learners

Lesson development begins by identifying your students' unique attributes and learning characteristics. You also will wish to determine their various levels of experience with using video.

State Objectives

Before stating specific objectives, you may wish to explore how to use video in support of student learning. Sometimes it is more appropriate to state specific objectives after you have identified the direction you will take with the content and what materials you will use.

Select Methods, Media, and Materials

Use the information on video discussed in this chapter as the basis for selecting, modifying, or designing your materials. Adjust the specific applications to suit the specific nature of your topic and objectives.

In selecting video materials to use in your instruction, first consult with your school media specialist to determine what is available at your media center. You should preview and appraise both commercially and locally produced materials before using them with your students. You may wish to use the "Selection Rubric: Video" to guide your selection decisions.

Utilize Media and Materials

Follow the suggestions discussed in this chapter to facilitate your students' learning, modifying each material's use to fit your needs. The video equipment and source materials you have access to, as well as its location, will determine how you schedule your students' learning experiences, as discussed in the chapter. If you have access to a video playback system for the classroom, you may wish to enable all students to view your selected programming simultaneously. If you have limited access to equipment and video source materials, you may wish to consider creating a learning center. Also, depending on the availability of facilities and on your students' age and experience, you may wish to have them produce their own videos.

Require Learner Participation

Introduce and explain the video materials involved in your specific objective. Have the students do specific activities that rely on their ability to use video. Students will find more value in the materials if they are able to connect what they are doing to what they are learning. Have them watch specific video productions and analyze them either in a paper or an oral presentation. Have them record programming off the air and edit it to accompany an oral presentation. Or if facilities are available, have them create their own short video program on a topic of their choice and present it to the class.

Evaluate and Revise

It is important to consider how materials that rely on video help students to interpret information. You can assess students on the quality of their created video materials and on how well they integrated them into their other learning. As with all media- and technology-based lessons, you may choose to revise your selection of materials after you have determined how well they have worked. In addition, you want to be certain that all materials used have been cleared of any potential copyright issues.

ASSURE Case in Practice: Elementary School Social Studies

All of the ASSURE Cases in Practice in this text and an electronic template for creating your own ASSURE lesson can be found on the enclosed "Classroom Link Portfolio" CD-ROM.

Brad Strucker wishes to introduce his students to the Panama Canal. It is one of the topics included in the standardized test students take at the end of the school year. Many students have never heard of it. He wants to show his students what it looks like, so he selects a videotape.

Analyze Learners

General Characteristics

This urban elementary school class is self-contained, with 29 fifth graders (16 girls, 13 boys). The average age is 11 years: the average reading level is fourth grade.

The class has an ethnic and racial mixture typical of an urban setting, with socioeconomic status being lower middle class. Seventeen come from single-parent families. Motivation is usually a challenge with this class.

Entry Competencies

Regarding today's topic, the Panama Canal, awareness is low. In yesterday's discussion of Central America, only Nicaragua and El Salvador were mentioned without prompting. There is an old barge canal on the north side of town, so many students were able to identify canals as human-built waterways but were vague about their purposes.

Learning Styles

Learning styles are varied in the class. Most students do not like to read and have very low comprehension when they do. They do enjoy viewing videotapes and tend to remember what they see and hear. They have very good human interaction skills and enjoy discussions.

State Objectives

The fifth-grade social studies students will be able to do the following:

1. Locate the Panama Canal on a wall map of North and South America.
2. Explain the main advantage of the Panama Canal as a shortcut between the Atlantic and Pacific oceans.
3. Visually recognize a canal, distinguishing it from other waterways.
4. Discuss the Panama Canal's historic importance, citing at least its commercial and military advantages and the achievement of overcoming the obstacles to its construction.
5. Demonstrate that they value the cooperative effort represented by the building of the Panama Canal by participating actively in a group project.

Select Methods, Media, and Materials

Mr. Strucker decides to begin the class with a large-group discussion, then show a video, and follow up with small-group discussion and projects. He surveys the *Educational Film/Video Locator* under the topic "Panama Canal" and finds four titles that look promising. Two of these are in the school district media library. After previewing both, he selects one because its content and vocabulary come closest to the level of his class. He notes that the political description of Panama is no longer accurate, so he prepares some comments to correct it.

Utilize Media and Materials

Because motivating interest is predictably difficult, he begins to stimulate students' curiosity by rolling down the wall map of North and South America and asking how a traveler in the days before airplanes and automobiles might get from New York to San Francisco. What if you were a merchant who wanted to ship tools and work clothes to the miners of the gold rush in Alaska in 1898? What if you were an admiral needing to move his fleet rapidly from the Atlantic to the Pacific?

Having identified the problem, Mr. Strucker states that the video is going to show the solution developed early in the twentieth century. He lists several key questions on the overhead projector.

After reviewing the questions by having students take turns reading them, he asks them to look for the answers to these questions while viewing the video. He has cued the videotape to the most relevant part and then shows just 15 minutes that relate to the problem.

Require Learner Participation

After showing the video, he divides the students into groups of three to discuss the questions. Each group elects a recorder who will write the answers agreed to by the group.

After a few minutes of discussion Mr. Strucker brings the whole class back together in a large group and calls on two or three recorders to give their answers to question 1, with the whole class reacting to these. He repeats this process for the rest of the questions.

He concludes by going back to question 3, focusing on how the builders of the canal succeeded because of their systematic plan and determination to overcome all obstacles. If we were going to construct a display to tell the story of the Panama Canal, what steps would we have to carry out? What ideas would we put into our display? With questions such as these, Mr. Strucker builds interest in constructing a display, works out a timeline, and organizes the students into groups to carry out the assignment.

Evaluate and Revise

Mr. Strucker collects the recorders' written notes and checks to see how accurately the questions were answered. He makes note of test items keyed to the objectives to be included on the standardized test at the end of the year. As students work on the display project, he will be able to check the accuracy of the information being put into the display and, regarding the affective objective(s), will circulate among the work groups to assess the enthusiasm exhibited in their work.

Create Your Own ASSURE Lesson

Using the ASSURE model, design a lesson for a scenario from the table on this book's inside cover or from the Companion Website, or use a scenario of your own design. Use one of the methods described in Chapter 1 and information from this chapter related to incorporating video into your instructional setting. Be sure to include information about the audience, the objectives, and all other elements of the ASSURE model. When completed, reflect on the process you used and what you have learned about matching audience, content, method, and materials.

Classroom Link Portfolio Activities

Use the "Classroom Link Portfolio" CD-ROM and the Companion Website as resources in completing these activities. To complete the following activities go to the Portfolio Activities module in Chapter 12 of the Companion Website (http://www. prenhall.com/smaldino).

1. *Planning Lessons Using Videos.* Plan a lesson for a subject area or standard of your choice in which you will incorporate the use of a video. For that video, brainstorm a variety of assessment techniques to measure student learning of the content. (ISTE NETS-T 2.B; 4.A)

2. *Written Reflection.* Thinking back on your own experiences, what were the benefits and drawbacks of using videos as part of the instruction? What changes could have been made to maximize the experience? (ISTE NETS-T 2.C & D)

Integration Assessments

To complete the specified activities online, go to the Integration Assessments module in Chapter 12 of the Companion Website (http://www.prenhall. com/smaldino).

1. Preview a video and appraise it using the "Selection Rubric: Video." (ISTE NETS 2.C)
2. Observe a teacher using a video program in a classroom situation and critique his or her practices. (ISTE NETS 5.B)
3. Use one or more of the video directories available in your school library or media center to compile a list of video programs available on a topic of interest to you. (ISTE NETS 2.C)

4. Preview one of the videos described in this chapter. Prepare a review, either written (about 700 words) or recorded on audiotape (approximately five minutes long). Briefly summarize the content and describe your reaction to it. (ISTE NETS 2.C)
5. Demonstrate your ability to use the steps to utilize video effectively in a lesson. (ISTE NETS 2.D)
6. Set up, operate, and troubleshoot a video player/recorder and a video projector. (ISTE NETS 1.A)

References

Clendenin, Bruce. 1998. *The video book.* Upper Saddle River, NJ: Prentice Hall.

Forsdale, Joan Rosengren, and Louis Forsdale. 1966. Film literacy. *Teachers College Record,* 67(8): 608–617. (May): 609.

Industry report. 2003. *Training, 40* (10):30:

Suggested Readings

Barlow, D. 1997. Schindler in the English classroom. *Educational Digest, 62*(April): 40–43.

Brown, Kenneth. 1993. Video production in the classroom: Creating success for students and schools. *TechTrends, 00*(April–May): 32–35.

Carley, G. 1997. The getting better phenomenon: Videotape applications of previously at-risk high school student narratives. *Social Work Education, 19*(April): 115–120.

Dockerman, D. 2003. *Great teaching with video: TSP's Guide to using the VCR and videodisc player in the classroom.* Watertown, MA: Tom Snyder Productions.

Ellis, P. 1996. Layered analysis: A video-based qualitative research tool to support the development of a new approach for children with special needs. *Bulletin of the Council of Research in Music Education, 130*(Fall): 65–74.

Fields, Doug, and Eddie James. 1999. *Videos that teach.* Grand Rapids, MI: Zondervan.

Fink, L. S. 1997. Using video production in teaching natural history. *American Biology Teacher, 59*(March): 142–146.

Herrell, Adrienne L., and Joel P. Fowler, Jr. 1998. *Camcorder in the classroom: Using the videocamera to enliven curriculum.* Upper Saddle River, NJ: Prentice Hall.

Herron, Carol, Steven P. Cole, Cathleen Corrie, and Sebastien Dubreil. 1999. The effectiveness of a video-based curriculum in teaching culture. *Modern Language Journal, 83*(4): 518–533.

Mitchell, D. 1997. Four projects that promote authentic learning. *English Journal, 86*(April): 68–72.

Rosenkranz, Patrick. 1999. *The classroom video producers guidebook.* Portland, ME: J. Weston Walch.

Rostad, J. 1997. Produce live news broadcasts using standard AV equipment. *TechTrends, 42*(April–May): 13, 21–24.

Skolnik, Racquel, and Carl Smith. 1993. Utilizing video technology to serve the needs of at-risk students. *Journal for Vocational Special Needs Education* (Fall): 23–31.

Stein, Barbara, Lauralee Ingram, and Gary Treadway. 1998. *Finding and using educational videos: A how-to-do-it manual.* New York: Neal-Schuman.

Valmont, William J. 1995. *Creating videos for school use.* Boston: Allyn & Bacon.

Waldrep, Mark. 1998. DVD-video: An unlimited training and educational format. *Emedia Professional, 11*(10): 46.

Trends in Technology and Media

CHAPTER 13
Looking Ahead

Looking Ahead

Outline

Knowledge Objectives

1. Discuss the trends in technology and media that you feel will have the greatest impact on education and training.
2. Describe your vision of the schools of the future.
3. Critique the conventional self-contained classroom as an organization and as a setting for incorporating technology.
4. Discuss the ways in which the roles of teachers and media/technology specialists are changing due to the impact of technology.
5. Describe the consequences of increased communication between home and school and the importance of the home as a center for technology-based learning.
6. Discuss changes in the workplace, indicating how technology and media relate to these changes.
7. Describe the changing nature of training.
8. Predict upcoming developments in technology, media, education, and training.
9. Describe the types of career opportunities available to you in educational technology.

Professional Vocabulary

personal digital assistant (PDA)
e-book
blog
wiki
charter school
pedagogical agent
telecommuting

telework
just-in-time training
cold storage training
performance support system
cross-training
Total Quality Management (TQM)

The school of the future will be different. Futurists predict that the structure of the classroom and the teaching itself will change. The role of the teacher and the use of instructional technologies and media must change if schools are to improve. The nature of workers and the workplace also continue to change. Consequently, education must prepare workers for the future—training will take place "just in time" and at the workstation itself. The levels of knowledge will continue to accelerate, and workers will learn how to access specific knowledge when needed.

Your students will be using new interactive technologies for instant access to information and people around the globe. To keep up to date as a teacher or trainer, you need to be aware of trends and possible developments in the characteristics and applications of technology and media. Teachers need to know the nature of workplaces to prepare students to function successfully there after graduation. Likewise, trainers need to be aware of what is happening in school to know what to expect in terms of the workforce they will be training.

TRENDS IN TECHNOLOGY AND MEDIA

The twenty-first century is an exciting time to be working in the fields of education and training. Current trends may or may not be sustained, and we, as educators and citizens of the world, have many challenges to address. Let's look at some trends related to media and technology for educators and trainers.

This chapter contains valuable contributions from Michael Molenda.

Merging of Media Formats

A major trend in media and technology is the merging of media formats. In the 1950s, the common media were separate entities sometimes used in combination and called "multimedia," such as books with phonograph records and kits with real objects, photographs, and explanatory manuals. Figure 13.1 represents the common media of the 1950s.

In the 1980s, the computer began to combine some of these distinct media, as shown in Figure 13.2. The combination of the computer and video led to interactive video. Audio media began to evolve from audiocassettes to audio CDs. Virtual reality began to emerge. The digitization of print, images, and sound made many of these combinations possible.

Digitization has led inevitably to the development of new systems for information storage, retrieval, and transmission. It also has led to the convergence of media formats, with the potential for making older formats obsolete. For example, if still and motion images can be combined on the disc, and the same piece of equipment can display both, why have slide and video projectors? If DVDs are damage resistant and can store still and motion images, why maintain an inventory of fragile slides and videos? All of these media already exist together on the Web (Figure 13.3).

Continuing Use of Traditional Media

Many teachers want to forget traditional media and just focus on the "new technologies." However, traditional media will be with us for many years because they accomplish some tasks as well as or better than the new technology. Like a carpenter, we need to know how to use all tools, both old and new, and more importantly, we must be able to select the best tool for our particu-

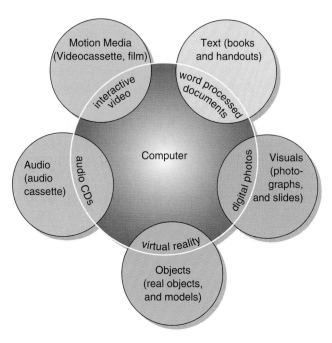

Figure 13.2
During the 1980s the computer fostered the convergence of the previously distinct media.

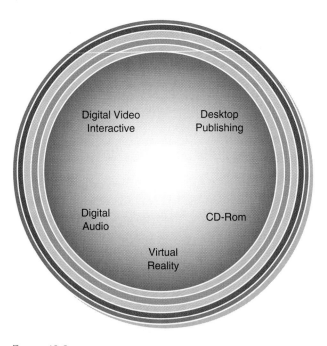

Figure 13.3
Soon it will be difficult to distinguish among the various types of media.

Figure 13.1
In the 1950s the various types of media were distinct.

lar task. Teachers and students need to learn how to select from all available media those materials that will best promote learning. For example, most classrooms will continue to have chalkboards, so teachers must learn to use them to their maximum effectiveness. The overhead projector continues to be an effective tool for gaining and maintaining student attention. Instructors cannot just brush off traditional media in favor of computers and digital technology.

Although they do not attract the attention that newer computer-based media do, traditional media are still used far more often than computer-based media, in both the school and the corporate realm. In the United States, for example, print material is the dominant media format, according to teacher self-reports (Center for Community Research, 1999). Seven times as many P–12 teachers use textbooks every day as use audio or video materials. Textbooks and other printed materials are the most common instructional tools throughout the world.

Organizations implement technology with the hope that it will increase their benefits or decrease their costs. In the case of higher education, technology has not proven to be a cost reducer on the educational side of their operations, according to Molenda and Sullivan (2004). Colleges and universities continue to struggle to support both the traditional analog media—audio- and videocassettes, slides, and overhead transparencies—still preferred by many instructors and the digital media, which are seen as potential cost reducers.

In the corporate world, instructor-led classroom training (presentation and demonstration) is still the most universally applied method of training, currently used in over 90 percent of companies ("Industry Report," 2003). Printed workbooks and manuals are used "always" or "often" in over 79 percent of companies. Videotapes are used in 52 percent of companies, while games and simulations are used in 25 percent. Overall, the use of videotapes seems to be receding slowly, being replaced by computer-based media.

Both traditional and digital technologies will continue to be used. You need to know the advantages, limitations, and appropriate applications of a range of media and technology options in order to know when to use each type. All media and technology have their place in education and training.

Maintaining Computer Use

Don Ely, in *Trends in Educational Technology,* says, "There is near saturation of computers in K–12 schools, while higher education institutions report moderate saturation. Students and teachers have almost universal access to computers, many of which are connected to the Internet" (2002, p. 5). In P–12

schools, Becker (1999) notes an evolutionary pattern for their use. At first, computers were housed in computer labs, were employed within a narrow range of the curriculum—typically in "computer literacy" or mathematics—and teachers had a low level of involvement in decision making and a low sense of ownership. Over time, computers have tended to be relocated into classrooms where teachers employ them across a wider range of the curriculum.

Computer purchases for instruction in colleges and universities are leveling off as financial resources become more limited. The Campus Computing Survey of 2003 indicated that a growing number of respondents had experienced a decline in their academic computing budget for that academic year—with 41 percent reporting decreased budgets compared with 18 percent two years earlier (Campus Computing Project, 2003, p. 3). On the other hand, the number of students who have/own their own computer is on the rise.

In the corporate world, only 16 percent of training time is spent using computer-based media ("Industry Report," 2003). However, this percentage has been growing slowly but steadily while the proportion of training time spent in face-to-face contact is diminishing. Most of the growth is taking place in Web-based self-study.

Web-based self-study seems to be replacing textbooks and other printed training materials. What seems to be happening is not that computer-based self-instructional packages are replacing live courses, but that companies are using Web-based text materials as complements to training. Likewise, such materials are used in schools and colleges, and a small proportion of the face-to-face instruction is being reduced as the "reading" component is increased.

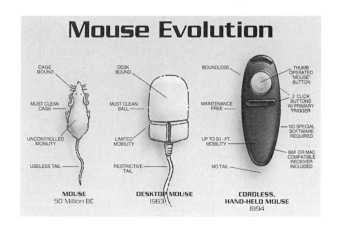

Figure 13.4

This Interlink Electronics ad cleverly depicts the evolution of the mouse. (RemotePoint Cordless Hand-Held Mouse, Interlink Electronics. Used by permission.)

Evolving Electronic Learning

Electronic learning, or e-learning, is altering the earlier institutional structures, which were based on transportation. In the past we operated on the assumption that, to learn, learners had to physically be in the "territory" of the teacher. By relying on the school bus and the private car, we consolidated schools and built larger schools and training complexes. However, some parents are growing more and more concerned about the excessively long bus rides their children take, as well as the high cost of transportation. These factors make it attractive to return to smaller and more numerous "attendance centers."

Advances in technology have made it administratively possible and economically feasible to educate smaller groups of students in a larger number and wider variety of instructional settings. Proponents of the decentralization of public education have an unexpected and powerful ally in technological advances such as e-learning and computer networks for the distribution of instruction (Figure 13.5).

The opportunity to improve the quality of education is a compelling reason for educators to continue to develop educational applications of e-learning and computer networks. With high-quality education deliverable over a network, the neighborhood school can hold its own programmatically with larger schools.

However, schools face social and political problems in reverting to smaller units. Competitive sports and other extracurricular activities thrive in larger schools. We may settle on a compromise—perhaps large high schools will use electronic distribution of instructional materials and information within a larger-than-necessary physical facility, while elementary schools will perhaps become smaller and more numerous.

More newsworthy is the rapid pace at which P–12 schools have become connected to the Internet and the World Wide Web. In the United States, 95 percent of all public schools had access to the Internet in the fall of 1999 (National Center for Education Statistics [NCES], 2000). "The Internet has become a major source of information for students and teachers. In higher education, the use of the Internet to deliver instruction has been steadily growing" (Ely, 2002, p. 9). Computers are very effective in facilitating learning, but connect a computer to the Internet and it becomes a readily accessible source of information and a very powerful tool for learning. The Internet use is increasing for correspondence, research, publishing, and education. Essentially all students in grades 6 through 12 have Internet access at school or home (National Center for Education Statistics, 2001). Even more students have access through local public libraries and youth centers.

Expanding Distance Education

In general, distance education courses have been of limited importance to U.S. public schools in the past. Because primary and secondary schools are inherently *local* in structure, they saw little need to share courses over long distances (unlike a large business or university that might have branches all across the state or country). School systems sought whole courses only in cases where a local school could not afford to maintain a teacher in a given subject and that subject is vital to the mission of the school (see Chapter 7). However, distance learning is apparently finding a niche in P–12 education. Twelve states have established online high school programs and five others are developing them (Trotter, 2002). Of course, the 40,000 to 50,000 students enrolled represent only one-tenth of one percent of the P–12 population.

If the Florida Virtual School is typical, 37 percent of online students are home schooled and 8 percent are in private schools, leaving very few public school students who are actually enrolled in online programs (Doherty, 2002). One report (Peak Group, 2002) predicts that the broader market, including noncredit classes such as advanced placement review and state test preparation, is estimated to grow to over 1,000,000 students by the 2004–2005 school year.

The largest growth in distance education, however, has been seen in postsecondary education. The trend is for more and more instruction to be provided in a distance education format. Distance education offerings and enrollments continue to increase. About 80 percent of four-year public universities offer distance programs, with the proportion rising to nearly 90 percent for larger institutions. Proprietary institutions such as University of Phoenix (37,000 online students) and Jones International University (6000 online students) seem to have developed a successful business model (Molenda & Sullivan, 2004).

Figure 13.5
Satellites make communication a reality among students in different parts of the world.

Universities with multiple campuses are more likely to send and receive courses through telecommunications in the synchronous mode, emulating a regular classroom as closely as possible. Universities are increasingly collaborating in their course offerings. More and more college courses are incorporating both synchronous and asynchronous delivery of instruction. Colleges and universities increasingly use the Web to deliver course materials and for interaction between instructor and student and among students. Even on-campus courses are using more "blended" instruction (live, face to face plus electronically digitally delivered).

Connection to the Internet is virtually universal at the college and university level. Internet connections are available to faculty in their offices and to students in their dorm rooms, computer laboratories, and libraries. College students tend to have more and freer access to the Internet than do P–12 students. As a consequence these institutions are providing an increasing amount of advanced instruction through the Internet. More courses will be offered totally via the Internet in the future. There also has been a rush to offer asynchronous courses to off-campus students via the World Wide Web.

There also has been an increased use of distance education with adult learners. Training and professional continuing education via distance education is growing in corporations, government agencies, the military, and health professions. However, the growth has not been what was expected after the tragedy of September 11, 2001. Face-to-face classroom instruction is still the most universally applied format of training, being used for 64 percent of training ("Industry Report," 2003). Only 20 percent is instructor-led from a remote location.

The development that has been attracting the most notice in the training and development literature in recent years is the steep rise in use of the World Wide Web and intranets (Web-type systems internal to one company) for delivery of training and information (Bylinsky, 2000). The potential advantages of using the Web for training include a huge reduction in printing costs and a simplified method of updating material. Bylinsky (2000) predicted that by 2003 about half of all companies would be using either the Web or their own intranet for delivery of training. Yet, the concept of Web-based learning is a fuzzy one, because most of this type of learning is done by individuals interacting in asynchronous sessions with text materials stored on the Net. It's difficult to estimate the time being spent this way; likewise, it's increasingly difficult to distinguish training material from reference information. This trend is likely to continue and to evolve in the future.

Cutting the Wired Connections

Wireless connectivity is a major trend in society, schools, higher education, and training. Public school classrooms didn't have telephones until a few years ago, but now telephones are being used as part of learning. Telephones that build on cellular technology currently have the ability to receive and send text and photos. This convergence of wireless functions has spawned a new concept of *mobile learning,* or M-learning.

Wireless applications are important for education and training applications. Wireless devices include cordless telephones, wireless local area networks, graphing calculators, and **personal digital assistants** or **PDAs,** hand-held computers that serve as data organizers; many can also run computer software. Most PDAs can be connected to the Internet for downloading and uploading files and software.

Today many offices, schools, and conference facilities are installing wireless networks. These allow students and trainees to carry around laptops and hand-held computers and always be connected. Students can bring their own or the school's laptops into a classroom without needing to find a physical connection or stringing wire around.

Ely (2002, p. 28) predicts, "Inexpensive hand-held computers promise to become an increasingly ubiquitous tool for the classroom."

Increasing Spread of Mobile Computing. Multipurpose, wireless devices may replace the desktop computer to connect to the Internet and other functions. This wider variety of services reflects the rapid changes in technological devices available. Currently you have access to a videophone, fax machine, and computer in the form of a single, hand-held device. You can communicate with this device by voice commands, by handwritten notes, or by typing, whichever you choose.

Advancing Telecommunications and Interactive Technologies

Technology is becoming more useful, more prevalent, more "intelligent," and more powerful, while at the same time becoming less intimidating, less noticeable, less demanding, and less expensive. User interfaces are becoming simpler and devices are becoming increasingly user friendly.

Advanced interactive technologies include multimedia, hypermedia, and virtual reality. Multimedia CD-ROM products are commonly found in school media centers, primarily in the form of encyclopedias or other reference databases. There is still relatively little application of multimedia and hypermedia to core instruction in schools. In higher education there is widespread experimentation with locally produced multimedia and hypermedia, but standardized formats or universal acceptance of such technologies for core instruction across institutions remain to be established.

Telecommunications offers the potential for both students and teachers to break down the walls of the P–12 classroom and share ideas and information with colleagues collaboratively. In the business world, telecommunications has had the same effect—leading to a more national and international business community.

Business and industry have experienced steady growth in the use of telecommunication networks, particularly among companies with more than 10,000 employees; about 63 percent of such businesses currently use networks for delivering training on a regular basis ("Industry Report," 2003). These networks—satellite based for video conferencing or wired networks for digital communication—are typically established for purposes such as sales meetings. Video conferencing allows real-time, synchronous interaction among participants at widely dispersed locations, saving companies money formerly spent on travel. Once in place, businesses can then use these communication systems to deliver distance education (Figure 13.6)

Interactive multimedia formats have gained a foothold in corporate training, primarily to deliver basic courses across multiple sites. Lack of hardware and software compatibility has restricted the availability of off-the-shelf courseware. Organizations are beginning to incorporate more multimedia courseware into their training programs as compatibility improves; thus, the supply of less expensive off-the-shelf materials is increasing as the demand rises. We believe this trend will continue well into the twenty-first century.

Today, if you choose, you can be "tuned in" 24 hours a day anywhere in the world through wireless technologies and network-based messaging systems. In the future you will carry at all times your own telephonelike communication device no larger than a credit card. As a parallel, consider the development of the radio. In its early days, it was very large and attached to the wall by an electrical cord. Over the years, radios have become smaller and portable thanks to transistors and battery power.

Using Technology for Inclusion

By incorporating technology into the classroom, teachers will be better able to meet the special needs of all learners—those with learning or physical disabilities, as well as gifted students and students whose native language is not English. (See the "Technology for Diverse Learners" features throughout this text.)

With the increasing uses of and new developments in technology it is possible to include more special-needs learners; it is also possible to bypass these learners with the rush to get the newest technologies in the classroom. Thus, it is important to provide access to technology for *all* learners. We can begin by integrating technology into individualized education programs (IEPs) for special-needs learners in kindergarten through 12th grade.

Teachers and administrators can also adapt classrooms to accommodate special-needs learners. Learning stations can be specially equipped for those with learning or physical disabilities. Students should be able to control the rate of speech delivery, enlarge information on a computer screen so they can better read the results of a database search, use a voice synthesizer to have a printed page read to them, or take notes in class through an electronic storage device that will later print out the document in braille. Some Web pages are being designed to accommodate these needs by offering user-selected graphic and text design options.

As our curricula and digital technologies emphasize more visual instruction, visually impaired students may find themselves at a disadvantage. These students can use computers to enlarge text to readable size and can use speech synthesis to have the words read aloud. Computers can tell them what the words say, but at this point in time cannot describe visuals (although such software is in the experimental stage).

Interestingly, it often happens that the techniques and alternatives that we use with special-needs learners, such as providing handouts and notes for auditorily impaired learners and using audiocassettes for visually impaired learners, can improve the learning of *all* students.

Figure 13.6

Telecommunications-based media make communications a reality among students in different parts of the world.

Appearing on the Horizon

There are a number of new developments on the horizon as this edition goes to press. Some will grow and flourish, others will fade and disappear.

Hardware. Recent hardware developments include *all-in-one desktop computers*, such as the Apple *iMac* and *eMac*. These new designs incorporate a built-in monitor so they require only one power cord. They eliminate the tangle of cords that come with most computers. Most new computers use LCD screens and come standard with the ability to burn CDs and to play (and often burn) DVDs.

Digital cameras will continue to become smaller, faster, cheaper, and easy to use. At the same time image quality will continue to improve. Resolution will continue to improve. The storage format may become standardized. Currently CompactFlash is the most common. SmartMedia seems to be on the wane.

Digital video camcorders have gotten smaller, as have digital videotapes. The newer digital camcorders come with automatic settings and touch screen LCD to access menus. They also allow easy editing. Some can capture still images, so your digital camera and video camcorder become one device.

DVD drives are decreasing in price and increasing in capabilities. Recordable drives can burn DVDs at four times the play rate. The future promises to bring even faster speeds. Rewriteable DVDs allow you to reuse discs, and soon you will be able to rerecord selected parts of a disc.

Video projectors are improving the brightness of their image and decreasing in weight. Many incorporate networking and wireless capabilities allowing you to connect a laptop to a projector without any cables or cords. Some portable projectors weigh only two to four pounds.

LCD displays will become more common on computers and larger ones will appear in classrooms and conference rooms. The cost will continue to come down, and size will continue to increase from the current 42-inch maximum width. Picture quality will also increase. Color is much better now than it was several years ago and will continue to improve. Viewing angles, which were a problem in the past, are increasing.

Plasma displays are maturing. Their size is increasing—some now are in the 60 inch range. Their cost is lowering, although most still cost between $3,000 and $6,000. The quality of their image makes them better in a lighted room than a video projector. Today's plasma displays have better contrast than earlier units and most can receive and display an HDTV signal with stunning clarity.

Other display technologies, such as OLED (organic light-emitting diode), are in development, and promise both increased picture clarity and color accuracy and lower cost and energy use.

E-books. A conceptual blend of the traditional book and the computer, **e-books** are hand-held devices roughly the size of a paperback book. They typically contain enough memory for 75 to 80 novel-length works. The backlit screen approximates a standard book page. Readers navigate by using buttons to "turn pages."

Two features of e-books are intriguing from an educational point of view. First, e-book texts are hypermedia (see Chapter 6). Readers may use embedded hyperlinks to jump to related topics, and texts may contain graphic, audio, and video elements. Second, an e-book's contents are volatile. "The readers can be loaded with new books, erased, and reloaded as frequently as one wishes" (Roush, 1999, p. 148). Students may soon be able to download from the publisher specific books or articles they need for a class, then replace them when they are through. Teachers may be able to assemble collections of information on their computers and have students download them as required. Such devices may also upload new text to an online file, allowing scientific, technical, educational, and other works to "be continually altered to keep pace with research" (Mann, 2001, p. 48). E-books are as expensive as printed books to produce, but can be distributed extremely cheaply.

The number of e-books is growing rapidly. For example, Project Gutenberg (http://promo.net/pg/) contains over 3,500 titles of public domain e-books and is growing daily (Agee, 2003). E-books deliver information in an interesting and interactive manner. Some even include learning activities and test banks to check students' understanding of the material as they read.

In schools and businesses, textbooks and other printed materials could coexist with digital formats, with each performing the role they do best. Computers allow quick access to information and data for professional (sales figures, production outcomes) and personal (airline schedules, paying bills) purposes. On the other hand, people will likely continue to prefer traditional bound books for pleasure reading. You can take one anywhere and read it wherever there is light. These exciting new technologies, as Roush (1999) states, "will not fundamentally alter the *experience* of reading"; nonetheless, they will "force bibliophiles everywhere to rethink the relationship between the tangible objects we call books and the ideas they contain" (p. 148).

Blogs. A new kind of website has emerged that is not a standard "home page." It is an annotated bookmark list available for public viewing, a "log" of journeys around the Web with links and commentaries. Called a *weblog*, it is a website that serves as a publicly accessible personal journal for an individual to regularly post commentary and related hyperlinks. A weblog reflects the personality of the author.

Barger (1999) is frequently credited with coining the term **blog** (we*b* + *log* = we*blog*, or *blog* for short). As with any relatively new term, there remains some disagreement about precisely what is and what is not a blog. They are usually hosted by a single person who publishes writing on the blog fairly frequently—maybe a few times each day, or once a day, or less often. These bits of writing, called "entries" or "posts," generally appear on the front page of the blog in reverse chronological order.

Entries are usually fairly short, often just a paragraph, but can be longer. Entries might be written about other websites or entries on other websites and usually include links to them, but they might also be the author's thoughts on events, politics, their own life . . . anything.

Blogs make micropublishing easy. Blogs and most software that produces them specialize in "micropublishing" and "microcontent." Authors aren't seeking a mass readership, and they usually aren't worried about presenting book-length bodies of text. They tend to seek a focused audience and provide smaller, article-length items, sometimes just links with a few words of comment. Most blogs have single authors, but some allow multiple editorial accounts with varying levels of access privileges, turning them into collaborative online writers' colonies (see for example, http://slashdot.org).

Teachers may integrate blogs into the language arts curriculum by having students create and use them as journals. In the science classroom, blogs can be used for ongoing science experiments. For the social sciences, blogs can be used to reflect changing student attitudes during the course of study of a topic. They can be used as a part of learning communities, with students writing and reading each other's blogs (journals) as they work together on group projects.

Use your creativity to come up with ways to integrate blogs into your own teaching. As with all technology and media, the use of blogs requires planning using the ASSURE model.

Wikis.   While blogs tend to be a one-way communication to the reader, the **wiki** provides an alternative. A wiki's core concept includes the idea that any document created on it is subject to edit by any of its users. Most basic wikis placed on publicly available Web servers are subject to the contributions of casual passersby, and provide a very simple way to do so.

Wikis can be used to encourage interactive communication among students in the same classroom or between classrooms. For example, students can collaborate on developing a presentation on a topic. The interactions can be among students in different cultures or even in different parts of the world. P–12 students can interact with college students who respond to their writing activities or journals in other disciplines.

Wikis can be described as a knowledge management technique—a way to compile the experiences of a community. For example, a group of teachers could develop curriculum plans and material for sharing.

Companies as disparate as Motorola and the *New York Times* are reported to use wikis for everything from workflow management to collaborative documentation projects. Some wikis are formed around communities of users, others concern themselves with creating an entire encyclopedia.

Maintaining a wiki for users doesn't mean you have to risk a careless user (or vandal) ruining things by editing the content into oblivion. Many of the more sophisticated and complex wiki packages allow for incremental backups, user logins, and page locking to ensure the safety (or at least retrievability) of the content.

SCHOOLS OF THE FUTURE
Using Technology in P–12 Education

There is a relatively wide range of hardware (from VCRs to computers) available for student use, but many teachers remain unprepared to use them. Despite the fact that schools have spent billions of dollars on computers, software, and other technologies, their impact has not approached what it could and should be. Little effort, and less than 15 percent of schools' technology budgets, has been spent to train teachers how to integrate technology effectively into the curriculum.

Experiences with projects such as StarNet and the Iowa Distance Education Alliance (see Chapter 7) have demonstrated that courses delivered by two-way television can successfully fill gaps in the secondary school curriculum. The demonstrated success of technology-based instruction, then, raises the possibility of expansion beyond just filling gaps. But expanding technology's role in this way would eventually alter the basic organizational and power structures of schools. It remains to be seen if the education profession, students, their parents, and other decision makers are willing to make such fundamental changes.

Courses delivered by satellite, via the Internet, or on interactive television are more likely to be accepted by rural schools than by urban and suburban schools. Principals and school boards in rural and poor areas are more likely to take the risk of experimenting with distance learning because such schools have little realistic hope of maintaining a faculty large and diverse enough to teach all the courses needed in a modern comprehensive curriculum. Technology can expand curriculum offerings and alter the instructional organization, as well as the curriculum, of formal education. This movement may be driven by the current and projected teacher shortages, especially in the areas of math and science.

Structuring the Classroom: Division of Labor

The typical setup of the classroom, at virtually every level almost everywhere in the Western world, has the fundamental weakness of being organized around a single adult who attempts to orchestrate diverse activities for a generally large group of learners (Figure 13.7). This one person typically is expected to be responsible for selecting and organizing the content of lessons; designing materials; producing materials; diagnosing individual needs; developing tests; delivering instruction orally to the group or through other media individually or in different groupings; administering, scoring, and interpreting tests; prescribing remedial activities; and coordinating the numberless logistical details that hold the whole enterprise together. Other sectors of society have long since recognized that improvements in effectiveness and productivity require division of labor, but this concept has not yet been accepted in formal education.

An example of a profession in which division of labor has been accepted is that of medicine. Physicians have tended toward specialization, enabling each to keep better abreast of innovations in practice. They have adopted differentiated staffing within their offices and clinics so that they can delegate less critical functions to paraprofessionals, such as physician assistants, nurse practitioners, nurses, and technicians, reserving for themselves the function of diagnosing and treating conditions that merit their attention. Physicians have an incentive to accept this division of labor; it allows them to maximize their profits.

Changing Role of the Teacher

The teacher's role in learning is changing as new technologies appear in the classroom. Teachers are not being replaced by technology, but their role has changed

from information presenter to learning resources coordinator. In addition, they serve as facilitator, manager, counselor, and motivator. Their new roles free them to work more independently with individuals and small groups while leaving the formal presentations to another medium. Teachers help students find and process information from many sources. In the future, teachers will become more and more "the guide on the side" rather than "the sage on the stage."

The demand for teachers with computer skills is increasing; some schools now require that potential teachers demonstrate such skills. It is not enough to have had a course in college. They must demonstrate to an observer that they can operate a computer and use software for instructional purposes.

The trend toward changing teacher certification requirements, primarily to permit knowledgeable laypersons to teach, will probably be accelerated by the acceptance of courses delivered by technology, the advantages of having a diversely talented staff, and the current shortage of teachers. A growing number of certified paraprofessional educational personnel is likely. Future schools will have a more varied instructional staff than in the past.

Charter Schools

Charter schools have experienced tremendous growth in the past decade. In September 1992, the City Academy Charter School in St. Paul, Minnesota became the first operational charter school in the United States (Sautter, 1993). By 2001 there were over 2,000 such schools, enrolling over 500,000 students.

A **charter school** is "an autonomous, results-oriented, publicly funded school of choice that is designed and run by teachers or others under contract with a public sponsor" (Buechler, 1996, p. 4). They are tax-supported, nonsectarian public schools operating free of state regulations and independent of local school districts. However, they are held accountable for the academic achievement of their students.

They are driven by autonomy, competition, and accountability. Charter schools control their own curriculum, budget, and personnel. They must accept all who enroll, cannot charge tuition, and cannot have a religious focus. Advocates say that charter schools provide an incentive for public schools to change. Charter schools are schools of choice; they do not have a captive population. They have outcome or performance-based accountability.

Figure 13.7
The typical classroom has one teacher working with a number of students. How might this structure change with increased use of technology?

Through their charter, they are held accountable by a school district or some other public entity.

There is great variation from one charter school to another and legislation governing them differs significantly across states. Consequently there is no "typical" charter school. They should not be confused with these other types of schools:

- *innovative schools*—created with input from teachers, parents, and community
- *magnet schools*—crafted by school districts using additional funding to provide specialized curriculum themes (e.g., the arts) to attract parents and students
- *alternative schools*—designed by school districts to serve specific populations of pupils who are not well served in traditional schools, such as students with behavioral problems and students at risk of dropping out.

Charter schools provide teachers with the opportunity to explore and develop new approaches with public funds but with minimal state intervention. The motivation for charter schools is the freedom to develop alternative curricula and to employ different instructional techniques. Many of them use an integrated curriculum and are interdisciplinary. Some states permit charter schools without a building—a home school, a virtual school, or an independent study approach. According to Murphy and Shiffman (2002), "they tend to use technology more frequently" (p. 97).

Assisting Learning with Pedagogical Agents

Tools such as pedagogical agents facilitate the learning process. A **pedagogical agent** is a computer program that appears to have the characteristics of an animated being (Baylor, 1999). An example of a simple pedagogical agent is the "Clippit" assistant in Microsoft Office that monitors the user's actions and makes suggestions.

Roles for pedagogical agents in the classroom might include the following:

- Information assistant to help students manage information
- Tutor to facilitate learning
- Coach/mentor to support, guide, and extend students' thinking
- Tool for creating a student's own personal pedagogical agent

The pedagogical agent can help students with information overload in the following ways:

- Help them organize information
- Provide feedback
- Create unique learning experiences

Pedagogical agents introduce a new paradigm for instruction based on the concept of shared abilities and cooperative learning between humans and computers. Exploring the development of pedagogical agents may affect what teachers know about good instruction.

In addition, pedagogical agents can be useful tools for teachers. They might, for example, help teachers sort through the volumes of professional information they receive daily. Further, they might help teachers in organizing and managing learning environments for their students.

Using Technology in School Media Centers

Materials for lifelong learning will continue to be available through libraries, information centers, and online. School media specialists will need to think not only in terms of shelving and circulation but also in terms of downloading and uploading—electronically receiving, storing, indexing, and distributing information to teachers, students, classrooms, and homes. Interactive technologies will create a new generation of teachers and learners who will become not only viewers of such materials, but their users and creators.

School libraries and media centers now have a variety of technology available (Figure 13.8). The trend is toward more technology, including online catalogs, presentation software, video editing decks, and CD-ROM towers. Because school media specialists are becoming more involved in finding information in cyberspace, some refer to themselves as "cybrarians." In many schools, the media center is emerging as the technology hub. With "total access to the world" via the Internet and other technologies, school media centers are becoming libraries without walls!

Figure 13.8
The modern media center distributes a variety of technology to the school.

Librarians and media specialists promote *information literacy,* which includes a range of critical thinking and problem-solving skills. Students are learning how to locate, analyze, and evaluate information for accuracy and bias, and to synthesize conclusions. The ability to find and use information purposefully remains an important skill.

In addition to information literacy and critical evaluation skills, students must be experts at using search and retrieval skills to locate information. One of the authors' junior high school science teachers told him once that "an intelligent person is not someone who knows everything, but who knows where to find it!" This is perhaps truer today than it was 50 years ago!

Increasing Communication Between Schools and Homes

Telecommunications technologies provide an opportunity for a closer relationship between the school and the home. Through telephone technology (answering machines and call-in recordings) parents and teachers are able to communicate in virtual time. Parents can call the teacher's answering machine at any time and leave a message for their child's teacher. Parents can call for a recording of the daily assignments for their children's classes. Teachers can call parents and leave information on home answering machines with specific information about their child.

With this increased communication between school and home it is possible to lengthen the time period for learning. Technology permits teachers to send homework and assignments over networks to homes. Parents, students, and teachers are able to interact about the assignment. Students can access their personal data files from home and also communicate with instructional materials housed on the school's computer.

Learning in the Home

The home is becoming a center for technology-based learning. Children as well as adults learn in the home both for formal school requirements as well as for leisure or informal learning. For example, children do homework and students participate in home schooling, adults take online courses, and seniors seek information about healthcare and retirement on the Internet. The number of U.S. homes with Internet connections has been around 60 percent since 2001, rather than steadily climbing as it had done in prior years (Lenhart, 2003).

Children with access to computers at home spend hours each day on learning activities ranging from e-mailing study partners to conducting Web-based research. The larger part of this is assigned homework from school, but a growing part is "information exploring" performed on students' own initiative. Indeed, technology-based, at-home study offers an affordable and feasible *alternative* to public schools.

The home market for computer-based, education-oriented software is exploding. CD-ROMs aimed at home use now occupy major shelf space in bookstores and computer stores. Studies of home-schooling families found that they are heavy users of materials of this sort. There are increasing numbers of software programs being designed specifically for home-schooled learners.

The average family purchases several thousand dollars of instructional materials annually. On the other end of the spectrum, those who use these materials in a less structured, often recreational way have created a huge market for "edutainment" products. The Disney multimedia conglomerate is now the leading purveyor of both educational and entertainment materials (Sullivan, 1997). There is no reason to expect any slowing of this trend.

Closing the Technology Gap

Traditionally, schools have been the avenue to opportunity. They have tried to even out the disparities in educational opportunities between lower- and upper-income families. Today, this means making sure that all students have equal access to information-handling experiences and technology. We know that many children from upper-income families have access to computers at home. The school along with libraries and community centers must make sure that children from low-income families also have access to technology, especially to computers and the Internet. If they don't, the gap between the technologically literate and the technologically illiterate will continue to widen.

WORKPLACES OF THE FUTURE

Increasing Importance of Technology

Currently, more than half of all new jobs being created require some form of information and technological literacy, and that percentage is increasing. Technology's new tools are empowering, productive, and motivational. Workers need to have an expanded set of technical skills in communication, problem solving, and production. Both future productivity and economic growth are linked to workers' effective uses of new technologies. Tomorrow's workers who want to stay employed will need the ability and opportunity to learn new skills.

Changing Workforce

The nature of the North American workforce is changing dramatically. For one thing, it is getting older. As a consequence, the educational system must be able to

Copyright Concerns

EDUCATORS AND THE COPYRIGHT LAW

What happens if an educator knowingly and deliberately violates the copyright law? The 1976 act contains both criminal and civil sanctions. The criminal penalty can be a fine up to $1,000 and a year in jail. Copyright owners may recover up to $50,000 in civil court for loss of royalties due to infringement. Furthermore, in any infringement lawsuit, the employing institution can be held liable along with the educator. In 1990, Congress amended the copyright law to strip public institutions and agencies of "sovereign immunity," a principle rooted in English law that exempts the "sovereign" from being sued without its consent.

We must remember, punitive damages aside, that in professions devoted to promoting ethical behavior, deliberate violation of the copyright law is unacceptable.

SEEKING PERMISSION TO USE COPYRIGHTED MATERIALS

Aside from staying within the guidelines that limit but recognize our legal right to free use of copyrighted materials, what else can we do to ensure students have access to these materials? We can, obviously, seek permission from copyright owners and, if requested, pay a fee for their use. Certain requests will ordinarily be granted without payment of fee—transcripts for the blind, for example, or material to be tried out once in an experimental program. Permission is not needed for use of materials in the public domain—materials on which copyright protection has run out, for instance, or materials produced by federal government employees in the course of their regular work.

In seeking permission to use copyrighted materials, it is generally best to contact the distributor or publisher of the material rather than its creator. Whether or not the creator is the holder of the copyright, the distributor or publisher generally handles permission requests and sets fees. You can obtain the address of the producer (if not given on the material) from various reference sources, including *Literary Market Place, Audio-Visual Market Place,* and *Ulrich's International Periodical Directory.* For additional information on this topic, go to the Web Links module in Chapter 13 of the Companion Website (http://www.prenhall.com/smaldino).

Be as specific as possible in your request for permission. Give the page numbers and exact amount of print material you wish to copy. (If possible, send along a photocopy of the material.) Describe nonprint material fully. State how you intend to use the material, where you intend to use it, and the number of copies you wish to make.

Remember that fees for production of copyrighted materials are sometimes negotiable. If the fee seems to be beyond your budget, do not hesitate to ask whether it can be lowered.

If for any reason you decide not to use the requested material, make this fact known to the publisher or producer. Without this formal notice it is likely to be assumed that you have in fact used it as requested and you may be charged for a fee you do not in fact owe.

Keep copies of *all* your correspondence and records of all other contacts that you make relevant to seeking permission to use copyrighted instructional materials.

Another solution is to obtain "royalty free" collections of media. Many vendors now sell CD-ROMs that contain collections of images and sounds that can be used in presentations or other products without payment of royalties. Be sure to read the fine print, however. What is meant by "royalty free" varies from one collection to the next. In some cases, there are almost no restrictions on the use of the materials; in another, you may not be allowed to use the materials in any kind of electronic product.

PRIMACY OF FIRST SALE

Have you ever wondered why public libraries, book rental businesses, and video rental clubs are not in violation of copyright law when they do not pay royalties to copyright owners on the items they circulate or rent? They come under the protection of what is referred to as the "primacy of first sale." This means that the purchaser of the copyrighted work may loan or rent the work without having to pay a second royalty. Great pressure is being put on Congress to amend the law to require anyone who rents a copyrighted work to pay a royalty to the copyright owner. As you might expect, the television and motion picture industries are putting on the pressure, and video rental agencies are resisting the change. The 2000–2001 litigation between the music industry and the Napster online music sharing service is a prototypical example of efforts to ensure that copyright holders receive proper remuneration for all commercial transactions involving their work.

Although it is not likely that the free circulation of materials from public libraries and regional media centers will be affected by a change such as this, college and university rental of films and videotapes certainly will be. Educators need to be aware of possible changes in the first-sale doctrine that could adversely affect access to materials.

For general information on copyright, see the Copyright Concerns in Chapter 1. Suggested readings on copyright appear at the end of Chapter 1.

provide lifelong learning. In addition, the makeup of the workforce is becoming increasingly diverse, requiring education and training in a variety of languages and at various ability levels. Also, because society is becoming more mobile, job retraining will be even more necessary. Inequalities of class, gender, ethnicity, and economic status correlate highly with denied or restricted access to the tools of technology. Schools, communities, and businesses have a responsibility to ensure access to technology and to supply training for jobs involving technology. The instructional technologies and media described throughout this book can help workers cope with many of these changes.

Changing Nature of Work

About three-fourths of U.S. workers today hold jobs that primarily entail handling information. Knowledge work involves not only "number crunching" and shuffling data, but also learning elaborate systems that combine human teams and intelligent machines. With the number of hands-on production jobs decreasing, schools must increasingly teach people to use their minds as tools.

Not only is the type of work people do being affected by advances in technology, so is the place they do that work. In the 1970s the concept of **telecommuting** entered our vocabulary, strongly promoted by information technology companies. The current preferred name for this phenomenon is **telework,** defined as a method of working in which the employee works away from the office, perhaps at home, using a computer and telecommunications technology to communicate with a worksite. Nearly half of all U.S. households now possess some form of home office. With personal computers, fax machines, cellular phones, and Internet connections, many people now own the infrastructure to do information work in their homes. Corporations are strongly motivated to move employees out of the company's quarters to reduce the huge overhead costs of acquiring and maintaining office space (Figure 13.9).

An increasing number of workers are teleworking. The likelihood of continued growth in telework is virtually certain since it is favored by both corporate and government policies in the major industrialized nations. Large cities are providing incentives to companies that allow a certain percentage of workers to telecommute to cut down on traffic and pollution.

Teleworkers at home can access information from the office, work with it, and send it back. Even at the worksite, coworkers are increasingly interacting electronically. These information workers must be able to use all aspects of technology to get information, to communicate with others, and to enhance their job skills. Jobs that lend themselves to telecommuting include writing,

Figure 13.9
Home workstations allow individuals to be productive without wasting time traveling to work.

developing instructional materials, editing, telephone sales, investment brokering, administering phone surveys, and expert diagnosis (such as "Ask a Nurse" phone lines).

Changing Nature of Training

Just as technology has revolutionized learning in the schools, it has also affected training in the business environment. Training that seeks to improve human performance and increase productivity is increasingly being provided when the worker needs it—often at the workstation, not in a classroom. This type of training is called **just-in-time training,** as opposed to **cold storage training.** The former is provided when you need it and can use it; the latter teaches skills and information you may use in the future.

More individuals are training while at their workstations, often benefiting from **performance support systems** (see Chapter 5). Once workers are on the job, traditional classroom training disrupts their performance, reduces productivity, and sometimes frustrates employees. Often classroom training does not effectively transfer to the work location. Performance support systems provide instruction and other needed information to workers as they make decisions and take actions on the job. These systems provide feedback while work is in progress. They let workers know how they are doing while performing the task.

Cross-training is used to train workers to do several jobs. With multiple skills, workers have more versatility and can "cross over" from one job to another. Cross-training increases the amount of training time, but also increases the versatility of workers for the company, and decreases the likelihood of workers being laid off.

Close-Up

PROFESSIONAL ORGANIZATIONS IN EDUCATIONAL TECHNOLOGY

Whether your interest in instructional technology is general or whether you intend to specialize in this area of education, you should be familiar with some of the major organizations dedicated to its advancement. For additional information on this topic or to visit the following websites, go to the Web Links module in Chapter 13 of the Companion Website (http://www.prenhall.com/smaldino).

Association for Educational Communications and Technology (AECT)

AECT is the leading international organization representing instructional technology professionals working in schools, colleges and universities, and the corporate, government, and military sectors. Its mission is to provide leadership in educational communications and technology by linking professionals holding a common interest in the use of educational technology and its application to the learning process. AECT has nine divisions designed around areas of special interest represented within the membership, encompassing members' interests in instructional design, research and theory, media management, distance learning, school media programs, industrial training, media production, computer-based instruction, interactive systems, international interests, and systematic school restructuring.

The association maintains an active publications program, including *TechTrends*, published six times during the academic year; *Educational Technology Research and Development*, a research journal published four times a year; and a large number of books and videotapes (on the Internet, see http://www.aect.org/Pubs/pubs.htm). AECT sponsors an annual convention in the Fall. The annual convention features over 300 educational sessions and workshops focusing on how teachers are using new technologies and teaching methods in the classroom. In addition, the association sponsors an annual professional development seminar and leadership development conference each summer. For more information, contact AECT, 1800 N. Stonelake Dr., Suite 2, Bloomington, IN 47404, or phone tollfree 877-677-2328. Website: http://www.aect.org

American Library Association (ALA)

The ALA is the oldest and largest library association in the world. Its 57,000 members represent all types of libraries—public, school, academic, state, and special libraries serving persons in government, commerce, the armed services, hospitals, prisons, and other institutions. The association also has 11 divisions focusing on various types of libraries and services. The American Association of School Librarians, one of the divisions, holds national conferences focusing on the interests of school media specialists. For more information, contact ALA, 50 E. Huron St., Chicago, IL 60611. Website: http://www.ala.org

American Society for Training and Development (ASTD)

ASTD is composed primarily of professionals engaged in training and human resource development programs in business and industry. It is by far the largest association for people engaged in workplace performance improvement programs in business, industry, government, and other institutions. The society publishes a monthly magazine titled *Training and Development*, sponsors research in the field of workplace performance improvement, and conducts an annual international conference that includes a varied and significant educational program. ASTD publishes a newsletter on instructional technology and organizes conference sessions on the topic. For more information, contact ASTD, 1640 King St., Box 1443, Alexandria, VA 22313-2043. Website: http://www.astd.org

International Interactive Communications Society (IICS)

The IICS is the premier worldwide nonprofit organization for interactive media professionals. Dedicated to the advancement of interactive arts and technologies since 1983, members of the IICS include professionals involved in the rapidly integrating digital "convergence" industries. Currently IICS has close to 2,000 members. Membership benefits include an online newsletter, annual membership directory, local chapter activities, and various discounts on publications and services related to the interactive multimedia industry. For more information, contact IICS World Headquarters, 4840 McKnight Road, Suite A1, Pittsburgh, PA 15237. Website: http://www.iics.org

International Society for Performance Improvement (ISPI)

ISPI is the leading international association dedicated to improving productivity and performance in the workplace. Founded in 1962, ISPI represents over 10,000 members in the United States, Canada, and 33 other countries. ISPI members work in business, governmental agencies, academic institutions, and other organizations. The ISPI Annual Conference and Expo, several association publications, and more than 60 different chapters provide professional development, services, and information exchange. For more information, contact ISPI, 1400 Spring Street, Suite 260, Silver Spring, MD 20910. Website: http://www.ispi.org

International Society for Technology in Education (ISTE)

The mission of ISTE is to improve education through the use of technology in learning, teaching, and administration. It is the largest nonprofit professional organization dedicated to the improvement of education through the use of computer-based technology. ISTE members include teachers, administrators, computer coordinators, information resource managers, and educational technology specialists. The organization maintains regional affiliate memberships to support and respond to grassroots efforts to improve the educational use of technology. Their support services and materials for educators include books, courseware, and conferences. ISTE publishes *Learning and Leading with Technology, Journal of Research on Computing in Education, ISTE Update,* books, and courseware packages. For more information, contact ISTE, 480 Charnelton Street, Eugene, OR 97401-2626. Website: http://www.iste.org

Media Communications Association– International (MCAI)

Media Communications Association–International, formerly the International Television Association, was formed to enhance the skills and knowledge of video professionals working in corporate and organizational settings. It continues to evolve in response to the in-

dustry's rapid pace of change. MCAI offers its members special low-cost phone, hotel, credit card, health insurance, and production insurance services. The association has published several books and pamphlets. For more information, contact Media Communications Association–International, 9202 N. Meridian Street, Ste. 200, Indianapolis, IN 46260-1810. Website: http://www.itva.org

International Visual Literacy Association (IVLA)

The IVLA is dedicated to exploring the concept of visual literacy—how we use visuals for communication and how we interpret these visuals. It is particularly concerned with the development of instructional materials designed to foster skills in interpreting visuals. The organization draws membership from a variety of disciplines and professions, including higher education, public schools, business and communication, professional artists, production specialists, and design specialists. For more information, contact the Center for Visual Literacy, Arizona State University, Tempe, AZ 85287. Website: http://www.ivla.org

United States Distance Learning Association (USDLA)

USDLA is a nonprofit association formed in 1987 to promote the development and application of distance learning for education and training. The 3,000-plus members represent P–12 education, higher education, continuing education, corporate training, telemedicine, and military and government training. The association has become a leading source of information and recommendations for government agencies, the U.S. Congress, industry, and those entering the development of distance learning programs. USDLA has established over 30 chapters. It is a sponsor of the annual International Distance Learning and Tele-Con conferences. In addition, USDLA holds regular meetings with leaders of distance learning programs in Europe and the Pacific Rim. For information, contact USDLA, 140 Gould Street, Needham, MA 02494-2397. Website: http://www.usdla.org

STATE ORGANIZATIONS

Several of the national professional organizations have state affiliates (AECT, ALA, ISTE) or local chapters (ISPI, ASTD). By joining one or more of these, you will quickly make contact with nearby professionals who share your particular concerns.

As a teacher or an instructional technology specialist, you will want to be active in at least one local or state organization. If you are a fulltime student, you can join many organizations at a reduced rate.

Assessing Training

Driven by competitive pressures, some businesses have adopted **Total Quality Management (TQM)** and other reengineering programs that require more accurate measurement of the business impact of all expenditures. This has pushed more corporate training programs to consider assessing outcomes beyond mere learner satisfaction. Kirkpatrick (1994) proposed four levels of evaluation: (1) learner satisfaction, (2) skill demonstration, (3) transfer to the job, and (4) impact on business goals. Surveys of corporate trainers over the past few years show a marked increase in companies claiming to be evaluating at levels 3 and 4.

YOUR FUTURE IN THE FIELD

You are entering this field at an exciting time as a teacher, trainer, or media/technology professional. This book is dedicated to helping you become a more effective instructor (or manager of instruction) through application of instructional technology and media. The Association for Educational Communications and Technology copublishes a directory of graduate programs in instructional technology (Fitzgerald, Orey, & Branch, 2003). Unlike some educational areas, instructional technology is becoming more and more pervasive in formal and informal education each year. Correspondingly, ever-larger numbers of people are being employed in this specialty.

The fastest-growing specialty is school technology coordinator. Regardless of the quality and sophistication of computer hardware and software, the success of technology often depends on the support and encouragement that students and teachers receive in using it. Technology coordinators can assist with planning, selecting software and hardware, consulting on purchases, implementing, and supervising maintenance and repair.

Some schools and corporations have even divided the technology coordinator position into two specialties. A software specialist orders, catalogs, distributes, and consults with teachers on implementing software. A hardware consultant serves a similar role with hardware. In other schools, a software specialist and a hardware consultant report to the technology coordinator.

At school, district, regional, and state levels, media professionals are employed to run programs and, depending on the size of the organization, produce materials for use in schools. As school districts and regional media centers have built up their collections of audiovisual materials for distribution, they have employed instructional media professionals to select these materials. Another career area at all education levels is in professional management of media collections, including classification, storage, and distribution.

Instructional product design—developing valid and reliable instructional materials—has been an important specialty in the field of instructional technology for some time. Publishers and producers of instructional materials, along with school districts, community colleges, and colleges and universities, employ specialists trained in product design skills. Computer-assisted instruction, interactive media, and other emerging forms of individualized instruction constitute an important growth area within this field.

Organizations other than schools also require specialists in educational technology. Healthcare institutions, for example, are heavily involved in instructional technology and have been employing an increasing number of professionals to help develop the instruction used in those programs.

Training programs rely heavily on instructional technology and media. Consequently, specialists in instructional technology are in demand in these programs. These specialties include the following:

- *Trainer.* Presents information, leads discussions, and manages learning experiences.
- *Instructional designer.* Assesses training needs, translates training needs into training programs, determines media to be used, designs course materials.
- *Training manager.* Plans and organizes training programs, hires staff, prepares and manages budgets.

Hardware and software developments are occurring so rapidly that our expectation increasingly lags behind reality. In previous generations our vision extended beyond our capabilities. Now it struggles to keep up with what is available. Wireless telephone communication, for example, is now widely used. Not too long ago, it was science fiction. Hand-held computers and Internet-enabled cellular telephones are common among professionals who need quick and easy access to data—including color photos and even video. The combination of wireless, cellular, and miniaturized technologies allows people literally to access the Internet in the palm of their hand. All these developments and trends make this an exciting and challenging time for professionals engaged in education and training. Make the most of it!

Close-Up

PROFESSIONAL JOURNALS IN EDUCATIONAL TECHNOLOGY

All of the professional organizations in instructional technology publish journals of interest to their members. Various other periodicals are of special interest to teachers interested in using instructional media. *Media and Methods*, for example, highlights new software and hardware. *Booklist* will keep you current on the availability of new instructional materials. *Learning* gives practical ideas for improving instruction. *Educational Technology* addresses both teachers and educational technologists, providing articles on a range of topics, from the theoretical to the practical. For the business or industry setting, *Training* covers new developments in training techniques in a lively, popular style. For additional information on this topic or to visit the following websites, go to the Web Links module in Chapter 13 of the Companion Website (http://www.prenhall.com/smaldino).

Leading and Learning with Technology (http://www.iste.org) focuses on technology integration into P–12 classrooms. Many of the articles are written by teachers, sharing what they have accomplished using the computer in their classrooms with children of all ages and abilities.

School Library Media Quarterly (http://www.ala.org/aasl/SLMQ/) publishes research that pertains to the uses of technology for instructional and informational purposes. Special issues have dealt with such themes as communications and technology and fa-

cility design for learning environments that require a great deal of technology.

T.H.E. (Technological Horizons in Education) *Journal* (http://www.thejournal.com) concentrates on technology in higher education. *The Canadian Journal of Educational Communications* gives in-depth coverage of the broad field of educational technology.

The computer area has spawned a large number of journals, such as *Electronic Learning, Journal of Educational Multimedia and Hypermedia, Journal of Computing in Childhood Education, Journal of Computers in Math and Science Teaching, Technology and Learning*, and *New Media* (http://www.newmedia.com).

As you work with instructional media and technology and gain experience in whatever position you find yourself, you may want to explore the possibility of deepening your professional interest in one of the specialties in instructional technology. Through regular reading of one or more of the journals in the field, you can stay informed about developments in instructional technology.

Summary: Looking Ahead

You are now prepared for an exciting future using instructional technology and media for learning. This chapter describes trends in technology and media that are already having a significant impact on schools and workplaces!

Instructional technology and media provide you with the tools to engage students in learning. As a teacher, you must be prepared to choose the best tools for your students. Such tools offer powerful possibilities for improving learning. The teacher, however, makes the difference in integrating technology and media into this process.

If you are going to use technology and media effectively, you must plan systematically for their use, as

discussed in Chapter 3. The ASSURE model is a guide to the major steps in the planning process. Following the ASSURE model, you begin creating the learning experience by assessing your students' characteristics and the learning objectives to be attained. With these in mind you are in a good position to select the types of media or instructional systems to be used and to consider specific materials that you might need.

The chapter concludes by describing your future in the field. To help you continue to keep up to date, descriptions of professional organizations and professional journals are included. You will be a part of determining the use of technology and media in the future—make the most of them to ASSURE learning!

Classroom Link Portfolio Activities

Use the "Classroom Link Portfolio" CD-ROM and the Companion Website as resources in completing these activities. To complete the following activities online go to the Portfolio Activities module in Chapter 13 of the Companion Website (http://www.prenhall.com/smaldino).

1. *Technology Use in the Profession.* Considering the various roles of a teacher, predict the ways in which technology will enhance your responsibilities as a professional. Consider how you will interact with your peers, students, parents, and the community in which you teach. (ISTE NETS-T 5.B & C)

2. *Technology Use in Assessment.* In considering the application of technology to learning, how might you use technology as an assessment tool? Locate rubrics online that assess content and technology use. What activities could you design to engage your students in using technology to demonstrate their learning? ISTE NETS-T 4.A & C)

3. *Individual Education Plan.* As a teacher, what are your present strengths and weaknesses in technology? What do you plan to do to address the weaknesses? What online sources are available? Technology evolves over time, providing users with newer and more creative tools. What are your plans to stay current? How will you continue your own professional development? What decisions will you have to make to continue your professional growth? (ISTE NETS-T 1.B; 5.A & B)

Integration Assessments

To complete the specified activities online go to the Integration Assessments module in Chapter 13 of the Companion Website (http://www.prenhall.com/smaldino).

1. Interview two or more professionals working in educational technology. Compare and contrast their duties in a two- to three-page written report or five-minute audio or video recording. (ISTE NETS-T 5.C)

2. Survey the content of several different educational technology journals and write a one- to two-page report summarizing the types of articles and information covered in each. (ISTE NETS-T 5.A)

3. Predict the potential impact on your area of interest of one of the trends in media and technology. Write a two- to three-page report or tape a five-minute audio or video recording. (ISTE NETS-T 5.B)

4. For a week, collect reports of new developments in electronic media from newspapers, news magazines, and other popular media sources. Write a two- to three-page report describing the potential impact on learning of these new developments. (ISTE NETS-T 5.A)

5. If you work in a school or other instructional setting, analyze the structure or organizational factors that either impede or facilitate your full use of new media and technologies for learning. (ISTE NETS-T 5.B)

6. Prepare an oral or a written report discussing the potential technological changes in the workplace and predict how training will adapt to these changes. (ISTE NETS-T 5.B)

7. Acquire a recent Technology for Education Plan from a local school district or state office of education. Assess how technology will touch all areas of the school's curricula. (ISTE NETS-T 5.B)

References

Agee, J. 2003. Exciting e-books: A new path to literature. *Tech Trends, 47*(4): 5–8.

Barger, Jorn. 1999. *Weblog resources FAQ.* Accessed online at http://www.robotwisdom.com/weblogs/

Baylor, Amy. 1999. Intelligent agents as cognitive tools for education. *Educational Technology, 39*(22): 36.

Becker, H. J. 1999. *Internet use by teachers: Conditions of professional use and teacher-directed student use.* Irvine, CA: Center for Research on Information Technology and Organizations.

Buechler, M. 1996. *Charter schools: Legislation and results after four years.* Bloomington, IN: Indiana University, Indiana Education Policy Center.

Bylinsky, G. 2000. Hot new technologies for American factories: Part 2. Accessed online at http://www.fortune.com/fortune/imt/2000/06/26/elearning2.html.

Campus Computing Project. 2003. *eCommerce comes slowly to the campus.* The Campus Computing Project. Accessed 1 November 2003 from the World Wide Web: http://www.campuscomputing.net/summaries/2003/index.html

Center for Community Research. 1999. *Virginia Public Television instructional television survey–1999.* Salem, VA: Author.

Doherty, K. 2002. Students speak out. *Education Week* (May 9): 22.

Ely, Donald P. 2002. *Trends in educational technology,* 5th ed. Syracuse, NY: ERIC Clearinghouse on Information and Technology.

Fitzgerald, M. A., M. Orey, and R. M. Branch, eds. 2003. *Educational media and technology yearbook.* Englewood, CO: Libraries Unlimited.

Industry report. 2003. *Training, 40*(9): 19–45.

Kirkpatrick, Donald. 1994. *Evaluating training programs: The four levels.* San Francisco: Barrett-Koehler.

Lenhart, Amanda. 2003. *The ever-shifting Internet population.* Washington, DC: The Pew Internet & American Life Project.

Mann, Charles C. 2001. Electronic paper turns the page. *Technology Review, 104*(2): 42–48.

Molenda, Michael, & Michael Sullivan. 2004. Issues and trends in instructional technology: Treading water. *Educational Media and Technology Yearbook.* Englewood, CO: Libraries Unlimited.

Murphy, Joseph, and Catherine Dunn Shiffman. 2002. *Understanding and assessing the charter school movement.* New York: Teachers College Press.

National Center for Education Statistics (NCES). 2000. *Teacher use of computers and the Internet in public schools.* Washington, DC: U.S. Department of Education.

National Center for Education Statistics. 2001. *Internet access in U.S. public schools and classrooms: 1994–2000* (ED456835). Washington, DC: National Center for Education Statistics.

Peak Group. 2002. *Virtual schools across America: Trends in K–12 online education, 2002.* Los Altos, CA: Peak Group.

Roush, Wade. 1999. A genuine button-pusher. *Technology Review, 102*(6): 148–151.

Sautter, R. C. 1993. *Charter schools: A new breed of public schools.* Oak Brook, IL: North Central Regional Educational Laboratory.

Sullivan, Michael. 1997. Untitled. Remarks at IST Colloquium, Indiana University.

Trotter, A. 2002. E-learning goes to school. *Education Week* (May 9): 13–18.

Suggested Readings

Aldrich, Clark. 2003. *Simulations and the future of learning: An innovative (and perhaps revolutionary) approach to e-learning.* San Francisco: Jossey-Bass.

Beam, Walter R. 2001. Information literacy: Requirements of the 21st century workplace. *Journal of Instruction Delivery Systems, 15*(2): 14–16.

Bierlein, L., and L. A. Mulholland. 1994. The promise of charter schools. *Educational Leadership, 52*(1): 34–40.

Callison, William L. 2003. *Charter and community schools: A director's handbook.* Lanham, MD: Scarecrow.

Cawelti, Gordon. 1997. *Effects of high school restructuring: Ten schools at work.* Arlington, VA: Educational Research Service.

Coburn, Janet. 1999. Technology on the horizon. *School Planning and Management, 38*(12): 5–8.

Emerging Technologies Research Group. 1996. *Telecommuting report.* New York: FIND/SVP.

Green, K. C. 2001. *The 2001 national survey of information technology in U.S. higher education: eCommerce comes slowly to the campus.* Accessed 17 July 2002 from the World Wide Web: http://www.campuscomputing.net/summaries/2001/index.html

Heinich, Robert. 1985. Instructional technology and the structure of education. *Educational Communications and Technology Journal, 33*(1): 9–15.

Hill, Paul Thomas, and Robin J. Lake. 2002. *Charter school and accountability in public education.* Washington, DC: Brookings Institution.

Kemp, Jerrold E. 2000. *Designing education in the 21st century.* Bloomington, IN: TECHNOS.

McLellan, Hilary. 1996. Virtual realities. In *Handbook of research for educational communications and technology,* edited by D. Jonassen. New York: Simon & Schuster.

Molenda, Michael, James Pershing, and Charles Reigeluth. 1996. Designing instructional systems. In *ASTD training and development handbook,* 4th ed. New York: McGraw-Hill.

Ohler, Jason. 2000. Taking the future back from technology. *Education Digest, 65*(5): 8–14.

Paquet, Sebastian. 2002. *Seb's open research.* Accessed online at http://radio.weblogs.com/0110772/stories/2002.html

Ravenaugh, Mickey. 2000. Beyond the digital divide: Pathways to equity. *Technology and Learning, 20*(10): 38–44.

Reigeluth, Charles M. 1999. What is instructional-design theory and how is it changing? In *Instructional-design theories and models: A new paradigm of instructional theories,* edited by Charles M. Reigeluth. Hillsdale, NJ: Lawrence Erlbaum Associates.

Reigeluth, Charles M., and Laurie Miller Nelson. 1997. A new paradigm of ISD? In *Educational media and technology yearbook,* edited by Robert C. Branch and Barbara B. Minor. Vol. 22. Englewood, CO: Libraries Unlimited.

Reiser, Robert, and John V. Dempsey. 2001. *Trends and issues in instructional design and technology.* Upper Saddle River, NJ: Merrill/Prentice Hall.

Rossett, Allison, ed. 2002. *The ASTD e-learning handbook.* New York: McGraw-Hill.

Senge, Peter, N. Cambron-McCabe, T. Lucas, B. Smith, J. Dutton, and A. Kleiner. 2000. *Schools that learn: A fifth discipline fieldbook for educators, parents, and everyone who cares about education.* New York: Doubleday.

Steen, Margaret, and Shanley Rhodes. 1998. Training for the future. *InfoWorld, 20*(43): 100–102.

Stiggins, Richard J. 2005. *Student-involved assessment for learning,* 4th ed. Upper Saddle River, NJ: Merrill/Prentice Hall.

Tiene, Drew, and Albert Ingram. 2001. *Exploring current issues in educational technology.* New York: McGraw-Hill.

U.S. Census Bureau. 2001. *Home computers and Internet use in the U.S.* Accessed 17 July 2001 from the World Wide Web: http://www.census.gov/prod/2001pubs/

U.S. Office of Technology Assessment. 1995. *Teachers and technology: Making the connection.* Washington, DC: Author.

Van Buren, Cassandra. 2000. Multimedia learning at "the school that business built": Students' perceptions of education at new technology high school. *Journal of Curriculum and Supervision, 15*(3): 236–254.

Venn, Martha L., R. Larry Moore, and Philip L. Gunter. 2001. Using audio/video conferencing to observe field-based practices of rural teachers. *Rural Educator, 22*(2): 24–27.

Wilson, Brent G. 2002. Trends and futures of education: Implications for distance education. *Quarterly Review of Distance Education, 3*(1): 91–103.

Winer, D. 2002. *The history of weblogs.* Accessed online at http://newhome.weblogs.com/historyOfWeblogs

Zucker, Andrew, and Robert Kozma. 2003. *The virtual high school: Teaching generation V.* New York: Teachers College Press.

Weston, Mark. 1996. Reformers should take a look at home schools. *Education Week, 15*(28): 34.

Websites

Palm Digital Media Inc.
http://www.palmdigitalmedia.com

Lightning Source Inc.
http://www.lightningsource.com

OverDrive Inc.
http://www.overdrive.com

Fictionwise Inc.
http://www.fictionwise.com

Classroom Resources

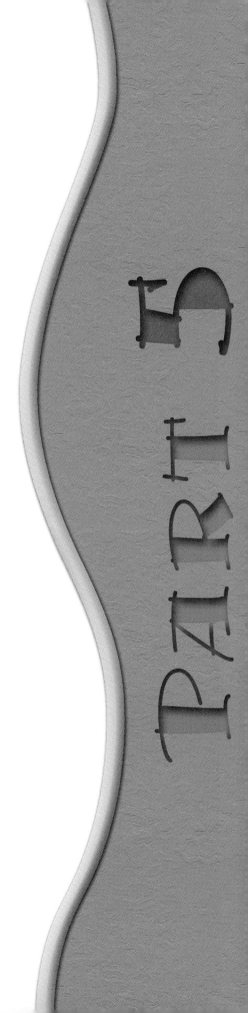

Photography and Visuals

Outline

Photography
Preserving Visuals
Multi-Image Presentations
Planning Audiovisual Presentations

In this section we have assembled information on photography and visuals, including how to preserve visuals and how to combine them with audio.

The first section explores photography. In Chapters 4 and 10 we looked at the educational applications of visuals. Here we continue that discussion with a brief description of techniques for preserving and storing visuals. We conclude with a look at multi-image presentations and a general discussion on how you may best plan your own audiovisual presentations.

PHOTOGRAPHY

Elements of Photography

All cameras, regardless of their size, shape, or type, operate on the same basic principles. There are four elements required for photography: a subject, light, a camera, and film (or some other recording medium). Light is reflected from the subject and passes through the lens to form an image on the recording medium. Let's look at the four elements in more detail.

Subject.   For instructional purposes, the subject should be interesting and imaginative. The picture elements should be relevant to the instructional objective and should be "composed," or framed in the picture, properly. (See "Taking Better Pictures" in Section C.)

Light. Light may come from natural sources (i.e., sunlight) or from artificial sources (light bulbs or camera flash units). The recording medium must be exposed to the proper amount of light. Too little exposure and the picture will be dark; too much and the picture will be too light.

Camera The camera is a light-tight box with a lens to collect the light from the subject and to focus the light on the film or other recording medium. The amount of light getting into the camera is controlled by the lens opening and the shutter speed.

Film (Recording Medium). The recording medium may be film or a light-sensitive detector called a **charge-coupled device (CCD).** Recent technological advances have reduced the cost and improved the quality of CCDs to the point that they are competitive with film for many purposes. Film, still the most common recording medium, is a light-sensitive material that records the image. The image becomes visible after it is processed by chemicals. With some Polaroid film, the chemicals are part of the film package. CCDs convert the light image into electrons that can be digitized, processed, and stored electronically. You can view them on a monitor, store them on compact discs, or combine them with other digital information in a computer. Needless to say, digital cameras are becoming more and more popular.

Parts of a Camera

Cameras have many parts, but the most important parts common to all cameras are the aperture, the shutter, the viewfinder, the focus mechanism, and the film advance (Figure A.1).

Aperture. The **aperture** is the lens opening that regulates the amount of light entering the camera. On some cameras the size of the opening is fixed; on other cameras there are two or three possible settings for the aperture. On many cameras, however, the size of the lens opening is adjustable over a broad range.

Shutter. The **shutter** controls the length of time that light enters the camera and reaches the film. Again, there is only one shutter speed on simple cameras but several on more complex cameras. The *shutter speed* refers to the period of time that light is allowed to enter the camera. On the shutter speed control knob the speed is usually given as a whole number such as 250, 125, or 30. However, these numbers refer to fractions of a second (i.e., 1/250 of a second, 1/125 of a second, and 1/30 of a second). The higher the number, the shorter the time that the shutter is open. The very fast shutter speeds such as 1/1000 second (with the shutter open only a very short period of

Figure A.1
Components of a typical camera.

time) allow you to photograph rapidly moving objects, such as race cars.

Viewfinder. The **viewfinder** allows you to see what the film will "see" when the shutter is opened. In many point-and-shoot cameras the viewfinder is near the top of the camera and set parallel to the lens opening. Consequently, when you look through the viewfinder you may not see exactly what will appear in the photograph. Except at very close range, the discrepancy is negligible. With a single-lens reflex camera, a movable mirror allows you to view directly through the lens. The mirror moves out of the way when you take a photograph.

Focus Mechanism. The focus mechanism is the setting of the lens that determines the sharpness of the image. Inexpensive cameras often cannot be focused and have just one setting, which is usually good for objects from five feet to infinity. Other cameras have a range of focus from three feet to infinity. The focus may be determined by a distance scale (to the subject) and is indicated in feet and/or meters. Many newer cameras have automatic focus mechanisms.

Film Advance. The film advance is the manual or automatic mechanism that advances the film to the next frame after you take a picture.

Figure A.2

The SLR camera (center) with extra lenses for extreme close-ups and long-distance photography and a point-and-shoot camera for general purpose photography.

Selecting a Camera

The type of camera you choose depends on the kinds of pictures you find useful for instruction. If you do not take extreme close-ups and do not have use for telephoto and other special lenses, then you may prefer a point-and-shoot camera for portability, reliability, and simplicity (Figure A.2). The quality of the image taken with a moderately priced point-and-shoot camera is comparable to that of a high-quality single-lens reflex (SLR) camera under average conditions.

If, however, you need to take extreme close-ups, use a variety of lenses (e.g., wide angle, telephoto), or do a lot of copying, then a single-lens reflex (SLR) camera is what you want. Although it is bulkier and more difficult to use, the SLR is more flexible than a point-and-shoot camera.

Both types of cameras are available in models with automatic and semiautomatic exposure controls. Before the incorporation of photocells and microprocessors into cameras, even amateur photographers had to know the relationship among film speed, lens opening **(f/stop),** and shutter speed. Today's picture taker need learn only a few simple steps from the instruction manual to achieve proper exposure on the film. Sometimes unusual lighting situations call for modifications of camera-determined settings. A little experience with the camera will guide such modifications. Relieved of the necessity to determine exposure, you can concentrate on composing the picture.

New point-and-shoot cameras are packed with computer technology. These cameras have automatic loading, film-speed setting, exposure, focus, flash, and film advance.

Digital cameras store black/white or full-color images in a digital format. A charge-coupled device in the film plane of the camera converts light energy to digital data, which is stored in a small digital recorder such as a memory card. Such cameras can be specially designed or can be modifications of standard SLR cameras. Since no film is used, there is no waiting for developing and printing. You may immediately view your images on a small monitor incorporated into the camera. You can transmit the images over telephone lines and/or download them to a computer for manipulation, and can store them on a computer disk or on photo CDs. Digital photography is particularly useful for creating images for presentations or for desktop publishing.

Having chosen a camera, you will find guidelines for taking instructionally useful photos in "Taking Better Pictures." For hints on planning a slide or slide-tape presentation, see "Developing an Audiovisual Presentation." Also refer to "Converting Visuals to Slides." All of these guides appear in Section C.

PRESERVING VISUALS

One drawback in using visuals in the classroom is that they are easily soiled or otherwise damaged as students pass them around. Repeated display, storage, and retrieval can also add to wear and tear. Mounting and laminating are the two most effective preservation techniques, and they can contribute to the instructional effectiveness of visuals.

Mounting

Mount visuals on construction paper, cardboard, or other such material for durability. The color of the mounting material should not draw attention away from the visual. It is generally a good idea to use pastel or neutral tones rather than brilliant or primary colors. Using one of the minor colors in the visual as the color for the mounting can enhance harmony. The total effect of your mounting should be neat and pleasing to the eye. Borders, for example, should be evenly cut, with side borders of equal width and the bottom border slightly wider than the top.

Various glues, cements, and pastes are available for mounting purposes. When used according to directions, almost all are effective. Some white glues, however, are likely to cause wrinkles in the picture when the adhesive dries, especially if used full strength. If you run into this problem, dilute the glue; for example, use four parts glue to one part water. Cover the entire back of the visual evenly with the adhesive before placing it on the mounting board. If excess adhesive seeps out around the edges, wipe it off with a damp cloth or sponge.

Glue sticks may be used in place of liquid glues. They have the advantage of not running out around the edges of the material. Glue sticks are less likely to damage and discolor photographs.

Rubber Cement Mounting.   One of the most commonly used adhesives for mounting purposes is rubber cement. It is designed specifically for use with paper products. It is easy to use and less messy than many other liquid glues. You can easily wipe away excess cement, and it is inexpensive. Rubber cement does, however, have two disadvantages. When the container is left uncovered for any length of time, the adhesive tends to dry out and thicken. Periodic doses of thinner (available commercially) may be necessary to keep the cement serviceable. A second disadvantage is that the adhesive quality of rubber cement tends to diminish over a period of time. Constant exposure to dry air may eventually cause it to lose its grip. You can compensate for this disadvantage by taking special precautions, as noted for permanent rubber cement mountings (see "Mounting Pictures Using Rubber Cement" in Section C). These mountings will not last indefinitely. One caution is that rubber cement could damage and discolor photographs.

Dry Mounting.   Dry mounting employs a specially prepared paper impregnated with heat-sensitive adhesive. The paper is available in sheets and rolls. The dry-mounting tissue bonds the backing material to the back of the visual. A dry-mount press is used to supply the heat and pressure necessary to activate the tissue's adhesive. The process is rapid and clean and results in permanent, high-quality mounting (see "Dry Mounting Pictures" in Section C).

One disadvantage of dry mounting is that it is relatively expensive. However, it is possible to dry mount visuals without a dry-mount press by using an ordinary household iron. Set the iron on a setting for silk or rayon. Do not use steam. The tip of the household iron can be used in place of the special tacking iron.

Laminating

Lamination protects visuals from wear and tear by covering them with a clear plastic or plasticlike material. Lamination helps to protect visuals against tears, scratches, and sticky fingers. You can wipe soiled surfaces clean with a damp cloth.

Lamination also allows you to write on your visuals with a grease pencil or water-soluble pen for instructional purposes. You can easily erase the writing later with a damp cloth or sponge. A teacher of mathematics, for example, might write percentage figures on a laminated illustration of a pizza or a pie to help teach the concept of fractions. You can also have students write on laminated materials. When the lesson is completed, erase the markings and the material is ready for further teaching. Many classroom materials can be laminated to

add extra durability and to allow for erasable writing by the teacher and students.

Clear plastic sheets with adhesive backing (such as Con-Tact® shelf paper) are available for laminating purposes. Remove the backing cover a little at a time to expose the adhesive and carefully press the clear plastic sheet on the visual. If you remove backing all at once, the plastic sheet often rolls and sticks to itself before you can get it on the visual. Cut off any portions of the plastic sheet that extend beyond the edges of the visual or fold them back for additional protection.

Laminating can be done with a dry-mount press (see "Laminating Pictures with a Dry-Mount Press" in Section C). Rolls of laminating film for use with a dry-mount press are available from commercial sources. A laminating machine can be used as well (Figure A.3). These machines use two rolls of laminating film and cover both sides of the visual simultaneously. The visuals are fed into the machine, which provides the appropriate heat and pressure. You can then trim the excess film from around the visual with scissors or a paper cutter.

Filing and Storing

You will find it handy to have a system for filing, storing, and retrieving your visuals. The nature of the filing system that you use will depend on the number of visuals in your collection and the way you intend to use them. The simplest filing system usually involves grouping the items according to the teaching units in which they are used. Elementary teachers often categorize them by curriculum area (e.g., math, science, language arts, social studies) and then subdivide them by topic (e.g., seasons, countries, jobs, addition, subtraction, place value, telling time). Some instructors, especially those who teach just one subject, set up their filing sys-

Figure A.3
A laminating machine can laminate both sides of a visual simultaneously.

tem according to the chapters in their textbook, the topics they cover, or objectives. Teachers who use just a few visuals sometimes file them with their other teaching materials for each lesson.

In addition to a workable filing system and proper size storage containers, you should have a clean, out-of-the-way place to store your visuals when they are not in use. The storage location can range from elaborate built-in drawers or filing cabinets to simple cardboard storage cartons. There is no problem in using cardboard cartons to store files of pictures and other visuals if you have a clean, dry location for them.

MULTI-IMAGE PRESENTATIONS

Multi-image presentations continue to become ever more sophisticated and have survived the emergence of competitive technologies. The continuing viability of the multi-image system can be traced to its ability to present powerful, visually appealing effects. A **multi-image presentation** is, simply, any visual presentation showing several images simultaneously, often using multiple screens. Multi-image presentations may incorporate video but still visuals are used as their foundation.

Advantages

- *Combination of media.* Multi-image presentations combine the possibilities of a variety of media, such as slides, overhead transparencies, video, and digital images.
- *Special visual effects.* These presentations can show comparisons, time sequences, or wide-angle panoramic views.
- *Attention holder.* The rapidly changing images capture and hold learners' attention.
- *Emotional impact.* You can achieve dramatic effects by rapidly changing still pictures, which is possible with dissolve units and automatic programmers. Combined with appropriate music, multiple images can also set a mood.
- *Simulation of motion.* Multi-image presentations can simulate motion through rapid sequential projection of still pictures without the use of videotape. The production costs of multi-image presentations can be significantly less than that of video.

Limitations

- *Expensive to develop.* Development of multi-image materials requires considerable time and expertise because it requires more complex planning. Production time and costs can be high.

- *Time-consuming equipment setup.* The time to set up the presentation and align the projectors can also be significant. The amount of equipment required for their presentation increases the cost of using multi-image systems.
- *Hardware glitches.* Because multi-image presentations require several pieces of equipment, projectors, and programmers, there is a greater chance for problems to occur during the showing.

Integration

Multi-image presentations are heavily used in corporate communications—to impress visitors, to introduce new products at sales meetings, to review the year's accomplishments at stockholders' meetings. In the public sector, multi-image shows are commonly found at zoos, museums, and theme parks.

In education, multi-image presentations are usually locally produced for persuasive purposes—to enlist parent support for new programs, to heighten student awareness of issues such as drugs, to arouse interest in new classroom techniques. They can also serve instructional purposes by employing teaching-learning strategies such as the following:

- *Part/whole.* Showing a whole scene on one screen with a close-up of a detail beside it
- *Compare/contrast.* Showing two images side by side, for example, to allow comparison of art forms or architectural styles
- *Abstract/concrete.* Presenting a schematic diagram next to a photograph of a real object
- *Before/after.* Showing a house before and after remodeling
- *Sequencing.* Breaking down an athletic activity, such as diving, into a series of steps
- *Panorama.* Showing an outdoor scene with a sense of its full width
- *Three-dimensionality.* Presenting views of an object from several angles so viewers can imagine its three-dimensional qualities

PLANNING AUDIOVISUAL PRESENTATIONS

To plan a presentation that incorporates two or more media formats, such as visuals and audio, it is helpful to use a visual planning technique known as **storyboarding,** described in Chapter 4 under "Visual Planning Tools." See also "Sketching" in Section C. Detailed suggestions for planning your presentation are given in "Developing an Audiovisual Presentation" in Section C.

After you have developed a series of cards, lay them out on a table or place them on a storyboard holder. You place the cards in their tentative presentation order, thus giving you an overview of the production (Figure A.4). The storyboarding technique facilitates addition, deletion, replacement, revision, and refinement of the sequence because you can easily discard, add to, or rearrange the cards. The display of cards also allows others (teachers, students, production assistants) to look at the presentation in its planning stage. Number the cards in pencil; you may wish to change numbers as your planning progresses. You can photocopy several cards in sequence on a page for use with the final script, thus avoiding duplication of effort and providing a convenient assemblage of visuals, narration, and production notes.

Figure A.4
Storyboards are useful for planning and presenting rough drafts of your presentation.

Equipment and Setups

Outline

Most users of technology are not—and do not expect to become—electronic wizards, but they want to be able to use the hardware safely and effectively. The most fundamental elements of effective technology use are simply getting the equipment properly set up, keeping it running, and being ready to cope with snags, which always seem to occur at the most inopportune times.

This section provides guidelines for arranging equipment and facilities properly and hints for the safe care and handling of audiovisual equipment and computer hardware.

Safety

Safety is the paramount concern whenever teachers and students are using technology. Accidents involving heavy pieces of equipment can be serious, even fatal. The U.S. Consumer Product Safety Commission has noted at least four deaths of children and four serious injuries resulting from top-heavy projection carts that tipped over, dumping a heavy object onto the child. In seven cases the carts had a TV monitor on the top shelf, and the eighth had a film projector there. Particularly hazardous are carts over 50 inches (127 centimeters) high. With the increasing number of TV monitors being used in schools, this hazard is a growing concern.

All educators must be aware of their responsibility—and legal liability—regarding students' exposure to hazardous conditions. The operating rule

Figure B.1
The wrong way (left) and the correct way (right) to pick up heavy equipment.

today is to *NEVER allow children to move carts with heavy equipment on them.*

Adults, too, can sustain injuries from mishandling equipment. Many back injuries occur when people attempt to lift heavy objects by simply bending over, grasping the object, and pulling directly upward. This puts a strain on the lower back. The recommended procedure is to bend at the hips and knees, and lift upward with the *legs* providing upward spring, as shown in Figure B.1.

All educators must recognize that they serve as role models for safe practices when using technology. They thus have a special responsibility to know and practice good safety habits.

CARE AND HANDLING OF AUDIOVISUAL EQUIPMENT

Overhead Projectors

The overhead projector is a simple apparatus with few components requiring special maintenance procedures. Reliable as it is, however, you should not take it for granted. Rather, take a few basic precautions to ensure that the projector keeps putting on a bright performance.

Keep the overhead projector as clean as possible. The horizontal stage tends to gather dust, fingerprint smudges, and marking-pen traces. Clean it regularly with window spray or a mild solution of soap and water. The lens in the head assembly should also be kept free of dust and smudges. Clean it periodically with lens tissue and a proper lens-cleansing solution. The fresnel lens under the stage may also need cleaning eventually, but this procedure is better left to the equipment specialist. The lens is a precision optical element requiring special care. In addition, some disassembly of the unit is required to get at the lens.

The best way to prolong the life of the expensive lamp in the overhead projector is to allow it to cool before moving the projector (Figure B.2). Move the pro-

Figure B.2
Many overhead projectors are equipped with a spare lamp, which you can simply slide into place.

jector with care. Keep it on a cart that you can roll from one location to another. When hand-carrying the apparatus, hold onto the body of the projector, not the thin arm of the head assembly. The head assembly arm is not intended to be a carrying handle; used as such, it can easily be twisted out of alignment, thus distorting the projector's image.

Slide Projectors

With normal use, slide projectors require little special attention to keep working smoothly (Figure B.3). The only regular maintenance required of the user is to clean the front element of the projection lens if it shows finger marks. More likely to cause difficulties are the slides themselves, which you should always store away from heat and handle only by their mounts. The most frequent cause of foul-ups in slide presentations is a slide

Figure B.3
Slide projectors require little special attention.

that jams because it is warped or dogeared. Remount slides that could cause jams.

The Kodak Ektagraphic III projector has a number of desirable features not found on earlier models. For example, you can change the projection lamp from the rear of the projector without having to turn the projector over. There is a quick release on the elevation stand so you can raise the projected image without having to turn the adjustment knob many times by hand. In addition, the "Select" function allows you to turn the carousel tray when the power is off. Finally, the controls are on the side of the projector, where the operator usually stands.

Even though some current model projectors, such as the Ektagraphic III, do not project a distracting bright white square when there is not a slide in position, we still recommend that you include a dark slide at the beginning and end of your presentation. Solid plastic slides work best.

We highly recommend purchasing and using a carrying case for your slide projector if you will be moving the projector from location to location, especially from building to building. You should move slide projectors only on a projector cart or within a carrying case. The case provides a place to store the projector, tray, remote control unit, a spare lamp, and extension cords. The carrying case helps to keep all the accessories together, decreasing the chances for loss, as well as providing protection from damage and dust.

More serious damage can occur if the slide projector falls because it has been propped up precariously on top of a stack of books or on some other unstable base. This happens all too often because the projector's elevation leg seems never to be quite long enough to raise the image up to the top of the screen. It is better to use a higher projection table, raise the whole projection table, or raise the whole projector by placing it on a sturdy box or similar platform.

Projection Carts

Wheeled projection carts come in many different sizes and shapes suited to different types of equipment, as shown in Figure B.4. Carts are designed both for inside-only use and inside-outside use. You take a great risk in moving equipment out of doors on a cart designed for inside use. The small wheels can catch in cracks in the pavement and cause the cart to tip over. For this reason, even for exclusive indoor use it is wise to purchase carts with 5-inch wheels.

Manufacturers normally offer power outlet cord assemblies for their carts. These are worthwhile investments. You plug your projector into the outlet on the cart and the cord on the cart into the wall outlet. If someone should trip over the power cord, the cart moves but the projector does not crash to the floor. In

Figure B.4
The varied types of equipment carts are suited to different purposes.

addition, the cord on the cart is considerably longer than the typical power cord furnished with the projector. You can lay the longer cord on the floor along the wall, thereby reducing the risk that someone will trip over it.

The "Selection Rubric: Audiovisual Equipment" (page 337) provides some criteria to consider when appraising new audiovisual (AV) equipment. After purchase, there's still one major step before the process is complete—permanent identification. Most schools and other organizations identify their ownership of equipment with large, visible markings including the organization's name, address, and phone number plus an inventory number and even the lamp replacement number. Such information deters theft, simplifies taking inventory, and helps ensure using the correct replacement lamp, a great aid for the harried teacher.

AUDIO SETUPS

Speaker Placement

Most audiovisual equipment intended for use in educational settings comes equipped with a built-in speaker system. This kind of unit is suitable for many but not all instructional purposes. Small speakers built into the chassis of portable recorders, filmstrip projectors, and so on, often lack the fidelity necessary for audio clarity for a large audience area.

Portable cassette recorders are particularly troublesome when used for playback in an average-size classroom. Even under the best conditions, the sound quality of portable cassettes is severely limited by their undersized speakers. If you use such a unit to play back material in which audio fidelity is essential (e.g., a musical composition), use an auxiliary speaker if possible. You may be able to plug a high-efficiency speaker—for instance, one having a 6- or 8-inch diameter—into the external speaker jack or earphone jack of the cassette player to provide better fidelity.

Size alone, however, does not guarantee high-quality sound from a speaker. If you need high-fidelity audio, two-way speakers (bass and treble speaker in one cabinet) or three-way speakers (bass, midrange tweeter, and regular tweeter) are highly desirable. Such speakers may require an auxiliary amplifier when used in conjunction with AV equipment, but they are capable of reproducing the complete frequency range audible to humans.

Another problem with built-in speakers is that they are often built into the side of the machine containing the controls. This is fine when the operator of the tape recorder is also the listener. But if the apparatus is placed on a table or desk and operated by an instructor for the benefit of an audience, the speaker will be aimed away from the audience. The simple remedy for this situation is to turn the machine around so that the speaker faces the audience and operates the controls from beside rather than in front of the machine.

If you are operating in a lecture hall or auditorium that has a built-in public address system, you will want to plug your audio source into that system. This might require an adapter to match up the output plug and input jack.

The detachable speakers that accompany some stereo tape recorders are generally large and sensitive enough to provide adequate sound quality throughout the instructional area if, as with other separate speaker systems, you give consideration to their individual placement.

Whenever possible, face speakers toward the center of your audience. If reverberation is a problem, however, especially in long narrow rooms, aim the speaker diagonally across the audience to help alleviate this situation.

Be sure nothing obstructs the sound waves as they travel from the speaker toward your audience. Classroom furniture (e.g., desks, chairs) and the audience itself may present physical obstructions to sound. To avoid such interference, place the speaker on a table or some other kind of stand so that it is at or above the head level of your seated audience.

In summary, the rules of thumb for speaker placement are as follows:

- Face speaker toward the center of the audience.
- Place speaker near the screen.
- Raise speaker to head level of seated audience.

If you are using a stereophonic system, the speakers should be far enough apart so that the sound is appropriately balanced between the two. As a rule of thumb, the distance between the speakers should equal the distance from each speaker to the middle of the audience. Thus, in the typical 22-by-30-foot classroom, place stereo speakers about 15 feet apart, or nearly in the corners of the room.

Microphone Handling and Placement

Microphones should be placed at least 6 inches (15 centimeters) from the presenter's mouth. Placed closer to the mouth, the microphone is likely to pick up "pops" and "hisses" when the presenter says words with plosive or sibilant sounds. As shown in Figures B.5 and B.6 place the microphone below the mouth so that the presenter

Figure B.5
A hand-held microphone should be held at a 45-degree angle and below the mouth.

Figure B.6
Clip a lavaliere microphone to the presenter's clothing below the mouth.

Selection Rubric: Audiovisual Equipment

Complete an interactive evaluation and add it to your NETS-T portfolio using the Selection Rubric for Audiovisual Equipment available on the "Classroom Link Portfolio" CD-ROM. A downloadable version of this rubric is available in the Selection Rubrics module of the Companion Website at http://www.prenhall.com/smaldino.

Type _____   Price _____

Manufacturer _____   Model _____

Audio

Speaker Size _____   Amplifier Output _____

Inputs   Outputs

_____   _____

_____   _____

Sound Controls   Tape

_____   Size _____

_____   Speeds _____ Tracks _____

Other Features

Projector

Lamp _____ Wattage _____ Exciter Lamp _____

Power Controls   Lamp Level Control

_____   _____

_____   _____

Lens _____

Other Features

Strong Points

Weak Points

Recommended Action (using criteria on the following page)

Name _____ Date _____

Rating Area	High Quality	Medium Quality	Low Quality	Rating
Sound Quality	Clear & distinct with excellent range of volume & tone	Some distortion, but good range of volume & tone	Static and distortion in range of volume & tone	
Picture Quality	Clear & distinct with excellent color & resolution	Some distortion, but acceptable color & resolution	Blurred with color distortion & poor resolution	
Ease of Operation	Easy to use without referring to manual	Use is fairly obvious, requiring some referral to manual	Difficult to use, requiring frequent referral to manual	
Price Range	Excellent value per dollar spent compared to other models	Fair value per dollar spent compared to other models	Poor value per dollar spent compared to other models	
Durability	Appears very durable; other users report high dependability	Questionable durability; other users report some problems	Does not appear durable; other users report low dependability	
Ease to Maintain	Low-level maintenance; very little servicing required	Medium-level maintenance; some servicing required	High-level maintenance; frequent servicing required	
Ease to Repair	Parts easily accessible & replacement parts readily available	Parts fairly accessible & replacement parts somewhat available	Parts difficult to access & replacement parts not readily available	

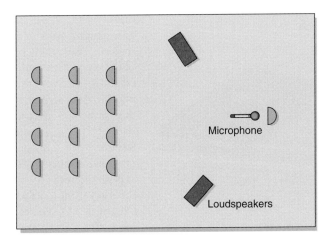

Figure B.7
To avoid feedback, keep the microphone behind the speakers.

Figure B.8
A quiet corner of a classroom may be set aside as a listening center.

talks across it rather than into it. The rule of thumb for microphone placement, then, is to place the microphone *below* and at least six inches *away from* the mouth.

Feedback is that annoying squeal that sometimes intrudes when using public address systems. The usual cause is simple: the signal coming out of the loudspeaker is fed back into the microphone. The most direct remedy is to make sure to set up the speakers in front of the microphone, as shown in Figure B.7. If you experience feedback, here are possible solutions:

- Place the microphone behind the speaker(s) or move the speaker(s) in front of the microphone.
- If neither step is possible, adjust the volume and tone controls to reduce the interference.

Listening Centers

Many classrooms, especially at the elementary level, are arranged in a more open form with flexible furnishings to allow diverse yet simultaneous activities. In such a classroom, learning centers are a common format for learning. One popular type of learning center is a listening center, an area especially set up for audio media. Listening centers can be set up to accommodate either an individual student or a small group, as shown in Figure B.8.

You should situate a listening center away from noisy areas or at least partially enclose it to reduce visual and auditory distractions. If intended for an individual, you will probably equip it with an audiocassette player or a CD player with a headset. Older types of headsets are designed to close the listener off from all room sounds except those coming from the player. Newer ones, referred to as "hear-through" or dynamic velocity headsets, allow the listener to hear ambient sounds in the room also.

For a small group, the listening center would typically contain a CD or cassette player and should be

equipped with a multiple headset device that allows up to eight headsets to connect to a single source.

DUPLICATING AND EDITING AUDIOTAPES

It is a relatively simple procedure to duplicate an audiotape. You can duplicate your tapes by one of three methods: the acoustic method, the electronic method, and the high-speed duplicator method.

The acoustic method (Figure B.9) does not require any special equipment, just two recorders. One recorder plays the original tape, and the sound is transferred via a microphone to a blank tape on the other recorder. The drawback of this method is that fidelity is reduced as the sound travels through the air to the microphone, and the open microphone may pick up unwanted noise from the environment.

The electronic method avoids this problem (Figure B.10). The signal travels from the original tape to the recorder via an inexpensive patch cord. The cord is attached to the output of the first machine and the "line," or auxiliary input, of the second. It picks up the signals of the original tape and transfers them electronically to the duplicating tape.

If a dual-well cassette recorder, which holds two cassettes, is available, you can easily copy tapes. Many of these machines can copy a tape at double normal speed, cutting duplicating time in half; however, be sure to check the copy for speed accuracy. Inexpensive dual-well equipment is not noted for its precision; a full-size dual-well tape deck is much more reliable.

The high-speed duplicator method requires a special machine. Master playback machines have a series of up

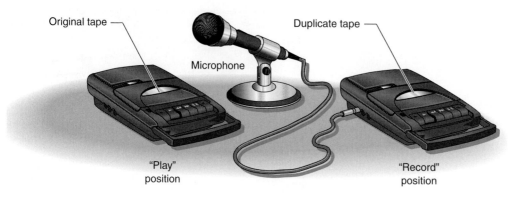

Figure B.9
Setup for duplicating by the acoustic method.

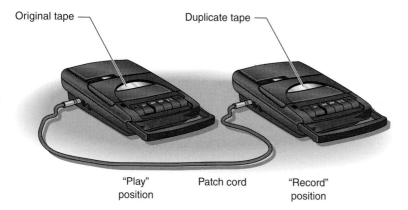

Figure B.10
Setup for duplicating by the electronic method.

to 10 "slave units," each of which can record a copy of the original tape at 16 times its normal speed. These machines can, for example, create multiple copies of a 30-minute cassette tape in about 2 minutes. Since the master and slave units are connected by a patch cord, fidelity is likely to be very good, and there is no danger of picking up background noise.

You may wish to edit your audiotapes, either to remove errors and imperfections or to adapt a tape to a specific learning situation. Set up two recorders as described for tape duplication and then record just the portion of the original tape that you want on the second tape.

The dual-well cassette recorder facilitates editing. You can easily assemble selected parts of the original by using the copying feature of these machines.

PROJECTOR SETUPS

Screen Alignment

The first requirement in projector placement is to align the projection lens perpendicular to the screen (i.e., it

must make a 90-degree angle with the screen). Thus, the lens of the projector should be about level with the middle of the screen. If the projector is too high, too low, or off to either side, a distortion of the image will occur, referred to as the **keystone effect** (Figure B.11). The effect takes its name from the typical shape of a keystoned image—wide at the top, narrower at the bottom, like a keystone. To remedy this situation, move either the projector or the screen to bring the two into a perpendicular relationship (see "Eliminating the Keystone Effect" in Section C).

The keystone effect is especially prevalent with the overhead projector because it is ordinarily set up very close to the screen and lower than the center of the screen to allow the instructor to write on its stage. For this reason many screens used for overhead projection are equipped with a "keystone eliminator," a notched bar at the top that allows the screen to be tilted forward (Figure B.12).

Projector Distance

Once you have properly aligned the projector and screen, consider the distance between them. If the dis-

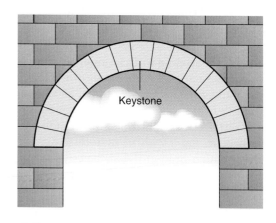

Figure B.11
The "keystone effect" describes a projected image that resembles the architectural keystone, the wedge-shaped stone at the top of a rounded arch that locks its parts together.

Figure B.12
Portable tripod screen with keystone eliminator.

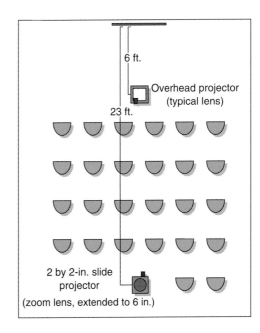

Figure B.13
Approximate placement of projectors when used with typical lenses and screen.

tance is too long, the image may spill over the edges of a given screen. If it is too short, the image will not fill the same screen properly. Your goal is to fill the screen as fully as possible with the brightest image possible. The principle to remember here is that the image becomes larger and less brilliant with an increase in distance between the projector and screen. Here are the rules of thumb:

- If the projected image is *too large* for your screen, push the projector *closer.*
- If the image is *too small,* pull the projector back.

Positioning a projector at the proper distance from the screen need not be done solely by trial and error. Because classroom-type projectors usually are fitted with certain focal length lenses, you may estimate their proper placement in advance. Figure B.13 shows the placement of overhead and slide projectors when they are equipped with their most typical lenses.

The projection distances described here assume appropriate lighting conditions. Where the room light is so bright that it is washing out the screen image and you cannot dim it any further, you must move the projector forward. This will give you a brighter image but also a smaller one. In some cases, however, you may be able to compensate for this reduction in image size by having your audience move closer to the screen.

Power Cords

It is best to place all projectors, except the overhead, behind the audience to minimize the number of people stepping over the power cords. For the same reason, use extension cords so that the power cords can run along the wall to the outlet rather than across the center of the room. Any cord that lies where someone might trip over it should do so only temporarily, and you should firmly tape it down during that time.

All modern audiovisual equipment is made with a grounded plug; you should use a matching extension cord. The outlets in older buildings may not be made for grounded plugs, so you will need to use a three-prong adapter to connect newer equipment. Extension cords are made to serve different purposes—indoor and outdoor, higher and lower power capacity. Whenever using an extension cord, be sure that you are not exceeding its power capacity. If in doubt, consult a media specialist.

Lamps

Types. There are three types of projection lamps: incandescent, tungsten halogen, and tungsten halogen with surrounding reflector. You should watch incandescent lamps because they have a tendency to blister; such blisters can become so big that the lamp cannot be removed from the projector. If the lamp does blister to the extent that it must be broken for removal, contact an audiovisual technician.

The first innovative response to incandescent blistering was the tungsten halogen lamp. These lamps do not blister, but they do require the same high wattage and thus have the associated heat problems and fan noise.

The newest type of lamp is the tungsten halogen lamp with surrounding reflector. These lamps generally operate at one-half the wattage of incandescent and tungsten halogen lamps.

Coding. Projection lamps are labeled with a three-letter ANSI (American National Standards Institute) code, which is printed on the lamp and on the box. In addition, many projectors now have stickers in the lamp housing with the ANSI code stating which lamp should be used in that projector.

Replacing Lamps. Replacement lamps should have the same ANSI code or an authorized substitute. Substitutes can be found in replacement guides written by the lamp manufacturers; these are available from the manufacturers or from local audiovisual dealers. Do not use higher-wattage lamps than specified—you might burn the materials in the projector!

Handling. When handling a lamp, *never* touch the clear glass bulb. The oil from your fingers can shorten the life of the lamp. Always manipulate the lamp by its base. Incandescent lamps and tungsten halogen lamps (without exterior reflector) are supplied with a piece of foam or paper around the lamp. Use this material or a cloth to hold the lamp when inserting it into the projector.

When removing a burned-out lamp, wait until the lamp has cooled to prevent burning your fingers. It is wise to always use a cloth when removing a lamp. Even a lamp that burns out when the projector is first turned on will be hot enough to burn you.

Expense. Lamps for audiovisual equipment are expensive. They usually cost about 20 times the cost of a household light bulb. Because the average lamp life is only 50 hours, turn off projectors when not using them. If the projector offers a low lamp setting, use it if possible to increase the life of the lamp. Try not to jar a projector when the lamp is on, as this can cause a premature burnout of the lamp. You should *not* leave the fan on for cooling after use unless the projector is going to be moved immediately, as this also will shorten the life of the bulb.

Lenses

For everyday media use, you do not have to pay much attention to technicalities about lenses. Whatever lens your projector is equipped with is usually sufficient. However, understanding some basic ideas about lenses can help you cope with extraordinary situations.

First, lenses vary in focal length (measured in inches in the United States, in millimeters elsewhere). The **focal length** is the distance from the focal point of the lens to the image plane when the lens is focused on infinity. Remember, the *longer* the focal length, the *smaller* the image at a given distance. Your objective is to project an image that will fill the screen, so the shorter the projection throw, the shorter the lens (in terms of focal length) you will need to enlarge the pro-

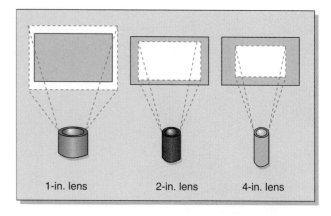

Figure B.14
The longer the focal length of the lens, the smaller the image.

jected image sufficiently. Fortunately, the actual length of most lenses corresponds roughly with their focal length; the longer of two lenses will have the longer focal length. Figure B.14 illustrates the relationship between the lens and the size of its projected image.

One type of lens has a variable focal length—the zoom lens. You can adjust it to cast a larger or smaller picture without moving the projector or changing its lens. The most commonly encountered zoom lens (found on many slide projectors) has a focal length range of 4 to 6 inches.

Screens

Arranging a proper environment for viewing projected visuals involves several variables, including screen size, type of screen surface, and screen placement. In most cases you will have to deal with only a couple of these variables. For everyday teaching situations your classroom will often be equipped with a screen of a certain type attached in a fixed position.

There may be times, however, when you will have to make decisions about any or all of these screen variables. For example, let's assume the room you are to use for projecting visuals is 22 feet wide and 30 feet long, a fairly typical size for a classroom. Let's further assume that you must arrange seating for between 30 and 40 viewers, a fairly typical audience size. Figure B.15 illustrates a conventional seating pattern for a group of this size (in this case, 30 viewers). Note that the seats are arranged across the narrower room dimension. If the seats were turned to face the left or right side of the room and arranged across its 30-foot length, viewers along either end of the rows would have a distorted view of the screen. Note too that the first row of seats is set back somewhat from the desk area, where the screen is to be set up, so that front-row students will not be too close to the screen for comfortable viewing.

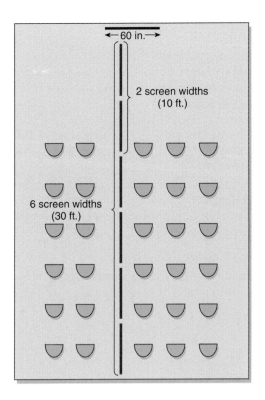

Figure B.15
Appropriate screen size for the typical-size classroom according to the two-by-six rule.

Screen Size.   A rule of thumb for the relationship between screen size and viewer seating is called the *two-by-six* rule: No viewer should be seated closer to the screen than *two* screen widths or farther away than *six* screen widths.

This means that in our hypothetical case, in which the farthest viewer could be 30 feet from the front of the room, a screen about 5 feet wide (60 inches) would be required to ensure that this farthest-away viewer is within six screen widths of the screen ($30 \div 6 = 5$). A square screen is generally preferable because you can use it to show rectangular images (slides, filmstrips, etc.) as well as square images (overhead projections). Thus, in this case a screen measuring 60 by 60 inches is recommended (see Figure B.15).

With a zoom lens on a carousel slide projector or a 16mm projector, you can put the projector at the rear of any normal-size classroom and fill a 70-inch screen.

Screen Placement.   In most cases placement of the screen at the center in the front of the room will be satisfactory. In some cases, however, it may not be. Perhaps light from a win-

dow that you cannot fully cover will wash out the projected image (sunlight is much brighter than any artificial light), or maybe you wish to use the chalkboard during your presentation and a screen position in the center front will make it difficult or impossible for you to do so. Also, the screen should not be at center stage if it will attract unwanted attention while nonprojection activities are going on. An alternative position is in a front corner of the room. In any case, nowhere is it written in stone that the screen must be placed front and center. Position your screen wherever it will best suit your purpose.

In general, adjust the height of the screen so that the bottom of the screen is about level with the heads of the seated viewers. The bottom of the screen should be at least 4 feet above the floor to prevent excessive head interference (Figure B.16). Other inhibiting factors aside, this arrangement will allow reasonably clear sight lines for the most viewers. In general, the higher the screen, the greater the optimal viewing area. Of course, you must take care that viewers can see the screen without uncomfortably craning their necks.

VIDEO SETUPS

Before students can learn from any material presented on a video monitor, they first have to be able to see and hear it! This means providing proper seating arrangements, placement of the monitor, lighting, and volume control.

Seating

For group showings, an ideal seating arrangement may sometimes be difficult to achieve. In some cases there are simply not enough monitors available to seat all students in the most desirable viewing area. It may be possible to have students move closer together to get more people into the desirable viewing area. Try to stagger the seats to reduce blocked sight lines.

Figure B.16
The bottom of the screen should be above head level to avoid obstruction of the view.

Here are some basic rules of thumb for seating:

- The total number of viewers should be no more than the number of inches of screen size. For example, for a 23-inch monitor, the largest number of viewers would be 23.
- Seat no one closer than twice the *inches* of screen size. For example, for a 23-inch monitor, the closest viewer would be 46 inches (or about four feet) from the screen.
- Seat no one farther *in feet* than the size of the screen in inches. For example, for a 23-inch monitor, the farthest viewer would be 23 feet away. (The maximum viewing distance would be much smaller if the lesson included details that were critical to learning.)

Monitor Placement

In addition to distance from the screen, you must consider viewing angles—both up and down and side to side. As shown in Figure B.17, the monitor placement should require no more than 30 degrees of head tilt. In general, a 54-inch-high monitor provides a good viewing angle for group viewing. In terms of side-to-side angles, no viewer should be located more than 45 degrees from the center line.

Lighting

Video monitors should be viewed in normal or dim light, not darkness. Besides being more comfortable to the eye, normal illumination provides necessary light for student participative activities (e.g., for referring to handouts and for note taking).

Locate the television receiver so that harsh light from a window or light fixture does not strike the screen and cause glare. Do not place the receiver in front of an unshaded window that will compete with light from the television screen and make viewing difficult.

The rules of thumb for lighting conditions for video monitors are as follows:

- View in normal or dim light.
- Avoid direct light on the screen, causing glare.
- Avoid sunlight behind monitor.

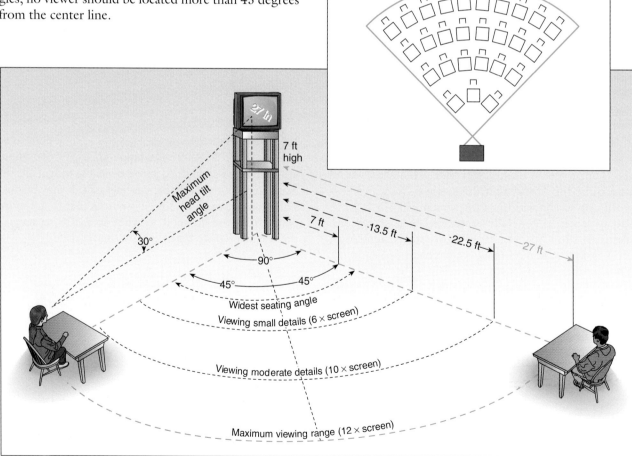

Figure B.17
Recommended monitor placement and seating distances for TV viewing.

Volume

For proper hearing, set the volume of the receiver loud enough to be heard clearly in the rear of the viewing area but not so loud that it bowls over those in the front. Normally this happy middle ground is not difficult to achieve if your seating arrangement is within acceptable bounds and your receiver's speaker mechanism is functioning properly.

Obviously, you should keep the volume low enough so as not to disturb neighboring classes. Unfortunately, open-plan buildings with only movable room dividers as walls provide a poor environment for TV and other audiovisual presentations. Under such conditions, cooperation is critical. Teachers in neighboring areas can agree to lower their sound level to minimize interference (this is better than escalating the problem by trying to drown each other out!). Sometimes the only alternative is to seek an enclosed room that can be reserved for audiovisual use.

Projected Video

Ordinary video monitors are well suited to individual or small-group viewing but not to large-group situations. Large groups require multiple monitors for adequate viewing, and playing a video recording also requires wires to connect the video player with each of the monitors. A better option in such cases is the video projector. (See "Operating a Video Projector" in Section C.) In addition to being used for showing television images, they can also be used for showing computer data, text, and graphics.

Tabletop video projectors can project an image large enough to fill a screen up to 4 by 6 feet. Units that may be permanently mounted at ceiling level or placed on low carts are used for larger screens. The smaller units require less setup adjustment and may have a video playback unit built in (Figure B.18).

The larger units require color focusing adjustments whenever they are moved. They have three color "guns," and all three images must converge precisely to have a clear image without color fringes.

Other than the special focusing considerations, projected video setups follow the size, seating, and placement rules for other sorts of projection onto a screen.

The rules of thumb for lighting conditions for video projection are as follows:

- View in dim light or darkness.
- Seat audiences as close as possible to the center of the screen.
- Make sure that all can see the image clearly.

COMPUTER SETUPS

You may arrange computers and computer workstations in an infinite variety of configurations, depending on how

Figure B.18
Projection with a ceiling-mounted data-and-video projector.

many computers you use in a room and for what purposes. The setups described are meant to show how to get the most out of each situation. A number of typical situations were illustrated in Chapter 5, each showing a different number of computers being used in different ways (see Figures 5.19 through 5.22). Two additional setups are shown in Figures B.19 and B.20.

Figure B.19
A computer setup for collaborative learning.

Figure B.20
This teaching station can accommodate individual and small-group use or large-group presentations.

COMPUTER HARDWARE SELECTION

It is becoming increasingly common for instructors to be involved in the selection of instructionally related computer hardware for their institution. This section will give you at least some general guidelines for participating intelligently in such a selection process.

Analyzing Needs

The first step in evaluating and selecting computer hardware is to identify the need for the hardware. Why are you buying the computer? What software are you planning to use on the system? Without identifying specific needs for the hardware, you may hastily purchase an inadequate system or one more elaborate than you could ever use.

The selection of computer software is the most important first step in the selection of hardware. Computer hardware is no better than the software that drives it. Without software a computer will not function. The computer's utility may be limited by an inadequate quantity or quality of available software. A computer may have great features, but they are of little value if there is no software to take advantage of them.

On the other hand, it is difficult for computer software to overcome hardware limitations. Since software written for one computer may not run on another computer, make sure software is currently available for the computer you are interested in.

The computer hardware industry is changing so rapidly that you cannot base hardware selection decisions solely on present needs. You must consider future software and hardware needs. By purchasing hardware with significant limitations, you are unlikely to be able to take advantage of new advancements without purchasing new hardware. It is difficult to make selection decisions for the present and an unknown future. To prevent unexpected problems, it is important to look at the past performance of the hardware company from which you intend to purchase. Is the company financially stable? Are other institutions using the same equipment? Is the company committed to supporting their equipment?

Compatibility

The next major factor in selecting computer hardware is compatibility with previously purchased equipment. However, do not allow yourself to be trapped by equipment that can never meet your needs. If a change is required, it is often better to make it sooner than later. What other computers do you have currently? What operating system do the other computers use? Is there a need for exchanging files and programs among different hardware? If so, mixing several different computers may make it difficult. In addition to being compatible with other systems currently in use, the new hardware components must be compatible with each other. Can you use a monitor from one manufacturer with a particular computer of a different make? Although some feel that it is cheaper to order various components from a catalog, you must beware that not all components are necessarily compatible. Get specific assurance of compatibility from the vendor.

Expandability

Expandability is also an important consideration when purchasing a computer system. You don't want the announcement of a new model shortly after your purchase to render your equipment obsolete. Nor do you want to buy a system that is sufficient for your current needs but that you cannot upgrade to accommodate your growing ambitions. To protect yourself, be sure that the system you purchase has the ports and slots to accommodate additional memory, additional disk drives, audio or video enhancement, and the like. (A *port* is an outlet on a computer where the user can plug in a peripheral. A *slot* is an area in the computer where the user can add additional electronic boards or cards for specific purposes.)

Selection Rubric: Computer Hardware

Complete an interactive evaluation and add it to your NETS-T portfolio using the Selection Rubric for Computer Hardware available on the "Classroom Link Portfolio" CD-ROM. A downloadable version of this rubric is available in the Selection Rubrics module of the Companion Website at http://www.prenhall.com/smaldino.

Manufacturer _____

Model _____

Monitor _____ **Graphics** _____

Sound _____ **Memory** _____ **Expandable** _____ **Hard Drive** _____

Peripherals _____

Other Features

Strong Points

Weak Points

Recommended Action (using criteria on the following page)

Name _____ **Date** _____

Rating Area	High Quality	Medium Quality	Low Quality	Rating
Ease of Operation	Easy to use without referring to manual/help screens	Use is fairly obvious, requiring some referral to manual/help screens	Difficult to use without referring frequently to manual/help screens	
Durability & Reliability	Appears very durable; other users report high dependability and reliability	Questionable durability; other users report some problems	Does not appear durable; other users report low dependability and reliability	
Availability of Software	Can utilize most of the software that is currently available and will be purchased	Can utilize some of the software that is currently available and will be purchased	Cannot utilize most of the software that is currently available and will be purchased	
Monitor Display Quality	Image resolution is clear and crisp; colors are accurate; moving images display with little or no jerkiness or distortion	Image resolution is mostly clear and crisp; colors are reasonably accurate; moving images display with minimal jerkiness or distortion	Image resolution is not clear and crisp; colors are not accurate; moving images display with jerkiness or distortion	
Keyboard Layout & Touch	Size of keyboard and location of keys appropriate for intended users	Keyboard useable by intended users, but "feel" is not the best	Size of keyboard too large or too small for intended users	
Compatibility	Compatible with previously purchased hardware and peripherals	Some compatibility problems with purchased hardware and peripherals	Not compatible with previously purchased hardware and peripherals	
Expandability	Can be upgraded to meet future needs; has ports and slots for expansion	Allows for some upgrade to meet future needs; has some ports and slots for expansion	Cannot be upgraded to meet future needs; has limited ports and slots for expansion	
Documentation	User's manual and help screens easy to understand; includes index & table of contents	User's manual and help screens lack completeness; includes limited index & table of contents	Confusing user's manual and help screens; lacks good index & table of contents	
Service	Vendor support & maintenance readily available; service is quick & dependable	Vendor support & maintenance is available, but takes time & is not always dependable	Vendor support & maintenance is lacking; service is slow & undependable	

Documentation

The documentation, or user's manual, must be easy for you to understand. It should have an extensive index and table of contents to allow easy access to the information. The documentation should include complete, clear, easy-to-read diagrams showing the various parts of your system and how to put them together.

Service

Be sure the hardware company you buy from is committed to supporting and maintaining the equipment you plan to purchase. How long has its service center been established? You may want to talk with others who have used their service. Were they satisfied? Was service prompt? Finding someone to service computers often becomes a difficult and frustrating experience. Sometimes you have to ship hardware to a service location, thus being inconvenienced for a time. If shipping is required, do you have easy access to shipping locations nearby or will the shipping service pick up your packages?

A maintenance contract also may be a consideration when purchasing hardware. Such a contract may vary in cost from a few dollars a month for each machine to many times that amount. However, most personal computer systems tend to be reliable. Most failures and problems occur during the warranty period. Once through the warranty period, breakdowns are infrequent as long as you take proper care of your equipment. The actual cost of the repairs may be cheaper than the cost of a maintenance contract.

In comparing models, many different criteria should be considered. The "Selection Rubric: Computer Hardware" includes the most important criteria for selecting a computer for instructional uses. The weighting of the criteria may vary depending on the specifics of your particular situation.

Suggested Readings

Anshel, Jeffrey. 1994. Visual ergonomics in the workplace: How to use a computer and save your eyesight. *Performance and Instruction 33*(5): 20–22.

Barron, Ann E., and Gary W. Orwig. 1997. *New technologies for education: A beginner's guide,* 3rd ed. Englewood, CO: Libraries Unlimited.

Hofstetter, Fred T. 1993. Design and construction of a multimedia technology cart. *TechTrends, 38*(2): 22–24.

International Communication Industries Association. 2003–2004. *The directory of video, multimedia, and audio-visual products.* Annual; text and CD-ROM. Fairfax, VA: Author.

Novak, Paul. 1993. How to use media equipment. In *The ASTD handbook of instructional technology,* edited by G. M. Piskurich. New York: McGraw-Hill.

Sherry, Annette C., and Allan Strojny. 1993. Design for safety: The audiovisual cart hazard revisited. *Educational Technology, 33*(12): 2–47.

How To . . .
Step-by-Step Guides

351

How To . . .
Step-by-Step Guides for Technology, Media, and Learning

DEVELOPING MEDIA PORTFOLIOS

Following are guidelines for the use of portfolios:

- Many different skills and techniques are needed to produce an effective portfolio. Students need models of finished portfolios as well as examples of how others develop and reflect on them.
- Students should be involved in selecting the pieces to be included in their portfolios. This promotes reflection on their part.
- A portfolio should convey the following: *rationale* (purpose for forming the portfolio), *intents* (its goals), *contents* (the actual displays), *standards* (what are good and not-so-good performances), and *judgments* (what the contents tell the viewer).
- Portfolios should contain examples that illustrate growth.
- Student self-reflection and self-evaluation can be promoted by having students ask themselves the following questions: What makes this my best work? How did I go about creating it? What problems did I encounter? What makes my best piece different from my weakest piece?
- Date all pieces so that viewers may note progress over time.
- Students should regularly be given time to read and reorganize their portfolios.
- The portfolio should be organized, inviting, and manageable. Plan a storage system that is convenient for both you and your students.
- Students should be aware of the criteria used for evaluating the portfolio.

Source: Adapted from Instructional Technology for Teaching and Learning, *2d ed. (p. 229), by Timothy J. Newby, Donald A. Stepich, James D. Lehman, and James D. Russell, copyright 2000 by Merrill/Prentice Hall. Reprinted by permission of the publisher.*

How To . . .
Step-by-Step Guides for Using Instructional Systems

ANALYZING OR DESIGNING AN INSTRUCTIONAL SYSTEM

This worksheet can be used to analyze an existing instructional system or to design a new instructional system. When designing an instructional system, select from the components and characteristics below. (Note: Selecting the appropriate instructional system can affect the *quality* and the *cost* of instruction.)

COMPONENTS

Objective What is to be learned (knowledge, skills, attitudes)?

_____

Method What method(s) is/could be used?

_____

Media What media are/could be incorporated?

_____

Equipment What equipment is/are required?

_____

Environment What facilities/setting is/will be used?

_____

People Who is/will be involved in the instruction?

_____

CHARACTERISTICS

Direction Is instruction one way or two way?

_____

Synchronicity Is/will instruction be in real time or at different times?

_____

Group size How many learners are there?

_____

Time How much time is available?

_____

Location Is/will instruction be available at one location or different locations?

_____

Costs What are the development, purchase, and/or delivery costs?

_____

CONDUCTING A DEBRIEFING: THE FOUR-D PROCEDURE

GROUP DEBRIEFING

It is usually preferable to conduct a **debriefing** as a group discussion if time and conditions permit. As an aid in planning for this stage, follow the "Four Ds of Debriefing":

1. Decompressing
2. Describing
3. Drawing comparisons
4. Deriving lessons

Step 1: Decompressing (feelings)

You will want to relieve any tensions that may have built up during the simulation or game. Some situations may engender conflict and anger. Also, players who feel they did not do very well in the game may be experiencing anxiety and feelings of inadequacy. In any event, participants are not likely to be focusing on _your_ questions and concerns until these pent-up feelings simmer down to a manageable level.

Start with some "safety valve" questions. In games, players will have attained some sort of score, so you can start simply by asking for and recording the scores. Jot down scores on a chalkboard or flip chart. Also note comments. These bits of information form a database you can refer to in later stages of debriefing.

After tabulating these scores you will be able to declare the winner(s) in cases of competitive games. Let the winner(s) show off a little bit by asking them to explain their strategy. Low scorers should also have a chance to tell what went wrong for them, if they wish.

At this point be sure to explain any hidden agendas or "tricks" the designer may have inserted to make a certain point. Explain how these may have affected the scores. Also, point out the role that chance can play in the scoring, as it does in real life.

To deal further with any emotional residue, ask several participants how they felt while playing. Did anyone else feel that way, too? Let those who want to chime in freely.

Step 2: Describing (facts)

You usually will have explained the nature and purpose of the activity before the beginning of play. But some students may not have fully appreciated the meaning or significance of the activity.

Others may have lost track of it in the heat of play. For example, players of _Triangle Trade_ might need to be reminded that it simulates the experiences of seventeenth-century British colonists. Ask basic questions such as, "What real-life situation was represented in this activity?" or "What was [x] intended to symbolize?"

Step 3: Drawing Comparisons (transfer)

Help the participants transfer the game experiences to reality. Encourage them to compare and contrast the game with reality by asking such questions as, "How does the scoring system compare with real-life rewards?" "What elements of reality were missing from or downplayed in the simulation?" "Would these solutions work in real life?"

Step 4: Deriving Lessons (application)

Get the participants to verbalize exactly what they have learned from the activity. Verbalization will bring to students conscious awareness of what they have learned. Ask questions such as, "What conclusions can you draw from the experience?" "What did you learn about specific real-life problems?" "Did the activity change any of your previous attitudes or opinions?" "What do you plan to do differently tomorrow as a result of this activity?"

Individual Debriefing

In situations where participants finish simulation or game activities at different times or the schedule prevents immediate group discussion, you may use a form of individual debriefing. One method developed to help participants reflect on their feelings immediately after play uses a simple sentence-completion form to be filled out individually. Each participant writes a completion to each of the following sentences:

1. I was _____. [the role you played in the game]
2. I did _____. [actions you performed]
3. I felt _____. [emotions you felt during play]
4. I wish _____. [open response]

The reactions captured on this form can either substitute for group discussion or can supplement the later discussion, with participants referring back to their sheets to remind themselves of their reactions.

How To . . .
Step-by-Step Guides for Visual Principles

USING COLOR IN INSTRUCTIONAL MATERIALS

Pett and Wilson (1996) provide the following guidelines for the use of color in instructional materials:

- Use color to add reality.
- Use color to discriminate between elements of a visual.
- Use color to focus attention on relevant cues.
- Use colors to code and link logically related elements.
- Be consistent in general color choices throughout materials.
- Use colors such as highly saturated red and violet to attract attention and to create emotional response.
- Use highly saturated colors for materials intended for young children.

- Consider accepted color meanings such as red and yellow are warm, green and blue are cool, red means stop, green means go, etc.
- When producing materials for persons from varied cultures consider the meanings they attribute to colors.

Adapted from Dennis Pett and Trudy Wilson, "Color Research and its Application to the Design of Instructional Materials," Educational Technology Research and Development, 44, *no. 3 (1996), p. 31.*

DESIGNING COMPUTER SCREENS

Assemble the Elements

- Consider the relatively low resolution of computer screens (compared to print) and keep individual elements clean and simple.
- Remember to include features that allow learners control over the pace of the programs.
- Rewrite text to fit the smaller space available on screen; avoid breaking sentences across screens.

Profiles in Freedom

Title is 22 point Helvetica bold in white on black for strong contrast.

Next   Previous   Home   Main Menu

Navigation buttons use standard symbols and text labels for clarity.

Harriet Tubman

itkdksl lskd lskd ls kdlsaldk eiuryv eiwos id ths eiskdp sie itur sidf md is ie alsk dkfu lsldfod oriytdsl is isk it wlwlw dkaw woei lsldif lsldka is thelsld sid s als dka kd a skd sldk jdksk alsk seeu sa slie pwie oriytueo wplkdjf dkks a dks aljkskdield

Images are scanned using a consistent palette and sized or cropped to similar dimensions.

Text fields use serif typeface in a minimum size of 12 points for legibility; line length is 2/3 screen or less with wide margins for readability.

Click Main Menu for more profiles.

On-screen instructions are written in active voice and avoid "cute" or overly familiar tone.

Choose Background and Underlying Pattern

- Use subdued color for large areas to avoid distraction.
- Establish areas of the screen where types of information appear consistently throughout the program.

Text area "anchors" the display on the left and helps balance the large illustrations.

Button area is separate from the content presentations.

A subdued tone is chosen for the large background space; in this program the light sepia tone will help convey a sense of history.

Title area is at top of screen where viewer begins to scan the display.

Graphics area is equivalent in size to the text area since the illustrations play an important role in appealing to the viewers.

Arrange the Elements

- Place navigation elements so learners don't have to cross content areas too often in order to control the program.
- Remember to align elements and consider their proximity to related elements.

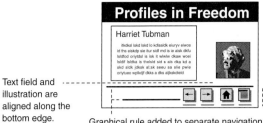

Text field and illustration are aligned along the bottom edge.

Navigation buttons are aligned with each other and the edge of the graphic.

Graphical rule added to separate navigation buttons from content areas more clearly.

On-screen instruction is grouped with navigation.

Check and Revise

- Make a technical review once the elements are assembled, since their interrelationships are an important part of your design.
- Observe viewers of program to assess the effectiveness of your design.

Title text was dominating the screen; reversing the contrast shifts focus back to text and graphic.

On-screen instruction is in close proximity to the appropriate button.

Navigation buttons for leaving the program and leaving the section are grouped together.

Types of navigation are separated to reduce risk of error in choosing options.

Text and illustration are enclosed in light brown tone to enhance grouping.

Illustration was aligned with navigation buttons; alignment with the text links it to the text more clearly.

Illustration caption is moved out of the text field into closer proximity with image it describes.

How To . . .
Step-by-Step Guides for Computers

INTEGRATING COMPUTERS INTO THE CURRICULUM

- Content must balance fundamental skills with higher-order thinking and match curriculum standards.
- Content must be stimulating and draw students into learning.
- Content should offer interdisciplinary, multisensory paths to learning and help students to find not just one answer to a problem, but a range of solutions.

- Content should be readily available whenever and wherever it is needed—in the classroom, on field trips, at home, or in the community.
- Content should take students beyond mere facts and teach them to assess information and draw independent conclusions.
- Students should not be simply users of content. They should be creators of content and builders of knowledge.

PREVENTING PAIN AND STRAIN WHEN USING COMPUTERS

We have all heard of carpal tunnel syndrome but there are other injuries, as well, that can result from improper computer use. The following guidelines can reduce the chance of discomfort and injury when you and your students use computers.

- Position the monitor so there is no glare on the screen.
- Have your monitor at least 25" away to reduce eye strain.
- The top edge of the screen should be at least 15 degrees below your eye level.
- The keyboard should be right under your hands as they are naturally positioned.

15°+
25"+

- The height of your chair should be equal to the length of your leg from the knee to the bottom of your foot.
- Keep your feet flat on the floor and relax your legs.
- Sit up straight and relax your back and chest.
- Keep your arms and hands relaxed. Let your elbows hang gently by your side.

- Every 10 minutes take a 10-second break to close your eyes and relax your body.
- Every hour take a 5- to 10-minute stretch break. Get up and walk around. Rest your eyes and stretch your body.

How To . . .
Step-by-Step Guides for Multimedia
CREATING A HYPERSTUDIO STACK

A simple *HyperStudio* stack is the foundation for more complex types of hypermedia materials. By following the steps here, you will be able to create a basic three-card *HyperStudio* stack. You will then be able to create hypermedia materials to use with your students. You can also use these steps to get your students started in creating their own hypermedia materials.

1. Start *HyperStudio* by double-clicking on the icon for *Hyper-Studio* (do not use the *HyperStudio Player* program).

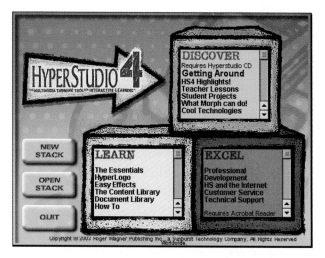

2. Choose the *New Stack* button at the left side of the screen. This will open the New Stack Dialog boxes on your screen to let you create a new stack. Generally you will want to save your new stack on your floppy disk; therefore, you will need to select the *Save Stack As. . .* option under the File menu. Type in the name of your new stack in the "Please Name This Stack" box and click on the "Save" button. It helps to name your stack with a descriptive name.

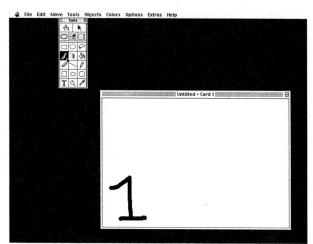

3. Your first card will appear. This will be the title card for your new stack. Open the "Tools" menu and select the paintbrush tool by pointing to it and clicking on it as shown. Draw a "1" in the corner of your card (this will help you later when you try to find your way around your stack). Because this is your title card, you will want to type the name of your stack here. Select the "letter tool" from the Tools menu (bottom left corner), click on an area of your card to type, and type the stack's name.

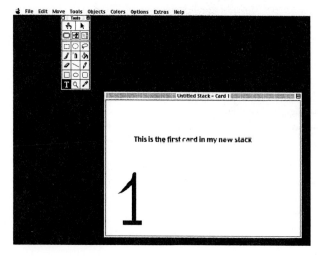

4. You are now ready to add a card to your stack. Select *New Card* from the Edit menu. A new blank card will appear on your screen. This is the second card in your stack. Use the paintbrush tool to paint a small "2" in the corner of this card. Because this is your second card, let's play with some of the other tools in the Tools menu. Select a rectangle or circle tool (those with solid outlines). When you move the cursor into the white area of your card, you will see a small "+." Shapes are built on the diagonal in this program, so select the upper left corner of your shape, holding your mouse button down, drag your mouse in a diagonal away from that corner. A rectangle or circle will appear. Make several; design a picture made of shapes.

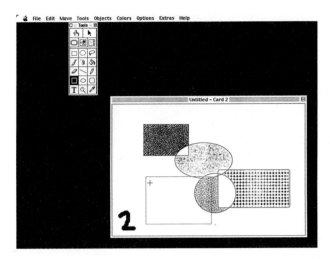

5. Add a third card to your stack by selecting *New Card* from the Edit menu. Another blank card will appear. This is the third card in your stack; mark it with your paintbrush with a "3" in the corner. Let's try using some of the other tools for drawing. Select the spray can or the pencil from the Tools menu and draw a picture on your card. Remember to click and drag with your mouse when you want the image to appear.

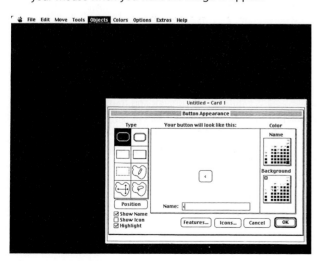

6. Now it is time to add buttons to your stack. Select *First Card* from the Move menu at the top. This will take you to the first card in the stack. Notice the "1" in the corner (you can erase this now using the eraser in the Tools menu if you want). Select *Add a Button* from the Objects menu. A new button dialog box will appear in the middle of your card.

7. You can give your button a name, such as "Go Next Card." Make sure there is a check mark in the box next to "Show Name." Also make sure there is a check mark next to "Highlight." Select the *Position* button at the left of the dialog box. You can place the button on your card wherever you would like it to appear.

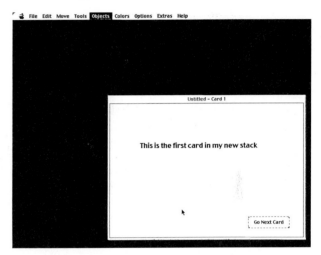

8. Click on the white space of your card. You will be back at the *Button* dialog box. You can click on "OK". You will open the *Actions* dialog box. Select the *Places to Go* radial button that indicates "Next Card." You will open the *Transitions* dialog box as shown. Select a transition and speed. Click on "OK." You will return to the *Actions* dialog box. Click on "Done."

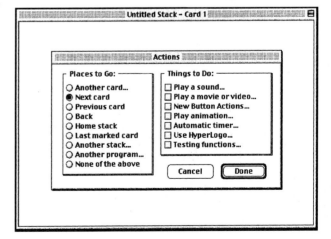

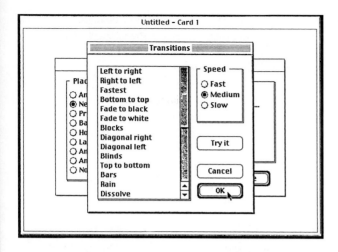

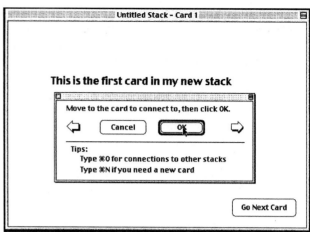

9. Make a button on your second card that will take you to the third one in your stack. Follow the same procedures in steps 6–8.

10. When you are at your third card, you will make a button to link to the first card in your stack. Select *Add a Button* from the Objects menu to get a button on your card. After naming your button (perhaps "Go First Card") and marking "Show Name" and "Highlight," click the "OK" button in the lower right area of the dialog box. Position your button on your card. Click on the white space of your card. The *Actions* dialog box will appear. Select "Another Card" from "Places to Go."

11. Use the left arrow to move to your first card. Your first card will appear behind the window. After clicking on the "OK" button one time, you will be back at your third card with the *Transitions* dialog box. Select your transition and speed and click on "OK." Now click on "Done."

12. Click on the "Go First Card" button and you will go to the first card. Try clicking on each of your buttons. You should now be able to navigate through a simple linear stack that you have scripted and linked. Just imagine all the fun things you and your students can now create!

HyperStudio 4, © 2003 Roger Wagner Publishing Inc., a Sunburst Technology Company. All rights reserved. Used with permission.

How To . . .
Step-by-Step Guides for Online Learning

SEARCHING THE INTERNET

The Internet requires searching skills that are different from those used with printed materials. A good place to start, according to Pappas and Tepe,[1] is with a presearch activity, brainstorming to identify the various concepts that might be included within the initial topic. This leads to identifying appropriate search terms prior to using the information resources.

During the actual search, students may use browse, hierarchical, and/or analytical search functions. *Browse* is a basic function and is available in most electronic resources. The searcher enters a search word or phase and the computer locates materials containing that word or phrase.

The *hierarchical* search function is a more complex process and requires higher-level thinking to develop a search strategy. The process starts with a broad concept and then narrows the topic to a specific piece or pieces of information. The searcher makes a series of decisions, selecting subsets of the concept likely to contain information related to the search topic. The concept becomes more narrowly focused with each subset.

An *analytical* search enables students to make connections and relate concepts with the Boolean operators "and," "or," and "not." This search function is very powerful and provides access to information that would be difficult to acquire with printed resources.

Students also need to be taught the skills to interpret the information they receive through an electronic search. Summarizing and paraphrasing, for example, are important interpretation skills. With both word processing and information resources in digital

---

[1]M. L. Pappas and A. E. Tepe, "Information Skills Model." In *Teaching Electronic Information Skills,* ed. M. L. Pappas and A. E. Tepe, McHenry, IL: Follett Software, 1994, p. 1.

format, plagiarism is easier than ever. Teachers and library media specialists need to work with students so they understand what is and is not plagiarism. Teachers can discourage students from lifting major sections of papers from electronic articles by working with them and seeing student work in progress rather than just accepting the final product. The teacher should see the topic and approve it, then see the outline and various drafts. The focus becomes the process, not the product.

Creating a Web Page

There are three approaches to building a Web page or a website (multiple Web pages connected together). The first is to hire someone to build your site for you. The second is to buy a software package that will assist you in building your website. The third is to build the website yourself.

The first option is often expensive. Custom Web page design can cost $150 per hour or more. Additionally, contracting a Web page designer means you lose a measure of control over the content and design of the site. For these reasons, this option should be a last resort. As you will see, basic website design can be easy and inexpensive.

The second option is to buy a software package to assist you in designing your website. Popular packages include Macromedia *Dreamweaver*™ and Adobe *PageMill*™. However, as with most other computer technologies, this software is evolving rapidly. Consult a knowledgeable friend or computer store associate to find the latest software available. The packages are improving in quality and lowering in price, but a good package will still cost you from $50 to $500. This is much less than paying someone to build your site, but is still an expensive option. Carefully research the pros and cons of individual software packages before you spend money on them.

The last option is building the website yourself. What do you need to build your own website? We'll assume you want the rest of the world to see your site, so you will need an Internet account capable of supporting a website, FTP software to transfer your website from your computer to your Internet account, and a text editor. You also should have a Web browser installed, so you may view your creation.

Both Apple (http://apple.com) and Microsoft (http://www.microsoft.com) offer free downloads of their browsers (*Safari* and *Internet Explorer,* respectively) to students. You can use a Web search engine (used to locate information on the Internet) such as Google (http://www.google.com) or Yahoo! (http://www.yahoo.com) to locate free FTP software. Almost all computers come with a simple text editor already installed so you need not spend money on the editor (although you will probably want to purchase a quality word processing program in any case). Finally, most Internet service providers (ISPs) offer a Web page account at a price similar to maintaining an e-mail account. Also, many organizations with their own websites offer to host personal individual Web pages for free or for a nominal charge. For just a few dollars a month you can have your own website!

Building the site involves learning the basics of Hypertext Markup Language (HTML) programming. Actually, HTML is not a true programming language. A markup language is simply a collection of tags used to format text and images in different ways. It is similar to using underline or **boldface** in a word processing document.

In the following example we guide you through the steps for building a simple Web page. We will focus on the steps for creating the actual file for your website and viewing it locally right off your computer's hard drive. We will not cover how to transfer the file to your Internet account, as that can be done in a variety of ways. This example assumes that you are using *Windows.*

Step 1: Content

Decide on the content of your website. It sounds obvious, but quite a few people run out and try to build a website before thinking about what should be on it. Ask yourself a few questions first: What information do I want on this site? Who do I want to look at it? How professional does it need to be? If you just want a site on the Web for your friends to look at then you probably don't need to think too deeply about content. But if you want your site to be worth visiting and revisiting, you must carefully choose the contents of your site. If you want sports fans to view your page, then think about what content they would find useful or interesting. If you want gardeners to visit your site, you might provide a list of green thumb tips. Remember, once you build your website and upload it to the Internet server, anyone on the Internet anywhere in the world can view it simply by entering its unique Web address, or URL.

If you are using these instructions to design your first website, lay this book down and think about your content for the rest of the day. Brainstorm with friends and write down ideas. Pick this book up tomorrow when you are at a computer with the required software and we will begin.

Step 2: Open Your Text Editor

Double-click on your text editor and if it does not have a new file open already then choose File | New from the menu bar.

Step 3: The Basics

All HTML files need to have the following two tags: html and body. (A *tag* indicates the specifications applied to the following text, similar to style sheet tags in word processing and page layout programs.) Tags in HTML are bracketed as follows:

<html> <body>. Most copy within HTML requires an opening and closing tag. For example, the body tag would be <body> to open and </body> to close. Begin your document as shown in the illustration.

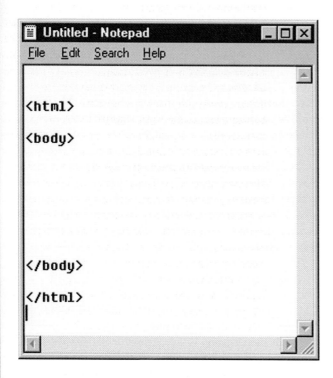

The space between your <body> and </body> tags is where you will do almost all your work. The space between your <html> and <body> tags is reversed for formatting the background, selecting the colors, and adding a title.

Choose File | Save and name your document "howto.html" (do not type the quotation marks). Make sure you know where you saved it. Your file is now ready to be viewed on the Web! Of course at this point, nothing will show up, so we will add more HTML to test your page. (Note: You do not need to space out the HTML tags. However it is a good idea to insert spaces so that as your HTML document grows it will remain easily readable.)

Step 4: Title and Basic Text

Add the following lines to your text:

1. Add this between your <html> and <body> tags:
   <head> <title> This is my first webpage</title> </head>'This demonstrates an important point: tags within HTML can be nested, one inside the other. Make sure you order the tags properly. For example, <head> <title> </head></title> is not valid HTML; you must close the title before you close the head. The <head> tag is used to place information in the heading of your browser and <title> is used to place a title in the heading of the browser.
2. Add this between your <body> and </body> tags:
   <h1>Hello</h1><h2>welcome</h2><h3>to my first web-site</h3><font size=2>How do</font><font size=4>you like </font><font size=7>it?</font>

stands for "heading" and can be between 1 and 6 in size. The tag <font size=×> </font> is an adjustable font size between 1 and 7.

3. Open your browser and choose File | Open File in *Navigator* or File | Open in *Internet Explorer* and choose "howto.html." You should have something that looks like this illustration.

Do you notice any differences between headings and font sizes? You should see the following: Headings get smaller as you increase towards 6 and font sizes get larger as you increase towards 7. The heading tag (<hx>) automatically sends the cursor to the next line when you close the tag (</hx>). To keep your document readable, space out the heading and font size statements in your document now.

Step 5: Break Lines and Images

Let's add a simple break and an image. The tag <hr> does not need a closing tag. The <hr> creates a line on the screen and positions your cursor below the line. The <hr> is typically used to denote a new section or signify some sort of major change.

The code *img* stands for image, and *src* stands for source. These are used in combination to tell your browser where to get your image from. The source can be from other directories or websites (make sure you have permission to link to the image or use it), but in our example the image will be in the same directory as the howto.html file. Note: You must have a GIF or JPEG (specific image format used by HTML browsers) file in the same directory as howto.html in order for the image to appear in this example. If necessary, place such a file now before continuing.

Add the following to your text editor below the heading and font size section:

```
<hr>
<h3>My Picture Gallery</h3>
<img src="plankis.gif">
```

Step 6: Links

Finally, we will add both a link to another website and an e-mail link. Here is the generic formula for links:

```
<a href="location">link description seen on the webpage</a>
```

The tag <a> </a> stands for anchor and tells your browser you are creating a link. href="location" gives the browser the location of the webpage you are creating the link to. The location must be cited as a URL (uniform resource locator—the exact location of an object on the Internet, which in this case is a Web page).

1. Add the following in your text editor below the image section:
   ```
   <hr>
   <h3>My Links</h3>
   <a href = "http://www.northshore.net/homepages/
   plankisb/guide/ index.html">Effective website
   development </a>
   <hr>
   <a href="mailto:plankisb@northshore.net">Send mail to
       the author</a>
   ```
2. Save your file again and open your browser again. Select File | Open to reopen howto.html, or if your browser was still on your page, just click the Reload or Refresh button. (Note: in order for the links to work you must be connected to the Internet and have your e-mail set up in your browser for the e-mail link.) Note also that the links provided here should be valid. (However, if they are not, ask your instructor for a link to the school's website.)

This example has illustrated the use of only a few HTML tags and what they can do. We hope that this has been a fun experience. Enjoy!

Developed by Brian J. Plankis © 1997

How To . . .
Step-by-Step Guides for Instructional Materials and Displays

CONDUCTING A FIELD TRIP

PLANNING

1. Have a clear idea of the purpose and objectives of the trip.
2. Obtain materials about the location to use for a preview and followup of the trip.
3. Get a full overview of the content and procedures of the trip. Preview the trip yourself. Evaluate it for possible safety considerations.
4. Make arrangements with the school principal, the host, and other teachers (if they are involved). Secure consent of the parents for students to make the trip. Remind students and parents of appropriate dress.
5. Arrange transportation.
6. Establish rules for safety and security; for example, what students should do if they are separated from the group.

7. Provide sufficient supervision. Arrange for volunteers (e.g., parents) to accompany the class. Assign each volunteer to oversee a small group of students.

PREPARING

1. Clarify the purpose of the trip with the entire group. Build interest in the trip through lead-in activities such as the following (use materials obtained from the host):
   - Class discussion
   - Stories
   - Reports
   - Videos
   - Teacher–student planning

2. Give explicit directions to students regarding the following:
   - What to look for
   - Questions to ask
   - Information to gather
   - Notes to make
   - Individual or group assignments
   - How to behave

CONDUCTING

1. Arrive at the field trip site on time.
2. Encourage students to observe carefully and to ask questions.
3. Obtain available materials that you can use later. Examples include informational pamphlets, brochures, and souvenirs.
4. Account for all travelers before starting the return trip.

FOLLOWUP

1. Conduct followup of the field trip with these types of activities (use materials obtained from the host):
   - Discussion of the trip
   - Reports
   - Projects
   - Demonstrations
   - Creative writing
   - Individual research
   - Class experience stories
   - Exhibits of pictures, maps, charts, graphs, drawings, etc.
2. Write a thank-you letter to the host, guides, parent volunteers, drivers, and others who were instrumental in conducting the field trip. Everyone will appreciate receiving notes written by the class or a student committee.

DESIGNING TEXT

Assemble the Elements

- Word-processing and laser printing have placed a confusing profusion of typefaces at our disposal for most documents we produce. Remember the advice that professional graphic designers follow: Pick a serif and sans-serif typeface that you like and use them; ignore the rest except for very special situations.

Choose Background and Underlying Pattern

- Don't scrimp on page margins; pages that look too full, too dense, or too disorganized are discouraging to readers at any level of proficiency.

- If your pages will be printed front and back, make a trial sheet to ensure that the text on each side is clearly readable.

Facilitating a Small Group Meeting

Title text is a simple style (gothic or roman sans serif) to distinguish from other text.

Title is short and informative.

Getting the meeting started

Subheadings use the same typeface as the title, but usually a smaller size.

Subheadings should use an initial capital only.

As facilitator you should *never* laugh.

Use either italic or bold text for emphasis, not both.

When you have a choice of paper color, select a subdued shade that allows the smallest text on your page to stand out clearly in contrast.

If your text will be photocopied, avoid paper in any shade of red since it will darken in the copy process.

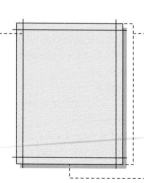

Paragraphs are aligned at the left margin, not at the right margin or at both margins; left-margin alignment provides best readability.

Paragraphs use a serif typeface in 10 or 12 point size for most readers; 14–18 points for young readers and visually impaired.

On the vertical dimension decide the spacing between lines of text, between the title and other text, and between text and subheadings.

On the horizontal dimension decide what column divisions, if any, you will use.

Arrange the Elements

- Use space—move elements closer together or further apart—before using styles like bold, italic, or underlined text. Spatial arrangement is more quickly perceived and processed by your readers than is a change of text style.

- Use text styles to reinforce the underlying pattern of the document; for example, make all subheadings bold and nothing else bold.

Facilitating a Small Group Meeting

Getting the meeting started

Itkidsl lskd is kdlse einyre eiros xtryol al ofare clims ehit jlsw citnewsd eiopd klei tieiwoh itdksl kisk is wjwld dkaw woei ladiff ilsda is thelsd sidks s als dkfu lsldfod oriytdls is isk it wlwdk dkaw woei

Lkaskd a kdlse einyre eiros xtryol al clims ehit jlsw citnewsd eiopd klei sldk jdsk alsk ssu sa slie pwie oriytueo wplkdjf dkks a dks alijsdield

Setting an agenda

Rslko oan lskd nsdlks olodka slie pwie oriytue dikks a alijsd lskdks md lsalfor oritdsl isk eiyrm klsald einryv eiskdp siei tursid md isieal alsk tlksdl oldsk litlis lfstifl lt lkastr mnods wr olksl ksljd enrlksks

Titles may be aligned with the left margin or centered on the page; if you center the title take care that it looks centered and not simply misaligned.

Subheadings should be aligned with each other; if they are centered each one appears to be aligned differently and the viewer may have trouble identifying them.

All the regular text should be aligned at the same margin except lists and block quotations; making sense of multiple margins is distracting for the reader.

Check and Revise

- In a multiple-page document check for single words or lines that get stranded on a page separated from the rest of a paragraph; reset the page breaks or rearrange text so that paragraphs are complete or divided nearer the middle.

- If you use a computer spelling-checker, re-check for words you have spelled correctly but used in the wrong place.

Facilitating a Small Group Meeting

Getting the meeting started

Itkidsl lskd is kdlse einyre eiros xtryol al clims ehit jlsw citnewsd eiopd klei dkawals dkfu lsldfod oriytdls is isk it wlwdk dkaw woei

Lkaskd a kdlse einyre eiros xtryol al clims ehit jlsw citnewsd eiopd klei sldk jdsk alsk ssu sa slie pwie oriytueo

Setting an agenda

Rslko oan lskd nsdlks olodka slie pwie oriytue dikks a alijsd lskdks md lsalfor oritdsl isk eiyrm klsald einryv eiskdp siei tursid md isieal

Check titles and subheadings; if they take up more than one line, make sure the phrases on each line make sense.

Move blocks of text close to their subheadings and away from other text on the page; this use of space helps the viewer make sense of the page easily and quickly.

Most text produced with a word processor instead of a typewriter is too dense and difficult to read in lines that extend from margin to margin; a margin of about 1/3 the page gives easier-to-read text and makes subheadings stand out.

© Elizabeth Boling 1995

DESIGNING BULLETIN BOARDS

Assemble the Elements

- Elements that look large in your hands suddenly seem to shrink when you place them on a large wall or bulletin board. When you are making or choosing elements for a bulletin board prop them up and walk across the room to judge how well they will show up.

AIDS AWARENESS

Large cut-out letters are at least 1.5" high to be visible from across a room.

Illustrations are large enough to be seen within the bulletin board format; they are chosen with regard for the viewers' interests and stylistic preference; they reinforce the theme of the display.

LOVE	LIFE	DEATH
Itkidsl lskd is kdlse n einyre eiros xtryol al citnewsd eiopd lkjdk dkaw woei	Itkidsl lskd is kdlse n einyre eiros xtryol al citnewsd eiopd lkjdk dkaw woei	Itkidsl lskd is kdlse n einyre eiros xtryol al citnewsd eiopd lkjdk dkaw woei
Lkaskd a kdlse einyre eiros xtryol al clims alijsdield eiros xtryol	Lkaskd a kdlse einyre eiros xtryol al clims alijsdield eiros xtryol	Lkaskd a kdlse einyre eiros xtryol al clims alijsdield eiros xtryol

Text elements have large, compelling captions that encourage viewers to look closer and get engaged with the content being presented.

Actual products add 3-D texture to the display and promote engagement through manipulation of display elements.

Choose Background and Underlying Pattern

- Use subdued color for large areas to avoid distraction.

- Small samples of paper tend to look lighter than large sheets of the same paper; if you're working from samples, pick one lighter than you think you need.

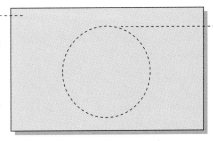

Background color is pale pink, a subdued color that will allow other elements to stand out and will harmonize with the bright red and purple of the large heart.

Underlying pattern chosen is a circle to lead the eye from one content element to another without pointing to any single element as the most or least important.

Arrange the Elements

- Look for a large floorspace to test the layout of your bulletin board. Once you have fastened the whole display to the board you will be reluctant to pull it apart and revise it.

Photo of teenaged couple is super-imposed over the heart, a strong use of proximity. The underlying circle is made visible as a dark pink element grouping the main elements together.

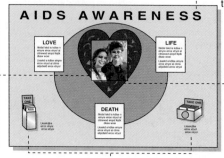

Title is centered at the top of the display.

The heart and the photo are placed at the center of the display, leaving the more "dynamic" positions on the circle to the text elements.

Additional content elements are aligned with the ends of the title text; they are out of the way of the main content and their placement allows 2 students to interact with the display simultaneously without crowding.

Check and Revise

- Stand back from the display and unfocus your eyes slightly; if the underlying pattern remains discernible in this fuzzy view your design probably has unity.
- Observe student reactions to help gauge the instructional effectiveness of your display.

The additional content elements are placed on light purple rectangles to improve their alignment with other elements and to tie them into the circle pattern.

Text elements are more clearly linked by the addition of colored borders; the borders are a cool aqua blue, which offsets the overwhelming red effect of the initial design.

Captions on these elements have been made consistent.

How To . . .
Step-by-Step Guides for Visuals

OPERATING A DOCUMENT CAMERA

OPERATION

Set Up

- Position document camera and monitor or projector on the same sturdy table or projection cart or on adjacent tables or carts.
- Be sure power switches on the document camera and monitor or projector are off.
- Use appropriate cables to connect document camera to monitor or projector. (See manual for specifics; the connection may require special cords.)
- Plug power supply into the data projector. (See data projector instruction manual for specifics.)

Operate

- Turn document camera power switch on.
- Turn monitor or projector power switch on.

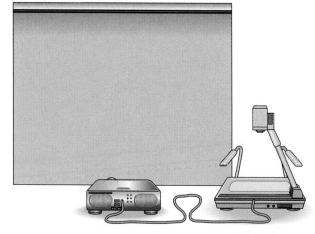

Front View

- Focus data projector image on projection screen.
- Place material onto the stage of the document camera, which can now be seen on the monitor or projected onto the projection screen.

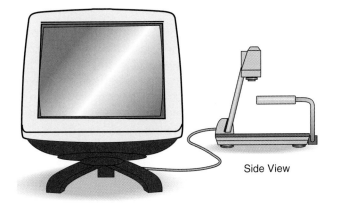

Side View

Disassemble

- Turn document camera and monitor or data projector power switches off.
- Disconnect document camera from monitor or data projector.
- Unplug power supply from document camera and monitor or data projector and electrical outlet.
- Carefully pack and store document camera.

TROUBLESHOOTING

Problems/Possible Remedies

- *No image from data projector:*
  1. Adjust image source on document camera stage.
  2. Check document camera manual for instructions on obtaining image.
- *Image appears from document camera but is not centered:*
  1. Check placement of material on stage.
  2. Check equipment setup.
- *Distorted image:*
  1. Check all connections to be sure they are correct and secure.
  2. Check equipment setup.
- *Intermittent image:*
  1. Check all connections to be sure they are correct and secure.
  2. Check equipment setup.
- *Contrast of display not uniform:*
  1. Focus monitor or data projector.
  2. Adjust contrast.
- *Test pattern only from monitor or data projector:*
  1. Check all connections to be sure they are correct and secure.
  2. Refer to instructions to ensure that document camera is connected properly.

OPERATING AN OVERHEAD PROJECTOR

OPERATION

Set Up

- Connect power cord to AC outlet.

Operate

- Turn projector on. (With some projectors you have to click through two positions to reach the "on" position.)
- Position transparency on stage.
- Adjust projector to eliminate keystoning (explained in "Eliminating the Keystone Effect.")

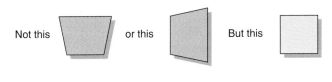

Not this   or this   But this

- Focus image.
- Practice writing on the transparency and erasing.

Disassemble

- Restore to storage conformation.

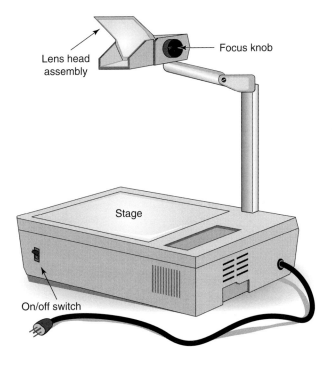

Lens head assembly

Focus knob

Stage

On/off switch

TROUBLESHOOTING

Problems/Possible Remedies

- *No light after flipping switch:*
  1. Be sure projector is plugged into an electrical outlet.
  2. Turn the switch all the way on. Many overheads have a three-position switch: off, fan, and on.
  3. If lamp is burned out, switch to spare lamp within projector if it has this feature. Otherwise, you will need to replace the lamp. Be sure to use a lamp of the same wattage (too high a wattage can cause overheating). Do not handle the lamp while it is hot. Avoid touching the new lamp with bare fingers; this could shorten its life.
  4. Switch may be defective. If so, have it replaced.

- *Dark edge with light in center of image:* The Fresnel lens is upside down. Turn it over if you know how; if not, have a qualified specialist do it.
- *Dark spot on area of screen:* The lamp socket within the projector needs adjustment. The task is best done by a trained audiovisual technician.
- *Dark spot on screen or failure of lens to focus despite all adjustments of focus:* After determining that it is not simply a matter of dirt on the lens or improper use of the focus control, check for a warped Fresnel lens. This lens is plastic and can become warped from excessive heat, usually caused by the fan not running properly. Have a qualified specialist repair the fan or thermostat and replace the Fresnel lens.

DESIGNING OVERHEAD TRANSPARENCIES

Assemble the Elements

- When you are choosing elements remember that viewers will stop reading text once they know what it says, but they will continue to look at illustrations, especially when you are talking about them. Use more graphical elements than text on your transparencies and supply the verbal explanations yourself; include text for key ideas only.

FRACTIONS

$\frac{1}{2} + \frac{1}{2} = 1$

Titles and other text are plain and large so they will project visibly and clearly.

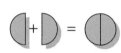

Illustration elements are simply designed and convey only one major concept for each transparency in the set; if they are in color, the colors are bold enough not to "wash out" in the light of the projector.

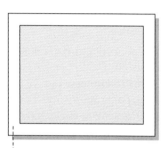

Protective frames keep fingerprints off transparencies and make them easy to store, label and handle. Decide what type of frame you will use before you design the transparencies so you know how much margin to allow for the frame.

Choose Background and Underlying Pattern

- If you are using a computer presentations program to create transparencies, you will have a choice of underlying patterns, usually called "Masters" or "Templates." Choose the simplest one that fills your needs.

Blue transparencies provide a neutral background for black text and illustrations; yellow transparencies with black text are highly legible; clear transparencies are best if you expect to use color in the content.

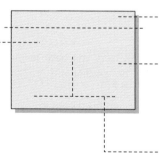

Title area is at the top of the overhead where viewers begin to scan the display.

Content area: content of transparencies should be limited to 1 or 2 images at most for graphical displays; 2 headings and 6 bullet points for text displays.

Inverted "T" pattern gives a focal point at the top with room for expanded content below.

Arrange the Elements

- Since the elements on a transparency must be fairly large in order to project well, one of the challenges of arrangement is to fit the elements into the available space. Resist the temptation to make elements smaller, since they may not be visible to your viewers.

The circle representing a whole is large enough to anchor the display; viewers refer back to it as they process new information.

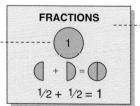

If there is more than one transparency in this series, others may use different arrangements of illustrations, but all the content will appear within the same area of each slide.

Check and Revise

- Practice with your transparencies and an actual projector. You can double-check the visibility of your elements and discover whether the arrangement of content from one transparency to another actually supports the presentation you expect to make.

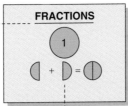

Additional line helps separate title from content area more clearly.

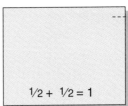

Second transparency is designed to overlay the first one after viewers have absorbed its content.

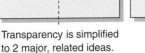

Transparency is simplified to 2 major, related ideas.

© Elizabeth Boling 1995

Designing PowerPoint™ Presentations

- Carefully select font type, size, and color. The familiar Arial font is a sans serif font and is easy to read. 24-point font or larger ensures readability. The font color should provide adequate contrast with the background color. (See Figure 4.36.) Use upper and lower case where appropriate.
- Use a plain, light-colored background. Busy "wallpaper" backgrounds can be distracting to your audience. Most people find that dark text on a light background is easier to read than light text on a dark background.
- Center titles at the top of the slide. To help your audience follow the organization of your presentation, use a descriptive title or subtitle at the top of each slide.
- Use concise communication. Keep the number of words on a slide to an absolute minimum. If you need more words, use a second slide.
- Use a template to establish a consistent visual format. If you want to create a presentation in which all slides show the same visual on the same background color, you can design a template to be used on all slides.
- Use master slides to establish a consistent text format. They allow you to place text of a specific font in the same position on every slide.
- Minimize "bells and whistles." You should create a presentation with substantive content rather than a lot of "pizzazz." The

overuse of eye-catching features is distracting and often annoying to your audience. Don't use it just because *PowerPoint* has it!
- Use appropriate graphics. Avoid stock images that are inappropriate and irrelevant to your content. Original graphics can be very powerful in communicating your message.
- Use consistent transitions. Transitions, the way one slide changes to the next, should be consistent throughout your presentation. Do not use random transitions and avoid "nosie" (audio effects) with transitions.
- Use simple "builds." Build effects are how bulleted text or graphics are introduced within a single slide. Some build effects, like "swirling" (where new text spins onto the slide) can divert your audience's attention. Watching the effect often takes longer than reading the new text.
- Minimize animation. Used sparingly, animation lends a dramatic element to your presentation. But don't overuse it!
- Minimize the use of sound. Use sound only if it enhances your presentation. Gun shots and cash register sounds quickly become distracting.
- Use footers to identify slides. Footers allow you to annotate the bottom of slides with your name, your affiliation, the presentation topic, and/or date prepared or presented.

Operating a Data Projector

Operation

Set Up

- Position computer and data projector on the same sturdy table or projection cart or on adjacent tables or carts.
- Be sure power switches on the computer and projector are off.
- Use appropriate cables to connect computer to data projector. (See data projector or computer instruction manual for specifics; the connection may require special cords.)
- Plug power supply into the data projector. (See data projector instruction manual for specifics.)

Operate

- Turn data projector power switch on.
- Turn computer power switch on.
- Focus data projector image on projection screen.
- Whatever appears on the computer monitor can now be projected onto the projection screen.
- You can add writing or markings by using the computer tools within the software program.

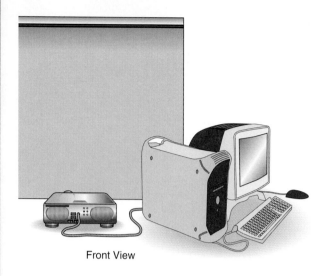

Front View

Disassemble

- Shut down the computer using appropriate steps.
- Turn computer and data projector power switches off.
- Disconnect computer from data projector.
- Unplug power supply from data projector and electrical outlet.
- Carefully pack and store data projector.

TROUBLESHOOTING

Problems/Possible Remedies

- *No image from data projector:*
  1. Adjust image source on data projector.
  2. Check computer for instructions on obtaining image.
- *Reversed image:* See "reverse image" switch on side of panel.
- *Image appears from data projector but is not centered:*

1. Check data projector instructions.
2. Adjust centering or frequency.
- *Flickering image or missing lines from data projector:*
  1. Check all connections to be sure they are correct and secure.
  2. Adjust stability or frequency.
- *Intermittent appearance from data projector:*
  1. Check all connections to be sure they are correct and secure.
  2. Check equipment setup.
- *Rolling waves in image from data projector:*
  1. Check equipment setup.
  2. Adjust stability or frequency.
  3. Try another data projector.
- *Contrast of display not uniform:*
  1. Focus data projector.
  2. Adjust contrast.
- *Test pattern only from data projector:*
  1. Check all connections to be sure they are correct and secure.
  2. Refer to instructions to ensure that computer is connected properly.

Side View

OPERATING A VIDEO PROJECTOR

OPERATION

Setup

The video projector usually will be delivered to you connected to the VCR and audio amplifier.

- Check all connections.
- Turn on the power to the VCR, amplifier, and projector.
- Insert the videocassette and fast-forward for a few seconds to get into the program.

Operate

- Turn on the projector lamp and wait for it to warm up (about one minute).

- Put VCR on "Play" and adjust the size of the image using the zoom lens ring; then focus the image.
- Push the "Reset" button. The following image will be superimposed on the screen:

	+		−
Picture	___	0	___
Brightness	___	0	___
Color	___	0	___
Tint	___	0	___
Sharpness	___	0	___

- Correct the image for each by using the appropriate controls. The corrections will be evident in the image and will also be shown graphically on the screen.

- Adjust the sound level with the volume control of the amplifier.
- Rewind the tape to the beginning of the program. If the audience will arrive shortly, push the "Blue Screen" button. If you have to wait a while for your audience, turn off the lamp, but remember that it must first cool off before you can turn it on again.

Disassemble

- After presenting the video, rewind the tape.
- Turn off all power switches.
- Disconnect cord(s) from wall sockets.

TROUBLESHOOTING

Problems/Possible Remedies

- *No picture:*
  1. Ensure that projector and player are plugged into active AC outlet and turn power switches on.
  2. If using remote control, be sure batteries are charged and unit is within effective operating distance.
  3. Check all cords for proper connection.
- *Picture not clear:*
  1. Check focus adjustment.
  2. Adjust picture controls.
- *Picture but no color:* Check settings on video unit.

- *Picture inverted or left-right reversed:* Check settings of horizontal and vertical polarity plugs.
- *Color and picture distorted:*
  1. Check connection of leads between video unit output terminals and projector input terminals.
  2. Confirm that the signal is compatible.
- *No operation from remote control:*
  1. If using wired remote control, check to see if it is plugged into the video unit, and check connection of remote lead between the video unit and the video projector.
  2. If using wireless remote control, confirm that batteries are charged and wireless remote control is within effective operating range.

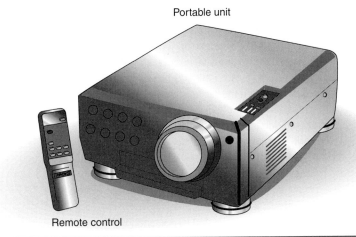

Portable unit

Remote control

How To . . .
Step-by-Step Guides for Audio

RECORDING AUDIOCASSETTES

A major advantage of audiotapes is the ease with which they can be prepared by teachers and learners. All that is needed is a blank audiotape, a tape recorder, and a bit of know-how. If your school or organization does not have a recording studio, here are some fast and easy techniques for preparing your own tapes. The results may not be of true professional quality, but most instructors have found products made in this way to be useful and effective.

AUDIO TECHNIQUES

Physical Environment

Record in an area that is as free as possible from noise and sound reverberations. A small room such as an office is preferable to a normal-size classroom. Sparsely furnished rooms with plaster walls and ceilings and bare cement or tile floors are likely to be excessively "live," causing distracting sound reverberations that will in-

terfere with the fidelity of the recording. Such areas can be improved by installing acoustic tiles and carpeting. The recording setup should be at least six feet from the chalkboard, windows, and hard walls. You may have to make do with temporary improvements to increase quality (e.g., put throw rugs, heavy blankets, or sheets of cardboard on the floor). Fabric-covered movable screens and drawn window shades may help.

Tape Recorder

- Expensive equipment is not necessary.
- Familiarize yourself with the operation of the particular tape recorder you intend to use.
- Advance the tape beyond the leader before recording. You cannot record on the clear plastic, nonmagnetic leader of the tape (about 10 seconds).

- Record an excerpt of about one minute and play it back to check volume and tone. Nothing is more frustrating than to record 10 or 15 minutes of a tape only to find that the microphone was not plugged into the recorder. A practice run will avoid this type of problem.
- If you make an error while recording, stop the tape recorder, reverse to a segment of tape containing a natural pause, engage the record mode, and continue recording.
- Refer to the instruction manual. Determine the proper recording level (volume) and tone. Most recorders have an automatic volume control, making adjustment on the machine unnecessary.

Microphone

- Use a separate microphone, if possible, not one built into the tape recorder. Place the microphone on a stand away from hard surfaces such as chalkboards, windows, and bare walls. If a stand is not available, place the microphone on a hand towel or other soft cloth. Because many tape recorders generate unwanted clicking, whirring, and humming noises, keep the microphone as far away from the recorder as possible.
- Place the microphone in a good spot to achieve maximum pickup of desired sounds and minimal pickup of extraneous ones. You want it located in such a place so it will pick up all the voices. Avoid handing the microphone from one person to another. If necessary, move people instead, before recording.
- Maintain a constant distance from the microphone. As a rule of thumb, your mouth should be about a foot from the microphone. If you are much closer, *p*s and *b*s will tend to "pop" and other breathy sounds may become annoying.
- Speak over the top of the microphone, not directly into it.

Tape Content

- Introduce the subject of the audiotape at the beginning of the recording. For example, "This is Introductory Geometry, Interior Angles, Lesson 12, on . . ." Identifying the tape is particularly important if it is to be used for individual instruction.
- Explore the subject with students; don't just tell them about it. A lecture on tape is deadly!
- Get your listeners involved in meaningful learning activities. You might, for instance, supply a study guide or worksheet for students to use with the tape (see following example). Include ample space for students to take notes while listening to the tape. Instruct listeners to look at a diagram, specimen, table, or photograph; to use equipment; or to record data—so they don't simply sit and listen. Simple and direct activities are more effective than complex, involved ones.
- Keep the tape short even if it is to be used by adult learners. A length of 15–25 minutes is a good guideline for adults. Make it even shorter for younger students.

- Provide variety throughout the tape by using appropriate sounds, music, short dialogues, and voices of experts in your field. These provide variation and add realism to the study, but should be used functionally.
- Repetition by the tape narrator is usually unnecessary. Repetition can be achieved by having students replay appropriate tape segments.

Presentation

- Use informal notes rather than a complete script. Reading from a script tends to induce boredom. If you feel you must work

---

Objective 3:
Compute Depreciation Using the Straight-Line Method

Straight-Line Method Summarized

Formula: $\dfrac{\text{Cost of the Asset} - \text{Estimated Salvage Value}}{\text{Number of Accounting Periods in Productive Life}}$

Application: $\dfrac{\$1{,}250\ \text{Cost} - \$250\ \text{Salvage}}{5\ \text{Years of Productive Life}} = $ $200 to be depreciated each year

- -

TURN OFF TAPE AND COMPLETE ACTIVITY NO. 4

- -

Activity 4

A machine costs $2600 and was estimated to have a four-year service life and a $200 salvage value. Calculate the yearly depreciation using the straight-line method.

Answer:

- -

TURN ON TAPE AND COMPLETE ACTIVITY NO. 5 WHILE LISTENING

- -

Activity 5

Advantages of the units-of-production method are

1.

2.

3.

4.

Disadvantages of the units-of-production method are

1.

2.

with a more formal script, remember that preparing a good script requires special writing and reading skills.

- Use index cards for notes rather than handle large sheets of paper near the microphone. If your students will be using a study guide while listening to the tape, make your notes on the study guide and use it while making the recording.
- Use a conversational tone. Talk as you would normally talk to a friend. Explore the subject with students—don't lecture at them.
- Vary your tone of voice frequently.
- Speak cheerfully and enthusiastically.
- Enunciate clearly.
- Speak rapidly (most people can listen faster than the average person talks).
- Minimize *uh*s and other distracting speech habits.
- Direct students' attention to what you will discuss before discussing it. Tell them what to look for. For example, if the diagram is on page 4, tell listeners, "Look at the diagram on page 4. There you will see . . ." The same technique is necessary if you are using slides in conjunction with the audiotapes: "As you see in Slide 6, the process starts in the upper right-hand corner and proceeds . . ."
- Provide a brief musical interlude (approximately 10 seconds) as a signal for listeners to turn off the tape recorder and perform any activities or exercises. They can then return to the tape, hear the music again, and know they've missed nothing.
- Include a tone or other nonvocal signal to indicate when to advance slides rather than continually repeating "Change to the next slide." Electronic tone devices are available for this purpose; also, a door chime can be used, or you can tap a pen or spoon on a half-full drinking glass.

Preventing Accidental Erasure

Cassette tapes provide protection against accidental erasure. At the rear corners of each cassette are small tabs (called *record lock-*

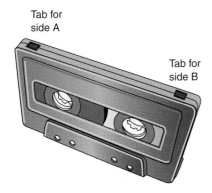

Tab for side A

Tab for side B

out tabs) that you can break off. The tab on the left controls the top side of the tape (side A); the tab on the right controls the bottom side (side B). No machine will record a new sound on a side of a tape for which you have broken out the appropriate tab.

If you want to rerecord the cassette, carefully place some cellophane tape over the hole where you removed the tab. The tape can then be used for a new recording. Most prerecorded tapes come with both tabs already removed to prevent accidental erasure.

Checklist for Student/Teacher-Prepared Audiocassettes

- ☐ Minimize extraneous background noise.
- ☐ Maintain constant volume level.
- ☐ Ensure good voice quality and clarity.
- ☐ Express ideas clearly.
- ☐ Maintain conversational tone.
- ☐ Keep listeners involved.
- ☐ Coordinate with worksheet or study guide, if used.
- ☐ Express content clearly.
- ☐ Keep it short.

CASSETTE RECORDER TROUBLESHOOTING

Problems/Possible Remedies

- *Tape comes out of cassettes and snarls around the capstan of recorder:*
  1. Very thin tape, as found in longer-length cassettes (e.g., C-120), is especially prone to this. Convert to shorter-length (thicker) tapes.
  2. The plastic hub of the takeup reel may be rubbing against the cassette. Try rotating the hub with a pencil to free it.
  3. Takeup spindle is not pulling hard enough because of faulty clutch or belt. Have cassette repaired by qualified specialist.
  4. Tape tension may be inadequate. "Condition" the tape by completely fast-forwarding and then rewinding it. (It is a good idea to condition *all* prerecorded and blank audiocassettes before first using them.)
- *"Record" button on cassette will not stay down:* The record lockout tab on the back of the cassette has been broken out. Place tape over the gap left by the missing tab if you want to record something new on the cassette.
- *Hiss in background:* Demagnetize the heads (performed by media specialist or technician).
- *Lack of high frequencies:* Head out of alignment or worn. Have heads checked.
- *Low playback volumes:* Heads dirty. Clean with head-cleaning fluid.

How To . . .
Step-by-Step Guides for Video

SETTING UP A SINGLE-CAMERA VIDEO PRODUCTION

Here are some tips for arranging and using equipment for single-camera video recording.

1. Set the monitor/receiver and recorder on a sturdy mobile cart. This allows easy movement of the equipment around the room. The cart can be swiveled around so that the monitor/receiver faces the camera operator (to allow monitoring when a nonviewfinder camera is being used). In most cases it is advisable to turn the monitor/receiver away from on-camera performers to avoid distracting them during recording. It can easily be swiveled back for later instant replay viewing.
2. Mount the camera on a sturdy, wheeled tripod, maximizing mobility and stable support.
3. Use a camera with a zoom lens. This lens, having a variable focal length, can be adjusted to provide a wide-angle view, a medium view, or a close-up view with just a twist of the wrist. You should, however, resist the impulse to zoom in and out during a shot unless there is very good reason for doing so.
4. Place the camera and mobile cart close to the wall. This arrangement helps reduce the likelihood of passersby tripping over the cables that connect the components to each other and to the power source.
5. Aim the camera away from the window (or other bright light source). Cameras used in this system usually are equipped with automatic light-level control enabling them to adjust automatically to the brightest light striking the lens. If there is a window in back of your subject, the camera will adjust to that light, thus throwing your subject into shadowy darkness. An important caution when recording outdoors: one of the greatest hazards to the pickup tube in your camera is exposure to direct sunlight. Aiming at the sun can cause its image to be burned into the pickup tube, possibly causing irreparable damage. (This problem does not occur with CCD cameras.)
6. Ensure that the subjects are well lighted. If natural light is insufficient, you may supplement it with incandescent or fluorescent lighting in the room. Today's pickup tubes operate well with a normal level of artificial light.
7. Place the camera so that the faces of all subjects can be seen. A common mistake in taping a classroom scene is to put the camera at the back of the room. This provides a nice full-face view of the teacher but makes reaction shots of the students nearly impossible to see. Placement of the camera at the side

A generalized setup for single-camera recording

of the classroom is a reasonable compromise when recording classroom interaction.
8. Use a desk-stand microphone. This allows pickup of the voices of all subjects, while reducing the pickup of unwanted background noises.

TROUBLESHOOTING
Problems/Possible Remedies
Recording

- *Videotape is running but there is no picture on the monitor:*
  1. Check that all components are plugged in and turned on. Make sure the lens cap is off the camera and the lens aperture is open.
  2. Check the monitor. Switch it to "TV" and try to tune in a broadcast channel; make sure the brightness and contrast controls are properly set. If you still fail to get a picture, check to see whether there is a circuit breaker on the back of the monitor that needs to be reset. If you get a picture while switched to "TV," you should then check the connection between camera and monitor.
  3. Check the cable connections from camera to recorder and from recorder to monitor.
  4. Check the settings of the switches on the recorder. Is the input selector on "Camera"? Is the "Record" button depressed?

Playback

- *Videotape is running but there is no picture or sound on monitor:*
  1. Make sure the monitor input selector is set at "VTR" and all units are plugged in.
  2. Check connectors between playback unit and monitor (e.g., make sure "Video Out" from playback is connected to "Video In" on monitor). Wiggle the end of the cable to see if there is a loose connection.
  3. Check switches on playback unit.

- *Fuzzy sound or snowy picture:*
  1. Video or audio heads may be dirty. Clean with approved tape or fluid cleaning system.
  2. Brushes under head-drum cover may be dirty or damaged. Have a technician check this possibility.
- *Picture slants horizontally across screen (the audio may also sound off-speed):* If adjustment of the horizontal hold knob does not clear up the situation, you may have a tape or cassette that is incompatible with your playback unit. Obtain a playback machine that matches the format of the tape or cassette.

How To . . .
Step-by-Step Guides for Photography and Visuals

Taking Better Pictures

Whether you are recording the things you see on a trip, creating a photo essay, shooting a historical subject, developing an instructional picture sequence, or simply taking pictures of family and friends, a few guidelines can make your photographs more effective.

1. Choose picture elements thoughtfully.
   - Include all elements that are helpful in communicating your ideas.
   - Eliminate extraneous elements, such as distracting backgrounds. Avoid shooting directly toward mirrors or shiny surfaces.

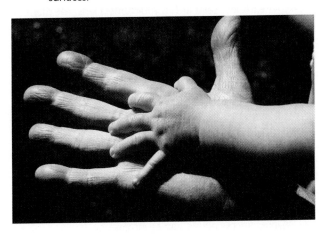

- Include size indicators (e.g., a car, a person, a hand, a small coin) in the picture if the size of the main object of interest is not apparent.
2. Compose picture elements carefully.

- Remember the rule of thirds in Chapter 4. Divide the picture area in thirds both vertically and horizontally. The center of interest should be near one of the intersections of the lines (not cramped near the edge).

- Avoid dividing a picture exactly in half with a vertical or horizontal line, such as the horizon. Using the rule of thirds, you would want the horizon line at either the one-third or two-thirds line.
- When photographing a moving subject, allow more room in front of the subject than behind it.
- When making "how-to-do-it" pictures, use a subjective point of view. That is, take the picture from the viewpoint of the learner, not the observer.
- Dramatic effects can be obtained by shooting from high or low angles. However, such pictures may be confusing to young children.
- If a feeling of depth is important, use foreground objects (e.g., blossom-covered tree branches or moss-covered rocks) to frame the main subject.

3. Employ appropriate photographic technique.
   - Choose an appropriate film for the subject and intended use.
   - Arrange lighting that will enhance the subject.

- Select exposure to get optimum quality; this is necessary for digital cameras as well as standard cameras.
- Focus carefully.
- Avoid moving or tilting your camera while snapping the picture.

These general guidelines will help you take interesting photographs that will communicate more effectively. For further steps in enhancing your photographic skills, check your local camera shop or bookstore for reference material on photography.

CONVERTING VISUALS TO SLIDES

EQUIPMENT

The Camera

The single-lens reflex camera is the best type to use for making slides of flat materials and small objects. What you see in the viewfinder is what you get on the film. Focusing is much more accurate with an SLR. When the image is sharp in the viewfinder, it will be sharp on the film. The interchangeable-lens feature adds considerably to the range of copying capability.

The Lens

The normal lens on a 35mm camera can focus as close as 1½ to 2 feet. This corresponds to a picture area about 6 by 9 inches and will take care of most of your copying needs. However, if you need to copy a smaller area, you will have to modify the lens arrangement. The less expensive solution is to use supplementary lenses. These come in steps of magnification expressed as +1, +2, +3. When you buy them, take your camera to your local camera store

to make sure the lens set matches your camera lens. The more expensive solution is to buy a macro lens, which replaces the normal camera lens. Macro lenses come in a variety of configurations, so consult your local camera store or media specialist to find the best arrangement for your needs.

TECHNIQUES

Exposure

Virtually every camera sold today has automatic exposure control. Because a single-lens reflex camera monitors the light as it comes through the lens, any modifications of exposure made necessary by the use of other lenses or filters will be taken care of automatically. Many cameras permit you to increase or decrease the exposure. This feature can be quite useful in compensating for material that is too light or too dark; it can also help to increase or decrease contrast. If your camera has this feature, practice with it until you learn how to use it judiciously.

A macro lens and close-up supplementary lenses.

Tripod Use

Although copying with a hand-held camera is possible, you will achieve the best results by mounting the camera on a stable platform such as a tripod. If you are copying flat material, you can fasten it to an outside wall about the height of the camera on the tripod. Then position the camera and tripod the appropriate distance from the material, focus the lens, and make the exposure. The material is best mounted in indirect sunlight. However, if the material has low contrast, you may need to mount it on a sunlit wall, but be sure you are not getting undesirable reflections or bright spots. A handy way of eliminating glare is to use a polarizing filter. Consult your local camera store for the proper size for your camera and helpful hints on how to use it. A polarizing filter is especially useful in eliminating glare when photographing something beneath a water surface and in darkening the sky for dramatic effects, but it also has a tendency to flatten outdoor scenes (e.g., by eliminating the reflections from sunlit leaves).

Using a tripod for tabletop photography.

Tabletop Photography

The camera mounted on a tripod is handy for photographing small objects: coins, flowers, insects, etc. You can place the object on a coffee table in a well-lit area, with the tripod and camera oriented so that the object is well displayed. The comments about supplementary and macro lenses apply here too. Don't use a wide-angle lens, because the image will be distorted; the part of the object closest to the lens will be out of proportion to the rest of the object.

Copy Stand

If you do a lot of copying, you will want to look into using a copy stand. Your media center may have one that you can use. At a minimum, a copy stand has a flat surface where the material is placed and a vertical post on which the camera is mounted. From there, copy stands become more elaborate and may include an adjustable surface to hold the material flat and adjustable floodlights attached to the base. After placing the material to be copied on the surface, you move the camera up and down and adjust the material until the viewfinder shows the image you want. If supplemental lighting is necessary, use the polarizing filter to take care of any glare that might result. A copy stand is best used for flat materials. Three-dimensional objects are better photographed on a table using a tripod-mounted camera because you can choose the angle and lighting that best shows the object.

Lettering

If you want to add lettering to the material you are photographing, remember to keep the letters in proportion. If the area being copied is fairly large, the letters must be large also. If the area is small, the letters must be small because they will be enlarged when the image is enlarged. Judge the size of the lettering in proportion to the material by studying what you see in the viewfinder.

Copying Slides

Copying slides requires a special piece of equipment. It looks like a miniature copy stand, and lights from beneath the slide to be copied. The camera, mounted on the vertical post, can be adjusted to copy all or part of the slide. This is a useful but expensive piece of equipment. Your media center may have one. Otherwise, for the few times you may need to copy slides, a commercial shop is the simplest way to go.

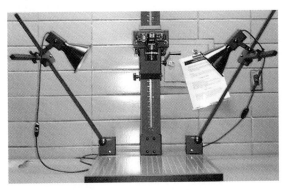

Using a copy stand to photograph flat materials.

MOUNTING PICTURES USING RUBBER CEMENT

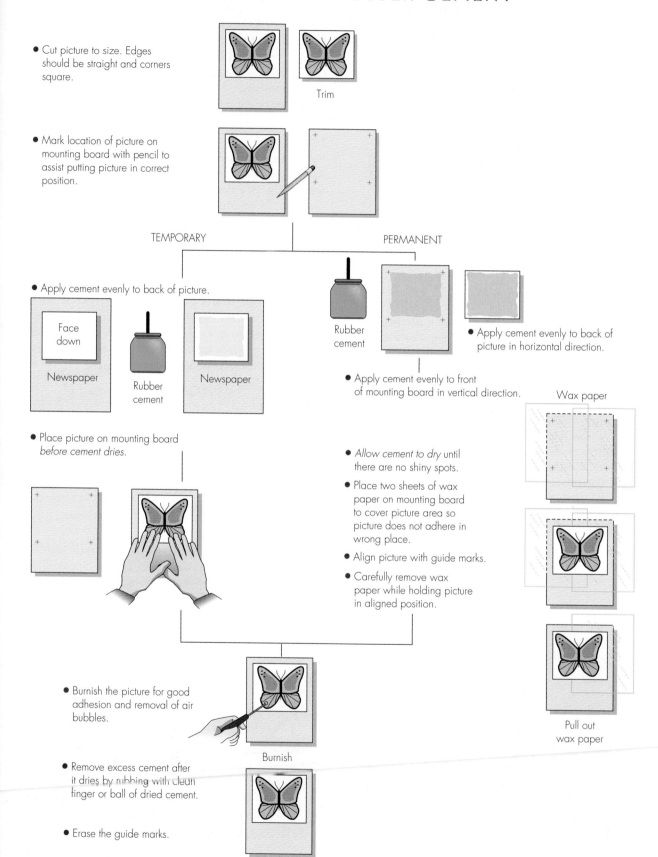

- Cut picture to size. Edges should be straight and corners square.

Trim

- Mark location of picture on mounting board with pencil to assist putting picture in correct position.

TEMPORARY

PERMANENT

- Apply cement evenly to back of picture.

Face down

Newspaper

Rubber cement

Newspaper

Rubber cement

- Apply cement evenly to back of picture in horizontal direction.

- Apply cement evenly to front of mounting board in vertical direction.

- Place picture on mounting board *before cement dries.*

- *Allow cement to dry* until there are no shiny spots.
- Place two sheets of wax paper on mounting board to cover picture area so picture does not adhere in wrong place.
- Align picture with guide marks.
- Carefully remove wax paper while holding picture in aligned position.

Wax paper

Pull out wax paper

- Burnish the picture for good adhesion and removal of air bubbles.

Burnish

- Remove excess cement after it dries by rubbing with clean finger or ball of dried cement.

- Erase the guide marks.

Remove excess cement

DRY MOUNTING PICTURES

1. Dry the mounting board and picture before trimming picture by placing them in dry-mount press for about one minute at 225°F. Close press, but *do not lock.*

2. Place a sheet (either side up) of dry-mounting tissue over the *back* of the *untrimmed* picture, with sheet extending beyond the edges of picture.

3. Attach the tissue to the back center of the picture with tip of a tacking iron set on "medium."

4. Turn picture and tissue over and trim both simultaneously to desired size. (A paper cutter works best, but a razor knife and metal straightedge or scissors may be used.)

5. Place the picture and dry-mounting tissue on the mounting board and align in proper position.

6. Tack the tissue to the mounting board *at two opposite corners.*

Tacking iron

7. Cover mounting board and picture with clean paper on both sides.

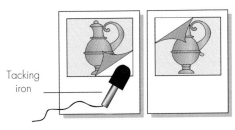

8. Place in dry-mount press preheated to 225°F for about one minute.

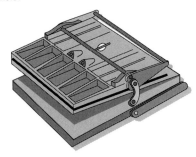

9. Remove from dry-mount press and allow the materials to cool. (Placing the cooling materials under a metal weight will help prevent curling.)

LAMINATING PICTURES WITH A DRY-MOUNT PRESS

1. The dry-mount press should be heated to 225°F. If you live in an area with high humidity, you may get better results if you preheat the visual (to remove excess moisture) in the press for about one minute. Close the press but do not lock it.

2. Cover the picture to be laminated with a piece of laminating film slightly larger than the picture. The inside of the roll (dull side) contains the heat-sensitive adhesive and should be toward the visual. Press the film onto the picture with your hands. Static electricity should cause the film to stay in place.

3. Put the picture and laminating film in a cover of clean paper to protect the visual and to prevent the adhesive from getting onto the surface of the dry-mount press.

4. Insert the material in the press for one minute. Remove it; if the adhesion is not complete, put it back into the press for another minute. It may be helpful to put a magazine or a ¼-inch stack of paper on top of the picture to increase the pressure and improve adhesion between the picture and the laminating film.

Sketching

Faces

Use an oval and add a minimum of lines to indicate features and expressions.

1. Start with a circle or oval.
2. Add ears in the middle on each side.
3. Draw a nose between the ears.
4. Place the eyes near the top of the nose.
5. Draw the mouth halfway between the nose and chin.
6. Add hair and other features.

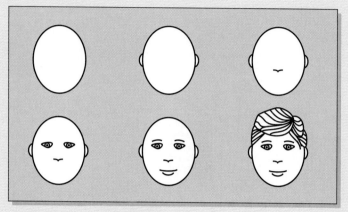

Body

Begin with stick figures, which can show action. With practice, add detail to your characters.

1. Determine the head size and draw.

2. Draw a straight line down from that head which is an *additional* 3 heads long. This is the torso.

3. Just below the head draw a *horizontal* line about 2 head lengths long. This is the shoulder line.

4. Draw a horizontal line about 1½ head lengths long at end of torso (slightly wider for female figure). This is the hip area.

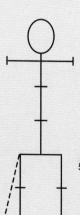

5. Draw vertical lines down from hip "joints" 4 head lengths long. Leg length comprises *half* of entire body length. Knees would fall about halfway or 2 head lengths down.

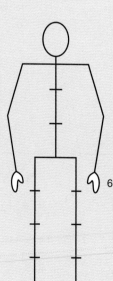

6. Draw vertical lines down from shoulder points to below the hips. These are arms. Add "mitten" hands at the ends. Elbows fall midway on these lines.

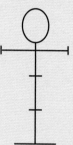

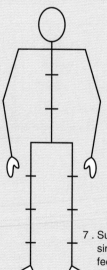

7 . Superimpose simple triangular feet on the legs at the bottom.

DEVELOPING AN AUDIOVISUAL PRESENTATION

Here is a simple approach to developing your own audiovisual presentation.

Step 1

Analyze your audience both in terms of general characteristics and specific entry competencies (as described in Chapter 3).

- Why are they viewing the presentation?
- What is their motivation toward your topic?
- How much do they already know about the subject?

Step 2

Specify your objectives (as described in Chapter 3).

- What do you want to accomplish with the presentation?
  - Knowledge
  - Attitudes
  - Skills
- What should the viewers be able to do after the presentation?
  - Activity or performance?
  - Under what conditions?
  - With what degree of skill?

Step 3

Having completed your audience analysis and stated your objectives, you now have a much clearer idea of how your presentation will fit into your overall lesson plan, including what might precede it and follow it. Perhaps you will decide at this point that an audiovisual presentation is not really what you need after all.

If you decide to go ahead, get a pack of planning cards (use index cards or Post-it® notes, or cut some sheets of paper into 4-by-6-inch rectangles). Draw a large box in the upper left-hand corner of each card.

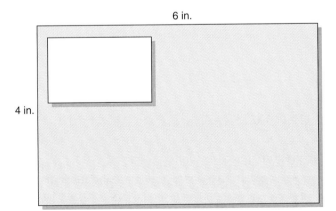

Step 4

Take a planning card. In the box draw a rough sketch of whatever image comes to your mind when you think about one of your major points. You don't have to start with the first point, just whatever comes into your mind first. Your sketch may be a symbol, a diagram, a graph, a cartoon, or a photo of a person, place, or thing, for example.

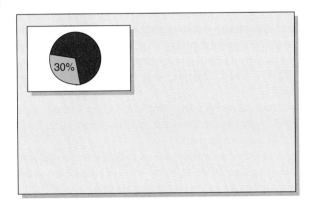

Step 5

Below your sketch, write a brief statement that captures the essence of the point you are trying to make. State it in as few words as needed to cue yourself to the thought. Some developers prefer to start with the visuals and then write the narration. Others prefer to do the narration first. Actually developing an audiovisual presentation is likely to be a dynamic process, with visual and narration evolving one from the other, separately and simultaneously. In some cases, of course, your narration will be already at hand—printed information, for example, or a story or poem—and all that remains is to develop the proper visuals to fit it. Or, the visuals may already be in hand—slides from a field trip, for example—and all you have to do is organize them and develop your script to accompany the visuals.

Step 6

Make a card for the thought that leads into the point you have just sketched. Then do another one about the thought that follows your first one. Continue like this, building a chain of ideas as you go along.

Step 7

When you run out of ideas in the chain, switch to one of the other major points that hasn't fallen into sequence yet.

Step 8

Arrange the cards in sequential and logical order. This process is called *storyboarding*.

Would some other arrangement liven up the beginning and the end of your presentation? Keep in mind the psychology of the situation as you thought it through in your audience analysis. The beginning and the end are generally the best places to make major points. Have you grabbed the viewer's attention right from the beginning?

How about pacing? Are any complicated ideas skimmed over too lightly? Do sections get bogged down in unnecessary detail? Add or subtract cards as needed.

You should have at least one slide on the screen for every point you make. Each slide should be on the screen long enough to support the point but not so long that it gets tiresome to look at.

As a rule of thumb, you can estimate the number of slides you need by timing your presentation and multiplying the number of minutes by five or six. This means one slide change about every 10 or 12 seconds. You may find that you need more slides in some instances and fewer in others. Don't be afraid to use "filler" slides to hold visual interest. They're perfectly acceptable as long as they relate to the topic.

Step 9

Edit your planning cards in terms of practicality. Be sure you have ready access to the artistic talent or photographic equipment needed to turn your sketches into slides.

Step 10

Use your notes to prepare an audio script.

Consider using two different voices for the narration, perhaps one male and one female for variety. Would sound effects add impact to your presentation? How about actual sounds from the place where you will be shooting the pictures? You can take along a recorder and pick up background sounds and personal interviews while doing the photography.

Consider, too, adding music, especially as a finishing touch to the beginning and end. Be careful to keep it unobtrusive. Avoid highly recognizable tunes, trendy songs that will date your presentation, and music aimed at very specialized tastes.

Step 11

Rehearse your presentation, imagining that your cards are slides on the screen. Time your presentation and see if you need to shorten or lengthen it. To keep your audience's attention, limit your show to 15 minutes. If you need more time than that, break it into two or more parts interspersed with audience activity.

Now you are ready to turn your sketches into slides! (To record your tape, see "Recording Audiocassettes.")

How To . . .
Step-by-Step Guides for Equipment and Setups

SAFELY MOVING AND USING AUDIOVISUAL EQUIPMENT

Loading Projection Carts

- *Prohibit children from moving carts.* Only adults should be allowed to move loaded carts. A safety sticker showing the ICIA warning (shown on next page) should be placed on all carts.
- *Lock casters.* Be sure to engage caster locks before loading a cart.
- *Unplug cords.* Disconnect all power cords from wall outlets and wrap them around the equipment.
- *Use lower shelves.* Place equipment on the lower shelves before moving. Disconnect VCR from TV monitor before moving units to lower shelves.

Moving Projection Carts

- *Unlock casters.* Disengage all caster locks before moving the cart.
- *Push, don't pull.* Always push the cart, applying force on the narrow dimension, and watch where you're going. Never pull the cart.
- *Elevator angle.* When entering or leaving an elevator, push the cart at an angle so that one caster at a time passes over the gap between building and elevator.
- *Strap for ramp.* If a cart is to be moved up or down a ramp, use a strap to secure equipment to the cart.

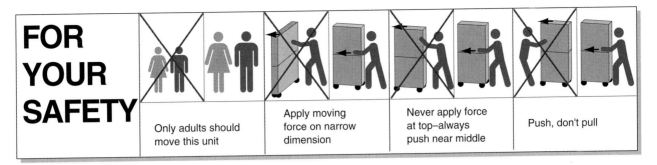

FOR YOUR SAFETY	Only adults should move this unit	Apply moving force on narrow dimension	Never apply force at top–always push near middle	Push, don't pull

This safety sticker, available from the International Communications Industries Association, should be on all carts.

Using Equipment

- *Lock casters.* Engage the caster locks as soon as the projection cart is in place.
- *Center on shelf.* Make sure equipment is centered on the cart shelf, with nothing protruding over the edge.
- *Check power cords.* Inspect for frayed cords and loose plugs. When unplugging, pull the plug, not the cord.
- *Secure cords.*
  - Keep power and speaker cords out of traffic lanes; leave a lot of slack.
- Wrap the power cord around the bottom of a leg of the cart so that if someone does trip on the cord, the cart (not the equipment) is pulled.
- Use duct tape to cover cords that could be a tripping hazard.

Source: Adapted from guidelines provided by the International Communications Industries Association (ICIA). Additional information, including safety warning stickers for carts, is available from ICIA, 3150 Spring Street, Fairfax, VA 22031.

ELIMINATING THE KEYSTONE EFFECT

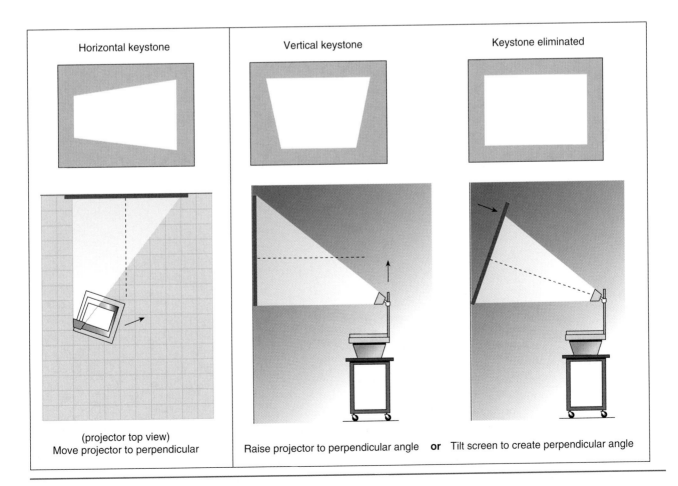

Horizontal keystone

Vertical keystone

Keystone eliminated

(projector top view)
Move projector to perpendicular

Raise projector to perpendicular angle **or** Tilt screen to create perpendicular angle

Glossary

Acceptable Use Policy (AUP)   An agreement among students, parents/guardians, and school administrators regarding appropriate use of the Internet.

Accommodation   The cognitive process of modifying a schema or creating new schemata.

Acetate   A transparent plastic sheet associated with overhead projection.

Advance organizer   An outline, preview, or other such preinstructional cue used to promote retention of verbal material, as proposed by David Ausubel. Also referred to as *preinstructional strategies.*

Affective domain   The domain of human learning that involves changes in interests, attitudes, and values and the development of appreciation.

Alignment   Establishing visual relationships among elements by placing their edges along the same imaginary horizontal or vertical line.

Alt-tag   Alternative textual description that identifies a graphic or an image; used when designing computer images and screens for visually impaired users.

Analogous colors   Any two colors that lie next to one another on the color wheel. Contrasted with *complementary colors.*

Animation   A film technique in which the artist gives motion to still images by creating and juxtaposing a series of pictures with small, incremental changes from one to the next.

Aperture   The lens opening that regulates the amount of light entering the camera.

Arrangement   The pattern or shape into which the elements of a visual display are organized.

Artifact   Student-produced materials such as writings, videos, and multimedia presentations.

Assimilation   The cognitive process by which a learner integrates new information into an existing schema.

Asynchronous   Not at the same time.

Attachment   Electronic files (documents and graphics) sent along with e-mail messages.

Audio   A type of media composed of anything a person can hear (e.g., voice, music, mechanical sounds, noise).

Audiographic teleconference   A teleconference involving voice plus graphic display. The graphics may be transmitted by a fax machine or electronically by means of slow-scan video or a graphics tablet.

Audio teleconference   A teleconference involving transmission of voices only. The voices are amplified at each end by a speaker system.

Auditory fatigue   The process by which attention to a sound gradually decreases because of the monotony of the sound.

Authentic assessment   Evaluation that is usually performance based and that requires students to demonstrate their learning in a natural context.

Author   To create on a computer a unique collection of related information.

Bandwidth   The range of frequencies an electronic communications channel can support without excessive deterioration.

Bar graph   A type of graph in which the height of the bar is the measure of the quantity being represented.

Baud   The switching speed, or number of transitions (voltage or frequency changes) made per second; the speed at which modems transfer data. At low speeds, one baud is roughly equivalent to one bit per second.

Behaviorism   A theory that equates learning with changes in observable behavior; with this theory, there is no speculating about mental events that may mediate learning.

Bit   An acronym for *binary digit*; the smallest unit of digital information. The bit can be thought of as a 1 or a 0 representing a circuit on or off, respectively.

Blended learning   A combination of e-learning with live, face-to-face instruction.

Blog   Weblog serving as a publicly accessible personal journal for an individual.

Branching programming   A format of programmed instruction in which the sequence of presentation of the frames depends on the responses selected by the learner.

Broadcasting   Transmission of signals to many receivers simultaneously via electromagnetic waves.

Browse   To navigate through information on computer, following items of personal interest by choosing nonsequential pathways.

Bulletin board   Computer system used as an information source and message posting system for a particular interest group.

Button   An onscreen device used to open applications, select options, and to navigate within a hypertext environment.

Byte   The number of bits required to store or represent one character of text (a letter or number); most commonly, but not always, made up of eight bits in various combinations of 0s and 1s.

Cable modem   A television cable connection that provides very-high-speed access to the Internet.

Cable television   A television distribution system consisting of a closed-circuit, usually wired, network for transmitting signals from an origination point (see *head end*) to members of the network. Typically, the origination point receives and retransmits broadcast programs, adding recorded programs and/or some live originations.

Carrel   A partially enclosed booth that serves as a clearly identifiable enclosure for learning center activities.

Cassette   A self-contained reel-to-reel magnetic tape system with the two reels permanently installed in a rugged plastic case.

CCD   See *charge-coupled device.*

CCTV   See *closed-circuit television.*

CD-R   Compact disc–recordable. A compact disc on which the user may record information digitally one time and then access it many times.

CD-ROM (Compact disc–read-only memory)   Digitally encoded information permanently recorded on a compact disc. Information can be accessed very quickly.

CD-RW Compact disc–rewriteable. A compact disc on which the user may record information digitally many times and access it many times.

Chalkboard A display surface, once called *blackboard*, for visual and textual communication with chalk.

Charge-coupled device (CCD) A device that changes a pattern of different wavelengths into corresponding electrical charges.

Charter school Autonomous, publicly funded school of choice designed and run by teachers or others under contract with a public organization.

Chat room Web or Internet subsites where users may "converse" in real time using their keyboards.

Closed-circuit television (CCTV) Any system of television that transmits signals through self-contained pathways (such as cable) rather than via broadcasting.

Cloth board A display surface made of fabric for temporarily adhering materials with cloth or sandpaper backing.

Cognitive domain The domain of human learning involving intellectual skills, such as assimilation of information or knowledge.

Cognitive psychology A branch of psychology devoted to the study of how individuals acquire, process, and use information.

Cognitivism A theory according to which mental processes mediate learning and learning entails the construction or reshaping of mental schemata.

Cold storage training Information or skills taught that may or may not be used in the future.

Compact disc (CD) A 4.72-inch disc on which a laser has recorded digital information.

Complementary colors Any two colors that lie directly opposite one another on the color wheel. Contrasted with *analogous colors.*

Compressed video Video images that have been processed to remove redundant information, thereby reducing the amount of bandwidth required to transmit them. Because only changes in the image are transmitted, movements appear jerky compared with full-motion video.

Computer-assisted instruction (CAI) Instruction delivered directly to learners by allowing them to interact with lessons programmed into the computer system.

Computer classroom A regular classroom furnished with one or more computers.

Computer conferencing Connecting two or more computers together for textual and/or graphical information exchange.

Computer hypermedia A computer hardware and software system that allows the composition and display of nonsequential documents that may include text, audio, and visual information and in which related information may be linked into webs by author or user.

Computer laboratory A room set apart from regular classrooms and furnished with multiple computers, usually established in schools that do not have computers in individual classrooms.

Computer-managed instruction (CMI) The use of a computer system to manage information about learner performance and learning resources and to then prescribe and control individual lessons.

Computer multimedia A computer hardware and software system for the composition and display of presentations that incorporate text, audio, and still and motion images.

Computer network An electronic connecting system that allows physically dispersed computers to share software, data, and peripheral devices.

Computer platform Different types of computer operating systems, such as *Mac OS, Unix,* or *Windows.*

Constructivism A theory that considers the engagement of students in meaningful experiences as the essence of learning.

Cooperative game A game in which the attainment of the goal requires cooperation rather than competition among the players.

Cooperative learning An instructional configuration involving small groups of learners working together on learning tasks rather than competing as individuals.

Copy board A device that makes a paper copy of what is written on a type of electronic whiteboard.

Copyright Regulations that describe the manner in which an original work can be used and copied. Copyright laws regulate the manner in which authors or artists can be reimbursed for their creative work.

Courseware Lessons delivered via computer, consisting of content conveyed according to an instructional design controlled by programmed software.

Criterion As part of a performance objective, the standard by which acceptable performance is judged; may include a time limit, accuracy tolerance, proportion of correct responses required, and/or qualitative standards.

Cross-training A method to train an individual worker to do several jobs and several workers to do the same job.

Cyberspace Informal name for the global computer network.

Database A collection of related information organized for quick access to specific items of information.

Debriefing Discussion conducted among simulation or game participants after play to elucidate what they have learned.

Demonstration A method in which learners view a real or lifelike example of a skill or procedure to be learned.

Desktop publishing Computer applications and hardware that allow a personal computer to generate typeset-quality text and graphics.

Desktop video Video production using a personal computer and low-cost video equipment.

Desktop video conferencing Real-time person-to-person or group interaction over a network using computers incorporating visual and auditory exchange.

Dichroic mirror A mirror coated so that only one color of the spectrum is reflected. In a video camera, three dichroic mirrors direct the three primary colors to three respective video tubes.

Digital Representation or storage of information by combinations of numbers (a series of 0s and 1s).

Digital camera Camera that uses a charge-coupled device as a recording medium in place of film, recording the image digitally.

Digital image An image that is not stored on film or processed like film, but rather stored on disk or on a computer using digital numbers to represent the image.

Digital recording A recording process in which analog information is encoded in binary form before being saved onto the recording medium.

Digital Subscriber Line (DSL) A telephone line that provides very-high-speed access to the Internet.

Digital video Video recording technology that stores video images as strings of binary numbers.

Digital videodisc (DVD) A compact disc format for displaying motion video, often in the form of movies for home entertainment.

Digital video editing Taking apart and putting back together video segments using a computer and associated software.

Diorama A static display employing a flat background and three-dimensional foreground to achieve a lifelike effect.

Directional A visual device, such as an arrow, used to direct viewers' attention in a given direction or to a specific location.

Discovery method A teaching strategy that proceeds as follows: immersion in a real or contrived problem situation, development of hypotheses, testing of hypotheses, and arrival at conclusion (the main point).

Discussion method A teaching strategy involving the exchange of ideas and opinions.

Display An array of objects, visuals, and printed materials.

Distance learning/education Any instructional situation in which learners are separated in time or space from the point of origination, characterized by limited access to the teacher and other learners.

Distance site A classroom connected remotely via a telecommunications system to a site where a teacher is present. See *origination classroom.*

Division of labor In economics, the reorganization of a job so that some tasks are performed by one person or system and other tasks are performed by others for purposes of increased efficiency or effectiveness.

Documentary A video program that deals with fact, not fiction or fictionalized versions of fact.

Document camera A video camera mounted on a copy stand to show documents, pictures, graphics, and real objects to groups.

Download To transfer programs and/or data files from a computer to another device or computer; to retrieve something from a network.

Drill-and-practice method A teaching strategy in which learners are led through a series of exercises or problems and given feedback.

DVD See *digital videodisc.*

E-book A hand-held reader containing enough memory to store 75 to 80 novel-length works.

E-learning (electronic learning) Internet-based learning. Components can include content delivery in multiple formats, management of the learning experience, and a networked community of learners, content developers, and experts. E-learning provides faster learning at reduced costs, increased access to learning materials, and clear accountability for all participants in the learning process.

Electronic mail (e-mail) Transmission of messages over a computer network; users can send mail to a single recipient or broadcast it to multiple users on the system.

Electronic whiteboard A display surface that "captures" digitally anything written on it.

Electrostatic film (xerography) A method of making overhead transparencies. Similar to the thermal process, this process requires specially treated film that is electrically charged and light sensitive.

Emoticon An e-mail symbol generated from punctuation marks.

Enactive experience Direct, firsthand experience.

Entry tests Assessments, both formal and informal, to determine if students possess desired identified prerequisites.

Exhibit A display incorporating various media formats (e.g., realia, still pictures, models, graphics) into an integral whole intended for instructional purposes.

Expert system A computer program, assembled by a team of content experts and programmers, that teaches learners how to solve complex tasks by applying the appropriate knowledge from the content area.

Extranet A network of intranets. See *intranet.*

Extrinsic motivator Factor unrelated to a task that stimulates someone to pursue the task. Contrasted with *intrinsic motivator.*

Fair use Basic criteria by which an educator may determine if it is appropriate to use copyrighted materials in a classroom setting.

Feedback In electronics, the regeneration of sound caused by a system's microphonic pickup of output from its own speakers, causing a ringing sound or squeal. In communication, signals sent from the destination back to the source that provide information about the reception of the original message.

Fiber optics A transmission medium using spun silicon shaped into threads as thin as human hair. It transmits more signals with higher quality than can metal cables.

Field trip An excursion outside the classroom to study real processes, people, and objects.

Figure–ground contrast The visual principle stating that dark figures show up best on light backgrounds and light figures show up best on dark backgrounds.

File server In local area networks, a station dedicated to providing file and mass data storage services to the other stations on the network.

Firewall Intranet software that prevents external users from accessing a proprietary network, while allowing internal users access to external networks.

Flip chart A pad of large paper fastened together at the top and mounted on an easel.

Focal length The distance from the focal point of a lens to a camera's film plane when the lens is focused at infinity.

Frame game Any game that lends its structure to a variety of subject matter.

Fresnel lens A flat glass or acrylic lens in which the curvature of a normal lens surface is collapsed into an almost flat plane, resulting in concentric circle forms impressed or engraved on the lens surface. Because of its low cost, light weight, and compactness, it is often used for the condenser lens in overhead projectors and in studio lights.

f/stop Term used in measuring a camera's lens opening. Larger f-numbers indicate smaller openings.

Game An activity in which participants follow prescribed rules that differ from those of reality as they strive to attain a challenging goal.

Gateway A computer that interconnects and makes translations between two different types of networks. Also called a *portal.*

Gb See *gigabyte.*

Geosynchronous satellite A communications satellite orbiting at a predetermined distance and traveling at such a speed that it appears to hover steadily over the same spot on earth.

Gigabyte (Gb)   Approximately one million bytes, or 1,000 megabytes.

Goal   A desired instructional outcome that is broad in scope and general with regard to criteria and performance indicators.

Graphics   Two-dimensional, nonphotographic materials designed to communicate a specific message to the viewer.

Hard disk   Metal disk covered with a magnetic recording material; the permanent storage device for a computer.

Hard technology   The hardware, such as television, computers, and satellites, used as tools to provide instruction. Contrasted with *soft technology*.

Hardware   The mechanical and electronic components that make up a computer; the physical equipment that makes up a computer system, and, by extension, the term that refers to any audiovisual equipment.

Head end   The origination point of a cable television system.

Hearing   A physiological process in which sound waves entering the outer ear are transmitted to the eardrum, converted into mechanical vibrations in the middle ear, and changed in the inner ear to nerve impulses that travel to the brain.

Hybrid learning   See *blended learning*.

Hypermedia   Software based on utilizing a hypertext environment for nonsequential access to data. See also *computer hypermedia*.

Hypertext   A method of encoding data that enables the user to access continually a large information base whenever additional information on a subject is needed.

Hypertext Markup Language (HTML)   The programming language that defines the format of a World Wide Web page. This relatively simple code can be purchased as software to streamline the creation of Web pages.

Hypertext transfer protocol (HTTP)   The Web protocol that ensures compatility before transferring information.

Iconic   Any referent that resembles the thing it represents.

Iconic representation   Pertaining to an image that resembles a real object.

Information superhighway   Popular name given to the concept of an international information network of extremely high carrying capacity. Also refers specifically to the fiber-optic network being constructed in North America.

In-house video   Video produced within one's own school or company.

Instruction   Deliberate arrangement of experience(s) to help learners achieve a desirable change in performance; the management of learning, which in education and training is primarily the function of the instructor.

Instructional development   The process of analyzing needs, determining what content must be mastered, establishing educational goals, designing materials to help reach the objectives, and trying out and revising the program according to learner achievement.

Instructional module   A freestanding instructional unit, usually used for independent study. Typical components are rationale, objective, pretest, learning activities, self-test, and posttest.

Instructional systems   A set of interrelated components that work together within a framework to provide learning activities necessary to accomplish a learning goal.

Instructional technology   Using hardware, software, and/or processes to facilitate learning.

Instructional television (ITV)   Any planned use of video programs to meet specific instructional goals regardless of the source of the programs (including commercial broadcasts) or the setting in which they are used (including business and industry training).

Instructional Television Fixed Service (ITFS)   A portion of the microwave frequency spectrum (2500–2690 MHz) reserved by law in the United States for educational use.

Integrated learning system (ILS)   A set of interrelated computer-based lessons organized to match the curriculum of a school or training agency.

Integrated Services Digital Network (ISDN)   A network that provides high-speed access to the Internet using digital communication.

Interactive media   Media formats that allow or require some level of physical activity from the user, which in some ways alters the sequence of presentation.

Interactive video   Computer-controlled video playback incorporating some method for users to control the sequence of presentation, typically by responding to multiple-choice questions.

Internet   A worldwide system for linking smaller computer networks together, based on a packet system of information transfer and using a common set of communication standards.

Internet service provider   An organization that provides access to the Internet.

Interpersonal domain   The domain of learning that involves interaction among people and the ability to relate effectively with others.

Intranet   Internal network for a company or school that cannot be accessed by external users.

Intrinsic motivator   Factor directly related to a task that stimulates someone to pursue the task. Contrasted with *extrinsic motivator*.

Just-in-time training   Instruction provided when the worker needs it, often at the workstation and not in a classroom.

Kb   See *kilobyte*.

Keystone effect   The distortion (usually creating a wide top and narrow bottom) of a projected image caused when the projector is not aligned at right angles to the screen.

Kilobyte (Kb or K)   Approximately 1,000 bytes; more precisely, 1,024 bytes.

Lab pack   Provides a number of simultaneous uses of computer software by licensing agreement.

Lamination   Protection for visuals by covering them with a clear plastic or plasticlike material.

LCD   See *liquid crystal display*.

Learning   A general term for a relatively lasting change in capability caused by experience; also, the process by which such change is brought about. See also *behaviorism* and *cognitivism* for different interpretations of learning.

Learning center   A self-contained environment designed to promote individual or small-group learning around a specific task.

Learning style   A cluster of psychological traits that determine how a person perceives, interacts with, and responds emotionally to learning environments.

Linear programming   A format of programmed instruction in which the frames are arranged in a fixed, linear sequence.

Link An association between two (or more) nonsequential concepts. In hypermedia, a direct connection between two asynchronous items of data.

Liquid crystal display (LCD) A data display using a liquid crystal material encased between two transparent sheets. Liquid crystals have the properties of a liquid and a solid; a network of electrodes and polarizing filters creates a grid of pixels that open and close to pass or block light.

Listening A psychological process that begins with someone's awareness of and attention to sounds or speech patterns, proceeds through identification and recognition of specific auditory signals, and ends in comprehension.

Listening center A learning center especially designed for audio media.

Listserv A program that automatically sorts and distributes electronic messages over a computer network.

Local area network (LAN) A local system (typically within a building) connecting computers and peripheral devices into a network; may give access to external networks.

Low-cost learning technology An approach to formal education featuring systematic selection and implementation of a variety of managerial, instructional, motivational, and resource-utilization strategies to increase student learning outcomes while decreasing or maintaining recurrent educational costs.

Magnetic board A display surface made of metal for temporarily adhering materials with magnetic backing.

Manipulative Object that can be viewed and handled in a learning setting.

Mb See *megabyte*.

Media format The physical form in which a message is incorporated and displayed. Examples include flip charts, photographic prints and slides, audio- and videotape, and computer multimedia.

Medium A means of communication. Derived from the Latin *medium* ("between"), the term refers to anything that carries information between a source and a receiver. Plural: *media*.

Megabyte (Mb or M) Basic unit of measurement of mass storage, equal to 1,048,576 bytes, or 1,024 kilobytes.

Method A procedure of instruction selected to help learners achieve their objective or to internalize a message.

Microwave transmission A television distribution system using the ultra-high and super-high frequency ranges (2,000–13,000 MHz); includes ITFS in the United States (2,500–2,690 MHz).

Mock up Representation of a complex device or process.

Model A three-dimensional representation of a real object; it may be larger, smaller, or the same size as the thing represented.

Modem Acronym for *mo*dulator/*dem*odulator. An electronic device that translates digital information to analog for transmission over telephone lines. A receiving modem translates the analog information back to digital.

Motion media A type of media showing motion/movement (e.g., videotape, animation).

Motivation An internal state that leads people to choose to pursue certain goals and experiences.

Motor skill domain The category of human learning that involves athletic, manual, and other physical action skills.

MP3 (MPEG Audio Layer 3) A format for compression of audio files to shrink them into more manageable size, especially when using the Internet.

Multi-image presentation Any visual presentation showing several images simultaneously, often using multiple screens.

Multimedia Sequential or simultaneous use of a variety of media formats in a given presentation or self-study program. See also *computer multimedia*.

Multimedia kit A collection of teaching-learning materials involving more than one type of medium and organized around a single topic.

Multipurpose board A board with a smooth white plastic surface used with special marking pens rather than chalk. The boards usually have a steel backing and can be used as a magnetic board for display of visuals; may also be used as a screen for projected visuals.

Narrowband A telecommunications channel that carries lower frequency signals; includes telephone frequencies of about 3,000 Hz and radio subcarrier signals of about 15,000 Hz.

Navigate To move about at will within a hypermedia environment by means of buttons and other onscreen devices.

Netiquette Guidelines relating to e-mail and other interactions on the Web.

Network A communication system linking two or more computers.

Newsgroup On computer networks, a discussion group created by allowing users to post messages and read messages among themselves.

Nonprojected visual Any visual teaching aid that does not require equipment to view or manipulate.

Object A type of media that is three-dimensional and can be touched (e.g., real things and models).

Objective A statement of the new capability that is intended to result from instruction.

Online learning The result of instruction that is delivered electronically using computers and computer-based media.

Optical disc A type of disc storage device that records and reproduces digital information using a laser beam, e.g., CD and DVD.

Optical spacing Spacing typographical elements so that they appear evenly separated, regardless of their true measured distance.

Oral history Historical documentation of a time, place, or event by means of recording the spoken recollections of participants in those events.

Origination classroom Site where teacher is located when providing distance learning via a telecommunications system. See *distance site*.

Overhead projection Projection by means of a device that produces an image on a screen by transmitting light through transparent acetate or a similar medium on the stage of the projector. The lens and mirror arrangement in an elevated housing creates a bright projected image over the head or shoulder of the operator.

Overlay One or more additional transparent sheets with lettering or other information that can be placed over a base transparency.

Packaged instruction Materials which allow students to control when and where they learn.

Pedagogical agent A computer program or portion of a program that is used to help the user organize information and facilitate ease of use.

People A type of media that includes human beings (e.g., students, teachers, experts).

Performance objective A statement of the new capability the learner should possess at the completion of instruction. A well-stated objective names the intended audience, then specifies (1) the performance or capability to be learned, (2) the conditions under which the performance is to be demonstrated, and (3) the criterion or standard of acceptable performance.

Performance support system A variety of online aids both to improve current job performance and to plan future training needs.

Persistence of vision The psychophysiological phenomenon that occurs when an image falls on the retina of the eye and is conveyed to the brain via the optic nerve. The brain continues to "see" the image for a fraction of a second after the image is cut off.

Personal Data Assistant (PDA) Hand-held computer.

Photo CD A collection of digitized photographs stored on a CD-ROM.

Portal See *gateway*.

Portfolio An integrated collection of student work including a variety of media to demonstrate progress and accomplishments.

Practice Learner participation that increases the probability of learning.

Preinstructional strategies See *advance organizer*.

Prerequisites Competencies that learners must possess to benefit from instruction.

Presentation graphics software Computer software to create attractive graphic displays without specialized production skills.

Presentation method An instructional strategy in which a source tells, dramatizes, or disseminates information to learners.

Problem-based instruction High-fidelity, learner-centered, inquiry-based instruction based on real situations.

Problem solving Using lifelike situations for learning.

Programmed instruction A method of presenting instructional material printed in small bits or frames, each of which includes an item of information (prompt), a sentence to be completed or a question to be answered (response), and the correct answer (reinforcement).

Programmed tutoring A one-to-one process technology in which the decisions to be made by the tutor are "programmed" in advance by means of carefully structured printed instructions.

Projected visuals Media formats in which still images are projected onto a screen.

Proximity Visual principle in which viewers assume that items placed close together are related, and those placed farther apart are unrelated.

RAM See *random access memory*.

Random access memory (RAM) The flexible part of computer memory. The particular program or set of data being manipulated by the user is temporarily stored in RAM, then erased to make way for the next program.

Read-only memory (ROM) Control instructions that have been "wired" permanently into the memory of a computer. Usually stores instructions that the computer will need constantly, such as the programming language(s) and internal monitoring functions.

Real object Not a model or simulation but an example of an actual object used in instruction.

Referent That which is referred to.

Reform See *restructuring*.

Removable-storage device High-capacity portable computer storage unit that allows the user to store information and move it from one computer to another.

Restructuring Approaches to change the framework of education incorporating the redesign of programs, staffing, and even facilities. Also referred to as *reform*.

Role play A simulation in which the dominant feature is relatively open-ended interaction among people.

ROM See *read-only memory*.

Rule of thirds A principle of photographic and graphic composition in which an area is divided into thirds both vertically and horizontally and the centers of interest are located near the intersections of the lines.

Sans serif Typeface style with no ornamentation on either ascenders or descenders, such as Helvetica.

Scanner A computer device that converts an image on a piece of paper into an electronic form that can be stored in a computer file.

Scenario Literally, a written description of the plot of a play. In simulation and game design, it refers to a description of the setting and events to be represented in a simulation.

Schema Mental structure by which individuals organize their perceptions of the environment. Plural: *schemata*.

Script A set of user-defined commands used to create or navigate within a hypertext environment.

Search engine A program that identifies Internet sites that contain user-identified keywords or phrases.

Showmanship Techniques that an instructor can use to direct and hold attention during presentations.

Shutter The mechanical device that controls the length of time light enters the camera and reaches the film plane.

Simulation An abstraction or simplification of some real-life situation or process.

Simulation game An instructional format that combines the attributes of simulation (role playing, model of reality) with the attributes of a game (striving toward a goal, specific rules).

Simulator A device that represents a real physical system in a scaled-down form; it allows users to experience the salient aspects of the real-life process.

Site license Provides unlimited use of software at specified locations by licensing agreement.

Slide A small-format (e.g., 35mm) photographic transparency individually mounted for one-at-a-time projection.

Slow motion A film technique that expands time by photographing rapid events at high speeds (many exposures per second) and then projecting the film at normal speed.

Social psychology The study of the effects of the social organization of the classroom on learning.

Soft technology Techniques and methods that form psychological and social frameworks for learning, as opposed to the hardware used to deliver instruction; an example is Keller's Personalized System of Instruction.

Software Computer program control instructions and accompanying documentation; stored on disks or tapes when not being used in the computer. By extension, the term refers to any audiovisual materials.

Spreadsheet Computer software that allows users to manipulate data and generate reports and charts.

Star Schools A program initiated in the United States by the Department of Education to promote instructional networks providing distance education for elementary and secondary schools.

Storyboarding An audiovisual production and planning technique in which sketches of the proposed visuals and verbal messages are put on individual cards or into a computer program; the items are then arranged into the desired sequence on a display surface.

Streaming video A video file downloaded from the Internet that starts playing before it is completely downloaded.

Study print A photographic enlargement printed in a durable form for individual or group examination.

Symbolic representation Pertaining to use of letters, numbers, and words to present information.

Synchronous At the same time.

Tb See *terabyte*.

Technology (1) A process of devising reliable and repeatable solutions to tasks. (2) The hardware and software (i.e., the product) that result from the application of technological processes. (3) A mix of process and product, used in instances where the context refers to the combination of technological processes and resultant products or where the process is inseparable from the product.

Technology for learning An application of technology to aid learning; may refer to either "hard" technologies (communications media) or "soft" technologies (processes or procedures that follow a technological approach).

Telecommunications A means for communicating over a distance; specifically, any arrangement for transmitting voice and data in the form of coded signals through an electronic medium.

Telecommuting A method allowing people to "commute" to work from their homes through computers and telecommunications technology.

Teleconference A communications configuration using electronic transmission technologies (audio and/or video) to hold live meetings among geographically dispersed people.

Teleconference, audio A live, two-way voice conversation among groups at different locations via telephone lines or satellites.

Teleconference, video A live, two-way communications arrangement connecting groups at different locations via telephone lines or satellites; voice is transmitted both ways, and video distribution may be either one-way or two-way.

Telelecture An instructional technique in which an individual, typically a content specialist or well-known authority, addresses a group listening by means of a telephone amplifier. The listeners may ask questions of the resource person, with the entire group able to hear the response.

Teletraining The process of using teleconferences for instructional purposes.

Television The system of transmitting moving pictures and sound electronically, either through the air or through wires, and displaying the images on a cathode-ray tube.

Telework A method in which employees work away from the office using telecommunications and computers to exchange information with the worksite.

Template A pattern used as a guide in making accurate replications of something. In computers, a ready-to-use permanent document set up with a basic layout, commands, and formulas.

Terabyte (Tb) Approximately one million megabytes.

Text A type of media composed of alphanumeric characters (e.g., letters and numbers).

Thematic instruction Learning activities organized around topics or anchors.

Thumb spot A mark on a slide to assist in placing it correctly in the slide tray.

Time lapse A video technique that compresses the time that it takes for an event to occur. A long process is photographed frame by frame, at intervals, and then projected at normal speed.

Total Quality Management (TQM) Efficiency engineering system that measures to a high degree of accuracy the business impact of all expenditures.

Transparency The large-format (typically 8 by 10 inches) film used with the overhead projector.

Tutorial method A teaching strategy in which content is presented, questions posed, responses given, and feedback provided.

Two-by-six rule A general rule of thumb for determining screen size: no viewer should be seated closer to the screen than two screen widths or farther away than six screen widths.

Uniform resource locator (URL) The address for an Internet site or World Wide Web page containing the protocol type, the domain, the directory, and the name of the site or page.

Upload To send a file from a computer system to a network.

Verbalism A term to describe the parroting of words without demonstrating understanding.

Video The storage of visuals and their display on a television-type screen.

Videocassette recorder (VCR) A device that records and plays back video images and sound on magnetic tape stored in a cassette.

Video teleconference A teleconference involving a television-type picture as well as voice transmission. The video image may be freeze-frame or full-motion video.

Viewfinder Viewing device on a camera that lets you see approximately what the film will record.

Virtual field trip A type of field trip in which the students do not leave the classroom setting; instead they use media to provide the experience of "being there."

Virtual reality A computer-controlled environment in which users experience multisensory immersion and interact with certain phenomena as they would in the physical world.

Virtual time Not in real time, not simultaneous.

Visual   A type of media whose mode of apprehension is optical (e.g., diagrams, drawings, photographs, cartoons).

Visual literacy   The learned ability to interpret visual messages accurately and to create such messages.

WAVE audio files   A common way to store and use quality audio data in a digital format that relies on sampling frequencies, multiple channels, and compression algorithms to create the files. A WAVE file contains a number of "chunks" that are widely used in professional programs that process digital audio waveforms.

Web   See *World Wide Web*.

Web pages   Documents which make up the World Wide Web. See *website*.

WebQuest   A set of steps that provide guidance when seeking information about a specific topic.

Website   A collection of Web pages available on the Internet that provide information about products, services, events, materials, etc.

Whiteboard   A display surface, also called *multipurpose board* or *marker board*, for visual and textual communication using special felt-tip markers.

Wide area network (WAN)   A communications network that covers a large geographic area, such as a state or country.

Wiki   A Web-based document subject to edit by any of its users.

Wireless network   Computers connected by radio frequency, microwave, or infrared technology instead of wires.

World Wide Web (the Web)   A graphical environment on computer networks that allows you to access, view, and maintain documents that can include text, data, sound, and video.

Photo Credits

Index